MEDIEVAL POLITICAL PHILOSOPHY

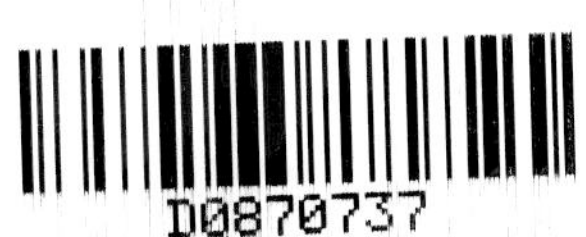

A volume in the series

AGORA

Edited by
THOMAS L. PANGLE

Founding Editor
ALLAN BLOOM

For a list of titles in the series, visit our website at www.cornellpress.cornell.edu.

MEDIEVAL POLITICAL PHILOSOPHY

A Sourcebook

SECOND EDITION

EDITED BY

JOSHUA PARENS *and*
JOSEPH C. MACFARLAND

1st edition edited by Ralph Lerner and Muhsin Mahdi

CORNELL UNIVERSITY PRESS · ITHACA AND LONDON

Cornell University Press gratefully acknowledges receipt of a grant from the Earhart Foundation, which assisted in the publication of this book.

First edition published 1963 by Agora Editions
Second edition published 2011 by Cornell University Press

First Cornell Paperbacks printing, first edition, 1972
First Cornell Paperbacks printing, second edition, 2011

Printed in the United States of America

Library of Congress Cataloging-in-Publication Data

Medieval political philosophy : a sourcebook. — 2nd ed. / edited by
Joshua Parens and Joseph C. Macfarland.
p. cm. — (Agora)
Selections translated from Arabic, Hebrew, Judeo-Arabic and Latin.
"1st edition edited by Ralph Lerner and Muhsin Mahdi."
Includes bibliographical references and index.
ISBN 978-0-8014-4962-8 (cloth : alk. paper)
ISBN 978-0-8014-7681-5 (pbk. : alk. paper)
1. Political science—Early works to 1800. 2. Philosophy, Medieval. I. Parens, Joshua, 1961–
II. Macfarland, Joseph C. III. Series: Agora editions (Cornell University Press)
JA82.M39 2011
320.09'02—dc22 2010053811

Cornell University Press strives to use environmentally responsible suppliers and materials to the fullest extent possible in the publishing of its books. Such materials include vegetable-based, low-VOC inks and acid-free papers that are recycled, totally chlorine-free, or partly composed of nonwood fibers. For further information, visit our website at www.cornellpress.cornell.edu.

Cloth printing 10 9 8 7 6 5 4 3 2 1
Paperback printing 10 9 8 7 6 5 4 3 2 1

CONTENTS

PART II

POLITICAL PHILOSOPHY IN JUDAISM

Edited by Joshua Parens

PART III

POLITICAL PHILOSOPHY IN CHRISTIANITY

Edited by Joseph C. Macfarland

ACKNOWLEDGMENTS

Medieval Political Philosophy: A Sourcebook, edited by Ralph Lerner and Muhsin Mahdi, was published in 1963 by The Free Press of Glencoe, in the Agora Editions series. Cornell University Press issued a paperback edition in 1972. The volume editors, in collaboration with the Reverend Ernest L. Fortin, AA, began preliminary work on a revised edition in 1986. They passed all accumulated rights and editorial responsibilities to Joshua Parens and Joseph C. Macfarland in the late 1990s. Parens and Macfarland, with the advice of the current editor of the Agora series, Thomas L. Pangle, have thoroughly revised and amplified the first edition of the book.

Parens and Macfarland thank with profound gratitude Ralph Lerner and the late Muhsin Mahdi for entrusting the *Sourcebook* to us, as well as the late Ernest L. Fortin, for helping us to get under way. We also thank Thomas L. Pangle for his constructive criticism and advice and the following scholars for their advice: Charles E. Butterworth, Christoph Flüeler, Steven Harvey, Joel L. Kraemer, Lidia Lanza, and Marco Toste. We acknowledge with gratitude the generous financial support of the Earhart Foundation both for research and for permissions costs. Joshua Parens thanks the University of Dallas for sabbatical leave time and financial support as well as financial assistance with permissions costs. He also thanks the library staff of the University of Dallas for technical assistance, especially Cherie Hohertz and Robert (Scott) Dupree. Joseph Macfarland thanks St. John's College, Annapolis, MD, for generous sabbatical leave time. He also thanks the Institute of Medieval Studies at the University of Fribourg, Switzerland, for providing a hospitable location for pursuing research and the National Association of Scholars for a John M. Olin Faculty Fellowship that supported research. We thank Roger Haydon of Cornell University Press for his patience with the project over so many years.

Selections appear here with the permission of the original publisher or of the translator.

Alfarabi, *Enumeration of the Sciences,* and Alfarabi, *Book of Religion,* are reprinted from *Alfarabi: The Political Writings; "Selected Aphorisms" and Other Texts,* translated and annotated by Charles E. Butterworth, copyright © 2001 by Cornell University, and are used by permission of the publisher, Cornell University Press. Alfarabi, *Political Regime,* translated by Charles E. Butterworth, appears by courtesy of the translator. Avicenna, *The Metaphysics of "The Healing,"* 10, translated by Michael E. Marmura (Provo, UT: Brigham Young University Press, 2004), is reprinted with permission from the publisher. Alghazali, *The Deliverer from Error,* translated by Richard J. McCarthy, SJ, appears by courtesy of Fons Vitae. Ibn Bajja, *The Governance of the Solitary,* translated by Lawrence Berman, appears by permission of Hanna Berman. Ibn Tufayl, *Hayy the Son of Yaqzan,* translated by George N. Atiyeh, appears by courtesy of the translator. Averroes, *Decisive Treatise,* translated by Charles E. Butterworth (Provo, UT: Brigham Young University Press, 2001), is reprinted with permission from the publisher.

Saadya Gaon: The Book of Doctrines and Beliefs, Tr. 3, ch. 2, translated by Alexander Altmann, edited by Daniel H. Frank (Indianapolis: Hackett Publishing Company, Inc., 2002), is reprinted by permission of Hackett Publishing Company, Inc., all rights reserved. Judah Halevi, *Kuzari,* translated by Barry Kogan and Lawrence Berman, is published with permission of Barry Kogan and Hanna

Berman, and of Ivan Marcus of the Yale Judaica Series of Yale University. Isaac Polgar, *The Support of Religion,* translated by Charles H. Manekin, appears by courtesy of the translator. Abravanel, *Commentary on the Bible,* translated by Robert Sacks, appears by courtesy of the translator.

Roger Bacon, *Opus Maius: Moral Philosophy,* translated by Richard McKeon, Donald McCarthy, and Ernest Fortin, from *Selections from Medieval Philosophers,* vol. 2, edited by Richard McKeon, is reprinted with the permission of Scribner, an imprint of Simon & Schuster Adult Publishing Group, copyright © 1930 by Charles Scribner's Sons; copyright renewed © 1958 by Richard McKeon. Thomas Aquinas, *Commentary on Aristotle's Nicomachean Ethics,* translated by C. I. Litzinger, OP; foreword by Ralph McInerny (Notre Dame, IN: Dumb Ox Books, 1993), appears by permission of the publisher. Boethius of Dacia, *On the Supreme Good, On the Eternity of the World, On Dreams,* translated by John F. Wippel, pp. 28–35, appears by permission of the publisher, © 1987 by the Pontifical Institute of Mediaeval Studies, Toronto. *Giles of Rome's On Ecclesiastical Power,* translated by R. W. Dyson, copyright © 2004 Columbia University Press, is reprinted with permission of the publisher. Ptolemy of Lucca, *On the Government of Rulers: De regimine principum,* translated by James M. Blythe (Philadelphia: University of Pennsylvania Press, 1997), is reprinted with permission of the University of Pennsylvania Press. Marsilius of Padua, *The Defender of the Peace,* translated by Alan Gewirth, appears by permission of Ayer Company Publishers. William of Ockham, *The Dialogue,* from *A Letter to the Friars Minor and Other Writings,* edited by Arthur Stephen McGrade, translated by John Kilcullen (Cambridge: Cambridge University Press, 1995), is reprinted with the permission of Cambridge University Press.

MEDIEVAL POLITICAL PHILOSOPHY

GENERAL INTRODUCTION

Over the decades since the first publication of the *Sourcebook* (1963), various events have brought to light the uneasy relation between religion and politics. Conflicts between Islamic radicals and the West, for example, have made it tempting to divide the world into a secular West and a radicalized Islamic world, despite the fact that neither side is simply secular or religious. In the West we often experience doubts about the progress of secularism, while the Islamic world seeks the benefits of modernization without its attendant ills. In a time in which we alternate between safeguarding secularism and questioning it (especially along its indistinct boundaries), medieval political philosophy offers a striking vantage point from which to view these political challenges, as it stands prior in time to the modern project of secularization and to a large extent outside it. Indeed, the separation of religion from politics, as established in liberal democratic regimes, is a modern solution to a problem that had been recognized and investigated by thinkers in the medieval period. And even though the modern, liberal democratic solution took hold in predominantly Christian countries, in the medieval period the theoretical questions inherent to this problem were investigated by diverse Muslims, Jews, and Christians, many of whom learned from their counterparts in the other religious communities.

For the authors gathered in this volume, there is perhaps a greater uniformity of general intention than at any other period: all of these authors studied the works of classical political philosophy and sought to think through the implications of this political thought for their contemporary situation in a monotheistic religious community. Coming to know political philosophy from the ancients, these authors, for the most part, understood political philosophy as extending well beyond the relatively narrow range of "politics" as it is understood in modern, liberal regimes. Yet monotheism posed for them challenges not addressed by classical political philosophy: for example, monotheism, especially Christianity and Islam, reoriented human strivings toward the next life, and so fueled the conflict between secular and ecclesiastical powers in favor of the latter. More importantly, monotheism led at the end of the medieval period toward a conflict between monotheistic sects—in other words, toward religious intolerance. Medieval political philosophy thus combines the comprehensiveness of ancient political philosophy with deep reflection about the challenges posed by monotheism.

We study these authors with the intention of coming to understand the recovery and reemergence of political philosophy in these three monotheistic religious communities. How is political philosophy affected or reshaped when it is articulated and explored within this new context? Might the practice of political philosophy come to be governed by the laws, counsels, or doctrines of the relevant religion? Or, conversely, how might political philosophy affect or reshape religious doctrines and interpretations of divine laws or counsels? Might the insights of political philosophy govern in some fashion the practice of religion? Without yet attempting to bring precision to these questions, we note that, in studying medieval political philosophy, we inevitably encounter the question concerning the confrontation between reason and faith or, we might say, provisionally, between philosophy and theology. In fact, we are drawn to the study of medieval political philosophy precisely because we expect it to enrich our thoughts on this confrontation.

In this introduction we intend to provide some preliminary guidance in pursuing these questions when reading these texts, but these questions, articulated in this fashion, lack precision, because their formulation does not apply equally well to authors situated in all three religious communities. For example, if we express this confrontation in the rubric of the opposition of "reason and faith," we tacitly presume that a life in accord with the precepts of the sacred text is succinctly understood more in terms of what one believes and adheres to privately than how one acts within one's community. If we express it in the rubric of "reason and revelation," we may permit ourselves to drop authors summarily into one category or another, as if were not possible for one who adheres vigorously to revelation or divine law to inquire deeply and rationally about matters outside of—or even contrary to—what is affirmed by that revelation or law. If we express this confrontation in the rubric of "philosophy and theology," we tacitly presume that the discipline or science that stands before or opposed to philosophy but calls upon the sacred text is "theology." The word *theology* may be used to refer to a discipline in each of the three religious communities (Latin: *theologia;* Arabic: *kalām*), but the disciplines so indicated are not conceived in the same manner. If we have distantly inherited from Christian medieval thought a familiar but imprecise notion of the opposition of philosophy and theology, and if we project this opposition, without further thought, back upon Islamic or Jewish medieval thought, we are likely to fall into a fundamental misunderstanding. The contemporary reader must resist the temptation to interpret medieval Islamic and Jewish political philosophy through the lens of Scholastic thought. As a preliminary, we should therefore first ask: When philosophy is pursued in a community defined by a monotheistic religion, what is the authoritative religious discipline against which it is likely to be measured?

In Islam and Judaism, the most authoritative religious science is jurisprudence (*fiqh* and *talmud*), as the divine text is a law, and the principal prophet is a legislator; whereas in Christianity, in which the central figure is not a legislator, the authoritative religious science is not jurisprudence, but theology. The focus of Christianity is the Son's role as the mediator in a Christian's journey to the kingdom of God. The closest parallel focus in Islam and Judaism is the prophet: the prophet, of course, should never be confused with God in either of these religions, even if the prophet does serve as more (Islam) or less (Judaism) the exemplary case of imitation of God. Jesus' earthly role is principally that of a teacher and moral counselor; his teaching, the Gospel, is related to and perhaps elaborates upon a divine law but is not itself given as a law. The closest parallel in Islam and Judaism is once again the prophet but now with the clarification that the prophet plays an even more important role as legislator than as moral exemplar. In the modern world, commentators on Islam often claim that Islam is more like Christianity than Judaism because Muhammad is more a bringer of counsels than a legislator. One thing is certain: none of the medieval political philosophers viewed Islam this way. Divine Law (*sharīʿa*) was the central concern of the political philosophers we present in this book.

Thus, to repeat, in Islam and Judaism, the most authoritative religious science is jurisprudence (*fiqh* and *talmud*), the discipline in which the divine text is studied as law, whereas in Christianity, the most authoritative religious science is theology. In Islam during the period with which we are concerned, theology (*kalām*) was a more marginal inquiry than jurisprudence. It was primarily apologetic in character, as will become obvious upon reading our selection from Alfarabi's *Enumeration of the Sciences.* In Judaism, jurisprudence (*talmud,* esp. *halakhah*) had undergone very extensive development for over a thousand years before theology began to develop as an independent discipline (exemplified by Saadya Gaon), shortly before political philosophy made its first significant appearance in the towering figure of Maimonides. The very fact that Maimonides felt it incumbent upon himself to write a commentary on the Talmud and then to codify it testifies to the centrality of jurisprudence in Judaism.

In Christendom, one could say that theology began in late antiquity, as soon as the fathers of the church began to engage the Stoic and Neoplatonic traditions. Yet at the close of antiquity the word *theology* was borrowed from pagan philosophers and used by Augustine to refer to the attempts of philosophers to reconcile the absurdities of the pagan religion with philosophy (*City of God* 6.4–10, 7.5, 23, 27–29). In Augustine's view, Christianity had no need of this "theology," since it, no less than natural philosophy, was opposed to the absurdities of pagan religion and, furthermore, it brought to fulfillment what various competing philosophies had sought for in vain. Theology as a systematic discipline, alongside the disciplines of canon law and jurisprudence, developed rapidly in the twelfth and thirteenth centuries in the schools and universities. Teachers compiled passages from scripture, the writings of the church fathers, and church decrees and organized them thematically, often laying out opposing arguments (*sic et non*) and seeking to bring them into harmony: these compilations resulted in the foundational documents of Scholastic theology and canon law (e.g., Peter Lombard's *Book of Sentences* and Gratian's *Decretum*). (The discipline of jurisprudence treated Roman civil law in a similar fashion but is otherwise not relevant to the present concern with the authoritative religious science.) In retrospect the labors of earlier authors such as Augustine in clarifying and elaborating Christian doctrine could then be viewed as belonging to this developing discipline of theology. The discipline of canon law exercised a great influence over the administration of the church as a comprehensive, extrapolitical community, and an indirect influence over nonecclesiastical politics, but as the Gospel is not a law, theologians maintained the superior dignity of their science in articulating sacred doctrine with precision.

Having surveyed the differences between the three religions with respect to the authoritative religious discipline, we are now in a better position to consider what we provisionally referred to as the confrontation between "philosophy and theology." That jurisprudence was the most authoritative religious science in Judaism and Islam shaped political philosophy therein decisively. Even if the consequences are far reaching, it is not difficult to argue that philosophy works at a higher level of inquiry than jurisprudence. After all, the primary focus of jurisprudence is correct action, while the primary focus of philosophy is the ascent from right opinion to knowledge. It was at least plausible for the Islamic and Jewish medieval political philosophers to argue for the leading role of political philosophy vis-à-vis jurisprudence. Moreover, they could argue for the leading role of philosophy in the ascent from opinion to knowledge without manifestly subverting obedience to the Law or the authority of jurisprudence in determining correct action. The situation is different in the context of Christianity, where philosophy is measured directly against theology, inasmuch as both disciplines concern themselves with right opinion or belief, and knowledge. The overlapping domains of theology and philosophy necessitated that a hierarchical relationship be made explicit, exemplified in Thomas Aquinas's characterization of philosophy as the handmaiden of theology (*Summa Theologiae* 1.1.5). While the so-called Latin Averroists were accused of having taught that in some cases philosophy contradicted theology, and that in these cases the theological teaching was false and the philosophical true, in the extant writings of the authors thus accused, where such contradictions do appear, the authors inevitably maintain that the Bible is true and must be believed. Moreover, in the Christian community, as opposed to the other two, there often existed officers in the church hierarchy or religious orders, and committees in the university, that supervised educators and guarded against heresy and heterodoxy. Thus, allowing for exceptions to the rule, we may say as a generality that theology in medieval Christianity enjoyed a higher regard vis-á-vis philosophy than did jurisprudence in Islam and Judaism. One of the puzzles of theology's predominance over philosophy in Christianity and political philosophy's relative independence from theology and jurisprudence in Islam and Judaism is the undeniably greater longevity of philosophy in the Christian West than in the Islamic world. Independence for philosophy, it would seem, spells not security but rather precariousness.

Before considering the distinct ways in which particular authors understood the relationship between philosophy and the authoritative religious disciplines, it is necessary to consider one further general difference between the three religious communities with regard to how classical political philosophy was studied. The aforementioned distinction between the religions—as divine Law or as a sacred teaching and moral counsel—unexpectedly corresponds to a difference in the ancient philosopher who served as the primary guide in the recovery of political philosophy: the Muslim and Jewish focus on the prophet as legislator suited the reliance of these authors upon Plato as their primary guide. The philosopher-king in the *Republic* serves as the model against which the prophet-legislator is measured throughout Islam and Judaism, from Alfarabi to Averroes and Maimonides to Isaac Polgar. To be capable of legislating a divine Law ready to stand the test of time, the prophet-legislator must possess every conceivable theoretical and practical virtue. The philosophical inquiry into the divine Law concerns not only the virtues of the legislator, but also the content that is characteristic of a divine Law, or that reveals a law as divine. Whether the law is of human or divine origin is the starting point of the conversation in Plato's *Laws,* in which the interlocutors discuss at length the content of a law that is said to be divine. In contrast, Aristotle's *Politics* would have suited much less well the development of political philosophy in Islam or Judaism, for several reasons. The *Politics* offers a meager treatment of religion, and it does not discuss the possibility of a divine law, let alone the content of such a law. Furthermore, given that Aristotle, in the *Nicomachean Ethics,* develops the distinction between theoretical and practical wisdom further than Plato and, in the *Politics,* cordons off politics from direct or overt dependence upon philosophy (as the *Politics*—even in commenting on the *Republic*—refrains from discussing the philosopher-king or metaphysical questions), Aristotle's ethical and political teaching was ill suited to the development of political philosophy in the context of Islam and Judaism. Aristotle's *Politics* proved very well suited, however, to the recovery of political philosophy in the context of (Western) Christianity. Because Jesus acted principally as a teacher and moral counselor, prior to the reemergence of classical political philosophy in the thirteenth century there already existed in canon law (and in the documents it was built upon) an ill-defined and much disputed, but nevertheless fundamental, distinction between the spheres of politics and religion—that is, between the temporal and the spiritual powers. Therefore, it was not expected that the study of political things as conducted in the *Politics* should extend to divine law or the characteristics of a prophet. This narrowing of the field of politics, by excluding divine law and neglecting religion, also suited the aforementioned separation of theoretical and practical wisdom in the *Ethics.* Because practical wisdom is evidently sufficient for governing the polity, the study of politics need not aspire to or rely upon theoretical wisdom, which in Aristotle's account touches upon the unchanging and divine, nor ought the study of politics aspire to any other virtue commonly thought to be divine.

Was the Islamic focus on Plato the result of a lacuna in the Aristotelian corpus available to Alfarabi, the founder of political philosophy in Islam? Although Alfarabi evinces extensive knowledge of the *Nicomachean Ethics,* he demonstrates little knowledge of the *Politics.* At first glance, the matter would seem to be settled in favor of the chance historical fact of limited Muslim access to the *Politics.* Almost as soon as one settles the matter, however, one begins to wonder whether the *Politics* was rarely commented upon because medieval political philosophers in Islam had few reasons to be interested in the text. Much of the Aristotelian corpus, of course, was or became available in all three religious communities in the course of the medieval period (e.g., *Nicomachean Ethics, Physics, Metaphysics, De Anima,* etc.), and several of the earliest (often incomplete) translations into Latin were made from Arabic translations rather than from the Greek: why should the fortune of the *Politics* in the religious communities have differed so greatly from that of the *Ethics*? Conversely, it is curious in the Christian tradition that Plato's *Timaeus* should be so widely known, that Neoplatonic metaphysics should have such a wide influence and deep hold on Christian theology, that Plato himself be held in such high regard, and yet, overtly political works, such as the *Republic* and the *Laws,* in which these metaphysical teachings are discussed, should be unknown. We suspect that some combination of chance events and human deliberation played a role in the development of these two trends in medieval political philosophy, though we can by no means be certain of this.

This difference between Islam and Judaism, on the one hand, and Christianity, on the other, regarding whether the primary guide to ancient political philosophy is Plato or Aristotle, proves highly significant for the generally accepted scope and goals of political philosophy in each tradition. For example, from a reading of the *Politics* or the *Ethics,* political philosophy will appear to be a part or a branch of philosophy as a whole, separate from the other parts of philosophy, and especially separate from and possibly subordinate to first philosophy (*Ethics* 6.7 1141a16–23), whereas this separation and subordination are not at all apparent from a study of the *Republic* and the *Laws.* Among the Christian authors, political philosophy may often be limited in scope to political questions narrowly conceived, such as the advantages and disadvantages of the types of regime (especially the mixed regime and the types of kingship) or the relation of civil law to natural law. In this milieu, the relationship between human governance of the city and divine governance of the whole would not belong to political philosophy narrowly understood, and it could belong to philosophy more broadly only on the understanding that the conclusions of philosophy on the governance of the whole conform to the conclusions of theology. By contrast, political philosophy among the Muslim and Jewish authors is manifestly more comprehensive, as comprehensive as the divine Law that it endeavors to comprehend, considering therefore questions such as what is prophecy, and the divine governance of the whole.

Having considered some general differences between the three religious communities in the authoritative religious disciplines and in the typical study of classical political philosophy, we are in a position to consider briefly and with some precision how representative authors treated the relationship of political philosophy to the authoritative religious disciplines. Our objective here is limited to sketching several salient, fundamental possibilities. For Alfarabi, political philosophy is the comprehensive theoretico-practical inquiry. He attempts to bring the politically relevant religious sciences (dialectical theology and jurisprudence) under the control and guidance of political philosophy. In the *Book of Religion,* he transforms theology (*kalām*), which had always been apologetic and dialectical or disputatious (and for this reason *kalām* is often translated "dialectical theology"), into dialectic (*jadal*)—that is, a specific form of argumentation subordinate to the putatively demonstrative methods of philosophy. Jurisprudence is from the start a dependent science: it argues by analogy from the previously existing laws set forth by a legislating prophet—without inquiring into whether that prophet is divinely inspired or a philosopher-king. Political philosophy, by contrast, inquires into the diverse natures of legislating prophets and the laws that they give, including the nature and conditions for the possibility of the existence of the philosopher-king. In short, political philosophy plays the leading role among the sciences, a role that befits its comprehensiveness.

Because Alfarabi conceives of political philosophy as comprehensive, he engages in inquiries into political matters both narrowly and very broadly conceived. For example, in his *Political Regime* he discusses the better and the worse regimes as well as a best political order that arises from this philosophical inquiry, the subject matter of politics in the narrow sense. Yet in the first part of this same work he describes a theological order that befits that best political order in a manner reminiscent of Plato's *Timaeus* as an account of the natural order that might make the *kallipolis* of the *Republic* possible. (Although the first half of the *Political Regime* is not included in the *Sourcebook* due to length constraints, a description of this theological order is found in the *Book of Religion.*) In this case, political philosophy can hardly be confused with "political science" in the contemporary sense: Alfarabi includes in his political works elements of metaphysics that most modern political scientists would consider wholly out of place. In other words, for Alfarabi the comprehensiveness of political philosophy is never in doubt; and its focus on the theoretico-practical heights of human inquiry is never in doubt.

The only challenge to the comprehensiveness of political philosophy are the doubts Alfarabi himself raises concerning the wisdom political philosophy would seem to need to possess if the rule of the prophet-king-legislator were to be just. He does not, as one might expect, defer to the claims to wisdom of revelation. He plunges ever deeper into debates about the origin of divine Law: whether its origin is imagination, prudence, or revelation. Such inquiries lead him into what an insightful twentieth-century interpreter of Alfarabi and Maimonides called "prophetology." Such inquiries can lead one deep into theoretical inquiries about the nature and fate of the soul. Again, the very comprehensiveness of political philosophy means that medieval Islamic and Jewish political philosophy can never seem to segregate practical inquiries into best rule from theoretical inquiries into the nature of the beings.

Alfarabi's stand on the status and scope of political philosophy can be contrasted sharply with the views of Thomas Aquinas. For Aquinas, philosophy, especially political philosophy, is less noble than sacred doctrine or revealed theology; theology is the most comprehensive science, since it is simultaneously theoretical and practical (*Summa Theologiae* 1.1.4, 5). In this regard Aquinas adhered to the Aristotelian division of the sciences, in which politics is a practical science, together with ethics and household management (economics), and is therefore segregated from the theoretical sciences of mathematics, physics, and metaphysics (i.e., "first philosophy" or "theology" [*Metaphysics* 6.1 1026a18–24]). Indeed, it could be argued that Aquinas and some other Christian authors deepen the Aristotelian distinction between theoretical and practical science and separate political science more thoroughly from theology or metaphysics than Aristotle intended (consider Aquinas's commentary on Aristotle's assertion that politics is the architectonic or master-craft [*Ethics* 1.2 1094a29; *Commentary on the Nicomachean Ethics* 1.2]). This ordering of philosophy as a "handmaiden" to theology does not mean that Aquinas demeans the activity of philosophizing or sets narrow limits upon what reason may discover through philosophical inquiry. Indeed, readers new to Aquinas's *Summa Theologiae* are more likely to be surprised by what he maintains philosophy is able to establish than by what lies beyond its scope (e.g., philosophical argumentation establishes that the world is created by God, although not that it is created in time [*Summa Theologiae* 1.46.1, 2]). In his commentaries on Aristotle's works, selections of which are found here, Aquinas rarely appeals to authorities outside of the text he is explicating, and he never makes his explication contingent upon an article of faith. Aquinas appreciates the capacity of philosophy to bring clarity to political and ethical questions; such reasoning is simply not the highest or most comprehensive kind.

The political philosophy of Aquinas, in its scope and content, is closer to what we might recognize as political science. Whereas for Alfarabi subjects such as the nature and conditions of prophecy and giving divine Law fall within the scope of political philosophy, for Aquinas these subjects, insofar as they bear on sacred doctrine, clearly belong to theology (*De Veritate* q. 12 a. 3, 4, 12). Perhaps this segregation of the practical and theoretical sciences, of political philosophy and metaphysics, ought not to be stated too strongly: outside of the philosophical commentaries, one does find in the works of Aquinas that metaphysical truths have a bearing on politics. For example, in the *Summa Theologiae,* the natural law is the providence of God insofar as it can be discerned by human reason (1–2.91.2), and this providence is in part discernible on the basis of a developed form of classical metaphysics. Within this volume, a similar intersection of metaphysics and political philosophy is discernible in the works of other authors (Roger Bacon, Ptolemy of Lucca, Giles of Rome, Dante Alighieri). One must ask the following questions in order to compare these authors with Alfarabi: Does the metaphysical account belong to political philosophy as part of a comprehensive theoretico-practical inquiry into the best life? Or is the practical philosophical account dependent upon metaphysics as a separate, theoretical, and higher discipline?

If Alfarabi and Aquinas may stand as paradigms for the emergence of political philosophy in their respective religious communities, this is not to say that other thinkers in each of their religious communities necessarily adopted the same views with respect to the relative status and comprehensiveness of political philosophy, theology, and jurisprudence. We will here only briefly discuss two authors who provide a stark contrast to Alfarabi and Aquinas: Alghazali and Marsilius of Padua. Alghazali vigorously attacked the philosophical arguments that brought into question the scriptural teaching on the creation of the world by God. Much more radically than Aquinas, Alghazali subordinates philosophical inquiry to divine Law. He also maintains that political philosophy does not add anything to the political teachings already manifest in divine Law: political philosophy is decidedly not comprehensive. This is not to say, however, that Alghazali regards theology as the highest and a comprehensive science in the place of political philosophy; he is likewise suspicious of theology as having attempted only superficially and inadequately to use the arguments of some philosophers against other philosophers. Despite Alfarabi's profound influence upon other philosophers in the Islamic world, such as Avicenna and Averroes, as well as beyond it, it was, nevertheless, Alghazali who had the greater influence upon the Muslim world as a whole. In the introduction to the Islamic part of the *Sourcebook* will be found a more detailed picture of the vigorous debates between Islamic authors.

Analogous to the opposition of Alfarabi and Alghazali is the opposition between Aquinas and Marsilius. Seeking to refute arguments advanced in theology and canon law that, in his view, attributed a tyrannical power to the papacy, Marsilius wrote the *Defender of the Peace* with two principal discourses: the first is philosophical; the second could be called theological, as it is often based upon passages from scripture and the works of the church fathers. What results is an unambiguous liberation of political philosophy from theology, without, it seems, bringing about a full subordination of theology in return. On the one hand, the conclusions of the Second Discourse regarding the structure and authority of the church invariably conform to the philosophical arguments of the First Discourse. Moreover, the ultimate authority for determining all doubtful meanings in scripture is said to lie with a general council, which is convoked by a political authority, and whose members, secular as well as ecclesiastical, are appointed by political authorities (*Defender of the Peace* 2.17, 2.20-21); the source of such political authority is, of course, made fully evident in the First Discourse. On the other hand, Marsilius allows that, by the New Law, priests may pursue a form of perfection exemplified by Christ (2.13), and that all priests have an "essential" authority that is caused by God and is inaccessible to philosophy (2.15). Thus, although many questions that formerly seemed theological are brought under the direction of political philosophy—and in the process, political philosophy is rendered independent of theology—nevertheless, the core teachings of theology evidently retain their independence from political philosophy. In addition, political philosophy, as well as the prudence of the good ruler, appears entirely separate from the theoretical philosophical disciplines, including metaphysics. For Marsilius, political philosophy has an independence and scope entirely unlike what one finds in the writings of Aquinas; nevertheless, it appears to lack the comprehensive character attributed to it by Alfarabi.

In this brief look at four medieval thinkers, in two of the religious communities, we naturally find that in neither religious tradition is philosophy uniformly subordinated to the religious sciences or the religious sciences to philosophy; a diversity of opinion and lively debates may be traced in all three traditions. But we also note that the subordination of philosophy to divine law, or of the religious sciences to philosophy, does not take the same form in the different traditions. Within the limited range offered by these four thinkers, in the Islamic tradition one finds both a more robust claim for the comprehensiveness of political philosophy and a more vigorous and radical criticism of that philosophy, while in neither case is theology strongly defended; in the Christian medieval tradition, by contrast, while authors disagree over the relative merits and scope of philosophy and of theology, philosophical inquiry is not criticized as radically as it is by Alghazali, nor is theology so plainly subordinated to philosophy as one finds in Alfarabi. This limited schema, of course, will have to be modified and elaborated in the light of a study of many more authors. Differences among their works must originate, in part, in the individual genius of those authors but may also be due, in part, to the rather different communal and intellectual environments in which classical political philosophy was discovered, and in which political philosophy was practiced anew.

PART I

POLITICAL PHILOSOPHY IN ISLAM

Edited by Joshua Parens

INTRODUCTION

When the *Sourcebook* was originally published in 1963, perhaps its most outstanding feature was the inclusion of a large body of medieval Islamic political philosophy not previously translated into English. To this day, the *Sourcebook* has few, if any, competitors in English for coverage of this area of political philosophy. When the *Sourcebook* was originally conceived, one of the primary interests of the Islamic material was the light it could shed, by means of comparison, on traditions "closer to home," namely, medieval Christian political philosophy. Since the Islamic resurgence of the 1980s and 1990s, not to mention the conflicts of the 2000s, however, this motive has been superseded in importance by others. For the educated student in the United States and beyond, a better understanding of the Islamic world has become a necessity. To understand contemporary Islamic politics, it is necessary to understand its premodern background.

The suggestion that the *Sourcebook* will contribute to the student's understanding of the premodern background of contemporary Islamic politics does not, however, imply that contemporary Islamic societies should be viewed as emerging directly out of the teachings of Alfarabi and Avicenna. Medieval Islamic political philosophy never had the kind of influence on Islamic society that, for example, Locke had on the founding of the United States. Furthermore, much of the influence of medieval Islamic political philosophy had already been spent when it ceased to be a vital area of study upon Averroes's death (in 1198). Yet, in the last two centuries, renewed importance has been attached to this period of political philosophy in the Islamic world itself. Some of the architects of modern Islamic politics in the late nineteenth and early twentieth centuries (e.g., Jamal al-Din al-Afghani) were eager to search out the resources of their own medieval tradition in lieu of, or at least in addition to, the imported political thought of the colonial powers. For this additional reason, an understanding of the premodern background of contemporary Islamic politics is especially important today.

Leaving aside the issue of motives for study, let us turn to four of the most prominent themes that will appear in the Islamic part of this volume: the identification of the Platonic philosopher-king with the legislating prophet, the division of the sciences, Alghazali's attack on the philosophers, and the solitary. Of course, the teacher and student will find many additional themes. These are merely a few of the most prominent.

Most readers are familiar with the philosopher-king theme from Plato's *Republic*. As part of an effort to find justice in the soul, in Book 2 of the *Republic,* Socrates persuades his young interlocutors to examine the just city. To produce the just or beautiful city, they must turn it into a family and establish philosophers as kings. Philosophic rule is supposed to guarantee that the person who is least interested in money and honor rules (347B), and does so not for his own private advantage but for the common good. Doctors, judges, and written laws are conspicuous by their absence from the just city—so healthy in both body and soul are its denizens. In lieu of laws, living intelligence rules.

Alfarabi identifies the philosopher-king with the legislating prophet in various ways throughout his corpus. Prophecy's political role is central in Islam (as in Judaism). Muhammad is the bearer of a divine Law (*sharīʿa*). The most notable divergence between Alfarabi and the *Republic* is that Muhammad wrote down a law for his adherents to follow when he died—rather than banking on the fantastic hope of an unending series of philosophic rulers.[1] Thus Alfarabi draws on not only the *Republic,* but also the *Laws.* In that dialogue, a group of old men have gathered to participate in the founding of a city based on written law. Over the course of the conversation, the lead character, the Athenian Stranger, makes it amply evident that the best city ruled by written law can only be second-best, after the city ruled by living human or divine intelligence (739C–E). The city in the *Laws* constitutes a greater compromise with reality than the city in the *Republic.*

In Alfarabi's various accounts of the virtuous city ruled by the legislating prophet or philosopher-king, there is little or no evidence that written law constrains the rulers. In a sense, Alfarabi combines the stability of Law with the flexibility of philosopher-kingship. (The theme of stability, or at least rigidity, and flexibility is by no means foreign, even to the *Republic.*) The combination solves certain problems and raises others. Revelation or divine aid makes possible what is otherwise impossible, namely, the virtuous city itself. Yet by making the legislating prophet a philosopher-king with all the natural gifts and extraordinary potential for cultivation that go along with it, Alfarabi raises the question of whether the prophet works by means of revealed or natural powers. As if Plato's account of the philosopher's virtues (*Republic* bk. 6, opening) were not enough (echoed for example in Alfarabi's *Attainment of Happiness* and *Virtuous City*), Alfarabi makes it readily apparent that combining philosophy with kingship is tantamount to ascribing to one man the possession of all of Aristotle's theoretical and practical sciences and virtues.

Some readers may have withheld assent when I claimed that Islam is a divine Law rather than a religion primarily comprised of dogmas or beliefs. (One reason this definition of Islam is frequently denied in contemporary discussions is that scholars believe identifying Islam as a religion of law will condemn them to obedience to an unchanging law. In the face of modern challenges, such an understanding can appear extremely stultifying.)[2] Yet I am not the originator of this interpretation of Islam. All major medieval Islamic political philosophers held this view. In both Alfarabi's and Avicenna's divisions of the sciences, there is abundant evidence that they viewed Islam as a theologico-political phenomenon, not a merely theological one.

In Avicenna's *On the Divisions of the Rational Sciences,* his conviction that Islam is essentially a divine Law is evident in his claim that the proper treatment of prophecy and divine Law (*sharīʿa*) appears in the third division of practical science. And Plato's *Laws* contains this treatment. Of course, the *Laws* could not be construed as a primarily theological work, even based on its title alone.

Among the religious sciences, *kalām* or dialectical theology has never played the central role in Islam that theology played in Christian thought. Indeed, at times *kalām* has been viewed with suspicion even by more traditional Muslims (see, for example, Alghazali's *Deliverer*). Another science, *fiqh* or jurisprudence, has long been more esteemed and more central in Islam. Furthermore, even theology can be seen within a political framework. To begin with, it was from the start an apologetic art. In Alfarabi's *Enumeration of the Sciences,* the bulk of the religious sciences, such as Qur'anic commentary and the study of the authenticity of the Tradition (*sunna*) of the Prophet, are discussed, if at all, in his account of the sciences of language.[3] In contrast, jurisprudence and theology are included in his chapter on political science—thus confirming that theology must be seen within a political framework. Alfarabi's *Book of Religion* gives further evidence of the ongoing centrality of jurisprudence. There, a much more expansive account of jurisprudence is given than in the *Enumeration* (see *Book of Religion* 9–10). In the *Book of Religion,* Alfarabi attributes the tasks of *kalām* to dialectic, viewed as a part of religion, which is in turn subordinated to philosophy (5–6). Averroes, a renowned jurist in his own right, continues to establish the subordination of *kalām* to philosophy. It is precisely because theology employs dialectical arguments that it needs to be guided by philosophy. One might argue that

1. Cf. *Averroes on Plato's "Republic,"* trans. Ralph Lerner (1974; repr., Ithaca, NY: Cornell University Press, 2005), 75.

2. Cf. Fazlur Rahman, *Islam,* 2nd ed. (Chicago: University of Chicago Press, 1979), 32, 115–16.

3. See the outline of the *Enumeration* (esp. chap. 1) in the introduction to that selection. Also cf. the opening pages of the *Philosophy of Plato* in *Alfarabi: The Political Writings; Philosophy of Plato and Aristotle,* ed. and trans. Muhsin Mahdi (New York: Free Press of Glencoe, 1962; rev. ed., Ithaca, NY: Cornell University Press, 1969, 2002). Cf. Muhsin Mahdi, *Alfarabi and the Foundation of Islamic Political Philosophy* (Chicago: University of Chicago Press, 2001), chap. 4, esp. 68–69.

the political philosophers attempt to establish theology's role as the "handmaiden" of philosophy. It would be well worth comparing this view with the opposing Christian view. In addition, one might well consider the political effects (if any) of each of these views.

Alghazali's attacks on philosophy in general, and on political philosophy in particular, had a profound effect on the latter, and on political philosophers. Because of his decisive influence on political philosophy, a selection from Alghazali's *Deliverer from Error* has been included in the *Sourcebook.* He expresses two basic criticisms of philosophy: the philosophers believe in and argue for the eternity of the world, against the revealed teaching that the world is created; and political philosophy borrows its ethical and political teachings from Sufism and scripture, respectively. Alghazali reserves his criticism of the belief in eternity for last, following his criticisms that philosophers deny reward and punishment (providence) and divine knowledge of particulars. By placing the belief in the eternity of the world last, he downplays that it leads to these criticisms. After all, the traditional Muslim can understand the necessity of providence and divine knowledge of particulars without understanding how they follow from creation of the world.

It is difficult to gainsay the claim that philosophers avow the eternity of the world. It is worth wondering, however, whether all the philosophers were equally responsible for opening philosophy up to such criticism. Avicenna, the philosopher who, more than any other, in a bid to protect philosophy, blurred the lines between it and traditional *kalām,* may have inadvertently opened up philosophy to Alghazali's attack. Avicenna attempted to blur the line between reason and revelation by developing his necessary existence argument, which could be interpreted in the light of either eternity or creation. Put as simply as possible, according to this argument, there are two kinds of existence: necessary, and contingent or possible. Beings whose existence is possible require a cause of their existence; beings whose existence is necessary do not. God is the necessary existent. Other beings have merely possible existence. Because other beings require a cause of their existence, God must exist. At least in its most rudimentary form, this argument can be made to fit arguments for God's existence from eternity as well as from creation.[4] Alghazali attacks this argument at great length in the *Incoherence of the Philosophers,* attempting, with success, to show that it is nondemonstrative. In doing so, he believes himself to be defending revelation against philosophy. Averroes criticizes Avicenna for blending philosophy with *kalām* in such a way as to leave philosophy open to such attacks. It appears that Avicenna believed he might smooth relations between philosophy and *kalām* by blending the two. Unfortunately, that plan seems to have failed, with almost incalculable consequences for philosophy and Islam. Although Averroes would come to the defense of philosophy in his *Incoherence of the Incoherence,* this effort, in view of Alghazali's popular appeal, had little effect, at least in the Islamic world.

One can raise objections to Alghazali's claim that political philosophers borrow their ethical and political teaching from revelation. To begin with, his claim conflicts with the fact that philosophers interpret everything in relation to nature. Do the Sufis and scripture do this as well? Furthermore, as we will see, the ethical teaching of the philosophers is far more compatible with politics than is that of the Sufis.

After Alghazali (1058–1111), political philosophers such as Ibn Bajja (1085–1138) and Ibn Tufayl (1100–1185) seemed to see at least a grain of truth in Alghazali's suggestion that affinities exist between Sufism and philosophy. Contrary to Alghazali, however, they used those affinities to defend both philosophy and the political well-being of the city. The most obvious affinity between Sufism and philosophy is the place of solitude in the mystical and philosophic ways of life. In some respects, the most famous philosophic drama, that of Socrates' death in Athens, is emblematic of the solitary character of philosophy. At a minimum, philosophers are at risk in society at-large because they challenge received views. Although the Platonic Socrates spent a great deal of time in the marketplace and, indeed, appeared to be concerned with inquiries into virtue, if not with holding office, rumors of the solitary, secretive, and possibly politically corrosive ways of Socrates

4. See Maimonides *Guide* 1.74, fifth and sixth method; and 2.1, third and fourth speculation. Also see *Guide* 1.71 (trans. Pines) 181; and Aristotle *Metaphysics* 1050b6 ff. and 1071b5–10.

can be traced back to Aristophanes' comedy *The Clouds*. Like the Platonic political philosophy that inspired him, Alfarabi was highly attuned to such accusations, as is evident in his parable of the abstemious ascetic in the introduction to his *Summary of Plato's "Laws."* Just as the ascetic must hide from the corrupt ruler who seeks to kill him, by appearing to be a drunk, so the philosopher Plato must dress up his true teaching in symbolic garb. Philosophers must hide—if not through physical solitude, at least through a kind of mental withdrawal.

The primary activity in both mysticism and philosophy is solitary. While the two endeavors share this characteristic, the same experiences or circumstances are not necessary in order for philosophers to be able to take advantage of it. This similarity is exploited to the fullest in Ibn Bajja's *Governance of the Solitary*, as the title demonstrates. Indeed, Ibn Bajja never indicates who or what the solitary is. Rather than identify the solitary as a philosopher, he merely describes him as someone with "true opinions." Admittedly, Ibn Bajja echoes the founding of *kallipolis* (the beautiful city) in Plato's *Republic*—or the perfect (*kāmila*) city, as Ibn Bajja refers to it—and had already established a reputation as a philosopher. Nevertheless, when it comes time to identify who is the solitary, he refers the reader to what the Sufis mean by "strangers," those who travel elsewhere in spirit if not in body—thereby leaving the impression that he is sympathetic to mysticism.

We must clarify further the different causes of solitude in mysticism and philosophy. Mystical solitude derives from the private character of the unification with God. It is not by chance that Sufism, even before Alghazali, had attempted to communicate this experience beyond words by analogy to erotic love. Such love and the actions expressing it are among the most private in human experience. The love of God is viewed as even more fundamentally private. In his *Deliverer from Error*, Alghazali signals the private character of the experience by undergoing ascetic detachment as a necessary prerequisite to mystical union. Certainly, mystical union is purported to involve incommunicable intuitions. In contrast, although philosophy may lead to experiences involving some form of intuition, for the most part it emphasizes communicable knowledge. (Even if the highest intellectual intuitions in philosophy are incommunicable, the path leading to them is fully open to disclosure—unlike the higher reaches of the path to mystical union.) As was already adumbrated in our reference to the parable of the abstemious ascetic in Alfarabi's *Summary*, the philosopher's proclivity toward solitariness derives from the danger of openly communicating his own views. Philosophic solitude, then, derives primarily from the gap between the philosopher and the community to which he belongs, especially regarding the divine. Mysticism, then, is private essentially or by nature; philosophy is, even if permanently, only accidentally private.

The very solitariness that mysticism and philosophy share has contributed significantly to the view that Ibn Bajja and Ibn Tufayl are, like the mystics, fundamentally antipolitical thinkers.[5] Ibn Bajja and Ibn Tufayl have been included in the *Sourcebook* because we believe they are not only philosophers but also political philosophers. To persuade the reader that this at least *might* be the case, let us pursue further what I refer to as the conditional or accidental solitude of the philosopher.[6] In the *Governance*, Ibn Bajja argues that the solitary would be completely at home in the perfect city (again, highly similar to the beautiful or noble city ruled by philosopher-kings in the *Republic*). But, alas, when the philosopher finds himself in an imperfect city, he should stay away from other men insofar as it is possible. If the sciences are not at all cultivated in that city, then he should emigrate (Palacios ed., 78). The isolation of the solitary is an extreme or medical cure, due to some disorder in the nature of the city (11). In contrast, the mystic's withdrawal is a natural and inevitable feature of mysticism.

5. See E. I. J. Rosenthal, "The Place of Politics in the Philosophy of Ibn Bajja," *Islamic Culture* 25 (1951): 187–211; reprinted in *Studia Semitica*, vol. 2 (Cambridge: Cambridge University Press, 1971), 41, 50, 52 [pages cited below for this article by Rosenthal refer to *Studia Semitica*, vol. 2]. Also see Majid Fakhry, *A History of Islamic Philosophy*, 3rd ed. (New York: Columbia University Press, 2004), 267–80, esp. 272–73, though consider his reservations about Ibn Tufayl's apparent reconciliation of religion (mysticism) and philosophy (278–80).

6. My necessarily sketchy argument here should be compared with a very different approach to Ibn Bajja from that of Rosenthal in Steven Harvey's "The Place of the Philosopher in the City according to Ibn Bājjah," in *The Political Aspects of Islamic Philosophy: Essays in Honor of Muhsin S. Mahdi*, ed. Charles E. Butterworth (Cambridge, MA: Harvard University Press, 1992), 199–233.

Even among scholars who do not view Ibn Bajja as a mystic, some claim that his turn toward the solitary is deeply antipolitical. They maintain that in the Platonic and Aristotelian traditions, which Alfarabi followed out and cultivated, philosophers argue that man is so political by nature that the virtuous or Ideal city is the indispensable minimum without which philosophy cannot achieve its full realization. Furthermore, they contend that Ibn Bajja's claim that philosophy can reach its fulfillment even in imperfect cities is fundamentally opposed to such a view of political philosophy.[7] Although Socrates does argue at times as if philosophy needs the beautiful city to become fully developed (*Republic* 497A), evidence abounds that it does not. Of course, the most obvious piece of evidence is too obvious to be ignored, namely, that Socrates, Plato, and Aristotle lived and thrived philosophically in cities falling far short of the beautiful city. More importantly, Socrates argues that although decent rulers rule for the sake of the ruled, as regards their wage they rule to avoid the penalty of being ruled by the worse (347A–E). Philosophers rule not out of a proto-Stoic sense of duty, as some have suggested—at odds with their claim that they rule in order that they might live where they can reach their full development[8]—but for the sake of this strange wage. Of course, one kind of regime does exist in which philosophers can avoid being ruled by the worse because they can avoid being ruled by anybody—democracy. It is also the best city for the philosopher because there he can experience all types of human souls (557C–E). The city in the *Republic* is envisioned, then, for the sake of two nonphilosophers, Glaucon and Adeimantus, and would be of minimal, if any, benefit to philosophers. If philosophers would not benefit from the realization of such virtuous cities, then why do they devote so much time to imagining them as cities in speech? To answer this question, though perhaps only partially, we must recall the motive behind the solitariness of philosophers. They are solitary because they hold heterodox views on religion; the construction of virtuous cities in speech adds protection to that solitude.[9]

Behind an impregnable wall of good opinions, philosophers can guard their own beliefs, which may be for the most part only questions. What I have referred to here vaguely as "good opinions," Ibn Bajja refers to as "true opinions," and Plato's Socrates as "noble lies." That is, Ibn Bajja claims the solitary is solitary in imperfect cities because he holds "true opinions." What appears at first to be a significant departure from Plato's *Republic* may not be. Socrates criticizes severely traditional Greek religion in Books 2 and 3 of the *Republic;* he criticizes it for propounding base lies. He replaces these with noble lies. Of course, the reader expects Socrates to replace base lies with the noble truth. He implies through his persistent reference to lies that he lacks some significant knowledge about the gods, though he may be confident of the ignorance behind or the inaccuracy of the traditional beliefs. We should have some reservations, however, about assuming that by "true opinions" Ibn Bajja means the unvarnished truth.[10] Because Ibn Bajja wrote so much on such metaphysical matters (especially on conjunction with the Active Intellect), it is tempting to assume that the only thing he deems important is the metaphysical knowledge that the solitary seeks.[11] Indeed, it becomes tempting to assume that he thought he possessed the highest metaphysical knowledge. If, on the contrary, by "true opinions" he means something like Socrates' noble lies, he might still be engaged in a surprisingly central activity of political philosophy, defending philosophy before the city.

With Ibn Bajja's musings on the relation between the solitary and society's opinions in mind, we turn to Ibn Tufayl's subtle treatment of the issue that proved so central in Alghazali's attack on the

7. See Rosenthal, "Place of Politics," 39.

8. Cf. Rosenthal, "Place of Politics," esp. 58 and 42.

9. For additional discussion of the strange logic of the claim that philosophy should rule the best regime, see Joshua Parens, *An Islamic Philosophy of Virtuous Religions: Introducing Alfarabi* (Albany: SUNY Press, 2006), chaps. 2 and 3, esp. 35–37.

10. Cf. Michael S. Kochin, "Weeds: Cultivating the Imagination in Medieval Arabic Philosophy," *Journal of the History of Ideas* 60.3 (1999): 399–416, esp. 407.

11. See Rosenthal, "Place of Politics," 39; Alexander Altmann, "Ibn Bājja on Man's Ultimate Felicity," in *Harry Austryn Wolfson Jubilee Volume* (Jerusalem: American Academy of Jewish Research, 1965), 47–87; reprinted in *Studies in Religious Philosophy and Mysticism* (Ithaca, NY: Cornell University Press, 1969; London: Routledge and Kegan Paul, 1969), 73–107, esp. 78–79. But cf. Shlomo Pines, "The Limitations of Human Knowledge according to al-Fārābī, Ibn Bājja, and Maimonides," in *Studies in Medieval Jewish History and Literature*, ed. I. Twersky (Cambridge, MA: Harvard University Press, 1979), 82–109, reprinted in *Collected Works of Shlomo Pines*, ed. W. Z. Harvey and Moshe Idel (Jerusalem: Magnes Press, 1997), 5:404–31. Finally, see Harvey's more balanced view in "Place of the Philosopher," 225–29.

philosophers, namely, creation versus eternity. The delicacy with which this topic is handled in *Hayy the Son of Yaqzan* has led interpreters for many years to assume that Ibn Tufayl sides with creation and is a mystic.[12] The facts that philosophers embrace eternity, Hayy appears to be a mystic, and mystics oppose the philosophers would seem to warrant such an interpretation. Hayy's quasi-mystical experiences take the form of inquiries into the world, involving ascent and descent through various heavenly spheres; in other words, they are laden with emanationist meaning. Emanationism, more than any other element of the metaphysical teaching of Alfarabi and his followers, promotes harmony between philosophy and revealed religion.[13] Emanationism gives eternity the appearance of creation by presenting the world as if it unfolded in time, even if from eternal matter.

In a pathbreaking new interpretation, Hillel Fradkin has given those who assume that Ibn Tufayl favors mysticism and creation pause. *Hayy* opens with two possible accounts of Hayy's origins: he was either generated spontaneously on a remote island, or he was exiled there because he was heir to the throne of a tyrant. Again, many interpreters infer that Ibn Tufayl is a mystic and must favor spontaneous generation. In contrast, Fradkin has shown that Ibn Tufayl indicates, ever so subtly and in passing, a preference for the latter rather than the former account. Of course, the more political account, if it is Ibn Tufayl's own, offers ample evidence that he is far more concerned with political matters, perhaps the political effects of mysticism or the turn toward the solitary life, than most readers assume.[14] The parallels between spontaneous generation and exile, on the one hand, and creation and eternity, on the other, are obvious. When it comes time for Hayy to decide between creation and eternity, he leaves the matter undecided,[15] just as the narrator left the decision between spontaneity and exile undecided. Could it be that Ibn Tufayl is in fact a proponent of eternity who cloaks such truths in the garb of emanationism? Had Ibn Tufayl avowed belief in eternity explicitly, his audience could never have taken him to be a proponent of revealed mysticism. And if he had been easily recognizable as a critic of mysticism, mystics might not have been as receptive to *Hayy*, a critique of mysticism wrapped subtly in the garb of mysticism.

Wherever the truth may lie on the metaphysical issue of creation or eternity, all readers can detect reasons for doubting the political prudence of mystics in the closing section of *Hayy*. Through his ignorance of his fellow human beings, Hayy is rendered unfit to rule a city. When he returns to civilization, he believes that he can convert all human beings to the truths he has discovered through his own inquiry. When he fails, he realizes that the divine Law is far wiser than he for responding to the fact that all human beings are not capable of the same knowledge and virtue. Rather than focusing exclusively on beliefs and experiences of God, the Law focuses on punishing unjust actions. Because mysticism treats solitude as natural, it leads toward either quietism or unrealistic hopes for politics—neither of which is desirable for political life. By the end of *Hayy* both Asal and Hayy retreat to Hayy's island, and many readers have unfortunately assumed that this indicates Ibn Tufayl's support for mysticism. Yet even this community of two attests that solitude need not be viewed as natural or a best way of life.

In addition to the timeless questions of political philosophy raised by our brief foray into medieval Islamic political philosophy, a series of historical questions come to the fore. Why is medieval Islamic political philosophy so short-lived (spanning roughly only the tenth to twelfth centuries)?

12. See Fakhry, *History of Islamic Philosophy*, 278. See many of the selections in Lawrence I. Conrad, ed., *The World of Ibn Tufayl* (Leiden: Brill, 1996), but cf. in that same collection Vincent J. Cornell's critique of this popular view: "Ḥayy in the Land of Absāl: Ibn Ṭufayl and Ṣūfism in the Western Maghrib during the Muwaḥḥid Era," 133–64. Compare the view of Lenn E. Goodman both in his translation and commentary, *Ibn Tufayl's Hayy Ibn Yaqzān*, updated ed. (Chicago: University of Chicago Press, 2009), and in his brief synoptic piece on Ibn Tufayl, in *History of Islamic Philosophy*, ed. Seyyed Hossein Nasr and Oliver Leaman, vol. 1 (London: Routledge, 1996), 313–29. Goodman argues that Ibn Tufayl sought to harmonize creation and eternity—in other words, to harmonize reason and revelation, as he argues Maimonides and Aquinas do (318–19). I believe that the history of philosophy shows that in any such harmonization, revelation, here mysticism, cannot help but become the senior partner.

13. See Alfarabi's *The Harmonization of the Two Opinions of the Two Sages: Plato the Divine and Aristotle* in *Alfarabi: The Political Writings; "Selected Aphorisms" and Other Texts*, ed. and trans. Charles E. Butterworth (Ithaca, NY: Cornell University Press, 2001), 115–67.

14. See Hillel Fradkin, "The Political Thought of Ibn Ṭufayl," in *The Political Aspects of Islamic Philosophy*, ed. Charles Butterworth, Harvard Middle East Monographs 27 (Cambridge, MA: Harvard University Press, 1992), 234–61, esp. 253.

15. See "Summary of the Tale," in selection 10 below, p. 112; Gauthier ed., 86.

And why does Alfarabi cast such an enormous shadow over its entire history? The first question has been the cause of much soul searching. Those with an animus against Islam jump readily to the conclusion that some defect in Islam must account for the brevity of its history. Others have suspected that some defect in the political philosophy of Islamic political philosophers must account for its demise. Still others have speculated that certain, possibly inevitable historical events, such as the invasion of the Mongols in 1258, led to the decline of this tradition. Some combination of these factors, rather than any single one, may come closer to the truth. Implicit in the first question is a comparison of medieval Islamic political philosophy with medieval Christian political philosophy. Why has the history of political philosophy been continuous in the Christian West, but not in the Islamic world? Yet one may overstate the extent of the continuity of political philosophy in the Christian West. The chasm between medieval and modern is sufficiently deep in the Christian West to raise doubts about whether the Christian political tradition should be viewed as continuous.

Regarding the second question, the disproportionate contribution of Alfarabi is not unlike that of Maimonides in the Jewish tradition of thought. The appearance of a towering figure at the beginning of a tradition can lead to the hasty conclusion that that whole tradition is (sadly) reducible to that one figure. Alfarabi's stature is magnified by his many works of political philosophy. It is also magnified by a crucial turn in the history of medieval Islamic political philosophy, initiated by Alghazali's searing attacks on the philosophers. Alghazali attacked Alfarabi and Avicenna (among others) for defending the eternity of the world and for offering a practical teaching that, he claimed, merely replicated the teachings of the Qur'an and Sufism. In the wake of this attack and in light of Alghazali's immense popularity and influence, medieval Islamic political philosophers adopted a far lower profile. Ibn Bajja and Ibn Tufayl wrote works focusing less on ranking political regimes than on the relation between the solitary and society. At times, these philosophers appear to be such staunch defenders of solitude that one might be tempted to suppose they advocate withdrawal. Indeed, in the case of Ibn Tufayl, some interpreters have inferred that he is a mystic rather than a philosopher—not to mention a *political* philosopher. A more nuanced understanding of the special challenge Alghazali posed to medieval Islamic political philosophy will enable us to see the tradition culminating in Averroes in a new light.

ONE

ALFARABI

The Enumeration of the Sciences

Translated by Charles E. Butterworth

Alfarabi (Abū Naṣr Muḥammad al-Fārābī, ca. 870–950) was born in Fārāb, a district straddling the Syr Darya (Jaxartes River) (in what is today southern Kazakhstan). He was the son of a military officer serving the Samanids. In one of the principal cities of the region, Bukhara, he studied the Islamic sciences, especially jurisprudence (*fiqh*), and music. He moved to Marv, where he studied logic with a Nestorian Christian monk, Yūḥannā Ibn Haylān. In his twenties, he followed his teacher to Baghdad where he continued to study logic and philosophy. His native language was probably Sogdian, an Iranian dialect; his teacher's principal language was Syriac. In Baghdad, Alfarabi cultivated his grasp of Arabic by studying it with the renowned philologist Ibn al-Sarrāj. He likely also attended lectures by the translator and Nestorian student of Aristotelian philosophy Mattā Ibn Yūnus. Alfarabi reports, and the historian al-Khaṭṭābī took it seriously enough to report, that Alfarabi traveled to Constantinople to study philosophy for eight years. He seems to have stopped along the way in Ḥarrān, one of the last way stations of the Athenian Academy, with his teacher Ibn Haylān. When Alfarabi returned to Baghdad, he became the renowned teacher and author known to us. He appears to have been compelled by political events to leave Baghdad for Damascus in 942, and for similar reasons a few years later to leave Damascus for Cairo. Meanwhile, Sayf al-Dawla, the prince of Aleppo, surrounded himself with learned men. Alfarabi traveled to Aleppo to join the prince a year before his death and was buried there with full honors.

Alfarabi was the first Muslim philosopher to head a "school" and to become known as a "teacher." He was acknowledged by subsequent Muslim philosophers as the true founder of philosophy in Islam, and Muslim historians of philosophy called him *the* Muslim philosopher and the "second Master" (after Aristotle). His commentaries on Aristotle's works established the latter's authority in logic, physics, and metaphysics. At the same time he recovered the significance of Plato and introduced him as the supreme authority on political philosophy and the investigation of human and divine laws.

In his preface to *The Enumeration of the Sciences,* Alfarabi states that his intention is to give an enumeration of the well-known sciences and make known the basic themes of each, its subdivisions, and the basic themes of each subdivision. This will be done in five chapters: (1) the science of language, (2) logic, (3) mathematics, (4) physics and metaphysics, and (5) political science, jurisprudence (*fiqh*), and dialectical theology (*kalām*).

Alfarabi concludes the preface by enumerating the uses of the book's content. It enables the student who wishes to study a particular science to know where to begin, what he will gain from his study, and so forth, and to be aware of what he is undertaking rather than plunging into it blindly. It enables one to compare the various sciences and learn which of them is more excellent, more useful, more precise, and so forth. It enables one to uncover the ignorance of whoever pretends to know a particular science; by asking about its subdivisions and basic themes, one will be able to expose a false claim. It enables one who knows a particular science to find out whether he knows all or only certain parts of it, and to what extent he knows it. Finally, it is useful to the educated man who intends to acquaint himself with only the basic themes of every science, and to the man who seeks to resemble the men of science and be considered one of them. Chapter 5 of *The Enumeration of the Sciences* contains the earliest comprehensive account of the basic themes and subdivisions of political philosophy in the Islamic tradition. As we will see when we consider the *Book of Religion,* that work is similar in broad outlines to the *Enumeration,* and the two beg to be compared with one another.

In the Arabic original, the *Enumeration* became an indispensable introduction to the study of the sciences and was freely copied and paraphrased by many encyclopedists and historians of the sciences. Judeo-Arabic authors used it in the Arabic original, and substantial extracts from it were translated into Hebrew by Shem Tov Ibn Falaquera (who lived in Spain and Provence, ca. 1223/8–1290) and by Kalonymos ben Kalonymos of Arles (in 1314). Dominicus Gundisalvi (perhaps in collaboration with John of Spain [Iohannes Avendauth, Ibn Dāwūd]) extracted about half of it in his composite work *De Scientiis* (middle of the twelfth century; printed in Paris, 1638); and Gerard of Cremona made a complete Latin translation from the Arabic in Toledo ca. 1175. The first modern edition of the Arabic was 'Uthmān Amīn's *Iḥṣā' al-'Ulūm li-al-Fārābī,* 2nd ed. (Cairo: Dār al-Fikr al-'Arabī, 1949). In the original *Sourcebook,* Fauzi M. Najjar provided the translation based on that edition. Later, Muhsin Mahdi corrected the section from Chapter 5 running through the first two paragraphs of Section 5 in his *Abū Naṣr al-Fārābī, Kitāb al-Milla wa Nuṣūṣ Ukhrā* (Beirut: Dar al-Mashriq, 1968), 67–76. Mahdi's corrections were based in part on Angel González Palencia's second edition of *Iḥṣā' al-'Ulūm-Catálogo de las ciencias* (Madrid: Consejo Superior de Investigaciones Científicas, 1953) and in part on a manuscript unknown to Amīn or Palencia—namely, Istanbul Köprülü Library, Mehmet, no. 1604.

CHAPTER FIVE: ON POLITICAL SCIENCE, THE SCIENCE OF JURISPRUDENCE, AND THE SCIENCE OF DIALECTICAL THEOLOGY

1. Political science investigates the sorts of voluntary actions and ways of life; the dispositions, moral habits, inclinations, and states of character from which those actions and ways of life come about; the goals for the sake of which they are performed; how they ought to exist in a human being; how to order them in him according to the manner they ought to exist in him; and the way to preserve them for him.

It distinguishes among the goals for the sake of which the actions are performed and the ways of life practiced.

It explains that some of them are truly happiness and that some are presumed to be happiness without being so and that it is not possible for the one which is truly happiness to come to be in this life, but rather in a life after this one, which is the next life, whereas what is presumed to be happiness—like affluence, honor, and pleasures—is what is set down as goals only for this life.

It distinguishes the actions and the ways of life.

It explains that the ones through which what is truly happiness is obtained are the goods, the noble actions, and the virtues; that the rest are evils, base things, and imperfections; and that the way they are to exist in a human being is for the virtuous actions and ways of life [103] to be distributed in cities and nations in an orderly manner and to be practiced in common.

It explains that those do not come about except by means of a rulership that establishes those actions, ways of life, states of character, dispositions, and moral habits in cities and nations and strives to preserve them for the citizens[1] so that they do not pass away; that this rulership does not come about except by a craft and a disposition that bring about the actions for establishing them among the citizens[2] and the actions for preserving for them what has been established among them. This is the kingly craft, or kingship, or whatever a human being wants to call it; and the regime is the work of this craft.[3] And [it explains] that rulership is of two kinds: (a) A rulership that establishes the voluntary actions, ways of life, and dispositions such that by them one obtains what is truly happiness; it is virtuous rulership, and the cities and nations subject to this rulership are the virtuous cities and nations. (b) And a rulership that establishes in cities and nations the actions and states of character by which one obtains what is presumed to be happiness without being such, namely, ignorant rulership. This rulership admits of several divisions, each one of which is called by the purpose it is intent upon and pursues; thus there are as many of them as there are things this rulership seeks as goals and purposes. If it seeks to acquire wealth, it is called a vile rulership; if honor, it is called timocracy; and if something other than these two, it is called by the name of that goal it has.

It explains that the virtuous kingly craft is composed of two faculties. One of these is the faculty for [104] universal rules. The other is the faculty a human being acquires through lengthy involvement in civic deeds, carrying out actions with respect to individuals and persons in particular cities, and skill in them through experience and long observation, as it is with medicine. Indeed, a physician becomes a perfect healer only by means of two faculties. One is the faculty for the universals and the rules he acquires from medical books. The other is the faculty he attains by lengthy involvement in practicing medicine on the sick and by skill in it from long experience with, and observation of, individual bodies. By means of this faculty the physician is able to determine the medicaments and cure with respect to each body in each circumstance. Similarly, the kingly craft is able to determine the actions with respect to each occurrence, each circumstance, and each city in each moment only by means of this faculty, which is experience.

2. Political philosophy is limited—in what it investigates of the voluntary actions, ways of life, and dispositions, and in the rest of what it investigates—to universal rules. It gives patterns for determining them with respect to each circumstance and each moment; how, by what, and to what extent they are to be determined. Then it leaves them undetermined, because determining in actuality belongs to a faculty other than this science and is such as to be added to it. Moreover, the circumstances and occurrences with respect to which determination takes place are indefinite and without limitation.

3. This science has two parts.

One part comprises bringing about cognizance of[4] what happiness is; distinguishing between what it truly is and what it is presumed to be; enumerating the universal voluntary actions, ways of life, moral habits, and states of character that are such as to be distributed in cities and nations; and distinguishing the virtuous ones from the non-virtuous ones.

Another part comprises the way of ordering the virtuous states of character and ways of life in the cities and nations; bringing about cognizance of the royal actions by which the virtuous ways of life and actions are established [105] and ordered among the inhabitants of the cities and of the actions by which what has been ordered and established among them is preserved.

Then it enumerates the non-virtuous sorts of kingly crafts, how many they are and what each one is. It enumerates the actions each one of them performs and what ways of life and dispositions each one of them seeks to establish in the cities and nations so as to obtain its purpose from the inhabitants of the cities and nations under its rulership. It explains that all of those actions, ways of life, and dispositions are like sicknesses for the virtuous cities. The actions that particularly characterize these kingly crafts and their ways of life are like sicknesses for the virtuous kingly craft. The ways of life and dispositions that particularly characterize their cities are like sicknesses for the virtuous cities.

Then it enumerates how many reasons and tendencies there are because of which the virtuous

1. Literally, "for them" (*ʿalaihim*).

2. Literally, "among them" (*fīhim*).

3. Or, alternatively, "and politics is the activity of this craft" (*wa al-siyāsa hiya fīʾl hādhihī al-mihna*). The term *siyāsa* could just as well mean "politics" as "regime."

4. Here and in what follows, cognates of "cognizance" are used to render forms of the verb *ʿarafa*. This is a matter of making citizens aware of something rather than providing them with scientific knowledge (*ʿilm*) of something.

rulerships and the ways of life of virtuous cities are in danger of being transformed into ignorant ways of life and dispositions. Along with them, it enumerates the sorts of actions by which virtuous cities and rulerships are restrained lest they become corrupted and transformed into non-virtuous ones. It also enumerates ways of ordering, tricks, and things to be used to restore them to what they were when they have been transformed into ignorant ones.

Then it explains the number of things that constitute the virtuous kingly craft; [106] among them are the theoretical and practical sciences, and added to them is the faculty attained through experience arising from long involvement in actions with respect to cities and nations, namely, the aptitude for excellently inferring the stipulations by which the actions, ways of life, and dispositions are determined with respect to each community, each city, or each nation in accordance with each circumstance and each occurrence. It explains that the virtuous city remains virtuous and is not transformed only when its kings succeed one another through time and have the very same qualifications[5] so that the successor has the same attributes and qualifications as his predecessor and their succession is without interruption or break. It brings about cognizance of what ought to be done so that there is no interruption in the succession of kings. It explains which natural qualifications and attributes ought to be sought in the sons of the kings and in others so that the one in whom they are found will qualify for kingship after the one who is now king. It explains how the one in whom these natural qualifications are found is to be raised and in what way he ought to be instructed so that he attains the kingly craft and becomes a complete king.

It explains, moreover, that those whose rulership is ignorant ought not to be called kings at all and that they have no need of either theoretical or practical philosophy in any of their circumstances, activities, or ways of ordering; rather, each one of them can achieve his purpose with respect to the city or nation under his rulership by means of the experiential faculty he attains by pursuing the kind of actions with which he obtains what he is intent upon and arrives at the good that is his purpose, [107] providing he happens to possess a deceitful faculty and genius good for inferring the actions he needs for obtaining the good he is intent upon—pleasure, honor, or whatever—and to that is added his being good at imitating those kings who preceded him and were intent upon the same thing as he.

4. The art of jurisprudence is that by which a human being is able to infer, from the things the lawgiver declared specifically and determinately, the determination of each of the things he did not specifically declare. And he is able to aspire to a verification of that on the basis of the purpose of the lawgiver in the religion (*al-milla*) he legislated with respect to the nation for which it was legislated.

Every religion has opinions and actions. The opinions are like the opinions that are legislated with respect to God, how He is to be described, the world, and other things. The actions are like the actions by which God is praised and the actions by which there are mutual dealings in cities. Therefore the science of jurisprudence has two parts: a part with respect to opinions and a part with respect to actions.

5. The art of dialectical theology is a disposition by which a human being is able to defend the specific opinions and actions [108] that the founder of the religion declared and to refute by arguments whatever opposes it. This art is also divided into two parts: a part with respect to opinions and a part with respect to actions.

It is different from jurisprudence in that the jurist takes the opinions and actions declared by the founder of the religion as given and sets them down as fundamentals from which he infers the things that necessarily follow from them, whereas the dialectical theologian defends the things the jurist uses as fundamentals without inferring other things from them. If it happens that there is a certain human being who has the ability to do both matters, he is a jurist and a dialectical theologian. He defends them insofar as he is a dialectical theologian, and he infers them insofar as he is a jurist.[6]

As for the ways and opinions by which religions are to be defended, (a) one group of dialectical theologians is of the opinion they should

5. Literally, here and in what follows, "stipulations" (*sharā'iṭ*).

6. This marks the end of the Arabic text edited by Muhsin Mahdi. For what follows, the translation is based on 'Uthmān Amīn's edition.

defend religions by saying that the opinions of religions and all that is posited in them are not such as to be examined by opinions, deliberation, or human intellects. For they are of a higher order insofar as they are taken from divine revelation and because there are divine secrets in them that human intellects are too weak to perceive and do not reach. Moreover, a human being is such that by revelation religions provide him with what he is not wont [109] to perceive by his intellect and what his intellect is too languid [to grasp]. Otherwise, were revelation to provide a human being only with what he knew and could perceive by his intellect if he considered it, there would be no sense to, or benefit from, it. If it were thus, people would trust in their intellects and they would have no need for prophecy or revelation. But that is not what is done with them. Therefore, with respect to the sciences, religions ought to provide what our intellects are not able to perceive. Not only this, but also what our intellects object to; for whatever we more strongly object to is more likely to be of greater benefit. That is because what religions bring forth that intellects object to and fancies find repugnant is not objectionable or absurd in truth, but is valid according to the divine intellects.

If a human being were to reach the end of perfection with respect to humanity, his position with respect to those who have divine intellects would be that of a child, an adolescent, and an immature youth with respect to a perfect human being. Many children and immature youths object to many things by their intellects that are not objectionable or impossible in truth, although to them they happen to be impossible. And that is like the position of the one at the end of the perfection of the human intellect with respect to the divine intellects. Before being educated and trained, a human being objects to many things, [110] finds them repugnant, and imagines that they are impossible. When he is educated by means of the sciences and given training in experiments, those presumptions disappear: the things that were impossible for him are transformed and become necessary, and he now comes to wonder about the opposite of what he formerly used to wonder about. Similarly, it is not impossible that the human being who is perfect in humanity may object to[7] things and imagine they are not possible without them being like that in truth.

So for these reasons,[8] these [dialectical theologians] were of the opinion that religions are to be set down as valid. Indeed, he who brought us revelation from God, may He be exalted, is truthful; it is not permissible that he ever have lied. That he is like this can be validated in one of two ways: either by the miracles he performs[9] or that appear through his hands, or by the testimonies of those truthful ones who preceded him whose statements about his truthfulness and his standing with respect to God, may He be exalted and magnified, are accepted, or by both together. Once we validate his truthfulness and that it is not permissible for him ever to have lied in these ways, there ought to remain no room for intellecting, consideration, deliberation, or reflection with respect to what he says. So by these and similar [ways], these [dialectical theologians] were of the opinion that they would defend religions.

(b) Another group is of the opinion that they defend religion by first setting forth everything stated explicitly by the founder of the religion in the very utterances he expressed. Then they pursue the sense-perceptible, generally accepted, and intelligible things. When they find one of these things or their consequences, [111] however remote, testifying to what is in the religion, they defend it by means of that thing. When they find one contradicting[10] anything in the religion, and they are able to interpret—even by a very remote interpretation—the utterance by which the founder of the religion expressed it in a way agreeing with that contradiction, they interpret it so. If that is not possible for them, yet it is possible to treat the contradiction as spurious or construe it so as to agree with what is in the religion, they do so. If the testimony of the generally accepted things is opposed to that of the sense-perceptible things, as when the sense-perceptible things or their consequences require one thing and the generally accepted things or their consequences require its opposite, they look to the one that has the most powerful testimony for what is in the religion and take it while rejecting the other and treating it as spurious. If it is not possible to construe the utterance in the religion so as to agree with one of these,

7. Reading *lā yamtani' an yastankir* with the Madrid Escurial MS.

8. Reading *al-asbāb* for sense, instead of *al-ashyā'* with Amīn and the other MSS.

9. Reading *ya'maluhā* with the Madrid Escurial MS.

10. Correcting *mutāqiḍan* (which has no meaning) in the text to *munāqiḍan*.

nor to construe one of these so as to agree with the religion, and it is not possible to reject or treat as spurious any of the sense-perceptible, generally accepted, or intellected things that are opposed to anything in it, they are then of the opinion that the thing may be defended by it being said to be true because it was reported by one for whom it is impermissible to have ever lied or erred. And these [dialectical theologians] say about this part of the religion what those first ones said about all of it. So these [dialectical theologians] are of the opinion that they defend religions in this way.

[112] A group of these [dialectical theologians] are of the opinion that they may defend things like this—that is, ones imagined to be repulsive—by pursuing the rest of the religions and finding what is repulsive in them. If a follower of those religions wants to blame something in the religion of these [dialectical theologians], they confront him with the repulsive things in his religion[11] and thereby ward him away from their religion.

Others came to the opinion that the arguments they brought forth to defend things like this were not sufficient to validate them completely so that their adversary's silence would be due to his holding them valid, rather than to his being incapable of countering them by argument. So they were obliged to use things that would compel him to refrain from encounter either from shame and being outmaneuvered or from fear of something abhorrent befalling him.

With others, when the validity of their religion was such they had no doubts about it, [113] they were of the opinion that they would defend it before others, make it attractive, remove suspicion from it, and ward their adversaries away from it by any chance thing. They did not care whether they used falsehood, deceit, slander, or disdain, for they were of the opinion that one of two [kinds of] men would oppose their religion. He would either be an enemy, and it is permissible to use falsehood and deceit to warn him off and conquer him, as is the case in struggle (*al-jihād*) and warfare (*al-ḥarb*). Or he would not be an enemy but one who, due to the weakness of his intellect and discernment, is ignorant of the good fortune for him from this religion; and it is permissible to bring a human being to his good fortune by means of falsehood and deceit, just as that is done with women and children.

11. Literally, "in the religion of those" (*fī milla ulā'ika*)—that is, "of those other people."

TWO

ALFARABI

The Book of Religion

Translated by Charles E. Butterworth

The Book of Religion parallels Chapter 5 of *The Enumeration of the Sciences* to a striking degree. Indeed, the casual reader might fail to detect any differences. Although the differences are subtle, they are ultimately more striking than the similarities. The *Enumeration* proceeded in the following order: political science 1, political science 2, jurisprudence, and dialectical theology. In contrast, *The Book of Religion* proceeds in the following order: an account of virtuous religion and its relation to philosophy (1–5), dialectic (6; cf. dialectical theology in *Enumeration*), jurisprudence (7–10), political science 1 (11–15.1), political science 2 (15.2–18), and what Charles Butterworth, citing Mahdi, has called "a practical or political divine science or theology that keeps an eye on the theoretical sciences and another eye on human ends" (19–27).[1] *The Book of Religion* not only reverses the order in which Alfarabi treats political science and the religious sciences, jurisprudence and dialectical theology in the *Enumeration,* but it also reverses the usual order in which Alfarabi treats politics and metaphysics or divine science (compare *Political Regime* and the *Principles of the Opinions of the Inhabitants of the Virtuous City*). The most obvious question that such a reversal of order raises is, What should we think of as the ground of what? Is metaphysics the ground of politics, as the *Virtuous City* would lead us to believe? In *The Book of Religion,* jurisprudence and dialectical theology are tethered to or shaped by the virtuous religion that Alfarabi derives from philosophy. In contrast, in the *Enumeration,* Alfarabi presented jurisprudence and dialectical theology as they came down to him, as autonomous religious sciences likely at odds with either or both political sciences presented therein. As Muhsin Mahdi and Charles Butterworth have argued, *The Book of Religion* solves problems or questions that the *Enumeration* is intended to pose.

The following is a translation of the critical Arabic edition by Muhsin Mahdi in *Abū Naṣr al-Fārābī, Kitāb al-Milla wa Nuṣūṣ Ukhrā* (Beirut: Dar al-Mashriq, 1968), 41–66. The bracketed numbers refer to the page numbers in that edition.

[43] 1. Religion is opinions and actions, determined and restricted with stipulations and

1. Muhsin S. Mahdi, "Science, Philosophy, and Religion," in *Alfarabi and the Foundation of Islamic Political Philosophy* (Chicago: University of Chicago Press, 2001), 96; qtd. in Butterworth's translation of *The Book of Religion,* 108 n. 22.

prescribed for a community by their first ruler,[2] who seeks to obtain through their practicing it a specific purpose with respect to them or by means of them.

The community may be a tribe, a city or district, a great nation, or many nations.

If the first ruler is virtuous and his rulership truly virtuous, then in what he prescribes he seeks only to obtain, for himself and for everyone under his rulership the ultimate happiness that is truly happiness; and that religion will be virtuous religion. If his rulership is ignorant,[3] then in what he prescribes he seeks only to obtain, for himself by means of them, one of the ignorant goods—either necessary good, that is, health and bodily well-being; or wealth; or pleasure; or honor and glory; or conquest—to win that good, be happy with it to the exclusion of them, and make those under his rulership tools he uses to arrive at his purpose and to retain in his possession. Or he seeks to obtain this good for them to the exclusion of himself, or both for himself and them; these two are the most virtuous of the ignorant rulers. If that rulership of his is errant, in that he presumes himself to have virtue and wisdom and those under his rulership presume and believe that of him without him being like that [in fact], then he seeks that [44] he and those under his rulership obtain something presumed to be ultimate happiness without it being truly so. If his rulership is deceptive, in that he purposely strives for that[4] without those under his rulership noticing it, then the people under his rulership believe and presume that he has virtue and wisdom; on the surface he seeks in what he prescribes that he and they obtain ultimate happiness, whereas[5] underneath it is that he obtain one of the ignorant goods by means of them.

Now the craft of the virtuous first ruler is kingly and joined with revelation (*al-waḥy*) from God. Indeed, he determines the actions and opinions in the virtuous religion by means of revelation. This occurs in one or both of two ways: one is that they are all revealed to him as determined; the second is that he determines them by means of the faculty he acquires from revelation and from the Revealer, may He be exalted, so that the stipulations with which he determines the virtuous opinions and actions are disclosed to him by means of it. Or some come about in the first way and some in the second way. It has already been explained in theoretical science how the revelation of God, may He be exalted, to the human being receiving the revelation comes about and how the faculty acquired from revelation and from the Revealer occurs in a human being.

2. Some of the opinions in virtuous religion are about theoretical things and some about voluntary things.

Among the theoretical are those that describe God, may He be exalted. Then there are some that describe the spiritual beings, their ranks in themselves, their stations in relation to God, may He be exalted, and what each one of them does. Then there are some about the coming into being of the world, as well as some that describe the world, its parts, and the ranks of its parts; how [45] the primary bodies were generated and that some of the primary bodies are the sources of all the other bodies that are gradually generated and pass away; how all the other bodies are generated from the ones that are the sources of bodies and the ranks of these; how the things the world encompasses are linked together and organized and that whatever occurs with respect to them is just and has no injustice; and how each one of them is related to God, may He be exalted, and to the spiritual beings. Then there are some about the coming into being of the human being and soul occurring in him, as well as about the intellect, its rank in the world, and its station in relation to God and the spiritual beings.[6] Then there are some that describe what prophecy is and what revelation is like and how it comes into being. Then there are some that describe death and the afterlife and, with respect to the afterlife, the happiness to which the most virtuous and the righteous proceed and the misery to which the most depraved and the profligate proceed.

Among the second type of opinions are those that describe the prophets, the most virtuous

2. A "first ruler" (*ra'īs awwal*) may or may not be first in time but is always first in rank. That is, he may be the supreme ruler who founds the religion, or the one who succeeds the founder but has full powers as a lawgiver; see below, secs. 7–9, 14b, and 18.

3. See the discussion of the different kinds of ignorant cities below in Alfarabi's *Political Regime* 93–119.

4. As becomes clear at the end of this sentence, this refers to the deceptive ruler striving to "obtain one of the ignorant goods."

5. Reading *ammā* for *immā*, "either."

6. If the pronoun refers to "human being" rather than "intellect," the sentence would read: "Then there are some about the coming into being of the human being and soul and intellect occurring in him, his rank in the world, and his station in relation to God and the spiritual beings."

kings, the righteous rulers, and the leaders of the right way and of truth who succeeded one another in former times; and those that relate what they had in common, what good actions were characteristic of each one, and where their souls and the souls of those who followed and emulated them in cities and nations ended up in the afterlife. There are those that describe the most depraved kings, the profligate rulers exercising authority over the inhabitants of ignorant communities, and the leaders of the errant way who existed in former times; and those that relate what they had in common, what evil actions were characteristic of each one, and where their souls and the souls of those who followed and emulated them in cities and nations ended up in the afterlife. There are those that describe the most virtuous kings, righteous men, and leaders of truth in the present time; and those that mention what they have in common with those who went before and what good actions are characteristic of them. There are those that describe the profligate rulers, the leaders of the errant way, and the inhabitants of ignorant communities in the present time; and those that relate what they have in common with those who went before, what evil actions are characteristic of them, and where their souls will end up in the afterlife.

The descriptions of the things comprised by the opinions of religion ought to be such as to bring the citizens to imagine everything in the city—kings, rulers, and servants; their ranks, the way they are linked together, and the way some yield to others; and everything prescribed to them—so that what is described will be likenesses the citizens will follow in their ranks and actions.

These, then, are the opinions that are in religion. [46]

3. As for actions, they are, first of all, the actions and speeches by which God is praised and extolled. Then there are those that praise the spiritual beings and the angels. Then there are those that praise the prophets, the most virtuous kings, the righteous rulers, and the leaders of the right way who have gone before. Then there are those that blame the most depraved kings, the profligate[7] rulers, and the leaders of the errant way who went before and that censure their activities. Then there are those that praise the most virtuous kings, the righteous rulers, and the leaders of the right way in this time and that blame those of this time who are their opposites.

Then, after all this, are determining the actions by which the mutual dealings of the inhabitants of the cities are regulated—either regarding what a human being ought to do with respect to himself[8] or regarding how he ought to deal with others—and bringing about cognizance[9] of what justice is with respect to each particular instance of these actions.

This, then, is the sum of what virtuous religion comprises.

4. "Religion" (*milla*) and "creed" (*dīn*) are almost synonymous, as are "law" (*sharīʿa*)[10] and "tradition" (*sunna*). Most often, the latter two signify and apply to the determined actions in the two parts of religion. It may be possible, as well, for the determined opinions to be called "law," so that "law," "religion," and "creed" would be synonymous, given that religion consists of two parts: specifying opinions and determining actions.

The first type of opinions specified in religion is twofold: an opinion designated by its proper name, which customarily signifies it itself; or an opinion designated by the name of what is similar to it.[11] Thus the determined opinions in the virtuous religion are either the truth or a likeness of the truth. In general, truth is what a human being ascertains, either by himself[12] by means of primary knowledge, or by demonstration. Now any religion in which the first type of opinions does not comprise what a human being can ascertain either from himself[13] or by demonstration and in which there is no likeness of anything he can

7. Reading *al-fajār* with Dunlop, instead of *al-fujjār* with Mahdi.

8. Or, alternatively, "by himself" (*bi-nafsih*).

9. "Cognizance" derives from the second form of *ʿarafa*. Alfarabi's point here concerns making the inhabitants of the city aware of, or acquainting them with, something, rather than providing them with knowledge or science about it.

10. Throughout this translation, *sharīʿa* is rendered as "law," the verb *sharraʿa* as "legislate," and the phrase *wāḍiʿ al-sharīʿa* as "lawgiver." The term *nāmūs* does not occur in this work. For *dīn*, see sec. 7 of the *Philosophy of Plato* in *Alfarabi: The Political Writings; The Philosophy of Plato and Aristotle,* trans. Muhsin Mahdi (New York: Free Press of Glencoe, 1962; rev. ed., Ithaca, NY: Cornell University Press, 1969, 2002). The term *sunna* usually refers to the practices that have come to be traditionally accepted within the religion, because they can be traced back to something the Prophet said or did.

11. Alfarabi is referring to the first kind of opinions set forth in sec. 2, those about theoretical things. When speaking of the way humans are brought into being, it is possible to use the proper name for what occurs. When speaking about God or the spiritual beings, similes are used.

12. Or, alternatively, "directly" (*bi-nafsih*).

13. Or, alternatively, "immediately" (*min dhātih*).

ascertain in one of these two ways is an errant religion.

5. Thus, virtuous religion is similar to philosophy. Just as philosophy is partly theoretical and partly practical, so it is with religion: the calculative theoretical part is what a human being is not able to do when he knows it, [47] whereas the practical part is what a human being is able to do when he knows it. The practical things in religion are those whose universals are in practical philosophy. That is because the practical things in religion are those universals made determinate by stipulations restricting them, and what is restricted by stipulations is more particular than what is pronounced unqualifiedly without stipulations: for instance, our saying "the human being who is writing" is more particular than our saying "the human being." Therefore, all virtuous laws are subordinate to the universals of practical philosophy. The theoretical opinions that are in religion have their demonstrative proofs in theoretical philosophy and are taken in religion without demonstrative proofs.

Therefore, the two parts of which religion consists are subordinate to philosophy. For something is said to be a part of a science or to be subordinate to a science in one of two ways: Either the demonstrative proofs of what is assumed in it without demonstrative proofs occur in that science, or the science comprising the universals is the one that gives the reasons for the particulars subordinate to it. The practical part of philosophy is, therefore, the one that gives the reasons for the stipulations by which actions are made determinate: that for the sake of which they were stipulated and the purpose intended to be obtained by means of those stipulations. Further, if to know something is to know it demonstratively, then this part of philosophy is the one that gives the demonstrative proof for the determined actions that are in virtuous religion. And since it is the theoretical part of philosophy that gives demonstrative proofs for the theoretical part of religion, it is philosophy, then, that gives the demonstrative proofs of what virtuous religion encompasses. Therefore, the kingly craft responsible for what the virtuous religion consists of is subordinate to philosophy.

6. Dialectic yields strong presumption about all or most of what demonstrative proofs yield certainty about, and rhetoric persuades about most of what is not such as to be proven by demonstration or looked into by dialectic. Moreover, virtuous religion is not only for philosophers or only for someone of such a station as to understand what is spoken about only in a philosophic manner. Rather, most people who are taught the opinions of religion and instructed in them and brought to accept its actions are not of such a station—and that is [48] either due to nature or because they are occupied with other things. Yet they are not people who fail to understand generally accepted or persuasive things. For that reason, both dialectic and rhetoric are of major value for verifying the opinions of religion for the citizens and for defending, supporting, and establishing those opinions in their souls, as well as for defending those opinions when someone appears who desires to deceive the followers of the religion by means of argument, lead them into error, and contend against the religion.

7. It may happen accidentally that the first ruler does not determine all of the actions and give an exhaustive account of them, but determines most of them; and with some of those he does determine, it may happen that he does not give an exhaustive account of all their stipulations. On the contrary, for diverse reasons that occur, many actions such as to be determined may remain without determination: death may overtake him and carry him away before he has covered all of them; necessary occupations, such as wars (*ḥurūb*) and other things, may keep him from it; or it may be that he only determines actions for each incident and each occurrence he observes or is asked about, at which time he determines, legislates, and establishes a tradition regarding what ought to be done for that kind of incident. Since not everything that can occur does occur in his time or in his country, many things remain that could occur in another time or in another country, each needing a specifically determined action, [49] and he will have legislated nothing about them. Or else he devotes himself to those actions he presumes or knows to be fundamental, from which someone else can extrapolate the remaining ones: he legislates about the manner and amount of what ought to be done with these and leaves the rest, knowing that it will be possible for someone else to extrapolate them by adopting his intention and following in his footsteps. Or he decides to begin with legislating and determining the actions that are of the greatest efficacy, use, value, and benefit, so that the city will cohere and its affairs will be linked and organized: he legislates about those things alone and leaves the rest for a moment of leisure or so that someone else—a contemporary

or a successor—can extrapolate them by following in his footsteps.

8. If, after his death, someone succeeds him who is like him in all respects, then the successor will be the one who determines what the first did not determine. And not only this, but it is also up to him to alter much of what the first had legislated and to determine it in another way, when he knows that this is best for his time—not because the first erred, but because the first made a determination according to what was best for his time and this one makes a determination according to what is best subsequent to the time of the first, this being the kind of thing the first would alter also, were he to observe it. It is the same if the second is followed by a third [50] who is like the second in all respects, and the third by a fourth: it is up to the one who comes after to determine, on his own, what he does not find determined and to alter what his predecessor determined; for, were his predecessor still here, he too would alter what the one who came after altered.

9. Now if one of those righteous leaders who are really kings should pass away and not be succeeded by one who is like him in all respects, it will be necessary—concerning everything done in the cities under the rulership of the predecessor—for the successor to follow in the footsteps of the predecessor with respect to what he determines; he should not do anything differently nor make any alteration, but should let everything the predecessor determined remain the way it was and look into anything that needs to be given a determination and was not declared by the predecessor, inferring and extrapolating it from the things the first determined by declaring them.

Thus, the art of jurisprudence would then be requisite. It enables a human being to make a sound determination of each thing the lawgiver did not declare specifically by extrapolating it or inferring it from the things he determined by declaring them and to verify that on the basis of the lawgiver's purpose in the religion he legislated with respect to the nation for which it was legislated. Now this verification is not possible unless his belief in the opinions of that religion is correct and he possesses the virtues that are virtues in that religion. Whoever is like that is a jurist.

10. Since a determination takes place with respect to two things—opinions and actions—the art of jurisprudence must have two parts: a part concerning opinions and a part concerning actions.

Thus, the jurist concerned with [51] actions must have exhaustive knowledge of all the actions the lawgiver has declared specifically. Declaration sometimes takes place through a statement and sometimes through an action of the lawgiver, his action taking the place of saying that a particular thing ought to be done in such and such a way. In addition, the jurist must be cognizant of the laws legislated by the first ruler for a certain moment and then replaced with others he retained so that in his own time the jurist follows in the traces of the latter ones, not the former. The jurist must further be cognizant of the language spoken by the first ruler; of the customary ways in which the people of his time used their language; and of what was used in it to signify something metaphorically, while in reality being the name of something else, so that he does not presume that when the name of one thing was used metaphorically for another thing, the first thing was meant, or presume this thing to have been the other thing. In addition, the jurist must be quite clever at recognizing the meaning intended by an equivocal name in the context in which it is used, as well as at recognizing equivocalness in speech. Also, he must be quite clever at recognizing when an expression is used in an unqualified sense, whereas the intention of the speaker is more restricted; at recognizing when an expression, taken literally, has a restricted meaning, whereas the intention of the speaker is more general; and at recognizing when an expression is used in a restricted, or general, or unqualified sense, whereas the intention of the speaker is what it means literally. He must be cognizant of what is generally accepted and what is customary. In addition, he must have a capacity for grasping similarities and differences in things, as well as a capacity for distinguishing what necessarily follows something from what does not. This comes about through a good natural disposition and through familiarity with the art. He must find out the lawgiver's utterances for everything he legislated in speech and his actions for whatever he legislated by doing it rather than by uttering it: by observing and listening to him, if he is [52] his contemporary and companion, or by having recourse to reports about him; and reports about him are either generally accepted or persuasive, each of these being either written or unwritten.

The jurist concerned with the opinions determined in religion ought already to know what the jurist concerned with practices knows.

Jurisprudence about the practical matters of religion therefore comprises only things that are particulars of the universals encompassed by political science; it is, therefore, a part of political science and subordinate to practical philosophy. And jurisprudence about the [theoretical or] scientific matters of religion comprises either particulars of the universals encompassed by theoretical philosophy or those that are likenesses of things subordinate to theoretical philosophy; it is, therefore, a part of theoretical philosophy and subordinate to it, whereas theoretical science is the source.

11. Political science investigates happiness first of all. It brings about cognizance that happiness is of two types: happiness presumed to be happiness without being such, and happiness that is truly happiness. The latter is the one sought for its own sake; at no time is it sought in order to obtain something else by it; indeed, all other things are sought in order to obtain this one, and when it is obtained, the search is given up; it does not come about in this life, but rather in the next life which is after this one; and it is called ultimate happiness. Examples of what is presumed to be happiness but is not such are affluence, pleasures,[14] honor and being glorified, or anything else sought and acquired in this life that the multitude calls goods. [53]

12. Then it investigates the voluntary actions, ways of life, moral habits, states of character, and dispositions until it gives an exhaustive account of all of them and covers them in detail.

13. Then it explains that these cannot all be found in one human being nor be done by one human being, but can be done and actually manifest themselves only by being distributed among an association of people.

It explains that when they are distributed among an association of people, the one charged with one kind cannot undertake or do it unless another person assists him by undertaking the kind the latter has been charged with; nor can the latter undertake what he has been charged with unless a third person assists him by undertaking the kind he has been charged with. Moreover, it is not impossible to find a person who cannot undertake the task he has been charged with unless assisted by an association of people, each one of whom undertakes the kind of thing he has been charged with: for example, someone charged with undertaking agriculture cannot complete his task unless a carpenter assists him by preparing wood for the plow, a blacksmith by preparing steel for the plow, and a cowherd by preparing oxen for the yoke.

Thus it explains that it is not possible to reach the purpose of voluntary actions and dispositions, unless they[15] are distributed among a very large association of people—either each assigned to a single individual in the association or each assigned to a single group in the association—so that the groups in the association cooperate, through the actions and dispositions in each, to perfect the purpose of the whole association in the same way that the organs of a human being cooperate, through the capacities in each, to perfect the purpose of the whole body.

[It explains] that it is therefore necessary for the association of people to live close together in a single place. And it enumerates the sorts of associations of people that live close together in a single place: there is a civic association, a national association, and others. [54]

14. Then it distinguishes the ways of life, moral habits, and dispositions that, when practiced in cities or nations, make their dwellings prosper and their inhabitants obtain goods in this life here below, and ultimate happiness in the afterlife; and it sets them apart from those not like that. Only those voluntary actions, ways of life, moral habits, states of character, and dispositions by which ultimate happiness is attained are virtuous; only they are goods; and they are the ones that are truly noble. Any other actions and dispositions are presumed to be goods, virtues, or noble, but are not such—on the contrary, they are truly evils.

14a. It explains that the things such as to be distributed in a city, in cities, in a nation, or in nations so as to be practiced in common are only brought about by means of a rulership that establishes those actions and dispositions in the city or nation and strives to preserve them for the people so that they do not disappear or become extinct. The rulership by which those ways of life and dispositions are established in a city or nation and preserved for the people cannot come about except by a craft, art, disposition, or faculty that gives rise to the actions by which they are established and preserved. This craft is the craft of the king and the kingly craft, or whatever a human being wants to call it instead of

14. Reading *aw al-ladhdhāt* with Leiden MS Or. 1002, rather than *wa al-ladhdhāt* with Mahdi.

15. Literally, "their kinds" or "kinds of them" (*anwāʿuhā*).

"kingly." And the regime is the work of this craft; that is, it performs the actions by which those ways of life and those dispositions are established in a city or nation and preserved for the people. This craft consists of cognizance of all the actions with which one goes about establishing, first, and preserving afterwards.

The rulership that establishes in a city or nation and preserves for the people the ways of life and dispositions [55] by means of which ultimate happiness is obtained is virtuous rulership. The kingly craft by means of which this rulership comes about is the virtuous kingly craft. The regime that comes into being through this craft is the virtuous regime. The city or nation subject to this regime is the virtuous city and the virtuous nation. The human being who is a part of this city or nation is the virtuous human being.

The rulership, the kingly craft, and the regime that do not aim at obtaining the ultimate happiness that is truly happiness but rather aim at attaining one of the goods particularly characteristic of this world here below—that is, the ones the multitude presumes to be goods—are not virtuous; on the contrary, they are called ignorant rulership, ignorant regime, and ignorant craft: indeed, they are not called "kingly" because, according to the Ancients, kingship was what came about through virtuous kingly craft. The city or the nation subject to the actions and dispositions established in it by the ignorant rulership is called the ignorant city or nation. The human being who is part of this city is called an ignorant human being.[16] This rulership and these cities and nations are divided in several ways; each one of them is called by the name of the purpose it is intent upon among the things presumed to be good: either pleasures, honors, wealth, or something else.

Now it is not impossible for a human being who is part of the virtuous city to be living [56] in an ignorant city, voluntarily or involuntarily. That human being is a part foreign to that city, and he may be likened to an animal that happens to have the legs of an animal belonging to an inferior species. Similarly, when someone who is part of an ignorant city lives in a virtuous city, he may be likened to an animal that has the head of an animal belonging to a superior species.[17] For this reason, the most virtuous persons, forced to dwell in ignorant cities due to the non-existence of the virtuous city, need to migrate to the virtuous city, if it happens to come into being at a certain moment.

14b. [Political science explains] that virtuous rulership is of two types: a first rulership and a rulership dependent on it. First rulership is the one that first establishes the virtuous ways of life and dispositions in the city or nation without their having existed among the people before that, and it converts them from the ignorant ways of life to the virtuous ways of life. The person undertaking this rulership is the first ruler.

The rulership dependent on the first is the one that follows in the steps of the first rulership with regard to its actions. The one who undertakes this rulership is called ruler of the tradition and king of the tradition. His rulership is based on an existing tradition.

The first virtuous kingly craft consists of cognizance of all the actions that facilitate establishing the virtuous ways of life and dispositions in cities and nations, preserving them for the people, and guarding and keeping them from the inroad of something from the ignorant ways of life—all of those being sicknesses that befall the virtuous cities. In this sense, it is like the medical craft; for the latter consists of cognizance of all the actions that establish health in a human being, preserve it for him, and guard it from any sickness that might occur. [57]

14c. It is clear that the physician ought to be cognizant that opposites ought to be combated by opposites, be cognizant also that fever is to be combated by chill, and be cognizant further that jaundice should be combated by barley-water or tamarind-water. Of these three, some are more general than others: the most general is that opposites ought to be combated by opposites; the most particular is that jaundice ought to be combated by barley-water; and our saying that "fever is to be combated by chill" is a mean between the more general and the more particular.

However, when the physician cures, he cures the bodies of individuals and of single beings—Zayd's body, for instance, or Amr's body. In curing Zayd's jaundice, he is not content with what he is cognizant of concerning opposites being

16. Or, perhaps, "a human being in a state of ignorance" (*insān jāhilī*).

17. Literally, "another, more venerable species" (*naw' ākhar ashraf minh*). Similarly, a literal translation of the contrasting phrase, "inferior species," would be "another species subordinate to it" (*naw' ākhar dūnah*).

combated by opposites, nor about jaundice needing to be combated by barley-water unless, with respect to the fever of this Zayd, he has, in addition, cognizance that is more particular than those things he is cognizant of through [the study of] his art. So he investigates whether this jaundice of his ought to be combated by barley-water because his body is cold and moist, or whether barley-water will heal the bodily humor, but not let him perspire, and similar things. If barley-water ought to be drunk, he is not content to be unqualifiedly cognizant of this unless he is cognizant, in addition, of what amount of it ought to be drunk, what consistency what is to be drunk ought to have, at what moment of the day it ought to be drunk, and in which one of Zayd's feverish states it ought to be drunk. So he will have determined that with regard to quantity, quality, and time. Nor is it possible for him to make that determination without observing the sick person, so that his determination accords with what he observes about the state of this sick person, namely, Zayd.

Clearly, he could not have acquired this determination from the books of medicine he studied and was trained on, nor from his ability to be cognizant of the universals and general things set down in medical books, but through another faculty developing from his pursuit of medical practices with respect to the body of one individual after another, from his lengthy observation of the states of sick persons, [58] from the experience acquired by being occupied with curing over a long period of time, and from ministering to each individual. Therefore, the craft of the perfect physician becomes complete, to the point of performing with ease the actions proceeding from that craft, by means of two faculties: one is the ability for unqualified and exhaustive cognizance of the universals that are parts of his art so that nothing escapes him; then there is the faculty that develops in him through the lengthy practice of his art with regard to each individual.

14d. And the first kingly craft is like that. First of all, it comprises universal things. In performing those actions particular to it, the ruler is not content to have comprehensive cognizance of universal things, or the ability to grasp them, unless he has another faculty as well, one acquired through lengthy experience and observation that enables him to determine actions with regard to their quantity, quality,[19] times, and the rest of what actions may be determined by and stipulations placed on them—either with respect to each city, nation, or person, or with respect to an event that occurs or something that happens at particular times. For the actions of the kingly craft are only concerned with particular cities: I mean, this city and that city, this nation and that nation, or this human being and that human being.

Now the faculty by means of which a human being is able to infer the stipulations with which to determine actions with respect to what he observes in each community, each city, each nation,[18] each group, or each person, and with respect to each occurrence in a city, a nation, [59] or a person, is what the Ancients call "prudence." This faculty is not acquired through cognizance of the universals of the art or through exhausting all of them, but through lengthy experience with individual instances.

15. Political science that is a part of philosophy is limited—in what it investigates of the voluntary actions, ways of life, and dispositions, and in the rest of what it investigates—to universals and to giving their patterns. It also brings about cognizance of the patterns for determining particulars: how, by what, and to what extent they ought to be determined. It leaves them undetermined in actuality, because determining in actuality belongs to a faculty other than philosophy and perhaps because the circumstances and occurrences with respect to which determination takes place are infinite and without limitation.

This science has two parts. One part comprises bringing about cognizance of what happiness is—that is, what happiness truly is and what is presumed to be happiness—and enumerating the universal voluntary actions, ways of life, moral habits, states of character, and dispositions that are such as to come about in cities and nations; and it distinguishes the virtuous ones from the non-virtuous. Another part comprises bringing about cognizance of the actions by which virtuous actions and dispositions are established and ordered among the inhabitants of the cities, as well as of the actions by which what has been established among them is preserved for them.

16. Then it[19] enumerates how many sorts of non-virtuous kingly crafts there are. It also gives

18. Adding *aw umma umma* with Leiden MS Or. 1002 and Dunlop.

19. The subject of all the enumerations, explanations, and so forth in what follows is the "political science that is a part of philosophy" of sec. 15.

the patterns of the actions performed by each one of these kingly crafts in order to obtain its purpose from the inhabitants of the cities under its rulership. It explains that those actions, ways of life, and dispositions that are not virtuous are the sicknesses of virtuous cities and that their ways of life and regimes are the sicknesses of the virtuous kingly craft. The actions, ways of life, and dispositions that are in the non-virtuous cities are the sicknesses of virtuous cities.

17. Then it enumerates how many reasons and tendencies there are because of which the virtuous rulerships and the ways of life of virtuous cities are frequently in danger of being transformed into [60] non-virtuous ways of life and dispositions and how they are transformed into the non-virtuous. It enumerates and brings about cognizance of (a) the actions by which virtuous cities and regimes are restrained so that they not be corrupted and not be transformed into non-virtuous ones and (b) the things by which it is possible to turn them back to health, if they are transformed and become sick.

18. Then it explains that the actions of the first virtuous kingly craft cannot come about completely except through cognizance of the universals of this art; that is, by theoretical philosophy being joined to it and prudence being added to it. Prudence is the faculty acquired through experience arising from long involvement in the actions of the art with respect to single cities and nations and with respect to each single community: it is the ability for excellently inferring the stipulations by which the actions, ways of life, and dispositions are determined with respect to each community, each city, or each nation, either with respect to a short period of time, with respect to a long but limited period of time, or—if possible—with respect to particular times,[20] and for determining them as well with respect to each state that may emerge and each occurrence that may happen in a city, nation, or community. This is what the first virtuous kingly craft consists of. The one dependent on it, whose rulership is based on tradition, does not by nature need philosophy.

It explains that what is best and most virtuous in virtuous cities and nations is for their kings and rulers who succeed one another through time to possess the qualifications[21] of the first ruler. It brings about cognizance of (a) how it ought to be worked out so that these kings who succeed one another possess the very same states of virtue and (b) which qualifications are to be sought for in the sons of the city's kings so that if they are found in one of them, it is to be hoped that he will become the same kind of king as the first ruler. In addition, it explains how he ought to be educated, how he is to be raised, and in what way he is to be instructed so that he might become a king completely.

It explains, moreover, that the kings whose rulerships are ignorant need neither the universals of this art nor philosophy. [61] Rather, each one of them can achieve his purpose with respect to the city by means of the experiential faculty he attains through the kind of actions with which he obtains what he is intent upon and arrives at the presumed good that is his purpose, providing he happens to possess a thoroughly deceitful genius capable of inferring what he needs for determining the actions he is to perform and for determining the actions in which he will employ the inhabitants of the city. The craft by which he is a king consists of (a) things attained through experience—either through his own experience or through the experience of some other king who shares in his intention, pursuing his experience or schooling himself in it, and combining that with what he himself has acquired through experience—and (b) matters that he, by the deceitfulness of his genius and cunning, has inferred from the principles he has acquired by experience.

19. Then, after that, it brings about cognizance of the ranks of the things in the world and of the ranks of the beings in general. It begins with the parts of the world that are most inferior, namely, the ones that have no rulership over anything at all and that give rise only to actions used for serving, not to actions used for ruling.

From these, it ascends to the things that rule them without an intermediary, namely, the things that rule them directly. It brings about cognizance of their ranks with respect to rulership: what ranks they have; what the extent of their rulership is; that they do not yet have complete rulership; and that their natural traits and faculties are not sufficient for them on that account to have rulership of themselves so that they can dispense with being ruled by others, but that there must necessarily be rulerships over them governing them.

20. This might also mean "or with respect to all time—if possible." The phrase is quite elusive: *aw bi-ḥasab al-zamān in amkan.*

21. Literally, "stipulations" (*sharā'iṭ*).

From these, it ascends to the things that rule them directly. It brings about cognizance of their ranks with respect to rulership: what ranks they have; what the extent of their rulership is; that they do not yet have complete rulership; and that their natural traits and faculties are not sufficient for them on that account to have rulership of themselves so that they can dispense [62] with being ruled by others, but that there must necessarily be rulerships over them governing them.

From these, it ascends to the things that rule them directly.[22] It brings about cognizance of their ranks with respect to rulership: what ranks they have; what the extent of their rulership is; and that they are not complete either, except that they are more complete than the rulerships below them. It also brings about cognizance that their natural faculties and traits are not yet sufficient for them to have rulership of themselves so that they have no ruler at all, but that there must necessarily be other rulerships over them governing them.

It ascends, as well, to the things that also rule these directly. With regard to them, it brings about the same cognizance it brought about concerning the former ones.

It does not cease ascending like this from things in lower ranks to things in higher ranks having more complete rulership than those below. In this way, it ascends from the more perfect to more and more perfect beings. It brings about cognizance that whenever it ascends to a higher rank and to a being more perfect in itself and of more perfect rulership, the number of beings in that rank must be fewer and each one of the beings in it must have greater unity in itself and less multiplicity. In addition, it explains the multiplicity and unity that are in a thing.

It does not cease ascending in the perfection of this order from one level of rulership to a more perfect level of rulership until it finally reaches a level at which it is impossible for there to be anything but one being—one in number and one in every aspect of oneness. It is impossible as well for there to be a rulership above it; on the contrary, the ruler at that level governs everything below him—it not being at all possible for another to govern him—and rules everything below him. It is not possible [63] for there to be any deficiency in him, not in any way at all; nor is it possible for there to be any perfection more complete than his perfection, nor any existence more excellent than his existence—whereas everything below him has deficiency in some way—and the ranks directly next to him are the most perfect ranks below his level.

20. Then, as it descends, it does not cease [bringing about cognizance that] the beings in each level have more multiplicity and less perfection, until it finally reaches the last beings, namely, the ones that perform servile actions. There is nothing more inferior in existence than these, nor is it at all possible for them to perform ruling actions. The action of the first, the sempiternal one, to whom nothing can be prior, cannot be a servile action at all. And every one of the intermediate ones in the ranks below the first ruler performs ruling actions toward what is below itself by which it serves the first ruler.

In addition, it brings about cognizance of their harmony, of how they are linked together, how they are organized, how their actions are organized, and how they mutually support one another so that despite their multiplicity they might be like one thing. This comes about due to the power with which that one governs them, his governance extending in each of them commensurate with its rank and in accordance with the amount of natural worth a being[23] at that level of existence must have, as well as with the actions that must be entrusted to it for serving, ruling, or doing both.

21. Then it indicates what corresponds to these with respect to the faculties of the human soul.

22. Then it indicates what corresponds to these with respect to the organs of the human body.

23. Then, it also indicates what corresponds to these with respect to the virtuous city, placing the king and the first ruler in the same station as the deity who is the first governor of the beings and of the world and the classes [of beings] in it.

24. Then, it does not cease going down through the ranks among them until it finally reaches groups within the divisions of the inhabitants of the city whose actions are such that it is not possible for them to rule by means of them, but only to serve, [64] and whose voluntary dispositions are such that it is not possible [for them] to rule

22. Dunlop suggests that the immediately preceding passage, from "It brings about cognizance..." to this sentence ending in "directly" be deleted, believing it to appear as the result of dittography.

23. Reading *mā* ("what," understood here as a "being") for sense, instead of *man* ("one" or "someone").

by means of them, but only to serve. The groups in the intermediate ranks have actions by means of which they rule what is below them and serve whomever is above them; as they move closer and closer to the level of the king, they are more perfect in traits and actions and, therefore, more perfect in rulership, until the level of the kingly craft is finally reached. It is clear that this is not at all a craft by which a human being can serve; no, it is a craft and a disposition only for ruling.

25. Then, after that, it begins to ascend from the first ranks [in the city], namely, the ranks of serving, to the ranks of rulership directly above them. It does not cease ascending in speech and description from a lower level to a higher level until it finally reaches the level of the king of the city who rules and does not serve.

26. Then it ascends from that level to the level of the spiritual being governing the king who is the first ruler of the virtuous city, namely, the one set down as the trustworthy spirit[24] and this is the one through which God, may He be exalted, communicates the revelation to the first ruler of the city. Thus it looks into what its level is and which one of the ranks of the spiritual beings it is.

27. Then it does not cease ascending like this in bringing about cognizance of things until it finally reaches the Deity, may His praise be magnified.

It explains how revelation descends from Him level by level until it reaches the first ruler who thus governs the city or the nation and nations with what revelation from God, may He be exalted, brings, so that the first ruler's governance also extends to every one of the divisions of the city in an orderly manner until it finally reaches the last divisions. It explains this in that God, may He be exalted, is also the governor of the virtuous city, just as He is the governor of the world, [65] and in that His, may He be exalted, governance of the world takes place in one way, whereas His governance of the virtuous city takes place in another way; there is, however, a relation between the two kinds of governing, and there is a relation between the parts of the world and the parts of the virtuous city or nation.

And [it explains that] there must also be harmony, linkage, organization, and mutual support in actions among the parts of the virtuous nation; something similar to the harmony, linkage, organization, and mutual support in actions that exist in the parts of the world due to their natural traits must [also] exist in the divisions of the virtuous nation due to their voluntary traits and dispositions. The Governor of the world places natural traits in the parts of the world by means of which they are made harmonious, organized, linked together, and mutually supportive in actions in such a way that, despite their multiplicity and the multiplicity of their actions, they become like a single thing performing a single action for a single purpose. In the same manner, the governor of the nation must set down and prescribe voluntary traits and dispositions for the souls in the divisions of the nation and city that will bring them to that harmony, linkage of some to others, and mutual support in actions in such a way that, despite the multiplicity of their divisions, the diversity of their ranks, and the multiplicity of their actions, the nation and the nations become like a single thing performing a single action by which a single purpose is obtained. What corresponds to that becomes clear to anyone who contemplates the organs of the human body.

Along with the natural constitutions and instincts that He implanted in the world and its parts, the Governor of the world provided other things that make the existence of the world and its divisions persevere and continue in the way He constituted it for very long periods of time. The governor of the virtuous nation ought to do the very same thing: he ought not to limit himself to the virtuous traits and dispositions that he prescribes for their souls so that they will be made harmonious, linked together, and mutually supportive in actions unless he provides, in addition, other things through which he seeks their perseverance and continuation in the virtues and good things he implanted in them from the outset.

In general, he ought to follow God and pursue [66] the traces of the Governor of the world concerning His provision for the [different] sorts of beings and His governance of their affairs: the natural instincts, constitutions, and traits He set down and implanted in them so that the naturally good things are fully realized in each of the realms according to its level as well as in the totality of the beings. So, too, should he set down in the cities and nations the corresponding arts, and voluntary traits and dispositions, so that the voluntary good things might be fully realized in every single city

24. See Qur'an 26:193.

and nation to the extent that its rank and worth permit, in order that the associations of nations and cities might thereby arrive at happiness in this life and in the afterlife. For the sake of this, the first ruler of the virtuous city must already have thorough cognizance of theoretical philosophy; for he cannot understand anything pertaining to God's, may He be exalted, governance of the world so as to follow it except from that source.

It is clear, in addition, that all of this is impossible unless there is a common religion in the cities that brings together their opinions, beliefs, and actions; that renders their divisions harmonious, linked together, and well ordered; and at that point they will support one another in their actions and assist one another to reach the purpose that is sought after, namely, ultimate happiness.

THREE

ALFARABI

The Political Regime

Translated by Charles E. Butterworth

In a famous letter to his translator Ibn Tibbon, Maimonides wrote: "Do not busy yourself with books on the art of logic except for what was composed by the wise man Abū Naṣr al-Fārābī [Alfarabi]. For, in general, everything that he composed—and particularly his book on the *Principles of Beings*—is all finer than fine flour. His arguments enable one to understand and comprehend, for he was very great in wisdom." (The *Principles of Beings* was a nickname given to Alfarabi's *The Political Regime.*) Like Maimonides, a number of Muslim authors cite the *The Political Regime* as one of the fundamental works of Alfarabi. Its importance for the Jewish tradition beyond Maimonides is also apparent, as it was translated into Hebrew in the middle of the thirteenth century.

As noted in the introduction to *The Book of Religion,* that work reverses the procedure of the *Principles of the Opinions of the Inhabitants of the Virtuous City* (*Virtuous City*) and the present work. That is, in *The Book of Religion,* politics comes first, and metaphysics or theology comes second, but in the *Virtuous City* and *The Political Regime* the order is reversed. (Because of space limitations, we have excluded the metaphysical first half of *The Political Regime,* providing an outline of the first half below.) Once again, the reader is confronted with the question, Which inquiry is more foundational, that into politics or that into theology? In addition, the similarity of structure of the *Virtuous City* and *The Political Regime* leads one to wonder: Why write two so similarly structured works? This is not to say that there are not important differences between the *Virtuous City* and *The Political Regime.* The former focuses on opinions, and the latter on regimes or constitutions.

Whatever its proper title, *The Political Regime* is highly similar to Plato's *Republic,* especially Book 8, and comparison of the two works is fruitful. An outline of the first half of *The Political Regime* follows.

PART 1

I. The World around Us (1–63)
- A. General Principles (1–14)
  - 1. The six principles and their six rankings (1)
  - 2. The first cause and the secondary causes (2)
  - 3. The active intellect (3)
  - 4. The ranking of the soul (4–9)
  - 5. Form and matter (10–14)
- B. Particulars concerning the Incorporeal Substances (15–35)
  - 1. Incorporeal substances other than the first cause (15–19)

2. The first cause (20–33)
3. The relation between the secondary causes, the active intellect, and the first cause (34–35)

C. Particulars concerning the Corporeal Substances and Existence in General (36–63)

1. Basic difference between the heavenly bodies and the nonheavenly bodies (36–38)
2. How accidental contraries arise among the heavenly bodies (39–40)
3. About possible existence (41–43)
4. The role of form and matter in possible existence (44–52)
5. How the different realms of being come into existence and assist one another (53–63)

This translation is based on Fauzi Najjar's edition of the Arabic text, *Abū Naṣr al-Fārābī, Kitāb al-Siyāsa al-Madaniyya, al-Mulaqqab bi-Mabādi' al-Mawjūdāt* (Beirut: al-Maṭba'a al-Kāthūlīkiyya, 1964). Although Najjar indicates the page numbers of the older Hyderabad version (*Kitāb al-Siyāsa al-Madaniyya* [Ḥaidar Ābād al-Dukn: Maṭba'a Majlis Dā'irat al-Ma'ārif al-'Ūthmāniyya, 1346 AH (1927)] in his own text, his is so much more reliable and readable that it renders the older version obsolete. Thus in this translation the pages of Najjar's edition appear in square brackets. Although this translation usually follows Najjar's division of the text into major paragraphs or sections, there are occasions when it departs from it. The numbering of the sections is that of the present translator, as is the further division of these sections or paragraphs into unnumbered paragraphs. Moreover, while accepting Najjar's division of the text into two major parts, the translator has further divided it into subparts and divisions of subparts—enclosing these in square brackets—in an attempt to make sense of Alfarabi's larger exposition.

[PART TWO: THE POLITICAL WORLD]

[A. The Divisions of Human Associations]

[1. Perfect and Defective Associations]

64. Human beings are of the species that cannot complete its necessary affairs nor gain its most excellent state except by coming together as many associations in a single dwelling-place. Some human associations are large, some medium, and some small. The large association is an association of many nations coming together and helping one another. The medium is the nation. And the small are those the city has mastery over. These three are the perfect associations.

Thus the city is first in the rankings of perfections. Associations in villages, quarters, streets, and houses are defective associations. Of these, one is very defective, namely, the household association. It is part [70] of the association in the street, and the association in the street is part of the association in the quarter. And this latter association is part of the civic association.[1] The associations in quarters and the associations in villages are both for the sake of the city. However, the difference between them is that quarters are parts of the city, while villages serve the city. The civic association is part of the nation, and the nation is divided into cities. The unqualifiedly perfect human association is divided into nations.

[2. How Nations Are Distinguished from One Another]

65. A nation is distinguished from another by two natural things—natural temperaments and natural states of character—and by a third, conventional, thing having some basis in natural things, namely, the tongue—I mean, the language through which expression comes about. And among nations, some are large and some small.

The first natural cause for the difference in nations with respect to these objects are [various] things. One of them is the difference in the parts of the heavenly bodies that face them with respect to the first sphere, then with respect to the sphere of the fixed stars. Then, there is the difference in the positions of the oblique spheres

1. Or "part of the political association" (*juz' li-al-ijtimā' al-madanī*). Because Alfarabi is pointing merely to the size of the association, "civic" seems to convey the sense of the argument better than "political."

from parts of the earth and what occurs in those parts because of the sphere's proximity and distance. Following that is the difference in the parts of the earth that are the dwelling-places of the nations. For from the outset, this difference follows from the difference in the parts of the first sphere facing them, then the difference in the fixed stars facing them, and then the difference in the positions of the oblique spheres with respect to them.

66. From the difference in the parts of the earth follows the difference in the vapors that arise from the earth. Because every vapor is generated from a soil, it resembles that soil. Following from the difference in the vapors is the difference in air and the difference in water, due to the water in every country coming into being from the vapors that are beneath the soil of that country. And the air in each country is mixed with the vapor that rises up to it from the soil. [71] Likewise, from the difference in the sphere of the fixed stars facing it, the difference in the first sphere, and the difference in the positions of the oblique spheres follow the difference in air and the difference in water.

From these follow the difference in plants and the difference in the species of non-rational animals; thus, the nutriments of the nations differ. Following from the difference in their nutriments is the difference in the materials and crops from which the people come to be who succeed those who pass away. Following from that is the difference in temperaments and the difference in natural states of character. Moreover, the difference in the parts of the heavens that face their heads is also a cause for the difference in temperaments and states of character in a way other than what was mentioned. Likewise, the difference in air is also a cause for the difference in temperaments and states of character in a way other than what was mentioned.

67. Then from the mutual help of these differences and their being mixed follow different minglings according to which the temperaments of nations and their states of character differ. In this way and according to this manner there is a concordance of these natures, a tying of some to others, and rankings of them. And this is the extent reached by the heavenly bodies in perfecting them. Now it is not up to the heavenly bodies to give the other perfections that remain; rather, that is up to the active intellect. To no species other than the human being is it possible for the active intellect to give the remaining perfections.

[B. The Active Intellect and Human Happiness]

[1. The Active Intellect, the Heavenly Bodies, and Will]

68. In what the active intellect gives the human being, it proceeds in the way the heavenly bodies do. For it first gives the human being a faculty and a principle by which he strives, or by which a human being is able to strive on his own, to the rest of the perfections that remain for him. That principle is the primary sciences and the primary intelligibles [72] attained in the rational part of the soul. It gives him those cognitions and those intelligibles only after the human being first proceeds and attains the sense-perceptive and the appetitive parts of the soul through which there come about the longing and loathing following upon sense-perception, as well as the instruments of these two from the parts of the body. Through these two, will is attained.

[2. Will and Choice]

69. Will is at first only a longing [that comes] from sensation. Longing comes about through the appetitive part and sensation through the sense-perceptive part. Then, by attaining the imaginative part of the soul and the longing that follows upon it after that, a second will is attained after the first. So this will is a longing [that comes] from imagination. After these two are attained, it is possible to attain the primary cognitions from the active intellect in the rational part.

At this point, a third kind of will is generated in the human being, namely, the longing [that comes] from reason. This is what is particularly characterized by the name "choice." This is what is in the human being in particular, apart from the rest of the animals. Through this, a human being is able to do what is praiseworthy or blameworthy, noble or base. And because of this, there is reward and punishment. Now the first two wills may come about in non-rational animals. When this [third will] is attained by the human being, it enables him to strive toward happiness or not to do so. Through it he is able to do good or to do bad, the noble or the base.

[3. Happiness]

70. Happiness is unqualified good. Whatever is useful for obtaining happiness and gaining it is also good, not for its own sake but for the sake of its usefulness with respect to happiness. Whatever impedes from happiness in any way is unqualified evil. The good useful for obtaining happiness may be something [73] existing by nature, and that may come about by will. The evil that impedes from happiness may be something that exists by nature, and it may come about by will.

That which is by nature is given only by the heavenly bodies, but not from an intention on their part to help the active intellect toward its purpose nor as an intention to hamper it. For the things useful for the active intellect's purpose, as given by the heavenly bodies, come not from an intention on their part to help the active intellect in that; nor are the natural things that impede it from its purpose due to the heavenly bodies having an intention contrary to the active intellect with respect to that. Rather it is in the substance of the heavenly bodies to give whatever is in the nature of matter to receive without their caring about what is useful or harmful to the purpose of the active intellect. Therefore, it is not impossible that in the sum of what is attained from the heavenly bodies there at times be what is suitable to the purpose of the active intellect and at times what is contrary to it.

[4. Voluntary Good and Evil]

71. Voluntary good and voluntary evil—namely, the noble and the base—are both generated by the human being in particular. Voluntary good is generated in only one way. That is because the faculties of the human soul are five: the theoretical-rational, the practical-rational, the appetitive, the imaginative, and the sense-perceptive. Happiness, which only the human being can intellect and be conscious of, is [attained] by means of the theoretical-rational faculty—not by any other of the rest of the faculties—and that is when he uses the principles and the first cognitions that the active intellect gave him.

For when he is cognizant of it,[2] he then longs for it by means of the appetitive faculty. He deliberates by means of the practical-rational [faculty] about what he ought to do so as to gain it. By means of the instruments of the appetitive [faculty], he does the actions he infers by means of deliberation. The imaginative and the sense-perceptive [faculties] contribute to and are led by the rational [faculty]. They assist it in arousing the human being to the actions by which he gains happiness. Then, everything that a human being generates is good. In this way alone is voluntary good generated. [74]

72. Voluntary evil is generated in the way I shall state. Now neither the imaginative nor the sense-perceptive [faculty] is conscious of happiness. Nor is the rational [faculty] conscious of happiness in every state. Rather, the rational [faculty] is conscious of happiness only when it strives to apprehend it. There are many things here that make it possible for the human being to imagine that they are what ought to be the aim and the end in life—like the pleasant and the useful, honor, and similar things.

When a human being slackens in perfecting the theoretical-rational part, he is not conscious of happiness so as to have an appetite for it. He sets up as the goal he is intent upon in his life something other than happiness—such as what is useful, what is pleasant, domination, or honor. He longs for it with the appetitive [faculty]. By means of the practical-rational [faculty] he deliberates so as to infer what will gain that end. By means of the instruments of the appetitive faculty, he does those things he has inferred. And the imaginative and the sense-perceptive [faculties] contribute to that. Then, everything that he generates is evil.

Likewise, a human being may have apprehended happiness and become cognizant of it. Yet he does not set it down as his aim and end. He does not long for it or has only a weak longing for it. He sets down as the end he longs for in life another thing

2. That is, happiness. Yet the pronoun *hā* could also refer to the principles and first cognitions just mentioned.

other than happiness. And he uses all the rest of his faculties to gain that end. Everything that he generates is evil.

[5. On Attaining Human Happiness]

73. Since what is intended by the existence of the human being is that he obtain happiness, that being the ultimate perfection remaining to be given to the possible beings able to receive it, the way by which it is possible for a human being to come to this happiness ought to be stated. Now that is possible only by the active intellect having first given the primary intelligibles, which are the primary cognitions. Not every human being is created so as to be disposed to receive the first intelligibles, because individual human beings are by nature generated with varied faculties and divergent preparations. So some of them do not by nature receive any of the primary intelligibles. [75] Others receive them, but not as they are—like mad persons. And others receive them as they are. These are the ones whose human innate character is sound. These, in particular, and not the others, are able to gain happiness.

74. People whose innate character is sound share in an innate character that disposes them to receive the intelligibles in which they all share and by which they strive toward objects and actions common to all of them. Then, afterwards, they diverge and differ, thereby coming to an innate character that particularly characterizes each one of them and each sect (*ṭā'ifa*). So one among them is disposed to receive certain other intelligibles that are not shared, but are particularly characteristic; and by them, he strives toward another genus. Another is disposed to receive other intelligibles that are fitting to be used in a certain other genus without one [person] sharing with his companion in any of what is particularly characteristic for him. One [person] is disposed to receive many intelligibles that are fitting for one thing in a particular genus, and another is disposed to receive many intelligibles that are fitting for everything in that genus.

Similarly, they may also differ and vary concerning the faculties by which they infer the objects that, concerning a particular genus, are such as to be apprehended by inference. Thus it is not impossible for there to be two [human beings] who are given the very same intelligibles that are fitting for a particular genus, while one of the two naturally infers fewer things with respect to that genus by means of those intelligibles and the other naturally has the ability to infer everything in that genus. Similarly, two [human beings] may have an equal ability to infer the very same things, while one of the two is quicker at inferring and the other slower, or one of the two is quicker at inferring what is most excellent with respect to that genus and the other what is most vile with respect to that genus. There also may be two [human beings] who have an equal ability for inference and for speed, while one of the two has in addition an ability to guide someone else and to instruct in what he has [76] already inferred, and the other[3] has no ability for guidance or instruction. Similarly, they may be equal with respect to ability for bodily actions.

75. The innate characters that come about by nature do not force anyone or make it necessary for anyone to do that. Rather, it is only that due to these innate characters it comes to be easier for them to do that thing toward which they are disposed by nature. And when an individual is left to his passion and nothing external moves him to its contrary, he is aroused to [do] that thing to which he was said to be disposed. When some external mover moves him to the contrary of that, he is also aroused to its contrary—but with adversity, distress, and hardship, whereas that to which he is accustomed is easy. Those for whom a certain thing is natural may happen to be very adverse to change from what they were created for; indeed, for many of them it may not be possible. That is because their brains were struck at birth by a disease and a natural chronic illness.

76. In addition to what was made natural for them, all of these innate characters need to have the will trained and be educated in the things toward which they are disposed in order that through those things they come to their final perfections or [come] close to the final ones. In a certain genus there may be extraordinary, superb innate characters that are neglected and not trained or educated in the things toward which they are disposed. So as time is drawn out in that way, their strength becomes nullified. And some among them may be educated in the vile things in that genus. Thus

3. Literally, "one of them" (*ba'ḍuhum*). Though less direct, this construction maintains the parallel between one human being and another.

they emerge as extraordinary in doing and inferring the vile things from that genus. [77]

77. By nature, people vary with respect to rankings in accordance with the variation in the rankings of the kinds[4] of arts and sciences toward which they are naturally disposed. Then, those who are disposed by nature toward a certain kind [of art and science] vary in accordance with the variation in the parts of that kind. For those who are disposed to a viler part of that kind [of art and science] are beneath those who are disposed to a more excellent part. Then, those who are naturally disposed to a certain kind [of art and science] or to a part of that kind also vary in accordance with the perfection or defectiveness of [their] being disposed.

Then, afterwards, inhabitants of equal natures vary with respect to the way they are educated in the things toward which they are disposed. Those who are equally educated vary according to their ability with respect to inference. For the one who has an ability to infer with respect to a certain kind [of art and science] is the ruler over one having no ability to infer what is in that kind. And one having the ability to infer more things is the ruler over one having the ability to infer only fewer things. Then, the latter vary with respect to the faculties they have procured from education for good or bad guidance and instruction. For the one who has the ability for good guidance and instruction is the ruler over one having no faculty for guidance.[5] Moreover, when those possessing natures more defective with respect to a particular kind [of art and science] than the extraordinary natures are educated in that kind, they become more excellent [in it] than one of the inhabitants with extraordinary natures not educated in anything. Those educated in what is most excellent with respect to that kind [of art and science] are rulers over those educated in what is most vile with respect to that kind.

So one having an extraordinary nature with respect to a certain kind [of art and science] who is educated in everything he is disposed to by nature is a ruler not only over one not having an extraordinary nature with respect to that kind [of art and science], but also over one having an extraordinary nature with respect to that kind [of art and science] who is not educated or is educated only in some trifling thing of what is in that kind [of art and science]. [78]

[C. Different Kinds of Rulers or Guides to Happiness]

[1. The Need for a Ruler and Qualification for Rulership]

78. Since what is intended by the existence of the human being is that he obtain ultimate happiness, to obtain it he needs to know happiness and to set it before his eyes as his end. Then, after that, he needs to know the things that ought to be done so as to gain happiness by means of them, then to perform those deeds.

Because of what was said with respect to the difference in innate characters in individual human beings, the innate character of every human being does not on its own know happiness or the things that ought to be done; rather, for that, there is need for an instructor and a guide. Some need slight guidance and some much guidance. Nor, when he is guided to these two,[6] does he inevitably do what he has been instructed and guided to do without an external spur and being aroused toward it. Most people are like this. Therefore, they need someone who acquaints them with all of that and arouses them to do it.

It is not within the power of every human being to guide someone else. Nor is it within the power of every human being to prompt someone else to do these things. One having no ability at all to arouse someone else to do one of the things nor to use him in it, having instead only the ability to do always what he is guided to, is in no way a ruler—not with respect to anything. Rather, he is always ruled in everything. One who has the power to guide someone else to a particular thing, to prompt him to do it, or to use

4. Literally, "genera" (*ajnās*). In this section and the next, the singular of this term—*jins*—is translated as "kind" rather than as "genus."

5. Reading *al-irshād* with Feyzullah 1279, rather than *al-istinbāṭ* (inference) with Najjar and the other MSS.

6. That is, to happiness and the things that ought to be done in order to achieve it.

him in it, is—with respect to that thing—a ruler over the one who is not able to do that thing by himself, but is able to when guided toward it and instructed in doing it. Then, one having the ability to arouse someone else toward that thing he was instructed in and guided toward and use him in it is a ruler over one human being and ruled by another human being.

The ruler may be a first[7] ruler, and he may be a secondary ruler. The secondary ruler is the one who is ruled by one human being while he rules another human being. [79] These two rulerships may be about a particular kind [of art and science], like farming, and like commerce and medicine. And they may be in relation to all the human kinds [of art and science].

[2. The First Ruler]

79. The first ruler without qualification is the one who does not need—not in anything at all—to be ruled by another human being. Rather, he has already attained the sciences and cognitions in actuality and has no need of a human being to guide him in anything. He has the ability for excellent apprehension of each one of the particular things that ought to be done and the faculty for excellently guiding everyone other than himself to all that he has instructed them in; the ability to use everyone as a means to do a particular thing pertaining to that action he is intent upon; and the ability to determine, define, and direct the activities toward happiness.

That comes about only in an inhabitant having a great, extraordinary nature[8] when his soul has joined with the active intellect. He obtains that only by having first attained the passive intellect then, after that, having attained the intellect called "acquired."[9] Through attaining the acquired [intellect] there comes about the conjunction with the active intellect that was mentioned in the book *On the Soul.*

80. This human being is the king in truth according to the ancients, and he is the one of whom it ought to be said that he receives revelation. For a human being receives revelation only when he obtains this rank, and that is when there remains no intermediary between him and the active intellect. Now the passive intellect is similar to matter and a subject for the acquired intellect. And the acquired intellect is similar to matter and a subject for the active intellect.

Then, there emanates from the active intellect to the passive intellect the faculty by which he is able to seize upon the definition of things and actions and direct them toward happiness. This emanation proceeding from the active intellect to the passive intellect by the intermediary [80] of the acquired intellect is revelation. Because the active intellect is an emanation from the existence of the first cause, it is possible due to this to say that the first cause is what brings revelation to this human being by the intermediary of the active intellect. The rulership of this human being is the first rulership, and the rest of the human rulerships are subsequent to this one and proceed from it. And that is evident.

[3. Those Governed by Such a Person]

81. The people who are governed by the rulership of this ruler are the virtuous, good, and happy people. If they are a nation, then that is the virtuous nation. If they are people who have come together in a single dwelling-place, then the dwelling-place that brings all these together under this rulership is the virtuous city. If they have not come together in a single dwelling-place, but are in separate dwelling-places whose inhabitants are governed by rulerships other than this one, then they are virtuous people who are strangers in those dwelling-places. They happen to be separate either because they have not yet chanced upon a city in which it is possible for them to come together or because they already were in a city but disasters happened to them—such as enemy aggression, epidemic, drought, or something else—forcing them to separate.

7. Or "primary" or even "supreme" (*awwal*).

8. Literally, "inhabitants having great, extraordinary natures" (*ahl al-ṭibāʿiʿ al-ʿaẓīma al-fāʾiqa*); but the context, as well as the following "his soul" (*nafsuh*), points to the singular.

9. Literally, "procured" (*al-mustafād*). So, too, in the next sentence and throughout the rest of this discussion. Though the discussion here centers on Aristotle's *On the Soul* 3.5 430a10–25 and 3.7 431a1–431b19, the term "acquired intellect" comes not from Aristotle's *On the Soul,* but from the commentary on it by Alexander of Aphrodisias.

[4. The Differences in Subordinate Rulers]

82. If there happens to be an association of these kings at a single moment in a single city, a single nation, or many nations, then their whole association is like a single king due to the agreement in their endeavors, purposes, opinions,[10] and ways of life. If they succeed one another in time, their souls will be as a single soul. The second will proceed according to the way of life of the first, and the one now present according to the way of life of the one who has passed away. Just as it is permissible for one of them to change a law[11] he legislated at one moment if he is of the opinion that it is more fitting to change it at another moment, [81] so may the one now present who succeeds the one who has passed away change what the one who has passed away has already legislated. For the one who has passed away would change [it] himself, were he to observe the [new] condition. When there does not happen to be a human being of this condition, the laws that the former [kings] prescribed or ordained are to be adopted, then written down and preserved, and the city is to be governed by means of them. So the ruler who governs the city by means of written laws adopted from past leaders is the king of traditional law.[12]

[D. What Acquiring Happiness Entails]

[1. True Happiness Occurring in a City]

83. When each of the inhabitants of the city does what is such as to be entrusted to him—having either learned that on his own or the ruler having guided and prompted him to it—those actions of his earn him good traits of the soul. So, too, does persistence in the good actions of writing earn a human being goodness in the art of writing, which is a trait of the soul. The more he persists in them, the more powerful goodness in writing becomes in him. His pleasure in the trait he attains in his soul is greater, and the delight of his soul in that trait is stronger. Similarly, the actions that are determined and directed toward happiness empower the part of the soul disposed by innate character toward happiness and make it become actual and perfect. So, from the power attained in becoming perfect, it manages to dispense with matter and gets to be free from it. Yet it does not perish when matter perishes, since in its constitution and its existence it has come not to need matter. Then it attains happiness.

84. It is evident that the happiness attained by the inhabitants of the city varies in quantity and quality in accordance with the variation in the perfections they procure through civic[13] actions. And in accordance with that, the pleasures they gain vary. For when the soul attains separation from matter and becomes incorporeal, the accidents that affect [82] bodies insofar as they are bodies are removed from it. So it cannot be said of it that it moves or that it rests. Then the sayings that are proper for what is not corporeal ought to be said of it. Everything befalling the human soul that describes body insofar as it is body ought to be negated of separated souls. To understand and to form a concept of this condition is difficult and not customary, in the way it is difficult to form a concept of substances that are not bodies nor in bodies.

85. When a sect passes away, and their bodies are nullified, and their souls are delivered and made happy, then other people follow after them, take their place in the city, and perform their activities; the souls of these [people], too, are delivered. When their bodies are nullified, they come to the rankings of those in this sect who have passed away. They are neighborly to them in the way that what is not corporeal is neighborly. And they join with the similar souls of the people of the unique sect, some with others. Whenever the similar separate souls multiply and some join with others, the pleasure of each one increases.

10. Reading *wa ārā'ihim* with Feyzullah 1279, rather than *wa irādātihim* (and their wills) with Najjar and the rest of the MSS.

11. The Arabic term is *sharī'a,* and the verb translated in what follows as "legislate" is *sharra'a.* The term *nāmūs* ("nomos" or "convention") does not occur in this work.

12. The term is *sunna,* which is usually used to refer to the sayings and deeds of the Prophet.

13. Or "political" (*al-madaniyya*); see above, note 1.

Whenever one of those who came after attaches to them, the pleasure of the one now attaching increases due to his encountering those who passed away. And the pleasures of those who passed away increase through joining with those who attach to them because each one intellects his essence and intellects the same as his essence many times. What is thereby intellected increases as the ones now present attach to them in future time. So there will be a boundless increase of pleasures for each one with the passing of time. That is the condition of each sect.

This, then, is the true ultimate happiness that is the purpose of the active intellect.

[2. What Happens When Bad Actions Are Established in a City]

86. When the actions of the inhabitants of a particular city are not directed toward happiness, they earn them traits [83] of the soul that are bad just as when the actions of writing are bad, they produce bad writing. Similarly, when the actions of any art are bad, they provide the soul bad traits with respect to that genus of those arts. And their souls become sick. Thus, they are pleased by the traits they earn through their actions just as, due to the corruption of their sense-perception, those with sick bodies—like those with fevers—take pleasure in bitter things, find them sweet, and are pained by sweet things which appear bitter to their palates. Similarly, due to the corruption of their imagination, those with sick souls take pleasure in bad traits.

Just as among the sick there is someone who is not conscious of his disease and someone who, in addition, presumes that he is healthy—and someone among the sick who is such as this does not at all heed what a physician says—so, too, is there among those with sick souls someone who is not conscious of his sickness and who, in addition, presumes that he is virtuous and has a sound soul. So he does not at all heed what a guide, instructor, or reformer says. Thus the souls of these people remain material[14] and do not come to a perfection such that they are separate from matter; so when their matter is nullified, they also are nullified.

[3. The Resemblance between the Ranks and Orders of the City and of the Universe]

87. The rankings of the inhabitants of the city vary with respect to rulership and service in accordance with the innate characters of its inhabitants and in accordance with the way they have been educated. The first ruler is the one who ranks the sects and each human being in each sect according to the ranking it or he merits—that is, either in a ranking of service or a ranking of rulership. Thus, there will be rankings close to his [own] ranking, rankings slightly distant from it, and rankings greatly distant from it. Those are the rankings of rulership, and they descend little by little from the highest rank until they come to be the rankings of service in which there is no rulership and beneath which there is no other ranking.

When the ruler, after making these rankings, then wants to define a command about an object he wants to prompt the inhabitants of the city or a sect among the inhabitants of the city to do [84] and arouse them toward it, he intimates that to the rankings closest to him; and they intimate it to whoever comes after them. Then it goes on like that until it arrives at the one who is ranked as serving that affair. Thus the parts of the city are then tied to one another, in concord with one another, and ranked with some having precedence and others being subordinate. It comes to resemble the natural beings, and its rankings also resemble the rankings of the beings that begin at the first [cause] and terminate at primary matter and the elements. The way it is tied together and its concord are similar to the way the different beings are tied to one another and to their concord. And the governor of that city is similar to the first cause through which is the existence of the rest of the beings.

Then, the rankings of the beings go on descending little by little, each of them coming to be ruler and ruled, until they terminate at the possible beings that have no rulership at all but only serve and exist for the sake of something else—namely, primary matter and the elements.

[4. The Need to Remove Natural and Voluntary Evils to Attain Happiness]

88. Happiness is obtained only by removing evils from the body and from nations—not just

14. Literally, "hylic" (*hayūlāniyya*).

the voluntary ones, but also the natural ones—and by their attaining all the goods—the natural ones and the voluntary ones. Now the function of the city's governor, that is, the king, is to govern cities so as to tie the parts of the city to one another and to give it concord and make a ranking such that the inhabitants assist one another in removing evils and attaining goods. And [his function is] to look into everything given by the heavenly bodies. Whatever assists or is suitable in a particular way, or in a particular way useful, for obtaining happiness, he retains and increases. Whatever is harmful, he struggles to render useful. And what he is unable to do that with, he nullifies or decreases. In general, he seeks to nullify both of the evils and to bring into existence[15] both of the goods.

Each of the inhabitants of the virtuous city needs to be cognizant[16] of the principles of the ultimate beings, their rankings, happiness, the first rulership that belongs to the virtuous city, and the rankings of its rulership. Then, after that, [85] [each needs to be cognizant of] the defined actions by which happiness is gained when they are performed. These actions are not to be restricted to being known without being done and the inhabitants of the city being brought to do them.

89. Now a human being either forms a concept of the principles of the beings, their rankings, happiness, and the rulership of the virtuous cities and intellects them or imagines them. To form a concept of them is to have their essences sketched in the human soul as they exist in truth. To imagine them is to have their images, their likenesses, and the objects representing them sketched in the human soul. That is similar to what is possible with objects that are seen—for example, a human being. Either we see him himself, we see a statue of him, we see an image of him in water, or we see an image of his statue in water or in other mirrors. Now our seeing him resembles the intellect's forming a concept of the principles of the beings, happiness, and the rest. And our seeing a human being in water or our seeing a statue of him resembles imagination. For our seeing a statue of him or our seeing him in a mirror is our seeing what represents him. Similarly, our imagining those things is in truth our forming a concept of what represents them, not our forming a concept of them in themselves.

90. Most people have no ability, either by innate character or by custom, to understand and form a concept of those things. For those people, an image ought to be made, by means of things that represent them, of how the principles, their rankings, the active intellect, and the first ruler come about.

While their meanings and essences are one and immutable, the things by which they are represented are many and different. Some are closer to what is represented and others more distant. That is just as it is with visible things. For the image of a human being seen in water is closer to the human being in truth than the image of the statue of a human being seen in water. Therefore it is possible to represent these things to one sect and one nation by objects other than those by which they are represented to another sect or another nation.

Thus it may be possible [86] for the religions of virtuous nations and virtuous cities to differ even if they all pursue the very same happiness. For religion is a sketch of these things or of their images in the soul. Since it is difficult for the public to understand these things in themselves and the way they exist, instructing them about these things is sought by other ways—and those are the ways of representation. So these things are represented to each sect or nation by things of which they are more cognizant. And it may be possible that what one of them is more cognizant of is not what another is more cognizant of.

Most people who pursue happiness pursue what is imagined, not what they form a concept of. Similarly, the principles such as to be accepted, imitated, extolled, and exalted are accepted by most people as they imagine them, not as they form a concept of them. Those who pursue happiness as they form a concept of it and accept the principles as they form a concept of them are the wise, whereas those in whose souls these things are found as they are imagined and who accept them and pursue them as though they are like that are the faithful.

91. The objects by which these things are represented vary so that some are wiser and more complete in imagination and others more defective, some are closer to the truth and others further from it. With some, the topics of contention are few or concealed; or it is difficult to contend

15. Reading *wa ījād* with Feyzullah 1279, instead of *wa ījāb* (and to affirm) with Najjar and the rest of the MSS. The two evils and goods in question are the voluntary and natural ones.

16. As in the previous two selections, "cognizant" renders a form of the verb *'arafa*.

against them. With others, the topics of contention are many or apparent; or it is easy to contend against and to refute them.

It is not impossible that the things by which these are presented imaginatively to the inhabitants be different objects and, in spite of their difference, be linked to one another—that is, that there be objects used to represent those things, other things to represent these objects, and yet a third group of objects to represent these things—or that the different objects used to represent those things (I mean, the principles of the beings, happiness, and its rankings) be equivalent in their representation.

If [87] all of them were equivalent with respect to the goodness of their representation or the topics of contention in them being few or concealed, all or any one of them chanced upon would be used. And if they were to vary, those chosen would be the ones most complete in representation or those in which the topics of contention were either nonexistent at all, trifling, or concealed; then would come those closest to the truth. Representations other than these would be discarded.

[E. The Different Kinds of Cities]

[Introduction: The Cities Contrary to the Virtuous City]

92. Contrary to the virtuous city are the (1) ignorant city, (2) immoral city, and (3) errant city. Then there are (4) the weeds in the virtuous city; for the station of weeds in cities is that of darnel in wheat, the thorns of plants within the crop, or the rest of the grasses that are useless or harmful to the crop or seedlings. Then there are the people who are bestial by nature. Now those who are bestial by nature are not citizens, nor do they have any civic associations at all. Rather, some of them are like domesticated beasts and some like wild beasts. And some of the latter are like predatory animals.

Similarly, among them are to be found those who live apart in the wilderness, those who live in associations while cavorting like predatory animals, and those who live close to cities. Among them are those who eat only raw meat, those who graze upon wild plants, and those who ravish [their prey] as do the predatory animals. These are found at the extremities of the inhabited dwelling-places, either at the northern or the southern tips. And they ought to be treated as beasts. Now any one of them who is domestic and useful in some way to the cities is to be spared, enslaved, and used as beasts are used. What is done to the rest of the harmful animals is to be done to any of them who is not useful or is harmful. The same ought to be done to any children of the inhabitants of the cities who happen to be bestial.

[1. The Different Categories of Ignorant City]

93. The inhabitants of the ignorant [cities] are citizens,[17] and their cities and civic associations are of many manners: [88] among them are (a) the necessary associations, (b) the association of depraved inhabitants in the depraved cities, (c) the vile association in the vile cities, (d) the association of [seekers of] honor in the timocratic cities, (e) the association of domination in the despotic cities, and (f) the association of freedom in the democratic city[18] and the city of the free.

[a. The Necessary City]

94. The necessary city or necessary association is the one in which there is mutual assistance for earning what is necessary to constitute and safeguard bodies. There are many ways of earning these things such as farming, herding, hunting, stealing, and others. Both hunting and stealing involve wiliness and openness. Among the necessary cities, there may be some that bring together all of the arts that procure what is necessary. With others, earning what is necessary comes about by a single art such as farming alone or another single one [of the arts].

According to them,[19] the most virtuous one is he who is most excellent at using stratagems for, governing, and making available the ways by which the inhabitants of the city arrive at earning what is necessary. Their ruler is the one who has fine governance and excellent stratagems for

17. Or "city people" (*madaniyyūn*).

18. Literally, "the associational city" (*al-madīna al-jamāʿiyya*). See below, secs. 113–19.

19. That is, the inhabitants of the necessary city or association.

using them so that they gain the necessary things and fine governance in preserving these things for them or who bestows these things upon them from what he has.

[b. The Plutocratic City]

95. The depraved city or association of depraved inhabitants is the one in which they assist one another in gaining prosperity and wealth, being excessive in acquiring the necessities and what takes their place with respect to dirhams and dinars, and accumulating them beyond [89] the extent they are needed. [This is] for nothing other than love of, and greed for, wealth, while spending of it only what is necessary to constitute bodies. That comes about either by all of the means of earning or by the means available in that country.

According to them, the one most virtuous is the most wealthy and most excellent at using stratagems to obtain prosperity. Their ruler is the human being capable of excellently governing them so that they earn wealth and preserve it always. Wealth is gained through all the ways by which what is necessary is gained—namely, farming, herding, hunting, and stealing—and then voluntary interactions such as commerce, leasing, and others.

[c. The Hedonistic City]

96. The city of vileness or association of the vile is the one in which they assist one another in the enjoyment of sensual pleasure or imaginary pleasure, such as play or jesting or both together, as well as in the enjoyment of the pleasure of eating, drinking, and sexual intercourse. The most pleasant of these is chosen in order to seek pleasure not, by means of it, to seek what constitutes the body or is useful to the body in some way, but only to be pleased by it. And so, too, with play and jesting.

According to the inhabitants of the ignorant [cities], this city is the happy and delightful one, because it is possible for them to obtain the purpose of this city only after having attained what is necessary and after having attained wealth.

[d. The Timocratic City]

97. The honor-seeking city or the association of [seekers of] honor is the one in which they aid one another to arrive at being honored in speech and in action. That is either by the inhabitants of other cities honoring them or by some of them honoring others. The honor some accord others is either equal or varied.

Equal honor is simply [90] that they exchange honor with one another by one bestowing one species of honor upon another at a particular moment so that at another moment the other bestows upon him that species of honor or another species whose power according to them is the same as that [first] species. The varied [exchange of honor] is for one to bestow upon another one species of honor and the other to bestow upon the first honor of greater power than the first species. All of this proceeds among them in that way according to merit in that the second merits honor of a certain extent and the first merits greater honor—that being in keeping with what is meritorious according to them.

98. Now according to the inhabitants of the ignorant cities, what is meritorious is not virtue, but (1) wealth, (2) making available for one another the causes of pleasure and play and obtaining the most of these two, (3) obtaining the most of what is necessary such that a human being is sufficiently served with all he needs of what is necessary, or (4) a human being acting in a useful manner, that is, doing good, to others with respect to these three things.

There is (5) another thing very beloved of many of the inhabitants of the ignorant cities, namely, domination. According to many of them, the one who masters it is to be envied. Therefore, that ought also to be counted among what is meritorious for the ignorant cities. For, according to them, the most exalted thing a human being is to be honored for is being well-known for domination over one, two, or many things; not being dominated either due to himself, because his supporters are many or powerful, or both of these; and not being subjected to what is loathsome, while subjecting someone else to what is loathsome when he wills. This, according to them, is one of the conditions of delight for which, according to them, a human being merits honor. The more virtuous he is in this [91] object, the more he is honored.

Or (6) for a human being to have distinguished ancestry, according to them. According to them, distinguished ancestry goes back to one of the things that preceded, that is, that his fathers and grandfathers were either wealthy, had much pleasure and the causes for making it available, had domination over many things, were useful to others with respect to these things—either to an association or to inhabitants of a city—or that available to them were the instruments for these such as nobility, endurance, or contempt for death. For these are the instruments of domination.

99. Equal honor sometimes has to do with merit coming from another, external thing. Sometimes honor itself is the merit, so that the human being who begins and honors another thereby merits being honored by the other, as takes place with market interactions. According to them, the one who merits more honor is the ruler over someone such as to be honored less. This variation does not cease ascending until it terminates at the one who merits more honor than anyone other than him in the city. That one comes to be the ruler of the city and its king. Since it is like that, that one ought to have more merit than anyone other than himself. What, according to them, are meritorious things are the ones we have enumerated.

100. If it is like that, then he ought to have more distinguished ancestors than anyone else. For, according to them, rulership comes only through distinguished ancestry and, similarly, honor according to them comes only through wealth. Then people vary and are ranked according to their extent of wealth and distinguished ancestry. Someone who has no wealth nor any distinguished ancestors has no access to rulerships or honors. It is like that when the meritorious things are [92] objects whose good does not extend beyond him, and these are the vilest among the rulers of honor. If he is honored only for the sake of his usefulness to the inhabitants of the city with respect to the endeavor and passion of the inhabitants of the city, that occurs insofar as he is useful to them with respect to wealth, pleasures, arriving at having others honor them or at other things among the desires of the inhabitants of the city—either bestowing these things upon them from what he has or gaining them for them through his fine governance and preserving them for them.

101. According to them, the most virtuous of these rulers is the one who gains these things for the inhabitants of the city and does not bother himself with anything other than honor alone—such as his gaining wealth for them and not seeking wealth, or his gaining pleasures for them and not seeking pleasures, but seeking only honor and being praised, extolled, and magnified in speech and action so that his name becomes well-known for that among the rest of the nations during his time and afterwards, and memory of him remains for a long time. This is the one who merits honor according to them. Many times, this one needs money and wealth to bestow in getting the inhabitants of the city to arrive at their desires concerning wealth or pleasure and in preserving it for them. When these deeds of his are greater, he ought to be wealthier; and that wealth of his comes to be a reserve for the inhabitants of the city.

102. So some of them seek wealth for this reason and are of the opinion that these expenditures of theirs are due to generosity and liberality. They take that money from the city either in the manner of a tax or they dominate a group other than the inhabitants of the city for their money, bring it to the treasure-house, and use it as a reserve for making great expenditures in the city so as to gain greater honor.

When someone loves honor by whatever means it chances to come about, it is not impossible for him to establish a [93] distinguished ancestry for himself and his offspring after him. And in order that memory of him remains after him through his offspring, he places possession in his offspring or in his family.[20] Then it is not impossible for him to establish wealth for himself to be honored for it, even if it is of no use to anyone else. Then he also honors a group so that they will also honor him. Thus, he brings together all the things for which it is possible that people will honor him, then keeps particularly for himself things for which, according to them, he will have splendor, radiance, eminence, and magnificence—such as buildings, clothing, medals, [and] then being inaccessible to the people.

Then he legislates traditional laws[21] concerning honors. When rulership devolves upon him and the people are accustomed to him and his family being their king, he then ranks the people in such a way as to attain honor and magnificence. For each ranking, he legislates a kind of honor and what merits honor—such as wealth, buildings, clothing, medals, mounts, or other things that make his command magnificent. And he sets that down according to an order. After that, he tends to prefer the people who honor him more or assist him more in that magnificence of his. And he honors and gives honors on that basis. Now, the inhabitants of his city who love honor interact in this way with him so that he will increase the honors he bestows upon them. Due to that, the inhabitants

20. Literally, "in his genus" (*fī jinsih*). When the term "family" occurs later in this section, it is also literally "genus."

21. Here and in what follows, the term is *sunna;* see above, note 12.

of the rankings beneath them and above them honor them.

103. Due to these things, this city is similar to the virtuous city, especially if the honors and the rankings of the people with respect to honors are for the sake of what is more useful for others—such as wealth, [94] pleasures, or any other thing the one who seeks useful things has a passion for. This city is the best among the ignorant cities.[22] It is the one whose inhabitants—unlike the inhabitants of the other cities—are [properly] called "ignorant" and similar names. However, if the love of honor in it becomes very excessive, it becomes a city of tyrants and is fit for being transformed into becoming a city of domination.

[e. The Despotic City]

104. The city of domination and the association of domination are the ones whose inhabitants assist one another so that they have domination. They are like that when they all have love of domination in common. Yet they diverge from one another insofar as they love it less or more, and they diverge from one another with respect to the kinds of domination and the kinds of things for which they dominate people. Some, for example, love to dominate to spill a human being's blood, some love to dominate for his money, and some love to dominate over his soul so as to enslave him. People are ranked with respect to it[23] according to the great extent of domination one person loves [to exercise] and the paucity of it that most love [to exercise]. Their love to dominate others is directed at their blood [so as to spill it] and their spirits [so as to extinguish them], their souls so as to enslave them, or their money so as to wrest it from them. Their love and their purpose in all of that are domination, conquest, humiliation, and that the conquered possesses neither himself nor any other thing for the sake of which he has been dominated but is subject to obeying the conqueror in whatever passion he has. Thus when one of those who love domination and conquest has an ambition or passion for a certain thing then gains it without conquering any human being for it, he does not take it and pays no attention to it.

105. Among them are those of the opinion that they should conquer by wiliness, those of the opinion that they should conquer only by severity, and some of the opinion [95] that they should conquer by both manners—by wiliness and by severity. Therefore, many of those who conquer so as to spill blood do not kill a human being when they find him sleeping nor take money from him until they awaken him; rather, they are of the opinion that they should take it by severity and have the other actively resist so that they conquer him and inflict upon him what he loathes. Every one of these loves domination and thus loves to dominate all others, whether they are inhabitants of the city or others. However, they refrain from dominating one another with respect to spilling their blood or taking their money due to the need they have of one another so as to survive, to assist one another in dominating others, and to prevent others from dominating them.

106. Their ruler is the one among them who is most powerful in governing well by using them to dominate others, the one most excellent at using stratagems, and the one most perfect in opinion about what they ought to do so as always to be seen as dominators and to prevent others from dominating them. He is their ruler and their king. And they are enemies of all others. All of their traditional laws are traditional laws and prescriptions such that, when adhered to, they are fit for dominating others. Their rivalry and boasting is either about the frequency of their domination, its greatness, or their abundant acquisition of the equipment and instruments of domination.

Equipment and instruments of domination consist either in a human being's opinion, in his body, or in what is external to his body—in his body, endurance, for example; external to his body, having weapons; and in his opinion, having excellent opinion about what allows him to dominate another. These human beings tend to be crude, cruel, irascible, haughty, and gluttonous in stuffing themselves with food and drink, overindulging in sexual intercourse, and dominating one another for all the goods—and that comes about through conquering and humiliating whoever has any of them. They are of the opinion that they should dominate everything and everybody. [96]

107. Sometimes the whole city is like this so that they are of the opinion that, due to their need

22. Bracketing, for sense, *ahl* (inhabitants), so that the phrase reads *khayr mudun al-jāhiliyya*, and not *khayr mudun ahl al-jāhiliyya* (best among the inhabitants of the ignorant cities).

23. Understanding the prepositional clause *fīhā* to refer to domination; but it can also be construed as referring to the city itself, in which case it should read "people are ranked in it."

for association and not for any other thing, they should be intent on dominating anyone not from the city.

Sometimes the ones dominated and the conquerors are neighbors in a single city. Then the conquerors either love to conquer and dominate in an equal way and have equal rankings in the city or they have [different] rankings, with each one dominating over the conquered neighbors about something and doing so less or more than another. Similarly, with respect to the powers and opinions by which they dominate, they draw close to the king who rules them and governs the conquerors' affairs as concerns the instruments by which they arrive at conquest.

Sometimes the conqueror is only a single person with a group as his instruments for conquering the rest of the people. Their endeavor is not to dominate something and take it for someone else, but to dominate a thing so that it will belong to that single person. In turn, what that single person uses to maintain his life and endurance is sufficient for him; he gives [the rest] to others and dominates for others, as do dogs and falcons. Likewise, the rest of the inhabitants of the city are slaves serving that single person in whatever he has a passion for; humiliated and submissive, they possess nothing of their own at all. Some of them cultivate the soil for him, others trade for him. His intention in that is nothing more than seeing a group be conquered, dominated, and humiliated by him alone, even though he gains no other use from them nor any pleasure except that they be humiliated and conquered.

By its king alone is this a city of domination. The rest of the inhabitants of the city are not ones who dominate. The one previous to this is a city of domination by half [of its inhabitants], and the first by all of them.[24]

108. So the city of domination may be of this sort in that it endeavors by one of these means only to dominate and to take pleasure in doing so. If it loves domination only so as to attain the necessary things, wealth, [97] enjoyment of pleasures, honors, or all of these, then that city of domination is of a different sort. These [inhabitants] belong to those other cities mentioned above. Though many people call these cities the city of domination, the one most deserving of this name is the one that wants [to obtain] all three of these by conquest.[25] And these cities are of three sorts, namely, [domination] by one of the inhabitants, by half of the inhabitants, or by all of the inhabitants.[26] Thus, these inhabitants pursue conquest and mistreatment, not for their own sake, but with an intention and a purpose for something else.

109. There are yet other cities intent upon these [things] along with domination. In the first, which is intent upon domination however it comes about and for any thing whatsoever, someone may chance to harm another without any benefit coming to him from that—such as killing for no reason[27] other than the simple pleasure of conquest. And in it there is domination for vile things, as is recounted about a group among the Arabs.

With the second, there is love of domination for the sake of things that, according to them, are highly praiseworthy and are not vile. When they gain these things without conquest, they do not resort to conquest.

In the third city, there is harming and killing only insofar as it is known that it is useful for one of the venerable things. When the things one [of the inhabitants] is intent upon are made available to him without domination or conquest—by, for example, a treasure existing, someone else sufficing, or some human being bestowing that thing upon him obediently—he does not destroy others, pay any attention to them, or take from them. These people are also called high-minded and prideful. [98]

110. The inhabitants of the first city restrict themselves to such conquest as is necessary so as to attain domination. Sometimes they contest and struggle[28] mightily when prevented from getting money or a soul, and they quarrel until they are triumphant and can implement their judgment and passion on it, then abandon it and do not take it. These, too, may be praised, honored, and extolled for this. Those who love honor may use

24. By "the one previous to this," Alfarabi means the city in which "the ones dominated and the conquerors are neighbors in a single city"; and by "the first city," he means the one where "the whole city is...of the opinion that...they should be intent on dominating anyone not from the city." For these, see the accounts in the first two paragraphs of this section.

25. Though Najjar thinks the word "three" (*al-thalāth*) may be an interpolation, he notes its presence in all the MSS and suggests an interpretation based on the punctuation of Feyzullah 1279, where the goods to be attained by domination—listed two sentences earlier—fall into three groups: "the necessary things, wealth, or enjoyment of pleasures; honors; or all of these."

26. See above, sec. 107 (end) and note 24.

27. The term is *sabab.*

28. The term here translated as "struggle" is *jihād.*

many of these things so as to be honored for them. The cities of domination are more often tyrannical than honor-seeking.

111. It may occur that the inhabitants of the city of wealth and the inhabitants of the city of play and jesting presume themselves to be delightful, happy, masterful, and more virtuous than the inhabitants of the rest of the cities. Because of what they presume of themselves, it may occur that they have contempt for the inhabitants of other cities, consider those other than them to have no value, and expect love and honor for what—according to them—makes them happy. So it occurs that they become conceited, haughty, boastful, praise-loving, that [they presume] others cannot reach what they have reached, and that they are therefore too stupid to get even one of these two kinds of happiness.[29] They create for themselves names that embellish their ways of life—for example, that they are the naturally gifted and elegant ones and that those other than them are the crude. Therefore it is presumed that they possess pride, magnanimity, and authority. Sometimes they are called high-minded.

112. When it chances that the lovers of wealth, pleasure, and play attain none of the arts by which wealth is earned except the power to dominate and they arrive at wealth and play by conquest and domination, they become more intensely prideful and enter into the troop of tyrants. The first are simpletons.[30]

Similarly, it is not impossible for there to be among those who love honor someone who loves it not for its own sake, but for wealth. Now many of them want others to honor them so as to gain wealth, either from those [who honor them] or from someone else. They want rulership over, and obedience from, the inhabitants of the city so as to arrive at wealth. And many [99] of them want wealth for play and pleasure. So it happens that many of them seek rulership and to be obeyed in order to attain wealth to use in play. They are of the opinion that the greater and more complete their rulership and the obedience of others to them, the more increase they will have in these things. So they seek to be the only ones to rule over the inhabitants of the city so as to attain the magnificence by which they can arrive at such great wealth that none of the inhabitants can approximate it, then to use that wealth in play and to gain from play and the pleasures of food, drink, and sexual intercourse what no one else gains with respect to both quantity and quality.

[f. The Democratic City]

113. The democratic city is the city in which every one of its inhabitants is unrestrained and left to himself to do what he likes. Its inhabitants are equal to one another, and their traditional law is that no human being is superior to another in anything at all. Its inhabitants are free to do what they like. One [inhabitant] has authority over another or over someone else only insofar as he does what removes that person's freedom.

Thus there arises among them many moral habits, many endeavors, many desires, and taking pleasure in countless things. Its inhabitants consist of countless similar and dissimilar sects. In this city are brought together those [associations] that were kept separate in all those [other] cities—the vile and the venerable ones. Rulerships come about through any chance one of the rest of those things we have mentioned. The public, which does not have what the rulers have, has authority over those who are said to be their rulers. The one who rules them does so only by the will of the ruled, and their rulers are subject to the passions of the ruled. If their situation is examined closely, it turns out that in truth there is no ruler among them and no ruled.

114. Yet those who are praised and honored among them are those who bring the inhabitants of the city to freedom and to all of their passions and desires and those who preserve their freedom and the diverging, differing desires [100] of some from others and from their external enemies while restricting their desires only to what is necessary. These are the ones among them who are honored, [deemed] most excellent, and obeyed.

Any of the other rulers is either equal to them or inferior to them. He is their equal when, in return for his producing the goods they will and desire, they bestow upon him honors and money equivalent to what he does for them. Then they are not of the opinion that he has superiority over them. They are superior to him when they bestow honors upon him and establish a share of their money for him without receiving any benefit from him.

29. Namely, wealth or play and jesting; see the beginning of this section.

30. That is, those discussed above in sec. 111.

So it is not impossible for there to be a ruler of this sort whose condition is that he chances to be magnified by the inhabitants of the city either because the inhabitants of the city have a passion for him or because the right of his forefathers, who had praiseworthy rulership over them, is preserved in him so that he rules. Then the public is in authority over the rulers.

All the endeavors and purposes of the ignorant [cities] are present in this city in the most perfect manner, and more.

115. Of [all] their cities, this is the admirable and happy city. On the surface, it is like an embroidered garment replete with colored figures and dyes. Everyone loves it and loves to dwell in it, because every human being who has a passion or desire for anything is able to gain it in this city. The nations repair to it and dwell in it, so it becomes great beyond measure. People of every tribe are procreated in it by every sort of pairing off and sexual intercourse. The children generated in it are of very different innate characters and of very different education and upbringing.

Thus this city comes to be many cities, not distinguished from one another but interwoven with one another, the parts of one interspersed among the parts of another. Nor is the foreigner distinguished from the native resident. All of the passions and ways of life come together in it. [101] Therefore, it is not impossible as time draws on that virtuous people emerge in it. There may chance to exist in it wise men, rhetoricians, and poets concerned with every type of object. It is possible to glean from it parts of the virtuous city, and this is the best that emerges in this city. Thus, of the ignorant cities this city has both the most good and the most evil. The bigger, more prosperous, more populous, more fertile, and more perfect it becomes for people, the more prevalent and greater are these two.[31]

116. What the ignorant rulerships are intent upon is as numerous as are the ignorant cities. For each ignorant rulership is intent upon gaining control over what is necessary; wealth; enjoyment of pleasures; honor, fame, and praise; domination; or freedom. Therefore, these rulerships are bought for money—especially the rulerships that come about in the democratic city. For no one there is more deserving of rulership than another. So when rulership in it is surrendered to someone, it is either because the inhabitants granted it to him or that they took money or some other recompense from him.

117. According to them, the virtuous ruler is the one who is excellent at deliberation and fine at using stratagems to gain them their different and variegated desires and passions, preserving that from their enemies, and not depriving [them] of any of their money but restricting himself only to what is necessary for his power.

The one who is virtuous in truth—namely, the one who, when he rules them, determines their actions and directs them toward happiness—is not made a ruler by them. If he chances to rule them, he is soon deposed or killed, or his rulership is disturbed and challenged. The same holds for [102] the rest of the ignorant cities: Each of them wants only to be ruled by someone who sets its choices and desires before it, makes the path to them easy, gains them for them, and preserves them for them. They reject the rulership of the virtuous and censure it. However, it is more possible and easier for the virtuous cities and the rulership of the virtuous to emerge from the necessary and democratic cities than from the other [ignorant] cities.

[Summary]

118. What is necessary, wealth, enjoyment of pleasures and play, and honor may be gained by conquest and domination and may be gained by other means. So the four cities[32] are divided in this manner. Similarly, of the rulerships intent upon these four [things] or [any] one of them, some are intent upon obtaining it by domination and conquest and some by means other than these. Those [individuals] who procure these things by domination and conquest and safeguard what they attained by resistance and conquest need to have strong and powerful bodies; to be cruel, crude, coarse, and contemptuous of death in their moral habits; to be of the opinion that it is not worth living without gaining what is important; to have an art of using weapons; and to be good in deliberating about how to conquer others. This is common to all of them.

119. In addition to these [things], those who pursue the enjoyment of pleasure happen to be voracious and to love eating, drinking, and sexual intercourse. Among them are those who are so

31. Namely, good and evil.

32. Namely, the necessary, depraved or plutocratic, vile or hedonistic, and timocratic cities.

dominated by softness and luxury that their irascible faculty disintegrates, and nothing of it at all or [only] a trifling extent is to be found in them.

And among them are those who are overwhelmed by anger, with its psychological and bodily instruments, and by desire, with its psychological and bodily instruments, to the point that these two are strengthened and increased thus making it possible to carry out their actions. Their deliberation is devoted to the actions of these two, and their souls are equally subservient to them.

And among these are those who are ultimately intent upon the actions of desire. They put their irascible faculties and actions as instruments for arriving [103] at the desires, thereby putting their higher and loftier faculties in the service of what is more vile. That is, they put their rational faculty in the service of the irascible and desiring [faculties] and then their irascible faculties in the service of their desiring faculties. They devote their deliberation to inferring what makes the actions of anger and desire complete; and they devote the actions of their irascible faculties and their instruments to what gains the pleasure to be savored from eating, drinking, and sexual intercourse, as well as to the rest of the things to be dominated and preserved for themselves—as is seen with the notables of the inhabitants of the steppes from among the Turks and the Arabs.

For common to the inhabitants of the steppes is love of domination and great gluttony with respect to eating, drinking, and sexual intercourse. Therefore, women are of great importance according to them. Many of them approve of licentiousness and are not of the opinion that it is degenerate and vile, since their souls are subservient to their desires. You see many of them being pleasing to women in all they do, doing so in order to magnify their standing among women. They hold as shameful what women deem shameful, and what women find fair is fair for them. In all things, they adhere to the desires of their women. Women are in authority over many of them and are responsible for the affairs of the household. For this reason,[33] many of them accustom their women to luxury and do not give them over to toil; rather, they keep them in luxury and comfort, while themselves undertaking everything that requires labor, toil, and undergoing hardship.

[2. The Immoral Cities]

120. The immoral cities are the ones whose inhabitants believed in, and formed a concept of, the principles [of the beings]. They had an image of happiness and believed in it. They were guided toward, were cognizant of, and believed in the actions by which they could gain happiness. Yet they did not hold fast to any of those actions, but through their passion and will inclined toward one of the purposes[34] of the inhabitants of the ignorant cities—either station,[35] honor, domination, or something else—and they established all of their actions and faculties to be directed toward those purposes.

The kinds of these cities are as numerous as the kinds of ignorant cities, because all the actions of their inhabitants are the actions [104] of the inhabitants of the ignorant cities and their moral habits the moral habits of those inhabitants. They are distinct from the inhabitants of the ignorant cities only by the opinions in which they believe. No one at all among the inhabitants of these cities gains happiness.

[3. The Errant Cities]

121. The errant cities are the ones whose inhabitants receive representations of objects other than the ones we have mentioned—that is, the principles set before them and represented for them are other than those we have mentioned. The happiness set before them is other than the one that is happiness in truth, and a happiness other than that one is represented for them. And the actions and opinions prescribed for them gain nothing of happiness in truth.

[4. The Weeds in the Virtuous Cities]

122. The weeds in the virtuous cities are of many sorts. Among them is a sort (1) that holds fast to the actions by which happiness is gained, except that in what they do they are intent not upon happiness but upon some other thing a human being may gain through virtue—such as honor, rulership, wealth, or something else. These [people] are called opportunists.[36]

33. The term is *sabab.*

34. Literally, "a particular thing from the purposes" (*shay' mā min aghrāḍ*).

35. Station (*manzila*), which has not heretofore been cited as one of the purposes of the ignorant cities, takes the place here of wealth (*yasār*).

36. Literally, "hunters" (*mutaqanniṣūn).*

And among them (a) are those who have a passion for one of the ends of the inhabitants of the ignorant cities, but the laws of the city and its religion prevent them from it. So they apply themselves to the utterances and statements of the law-giver[37] for his precepts and interpret them so as to agree with their passion, thereby embellishing that thing by their interpretation. These [people] are called distorters.

And among them are (b) those who are not intent upon distortion. But due to their poor understanding of the law-giver's intention and their defective grasp of his statements, they understand the laws of the city differently from the way the law-giver intended. So their actions fall outside the intention of the first ruler and they err without being conscious of it. These people are called schismatics (*māriqa*).

123. Another sort (2) has already imagined the things we have mentioned, except that they are not persuaded by what they have imagined. So, for themselves and for others, they show those things to be false by arguments. In doing so, [105] they are not contending against the virtuous city. Rather, they are asking for guidance and seeking the truth.

Whoever is like this has his level of imagination elevated to things that the arguments he brings forth do not show to be false. If he is persuaded in thus being elevated, he is left there. But if he is not persuaded by that either and falls upon topics he can contend against, he is elevated to another level. It goes on like this until he is persuaded by one of these levels. But if he does not chance to be persuaded by one of the levels of imagination, he is elevated to the ranking of truth and made to understand those things as they are. At that point, his opinion becomes settled.

124. Among them, another sort (3) shows what they imagine to be false. Whenever they are elevated in rank, they show it to be false—even when they obtain the ranking of truth. They do all this in seeking domination alone or in seeking to embellish one of the purposes of the inhabitants of the ignorant cities to which they are inclined. So they show [what they imagine] to be false in every way they can. They do not like to hear anything that firmly establishes[38] happiness and truth in the soul nor any argument that embellishes them and prescribes them for the soul, but meet them with sham arguments that they presume will discredit happiness. In doing that, many of them are intent upon appearing to be excused for inclining to one of the purposes of the inhabitants of the ignorant cities.

125. Among them is a sort (4) that imagines happiness and the principles [of the beings], but it is not within the power of their minds to form a concept of them at all. Or it is not within the power of their understanding to form a sufficient concept of them. So they show what they imagine to be false and seize upon the topics of contention in them. Whenever they are elevated to a level of imagination that is closer to the truth, they show it to be false. It is not possible for them to be elevated to the level of truth, because it is not within the power of their minds to understand it. It may chance that many of these people show much of what they imagine to be false, not because there are truly topics of contention in what they imagine, but because their imagination is defective. So, due to their poor understanding, they show that to be false—not because there is a topic of contention in it. [106]

When unable to imagine something sufficiently or to grasp the true topics of contention in the places in which there are topics of contention and when unable to understand the truth, many of them presume that the one who apprehends the truth and says he has apprehended it is lying deliberately in a quest for honor or domination. Or they presume that he is a deluded zealot who also wants to show the truth to be false and to vilify the one who has apprehended it. That leads many of them to presume that all people are deluded about everything they claim to have apprehended.

And that leads (a) some of them to perplexity about all objects.

And that leads (b) some of them to be of the opinion that there is nothing accurate at all in what is apprehended and that whenever someone presumes he has apprehended something, he is lying about that[39] without being sure or certain of what he presumes. According to intelligent persons and in relation to the philosophers, these people are in the position of ignorant simpletons. Due to that,

37. Here and in what follows the term translated as "laws" is *sharā'i'* (sing. *sharī'a*) and that translated as "law-giver" is *wāḍi' al-sunna*. See above, notes 11 and 12.

38. Literally, "strengthens" (*yuqawwī*).

39. At this point all of the MSS except Feyzullah 1279 end.

it is obligatory for the ruler of the virtuous city to watch over the weeds, keep them busy, and cure each sort by means of what is particularly suited to it—either expulsion from the city, punishment, imprisonment, or assigning them tasks even though they do not strive after them.

And (c) some of them presume that the truth is what appears to each person and what he presumes at each moment and that the truth about each thing is what someone presumes it to be.

And (d) some of them exert themselves in making it seem that whatever has been presumed to have been apprehended up to this point is completely false and that even if there is something accurate and true, it has not yet been apprehended.

And (e) some of them imagine—as in a sleeping person's dream or as with a thing seen from afar—that there is a truth here, and it occurs to them that those who claim to have apprehended it have perhaps apprehended it or that there is among them someone who has perhaps apprehended it. In themselves, they sense that it has eluded them either because [107] apprehending it requires a long time as well as toil and hardship whereas they do not have adequate time for it nor the power to toil and persevere, because they are busy with pleasures and other things to which they have become accustomed and which it is hard for them to discard, or because they have sensed that they would not [be able to] apprehend it even if all its causes were made available to them.

Sorrow and grief occur to them due to their presuming that it is possible someone else may have seized upon it. Due to jealousy about someone having perhaps apprehended the truth, they form the opinion to struggle[40] by means of sham arguments to make it seem that the one who says he has apprehended is either deluded or a liar who, in what he purports, is searching for honor, wealth, or some other thing such as to incite passion.

Many of these people sense their own ignorance and perplexity. They are pained and hurt by what they feel in themselves,[41] and that grieves and torments them. They find no way to remove this from themselves by means of a science that would seize upon the truth, the apprehension of which would earn them pleasure. So they form the opinion to take a respite from that through recourse to the rest of the ends of the ignorant cities and to jesting and playful things. They set those down as consolation until death comes to relieve them of their lot.

Some of these people—I mean those who seek to take a respite from the torments they find in ignorance and perplexity—sometimes fancy that the [true] ends are the ones they choose and prefer, that happiness consists of these, and that the remaining human beings are deluded in what they believe. They struggle[42] to embellish ignorant things and [ignorant] happiness. They fancy that they have come to prefer this after a long investigation of everything others purport to have apprehended, that they have rejected it only after grasping that it is not to be attained, and that they have come to this through an insight that these are the ends—not the ones those other people purport to be.

126. These, then, are the sorts [of weeds] growing among the inhabitants of the city. From their opinions, no city at all is attained, nor a large association from the populace. But they are embedded among the inhabitants of the city as a whole.[43]

40. The term here translated as "struggle" is from the same root as *jihād.*

41. That is, the inadequacy or lack they feel in themselves.

42. The term here translated as "struggle" is from the same root as *jihād.*

43. This marks the end of the discussion of the cities contrary to the virtuous city that began in sec. 92 above. Feyzullah 1279 contains an additional paragraph that is almost identical to a passage from Alfarabi's *Virtuous City.* In Richard Walzer's edition and translation, the passage occurs at the beginning of Section 6, Chapter 18, 286:2–288:3; and in Friedrich Dieterici's edition, *Risāla fī Ārā' Ahl al-Madīna al-Fāḍila* (1895; repr., Leiden: E. J. Brill, 1964), it occurs at 71:23–72:10.

As Najjar points out, the paragraph may simply be misplaced; and the text can therefore be considered as complete at this point. If it does belong to the text, then the work as a whole must be considered incomplete, since the paragraph terminates with an incomplete sentence and omits the part corresponding to the rest of the passage in the *Virtuous City,* namely, the rest of Section 6, Chapter 18, plus all of Section 6, Chapter 19 (288:3–328:12) in Walzer's edition and 72:10–85:7 in Dieterici's edition. Here is the passage in question:

"The errant cities are generated when religion is built on some of the ancient, corrupt opinions. Among them is a group that says: 'We see that the beings we observe are contrary to one another, and each seeks to destroy the other; and we see that when each of them attains existence, along with its existence it is given something with which to preserve its existence from destruction, something with which to defend and safeguard itself from its contrary, and something by which it is able to put the rest of things into its service concerning what is useful for its most excellent and continuous existence. And for many of them, there is set down that by which they conquer whatever resists them. That is set down for every contrary with respect to its contrary and whatever else is in this condition, so that each of them is intent upon safeguarding for itself the most excellent existence apart from the others. Therefore, there is set down for it what destroys. . .'"

FOUR

ALFARABI

The Attainment of Happiness

Translated by Muhsin Mahdi

The *Attainment of Happiness* is the first part of a trilogy entitled the *Philosophy of Plato and Aristotle,* of which the second part is the *Philosophy of Plato* and the third part is the *Philosophy of Aristotle.* The *Attainment of Happiness* has four subdivisions. The first gives an account of (1) the theoretical virtues or theoretical sciences (including "theoretical" political science) and explains the relationship among them. The second raises and answers the question of the need for something beyond theoretical science, which answer unfolds into an account of (2) prudence or deliberation, (3) the moral virtues, and (4) the practical arts; and discusses the relationship among these four things in an individual. The third gives an account of the methods through which these four are realized in a nation or a city, which unfolds into a discussion of the qualities of the ruler and the structure of the city, and its opinions and actions. The fourth begins with praise of theoretical science or philosophy, and then proceeds to discuss the relation between the philosopher and the prince, between philosophy and religion, and between true and false philosophy. This is perhaps Alfarabi's most fundamental work; it provides the philosophic framework on the basis of which his didactic and political works ought to be understood. The sections omitted here (2–15 [sec. 1 is given in note 6]) deal with logic, mathematics, and physics.

A Hebrew paraphrase of the *Attainment of Happiness* is included in Shem Tov Ibn Falaquera's *Introduction to Science,* which in turn was translated into Latin. The following translation is based on an edition in progress. The numbers inserted in the translation refer to the Hyderabad text: *Taḥṣīl al-saʿāda* (1345 AH), 12–47. The variants adopted here were given in "Notes to the Arabic Text of the *Attainment of Happiness,*" in *Alfarabi: The Political Writings; Philosophy of Plato and Aristotle,* ed. and trans. Muhsin Mahdi (New York: The Free Press of Glencoe, 1962; rev. ed., Ithaca, NY: Cornell University Press, 1969, 2002), 150–56.

SUBDIVISION 1

16. When one finally comes to inquire into the heavenly bodies and investigate the principles of their being, this inquiry into the principles of their being will force one to look for principles that are not natures or natural things, but beings more perfect than nature and natural things. They are also

not bodies or in bodies. Therefore, one needs another kind of investigation here and another science that inquires exclusively into beings that are metaphysical. At this point he is again standing between two sciences: the science of nature and [metaphysics, or] the science of what is beyond natural things [13] in the order of investigation and instruction and above them in the order of being.

17. When his inquiry finally reaches the stage of investigating the principles of the being of animals, he will be forced to inquire into the soul and learn about psychical [or animate] principles, and from there ascend to the inquiry into the rational animal. As he investigates the principles of the latter, he will be forced to inquire into (1) *what, by what,* and *how,* (2–3) *from what,* and (4) *for what* it is.[1] It is here that he acquaints himself with the intellect and things intelligible. He needs to investigate (1) *what* the intellect is and *by what* and *how* it is, and (2–3) *from what* and (4) *for what* it is. This investigation will force him to look for other principles that are not bodies or in bodies, and that never were or ever will be in bodies. This inquiry into the rational animal will thus lead him to a similar conclusion as the inquiry into the heavenly bodies. Now he acquaints himself with incorporeal principles that are to the beings below the heavenly bodies as those incorporeal principles (with which he became acquainted when investigating the heavenly bodies) are to the heavenly bodies. He will acquaint himself with the principles for the sake of which the soul and the intellect are made, and with the ends and the ultimate perfection for the sake of which man is made. He will know that the natural principles in man and in the world are not sufficient for man's coming to that perfection for the sake of whose achievement he is made. It will become evident that man needs some rational, intellectual principles with which to work toward that perfection.

18. At this point the inquirer will have sighted another genus of things, different from the metaphysical. It is incumbent on man to investigate what is included in this genus: that is, the things that realize for man his objective through the intellectual principles that are in him, and by which he achieves that perfection which became known in natural science. It will become evident concomitantly that these rational principles are not mere causes by which man attains the perfection for which he is made. Moreover, he will know that these [14] rational principles also supply many things to natural beings other than those supplied by nature. Indeed, man arrives at the ultimate perfection (whereby he attains that which renders him truly substantial) only when he labors with these principles toward achieving this perfection. Moreover, he cannot labor toward this perfection except by exploiting a large number of natural beings and until he manipulates them to render them useful to him for arriving at the ultimate perfection he should achieve. Furthermore, it will become evident to him in this science that each man achieves only a portion of that perfection, and what he achieves of this portion varies in its extent, for an isolated individual cannot achieve all the perfections by himself and without the aid of many other individuals. It is the innate disposition of every man to join another human being or other men in the labor he ought to perform: this is the condition of every single man. Therefore, to achieve what he can of that perfection, every man needs to stay in the neighborhood of others and associate with them. It is also the innate nature of this animal to seek shelter and to dwell in the neighborhood of those who belong to the same species, which is why he is called the social and political animal. There emerges now another science and another inquiry that investigates these intellectual principles and the acts and states of character with which man labors toward this perfection. From this, in turn, emerge the science of man and political science.

19. He should begin to inquire into the metaphysical beings and, in treating them, use the methods he used in treating natural things. He should use as their principles of instruction[2] the first premises that happen to be available and are appropriate to this genus, and in addition, the demonstrations of [15] natural science that fit as principles of instruction in this genus. These should be arranged according to the order mentioned above,[3] until one covers every being in this genus. It will become evident to whoever investigates these beings that none of them can possess

1. These are the four ways of interpreting and asking the question *why,* which Alfarabi has indicated previously in secs. 5 ff.; they ask after (1) the form, (2–3) the agent and the material, and (4) the end.

2. For the source of the distinction between the "principle of instruction" and the "principle of being," between "what is better known to us" and "what is better known by nature," consider Aristotle *Physics* 184a16–23, 189a4 (cf. *Posterior Analytics* 71b34–72a6); *Nicomachean Ethics* 1095a30 ff., 1139b25 ff.

3. Secs. 4 ff.

any matter at all; one ought to investigate every one of them only as to (1) *what and how* it is, (2–3) *from what* agent and (4) *for what* it is. He should continue this investigation until he finally reaches a being that cannot possess any of these principles at all (either *what* it is or *from what* it is or *for what* it is) but is itself the first principle of all the aforementioned beings: it is itself that *by which, from which,* and *for which* they are, in the most perfect modes in which a thing can be a principle for the beings, modes free from all defects. Having understood this, he should investigate next what properties the other beings possess as a consequence of their having this being as their principle and the cause of their being. He should begin with the being whose rank is higher than the rest (that is, the one nearest to the first principle), until he terminates in the being whose rank is inferior to the rest (that is, the one farthest from the first principle). He will thus come to know the ultimate causes of the beings. This is the divine inquiry into them. For the first principle is the divinity, and the principles that come after it—and are not bodies or in bodies—are the divine principles.

20. Then he should set out next upon the science of man and investigate the *what* and the *how* of the purpose for which man is made, that is, the perfection that man must achieve. Then he should investigate all the things by which man achieves this perfection or that are useful to him in achieving it. These are the good, virtuous, and noble things. He should distinguish them from [16] the things that obstruct his achieving this perfection. These are the evils, the vices, and the base things. He should make known *what* and *how* every one of them is, and *from what* and *for what* it is, until all of them become known, intelligible, and distinguished from each other. This is political science.[4] It consists of knowing the things by which the citizens of cities attain happiness through political association in the measure that innate disposition equips each of them for it. It will become evident to him that political association and the totality that results from the association of citizens in cities correspond to the association of the bodies that constitute the totality of the world. He will come to see in what are included in the totality constituted by the city and the nation the likenesses of what are included in the total world. Just as in the world there is a first principle, then other principles subordinate to it, beings that proceed from these principles, other beings subordinate to these beings, until they terminate in the beings with the lowest rank in the order of being, so the nation or the city includes a supreme commander, followed by other commanders,[5] followed by other citizens, who in turn are followed by other citizens, until they terminate in the citizens with the lowest rank as citizens and as human beings. Thus the city includes the likenesses of the things included in the total world.

21. This, then, is theoretical perfection. As you see, it comprises knowledge of the four kinds of things[6] by which the citizens of cities and nations attain supreme happiness. What still remains is that these four be realized and have actual existence in nations and cities while conforming to the account of them given by the theoretical affairs (*al-umūr al-naẓariyya*).[7]

SUBDIVISION 2

22. Do you suppose that these theoretical [sciences] have also given an account of the means by which these four can be [17] actually realized in nations and cities, or not? They have indeed given an account of the latter as they are perceived by the intellect. Now if it were the case that to give an account of these things as they are perceived by the intellect is to give an account of their [actual] existence, it would follow that the theoretical sciences have given an account of them as actually existent.

4. That is, the "theoretical" part of it. Cf. below, sec. 26; cf. selection 1, *Enumeration of the Sciences* 1–3; and cf. selection 2, *Book of Religion* 5, 11–18.

5. Alfarabi says "first principle" and "principles," respectively; cf. the physical-metaphysical and political connotations of *archē* (*archōn*): *principium-princeps*, "principle"-"prince."

6. Enumerated by Alfarabi in sec. 1: "The human things by which nations and citizens of cities attain earthly happiness in this life and supreme happiness in the life beyond are of four kinds: theoretical virtues, deliberative virtues, moral virtues, and practical arts."

7. Alfarabi's choice of "affairs" (*al-umūr*) here, where one might expect "sciences" (*al-'ulūm*), becomes all the more striking because he delays using "sciences" until the middle of the next paragraph. Perhaps he avoids "sciences" at the end of sec. 1 to emphasize the inconclusiveness of the inquiry described therein.

(For instance, if it were the case that giving an intelligible account of architecture and perceiving by the intellect what constitutes architecture and what constitutes a building make an architect of the man who has intellected what manner of thing the art of building is, or, if it were the case that giving an intelligible account of a building is to give an account of its actual existence, then the theoretical sciences (*al-ʿulūm al-naẓariyya*) do both.) But if it is not the case that the intellection of a thing implies its existence outside the intellect, and that to give an intelligible account of it is to give an account of its actual existence; then, when one intends to make these four things exist, he necessarily requires something else beside theoretical science.

23. That is because things perceived by the intellect are as such free from the states and accidents that they have when they exist outside the [thinking] soul. In what remains numerically one, these accidents do not vary or change at all; they do vary, however, in what remains one, not numerically, but in the species. Therefore when it is necessary to make the things perceived by the intellect and remaining one in their species exist outside the soul, one must join to them the states and accidents that must accompany them if they are to have actual existence outside the soul. This applies to the natural intelligibles, which are and remain one in their species, as well as to the voluntary intelligibles.[8]

24. However, the natural intelligibles, which exist outside the soul, exist from nature only, and it is by nature that they are accompanied with their accidents. As for the intelligibles that can be made to exist outside the soul by will, the accidents [18] and states that accompany them when they come into being are willed too. Now voluntary intelligibles cannot exist unless they are accompanied with these accidents and states. Since everything whose existence is willed cannot be made to exist unless it is first known, it follows that when one plans to bring any voluntary intelligible into actual existence outside the soul, he must first know the states that must accompany it when it exists. Because voluntary intelligibles do not belong to things that are one numerically, but in their species or genus; the accidents and states that must accompany them vary constantly, increase and decrease, and fall into combinations that cannot be covered at all by invariable and unchangeable formal rules. Indeed for some of them no rule can be established. For others rules can be established, but they are variable rules and changeable definitions. Those for which no rule at all can be established are the ones that vary constantly and over short periods. The others, for which rules can be established, are those whose states vary over long periods. Those of them that come to exist are for the most part realized by the agency of whoever wills and does them. Yet because of obstacles standing in their way—some of which are natural and others voluntary, resulting from the wills of other individuals—sometimes none of them at all is realized. Furthermore, they suffer not only temporal variations, so that they may exist at a certain time with accidents and states different from those that accompany them at another time before or after; their states also differ when they exist in different places. This is evident in natural things, for example, Man. For when it [that is, the intelligible idea Man] assumes actual existence outside the soul, [19] the states and accidents in it at one time are different from the ones it has at another time, after or before. The same is the case with respect to different places. The accidents and states it has when existing in one country are different from the ones it has in another. Yet, throughout, the intellect perceives Man as a single intelligible idea. This holds for voluntary things as well. For instance, Moderation, Wealth, and the like are voluntary ideas perceived by the intellect. When we decide to make them actually exist, the accidents that must accompany them at a certain time will be different from the accidents that must accompany them at another time, and the accidents they must have when they exist in one nation will be different from those they must have when existing in another. In some of them, these accidents change from hour to hour, in others from day to day, in others from month to month, in others from year to year, in others from decade to decade, and in still others they change after many decades. Therefore, whoever should will to bring any of them into actual existence outside the soul ought to know the variable accidents that must accompany it, in the specific period at which he seeks to bring it into existence, and in the determined place in the inhabited part of the earth. Thus he ought to know the accidents that must accompany what is

8. The distinction between "natural" and "voluntary" intelligibles and the meaning of "voluntary" intelligibles is stated below, secs. 24 ff.

willed to exist from hour to hour, from month to month, from year to year, from decade to decade, or in some other period of determinate length, in a determined locality of large or small size. And he ought to know which of these accidents are common to all nations, to some nations, or to one city over a long period, common to them over a short period, or pertain to some of them specifically and over a short period.

25. The accidents and states of these intelligibles vary [20] whenever certain events occur in the inhabited part of the earth: events common to all of it, to a certain nation or city, or to a certain group within a city, or pertaining to a single man. Such events are either natural or willed.

26. Things of this sort are not covered by the theoretical sciences, which cover only the intelligibles that do not vary at all. Therefore, another faculty and another skill is required with which to discern the voluntary intelligibles [not as such, but] insofar as they possess these variable accidents: that is, the modes according to which they can be brought into actual existence by the will at a determined time, in a determined place, and when a determined event occurs. That is the deliberative faculty.[9] It is the skill and the faculty by which one discovers and discerns the variable accidents of the intelligibles whose particular instances are made to exist by the will; when one attempts to bring them into actual existence by the will at a determined time, in a determined place; and when a determined event takes place, whether the time is long or short, whether the locality is large or small.

27. Things are discovered by the deliberative faculty only insofar as they are found to be useful for the attainment of an end and purpose. The discoverer first sets the end before himself and then investigates the means by which that end and that purpose are realized. The deliberative faculty is most perfect when it discovers what is most useful for the attainment of these ends. The ends may be truly good, may be evil, or may be only believed to be good. If the means discovered are the most useful for a virtuous end, then they are noble and fair. [21] If the ends are evil, then the means discovered by the deliberative faculty are also evil, base, and bad. And if the ends are only believed to be good, then the means useful for attaining and achieving them are also only believed to be good. The deliberative faculty can be classified accordingly. Deliberative virtue is that by which one discovers what is most useful for some virtuous end. As for the deliberative faculty by which one discovers what is most useful for an evil end, it is not a deliberative virtue but ought to have other names. And if the deliberative faculty is used to discover what is most useful for things that are only believed to be good, then that deliberative faculty is only believed to be a deliberative virtue.

28. (1) There is a certain deliberative virtue that enables one to excel in the discovery of what is most useful for a virtuous end common to many nations, to a whole nation, or to a whole city, at a time when an event occurs that affects them in common. (There is no difference between saying "most useful" for a virtuous end and "most useful and most noble," because what is both most useful and most noble necessarily serves a virtuous end, and what is most useful for a virtuous end is indeed the most noble with respect to that end.) This is political deliberative virtue. The events that affect them in common may persist over a long period or vary within short periods. However, political deliberative virtue is the deliberative virtue that discovers the most useful and most noble that is common to many nations, to a whole nation, or to a whole city, irrespective of whether what is discovered persists there for a long period or varies over a short period. When it is concerned exclusively with the discovery of the things that are common to many nations, to a whole nation, [22] or to a whole city, and that do not vary except over many decades or over longer periods of determinate length, then it is more akin to a legislative ability. (2) The deliberative virtue with which one discovers only what varies over short periods: this is the faculty that manages the different classes of particular, temporary tasks in conjunction with, and at the occurrence of, the events that affect all nations, a certain nation, or a certain city. It is subordinate to the former. (3) The faculty by which one discovers what is most useful and noble, or what is most useful for a virtuous end, relative to one group among the citizens of a city or to the members of a household: it consists of a variety of deliberative virtues, each associated with the group in question; for instance, it is economic deliberative virtue or military deliberative virtue. Each of these, in turn, is subdivided inasmuch as

9. The "rationative," "thinking," "calculative," or "reflective" faculty (*fikriyya*).

what it discovers (a) does not vary except over long periods or (b) varies over short periods. (4) The deliberative virtue may be subdivided into still smaller fractions, such as the virtue by which one discovers what is most useful and noble with respect to the purpose of particular arts or with respect to particular purposes that happen to be pursued at particular times. Thus it will have as many subdivisions as there are arts and ways of life. (5) Furthermore, this faculty can be divided also insofar as (a) it enables man to excel in the discovery of what is most useful and noble with respect to his own end when an event occurs that concerns him specifically, and (b) it is a deliberative virtue by which he discovers what is most useful and noble with respect to a virtuous end to be attained by somebody else—the latter is consultative deliberative virtue. These two may be united in a single man or may exist separately.

29. It is obvious that the one who possesses a virtue by which he discovers what is most useful and noble, and this for the sake of a virtuous end that is good (irrespective of whether what is discovered is a true good that he wishes [23] for himself, a true good that he wishes someone else to possess, or something that is believed to be good by whomever he wishes it for), cannot possess this faculty without possessing a moral virtue. For if a man wishes the good for others, then he is either truly good or else believed to be good by those for whom he wishes the good although he is not good and virtuous. Similarly, he who wishes the true good for himself has to be good and virtuous, not in his deliberation, but in his moral character and in his acts. It would seem that his virtue, moral character, and acts, have to correspond to his power of deliberation and ability to discover what is most useful and noble. Hence, if he discovers by his deliberative virtue only those most useful and noble means that are of great force (such as what is most useful for a virtuous end common to a whole nation, to many nations, or to a whole city, and does not vary except over a long period), then his moral virtues ought to be of a comparable measure. Similarly, if his deliberative virtues are confined to means that are most useful for a restricted end when a specific event occurs, then this is the measure of his [moral] virtue also. Accordingly, the more perfect the authority and the greater the power of these deliberative virtues, the stronger the authority and the greater the power of the moral virtues that accompany them.

30. (1) Since the deliberative virtue by which one discovers what is most useful and noble with respect to the ends that do not vary except over long periods and that are common to many nations, to a whole nation, or to a whole city when an event that affects them in common occurs, has more perfect authority and greater power; the [moral] virtues that accompany it should possess the most perfect authority and the greatest power. [24] (2) Next follows the deliberative virtue with which one excels in the discovery of what is most useful for a common, though temporary end, over short periods; the [moral] virtues that accompany it are of a comparable rank. (3) Then follow the deliberative virtues confined to individual parts of the city—the warriors, the rich, and so on; the moral virtues that have to do with these parts are of a comparable rank. (4) Finally, one comes to the deliberative virtues related to single arts (taking into account the purposes of these arts) and to single households and single human beings within single households (with attention to what pertains to them as events follow one another hour after hour or day after day); they are accompanied by a [moral] virtue of a comparable rank.

31. Therefore one ought to investigate which virtue is the perfect and most powerful virtue. Is it the combination of all the virtues? Or, if one virtue (or a number of virtues) turns out to have a power equal to that of all the virtues together, what ought to be the distinctive mark of the virtue that has this power and is hence the most powerful virtue? This virtue is such that when a man decides to fulfill its functions, he cannot do so without making use of the functions of all the other virtues. If he himself does not happen to possess all of these virtues—in which case he cannot make use of the functions of particular virtues present in him when he decides to fulfill the functions of that virtue—that virtue of his will be a moral virtue in the exercise of which he exploits the acts of the virtues possessed by all others; whether they are nations, cities within a nation, groups within a city, or parts within each group. This, then, is the leading virtue that is not surpassed by any other in authority. [25] Next follow the virtues that resemble this one in that they have a similar power with respect to single parts of the city. For instance, together with the deliberative faculty by which he discovers what is most useful and noble with respect to that which is common to warriors, the general ought to possess a moral virtue. When he decides to fulfill the functions of the latter, he exploits the virtues possessed by the

warriors as warriors. His courage, for instance, ought to be such as to enable him to exploit the warriors' particular acts of courage. Similarly, the one who possesses a deliberative virtue by which he discovers what is most useful and noble for the ends of those who acquire wealth in the city ought to possess the moral virtue that enables him to exploit the particular virtues of the classes of people engaged in acquiring wealth.

32. The arts, too, ought to follow this pattern. The leading art that is not surpassed by any other in authority is such that when we decide to fulfill its functions, we are unable to do so without making use of the functions of all the arts. It is the art for the fulfillment of whose purpose we require all the other arts. This, then, is the leading art and the most powerful of the arts—just as the corresponding moral virtue was the most powerful of all the moral virtues. It is then followed by the rest of the arts. An art of a certain class among them is more perfect and more powerful than the rest in its class if its end can be fulfilled only by making use of the functions of the other arts in its class. Such is the status of the leading military arts. For instance, the art of commanding armies is such that its purpose can be achieved only by making use of the functions of the particular arts of warfare.[10] Similarly, the [26] leading art of wealth in the city is such that its purpose with regard to wealth can be achieved only by exploiting the particular arts of acquiring wealth. This is the case also in every other major part of the city.

33. Furthermore, it is obvious that what is most useful and noble is in every case either most noble according to generally accepted opinion, most noble according to a particular religion, or truly most noble. Similarly, virtuous ends are either virtuous and good according to generally accepted opinion, virtuous and good according to a particular religion, or truly virtuous and good. No one can discover what is most noble according to the followers of a particular religion unless his moral virtues are the specific virtues of that religion. This holds for everyone else; it applies to the more powerful virtues as well as to the more particular and less powerful. Therefore the most powerful deliberative virtue and the most powerful moral virtue are inseparable from each other.

34. It is evident that the deliberative virtue with the highest authority can only be subordinate to the theoretical virtue; for it merely discerns the accidents of the intelligibles that, prior to having these accidents as their accompaniments, are acquired by the theoretical virtue. If it is determined that the one who possesses the deliberative virtue should discover the variable accidents and states of only those intelligibles of which he has personal insight and personal knowledge (so as not to make discoveries about things that perhaps ought not to take place), then the deliberative virtue cannot be separated from the theoretical virtue. It follows that the theoretical virtue, the leading deliberative virtue, the leading moral virtue, and the leading [practical] art are inseparable from each other; otherwise the latter [three] will be unsound, imperfect, and without complete authority. [27]

35. But if, after the theoretical virtue has caused the intellect to perceive the moral virtues, the latter can only be made to exist if the deliberative virtue discerns them and discovers the accidents that must accompany their intelligibles so that they can be brought into existence, then the deliberative virtue is anterior to the moral virtues. If it is anterior to them, then he who possesses the deliberative virtue discovers by it only such moral virtues as exist independently of the deliberative virtues. Yet if the deliberative virtue is independent of the moral virtue, then he who has the capacity for discovering the (good) moral virtues will not himself be good, not even in a single virtue.[11] But if he himself is not good, how then does he seek out the good or wish the true good for himself or for others? And if he does not wish the good, how is he capable of discovering it without having set it before himself as an end? Therefore, if the deliberative virtue is independent of the moral virtue, it is not possible to discover the moral virtue with it. Yet if the moral virtue is inseparable from the deliberative, and they coexist, how could the deliberative virtue discover the moral and join itself to it? For if they are inseparable, it will follow that the deliberative virtue did not discover the moral virtue; while if the deliberative virtue did discover the moral virtue, it will follow that the deliberative virtue is independent of the moral virtue. Therefore, either the deliberative virtue itself is the virtue of goodness or one should assume that the deliberative virtue is accompanied by some other virtue, different from the moral virtue that is discovered by the deliberative faculty. If that other moral

10. "Warfare" here is from the root *ḥ.r.b.*

11. Cf. Aristotle *Nicomachean Ethics* 6.12, 13.

virtue is formed by the will also, it follows that the deliberative virtue discovered it—thus the original doubt recurs. It follows, then, that there must be some other moral virtue—other, that is, than the one discovered by the deliberative virtue—which accompanies the deliberative virtue and enables the possessor of the deliberative virtue to wish the good and the virtuous end. [28] That virtue must be natural and must come into being by nature, and it must be coupled with a certain deliberative virtue [that is, cleverness] which comes into being by nature and discovers the moral virtues formed by the will. The virtue formed by the will will then be the human virtue by which man, after acquiring it in the way in which he acquires voluntary things, acquires the human deliberative virtue.

36. But one ought to inquire what manner of thing that natural virtue is. Is it or is it not identical with this voluntary virtue? Or ought one to say that it corresponds to this virtue, like the states of character that exist in irrational animals?—just as it is said that courage resides in the lion, cunning in the fox, shiftiness in the bear, thievishness in the magpie, and so forth. For it is possible that every man is innately so disposed that his soul has a power such that he generally moves more easily in the direction of the accomplishment of a certain virtue or of a certain state of character than in the direction of doing the opposite act. Indeed man moves first in the direction in which it is easier for him to move, provided he is not compelled to do something else. For instance, if a man is innately so disposed that he is more prone to stand his ground against dangers than to recoil before them, then all he needs is to undergo the experience a sufficient number of times and this state of character becomes voluntary. Prior to this, he possessed the corresponding natural state of character. If this is so in particular moral virtues that accompany particular deliberative virtues, it must also be the case with the highest moral virtues that accompany the highest deliberative virtues. If this is so, it follows that there are some men who are innately disposed to a [natural moral] virtue that corresponds to the highest [human moral] virtue and that is joined to a naturally superior deliberative power, others just below them, and so forth. [29] If this is so, then not every chance human being will possess art, moral virtue, and deliberative virtue with great power.

37. Therefore the prince occupies his place by nature and not merely by will. Similarly, a subordinate occupies his place primarily by nature and only secondarily by virtue of the will, which perfects his natural equipment. This being the case, the theoretical virtue, the highest deliberative virtue, the highest moral virtue, and the highest practical art are realized only in those equipped for them by nature: that is, in those who possess superior natures with very great potentialities.

SUBDIVISION 3

38. After these four things are realized in a certain man, the realization of the particular instances of them in nations and cities still remains; his knowing how to make these particular instances exist in nations and cities remains: he who possesses such a great power ought to possess the capacity of realizing the particular instances of it in nations and cities.

39. There are two primary methods of realizing them: instruction and the formation of character. To instruct is to introduce the theoretical virtues in nations and cities. The formation of character is the method of introducing the moral virtues and practical arts in nations. Instruction proceeds by speech alone. The formation of character proceeds through habituating nations and citizens in doing the acts that issue from the practical states of character by arousing in them the resolution to do these acts; the states of character and the acts issuing from them should come to possess their souls, and they should be, as it were, enraptured by them. The resolution to do a thing may be aroused by speech or by deed.

40. Instruction in the theoretical sciences should be given either to the imams and the princes, or else to those who should preserve the theoretical sciences. The instruction of these two groups proceeds by means of identical approaches. These are the approaches [30] stated above.[12] First, they should know the first premises and the primary knowledge relative to every kind of theoretical

12. Secs. 4 ff.

science. Then they should know the various states of the premises and their various arrangements as stated before,[13] and be made to pursue the subjects that were mentioned. (Prior to this, their souls must have been set aright through the training befitting the youths whose natures entitle them to this rank in the order of humanity.) They should be habituated to use all the logical methods in all the theoretical sciences. And they should be made to pursue a course of study and form the habits of character from their childhood until each of them reaches maturity, in accordance with the plan described by Plato.[14] Then the princes among them will be placed in subordinate offices and promoted gradually through the ranks until they are fifty years old. Then they will be placed in the office with the highest authority. This, then, is the way to instruct this group; they are the elect who should not be confined to what is in conformity with unexamined common opinion. Until they acquire the theoretical virtues, they ought to be instructed in things theoretical by means of persuasive methods. They should comprehend many theoretical things by way of imagining them. These are the things—the ultimate principles and the incorporeal principles—that a man cannot perceive by his intellect except after knowing many other things. The vulgar ought to comprehend merely the similitudes of these principles, which should be established in their souls by persuasive arguments. One should draw a distinction between the similitudes that ought to be presented to every nation, and in which all nations and all the citizens of every city should share, and the ones that ought to be presented to a particular nation and not to another, to a particular city and not to another, or to a particular group among the citizens of a city [31] and not to another. All these [persuasive arguments and similitudes] must be discerned by the deliberative virtue.

41. They [the princes, the imams, etc.] should be habituated in the acts of the practical[15] virtues and the practical arts by either of two methods: first, by means of persuasive arguments, passionate arguments, and other arguments that establish these acts and states of character in the soul completely so as to arouse the resolution to do the acts willingly. This method is made possible by the practice of the logical arts—to which the mind is naturally inclined—and by the benefits derived from such practice. The other method is compulsion. It is used with the recalcitrant and the obstinate among those citizens of cities and nations who do not rise in favor of what is right willingly and of their own accord or by means of arguments, and also with those who refuse to teach others the theoretical sciences in which they are engaged.

42. Now since the virtue or the art of the prince is exercised by exploiting the acts of those who possess the particular virtues and the arts of those who practice the particular arts, it follows necessarily that the virtuous and the masters of the arts whom he [the prince] employs to form the character of nations and citizens of cities comprise two primary groups: a group employed by him to form the character of whoever is susceptible of having his character formed willingly, and a group employed by him to form the character of those who are such that their character can be formed only by compulsion. This is analogous to what heads of households and superintendents of children and youths do. For the prince forms the character of nations and instructs them, just as the head of a household forms the character of its members and instructs them, and the superintendent of children and youths forms their character and instructs them. Just as each of the last two forms the character of some of those who are in his custody [32] by being gentle to them and by persuasion and forms the character of others by compulsion, so does the prince. Indeed it is by virtue of the very same skill in [all three] classes of men who form the character of others and superintend them that they undertake both the compulsory formation of character and the formation of character received willingly; the skill varies only with respect to its degree and the extent of its power.[16] Thus the power required for forming the character of nations and for superintending them is greater than the power required for forming the character of children and youths or the power required by heads of households for forming the character of the members of a household. Correspondingly, the power of the princes who are the superintendents of nations and cities and who form their character, and the power of whomever and whatever they

13. Secs. 4 ff.

14. *Republic* 376E–427C, 521C–41B.

15. That is, deliberative and moral.

16. Note, however, the end of the section and the following sections, where the dual aspect of this skill is emphasized.

employ in performing this function, are greater. The prince needs the most powerful skill for forming the character of others with their consent and the most powerful skill for forming their character by compulsion.

43. The latter is the craft of war:[17] that is, the faculty that enables him to excel in organizing and leading armies and utilizing war implements and warlike people to conquer the nations and cities that do not submit to doing what will procure them that happiness for whose acquisition man is made. For every being is made to achieve the ultimate perfection it is susceptible of achieving according to its specific place in the order of being. Man's specific perfection is called supreme happiness, and to each man, according to his rank in the order of humanity, belongs the specific supreme happiness pertaining to his kind of man. The warrior who pursues this purpose is the just warrior, and the art of war that pursues this purpose is the just and virtuous art of war.

44. The other group, employed to form the character of nations and the citizens of cities with their consent, is composed of those who possess the natural virtues and arts. For it is obvious that the prince needs to return to the theoretical, intelligible things [33] whose knowledge was acquired by certain demonstrations, look for the persuasive methods that can be employed for each, and seek out all the persuasive methods that can be employed for it (he can do this because he possesses the power to be persuasive about individual cases). Then he should repair to these very same theoretical things and seize upon their similitudes. He ought to make these similitudes produce images of the theoretical things for all nations jointly, so establish the similitudes that persuasive methods can cause them to be accepted, and exert himself throughout to make both the similitudes and the persuasive methods such that all nations and cities may share in them. Next he needs to enumerate the acts of the particular practical virtues and arts that fulfill the above-mentioned requirements.[18] He should devise methods of political oratory with which to arouse the resolution to such acts [in nations and cities]. He should employ here: (1) arguments that support [the rightness of] his own character; (2) passionate and moral arguments that cause (a) the souls of the citizens to grow reverent, submissive, muted, and meek. But with respect to everything contrary to these acts he should employ (b) passionate and moral arguments by which the souls of the citizens grow confident, spiteful, insolent, and contemptuous. He should employ these same two kinds of arguments [a and b], respectively, with the princes who agree with him and with those who oppose him, with the men and the auxiliaries employed by him and with the ones employed by those who oppose him, and with the virtuous and with those who oppose them. Thus with respect to his own position, he should employ arguments by which souls grow reverent and submissive. But with respect to his opponents he should employ arguments that cause souls to grow spiteful, insolent, and contemptuous; arguments with which he contradicts, using persuasive methods, those who disagree with his own opinions and acts; and arguments that show the opinions and acts of the opponent as base and make their meanness and notoriety apparent. He should employ here [34] both classes of arguments: I mean the class that should be employed periodically, daily, and temporarily, and not preserved, kept permanently, or written down; and the other class, which should be preserved and kept permanently, orally and in writing. [The latter should be kept in two Books, a Book of Opinions and a Book of Actions.] He should place in these two Books the opinions and the acts that nations and cities were called upon to embrace, the arguments by which he sought to preserve among them and to establish in them the things they were called upon to embrace so that they will not be forgotten, and the arguments with which he contradicts the opponents of these opinions and acts. Therefore the sciences that form the character of nations and cities will have three orders of rank [the first belongs to the theoretical sciences themselves, the second to the popular theoretical sciences, and the third to the image-making theoretical sciences]. Each kind will have a group to preserve it who should be drawn from among those who possess the faculty that enables them to excel in the discovery of what had not been clearly stated to them with reference to the science they preserve, to defend it, to contradict what contradicts it, and to excel in teaching all of this to others. In all of this, they should aim at

17. All of the terms for "war" and their cognates in this section are from the root *ḥ.r.b.*

18. Secs. 41–43, perhaps also secs. 28 ff.

accomplishing the purpose of the supreme ruler with respect to nations and cities.

45. Then he [the supreme ruler] should inquire next into the different classes of nations by inquiring into every nation and into the human states of character and the acts for which all nations are equipped by that nature which is common to them, until he comes to inquire into all or most nations. He should inquire into that in which all nations share—that is, the human nature common to them—and then into all the things that pertain specifically to every group within every nation. He should discern all of these, draw up an actual—if approximate—list of the acts and the states of character with which every nation can be set aright and guided toward happiness, and specify the classes of persuasive argument (regarding both the theoretical and the practical virtues) that ought to be employed among them. He will thus set down what every nation is capable of, having subdivided every nation and inquired whether or not there is a group fit for preserving the theoretical sciences [35] and others who can preserve the popular theoretical sciences or the image-making theoretical sciences.[19]

46. Provided all of these groups exist in nations, four sciences will emerge: first, the theoretical virtue through which the beings become intelligible with certain demonstrations; next, these same intelligibles acquired by persuasive methods; subsequently, the science that comprises the similitudes of these intelligibles, accepted by persuasive methods; finally, the sciences extracted from these three for each nation. There will be as many of these extracted sciences as there are nations, each containing everything by which a particular nation becomes perfect and happy.

47. Therefore he [the supreme ruler] has to find certain groups of men or certain individuals who are to be instructed in what causes the happiness of particular nations, who will preserve what can form the character of a particular nation alone, and who will learn the persuasive methods that should be employed in forming the character of that nation. The knowledge which that nation ought to have must be preserved by a man or a group of men also possessing the faculty that enables them to excel in the discovery of what was not actually given to this man or this group of men but is, nevertheless, of the same kind for which they act as custodians, enables them to defend it and contradict what opposes it, and to excel in the instruction of that nation. In all of this, they should aim at accomplishing what the supreme ruler had in mind for the nation, for whose sake he gave this man or this group of men what was given to them. Such are the men who should be employed to form the character of nations with their consent.

48. The best course is that each member of the groups to which the formation of the character of nations is delegated should possess a warlike[20] virtue and a deliberative virtue for use in case there is need to excel in leading troops in war; [36] thus every one of them will possess the skill to form the [nation's] character by both methods. If this combination does not happen to exist in one man, then he [the supreme ruler] should add to the man who forms the character of nations with their consent, another who possesses this craft of war. In turn, the one to whom the formation of the character of any nation is delegated should also follow the custom of employing a group of men to form the character of the nation with its consent or by compulsion, either by dividing them into two groups or employing a single group that possesses a skill for doing both. Subsequently, this one group, or the two groups, should be subdivided, and so on, ending in the lowest divisions or the ones with the least power in the formation of character. The ranks within these groups should be established according to the deliberative virtue of each individual: that is, depending on whether this deliberative virtue exploits subordinate ones or is exploited by one superior to it. The former will rule and the latter have a subordinate office according to the power of their respective deliberative virtues. When these two groups are formed in any nation or city, they, in turn, will order the rest.

49. These, then, are the modes and methods through which the four human things by which supreme happiness is achieved are realized in nations and cities.

19. The latter two sciences are (derivatively) "theoretical" (or "philosophic"; cf. sec. 55 [40:12–13]) inasmuch as (a) they deal with opinions (vs. acts), and (b) their subjects were originally seized upon in the theoretical sciences properly so called (above, sec. 44; below, sec. 46).

20. All terms translated as "war" and their cognates in this section are derived from the root *ḥ.r.b.*

SUBDIVISION 4

50. Foremost among all of these [four] sciences is that which gives an account of the beings as they are perceived by the intellect with certain demonstrations. The others merely take these same beings and employ persuasion about them or represent them with images so as to facilitate the instruction of the multitude of the nations and the citizens of cities. That is because nations and the citizens of cities are composed of some who are the elect and others who are the vulgar. The vulgar confine themselves, or should be confined, to theoretical cognitions that are in conformity with unexamined common opinion. [37] The elect do not confine themselves in any of their theoretical cognitions to what is in conformity with unexamined common opinion, but reach their conviction and knowledge on the basis of premises subjected to thorough scrutiny. Therefore whoever thinks that he is not confined to what is in conformity with unexamined common opinion in his inquiries, believes that in them he is of the "elect" and that everybody else is vulgar. Hence, the competent practitioner of every art comes to be called one of the "elect" because people know that he does not confine himself, with respect to the objects of his art, to what is in conformity with unexamined common opinion, but exhausts them and scrutinizes them thoroughly. Again, whoever does not hold a political office or does not possess an art that establishes his claim to a political office, but either possesses no art at all or is enabled by his art to hold only a subordinate office in the city, is said to be "vulgar"; and whoever holds a political office or else possesses an art that enables him to aspire to a political office is of the "elect." Therefore, whoever thinks that he possesses an art that qualifies him for assuming a political office or thinks that his position has the same status as a political office (for instance, men with prominent ancestors and many who possess great wealth) calls himself one of the "elect" and a "statesman."

51. Whoever has a more perfect mastery of the art that qualifies him for assuming an office is more appropriate for inclusion among the elect. Therefore it follows that the most elect of the elect is the supreme ruler. It would appear that this is so because he is the one who does not confine himself in anything at all to what is in conformity with unexamined common opinion. He must hold the office of the supreme ruler and be the most elect of the elect because of his state of character and skill. As for the one who assumes a political office [38] with the intention of accomplishing the purpose of the supreme ruler, he adheres to thoroughly scrutinized opinions. However, the opinions that caused him to become an adherent[21] or because of which he was convinced that he should use his art to serve the supreme ruler, were based on mere conformity to unexamined opinions; he conforms to unexamined common opinion in his theoretical cognitions as well. The result is that the supreme ruler and he who possesses the science that encompasses the intelligibles with certain demonstrations belong to the elect. The rest are the vulgar and the multitude. Thus the methods of persuasion and imaginative representation are employed only in the instruction of the vulgar and the multitude of the nations and the cities, while the certain demonstrative methods, by which the beings themselves are made intelligible, are employed in the instruction of those who belong to the elect.

52. This is the superior science and the one with the most perfect [claim to rule or to] authority. The rest of the authoritative sciences are subordinate to this science. By "the rest of the authoritative sciences" I mean the second and the third, and that which is derived from them,[22] since these sciences merely follow the example of that science and are employed to accomplish the purpose of that science, which is supreme happiness and the final perfection to be achieved by man.

53. It is said that this science existed anciently among the Chaldeans,[23] who are the people of al-'Irāq,[24] subsequently reaching the people of

21. Or "follower," "successor" (*tābi'*). He functions as an "aide" or "subordinate" who is employed by the supreme ruler to apply and preserve his law (above, secs. 44, 47–48). In the absence of the supreme ruler, the "adherent" is envisaged as his "successor." This is a second-best arrangement, because the ruler will then lack theoretical knowledge and hence the ability to be a true lawgiver (above, secs. 45 ff.). Cf. Alfarabi *The Political Regime* 82, 87 (above, selection 3).

22. Above, sec. 46.

23. For an account of the "philosophic" sciences (mathematics, astronomy, etc.) of the "Chaldeans," cf., e.g., Ṣā'id al-Andalusī, *Classes of Nations* [*Ṭabaqāt al-umam*], ed. Louis Cheiko (Beirut, 1912) 4.3.

24. Southern Mesopotamia, the alluvial region bounded on the north by a line from al-Anbār to Takrīt. Cf. al-Andalusī *Classes of Nations* 1.

Egypt,[25] from there transmitted to the Greeks, where it remained until it was transmitted to the Syrians,[26] and then to the Arabs. Everything comprised by this science was expounded in the Greek language, later in Syriac, and finally in Arabic. The Greeks who possessed this science used to call it "unqualified wisdom" and the "highest wisdom." They called the acquisition of it "science" and the scientific state of mind "philosophy" (by which they meant the quest and the love for the highest wisdom). [39] They held that potentially it subsumes all the virtues. They called it the "science of sciences," the "mother of sciences," the "wisdom of wisdoms," and the "art of arts" (they meant the art that makes use of all the arts, the virtue that makes use of all the virtues, and the wisdom that makes use of all wisdoms). Now, "wisdom" may be used for consummate and extreme competence in any art whatsoever when it leads to performing feats of which most practitioners of that art are incapable. Here "wisdom" is used in a qualified sense. Thus he who is extremely competent in an art is said to be "wise" in that art. Similarly, a man with penetrating practical judgment and acumen may be called "wise" in the thing regarding which he has penetrating practical judgment. However, unqualified wisdom is this science and state of mind alone.

54. When the theoretical sciences are isolated and their possessor does not have the faculty for exploiting them for the benefit of others, they are defective philosophy. To be a truly perfect philosopher, one has to possess both the theoretical sciences and the faculty for exploiting them for the benefit of all others according to their capacity. Were one to consider the case of the true philosopher, he would find no difference between him and the supreme ruler. For he who possesses the faculty for exploiting what is comprised by the theoretical matters for the benefit of all others possesses the faculty for making such matters intelligible as well as for bringing into actual existence those of them that depend on the will. The greater his power to do the latter, the more perfect is his philosophy. Therefore, he who is truly perfect possesses with sure insight, first, the theoretical virtues, and subsequently the practical. Moreover, he possesses the capacity for bringing them about in nations and cities in the manner and the measure possible with reference to each. Since it is impossible for him to possess the faculty for bringing them about except by employing certain demonstrations, persuasive methods, [40] as well as methods that represent things through images—and this either with the consent of others or by compulsion—it follows that the true philosopher is himself the supreme ruler.

55. Every instruction is composed of two things: (a) making what is being studied comprehensible and causing its idea to be established in the soul and (b) causing others to assent to what is comprehended and established in the soul. There are two ways of making a thing comprehensible: first, by causing its essence to be perceived by the intellect, and second, by causing it to be imagined through the similitude that imitates it. Assent, too, is brought about by one of two methods, either the method of certain demonstration or the method of persuasion. Now when one acquires knowledge of the beings or receives instruction in them, if he perceives their ideas themselves with his intellect, and his assent to them is by means of certain demonstration, then the science that comprises these cognitions is philosophy. But if they are known by imagining them through similitudes that imitate them, and assent to what is imagined of them is caused by persuasive methods, then the ancients call what comprises these cognitions "religion." And if those intelligibles themselves are adopted, and persuasive methods are used, then the religion comprising them is called "popular," "generally accepted," and "external philosophy." Therefore, according to the ancients, religion is an imitation of philosophy. Both comprise the same subjects and both give an account of the ultimate principles of the beings. For both supply knowledge about the first principle and cause of the beings, and both give an account of the ultimate end for the sake of which man is made—that is, supreme happiness—and the ultimate end of every one of the other beings. In everything of which philosophy gives an account based on intellectual perception or conception, religion gives an account based on imagination. In everything demonstrated by philosophy, religion employs persuasion. Philosophy gives an account of the ultimate principles

25. Ibid. 4.6. Ṣāʿid al-Andalusī reports the popular myth of the "prophetic" origin of the philosophic sciences. In addition to claiming that philosophy *alone* is true wisdom, Alfarabi insists (below, sec. 55 [41:12]) that "philosophy is prior to religion *in time*."

26. *al-Siryān:* the Jacobite and Nestorian (Monophysite) Christians using Syriac as a literary medium in Syria, Mesopotamia, and the Persian Empire.

(that is, the essence of the first principle and the essences of the incorporeal second principles),[27] [41] as they are perceived by the intellect. Religion sets forth their images by means of similitudes of them taken from corporeal principles and imitates them by their likenesses among political offices.[28] It imitates the divine acts by means of the functions of political offices.[29] It imitates the actions of natural powers and principles by their likenesses among the faculties, states, and arts that have to do with the will, just as Plato does in the *Timaeus.*[30] It imitates the intelligibles by their likenesses among the sensibles: for instance, some imitate matter by [terms such as] "abyss" or "darkness" or "water," and nothingness by "darkness." It imitates the classes of supreme happiness—that is, the ends of the acts of the human virtues—by their likenesses among the goods that are believed to be the ends. It imitates the classes of true happiness by means of the ones that are believed to be happiness. It imitates the ranks of the beings by their likenesses among spatial and temporal ranks. And it attempts to bring the similitudes of these things as close as possible to their essences.[31] Also, in everything of which philosophy gives an account that is demonstrable and certain, religion gives an account based on persuasive arguments. Finally, philosophy is prior to religion in time.

56. Again, it is evident that when one seeks to bring into actual existence the intelligibles of the things depending on the will supplied by practical philosophy, he ought to prescribe the conditions that render possible their actual existence. Once the conditions that render their actual existence possible are prescribed, the voluntary intelligibles are embodied in laws. Therefore the legislator is he who, by the excellence of his deliberation, has the capacity to find the conditions required for the actual existence of voluntary intelligibles in such a way as to lead to the achievement of supreme happiness. It is also evident that only after perceiving them by his intellect should the legislator seek to discover their conditions, and he cannot [42] find their conditions that enable him to guide others toward supreme happiness without having perceived supreme happiness with his intellect. Nor can these things become intelligible (and the legislative craft thereby hold the supreme office) without his having beforehand acquired philosophy. Therefore, if he intends to possess a craft that is authoritative rather than subservient, the legislator must be a philosopher. Similarly, if the philosopher who has acquired the theoretical virtues does not have the capacity for bringing them about in all others according to their capacities, then what he has acquired from it has no validity. Yet he cannot find the states and the conditions by which the voluntary intelligibles assume actual existence, if he does not possess the deliberative virtue; and the deliberative virtue cannot exist in him without the practical virtue. Moreover, he cannot bring them about in all others according to their capacities, except by a faculty that enables him to excel in persuasion and in representing things through images.

57. It follows, then, that the idea of Imam, Philosopher, and Legislator is a single idea. However, the name "philosopher" signifies primarily theoretical virtue. But if it be determined that the theoretical virtue reaches its ultimate perfection in every respect, it follows necessarily that he must possess all the other faculties as well. "Legislator" signifies excellence of knowledge concerning the conditions of practical[32] intelligibles, the faculty for finding them, and the faculty for bringing them about in nations and cities. When it is determined that they be brought into existence on the basis of knowledge, it will follow that the theoretical virtue must precede the others—the existence of the inferior presupposes the existence of the higher. The name "prince" signifies sovereignty and ability. To be completely able, one has to possess [43] the power of the greatest ability. His ability to do a thing must not result only from external things; he himself must possess great ability because his art, skill, and virtue are of exceedingly great power. This is not possible except by great power of knowledge, great power of deliberation, and great power of [moral] virtue and art. Otherwise he is not truly able nor sovereign. For if his ability stops short of this, it is still imperfect. Similarly, if his ability is restricted to goods inferior to supreme happiness, his ability is incomplete and he is not perfect. Therefore the true prince is the same as the philosopher-legislator. As to the idea of Imam in the Arabic language, it signifies merely

27. The causes or principles of the heavenly bodies.

28. Alfarabi says "principles." Cf. above, note 5.

29. Alfarabi says "principles." Cf. above, note 5.

30. See *Timaeus* 19D, 21B–C, 29B ff.

31. See selection 3, Alfarabi *The Political Regime* 89–91.

32. "Practical" as distinguished from "incorporeal" and "natural." They are the intelligibles whose realization depends on deliberation, moral character, and art. Above, secs. 22 ff., 40.

the one whose example is followed and who is well received: that is, either his perfection is well received or his purpose is well received. If he is not well received in all the infinite activities, virtues, and arts, then he is not truly well received. Only when all other arts, virtues, and activities seek to realize his purpose and no other, will his art be the most powerful art, his [moral] virtue the most powerful virtue, his deliberation the most powerful deliberation, and his science the most powerful science. For with all of these powers he will be exploiting the powers of others so as to accomplish his own purpose. This is not possible without the theoretical sciences, without the greatest of all deliberative virtues, and without the rest of those things that are in the philosopher.

58. So let it be clear to you that the idea of the Philosopher, Supreme Ruler, Prince, Legislator, and Imam is but a single idea. No matter which one of these words you take, if you proceed to look at what each of them signifies [44] among the majority of those who speak our language, you will find that they all finally agree by signifying one and the same idea.

59. Once the images representing the theoretical things[33] demonstrated in the theoretical sciences are produced in the souls of the multitude and they are made to assent to their images, and once the practical things (together with the conditions of the possibility of their existence) take hold of their souls and dominate them so that they are unable to resolve to do anything else; then the theoretical and practical things are realized. Now these things are philosophy when they are in the soul of the legislator. They are religion when they are in the souls of the multitude. For when the legislator knows these things, they are evident to him by sure insight, whereas what is established in the souls of the multitude is through an image and a persuasive argument. Although it is the legislator who also represents these things through images, neither the images nor the persuasive arguments are intended for himself. As far as he is concerned, they are certain. He is the one who invents the images and the persuasive arguments, but not for the sake of establishing these things in his own soul as a religion for himself. No, the images and the persuasive arguments are intended for others, whereas, so far as he is concerned, these things are certain. They are a religion for others, whereas, so far as he is concerned, they are philosophy. Such, then, is true philosophy and the true philosopher.

60. As for mutilated philosophy: the counterfeit philosopher, the vain philosopher, or the false philosopher is the one who sets out to study the theoretical sciences without being prepared for them. For he who sets out to inquire ought to be innately equipped for the theoretical sciences—that is, fulfill the conditions prescribed by Plato in the *Republic*:[34] He should excel in comprehending and conceiving that which is essential. Moreover, he should have good memory and be able to endure the toil of study. He should love truthfulness and truthful people, and justice and just people; [45] and not be headstrong or a wrangler about what he desires. He should not be gluttonous for food and drink, and should by natural disposition disdain the appetites, the dirhem, the dinar, and the like. He should be great-souled (*kabīr al-nafs*)[35] and avoid what is disgraceful in people. He should be pious, yield easily to goodness and justice, and be stubborn in yielding to evil and injustice. And he should be strongly determined in favor of the right thing. Moreover, he should be brought up according to laws and habits that resemble his innate disposition. He should have sound conviction about the opinions of the religion in which he is reared, hold fast to the virtuous acts in his religion, and not forsake all or most of them. Furthermore, he should hold fast to the generally accepted virtues and not forsake the generally accepted noble acts. For if a youth is such, and then sets out to study philosophy and learns it, it is possible that he will not become a counterfeit or a vain or a false philosopher.

61. The false philosopher is he who acquires the theoretical sciences without achieving the utmost perfection so as to be able to introduce others to what he knows insofar as their capacity permits. The vain philosopher is he who learns the theoretical sciences, but without going any further and without being habituated to doing the acts considered virtuous by a certain religion or the generally accepted noble acts. Instead, he follows his own

33. "Things" (*ashyā'*). The term *shay'* is used throughout in a variety of senses (roughly corresponding to "being"). It can signify particulars or universals, what exists outside the mind or the intelligible ideas (as here), the objects of knowledge or of opinion and imagination (as in the rest of the section).

34. *Republic* 375A ff., 485B ff., passim.

35. Compare Ibn Bajja, selection 9, note 33.

inclination and appetites in everything, whatever they may happen to be. The counterfeit philosopher is he who studies the theoretical sciences without being naturally equipped for them. Therefore, although the counterfeit and the vain may complete the study of the theoretical sciences, in the end their possession of them diminishes little by little. By the time they reach the age at which [46] a man should become perfect in the virtues, their knowledge will have been completely extinguished, even more so than the extinction of the fire [sun] of Heraclitus mentioned by Plato.[36] For the natural dispositions of the former and the habit of the latter overpower what they might have remembered in their youth and make it burdensome for them to retain what they had patiently toiled for. They neglect it, and what they retain begins to diminish little by little until its fire becomes ineffective and extinguished, and they gather no fruit from it. As for the false philosopher, he is the one who is not yet aware of the purpose for which philosophy is pursued. He acquires the theoretical sciences, or only some portion of them, and holds the opinion that the purpose of the measure he has acquired consists in certain kinds of happiness that are believed to be so or are considered by the multitude to be good things. Therefore he rests there to enjoy that happiness, aspiring to achieve this purpose with his knowledge. He may achieve his purpose and settle for it, or else find his purpose difficult to achieve and so hold the opinion that the knowledge he has is superfluous. Such is the false philosopher.

62. The true philosopher is the one mentioned before.[37] If after reaching this stage no use is made of him, the fact that he is of no use to others is not his fault but the fault of those who either do not listen or are not of the opinion that they should listen to him. Therefore the prince or the imam is prince or imam by virtue of his skill and art, regardless of whether or not anyone acknowledges him, whether or not he is obeyed, whether or not he is supported in his purpose by any group; just as the physician is physician by virtue of his skill and his ability to heal the sick, whether or not there are sick men for him to heal, whether or not he finds tools to use in his activity, whether he is prosperous or poor—not having any of these things does not do away with his physicianship. Similarly, neither the imamate of the imam, [47] the philosophy of the philosopher, nor the princeship of the prince is done away with by his not having tools to use in his activities or men to employ in reaching his purpose.

63. The philosophy that answers to this description was handed down to us by the Greeks from Plato and Aristotle only. Both have given us an account of philosophy, but not without giving us also an account of the ways to it and of the ways to reestablish it when it becomes confused or extinct. We shall begin by expounding first the philosophy of Plato and the orders of rank in his philosophy. We shall begin with the first part of the philosophy of Plato, and then order one part of his philosophy after another until we reach its end. We shall do the same with the philosophy presented to us by Aristotle, beginning with the first part of his philosophy.

64. So let it be clear to you that, in what they presented, their purpose is the same, and that they intended to offer one and the same philosophy.

36. *Republic* 498B; cf. Aristotle *Meteorologica* 355a9 ff.

37. Secs. 53, 57, 59.

FIVE

ALFARABI

Plato's Laws

Translated by Muhsin Mahdi

Plato's Laws consists of an introduction and accounts of the first nine books of Plato's *Laws.* In the introduction, Alfarabi explains Plato's art of writing in general and the method he follows in writing the *Laws* in particular. Alfarabi also states his own method of summarizing Plato's *Laws,* points to the two groups of readers for whom the work was written, and indicates the benefit that each can derive from reading it. In the preceding selections Alfarabi examines the place of laws and legislation in the broader context of political philosophy. Here, the question of laws becomes the object of a specialized study. In the guise of a commentary on Plato's *Laws,* Alfarabi shows the relevance of Plato's investigation of Greek divine laws to the study and understanding of all divine laws; hence Avicenna's statement (below, selection 6) that Plato's *Laws* treat prophecy and the divine Law.

The Arabic text of Alfarabi's *Plato's Laws* was first published by F. Gabrieli in *Alfarabius, Compendium Legum Platonis* (London, 1952). This publication was examined in detail and additional evidence was presented with a view to a new edition by Muhsin Mahdi in "The *Editio Princeps* of Fārābī's *Compendium Legum Platonis,*" *Journal of Near Eastern Studies* 20 (1961): 1–24. The present translation is based on the revised edition by Therêse-Anne Druart, published as *Le sommaire du livre des Lois de Platon* [Jawāmi' Kitāb al-Nawāmīs li-Aflāṭūn] in *Bulletin d'Études Orientales* 50 (1998): 109–55. The numbers in brackets in the body of the translation refer to the pages of Gabrieli's text.

[INTRODUCTION]

1. Whereas the thing due to which man excels all other animals is the faculty that enables him to distinguish among the affairs and matters with which he deals and that he observes, in order to know which of them is useful so as to prefer and obtain it while rejecting and avoiding what is useless; and that faculty only emerges from potentiality into actuality through experience ("experience" means reflection on the particular instances of a thing and, from what one finds in these particular instances, passing judgment upon its universal characteristics)—therefore, whoever

acquires more of these experiences is more excellent[1] and perfect in being human. However, the one guided by experience may err in what he does and experiences so that he conceives the thing to be in a different state than it really is. (There are many causes of error, these have been enumerated by those who discuss the art of sophistry. Of all people, the wise are the ones who have acquired experiences that are true and valid.) Nevertheless, all people are naturally disposed to pass a universal judgment after observing only a few particular instances of the thing ("universal" here means that which covers all the particular instances of the thing as well as their duration in time); so that once it is observed that an individual has done something in a certain way on a number of occasions, it is judged that he does that thing in that way all the time. For instance when someone has spoken the truth on one, two, or a number of occasions, people are naturally disposed to judge that he is simply truthful; similarly when someone lies. Again, when someone is observed on a number of occasions to act with courage or as a coward, or to give evidence of any other moral habit,[2] he is judged to be so wholly and always.

Whereas those who are wise know this aspect of people's natural disposition, sometimes they have repeatedly shown themselves as possessing a certain character so that people will judge that this is how they always are. Then, afterwards, they would act in a different manner, which went unnoticed by people, who supposed they were acting as they had [4] formerly. It is related, for example, that a certain abstemious ascetic was known for his probity, propriety, asceticism and worship, and having become famous for this, he feared the tyrannical sovereign and decided to run away from his city. The sovereign's command went out to search for and arrest him wherever he was found. He could not leave from any of the city's gates and was apprehensive lest he fall into the hands of the sovereign's men. So he went and found clothing worn by vagabonds, put it on, carried a cymbal in his hand and, pretending to be drunk, came early at night out to the gate of the city singing to the accompaniment of that cymbal of his. The gatekeeper said to him, "Who are you?" "I am so and so, the ascetic!" he said jokingly. The gatekeeper supposed he was poking fun at him and did not interfere with him. So he saved himself without having lied in what he said.

2. Our purpose in making this introduction is this: the wise Plato did not feel free to reveal and uncover every kind of knowledge for all people. Therefore he followed the practice of using symbols, riddles, obscurity, and difficulty, so that knowledge would not fall into the hands of those who do not deserve it and be deformed, or fall into the hands of someone who does not know its worth or who uses it improperly. In this he was right. Once he knew and became certain[3] that he had become famous for this practice, and that it was widespread among people that he expresses everything he intends to say through symbols, he would sometimes turn to the subject he intended to discuss and state it openly and literally; but whoever reads or hears his discussion supposes that it is symbolic and that he intends something different from what he stated openly. This notion is one of the secrets of his books. Moreover, no one is able to understand what he states openly and what he states symbolically or in riddles unless trained in that art itself, and no one will be able to distinguish the two unless skilled in the discipline being discussed. This is how his discussion proceeds in the *Laws.* In the present book we have resolved upon extracting the notions to which he alluded in that book and grouping them together, following the order of the Discourses it contains, so that the present book may become an aid to whoever wants to know that book and sufficient for whoever cannot bear the hardship of study and reflection. God accommodates to what is right. [5]

1. "Excellent" or "virtuous" (*afḍal,* from *faḍīla:* "virtue, excellence").

2. "Moral habit" (*khulq*).

3. Reading *wa istayqana* with MS A.

SIX

AVICENNA

On the Divisions of the Rational Sciences

Translated by Muhsin Mahdi

Avicenna (Abū 'Alī al-Ḥusayn Ibn Sīnā, 980–1037) was born in Afshana, near Bukhara, where his father was governor. Bukhara (the capital of the Samanid kingdom, one of the many principalities into which Persia, nominally still a province of the caliph in Baghdad, was divided) was at the time a respectable center of learning. Here Avicenna had his early training, distinguished himself as a capable physician, was enrolled in the service of the sultan Nūḥ Ibn Manṣūr, and was able to make use of the excellent court library. In 999 the Samanid kingdom broke up, and Avicenna began to wander among the warring Persian principalities, entering the service of various princes. Between 1015 and 1022, he acted as the physician and, twice, as the vizier of the Buyid prince Shams al-Dawla in Hamadhan. He refused to take office under his son Tāj al-Mulk and made secret overtures to join the service of the Kakuyid prince 'Alā' al-Dawla (in Isfahan), who was preparing to overthrow the Buyids. After a short period in hiding and four months in prison, Avicenna finally succeeded in escaping—disguised in Sufi garb—from Hamadhan to Isfahan, where he pursued his scientific work as the intimate friend and learned courtier of the prince until his death. In Eastern Islam, Avicenna replaced Alfarabi as the leading philosopher, and Alghazali's attacks on him do not seem to have diminished his authority among students of philosophy, the sciences, and especially mysticism. In Western Islam, in contrast, he was criticized (by Averroes and others) as having departed from Aristotle and as having compromised with dialectical theology on a number of important issues. There, Alfarabi continued to be regarded as the great master, with Avicenna occupying an important but secondary position. This was true also of his place among Judeo-Arabic authors, as is evident from Maimonides' remarks. Among the Latins, the differences between Avicenna and Averroes had significant repercussions beginning in the twelfth century.

On the Division of the Rational Sciences (or the *Division of Wisdom*) is a short epistle composed by Avicenna in answer to someone who asked him to present a summary account of the rational sciences—an account that is short, complete, clear, true, easy to understand, well arranged, and well ordered. Avicenna begins with a definition of the essence of wisdom, followed by the account of the primary division of science (or wisdom); then he presents the divisions of theoretical science, followed by the divisions of practical science. The remaining part of the epistle deals with the principal parts and branches of natural science, mathematics, metaphysics, and logic. The "branches" of metaphysics or divine science deal again with revelation and prophecy (see below, selection 7). Unlike Alfarabi's classification in *The Enumeration of the Sciences* (above, selection 1), Avicenna here follows the more traditional Aristotelian classification of the sciences into theoretical and practical and subdivides the latter into ethics, economics, and politics. Nevertheless, it is noteworthy that he considers the study of prophecy and the divine Law as integral parts of political science.

This work, like Alfarabi's *Enumeration,* was popular among students of philosophy in Islam, and among historians of science and authors of scientific encyclopedias. It was translated into Hebrew and Latin. The following translation is based on a composite text resulting from the collation of a number of manuscripts of the original Arabic text preserved in the libraries of Constantinople. The two sections correspond to *Fī aqsām al-ʿulūm al-ʿaqliyya,* in *Tisʿ rasāʾil fī al-ḥikma wa-al-ṭabiʿiyat* (Cairo: Maṭbaʿa Hindiyya, 1908), 105 and 107–8, respectively.

ON THE PRIMARY DIVISIONS OF SCIENCE

Science is divided into a theoretical, abstract part and a practical part. The theoretical part is the one whose end is to acquire certainty about the state of the beings whose existence does not depend on human action. Here the aim is only to acquire an opinion. Examples of it are the science of [God's] unity and astronomy. The practical part is the one whose aim is not merely to acquire certainty about the beings; its aim can be the acquisition of a sound opinion about a matter that exists through man's endeavor, with a view to acquiring by it what is good. Thus, the aim here is not merely to acquire an opinion, but rather to acquire an opinion for the sake of action. Therefore, the end of the theoretical part is truth, and the end of the practical is the good.

On the Divisions of Practical Science

Because human governance either pertains to a single individual or does not pertain to a single individual, because the one that does not pertain to a single individual takes place through partnership, and because partnership is formed within the context of a household association or of a political association, there are three practical sciences.

One of these sciences pertains to the first division. Through this science one knows how man ought to be in his moral habits and in his actions so as to lead a happy life here and in the hereafter. This part is contained in Aristotle's book on ethics [that is, the *Nicomachean Ethics*].

The second science pertains to the second division. Through this science one knows how man ought to conduct the governance of his household—which is common to him, his wife, his children, his servants, and his slaves—so as to lead a well-ordered life that enables him to gain happiness. It is contained in Bryson's *On the Governance of the Household*[1] and in books by many others.

The third science pertains to the third division. Through this science one knows the kinds of political regimes, rulerships, and associations, both virtuous and bad; and it makes known the way of preserving each, the reason for its disintegration [108] and the manner of its transformation. Of this science, the treatment of kingship is contained in the book by Plato and that by Aristotle on the regime, and the treatment of prophecy and the Law is contained in their two books on the laws.[2] By the nomoi, the philosophers do not mean what the vulgar believe, which is that the nomos is nothing but a device and deceit.

1. On Bryson's *Economist,* see Martin Plessner, *Der Oikonomikos des Neupythagoreers 'Bryson' und sein Einfluss auf die islamische Wissenschaft* (Heidelberg: C. Winter, 1928).

2. Although in the case of Plato the references are unmistakably to the *Republic* and the *Laws,* the references to Aristotle are less certain. Avicenna may be referring to the two books given in the bibliographies of Aristotle's writings that bear the same titles as the two works by Plato.

Rather, according to them, the nomos is the law and the norm that is established and made permanent through the coming-down of revelation. The Arabs, too, call the angel that brings down the revelation, a nomos (*nāmūs*). Through this part of practical wisdom, one knows the necessity of prophecy and the human species' need of the Law for its existence, preservation, and future life. One knows through it the wisdom in the universal penalties that are common to all Laws and in the penalties pertaining to particular Laws, having to do with particular peoples and particular times. And one knows through it the difference between divine prophecy and false pretensions to it.

SEVEN

AVICENNA

Healing: Metaphysics 10

Translated by Michael E. Marmura

The *Healing* (or "Sufficiency," as it was called by some Latin writers) is perhaps Avicenna's most important, comprehensive, and detailed work. It is composed of four parts: *Logic, Physics, Mathematics,* and *Metaphysics* or *Divine Science.* In *Physics* 6 ("Psychology") Avicenna gives an account of practical intellect, of the prophetic faculties, and of certain related political questions, within the framework provided by natural science. The specific treatment of political science, however, is reserved for the end of the *Metaphysics,* with the implication that the understanding of political science has to be based on the conclusions arrived at in metaphysics. To the revised edition of the *Sourcebook,* we have added the first chapter of Book 10, which summarizes the metaphysical results of the preceding nine books.

Unlike Alfarabi's *Book of Religion,* Avicenna's *Healing* treats politics after metaphysics, again, implying that its metaphysics grounds its politics. In this respect, the *Healing* is more like, and may have to some extent inspired, the theological works of subsequent Christian authors such as Aquinas. This departure from Alfarabi should be compared with a related departure from Alfarabi: Avicenna adheres closely to the Aristotelian division of the sciences into theoretical and practical (see selection 6 and its historical introduction). The following is a translation of Book 10 of the *Metaphysics* part of the *Healing.*

The *Metaphysics (Philosophia Prima)* was translated into Latin about the middle of the twelfth century and was printed a number of times in Venice (first in 1495). The first critical edition of the Arabic original was made by G. C. Anawati and others: *al-Shifā': al-Ilāhiyyāt,* 2 vols. (Cairo, 1960). The following translation is based on the Anawati edition, 2:433–55. The numbers in brackets in the body of the translation refer to pages in this edition. Since the appearance of the first edition of the *Sourcebook,* Michael E. Marmura has published a complete English-Arabic edition of *The Metaphysics of "The Healing"* (Provo, UT: Brigham Young University Press, 2005), which includes, with minor differences, the following translation.

CHAPTER 1
A BRIEF STATEMENT ON THE BEGINNING AND "THE RETURN." ON INSPIRATIONS AND DREAMS AND PRAYERS THAT ARE ANSWERED AND CELESTIAL PUNISHMENTS. ON THE STATES OF PROPHECY AND ON THE STATE OF ASTROLOGICAL PREDICTIONS.

When existence commences from the First, every successive existent proceeding from Him continues to be of a lower rank than the first and continues to degenerate in rank. The first of these is the rank of the spiritual angels denuded [of matter] that are called "intellects," then the ranks of the spiritual angels called "souls," namely, the active angels, then the ranks of the celestial bodies, some being nobler than others, until the last [of these] is reached.

Thereafter begins the existence of matter receptive of the generable and corruptible forms. [Existence] first of all assumes the forms of the elements and then, little by little, [ascends in such a way] that the first existence in [matter] is more base and lower in rank than the one that comes after it. Thus the most base [of these] would be [prime] matter, then, [on a higher level], the elements, then the inanimate compounds, then the plants. The best [in this ascending, terrestrial order of existence] is the human, then, [below the human,] the animals, then the plants. The best of people is the one whose soul is perfected [by becoming] an intellect in act and who attains the morals that constitute the practical virtues. The best of [the latter] is the one ready [to attain] the rank of prophethood. This is the one who in his psychological powers has three distinctive properties which we had mentioned, namely, that he hears the speech of God, exalted be He, and sees His angels, that have been transformed for him into a form he sees. We have shown the manner of this.[1] We have shown that the angels take visible shape for the person who receives revelation and that there occurs in his hearing a voice, [coming] from the direction of God and His angels. He thus hears it without this being [436] speech [coming] from people and the terrestrial animal. This is the one to whom revelation is given.

Just as the first of beings [proceeding from the First], from the commencement [down] to the rank of the elements, had been intellect and then soul and then body, so here [in the terrestrial world] existence begins with bodies, then souls coming into being, then intellects. [All] these forms necessarily emanate from these [celestial] principles. The temporal events that take place in this [terrestrial] world come about [as a result] of the collision of the active celestial powers.[2] The passive terrestrial [powers] follow the collisions of the active celestial powers.

As for the powers of the terrestrial world, that which occurs therein is completed by reason of two things: One is the active powers in them, whether natural or voluntary; the second is the passive powers, either natural or psychological. As for the celestial powers, their effects in these bodies beneath them take place in three respects: One is by themselves such that there is no causal [action] in any manner whatsoever on the part of terrestrial things. [The second is that these effects] are due either (a) to the natures of [the celestial] bodies and their bodily powers, in accordance with the configurations [they cause] jointly with the terrestrial powers and the relations between them, or (b) to their psychological natures.

The third way involves some manner of sharing with the terrestrial states and causal activity in the manner I [now] state: It has become clear to you that the souls of these celestial bodies have a mode of doing things with particular meanings by way of an apprehension which is not purely intellectual, and that it is for the like of [such celestial souls] to arrive at an apprehension of particular events. This is possible by reason of apprehending the differences in their realized efficient and receptive causes—inasmuch as they are causes—and what these lead to. [It has also become clear to you] that these always terminate in a nature or a necessitating will, not a lukewarm will that is neither binding nor decisive. But they do not end up being compulsory. For the compulsory is either

1. Avicenna, *al-Shifā'* [Healing]: *al-Nafs* [Psychology], ed. G. C. Anawati and S. Zayid (Cairo, 1974) 4.2, pp. 151–52.

2. These "collisions" are not haphazard or accidental. See above, bk. 9, chap. 6 (Anawati ed., pp. 417–18).

compulsion [437] by nature or compulsion by will. At these two, all analysis in compulsory things terminates. [Now,] all voluntary [events] come to be after not being. They thus have sufficient causes that necessitate them. No will comes to be through another will; otherwise, this would lead to an infinite regress. Nor does it come about through a nature belonging to the one who wills; otherwise, the will becomes necessary as long as the nature exists. Rather, wills come about with the coming to be of causes that necessitate. Motives depend on both terrestrial and celestial [states] and necessarily necessitate that will. As for natural [causes], if they are permanent, they constitute a principle; and if coming to be in time, then they inevitably also depend on celestial and terrestrial matters.

All this you have previously known. [You have also known] that the crowding of these causes—their collisions and their continuance—has an order that is drawn in accordance with the celestial motion. Thus if you know the primary [causes], inasmuch as they are the primary [causes], and the way they lead toward the secondary,[3] you will necessarily know the secondary [causes]. From these things we know that the celestial souls and those above them have knowledge of particulars. As for those above them, their knowledge of particulars is in a universal way; but as for [the celestial souls, their knowledge of particulars] is in a particular way, similar to direct [apprehension], that which leads to direct [apprehension], or [similar] to that which is observed by the senses. Hence, [these latter] necessarily know what will be. And, in the case of many, they necessarily know between two possible things the one which is more correct, better, and closer to the absolute good.

We have shown that the conceptions (*al-taṣawwurāt*) possessed by these [celestial] causes are the principles for the existence of these forms here, (a) if [these latter] are possible [in themselves] and (b) if there were no celestial causes stronger than these conceptions among the things that are prior and that belong to one of the two divisions of the three (other than this third). If this is the case, then it follows necessarily that that possible thing should be realized as existing, not due to any terrestrial cause, nor to a natural cause in the heaven, but due to some influence of these matters in celestial things. In reality [however] this is not an influence; rather, the influence for the principles of the existence of that thing belongs to celestial things. For if they intellectually apprehend the primaries, they intellectually apprehend that thing; and if they intellectually apprehend that thing, they intellectually apprehend that which has the greater priority to be [438]; and if they apprehend this, then there is nothing to impede [its existence] other than the absence of a natural terrestrial cause or the existence of a natural terrestrial cause.

As regards the absence of the natural terrestrial cause, it is, for example, that that [celestial] thing should bring about the existence of warmth, [but] that there would be no natural terrestrial warming power. That warmth would occur to the celestial conception, in a manner in which the good lies, in the same way that [warmth] would come about in the bodies of people due to causes of people's conceptions and [in the ways] you have previously known. As for an example of the second, [this is] where the impediment is not only the absence of the cause of warming but also the existence of that which cools. Thus the celestial conception of the good, [as consisting] in the opposite of what is necessitated by that which cools [in it], also subdues that which cools in the way our conception of what induces anger subdues the cooling cause, whereby warmth comes to be. The kinds of this part would then consist of transformations of natural matters, inspirations that connect with the supplicant or some other, or combinations of these, which individually or collectively, lead to the useful end.

The relation of supplication to invoking this power is [similar to] the relation of cogitation to the summoning of clarification, all [of which] emanates from above. This does not follow the celestial acts of imaged representation (*al-taṣawwurāt*),[4] but the First Truth knows all this in the manner we have said is appropriate to Him. From Him begins the existence of all that comes to be, but through mediation—the same [applies to] His knowledge. It is by reason of these things that benefits are gained through prayers and offerings, particularly in the matter of seeking rain and other things. For this reason, [punishments] for evil are to be feared and recompense for the good is to be expected. For, in the establishment of the truth of this, evil is prevented. The establishment of the truth of

3. *Wa hay'at injirārihā ilā al-thawāni:* literally, "the disposition (or state, or manner) of their being drawn to the secondary."

4. Rendered "conception" above.

this is through the manifestation of His signs, and His signs consist in the existence of His particular [effects]. This state of affairs is intellectually apprehended [by] the principles, hence it must necessarily have existence. If [it] does not exist, then there is either an evil and a cause that we do not apprehend, or some other impeding cause. But the [former] has the greater claim to exist than this [latter], and the existence of both together is impossible.

If you wish to know that the things intellectually apprehended [439] as useful [and] conducive to benefits have been brought into existence in nature, in the manner of the bringing to existence which you have known and ascertained; contemplate the state of the usefulness of the organs in animals and plants and how each has been created. There is [for this] no natural cause at all, but its principle is necessarily [divine] providence in the way you know [it from our previous discussion]. In a similar way one arrives at the true belief in these meanings. For they are dependent on providence in the way you have known providence to attach to these.

Know that most of what the populace confesses, takes refuge in, and upholds is true. It is only those who are pseudo-philosophers who reject it, due to ignorance on their part of its causes and reasons. We have written on this subject *The Book of Piety and Evil.* Reflect on the explanation of these things there, and believe what is related about divine punishments that fall upon corrupt cities and unjust individuals. Perceive how right is rendered victorious. [Moreover, perceive] that the cause of supplication on our part, of almsgiving and other things, [and] similarly the coming to be of injustice and evil comes only from there. For the principles of all these matters terminate in nature, will, and coincidence. The principle of nature is from there. Our volitions come into being after not being, and everything that comes into being after not being, has a cause. Hence every will we have has a cause. The cause of this will is not a will that regresses in this *ad infinitum,* but consists of matters that occur from external [sources], terrestrial and celestial. The terrestrial terminates in the celestial and the combination of all that necessitates the existence of the will. As for coincidence, it comes into being due to the collisions of these. When all matters are analyzed, [they are found] to rest on the principles that necessitate them, descending from God, exalted be He. The decree from God, exalted be He, is the first simple placing [of things]. Predetermination is that toward which the decree gradually directs itself, as though necessitating aggregates of simple things that are attributed, inasmuch as they are simple, to the first divine decree and command.

If it were possible for some human to know all the temporal events on earth and in heaven, and their natures, he would comprehend the manner of all that will occur in the future. [But] this astrologer who professes astral [predictions]—in addition [to the fact] that his first positings and premises are not based on demonstration, although he may claim [for them] experiment or inspiration, and may attempt poetic and rhetorical syllogism to establish them—depends on [only] one genus of evidential indicator of the causes of generated things, namely, those that are in heaven. But he cannot guarantee for himself knowledge of all the states that are in heaven. And [even] if he were to guarantee this for us and to fulfill [his promise], he would be unable to make us and himself know the existence of all of them in every [moment of] time, even if all were known to him with respect to their [kind of] action and nature. This is not sufficient for one to know that [something] exists or does not exist. This is because, in order to know that [fire] has warmed [a particular thing], it is not sufficient for you to know that fire is hot and that it warms and enacts such and such a thing, as long as you [still] do not know that it is realized [in existence]. What method of calculation would yield to us the knowledge of every event and innovation that occurs in the [celestial] sphere? [But, even] if he were able to make us and himself such as to know all of this, it would not suffice to make the transition [to the knowledge of] the hidden. For things that are absent [but] on the path of coming to be are completed only through mixtures between celestial matters (which, out of tolerance, [we will grant] that we have achieved knowledge of in all their numbers); and terrestrial matters, anterior and posterior; that which enacts them; and that which receives their action, those that are natural and those that are voluntary. [These] do not become complete through celestial [matters] alone. Thus, the one who does not have knowledge of all that is present of the two states of affairs and [knowledge of] that which necessitates each of the two—particularly that which is connected with the hidden—will be unable to make the transition [in knowledge] to the hidden. Thus, we do not rely upon their statements, even if we admit as a concession that all that they give us of their philosophical premises are true.

CHAPTER 2
PROOF OF PROPHECY.
THE MANNER OF THE PROPHET'S CALL TO GOD, THE EXALTED.
THE "RETURN" TO GOD.

We now say: it is known that man differs from the other animals in that he cannot lead a proper life when isolated as a single individual, managing his affairs with no associates to help him satisfy his basic wants. One man needs to be complemented by another of his species, the other, in turn, by him and one like him. Thus, for example, one man would provide another with vegetables while the other would bake for him; one man would sew for another while the other would provide him with needles. Associated in this way, they become self-sufficient. For this reason men have found it necessary to establish cities and form associations. Whoever, in the endeavor to establish his city, does not see to the requirements necessary for setting up a city and, with his companions, remains confined to forming a mere association, would be engaged in devising means [to govern] a species most dissimilar to men and lacking the perfection of men. Nevertheless, even the ones like him cannot escape associating with the citizens of a city, and imitating them.

If this is obvious, then man's existence and survival require partnership. Partnership is only achieved through reciprocal transactions, as well as through the various trades practiced by man. Reciprocal transactions demand law (*sunna*) and justice, and law and justice demand a lawgiver and a dispenser of justice. This lawgiver must be in a position that enables him to address men and make them adhere to the law. He must, then, be a human being. Men must not be left to their private opinions concerning the law so that they disagree, each considering as just what others owe them, unjust what they owe others.

Thus, with respect to the survival and actual existence of the human species, the need for this human being is far greater than the need for such benefits as the growing of the hair on the eyebrow, the shaping of the arches in the feet, and many others that are not necessary [442] for survival but at best are merely useful for it. Now the existence of the righteous man to legislate and to dispense justice is a possibility, as we have previously remarked.[5] It becomes impossible, therefore, that divine providence should ordain the existence of those former benefits and not the latter, which are their bases. Nor is it possible that the First Principle and the angels after Him should know the former and not the latter. Nor yet is it possible that that which He knows to be in itself within the realm of possibility but whose realization is necessary for introducing the good order, should not exist. And how can it not exist, when that which depends and is constructed on its existence exists? A prophet, therefore, must exist and he must be a human. He must also possess characteristics not present in others so that men could recognize in him something they do not have and which differentiates him from them. Therefore he will perform the miracles about which we have been informed.

When this man's existence comes about, he must lay down laws about men's affairs by the permission of God, the Exalted, by His command, inspiration, and the *descent of His Holy Spirit* on him [cf. 16:102]. The first principle governing his legislation is to let men know that they have a Maker, One and Omnipotent; that *He knows the hidden and the manifest* [cf. 16:19]; that obedience is due Him since *command* must belong to *Him who creates* [cf. 7:54]; that He has prepared for those who obey Him an afterlife of bliss, but for those who disobey Him an afterlife of misery. This will induce the multitude to obey the decrees put in the prophet's mouth by God and the angels.

But he ought not to involve them with doctrines pertaining to the knowledge of God, the Exalted, beyond the fact that He is one, the truth, and has none like Himself. To go beyond this and demand that they believe in His existence as being not referred to in place, as being not subject to verbal classifications, as being neither inside nor outside the world, or anything of this kind, is to ask too much. This will simply confuse the religion (*dīn*) they have and involve them in something from which deliverance is only possible for the one who receives guidance and is fortunate, whose

5. See above, chap. 1 (Anawati ed., p. 435).

existence is most rare. For it is only with great strain that they can comprehend the true states of such matters; it is only the very few among them that can understand the truth of divine "unicity" and divine "remoteness." The rest would inevitably come to deny the truth of such an existence, fall into dissensions, and indulge in disputations and analogical arguments that stand in the way of their political duties. This might even lead them [443] to adopt views contrary to the city's welfare, opposed to the imperatives of truth. Their complaints and doubts will multiply, making it difficult for a man to control them. For divine wisdom is not easily acquired by everyone.

Nor is it proper for any man to reveal that he possesses knowledge he is hiding from the vulgar. Indeed, he must never permit any reference to this. Rather, he should let them know of God's majesty and greatness through symbols and similitudes derived from things that for them are majestic and great, adding this much—that He has neither equal, nor companion, nor likeness. Similarly, he must instill in them the belief in the resurrection in a manner they can conceive and in which their souls find rest. He must tell them about eternal bliss and misery in parables they can comprehend and conceive. Of the true nature of the afterlife he should only indicate something in general: that it is something that "no eye has seen and no ear heard," and that there are pleasures that are great possessions, and miseries that are perpetual torture.

Know that God, exalted be He, knows that the good lies in such a state of affairs. It follows, then, that that which God knows to be the good, must exist, as you have known [from the preceding discussion]. But there is no harm if the legislator's words contain symbols and signs that might stimulate the naturally apt to pursue philosophic investigation.

CHAPTER 3
ACTS OF WORSHIP: THEIR BENEFITS IN THIS WORLD AND THE NEXT.

Moreover, this individual who is a prophet is not one whose like recurs in every period. For the matter that is receptive of a perfection like his occurs in few bodily compositions. It follows necessarily, then, that the prophet (may God's prayers and peace be upon him) must plan with great care to ensure the preservation of the legislation he enacts concerning man's welfare. [444] Without doubt, the fundamental principle here is that men must continue in their knowledge of God and the resurrection and that the cause for forgetting these things with the passage of the generation succeeding [the mission of] the prophet (may God's prayers and peace be upon him) must be absolutely eliminated. Hence there must be certain acts and works incumbent on people that the legislator must prescribe to be repeated at frequent specified intervals.[6] In this way memory of the act is renewed and reappears before it can die.

These acts must be combined with what brings God and the afterlife necessarily to mind; otherwise they are useless. Remembering is achieved through words that are uttered or resolutions made in the imagination and by telling men that these acts bring them closer to God and are richly rewarded. And these acts must in reality be of such a nature. An example of these is the acts of worship imposed on people. In general, these should be reminders. Now reminders consist of either motions or the absence of motions that lead to other motions. An example of motion is prayer, of the absence of motion, fasting. For although the latter is a negative notion, it so greatly moves one's nature that he who fasts is reminded that what he is engaged in is not a jest. He will thus recall the intention of his fasting, which is to draw him close to God.

These conditions must, if possible, be mixed with others useful for strengthening and spreading the law. Adding these will also be beneficial to men's worldly interests, as in the case of war (*jihād*) and the pilgrimage (*ḥajj*). Certain areas of land must be designated as best suited for worship and as belonging solely to God, the Exalted. Certain acts, which people must perform, must be specified as belonging exclusively to God—as,

6. Literally, "to be repeated at such intervals that they recommence soon after they end."

for example, sacrificial offerings—for these help greatly in this connection. Should the place that is of such a benefit contain the legislator's home and abode, this will then also be a reminder of him. Remembrance of him in relation to the above benefits is only next in importance to the remembrance of God and the angels. Now, the one abode cannot be within proximate reach of the entire community (*umma*). It therefore becomes fitting [445] to prescribe a migration and a journey to it.

The noblest of these acts of worship, from one point of view, should be the one in which the worshiper considers himself to be addressing God, beseeching Him, drawing close to Him, and standing in His presence. This is prayer. The legislator should therefore prescribe for the worshiper in preparation for prayer those postures men traditionally adopt when they present themselves to human kings, such as purification and cleanliness (indeed, he must prescribe fully in these two things). He should also prescribe for the worshipers the behavior traditionally adopted in the presence of kings: reverence, calm, modesty, the lowering of the eyes, the contracting of the hands and feet, the avoidance of turning around, composure. Likewise, he must prescribe for each time of prayer praiseworthy manners and customs. These acts will benefit the vulgar inasmuch as they will instill in them remembrance of God and the resurrection. In this way their adherence to the statutes and laws will continue. For without such reminders they will forget all of this with the passing of a generation or two. It will also be of great benefit for them in the afterlife inasmuch as their souls will be purified in the manner you have known [in our discourse].[7] As for the elect, the greatest benefit they derive from these things pertains to the afterlife.

We have established[8] the true nature of the afterlife and have proved that true happiness in the hereafter is achieved through the soul's detaching itself by piety from the acquisitions of bodily dispositions opposed to the means to happiness. This purification is realized through moral states and habits of character acquired by acts that turn the soul away from the body and the senses and perpetuate its memory of its true substance. For if the soul continues to turn unto itself, it will not be affected by the bodily states. What will remind and help the soul in this respect are certain arduous acts that lie outside natural habit—indeed they are more on the side of exertion. These tire the body and curb the [natural] animal desire for rest, for laziness, for the rejection of toil, for the quieting of the hot humor, and for avoiding all exercise except that which is conducive [446] to bestial pleasure. In the performance of these acts the soul must be required to recall God, the angels, and the world of happiness, whether it desires to do so or not. In this way the soul is instilled with the propensity to be repelled from the body and its influences and with the positive disposition to control it. Thus it will not be affected by the body. Hence when the soul encounters bodily acts, these will not produce in it the propensities and positive disposition that they would normally produce when the soul submits to them in everything. For this reason, the one who speaks truth has said: *Surely the good deeds drive away the bad deeds* [11:114]. If this act persists in man, then he will acquire the positive disposition of turning in the direction of truth and away from error. He thus becomes well prepared to be delivered unto [true] happiness after bodily separation.

If these acts were performed by someone who did not believe them to be divine obligations and who, nonetheless, had to remember God in every act, rejecting everything else, this one would be worthy of some measure of this virtue. How much more worthy will be the one who performs these acts knowing that the prophet comes from God and is sent by God, that his being sent is necessitated by divine wisdom, that all the prophet's legislation is an obligation demanded of him by God, that all he legislates comes from God? For the prophet was obligated by God to impose these acts of worshiping Him. These acts benefit the worshipers in that they perpetuate in the latter adherence to the laws and religion (*sharīʿa*) that insure their existence and in that, by virtue of the goodness they inspire, they bring the worshipers closer to God in the hereafter.

Moreover, this is the man who is charged with administering the affairs of men, for insuring their livelihood in this world and their well-being in the world to come. He is a man distinguished from the rest of mankind by his godliness. [447]

7. *Healing: Metaphysics* 9.7.

8. Ibid.

CHAPTER 4
ESTABLISHMENT OF THE CITY, THE HOUSEHOLD (THAT IS, MARRIAGE), AND THE GENERAL LAWS PERTAINING TO THESE MATTERS.

The legislator's first objective in laying down the laws and organizing the city must be to divide it into three groups: administrators, artisans, and guardians. He must place at the head of each group a leader, under whom he will place other leaders, under these yet others, and so forth until he arrives at the common run of men. Thus none in the city will remain without a proper function and a specific place: each will have his use in the city. Idleness and unemployment must be prohibited. The legislator must leave the way open to no one for acquiring from another that share of a livelihood necessary for man while exempting himself from any effort in return. Such people he must vigorously restrain. If they fail to refrain from such a practice, he must then exile them from the land. But should the cause here be some physical malady or defect, the legislator must set aside a special place for such cases, under someone's charge.

There must exist in the city a common fund, part of it consisting of duties imposed on acquired and natural profits such as fruit and agricultural produce, part of it imposed as punishment, while another part should consist of property taken from those who resist the law, that is, of war-booty.[9] Thus the fund will serve to meet the exigencies of the common good, to meet the needs of the guardians who do not work in any craft, and those prevented from earning their livelihood by maladies and chronic diseases. Some people have held the opinion that the diseased whose recovery is not to be expected should be killed.[10] But this is base, for their sustenance will not hurt the city. If such people have relatives enjoying a superfluity of means, then the legislator must impose on these relatives the responsibility for their people. [448]

All fines must not be imposed on the criminal alone. Some of these must be imposed on the criminal's protectors and relatives who fail to reprimand and watch over him. But the fines legislated in the latter case should be mitigated by allowing delay in payment. The same should apply to crimes committed inadvertently. These must not be ignored even though they do occur by mistake.

Just as idleness must be prohibited, so should professions like gambling, whereby properties and useful things are transferred without any benefit rendered in exchange. For the gambler takes without rendering any service at all. Rather, what one takes must always be a compensation given in return for work, a compensation that is either substance, utility, good remembrance, or any other thing considered a human good. Similarly, professions that lead to the opposite of welfare and usefulness, such as the learning of theft, brigandage, pandering, and the like, must be prohibited. Professions that allow people to dispense with learning those crafts pertaining to the association—professions such as usury—must be prohibited. For usury is the seeking of excess profit without practicing a craft to achieve it, even though it does render a service in return. Also those acts—which, if once permitted, would be detrimental to the city's growth—like fornication and sodomy, which dispense with the greatest pillar on which the city stands, that is, marriage, must be prohibited.

The first of the legislator's acts must pertain to marriage resulting in issue. He must call and urge people to it. For by marriage is achieved the continuity of the species, the permanence of which is proof of the existence of God, the Exalted. He must arrange it in such a way that matrimony takes place as a manifest affair, so that there will be no uncertainties concerning progeny causing defects in the proper transfer of inheritances, which [449] are a source of wealth. For wealth is indispensable for a livelihood. Now wealth divides into source and derivatives. Sources consist of wealth that is inherited, found, or granted. Of these three sources, the best is inherited wealth; for it does not come by way of luck or chance but is of an order akin

9. *ghanā'im.*

10. Cf. Plato *Republic* 410A, 459E, 541A; *Laws* 627E ff.

to the natural. Through this also—I mean the concealment of marriage—defects in other respects occur: for example, in the necessity that one party should undertake expenditure over the other, in rendering mutual assistance, and in other matters that will not escape the wise person after reflection.

The legislator must take firm measures to assure the permanence of the union so that not every quarrel should result in a separation that disrupts the bond between children and parents and renews the need of marriage for everyone. In this there are many sorts of harm. Also, because what is most conducive to the general good is love. Love is only achieved through friendship; friendship through habit; habit is produced only through long association. This assurance, with respect to the woman, consists in not placing in her hands the right to make the separation. For in reality she is not very rational and is quick to follow passion and anger. But a way for separation must be left open and not all doors closed. To prevent separation under all circumstances results in all kinds of harmful consequences. Of these is the fact that some natures cannot adapt themselves to others: the more they are brought together, the greater the resulting evil, aversion, and unpleasantness. Or again, someone might get an unequal partner, or one who is of bad character, or repellent in nature. This will induce the other partner to desire someone else—for desire is natural—and this in turn leads to many harmful consequences. It also might so happen that the married couple do not cooperate for procreation and if exchanged for other partners they would. Hence some means for separation is necessary. But the law must be strict about it. [450]

The means for separation must not be placed in the hands of the less rational of the two, the one more prone to disagreement, confusion, and change. Instead, this must be relegated to the judges who will affect the separation when they ascertain the woman's mistreatment by [her] partner. In the case of the man, an indemnity must be imposed on him so that he will approach separation only after ascertainment and after he finds it to be the right thing for him in every way.

The legislator must, nevertheless, leave the way open for reconciliation, without, however, emphasizing it lest this encourage thoughtless action. On the contrary, he must make reconciliation more difficult than separation. How excellent was that which [Muhammad] the greatest of legislators commanded [cf. 2:229–30]—that the man, after thrice pronouncing the formula for divorce, is not allowed to remarry the woman until he brings himself to drink a cup unsurpassed in bitterness, which is, to first let another man marry her by a true marriage and have real relations with her. If such a prospect awaits a man, he will not approach separation recklessly, unless he has already determined that the separation is to be permanent, or unless he is of a defective character and takes perverted pleasure in scandal. But the likes of these fall outside the pale of men who deserve the seeking of their welfare.

Since woman by right must be protected inasmuch as she can share her sexual desire with many, is much inclined to draw attention to herself, and in addition to that is easily deceived and is less inclined to obey reason; and since sexual relations on her part with many men cause great disdain and shame, which are well-known harms, whereas on the part of the man they only arouse jealousy, which should be ignored as it is nothing but obedience to the devil; it is more important to legislate that the woman should be veiled and secluded from men. Thus, unlike the man, she should not be a bread-winner. It must be legislated that her needs be satisfied by the man upon whom must be imposed her sustenance. For this the man must be compensated. He must own her, but not she him. [451] Thus she cannot be married to another at the same time. But in the case of the man this avenue is not closed to him though he is forbidden from taking a number of wives whom he cannot support. Hence the compensation consists in the ownership of the woman's "genitalia." By this ownership I do not mean sexual intercourse. For both partake of its pleasure and the woman's share is even greater, as is her delight and pleasure in children. But by this I mean that no other man can make use of them.

It must be legislated with respect to the child that both parents must undertake his proper upbringing—the woman in her special area, the man by provision. Likewise it must be prescribed that the child must serve, obey, respect, and honor his parents. For they are the cause of his existence and in addition have borne his support, something we need not enlarge upon as it is evident.

CHAPTER 5
CONCERNING THE CALIPH AND THE IMAM: THE NECESSITY OF OBEYING THEM. REMARKS ON POLITICS, TRANSACTIONS, AND MORALS.

Next, the legislator must impose as a duty obedience to whosoever succeeds him. He must also prescribe that designation of the successor can only be made by himself or by the consensus of the elders.[11] The latter should verify openly to the public that the man of their choice can hold sole political authority, that he has independent judgment, that he is endowed with the noble qualities of courage, temperance, and good governance, and that he knows the law to a degree unsurpassed by anyone else. Such a verification must be openly proclaimed and must find unanimous agreement by the entire public. The legislator must lay down in the law that should they disagree and quarrel, succumbing to passion and whim, or should they agree to designate someone [452] other than the virtuous and deserving individual; then they would have committed an act of unbelief. Designation of the caliph through appointment by testament is best: it will not lead to partisanship, quarrels, and dissensions.

The legislator must then decree in his law that if someone secedes and lays claim to the caliphate by virtue of power or wealth, then it becomes the duty of every citizen to fight and kill him. If the citizens are capable of so doing but refrain from doing so, then they disobey God and commit an act of unbelief. The blood of anyone who can fight but refrains becomes free for the spilling after this fact is established in the assembly of all. The legislator must lay down in the law that, next to belief in the prophet, nothing brings one closer to God than the killing of such a usurper.

If the seceder, however, verifies that the one holding the caliphate is not fit for it, that he is afflicted with an imperfection, and that this imperfection is not found in the seceder; then it is best that the citizens accept the latter. The determining factor here is superiority of practical judgment and excellence in political management. The one whose attainment in the rest of the virtues [including knowledge] is moderate—although he must not be ignorant of them nor act contrary to them—but excels in these two is more fit than the one who excels in the other virtues but is not foremost in these two. Thus the one who has more knowledge must join and support the one who has better practical judgment. The latter, in turn, must accept the former's support and seek his advice, as was done by 'Umar[12] and 'Alī.[13]

He must then prescribe certain acts of worship that can be performed only in the caliph's presence, in order to extol his importance and make them serve his glorification. These are the congregational affairs, such as festivals. He must prescribe such public gatherings; for these entail the call for solidarity, the use of the instruments of courage, and competition. It is by competition that virtues are achieved. Through congregations, supplications are answered and blessings are received in the manner discussed in our statements.

Likewise, there must be certain transactions in which the imam participates. These are the transactions that lead to the building of the city's foundation, such as marriage and communal activities. He must also prescribe, in the transactions involving exchange, laws that prevent treachery and injustices. He must forbid unsound transactions where the objects of exchange change before being actually received or paid, as with moneychanging, [453] postponement in the payment of debt, and the like.

He must also legislate that people must help and protect others, their properties, and lives; without this, however, entailing that the contributor should penalize himself as a result of his contribution.

As for enemies and those who oppose his law, the legislator must decree waging war[14] against them and destroying them, after calling on them to accept the truth. Their property and women must be declared free for the spoil. For when such property and women are not administered according to the constitution of the virtuous city, they will

11. Literally, "forerunners" or "predecessors," a term usually applied to those who had been close to Muhammad.

12. 'Umar Ibn al-Khaṭṭāb, the second orthodox caliph (d. 644).

13. 'Alī Ibn Abī Ṭālib, the fourth orthodox caliph (d. 661).

14. The word translated "waging war" is from the root *q.t.l.*

not bring about the good for which property and women are sought. Rather, these would contribute to corruption and evil. Since some men have to serve others, such people must be forced to serve the people of the just city. The same applies to people not very capable of acquiring virtue. For these are slaves by nature as, for example, the Turks and the Zinjis and in general all those who do not grow up in noble [that is, moderate] climes where the conditions for the most part are such that nations of good temperament, innate intelligence, and sound minds thrive. If a city other than his has praiseworthy laws, the legislator must not interfere with it unless the times are such that they require the declaration that no law is valid save the revealed law. For when nations and cities go astray and laws are prescribed for them, adherence to the law must be assured. If the adherence to the law becomes incumbent, it might very well be the case that to ensure this adherence requires the acceptance of the law by the whole world. If the people of that [other] city, which has a good way of life, find that this [new] law, too, is good and praiseworthy and that the adoption of the new law means restoring the conditions of corrupted cities to virtue, and yet proceed to proclaim that this law ought not to be accepted and reject as false the legislator's claim that this law has come to all cities, then a great weakness will afflict the law. Those opposing it could then use as argument for their rejecting it that the people of that [other] city have rejected it. In this case these latter must also be punished and war (*jihād*) waged on them, but this war must not be pursued with the same severity as against the people utterly in error. Or else an indemnity must be imposed on them in lieu of their preference. In any case, it must be enunciated as a truth that they are negators [of the true law]. For how are they not negators, when they refuse to accept the divine Law, which God, the Exalted, has sent down? Should they perish, they would have met what they deserve. For their death, though it means the end of some, results in a permanent good, particularly when the new law is more complete and better. [454] It should also be legislated with regard to these, that if clemency on condition that they pay ransom and tax is desired, this can be done. In general, they must not be placed in the same category as the other nonbelievers.

The legislator must also impose punishments, penalties, and prohibitions to prevent disobedience to the divine Law. For not everyone is restrained from violating the law because of what he fears of the afterlife. Most of these [penalties and so forth] must pertain to acts contrary to law that are conducive to the corruption of the city's order: for example, adultery, theft, complicity with the enemies of the city, and the like. As for the acts that harm the individual himself, the law should contain helpful advice and warning, and not go beyond this to the prescription of obligatory duties. The law concerning acts of worship, marriage, and prohibitions should be moderate, neither severe nor lenient. The legislator must relegate many questions, particularly those pertaining to transactions, to the exercise of the individual judgment (*ijtihād*) of the jurists. For different times and circumstances call for decisions that cannot be predetermined. As for the further control of the city involving knowledge of the organization of guardians, income and expenditure, manufacture of armaments, legal rights, border fortifications, and the like; it must be placed in the hands of the ruler in his capacity as caliph. The legislator must not impose specific prescriptions concerning these. Such an imposition would be defective since conditions change with time. Moreover, it is impossible to make universal judgments that cover every contingency in these matters. He must leave this to the body of counselors.

It is necessary that the legislator should also prescribe laws regarding morals and customs that advocate justice, which is the mean. The mean in morals and customs is sought for two things. The one, involving the breaking of the dominance of the passions,[15] is for the soul's purification and for enabling it to acquire the power of self-mastery so that it can liberate itself from the body untarnished. [455] The other, involving the use of these passions, is for worldly interests. As for the use of pleasures, these serve to conserve the body and procreation. As for courage, it is for the city's survival. The vices of excess are to be avoided for the harm they inflict on human interests, while the vices of deficiency are to be avoided for the harm they cause the city. By wisdom as a virtue, which is the third of a triad comprising in addition temperance and courage, is not meant theoretical wisdom—for the mean is not demanded

15. Literally, "powers."

in the latter at all—but, rather, practical wisdom pertaining to worldly actions and behavior. For it is deception to concentrate on the knowledge[16] of this wisdom, carefully guarding the ingenious ways whereby one can attain through it every benefit and avoid every harm, to the extent that this would result in bringing upon one's associates the opposite of what one seeks for oneself and result in distracting oneself from the attainment of other virtues. To cause the hand to be thus fettered to the neck, means the loss of a man's soul, his whole life, the instrument of his well-being, and his survival to that moment at which he attains perfection. Since the motivating powers are three the appetitive, the irascible, and the practical—the virtues consist of three things: (a) moderation in such appetites as the pleasures of sex, food, clothing, comfort, and other pleasures of sense and imagination; (b) moderation in all the irascible passions such as fear, anger, depression, pride, hate, jealousy, and the like; and (c) moderation in practical matters. At the head of these virtues stand temperance, practical wisdom, and courage; their sum is justice, which, however, is extraneous to theoretical virtue. But whoever combines theoretical wisdom with justice is indeed the happy man. And whoever, in addition to this, wins the prophetic qualities, becomes almost a human god. Worship of him, after the worship of God, becomes almost allowed. He is indeed the world's earthly king and God's deputy in it.

16. Reading *ta'arrufihā* (n.) for *ta'rīfihā* (making it known).

EIGHT

ALGHAZALI

The Deliverer from Error

Translated by Richard J. McCarthy, SJ

Alghazali (Abū Ḥāmid Muḥammad Ibn Muḥammad al-Ṭusī al-Ghazālī, 1058–1111) was born in Ṭūs in northeast Persia. He studied there, in Jurjān, and finally in Nīshāpūr under the renowned Shāfi'ī jurist Abū al-Ma'ālī al-Juwaynī until his teacher's death in 1085. Alghazali was to become one of the most influential and prolific Muslim thinkers in the history of Islam. In addition to studying Islamic jurisprudence in his youth, he received wide training in the religious sciences, including *kalām*. Between 1085 and his appointment as the leading teacher of jurisprudence in the Niẓammiya in 1091, he seems to have spent time both at the court of the Seljuk sultan Niẓām al-Mulk, in Baghdad, and teaching in Nīshāpūr. In some of his writings of this period, he defends the Sunnī caliphate at Baghdad against the Shi'ī Fatimids in Egypt. According to the *Deliverer from Error*, from which our selection is taken, the period from 1091–1095 was marked by the rise of skepticism in Alghazali's thought, which was closely linked to his study of philosophy. During the same period, he wrote his renowned *Incoherence of the Philosophers*. In 1095 he experienced a profound spiritual and physical crisis, apparently brought on by his meteoric rise as a lecturer and author. Amid this crisis, he decided to withdraw from public life. He left Baghdad, traveling to Damascus, Jerusalem, Hebron, Medina, and Mecca, to return to Persia within four years. For another seven years, he remained withdrawn from public life. During these eleven years of withdrawal, he wrote among many other things his largest and most ambitious work, *The Revivification of the Religious Sciences*. At the request of the vizier of the Seljuk sultan, in 1106 he returned to teaching for roughly two more years. During this time, he wrote the *Deliverer*. Eventually, he withdrew to his home in Ṭūs, where he died in 1111.

The *Deliverer from Error* is an engaging, largely autobiographical work. Scholars disagree about how trustworthy it is as autobiography, but it is undoubtedly a very persuasive work. What it is supposed to persuade us of, however, is debatable. Is it intended merely to persuade Muslims to remain steadfast in their piety? Or does Alghazali walk a fine line between wholesale condemnation of philosophy and a subtle defense of philosophy for the freethinkers in his audience? Debate still swirls around Alghazali's intentions generally. The overall effect of our selection, however, is decidedly antiphilosophical. The general structure of the *Deliverer* is the following: (1) Alghazali presents himself as the true opponent, like the philosophers, of "servile conformism"; (2) he engages in a consideration of the sources of knowledge, challenging the view that reason on the basis of sensation can lead to true knowledge; (3) he describes the efforts of the four schools of those who seek the truth: (a) the *mutakallimūn,* (b) the philosophers, (c) the internalists/followers of the infallible Imam, and (d) the Sufis (his account of the Sufi path is blended with an account of his spiritual crisis, which resulted in ascetic withdrawal from worldly affairs and the pursuit of mystical knowledge); (4) he explains the Sufi path as a form of prophecy accessible to all Muslims, culminating in the taste (*dhawq*) of God; and (5) he defends his choice to resume teaching, reiterating and developing his condemnation of the learned, especially the philosophers, for their purported immorality and failure to seek the rewards of the afterlife.

McCarthy's translation is based on Shehid Ali Pasha MS no. 1712. This manuscript was copied roughly ten years after the composition of the *Deliverer.* McCarthy found this manuscript to be superior on many occasions to the most widely available Arabic edition, by Jamīl Ṣalībā and Kāmil ʿAyyād, which has served as the basis for other translations and includes a French translation by C. M. Jabre: *Al-Munqidh min al-ḍalāl [Erreur de délivrance]* (Beirut: Collection Unesco d'Oeuvres Représentatives, 1959). McCarthy's complete English translation of the *Deliverer* appears in *Deliverance from Error and Other Works* (Boston: Twayne, 1980; 2nd ed., Louisville, KY: Fons Vitae, 2004).

PHILOSOPHY

25. After finishing with the science of *kalām,* I then started on philosophy. I knew for sure that one cannot recognize what is unsound in any of the sciences unless he has such a grasp of the farthest reaches of that science that he is the equal of the most learned of those versed in the principles of that science; then he must even excel him and attain even greater eminence so that he becomes cognizant of the intricate profundities which have remained beyond the ken of the acknowledged master of the science. Then, and only then, will it be possible that the unsoundness he alleges will be seen as really such.

26. I noted, however, that not a single Muslim divine scholar had directed his attention and endeavor to that end. What the *mutakallimūn* had to say in their books, where they were engaged in refuting the philosophers, was nothing but abstruse, scattered remarks, patently inconsistent and false, which could not conceivably hoodwink an ordinary intelligent person, to say nothing of one familiar with the subtleties of the philosophical sciences.

27. I knew, of course, that undertaking to refute their doctrine before comprehending it and knowing it in depth would be a shot in the dark.[1] So I girded myself for the task of learning that science by the mere perusal of their writings without seeking the help of a master and teacher. I devoted myself to that in the moments I had free from writing and lecturing on the legal sciences—and I was then burdened with the teaching and instruction of three hundred students in Baghdad. As it turned out, through mere reading in those embezzled moments, God Most High gave me an insight into the farthest reaches of the philosophers' sciences in less than two years. Then, having understood their doctrine, I continued to reflect assiduously on it for nearly a year, coming back to it constantly and repeatedly reexamining its intricacies and profundities. Finally, I became so familiar with the measure of its deceit and deception, and its precision and delusion, that I had no doubt about my thorough grasp of it.

28. So hear now my account of them [the philosophers] and my report of the substance of their sciences. For I observed that they fell into several categories and noted that their sciences included several divisions. But to all of them, despite the multiplicity of their categories, cleaves the stigma of unbelief and godlessness.[2] Yet there is a marked difference between the older and the oldest of them and the more recent and the earlier in their distance from and closeness to the truth.

1. Literally, "a throwing in blindness."

2. *Al-kufr wa al-ilḥād: kufr* means "unbelief" and *ilḥād* means "heresy" or, literally, "deviation" from the true faith, Islam.

The Categories of the Philosophers and the Fact That the Stigma of Unbelief Is Common to All of Them

29. Know that the philosophers, notwithstanding the multiplicity of their groups and the diversity of their doctrines, can be divided into three main divisions: Materialists, Elementalists, and Deists.[3]

30. The first category, the Materialists (*dahriyyūn*), were a group of the most ancient philosophers who denied the existence of the omniscient and omnipotent Creator-Ruler.[4] They alleged that the world has existed from eternity as it is, of itself and not by reason of a Maker. Animals have unceasingly come from seed, and seed from animals: thus it was, and thus it ever will be. These are the godless[5] in the full sense of the term.

31. The second category, the Elementalists (*al-ṭabīʿiyyūn*), were men who devoted much study to the world of nature and the marvels found in animals and plants; they also were much taken up with the dissection of animal organs. In these they saw such marvels of God Most High's making and such wonders of His wisdom that they were compelled, with that in mind, to acknowledge the existence of a wise Creator (*fāṭir*) cognizant of the aims and purposes of all things. Indeed, no one can study the science of anatomy and the marvelous uses of the organs without acquiring this compelling knowledge of the perfect governance of Him Who shaped the structure of animals, and especially that of man.

32. However, it appeared to these philosophers, because they had studied nature so much, that the equilibrium of the mixture of humors had a great effect on the resulting constitution of the animal's powers. Hence they thought that man's rational power was also dependent on the mixture of his humors and that its corruption would follow the corruption of the mixture of his humors, and so that power would cease to exist. Once it ceased to exist, they alleged that bringing back the nonexistent would be unintelligible. So they adopted the view that the soul dies, never to return. Consequently they denied the afterlife and rejected the Garden and the Fire,[6] the Assembly and the Recall, and the Resurrection[7] and the Reckoning.[8] So in their view there would be no future reward for obedience, and no punishment for disobedience. Therefore they lost all restraint and abandoned themselves to their passions like beasts. These were also godless men, because basic faith is belief in God and the Last Day—and these men denied the Last Day, even though they believed in God and His Attributes.

33. The third category, the Deists (*al-ilāhiyyūn*), were the later philosophers, such as Socrates, the master of Plato, and Plato, the master of Aristotle. It was Aristotle who systematized logic for the philosophers and refined the philosophical sciences, accurately formulating previously imprecise statements and bringing to maturity the crudities of their sciences. Taken altogether, these refuted the first two categories of the Materialists and the Elementalists. Indeed, by the arguments they advanced to lay bare the enormities of the latter, they relieved others of that task: *And God spared the believers from fighting [the unbelievers]* [33:25] by reason of the unbelievers' own infighting.

34. Then Aristotle refuted Plato and Socrates and the Deists who had preceded him in such thorough fashion that he disassociated himself from them all. Yet he, too, retained remnants of their vicious unbelief and innovation which he was unsuccessful in avoiding. So they all must be taxed with unbelief, as must their partisans among the Muslim philosophers, such as Avicenna and Alfarabi and their likes. None, however, of the Muslim philosophers engaged so much in transmitting

3. *Al-dahriyyūn wa al-ṭabīʿiyyūn wa al-ilāhiyyūn:* McCarthy renders these as "Materialists, Naturalists, and Theists." He offers "Elementalists" as an alternative to "Naturalists." The editor has decided to use "Elementalists" because "naturalism" has come to have a relatively narrow meaning in contemporary thought in general. He has chosen to substitute "Deism" for "Theism," though it is also potentially misleading, because for contemporary readers "Theism" could not be something Alghazali attacks but what he defends—J. P.

4. Literally, "the artisan-governor and world decreer" (*al-ṣāniʿ al-mudabbir al-ʿālim al-qādir*).

5. *Al-zanādiqa* (pl. of *zindīq*), a more emphatic term than *ilḥād*, often rendered as "godlessness."

6. Heaven and hell.

7. The reunion of souls with bodies and their rising on the Last Day.

8. God's judgment of souls.

Aristotle's lore as did the two men just mentioned. What others transmitted is not free from disorder and confusion, and, in studying it, one's mind becomes so muddled that he fails to understand it—and how can the incomprehensible be rejected or accepted?

35. The sum of what we regard as the authentic philosophy of Aristotle, as transmitted by Alfarabi and Avicenna, can be reduced to three parts: a part that must be branded as unbelief; a part that must be stigmatized as innovation;[9] and a part that need not be repudiated at all. Let us now set this forth in detail.

The Divisions of the Philosophical Sciences

36. Know that the sciences of the philosophers, with reference to the aim we have in mind, include six divisions: mathematical, logical, physical, metaphysical, political, and moral.[10]

37. The mathematical sciences deal with arithmetic, geometry, and astronomy. But nothing in them entails denial or affirmation of religious matters. On the contrary, they concern rigorously demonstrated facts which can in no wise be denied once they are known and understood. From them, however, two evils have been engendered.

38. One of these is that whoever takes up these mathematical sciences marvels at the fine precision of their details and the clarity of their proofs. Because of that, he forms a high opinion of the philosophers and assumes that all their sciences have the same lucidity and apodeictic solidity as this science of mathematics. Moreover, he will have heard the talk of the town about their unbelief, their negative attitude, and their disdain for the Law. Therefore he ceases to believe out of pure conformism,[11] asserting: "If religion were true, this would not have been unknown to these philosophers, given their precision in this science of mathematics." Thus, when he learns through hearsay of their unbelief and rejection of religion, he concludes that it is right to reject and disavow religion. How many a man have I seen who strayed from the path of truth on this pretext and for no other reason!

39. One may say to such a man: "A person skilled in one field is not necessarily skilled in every field. Thus a man skilled in jurisprudence and *kalām* is not necessarily skilled in medicine, nor is a man who is ignorant of the speculative and rational sciences necessarily ignorant of the science of syntax. On the contrary, in each field there are men who have reached in it a certain degree of skill and preeminence, although they may he quite stupid and ignorant about other things. What the ancients[12] had to say about mathematical topics was apodeictic, whereas their views on metaphysical questions were conjectural. But this is known only to an experienced man who has made a thorough study of the matter."

40. When such an argument is urged against one who has become an unbeliever out of mere conformism he finds it unacceptable. Rather, caprice's sway,[13] vain passion,[14] and love of appearing to be clever prompt him to persist in his high opinion of the philosophers with regard to all their sciences. This, then, is a very serious evil, and because of it one should warn off anyone who would embark upon the study of those mathematical sciences. For even though they do not pertain to the domain of religion, yet, since they are among the primary elements of the philosophers' sciences, the student of mathematics will be insidiously affected by the sinister mischief of the philosophers. Rare, therefore, are those who study mathematics without losing their religion and throwing off the restraint of piety.

41. The second evil likely to follow from the study of the mathematical sciences derives from the case of an ignorant friend of Islam who supposes that our religion must be championed by the rejection of every science ascribed to the philosophers. So he rejects all their sciences,

9. Accepting what is worthy of *takfīr* (branding as unbelief) would excommunicate one from the community of Islam; the acceptance of what is worthy of *tabdī*ʿ (stigmatizing as innovation) would render one a "heretic," but not a non-Muslim.

10. Compare the historical introduction to Alfarabi, *Enumeration of the Sciences* (above, selection 1).

11. *Taqlīd:* an important motive claimed by Alghazali in the opening pages of the *Deliverer* for his inquiry into the competing claims of *kalām*, philosophy, internalism, Sufism. See the historical introduction.

12. *Al-awā'il.* Contrast W. Montgomery Watt (*The Faith and Practice of al-Ghazālī* [London: George Allen and Unwin Ltd., 1953]), who renders this as "elementary matters."

13. *Taḥmiluh ghalabtu* with Jabre.

14. *Al-shahwatu al-bāṭila* with Jabre.

claiming that they display ignorance and folly in them all. He even denies their statements about eclipses of the sun and the moon and asserts that their views are contrary to the revealed Law (*al-shar'*). When such an assertion reaches the ears of someone who knows those things through apodeictic demonstration, he does not doubt the validity of his proof, but rather believes that Islam is built on ignorance and the denial of apodeictic demonstration. So he becomes all the more enamored of philosophy and envenomed against Islam. Great indeed is the crime against religion committed by anyone who supposes that Islam is to be championed by the denial of these mathematical sciences. For the revealed Law nowhere undertakes[15] to deny or affirm these sciences, and the latter nowhere address themselves to religious matters.

42. The saying of Muhammad (God's blessing and peace be upon him): "The sun and moon are two of the signs of God Most High: they are not eclipsed for the death or life of any man; so when you see an eclipse, fly in fear to the mention of God Most High,"[16] contains nothing demanding the denial of the science of calculation which apprises us of the course of the sun and the moon and their conjunction and their opposition in a specific way. As for his (alleged) saying (Peace be upon him): "But when God manifests Himself to a thing, it humbles itself before Him," this addition is not found at all in sound tradition.[17] This, then, is the judgment to be made on the character of mathematics and its evil consequences.

43. Nothing in the logical sciences has anything to do with religion by way of negation and affirmation. On the contrary, they are the study of the methods of proofs, of syllogisms, of the conditions governing the premises of apodeictic demonstration, of how these premises are to be combined, of the requisites for a sound definition, and of how the latter is to be drawn up. Knowledge is either a concept, and the way to know it is the definition, or it is an assent,[18] and the way to know it is the apodeictic demonstration. There is nothing in this which must be rejected. On the contrary, it is the sort of thing mentioned by the *mutakallimūn* and the partisans of reflection[19] in connection with the proofs they use. The philosophers differ from them only in modes of expression and technical terms and in a greater refinement in definitions and subdivisions. Their manner of discoursing on such things is exemplified by their saying: "If it is certain that every A is B, then it necessarily follows that some B is A"—for instance: If it is certain that every man is an animal, then it follows necessarily that some animal is a man. This they express by saying that a universal affirmative proposition is convertible to a particular affirmative proposition.

44. What has this to do with the important truths of our religion, that it should call for rejection and denial? When it is rejected, the only effect of such a rejection in the minds of logicians is a low opinion of the rejecter's intelligence, and, what is worse, of his religion, which, he claims, rests on such rejection. To be sure, the philosophers themselves are guilty of a kind of injustice in the case of this science of logic. This is that in logic they bring together, for apodeictic demonstration, conditions known to lead undoubtedly to sure and certain knowledge. But when, in metaphysics, they finally come to discuss questions touching on religion, they cannot satisfy those conditions, but rather are extremely slipshod in applying them. Moreover, logic may be studied by one who will think it a fine thing and regard it as very clear. Consequently, he will think that the instances of unbelief attributed to the philosophers are backed up by demonstrations such as those set forth in logic. Therefore he will rush into unbelief even before reaching the metaphysical sciences. Hence this evil may also befall the student of logic.

45. The physical sciences are a study of the world of the heavens and their stars and of the sublunar world's simple bodies, such as water, air, earth, and fire, and composite bodies, such as animals, plants, and minerals. They also study the causes of [these bodies'] changing and being transformed and being mixed. That is like medicine's study of the human body and its principal and subsidiary organs and the causes of the alterations of the mixtures of its humors. And just as religion does not require the repudiation of the

15. Literally, "addresses itself to" (*ta'arruḍ*).

16. Sunna.

17. It is not found, for example, in Bukhārī's authoritative collection of traditions.

18. Compare Averroes's use of "concept" and "assent" in the *Decisive Treatise* (selection 11 below).

19. Literally, "those who engage in speculation" (*ahl al-naẓar*). Compare Averroes's use in the *Decisive Treatise* (selection 11 below).

science of medicine, so also it does not require the repudiation of the science of physics, except for certain specific questions which we have mentioned in our book *The Incoherence of the Philosophers.*[20] Apart from these, it will be clear upon reflection that any other points on which the physicists must be opposed are subsumed in those we have alluded to. The basic point regarding all of them is for you to know that nature is totally subject to God Most High: It does not act of itself but is used as an instrument by its Creator. The sun, moon, stars, and the elements are subject to God's command: none of them effects any act by and of itself.

46. It is in the metaphysical sciences that most of the philosophers' errors are found. Owing to the fact that they could not carry out apodeictic demonstration according to the conditions they had postulated in logic, they differed a great deal about metaphysical questions. Aristotle's doctrine on these matters, as transmitted by Alfarabi and Avicenna, approximates the teachings of the Islamic philosophers. But the sum of their errors comes down to twenty heads, in three of which they must be taxed with unbelief, and in seventeen with innovation. It was to refute their doctrine on these twenty questions that we composed our book *The Incoherence.*

47. In the three questions first mentioned they were opposed to [the belief of] all Muslims, that is, in their affirming [the following]:

(1) that men's bodies will not be assembled[21] on the Last Day, but only disembodied spirits will be rewarded and punished, and the rewards and punishments will be spiritual, not corporeal. They were indeed right in affirming the spiritual rewards and punishments, for these also are certain; but they falsely denied the corporeal rewards and punishments[22] and blasphemed the revealed Law in their stated views.

(2) The second question is their declaration: "God Most High knows universals, but not particulars." This also is out-and-out unbelief. On the contrary, the truth is that *there does not escape Him the weight of an atom in the heavens or in the earth* [34:3; cf. 10:62, 61].

(3) The third question is their maintaining the eternity of the world, past and future. No Muslim has ever professed any of [the philosophers'] views on these questions.

48. On other matters—such as the denial of the divine attributes, and their assertion that God is knowing by His essence, not by a knowledge superadded to His essence, and similar views of theirs—their doctrine is close to that of the Mu'tazilites.[23] But there is no need to tax the Mu'tazilites with unbelief because of such views. We have already mentioned that[24] in our book *The Clear Criterion for Distinguishing between Islam and Godlessness,* as well as what shows the error of anyone who precipitously brands as unbelief everything that clashes with his own doctrine.

49. In the political sciences all that the philosophers have to say comes down to administrative maxims concerned with secular affairs and the government of rulers. They simply took these over from the scriptures revealed to the prophets by God Most High and from the maxims handed down from the predecessors of the prophets.

50. All they have to say about the moral sciences comes down to listing the qualities and habits of the soul, and recording their generic and specific kinds, and the way to cultivate the good ones and combat the bad. This they simply took over from the sayings of the Sufis. These were godly men, who applied themselves assiduously to invoking[25] God, resisting passion, and following the way leading to God Most High by shunning worldly pleasures. In the course of their spiritual combat, the good habits of the soul and its shortcomings had been disclosed to them as well as the defects that vitiate its actions. All this they set forth plainly. Then the philosophers took over these ideas and mixed them with their own doctrines, using the luster afforded by them to promote the circulation of their own false teaching. There was indeed in their age, nay there is in every age, a group of

20. See the critical Arabic edition and translation by Michael Marmura, 2nd ed. (Provo, UT: Brigham Young University Press, 2002).

21. Resurrected.

22. Cf. Avicenna, *Healing: Metaphysics* 10.2 (selection 7 above).

23. One of the two main schools of dialectical theology. Alghazali is generally thought to be affiliated with the other school, the Ash'arites, who seem to allow for little or no mitigation of divine omnipotence, not even, for example, by divine goodness.

24. Following Duncan B. Macdonald's reading in "The Life of al-Ghazzālī with Especial Reference to His Religious Experiences and Opinions," *Journal of the American Oriental Society* 20 (1899): 71–132: *wa qad dhakarnā dhālika fī... wa mā yatabayyanu.*

25. *dhikr:* a reference to the Sufi practice of constantly repeating the name of God, as well as certain verses and formulas.

godly men of whom God Most High never leaves the world destitute. For they are the pillars of the earth,[26] and by their blessings the divine mercy descends upon earth dwellers as is declared in the tradition from Muhammad (God's blessing and peace be upon him!) in which he says: "Because of them you receive rain, and thanks to them you receive sustenance, and among them were the Companions of the Cave." Such godly men existed in ancient times, as the Qur'an declares [cf. Sura 18].

51. From the Islamic philosophers' mixing the prophetic utterances and the sayings of the Sufis with their own writings two evils have sprung: one in the case of the man who accepts their ethical teaching, the other in the case of the man who rejects it.

52. The evil in the case of the man who rejects their ethical teaching is very serious. For some dim-witted persons suppose, since that borrowed prophetic and Sufi doctrine has been set down in the philosophers' writings and mixed with their false doctrine, this doctrine must be eschewed and never cited and even disavowed whenever anyone cites it. This is their attitude because they have heard that doctrine in the first place only from the philosophers. So their weak minds straightway judge it to be erroneous because the one who voices it is in error on other matters. This is like the case of a man who hears a Christian say: "There is no God but God; Jesus is the Apostle of God," and then denies it, saying: "This is what the Christians say." Such a man does not defer judgment while he ponders whether the Christian is an unbeliever because of that statement, or because of his denial of Muhammad's prophethood (God's blessing and peace be upon him). Hence, if he is an unbeliever only because of his denial of the latter, he should not be contradicted in matters other than what he disbelieves—I mean something which is true in itself, even though the Christian also holds it to be true.

53. This is the practice of those dim-witted men who know the truth by men, and not men by the truth. The intelligent man, on the contrary, follows the advice of the Master of the Intelligent, ʿAlī (God be pleased with him) where he says: "Do not know the truth by men, but rather, know the truth and you will know its adherents." The intelligent man, therefore, first knows the truth; then he considers what is actually said by someone. If it is true, he accepts it; whether the speaker be wrong or right in other matters. Indeed, such a man will often be intent on extracting what is true from the involved utterances of the erring, since he is aware that gold is usually found mixed with dirt. The moneychanger suffers no harm if he puts his hand into the sack of the trickster[27] and pulls out the genuine pure gold from among the false and counterfeit coins, so long as he can rely on his professional acumen. It is not the expert moneychanger, but rather the inexperienced bumpkin who must be restrained from dealing with the trickster. Likewise, a clumsy and stupid person must be kept away from the seashore, not the proficient swimmer; and a child must be prevented from handling a snake, not the skilled snake charmer.

54. It is certainly true, since most men have an overweening opinion of their own competence and cleverness and think that they are perfectly equipped intellectually to discern truth from error, that the door must be blocked to prevent the generality of men, as far as possible, from perusing the works of those addicted to error. For they will by no means be safe from the second evil which we shall presently mention, even if they do manage to escape the evil which we have just noted.

55. Some of the remarks found here and there in our works on the mysteries of the religious sciences were objected to by a group of men whose minds were not thoroughly grounded in those sciences and whose mental vision was not open to the ultimate aims of our teachings. They alleged that those remarks were taken from things said by the early philosophers. As a matter of fact, some of them were my own original ideas—and it is not farfetched that ideas should coincide, just as a horse's hoof may fall on the [hoof] print left by another; and some are found in the scriptures; and the sense of most is found in the writings of the Sufis.

56. However, assuming that they are found only in the writings of the philosophers, if what is said is reasonable in itself and corroborated by apodeictic proof and not contrary to the Qur'an and the Sunna; then why should it be shunned and rejected? If we were to open this door and aim at forgoing every truth that had been first formulated by

26. *Awtād al-arḍ: watad* means, literally, "tent peg," "stake," "pole." The plural was applied to a group of theurgic "saints" in a hierarchy headed by the *quṭb* (Pole)—that is, the saint who, in each age, mysteriously supports and directs the world.

27. *Al-qallāb.*

the mind of one in error, we would have to forgo much of what is true. We would also have to give up a lot of the verses of the Qur'an and the traditions of the Apostle and the recitals of our pious forebears and the sayings of the sages and the Sufis. For the author of the book of "The Brethren of Purity" cites these in his own work, appealing to their authority and thereby enticing the minds of stupid men to embrace his false doctrine. That would be an invitation to those in error to wrest the truth from our hands by putting it into their own books.

57. The lowest level attained by an intelligent man is to be so different from the gullible man in the street that he feels no aversion to honey, even though he finds it in a cupper's glass, but realizes that the cupping glass does not alter the nature of the honey. For the natural distaste for such honey is based on a popular misconception arising from the fact that the cupping glass is made for blood deemed impure. Consequently, the man in the street supposes the blood is deemed impure because it is in the cupping glass and does not realize that it is deemed impure because of a property found in the blood itself. Because this property does not exist in the honey, its being found in such a vessel does not impart to it that property nor does it necessitate its being deemed impure. This is an empty fancy yet it is prevalent among most men. Thus, whenever you trace back a statement and attribute it to a speaker of whom they have a good opinion, they accept it, even though it be false; but whenever you attribute it to someone of whom they have a bad opinion they reject it, even though it is true. Thus they always know the truth by men, not men by the truth—which is the extreme of error! This, then, is the evil due to total rejection of the philosophers' ethical teaching.

58. The second evil is that due to total acceptance of their ethical teaching. For one who studies their books, such as that of "The Brethren of Purity" and others, and sees the prophetic maxims and Sufi sayings they interspersed with their own utterances, often approves of their writings and accepts them and forms a good opinion of them. Thereupon he may readily accept their errors mixed up with those borrowed truths because of a good opinion acquired about what he has seen and approved. That is a way of luring men into error.

59. Because of this evil the perusal of the philosophers' books must be prevented on the score of the deceit and danger they contain. Just as an unskilled swimmer must be kept away from slippery river banks, so men must be kept from perusing those books. And just as children must be kept from handling snakes, so the ears of men must be protected from the jumble of those sayings. And just as the snake charmer must not handle a snake in the presence of his little boy, since he knows that the boy will imitate him thinking he is like his father, but rather must caution his boy against that by being cautious himself in the boy's presence; so also the man of deep learning must comport himself. Furthermore, when a skilled snake charmer takes a snake and separates the antidote from the poison and draws forth the antidote and renders the poison harmless, he is not free to withhold the antidote from anyone in need of it. So, too, when the moneychanger skilled in picking out coins puts his hand in the trickster's sack and takes out the genuine pure gold and discards the spurious and counterfeit coins, he is not free to withhold the good and acceptable coins from anyone who needs them. The same holds good for the true scholar.

60. Moreover, a man in need of the antidote whose soul feels a great loathing for it, because he knows that it has been extracted from the snake which is the seat of the poison, must be properly instructed. Likewise, when a poor man in dire need of money is averse to accepting gold drawn from the trickster's sack he must be reminded that his aversion is pure ignorance, which will cause him to be deprived of the benefit he seeks. He certainly ought to be informed that the proximity of the counterfeit to the genuine coins does not make the genuine coins counterfeit, just as it does not make the counterfeit coins genuine. In precisely the same way, therefore, the close proximity of the true to the false does not make the true false, as it does not make the false true.

This, then, is as much as we wish to say about the evil and mischief of philosophy.

NINE

IBN BAJJA

The Governance of the Solitary

Translated by Lawrence Berman

Ibn Bājja or Avempace (Latin) (Abū Bakr Muḥammad Ibn Bājja [or Ibn al-Ṣā'igh], ca. 1085–1138) was born in Saragossa toward the end of the eleventh century, lived in Seville, Granada, and later in North Africa (where he seems to have enjoyed a favored position at the Almoravid court), and died in Fez. A striking feature of his life and thought is that, though the *Governance of the Solitary* would seem to recommend withdrawal from political affairs in imperfect regimes, Ibn Bajja spent much of his life in public service.[1] While in Saragossa, he is thought to have been the vizier to Abū Bakr Ibn Ibrāhīm al-Ṣaḥrāwī (known as Ibn Tīfalwīt) from ca. 1110 to 1117. And he is believed to have been appointed vizier, probably of Seville, for roughly twenty years, by Yaḥyā Ibn Abī Bakr, grandson of the founder of the Almoravids, Yūsuf Ibn Tāshfīn. To add to the complexity of Ibn Bajja's character and actions, all evidence indicates that he, like Avicenna before him, led a relatively dissolute life. He is celebrated as the first Spanish-Muslim philosopher and is credited with extensive knowledge of medicine, mathematics, astronomy, poetry, and music. Most of his surviving works are short treatises, many of which are incomplete and do not appear to have been properly revised by the author.

The *Governance of the Solitary* is noteworthy for having the character and position of the philosopher in the imperfect cities as its central theme. This theme, in a sense, complements Alfarabi's discussion of the solitary individuals (or Weeds) in the virtuous city in his *Political Regime* (above, selection 3). "Abū Bakr Ibn al-Ṣā'igh sought to establish a way for the 'Governance of the Solitary' in these lands," says Averroes, "but this book is incomplete, and besides, it is not always easy to understand its meaning.... He is the only one to treat this subject, and none of his predecessors surpassed him in this respect." The central theme of the work is interwoven with another theme, that of "spiritual" or incorporeal "forms." Only such parts as treat the main theme are given here.

Moses Narboni made a Hebrew paraphrase of the book in his commentary on Ibn Tufayl's *Hayy the Son of Yaqzan*, composed in 1349. This paraphrase was published by David Herzog: *Die Abhandlung des Abu Bekr Ibn al-Saig "Vom Verhalten*

1. For a perceptive and thought-provoking analysis of Ibn Bajja and his work, readers should consult Steven Harvey, "The Place of the Philosopher in the City according to Ibn Bājjah," in *The Political Aspects of Islamic Philosophy: Essays in Honor of Muhsin S. Mahdi*, ed. Charles E. Butterworth (Cambridge, MA: Harvard University Press, 1992), 199–233.

des Einsiedlers" nach Mose Narbonis Auszug (Berlin, 1896). The first edition of the Arabic text was published by Miguel Asín Palacios: *Tadbīr al-mutawaḥḥid* (Madrid and Granada, 1946). At about the same time, D. M. Dunlop published the first two chapters of the text: "Ibn Bājjah's Tadbīru'l-Mutawaḥḥid (Rule of the Solitary)," *Journal of the Royal Asiatic Society of Great Britain and Ireland,* 1945, 63–73 (corresponding to Asín Palacios's ed., 3–17). Both editions are based on the same manuscript (Bodleian, Pococke, No. 206) and present numerous difficulties, some of which are no doubt due to the unfinished character of the work as left by Ibn Bajja. Majid Fakhry published another edition based on the same MS in his *Opera Metaphysica* of Ibn Bājjah (Beirut: Dār al-Nahār, 1968), 35–96. And Ma'an Ziyādah published another edition (Beirut: Dār al-Fikr, 1978), which includes notes on the divergent readings of the previous editions based on this same single MS. As Dunlop explains in his *Encyclopaedia of Islam* entry for Ibn Bajja, new ed. (Leiden: Brill, 1971), 3:728–29, several other manuscripts are known to exist, though they have been lost track of. Until additional manuscripts are found and collated, Palacios's edition remains trustworthy, as does Berman's translation. This translation is based on Palacios's edition, pp. 3–12, 37, 54–55, 58–62, 78–79. The bracketed page numbers refer to the Palacios edition.

CHAPTER 1

1. The word "governance" (*tadbīr*) is used in Arabic in many senses, enumerated by the experts in that language. Most commonly, it is used to signify, in a general way, the ordering of actions to an end that is being pursued. Therefore they do not apply it to someone who performs a single action with a view to accomplishing a particular end: one does not call an activity "governance" if he believes that it consists of a single action; whereas the one who believes that the activity consists of many actions and considers it inasmuch as it possesses an order, he then calls that order a governance. (For this reason, they say of God that He is the "governor" of the world.) This [order] may be potential or actual; but the more frequent use of the word "governance" signifies the potential [order].

It is evident that when certain affairs are ordered potentially, they are so ordered by means of calculation; for this [kind of order] pertains to calculation and can exist through calculation alone. Therefore [4] it can exist in man alone, and the use of "governor" [cited above] is merely analogical. Hence governance is used in a primary and a derivative sense.[2] Governance may also designate the bringing of this [potential] order into being and insofar as order is on its way into being, which is more frequent and apparent in human action, less so in the actions of the irrational animal. Applied in this manner, governance has a general and a restricted sense. Used in a general sense, it designates all human activities of whatever kind. It is applied to the crafts as well as to the faculties, except that it is more frequent and common to apply it [in the restricted sense] to the faculties. Therefore it is applied to the ordering of military affairs and hardly ever to the arts of shoemaking and weaving. When applied in this [restricted] manner, again it has a general and a restricted sense. Used in a general sense, it designates all that is covered by the arts called "faculties." And they have been summarized in political science.[3] Used in a restrictive sense, it designates the governance of cities.

Governance is applied to matters some of which are prior to others in dignity and perfection. Of these, the most dignified are the governance of cities and the governance of the household. But governance is seldom applied to the household, to the extent that the expression "governance of the household" is used in a metaphorical and qualified sense. As for the governance of war (*ḥarb*) and so forth, they form parts of these two kinds of governance. As for God's governance of the world, this is certainly governance of a different kind, only distantly related to even that meaning of the word [that is, the one referring to the city], which resembles[4]

2. Literally, "is said in [in accordance with an order of] priority and posteriority."

3. The translation of this sentence, suggested by Charles E. Butterworth, replaces Berman's translation, especially his interpolation "I have given an account of this in [my work(s) on] political science."

4. With Dunlop.

it most closely. The latter is governance in the unqualified sense. It is also the most dignified, for it receives the designation [5] "governance" because of the supposed similarity between it and bringing the world into existence by God, the Exalted.

It is evident that this class of ambiguous nouns [to which "governance" belongs] is the farthest removed from univocity; it is almost completely equivocal. The multitude uses it ambiguously. The philosophers use it with complete equivocity; they consider it ambiguous only in the sense in which we give A the name of B because A contains something that is similar to B—a class of which they did not give an account in [their discussions of] ambiguous nouns because of its rarity. Therefore the multitude does not use the adjective "right" in connection with God's governance [of the world] and does not say of the governance of the world that it is "right" governance. Instead it says that it is "perfect," "precise," and the like, because these expressions imply the presence of rightness and some other dignified thing in addition. For in the eyes of the multitude, right activity is like a species of perfect and precise activity. The account of this matter is presented elsewhere.

2. When governance is used in an unqualified sense, as we have used it above, to designate[5] the governance of cities, and when used in a restricted sense [to designate the governance of the household], it is divided into right and wrong governance. It is sometimes supposed that governance may be free of these two opposite [qualifications], but investigation and close study will reveal that they adhere to it necessarily. This can be ascertained easily by anyone with a minimal understanding of political philosophy. Therefore the two types of governance properly so called can be divided into right and wrong governance.

As far as the governance of cities is concerned, Plato has explained it in the *Republic.* He explained [6] what is meant by the right governance of cities and the source of the wrongness that adheres to it. To trouble oneself with the task of dealing with something that has been adequately dealt with before is superfluous, a result of ignorance, or a sign of evil intent.

As for the governance of the household, the household as household is a part of the city. He [Plato] explained there that man alone forms the natural household [of which he spoke]. He explained that the most excellent existence of that which is a part is to exist as a part. Therefore he did not formulate the governance of the household as a [separate] part of the political art, since it is treated by him within the political art. He explained there what the household is and how it exists, that[6] it exists most excellently when the [city conducts a] common household, and he describes its communal character.

As for the household existing in cities other than the virtuous—that is, in the four [imperfect] cities enumerated [in the *Republic*[7]]—the household exists in them imperfectly, and there is something unnatural in it. Only that household is perfect to which nothing can be added without resulting in an imperfection, like the sixth finger; for the distinguishing feature of what is well constructed is that it becomes imperfect by adding to it. All other households are imperfect and diseased in comparison with the [natural] household, for the conditions that differentiate them from the virtuous household lead to the destruction of the household and its ruin. Therefore these conditions are like a disease. Certain authors have gone to the trouble of treating the governance of these imperfect—that is, the diseased—households. Those of them whose books on the governance of the household have reached us employ rhetorical arguments. In contrast, the position we stated is clear: except for the virtuous household, the households are diseased; they are all corrupt; and they do not exist by nature but only by convention. Therefore whatever virtue they may possess, [7] is by convention too, except perhaps so far as they have something in common with the virtuous household. The virtuous household can be treated following a fixed and necessary order of exposition. Understand,[8] then, that the treatment of that common element can be scientific as well, for no household is without many of the common features that are to be found in the virtuous household. For without them a household cannot endure or even be a household except equivocally. Let us, then, turn aside and leave the treatment of

5. Reading *[wa-]dall.*

6. Reading *wa-inn* for *fa'inn* (indeed).

7. That is, timocracy, oligarchy, democracy, and tyranny. See Plato *Republic* 8 and 9.

8. With Dunlop.

imperfect households to those who devote themselves to the treatment of such matters as exist at particular times.

Moreover, the perfection of the household is not something desired for its own sake, but only for the sake of rendering perfect either the city or the natural end of man; and the treatment of the latter clearly forms part of man's governance of himself [that is, ethics]. In any case, the household is either a part of the city and its treatment forms part of the treatment of the city, or a preparation for another end and its treatment forms part of the treatment of that end. This explains why the treatment of the household in the popular manner is pointless and does not constitute a science. If it has any advantage, then this is only temporary, as is the case with what the rhetoricians present in their works on "manners" (which they call psychological), such as *Kalila and Dimna* and the *Book of Arab Sages,* which contain maxims and sayings of counsel. For the most part, this topic is treated in certain sections of a book, such as in the chapters[9] dealing with the companionship of the sultan, the social relations with friends, and the like. In the majority of cases, these things are true[10] for a particular time and a particular [8] way of life. When that way of life changes,[11] those opinions—expressed as universal statements—change;[12] their application becomes restricted after having been universal; they become harmful or rejected after having been useful. You will understand this if you acquaint yourself with the contents of the books composed on this topic and try to apply what is said in each case to later times.

3. The virtuous city is characterized by the absence of the art of medicine and of the art of judication (*ṣināʿat al-qaḍāʾ*).[13] For friendship binds all its citizens, and they do not quarrel among themselves at all. Therefore it is only when a part of the city is bereft of friendship and quarrelsomeness breaks out that recourse must be had to the laying down of justice and the need arises for someone, who is the judge, to dispense it. Moreover, since all the actions of the virtuous city are right—this being the distinguishing characteristic that adheres to it—its citizens do not eat harmful foods. Therefore they do not need to know about the cures for the suffocation caused by mushrooms and the like, nor do they need to know about the treatment for excessive wine-drinking, for nothing there is not properly ordered. When the citizens forego exercise, this too, gives rise to numerous diseases; but it is evident that the virtuous city is not subject to such diseases. It may not even need any remedies aside from those for dislocation and the like, and, in general, for such diseases whose specific causes are external and that the healthy body cannot ward off by its own effort. For it has been observed in many a healthy man that his serious wounds heal [9] by themselves, and there are other kinds of evidence for this. It is, then, characteristic of the perfect city that there is neither doctor nor judge, while it is inherent in the four [imperfect simple regimes or] unmixed[14] cities that they are in need of doctor and judge. The more removed a city is from the perfect, the more it is in need of these two and the more dignified the station of these two types of men in it.

It is evident that in the virtuous and perfect city, every man is offered the highest excellence he is fit to pursue. All of its opinions are true and there is no false opinion in it. Its actions alone are virtuous without qualification. When any other action is virtuous, it is so only in relation to some existing evil. For instance, the amputation of a limb from the body is harmful in itself, but, by accident, it may prove beneficial to someone who has been bitten by a snake and whose body achieves health by that amputation. Similarly, scammony is harmful in itself, but it is beneficial to someone with a disease. An account of these matters is given in the *Nicomachea.*[15]

It is, then, evident that every opinion arising in the perfect city that is different from the opinions of its citizens is false, and every action arising in it that is different from the actions customarily performed in it is wrong. Now the false does not have a defined nature and cannot be known at all; this is explained in the *Book of Demonstration.*[16]

9. With Dunlop.

10. With Dunlop.

11. With Dunlop.

12. With Dunlop.

13. The difference between this art of judication and the art of jurisprudence (*fiqh*), as the latter is discussed by Alfarabi in the *Enumeration of the Sciences* and *Book of Religion,* is that the former is the activity of the jurisconsult or judge, and the latter is the activity of the jurisprudent. In Shlomo Pines's translation of the *Guide of the Perplexed* (Chicago: University of Chicago Press, 1963), jurisprudence (*fiqh*) is helpfully, if somewhat repetitively, rendered as the "legalistic science of the Law." Compare the following paragraph with Plato *Republic* 405A ff.

14. See above, note 7.

15. Aristotle *Nicomachean Ethics* 1138b1 and 7.5 ff. passim.

16. Aristotle *Posterior Analytics* 1.16 passim.

As to the wrong action, it may be performed in order to achieve some other end. There are books composed to enable one to study these actions, such as the *Book of Devices* by the Banū Shākir.[17] But everything contained in them has the nature of play—things intended to excite rather than to contribute [10] to the essential perfection of man. To discuss such things is a sign of evil intent and results from ignorance.

In the perfect city, therefore, one does not introduce arguments dealing with those who hold an opinion other than that of its citizens or perform an action other than their action. In the four [imperfect] cities, on the other hand, this can be done. For here, there may be an unknown[18] action that a man discovers by nature or learns from someone else, and does it. Or there may be a false opinion, and some man becomes aware of its falsehood. Or there may be erroneous sciences in all or most of which the citizens do not believe because they involve accepting[19] contradictory positions; and, by nature or instruction, a man may find which of the two contradictory propositions is the true one.

Now the ones who discover a right action or learn a true science that does not exist in the city belong to a class that has no generic name. As for the ones who stumble upon a true opinion that does not exist in the city or the opposite of which is believed in the city, they are called Weeds.[20] The more such opinions they hold and the more crucial the opinions, the more appropriate the appellation. Strictly speaking, the term applies to these men alone. But it may be applied, more generally, to anyone who holds an opinion other than the opinion of the citizens of the city, regardless of whether his opinion is true or false. The name has been transferred to these men from the weeds that spring up of themselves among plants. But let us restrict the use of this term to the ones who hold true opinions. It is evident that one of the characteristics of the perfect city is that it is free of Weeds [in both its strict and more general senses]; in the strict sense, because it is free of false opinions; and in the general sense, because their presence means that the city is already diseased and disintegrating and has ceased to be [11] perfect. The Weeds can, however, exist in the four [imperfect] ways of life. Their existence is the cause that leads to the rise of the perfect city, as explained elsewhere.[21]

All the ways of life that exist now or have existed before (according to the great majority of the reports reaching us about them, with the possible exception of what Abū Naṣr [Alfarabi] narrates concerning the early Persians' way of life) are mixtures of the five ways of life [that is, the perfect and the four imperfect ones], and for the most part we find them to be mixtures of the four [imperfect] ways of life. We leave it to those who devote themselves to the investigation of the ways of life that exist in this time to supply the details. We merely remark that the three types of men—the Weeds, the judges, and the doctors—exist or can exist, in these ways of life. The happy, were it possible for them to exist in these cities, will possess only the happiness of an isolated individual; and the only right governance [possible in these cities] is the governance of an isolated individual, regardless of whether there is one isolated individual or more than one, so long as a nation or a city has not adopted their opinion. These individuals are the ones meant by the Sufis when they speak of the "strangers"; for although they are in their homelands and among their companions and neighbors, the Sufis say that these are strangers in their opinions, having traveled in their minds to other stations that are like homelands to them, and so forth.

We intend to discourse here about the governance of this solitary man. It is evident that he suffers from something that is unnatural. We will therefore state how he should manage himself so that he may achieve the best existence proper to him, just as the doctor states how the isolated man in these cities should manage himself in order to be healthy: that is, either how to preserve his health (for instance, [12] what Galen writes in his *Preservation of Health*), or how to recover it once it is lost, which is laid down in the art of medicine. Similarly, this discourse is addressed to the isolated Weed: how he is to achieve happiness if he does not possess it, or how to remove from himself the conditions that prevent his achieving happiness or achieving the portion he can achieve of it, which in turn depends either on how far his insight takes him or on [a belief]

17. Aḥmad, al-Ḥasan, and Muḥammad, the sons of Mūsā Ibn Shākir, collaborated in writing numerous works on mathematics, astronomy, and mechanics. The *Book of Devices* is attributed to Muḥammad (d. 873).

18. Reading *yujhal* for *yuḥill* (permitted).

19. With Dunlop.

20. Cf. Alfarabi *Political Regime* secs. 92, 122 ff. (above, selection 3)

21. Cf., e.g., Alfarabi *Political Regime* secs. 114–15 (above, selection 3).

that had seized him. As to the preservation of his happiness, which is similar to the preservation of health, it is impossible in the three [four?] ways of life and those mixed of them; what Galen and others prescribe in this situation is similar to alchemy and astrology. What we are laying[22] down here is the medicine of the soul, as distinguished from the other medicine, which is the medicine of the body, and from judication, which is the medicine of social relations. It is evident that the latter two arts disappear completely in the perfect city and are, therefore, not to be reckoned among the sciences. Similarly, the subject we are treating would disappear if the city were perfect, and so would the utility of this subject, just as would the science of medicine, the art of judication, and every other art devised to meet [the predicaments characteristic of] the imperfect [kinds of] governance. Just as the true opinions contained in medicine revert [in the perfect city] to the natural sciences,[23] and those contained in the art of judication to the art of politics, similarly those contained in the present subject revert to natural science[24] and the art of politics.

CHAPTER 7

4. [37] Every one of these [particular spiritual forms, that is, the ones present in common sense, in the imagination, and in memory] is beloved of man by nature, and hardly a man can be found who does not have a liking for at least one of these spiritual forms. If man is a part of the city, then the city is the end that is served in all of his actions. But this obtains in the virtuous city alone. In the other four cities and the ones mixed of them, in contrast, each citizen establishes for himself any of these spiritual forms as an end and has a predilection for the pleasures resulting from them. Hence things that are mere preparations in the virtuous city become the ends in the other cities.

CHAPTER 12

1. [54] The ends that the solitary individual establishes[25] for himself are three: his corporeal form, his particular spiritual form, or his universal spiritual form [that is, his intellectual perception of the intelligible ideas]. The account of his ends when he[26] is a part of a lasting [that is, perfect or virtuous] city has been given in political science. As regards the ends he establishes for himself in each one of the other cities—insofar as he is a part of one of them—here, the solitary individual performs, among others, certain activities appropriate to him as he pursues any of these ends. Now these ends are pursued in the city,[27] and the general account of the city has been given in [55] political science. To achieve any of them, one has to use reflection, investigation, inference, and, in general, calculation; for without the use of calculation, an activity is bestial, not partaking of the human in any way beyond the fact that its object is a body that has a human form. When, in contrast, one pursues a bestial purpose—whether this purpose can be achieved through human calculation or not[28]—this kind of man is not different from the beast, and there is no difference at this point whether this being possesses a human form that conceals a beast or it is a beast living in isolation. It is also evident that no city can be formed from beings that act in the bestial manner, and that they cannot at all form parts of a city. Only the solitary individual can act in this manner, and we have stated the ends of the solitary. Hence the end of the bestial man is among these three ends. However, it cannot be the universal spiritual form; for this pertains to the intellect, which achieves it through inquiry. It is, then, evident that they must be two, that is, the particular spiritual and the corporeal forms.

22. With Dunlop.

23. Ibn Bajja says "arts" and "art," respectively. He is perhaps alluding to the arts that treat dislocation and the like; see above, p. 100.

24. With Dunlop.

25. Reading *yanṣubuhā* for *yataḍamanuhā* (embraces) with Narboni. Cf. the use of "establishes," just below.

26. Reading *wa-huwa* for *wa-hiya.*

27. Bracketing *al-fāḍila* (virtuous).

28. Adding *aw* before *lam.*

CHAPTER 13

1. [58] Some men, as we stated previously, are merely concerned with their corporeal form; they are the base. Others occupy themselves only with their [particular] spiritual form; they are the high-minded and the noble. Just as the basest among the men concerned with their corporeal form would be the one who disregards his spiritual form for the sake of the corporeal and does not pay any attention to the former, so the one who possesses [59] nobility in the highest degree would be the one who disregards his corporeal form and does not pay any attention to it. However, the one who disregards his corporeal form completely, reduces his longevity; like [the basest of men] he deviates from nature; and like him he does not exist. But there are men who destroy their corporeal form, in obedience to the demands of their spiritual form. Thus Ta'abbata Sharran[29] says:

> Our lot is either captivity to be followed by the
> favor [of manumission]
> Or to shed our blood; death is preferable for the
> free.

Thus he considers death better than having to bear the favor of manumission. Others choose to kill themselves. This they do either by seeking certain death on the battlefield, as did, for example, the Marwanite[30] in the war (*ḥarb*) with 'Abd Allāh Ibn 'Alī Ibn al-'Abbās; he is the author of the following lines:

> Life with dishonor and the dislike of death,
> Both I consider evil and hard.
> If there is no escape from one or the other,
> Then I choose to march nobly to death.

[Or else they choose to take their life with their own hands.] Zenobia did this when 'Amr was about to kill her: "I would rather do it with my own hands than let 'Amr kill me."[31] So did the queen of Egypt whose story[32] with Augustus is given in the histories. So also did certain peoples [60] whom Aristotle mentions when treating of the great-souled man:[33] they burned themselves and their city[34] when they became certain that their enemy was about to defeat them. All this borders on excess, except in certain situations in which the destruction of the corporeal form (but not the spiritual form) results from greatness of soul and magnanimity. This, for instance, applies to what Fāṭima the mother of al-Rabī' (and the rest of the Banū Ziyād) did when Qays Ibn Zuhayr caught up with her. She threw herself off the camel she was riding, and died.[35] But this is one of the special cases in which it is better to die than to live, and in which the choice of death over life is the right thing for man to do. We shall give an account of this later on.

2. There is another and lower type of the noble and the great-souled man, which forms the majority. This is the man who disregards his corporeal form for the sake of the spiritual, but does not destroy the former, either because his spiritual form does not compel him to do so, or—despite its compelling him to destroy his corporeal form—because he decides in favor of keeping it. We believe this to be what Ḥātim al-Ṭā'ī[36] did when he slaughtered his horse and sat hungry, not eating any of it himself or feeding any of it to his family, while his young children were convulsing with hunger. Another example is what thieves do [when they endure hardships and face danger]. However, in the former case, the purpose is to control the body and improve it, while these thieves expend[37] their bodies for the sake of their bodies and have a predilection for one corporeal state rather than another. In the former case—the case of Ḥātim al-Ṭā'ī and his like—no argument

29. A pre-Islamic poet.

30. The event took place in the decisive battle of the Greater Zab (in 750) in which the Abbasids, led by 'Abd (not 'Ubayd) Allāh, defeated the last Umayyad caliph, Marwān. The Umayyad (Marwanite) Yaḥyā Ibn Mu'āwiya refused 'Abd Allāh's offer of safety and preferred to die.

31. According to an apocryphal story (reported by al-Mas'ūdī, *Les prairies d'or,* ed. C. Barbier de Meynard and Pavet de Courteille [Paris, 1864], 3:189–96), the pre-Islamic Arab queen of Syria, Zenobia (captured by Aurelian in 272), was trapped by the Lakhmid king, 'Amr Ibn 'Adī, who was about to kill her in revenge for his maternal uncle, King Jadhīma, whom she had invited to her court and treacherously murdered. Zenobia sucked at her ring, which contained poisin, while addressing 'Amr (read *bi-yad* for *yā* with al-Mas'ūdī).

32. Reading *khabaruhā* for *ḥarruhā.*

33. Cf. Aristotle *Nicomachean Ethics* 4.3–4; *Eudemian Ethics* 3.5; *De Virtutibus et Vitiis* 3, 5; and esp. *Posterior Analytics* 97b15–25.

34. Reading *ḥaraqū anfusahum wa-madīnatahum* with Narboni.

35. The event took place during the pre-Islamic battle days of Dāḥis (second half of the sixth century).

36. Famous for his hospitality (d. ca. 605).

37. Reading *yabdhulūn* for *yubdilūn* (change).

can be adduced for not acknowledging that the action is noble and high-minded, and the nature responsible for it is honorable, sublime, [61] and spiritual; it occupies the most sublime position, next only to that occupied by wisdom; and it must necessarily be one of the qualities of the philosophic nature, for without it the philosophic nature would be corporeal and mixed.

To achieve its highest perfection, the philosophic nature must, then, act [nobly and with greatness of soul]. Therefore, whoever prefers his corporeal existence to anything pertaining to his spiritual existence will not be able to achieve the final end. Hence no corporeal man is happy and every happy man is completely spiritual. But just as the spiritual man must perform certain corporeal acts—but not for their own sake—and perform [particular] spiritual acts for their own sake; so the philosopher must perform numerous [particular] spiritual acts—but not for their own sake—and perform all the intellectual acts for their own sake. The corporeal acts enable him to exist as a human; the [particular] spiritual acts render him nobler; and the intellectual acts render him divine and virtuous. The man of wisdom is therefore necessarily a man who is virtuous and divine. Of every kind of activity, he takes up the best only. He shares with every class of men the best states that characterize them, but he stands alone as the one who performs the most excellent and the noblest of actions. When he achieves the final end—that is, when he intellects simple essential intellects, which are mentioned in the *Metaphysics, On the Soul,* and *On Sense and the Sensible*—he then becomes one of these intellects. It would be right to call him simply divine. He will be free from the mortal sensible qualities, as well as from the high [particular] spiritual qualities: [62] it will be fitting to describe him as a pure divinity.

All these qualities can be obtained by the solitary individual in the absence of the perfect city. By virtue of his two lower ranks [that is, the corporeal and the particular spiritual], he will not be a part, the end, the agent, or the preserver of this perfect city. By virtue of this third rank, he may not be a part of this perfect city, but he will nevertheless be[38] the end aimed at in this city. Of course, he cannot be the preserver or the agent of the perfect city while a solitary man.

CHAPTER 17

2. [78]...It is clear from the situation of the solitary that he must not associate with those whose end is corporeal nor with those whose end is the spirituality that is adulterated with corporeality. Rather, he must associate with those who pursue the sciences. Now since those who pursue the sciences are few in some ways of life and many in others—there even being ways of life in which they do not exist at all—it follows that in some of the ways of life the solitary must keep away from men completely so far as he can, and not deal with them except in indispensable matters and to the extent to which it is indispensable for him to do so; or emigrate to the ways of life in which the sciences are pursued—if such are to be found. This does not contradict what was stated in political science and what was explained in natural science. It was explained there [that is, in natural science] that man is political by nature, and it was explained in political science that all isolation is evil. But it is only evil as such; accidentally, it may be good, which happens with reference to many things pertaining to nature. For instance, bread and meat are by nature beneficial and nourishing, while opium and colocynth are mortal poisons. But the body may possess certain unnatural states in which the latter two are beneficial [79] and must be employed, and the natural nourishment is harmful and must be avoided. However, such states are necessarily diseases and deviations from the natural order. Hence the drugs are beneficial in exceptional cases and by accident, while [natural] nourishment is beneficial in the main and essentially. These states are to the body as the ways of life are to the soul. Just as health is believed to be one in opposition to these many [diseased] states, and health alone is the natural state of the body while the many [diseased states] are deviations from nature; similarly the lasting way of life is the natural state of the soul and is one in opposition to the rest of the ways of life, which are many, and these many [ways of life] are not natural to the soul.

38. Reading *yakūn* for *takūn*.

TEN

IBN TUFAYL

Hayy the Son of Yaqzan

Translated by George N. Atiyeh

Ibn Tufayl (Abū Bakr Muḥammad Ibn Ṭufayl, ca. 1110–1185) was born in Guadix near Granada. He practiced medicine in the city of Granada, became secretary to the governor of the province of Granada, and in 1154 was appointed by the founder of the Almohad dynasty, ʿAbd al-Muʾmin, as secretary to his son Abū Saʿīd, governor of Ceuta and Tangier. He became the chief physician and vizier of the second Almohad prince, Abū Yaʿqūb (r. 1163–1184), who "was most affectionate and friendly to him." "I was told," says the historian al-Marrākushī, "that he [Ibn Tufayl] used to stay with him for many days and nights without leaving the palace." In 1182 he retired as chief physician to be succeeded in this function by his protégé, Averroes, whom he had introduced to the prince in 1168/9. After Abū Yaʿqūb's death in 1184, his son and successor, Abū Yūsuf, seems to have kept Ibn Tufayl as vizier and honored courtier until the latter's death in Marrakesh.

Ḥayy the Son of Yaqẓān is an epistle addressed to a disciple and friend seeking information about the secrets of the Oriental or Illuminative philosophy mentioned by Avicenna. It consists of an introduction, which is a critical survey of the history of Islamic philosophy; the narrative relating the birth of *ḥayy* (alive) the son of *yaqẓān* (awake) and his development on a deserted island; the narrative of the development of *salāmān* (sound or whole?) and *āsāl* (questioner?) in a religious community on a neighboring island; and the narrative of Asal's retirement to Hayy's island, their meeting, their decision to go back to Asal's island to educate and improve the religious community, their failure in their mission, and their return to Hayy's island. A number of the names and the elements of the story are borrowed from popular Hellenistic stories and from Avicenna's story that bears the same title.

Ibn Tufayl's *Hayy the Son of Yaqzan* was translated into Hebrew by an unknown author, and Moses Narboni wrote a commentary on the work in 1349. The Arabic original was first published together with a Latin translation by Edward Pococke, Jr.: *Philosophus Autodictatus, sive Epistola Abi Jaafar ebn Tophail de Hai ebn Yokdan, quomodo ex Inferiorum contemplatione ad Superiorum notitiam Ratio humana ascendare possit* (Oxford, 1671, 1700). Pococke's Latin version was translated into English by the Quaker George Keith (1674) and by Ashwell (1686). A third English translation, made directly from the Arabic, was done by Simon Ockley: *The Improvement of the Human Reason, Exhibited in the Life of Hai Ebn Yokdhan* (London, 1708). The reason for the interest in this book during the late seventeenth and early eighteenth centuries may be detected in Ockley's subtitle: "in which is demonstrated, by what Methods one may, by the meer *Light of Nature,* attain the Knowledg of things *Natural* and *Supernatural;* more particularly the Knowledg of God, and the Affairs of another Life." Ockley found it useful to add an appendix "in which the Author's Notion concerning the Possibility of Man's attaining the True Knowledg of God, and Things necessary to Salvation, without the Use of external Means [Instruction], is briefly consider'd," because "the preceding History...contains several things co-incident with the Errors of some Enthusiasts of these present Times." The following translation and summary are based on the critical edition of the Arabic text by Léon Gauthier: *Ḥayy Ben Yaqdhān* 2nd ed. (Beirut, 1936).

[INTRODUCTION]

You have asked me, my noble, sincere, and affectionate brother (may God bestow upon you eternal life and infinite happiness), to convey to you what I can of [4] the secrets of the illuminative [or oriental] philosophy referred to by the Leading Master Abū 'Alī Ibn Sīnā [Avicenna]. Know, then, that he who desires to know the perfect truth should seek after this philosophy and assiduously endeavor to possess it.

Your question has awakened in me a noble intention that led me, praise be to God, to partake in the vision of a state I had not experienced before. It made me reach a point so extraordinary that words cannot describe and clear exposition cannot render an account thereof, because it is of an order and realm not belonging to them. Nonetheless, because of the joy, exuberance, and the pleasure radiating from that state, whoever attains it or reaches one of its limits is incapable of remaining reticent about it or of concealing its secret. He is overwhelmed with such rapture, liveliness, gaiety, and cheerfulness that drive him to divulge the gist, though not the details, of its secret.

Now, if the one who experiences this state lacks scientific skill, he will speak about it inconclusively. One such man went so far as to declare while in this state, "Glory to me, how great I am."[1] Another said, "I am the Truth."[2] And still another said, "He who wears this garment is none other than God."[3] As to the Master Abū Ḥāmid [Alghazali], when he attained this state, he described it by reciting the following verse:

> There was what was of what I do not mention;
> So think of it well, and ask for no account.[4] [5]

But then he was a man refined by knowledge and made skillful through the pursuit of science.

Consider, further, the discourse of Abū Bakr Ibn al-Ṣā'igh [Ibn Bajja] in connection with his doctrine on the character of conjunction (*ittiṣāl*).[5] He says, "If...someone comes to grasp the (intended) meaning, then it becomes evident to him that no knowledge of the ordinary sciences can be placed in the same category. His conception of that meaning takes place on a level in which he finds himself cut off from all that preceded, and holding new convictions free of corporeality, too sublime to be attributed to natural life, and free from the ephemeral composition inherent in natural life. They are rather worthy to be considered as divine states, bestowed by God upon whomsoever He pleases of His servants."[6] This level to which Abū Bakr [Ibn Bajja] has alluded is attained by way of theoretical science and by rational investigation. Doubtlessly, he must have attained such a level although he did not go beyond it.

Regarding the level to which we have alluded first, it is different although it is the same in the sense that there is nothing revealed in the first

1. Attributed to the Sufi al-Bisṭāmī (d. 875 or 877).
2. Attributed to the Sufi al-Ḥallāj (d. 922).
3. Attributed to the Sufi al-Ḥallāj.
4. The verse is by the poet Ibn al-Mu'tazz (d. 908). It is quoted by Alghazali in the *Deliverer from Error* in sec. 96 of the McCarthy translation.
5. A term used especially by philosophers to distinguish conjunction from unification (*ittiḥād*). Unification with God smacks of something that the Qur'an strictly forbids, namely, associationism (*shirk*). In spite of Sufism's wide mystical appeal, some Sufis seem to have crossed this line.
6. Ibn Bajja, *On Conjunction* (*Fī ittiṣāl al-'aql bi-l-insān*): M. Asín Palacios, "Tratado de Avempace sobre la unión del intelecto con el hombre," *Al-Andalus* 7 (1942): 22–23 (text), 46–47 (Spanish trans.). See also Ibn Bājjah, *Opera Metaphysica*, ed. Majid Fakhry (Beirut: Dār al-Nahār, 1968), 172–73.

that is not revealed also in the second. The first, however, differs by its superior clarity and in the way it is beheld through something that we call "force," but only metaphorically because we fail to find terms, [6] whether current or technical, that designate the thing by virtue of which that kind of vision is experienced. The state we have just described—of which, moved by your question, we have had a taste (*dhawq*)[7]—is one of the states indicated by the Master Abū ʿAlī [Avicenna] when he says, "Then, when by will and discipline one is carried to a limit where he catches delightful glimpses of the Truth, strokes of lightning as it were, which no sooner flash than they disappear.... Now, if he persists in his disciplinary practice, these ecstatic glimpses multiply. Then he goes deeper and deeper until he is capable of catching these glimpses without any more discipline. Every time he glances at a thing, he turns toward the August Divinity, and remembers something of that state. An ecstasy takes hold of him until he would see the Truth in almost all things.... Finally discipline leads him to the point where his [troubled] time turns into tranquility. What was only evanescent becomes common and what was just a gleam [7] becomes a shining star. He acquires a firm intimacy, a constant association as it were." He then goes on to describe the orderly gradation of the levels and how they terminate in attaining the goal as the seeker's most intimate soul turns into "a polished mirror facing the Truth." At this point the most sublime pleasures flow upon him, and "the traces left by the Truth" in his soul fill him with happiness. And at this level, he hesitatingly fluctuates between "looking at the Truth and at himself," until finally "all consciousness of himself is lost and he notices nothing but the August Divinity. If he ever happens to glance aside at his soul, he does so only inasmuch as his soul is the glancing agent.... It is then that true union takes place."[8] Now by these states that he described, Avicenna intended that he [the initiate] acquire a taste that is not acquired by way of theoretical perception, which results from syllogistic reasoning, the assumption of premises, and the drawing of conclusions.

If you wish a comparison to illustrate the difference between the perception attained by this group of men and that attained by others, then imagine the case of a man born blind, but endowed with keen innate intelligence, penetrating insight, tenacious memory, and determined will. From the day he is born, he grows up in a [8] certain town. By means of his other powers of perception, he continues to acquaint himself with the individual men living there, the many species of animate and inanimate beings, the streets of the city and alleys that cut through it, its houses, and its markets—to such an extent that he can walk around in that city without a guide, and recognize instantly everyone he meets. Colors form an exception; he knows them by means of the explanations of their names and by certain definitions designating them. Then, when he reaches this grade, his eyes are open of a sudden, and his eyesight is restored to him. He runs all over town only to discover that in fact nothing is different from what he has believed it to be, nor does he fail to recognize anything he lays eyes upon. He finds the colors truly corresponding to the descriptions given him. In all this he experiences, nevertheless, two great things, the one a consequence of the other: a greater lucidity and clarity, and an exalted pleasure. The state of the speculators who have not attained the level of sanctity is comparable to the first state of the blind man; the colors, which, [9] in this state, are known through the description of their names, are comparable to those things of which Abū Bakr [Ibn Bajja] said that they are too sublime to be attributed to natural life and that they are bestowed by God upon whomsoever He pleases of His servants. The state of the speculators who attain sanctity and to whom God grants that thing of which we said that it is not called "force" except metaphorically, is the second state.

In very rare cases, one may find someone with piercing intelligence, keen, and not in need of speculation. Here I do not mean—may God bestow His sanctity upon you—by "the perception of the speculators" what they perceive of the physical world and by "the perception of the men of sanctity" what they perceive of the metaphysical; for these two kinds of perception in themselves are very different from each other, and it is hardly possible to confound the one with the other. What we mean by the perception of the speculators is

7. A Sufi term meaning the first immediate experience of the intuition of God; it is characterized by its instability and furtiveness. Cf. note 4 above.

8. Note Avicenna's willingness to speak of "union." Avicenna, *Directives and Remarks (al-Ishārāt wa-al-tanbīhāt)*, ed. J. Forget (Leiden, 1892), 202–4 (French trans.: A.-M. Goichon, *Livre des directives et des remarques* [Paris, 1951], 493–97).

what they apprehend of the metaphysical order, such as was apprehended by Abū Bakr [Ibn Bajja]. When this perception is true and valid, it is possible to compare it with the perception of the men of sanctity who are concerned with these very same [metaphysical] things, but who perceive them with greater clarity and pleasure. However, [10] Abū Bakr [Ibn Bajja] censures the men of sanctity for this pleasure and ascribes it to the imaginative faculty. He promised to describe in a clear and precise manner how the state of the happy ones ought to be. One ought to answer him in this context with the saying: "Do not call sweet what you have not tasted, nor step over the necks of the veracious." Our man did not do any of the things he said he would do; he did not fulfill his promise. It seems, as he himself mentions, he was impeded by shortage of time and the trip he took to Wahrān [Oran]. Or, it could be he realized that if he described that state, he would find himself obliged to say things that decry his own conduct, and belie what he had continually maintained concerning the efforts one should exert to accumulate and hoard riches and the use of all kinds of artifices to obtain them.

We have deviated somewhat from the course to which your question had led us, as this seemed necessary. However, it is now clear from what has been said that your goal can only be one of two things: (1) That you are seeking to understand that which is beheld by those who experience the vision, the taste, and the presence [of God] in their moment of sanctity. This is one of those things whose real nature cannot be entrusted to the pages of a book; and once you try to do that, constraining yourself either through the spoken or the written word, the very nature of the experience is altered by passing to [11] the other realm, that is, the speculative. Because whenever such an experience is wrapped in sounds and letters and brought nearer to the sensible world, its nature does not remain the same, no matter how we look at it. Hence it lends itself to a great many different and varied expressions. As a result many are led astray from the right path, and others are thought to have gone astray although in reality they have not. This is because [one is trying to explain] an infinite entity within a divine epiphany of enormous dimensions, an epiphany that contains but is not itself contained. (2) The second of the two goals to which your question could possibly lead is that you are seeking that this thing be made known to you in accordance with the method of the speculators. This—may God honor you with sanctity—is a thing that could be entrusted to books and it lends itself to being expressed, although [this knowledge] is rarer than red sulphur, especially in the region we live in [that is, Andalusia and Northwest Africa]. Such [knowledge] is so extremely uncommon that only now and then someone acquires small portions of it. Moreover, whoever comes to acquire any portion of it does not communicate it to others except through symbols. The Ḥanīfite [Islamic] religion and the true [Islamic] Law have prohibited delving into it and warned against pursuing it.

Do not think that the philosophy that reached us [12] in the works of Aristotle, Abū Naṣr [Alfarabi], and in [Avicenna's] *Healing* is sufficient to achieve your purpose. Furthermore, no Andalusian has as yet written enough on the subject. This is because all those Andalusians with brilliant talent—and who received their education before the diffusion of logic and philosophy in that country—dedicated themselves to the science of mathematics, reaching a high degree in it. But they were not able to do more than that. The generation that succeeded them went beyond and into the science of logic. They studied it, but it failed to bring them to true perfection. One of them recited:

> Afflicted I am, because all that mortals know
> Are two things and no more;
>
> A truth whose acquisition is impossible,
> And a falsehood whose acquisition is of no use.[9]

Then followed another generation with a greater perspicacity and closer to the truth. There was none among them of a finer genius, of a greater understanding, or of a truer insight than Abū Bakr Ibn al-Ṣā'igh [Ibn Bajja]. Yet, the things of this world kept him busy until death overtook him before the treasures of his science could be brought to light and the secrets of his wisdom made available. The greatest part of his extant writings are in an imperfect state and incomplete, [13] such as *On the Soul* and the *Governance of the Solitary*, as well as his books on logic and physics. As for his finished works, they include

9. The verse is by the Toledan poet al-Waqqāshī (d. 1095).

only concise books and hastily written treatises. He himself declared this when he mentioned that the idea he meant to demonstrate in his treatise *On Conjunction* cannot be clearly understood without hard struggle and great effort; that the order of his explanations, in some places, is not the best; and that he was inclined to change them, had time permitted him to do so. This is what has come down to us concerning this man's knowledge; we never met his person. With regard to his contemporaries who are described as being of the same rank as he, we have not found any written works by them. Regarding their successors who are our contemporaries, they are either in the stage of development, or have stopped short of perfection, or else we are not sufficiently informed about them.

As to the books of Abū Naṣr [Alfarabi] that have reached us, the majority are on logic. The ones that deal with philosophy proper are plagued with doubts. For example, he affirms in the *Virtuous Religion*[10] that the souls of the wicked are doomed after death to infinite suffering for an infinite time. Then he declares in *The Political Regime* that they dissolve into nothingness and that only [14] the virtuous and perfect souls survive. Then in his commentary on [Aristotle's *Nicomachean] Ethics,* he describes an aspect of human happiness and affirms that this is achieved only in this life and in this very world. He then adds a remark whose meaning can be summed up as follows: all that is said contrary to this is senseless chatter and tales told by old women. A doctrine like this leads all men to despair of God's mercy, and places the wicked and the good in the same category since, according to this doctrine, all men are destined for nothingness. This is a slip that cannot be rectified, and a false step that cannot be remedied. This, aside from his declared disbelief in prophecy, namely, his assertion that it is the exclusive property of the imaginative faculty; and not to mention his preference for philosophy over prophecy, and many other things into which we need not now go.

As for the works of Aristotle, the Master Abū ʿAlī [Avicenna] undertook to explain their contents. He followed Aristotle's doctrine and philosophic method in his *Healing.* At the beginning of that book, he declares that the truth in his opinion is otherwise, that the above work expounds the peripatetic teaching, and that he who seeks pure truth should look for it in his [15] *Illuminative [or Oriental] Philosophy.* He who takes the trouble of reading the *Healing* and the books of Aristotle cannot but recognize their agreement on most points, though there are things in the *Healing* that have not come down to us as Aristotelian. Now, were one to accept the literal meaning of everything presented in the books of Aristotle as well as in the *Healing* without penetrating into the secret and esoteric sense, this would not enable him to attain perfection—as the Master Abū ʿAlī [Avicenna] warned us in the *Healing.*

As for the books of the Master Abū Ḥāmid [Alghazali], what he says in them depends on his audience; he says one thing in one place and a different thing in another. He charges others with unbelief because they hold certain doctrines, then turns about and accepts them as lawful. Among other things, he charges the philosophers with unbelief, in his *Incoherence [of the Philosophers],* for their denial of the resurrection of the body and their affirmation that only the souls receive rewards and punishments. But at the outset of his *Criterion [of Action],* he says that this very same tenet is definitely held by the Sufi masters. Then, in his *Deliverer from Error* and the *Explainer of the States,* he says that he himself holds the same belief as the Sufis and that he had arrived [16] at this conviction after a long and detailed study. His books are packed with things of this kind, and anyone who takes the pain to consider and examine them can see that for himself. In fact he apologizes for such conduct at the end of his *Criterion of Action,* where he maintains that opinion is of three classes: (1) an opinion in which one agrees with the multitude; (2) an opinion that is in conformity with the way one addresses all questioners and seekers of counsel; and (3) an opinion that one holds intimately within oneself and does not disclose except to those who share one's convictions. Then he says: "Even if there were no value in these words except to make you doubt your inherited beliefs, that in itself would be useful enough. He who does not doubt does not look, he who does not look does not see, he who does not see

10. This is apparently a reference to the *Virtuous City* (*The Principles of the Opinions of the Inhabitants of the Virtuous City*) chap. 16, possibly sec. 8, though nothing Alfarabi says there is quite as decisive as it is portrayed by Ibn Tufayl. See Richard Walzer, ed. and trans., *Al-Farabi on the Perfect State* (Oxford: Clarendon Press, 1985), 273–74.

remains blind and perplexed." Then he recites the following verse:

> Accept what you see and let go what you hear;
> When the sun comes out you will need no
> Saturn.[11]

So this is how he presents his teaching. It is mainly symbols and allusions of little use except for the one who is capable of grasping them first by his own perspicacity and then by listening to his [Alghazali's] explanations, or the one who is naturally disposed to understand and is endowed with great intelligence and for whom the slightest allusion is enough. He mentions [17] in his *Jewels [of the Qur'an]* that he composed some esoteric books in which he incorporated the unveiled truth. But as far as we know none of these books has reached Andalusia. The books that have in fact reached us and are alleged to be his esoteric works are in reality not so. These books are the *Intellectual Cognitions,* the *Blowing and Leveling,* and a work in which certain other problems are brought together. Although these books contain certain allusions here and there, they nevertheless contain little else that could reveal more than what is already to be found in his more familiar books. In fact one may find in his *Supreme Purpose* things that are more ambiguous than what is found in these [allegedly esoteric books]. Since he himself declares that the *Supreme Purpose* is not esoteric, it must follow if this is so, that these books that have reached Andalusia are not the esoteric books. A recent author imagines that what is said at the end of the *Niche [of Lights]*[12] presents a grave difficulty that supposedly caused al-Ghazālī to fall in a pit from which there is no salvation. The reference is to what [Alghazali] says after enumerating the different classes of those who are veiled by [divine] lights, and his passing to mention the ones who attained [union with God]. He says that the latter have learned that this Being is characterized by an attribute [18] incompatible with pure unity. [Our author] tries to infer from this that [Alghazali] must believe in some kind of multiplicity in the very essence of the First Truth (may God be exalted far and above what the unjust say of Him). We, on the other hand, do not doubt that the Master Abū Ḥāmid [Alghazali] was one of those who were blessed with supreme happiness and who have consummated that most honorable of unions [the union with God]. Yet his esoteric books, which contain the science of unveiling [the truth], have not come down to us.

Now the truth at which we have arrived, which was the end of our quest, would have been impossible to obtain had we not scrutinized his [Alghazali's] teaching and the teaching of Abū 'Alī [Avicenna], compared the one with the other, and then related both to the opinions that appeared in our times and are being professed by some who pretend to philosophize, until the truth dawned upon us—at first by means of investigation and speculation, and now we enjoy also this slight degree of the taste [that we experienced] through vision. It was at this stage that we felt ourselves worthy of saying something of our own. And we deem it an obligation that you be made the first to be presented with what we have and to be acquainted with what we possess, in recognition of your sincere loyalty and candor. However, to hand you the conclusions at which we arrived before making sure that you possess the principles upon which they rest, will be of as little value to you as giving you a conventional [19] summary. In return, we trust that you will approve what we say because of our intimate friendship rather than because we are worthy of saying things that ought to be accepted. However, we do not accept this level for you; and we will not be content until you achieve a higher one, since this level does not insure salvation, much less the winning of the highest dignities. It is our desire to take you along the same path through which we have passed, and to make you swim in the very sea we had to cross first, until you are carried to where we have been carried. You will then see what we have seen; you will ascertain for yourself all the things we ascertained for ourselves. In this way you will not need to make your knowledge dependent upon ours.

This requires an appreciable length of time, freedom from all concerns, and complete dedication to this art. Now, if you are sincerely decided and resolutely set on seeking this end, gratefully will you rise after *a nocturnal journey* [cf. 17:1] and blessed will be your endeavor. Both your Lord and your self will be *satisfied* [cf. 58:22]. I will be at your side as you

11. The verse is by the poet al-Taghrā'ī (d. 1120).

12. See David Buchman, ed., *Al-Ghazālī: The Niche of Lights* (Provo, UT: Brigham Young University Press, 1998).

expect,[13] to guide you along [20] the shortest road and the one safest from mishaps and accidents, although now I am only hinting at a little glimpse just to stimulate and exhort you to get going. I shall narrate to you the story of Hayy the son of Yaqzan and of Asal and Salaman, who are mentioned by the Master Abū ʿAlī [Avicenna].[14] In *their story is surely a lesson for men of understanding* [12:111], *and surely in that there is a reminder to him who has a heart, or will give ear with a present mind* [50:37].

[Summary of the Tale]

After this introduction, Ibn Tufayl proceeds to narrate the experiences of Hayy the son of Yaqzan. Starting with his birth, he offers the reader a choice between two alternative accounts. According to the first, Hayy would have been born on a desert island south of the equator, not from a father and a mother, but from clay in fermentation. The author expounds the importance of the island's perfect geographic position and temperate climate in order to indicate the possibility of spontaneous human generation without the need for mother and father. According to the second story, Hayy would be the illegitimate son of a princess who is daughter of the tyrant of a large inhabited island next to the desert island. To save Hayy from certain death if she were discovered, she puts him in a feather-lined box and entrusts him to the waves. Overnight the tides toss it on the desert island. The author then gives a detailed description, in accordance with the first story, of the successive phases in the spontaneous generation of the human embryo. First, the clay ferments, then sticky and aerated bubbles appear, a heart is formed from the bubbles, and finally a soul descends from heaven and enters the heart. There follows a comparison between the soul and the continually emanating light of the sun. The soul sheds its light on the human body, whereas the sun sheds its light on the different classes of substance that constitute this world. The two stories coincide from here on.

The author begins his description of Hayy's self-education. A gazelle who had lost her doe hastens to the sound of a crying baby. She adopts, feeds, and raises him, putting him to sleep every night in the feathers from the box he arrived in,[15] until he is over seven years old. As the boy, endowed with keen intelligence, grows up, he begins to observe nature and the animal world around him. To provide for his needs, he learns how to dress himself, how to shelter himself, and also how to domesticate animals. One day, however, the gazelle dies. Frightened, but wanting to save her, he reasons that the gazelle's inertness must be due to an invisible impediment. He decides to open her up and look for the seat of the impediment. He finds it in the left ventricle of the heart. He discovers that the obstacle is nothing but the permanent departure of a vital principle located in the ventricle. And that leads him to think of the body as the mere instrument of a life-sustaining principle, without which the body is nothing. After burying his "mother," he wonders what that principle is, what unites it to the body, and where it goes. For a time he roams around the island until one day he sees a fire break out in a bush. Taking a firebrand to the cave in which he now lives, he keeps it alive night and day. He studies the properties of the flame and observes that it tends to go upward and to radiate warmth. This convinces him that it belongs by nature to the celestial bodies and that it may somehow be related to the life-sustaining principle. To find out whether that principle possesses things like fire, light, and heat, he opens the heart of a living animal. In the left ventricle, which he had found empty in the heart of the gazelle, he senses with his finger a whitish vapor of such warmth that his finger is almost burned. The immediate death of the animal convinces him that the hot vapor is the principle of motion in all living beings, and that its absence spells death. Devoured with curiosity, he now wants to know how this vapor holds together and how it imparts life to all the bodily organs. Hayy dissects live and dead animals until his scientific knowledge equals that of the greatest natural philosophers. He recognizes that what gives unity to the body, in spite of the multiplicity of its parts and the variety of its sensations and movements, is the animal spirit radiating from a central abode and using the bodily organs as instruments to perform specific functions.

When Hayy reaches his twenty-first birthday, he has already learned how to stew meat, dress, use a knife made from the spines of fish, build himself a refuge, and domesticate animals. But then his mind begins to move from the consideration of the physical order of things to the metaphysical. He starts with the world of generation and corruption. After examining all kinds of objects such as animals, plants, and minerals, he notices that they possess a great variety of attributes and perform a number of varied functions; moreover, their movements are either concordant or discordant. Looking at them carefully, he notices that they coincide in certain attributes but differ in others. They form a unity if one looks at them with an eye to their congruencies, and form a multiplicity if one looks at them with an eye to their discrepancies. He observes in every animal a certain unity in spite of the multiplicity of its parts. Also, all classes of animals coincide in sensation, in the need for food, and in voluntary motion, all of which are functions of the animal spirit. This must be, he thinks, one in essence in spite of the small differences that exist between the species. He then mentally reduces the animal and vegetable kingdoms to their smallest units, and in the inanimate kingdom he observes a tighter unity in all corporeal bodies. From the attributes common to corporeal bodies, he infers the general notion of a body as a three-dimensional extension. He begins then to look for that quality which makes a body, that is, the essence of a body. He had observed that bodies are either

13. Or "He [that is, God] will enable you to reach where you want."

14. Avicenna, *Recital of Ḥayy Ibn Yaqẓān* (in Henri Corbin, *Avicenna and the Visionary Recital,* trans. W. R. Trask [New York, 1960], 137–50).

15. See the introduction to the Islamic part of this volume (part 1) for a discussion of Hillel Fradkin's interpretation of this moment in Hayy's story.

light or heavy. Nonetheless, these two attributes, lightness and heaviness, do not belong to the body as body, they are added to corporeality, which is common to all bodies. This is how Hayy arrives at the notion of form and thus comes nearer to the spiritual world. He comes to realize that a body, aside from being an extension, is also a form, and that a substance is made up of matter, extension, and form. He discovers along with this duality in substance the notion of a first matter that is apt to receive all forms through change. Now, if bodies change, that is, if the same matter receives different forms, this implies a giver of forms. He looks for a giver of forms among the bodies that surround him, but he realizes that they are all produced, which implies the existence of a producer.

When Hayy reaches his twenty-eighth year, he looks into the sky and among the stars but comes to the conclusion that the sky and what is in it are all corporeal since they all have length, width, and depth. He proves to himself that an infinite body is impossible. He later demonstrates to himself that the celestial body is finite and tries to find out what form the sky could have. He arrives at the conclusion that it is spherical in shape, but composed of a series of concentric spheres, the outermost of which causes the movement of the rest. He also infers that the world is a huge animal. Asking himself whether the world is eternal or produced, he finds that there are two plausible answers to this question, which he leaves unanswered. In each case, however, he is led to the conclusion that there exists a necessary being who is the maker of all other things and who is exempt from all corporeal qualities and inaccessible to the senses or the imagination. He maintains the world and is superior to it in the order of His being as well as by His eternity. Hayy then determines the degree of His power over all created things, also His eternity and omnipotency. He finds Him, furthermore, endowed with complete perfection and exempt from all imperfection.

When Hayy reaches his thirty-fifth year, he is completely absorbed in thinking about this producer. Sure of the existence of a Perfect Being, Hayy wants to find out how he came to know Him. He realizes that he could not have known Him through the senses. These, being divisible, are not capable of knowing what is indivisible, spiritual, and not subject to corruption. He must have come to know Him through something to which corporeality cannot be attributed, and that must be the very essence of his own being, that is, his soul. This, consequently, is indivisible, spiritual, and not subject to corruption. After he reaches the knowledge that his soul is not subject to corruption, he wants to know what happens to it after it departs from the body. Examining all the faculties of perception, he finds out that they perceive sometimes in actuality and at other times in potentiality. Whenever the perception is in a state of potentiality, it tends toward actuality, this being a state more perfect than potentiality. In fact, the more perfect a being is, the greater is the craving for actuality and the sadness at being deprived of it. He thus comes to know that the Necessary Being is perfect and exempt from all privation, and that He is known by something whose nature is unlike the corporeal bodies. This leads him to see that the perfection of the soul consists in the constant use of reason in this life. If one does not use reason, however, his soul becomes a nothingness after death. Also, if he has known the Necessary Being, but turned away from Him in order to follow his passions, he will be deprived of the intuitive vision and will suffer infinitely; however, if one turns wholly toward God and dies while enjoying the intuitive vision, he will enjoy eternal bliss. These considerations lead Hayy to seek divine ecstasy by concentrating his thoughts on the Necessary Being. However, the senses, sensible images, plus the physical needs of the body, would obstruct him. He is afraid death would overtake him while he is still being distracted from the Necessary Being. Hoping to find a remedy for his plight, he examines the actions and goals of all animals to find out whether they seek after God so that he could learn from them how to save himself. To his dismay, he discovers that they do not seek after God. He next examines the celestial bodies and finds out that they possess an intelligent substance, like his, and that they eternally behold the Necessary Being. Among all the animals, he thinks of himself as the only one who could know the Necessary Being. The reason lies in his possession of a perfectly balanced substance that abides in the heart and presents unmistakable similarities to the celestial bodies. Moreover, he realizes that he resembles, on the one hand, the Necessary Being through that noble part of himself—the immaterial intelligent substance, his soul—and, on the other, the animals through that vile part of himself that is his body. From this he concludes that his action should be carried out on three levels: (1) the actions emulating those of the animals, (2) those emulating the celestial bodies, and (3) those emulating the Necessary Being [20–107].

[HAYY'S THREE EMULATIONS]

He was obliged to undertake the first emulation by virtue of having a murky body with separable members, different faculties, and a variety of passions. He was obliged to undertake the second emulation by virtue of his animal spirit, which has its seat in the heart and which is a principle for the whole body and the faculties existing in it. He was obliged to undertake the third emulation by virtue of his being what he is, that is, by virtue of being the essence through which he came to know the Necessary Being. He had come to know before that his happiness and his triumph over misery consisted in a continuous intuitive vision of this Necessary Being and not parting from it for so much as the twinkling of an eye. Then he considered the means by which this continuity might be secured, and his considerations led him to conclude the necessity of continuous practice in the three levels of emulation. The first emulation, he realized, could not contribute to his acquiring any portion of [108] this vision, but on the contrary it was a deterrent and a hindrance to it because it concerned sensible things, and all sensible things are curtains that interfere with that vision. The reason for practicing such an emulation, therefore, was to preserve the animal spirit that makes possible the second emulation, namely, emulating the celestial bodies. Sheer necessity demands that one take this road, although it is not exempt from the harm indicated. Through the second emulation, he realized, he might obtain a great portion of this continuous vision. However, it is an adulterated vision since whosoever beholds after this manner of vision, remains, while experiencing the vision, conscious of his own essence and turns toward it, as will be shown afterwards. Finally, through the third emulation one might obtain pure vision and absolute absorption, without being diverted from it in any direction except in the direction of the Necessary Being. The very essence of the one who experiences this vision disappears from his consciousness, it melts and fades away, and so do all the other essences, irrespective of their number, except the essence of the One, the True, the Necessary [109] Being (may His name be exalted).

Now it became clear to him that his ultimate end consists in the third emulation, that this is not obtained without long exercise and practice in the second, and that the continuation of the second depends on his first emulation. And he also realized that the first emulation, although necessary, is as such a hindrance and a help only accidentally. Consequently, he forced himself to reduce the first emulation to bare necessity, that is, the strictly required amount below which the animal spirit would not subsist. He found two things necessary for the subsistence of the animal spirit. One, what maintains it internally by restoring what is wasted of it, namely, food. The other, what preserves it externally and guards it against all kinds of possible damage coming from cold, heat, rain, sunburn, harmful animals, and the like. And he perceived that if he were to take his necessities from these elements haphazardly, he would fall into excess and take more than the strictly required amount. He might thus [110] injure himself unawares. Whereupon he thought it prudent to set for himself certain limits that he would not pass and measures that he would not exceed; and it became clear to him that this prescription should apply to the kind, content, and quantity of his nourishment as well as its frequency.

Examining first the types of his food, he discovered that they are three in number: (1) Either plants that have not yet finished, or reached the limit of, their growth—that is, the different kinds of green vegetables proper for nourishment; (2) fruit of the plants that have reached their full growth and developed seeds for the reproduction of the same species—that is, the different kinds of fruit, fresh or dry; (3) or some kind of edible animal, either terrestrial or marine. Hayy had ascertained that all these types of food are made by the Necessary Being; and it had become evident to him that his happiness consists in the nearness to, and the desire to imitate Him. Doubtless, he thought, to eat these different foods [111] must prevent them from reaching their perfection and obstruct the realization of the end for which they are destined. This would be like an objection against the work of the Maker, an objection that is contrary to what he was seeking: the nearness to, and emulation of Him. He perceived that the correct thing for him to do, if possible, would be to abstain from eating altogether. But this was impossible. He found that by completely abstaining from eating, his body tended to dissolve, a thing that constituted a much greater objection against his Maker than the former; since he is nobler [by nature] than the other things whose very destruction is the cause of his preservation. He chose the lesser of the two evils and indulged in the milder of the two objections. Now, it seemed proper to him that, whenever some of these classes of food are not available, he should partake of whatever can be obtained, and in quantities that he will decide about later. But if all the classes of food are available, then he should make sure to choose those foods whose consumption will not constitute a major objection against the work of the Maker, such as the flesh of fully ripe fruit whose seeds have so matured as to produce [112] others of the same class. But always with the condition that he preserve the seeds by not eating them or spoiling them or throwing them in places not fit for plants to grow in, such as rocks, briny soil, and the like. And whenever such fruit with nourishing flesh—such as apples, plums, and the like—are not accessible, he should then eat of those fruits that had nothing edible in them but their seeds—such as walnuts and chestnuts or the vegetables that had not yet reached the limit of their perfect growth—but on condition in both cases that he should prefer the vegetables that are more abundant and endowed with greater force of reproduction. He was never to extract any of their roots or destroy their seeds. And if none of these [edible plants] was to be had, then he could take some animals or their eggs, on condition—inasmuch as the animals were concerned—that he take the more numerous and not exterminate any one species. This was what he considered prudent with regard to the kind of his nourishment. Regarding the quantity, he perceived that it should be in accordance with what satisfies a man's hunger and no more. As to the lapse of time between meals, he ruled that once he had satisfied [113] his needs, he was to remain content with that and not touch anything until he suffered a weakness that would hinder him from the performance of some of the actions to which he was committed in the second emulation and that will be mentioned afterwards. Regarding the necessities required for the subsistence of the animal spirit, protecting it from external harm, he had very little to worry about, for he clothed himself with skins and he had a dwelling that protected him against external harm. This satisfied him, and hence he did not see any further need to worry about it. And as far as his diet was concerned, he observed the rules he had set for himself, which we have already explained.

Then he applied himself to the second exercise—that is, to emulate the celestial bodies, imitate them, acquire their attributes, and look for their qualities, which he found to be of three kinds. First, the qualities the celestial bodies possess by virtue of the relations they maintain with what is below them in the world of generation and corruption: imparting heat (by essence), and cold (by accident), illumination, rarefaction, condensation, and the other actions [114] by means of which they dispose the things of this world to receive the overflow of the spiritual forms from the Agent, the Necessary Being. The second kind of qualities are qualities that belong to their very essence—such as that they are translucent, luminous, pure, free from turbidness and any kind of vileness, and that they move circularly, some of them moving around their own center and some around the center of another. The third kind of qualities are the ones they possess by virtue of their relation to the Necessary Being, such as that they possess continuous vision of Him without any deviation, and that they yearn for Him and act according to His command, constrain themselves in order to do His will, and do not move save in accordance with His wish and within His control. So he proceeded to emulate them [the celestial bodies] in every one of these three kinds of qualities to the utmost of his power.

In the first case, his emulation of the celestial bodies consisted in obliging himself, whenever he could, to remove [the cause of the plight] of every animal or plant he sees to be in need, diseased, injured, or facing an impediment. Thus, whenever he saw a plant that was deprived of sunlight by the interference of another object, or that was entwined with another harmful plant, or that was suffering from extreme dryness; he would remove the object [115] if it was something that could be removed, and he would separate the harmful plant from the other without injuring the harmful one, and he would take care to water it whenever that was possible. Whenever he happened to see any animal endangered by a wild beast, or trapped in a snare, or pricked with thorns, or that had something harmful fallen into its eyes or ears, or was hungry or thirsty; he would take infinite care to relieve it and give it food and drink. Or whenever he happened to see any watercourse, flowing to irrigate a plant or to quench the thirst of an animal, stopped by a stone that has fallen in it or by a fallen cliff; he took care to remove all that. He persisted in this kind of emulation until he attained its highest end.

In the second case, his emulation consisted in obliging himself to remain pure, to remove all dirt and filth from his body, washing himself often and keeping his nails, teeth, and the hidden parts of his body clean, and perfuming himself [116] with every kind of fragrant herb and all sorts of aromatic pomades that he could find. He took care to maintain his clothes clean and fragrant until he was resplendent with beauty, cleanliness, and fragrance. In addition, he took upon himself to perform all sorts of circular movements. One time he would walk around the island compassing its shores and journeying to its remotest areas. Sometimes he would walk or run around his house or a rock a number of times. At other times, he would spin himself until he lost consciousness.

In the third case, his emulation of the celestial bodies consisted in concentrating his thoughts on the Necessary Being and suppressing all connection with the sensible world. He would close his eyes, stop his ears, and restrain himself from following his imagination. He would wish, to the utmost of his power, to think of nothing else but Him, and to associate nobody with Him. To accomplish this, he would have recourse to spinning himself more rapidly. As his spinning increased, sensible objects would vanish out of his sight, his imagination would grow weaker and so would all the faculties that make use of [117] bodily organs. Meanwhile, the work of his essence, which is independent of the body, grew stronger; so that at times his thoughts freed themselves from all confusion, and he beheld the Necessary Being. But the corporeal faculties would return upon him and spoil this state for him, bringing him back to the lowest of levels; thus he would go back to his former condition. Whenever he felt any weakness that interrupted him from pursuing his purpose, he partook of some food, but always according to the established conditions. Henceforth he moved to the performance of his emulation of the celestial bodies in the three mentioned respects. He applied himself assiduously to this for some time, struggling against his corporeal faculties—just as they were resisting him. Whenever he got the better of them and his thoughts were free from confusion, he briefly experienced something of the state of those who have attained the third emulation.

Then he started to seek after the third emulation and tried hard to attain it by pondering over the attributes of the Necessary Being. He had come to know, during the period of his [118] scientific speculation on the subject before he had entered upon any action, that these attributes were of two kinds: positive, such as knowledge, power, and wisdom; and negative, such as His complete freedom from corporeality and from the bodily attributes, and from whatever adheres to these attributes or is related to them even remotely. The negative attributes are a condition that renders the positive attributes absolutely exempt from the attributes of the bodies, one of which is multiplicity, so that His essence would not be multiplied by these positive attributes, and so that all of them would be reduced to a single notion which is that of His real essence. He started thereupon to seek a way by which to emulate Him in both these kinds [of attributes]. As for the positive attributes, when he came to know that they are all to be reduced to His real essence and that they are free from multiplicity in every respect—since multiplicity is one of the attributes of bodies—and that His knowledge of His essence is not a notion superimposed on His essence, but that His essence is His knowledge of His essence and His knowledge of His essence is His essence; it became evident to him that if he could know his own essence, the knowledge with which he would come to know it could not be something superimposed on his essence, but identical with it. Therefore, he perceived that to emulate Him in His positive attributes would be to know Him alone without association with [119] any of the corporeal attributes. He took it upon himself to do exactly that. As for the negative attributes, they are all reduced to exemption from the corporeal.

He began therefore to strip himself of all corporeal attributes. He had cast off a great deal of them during his former exercises in which he sought to emulate the celestial bodies. However, a great many relics had been left, such as spinning around—and movement is one of the most characteristic attributes of bodies—and his care for animals and plants, the feeling of pity toward them, and the preoccupation he had to remove whatever inconvenienced them. The latter, too, are corporeal attributes. For, to begin with, they can be seen only with the help of a corporeal faculty. Furthermore, the hard labor they require is also performed with a corporeal faculty. Therefore, he began to rid himself of all this, for it in no way befits the state to which he now aspired. Henceforth he confined his activities to repose in the bottom of his cave with his head tilted down, his eyes closed, disregarding all sensible things and all corporeal faculties, concentrating all his effort and thoughts on the Necessary Being alone, without associating Him with anything whatsoever. Whenever a thought that was not of God crossed his imagination, he tried to drive it away [120] and put it off with all his force. He exercised himself in this, persisting for a long time, so much so that several days would pass without his having anything to eat and without ever stirring. At those moments when he would reach a high pitch in his exercise, all things might vanish from his memory and thought except his own essence, which would continue to be present when he was deeply immersed in the vision of the True Being, the Necessary Being.

This used to cause him great concern, for he knew that it was a mixture perturbing the sure vision and an intrusion in the observation [of Him]. Nevertheless, he kept seeking the disappearance of his soul and the utmost sincerity in his vision of the Truth, until finally he achieved what he was after. Thereupon, *the sky, the earth, and everything that is between* [15:85; 78:37] vanished from his memory and thought. And so did all the spiritual forms[16] and corporeal faculties and all the powers separate from the elements, namely, the essences that know the True Being. Also, his own essence disappeared like the other essences. The universe vanished and dwindled away, *a scattered dust*

16. See Ibn Bajja *Governance of the Solitary* chaps. 7 and 12 (above, selection 9).

[56:6]. There remained only the One, the True Being, the Permanent Being, and he recited his speech (which is not a notion superimposed on his essence): *Whose is the Kingdom today? God's, the One, the Omnipotent* [40:16]. He understood [121] His words and heard His call, and not even his ignorance of words and his inability to speak could hinder the understanding of Him. He immersed himself in this state, and beheld "that which no eye has ever seen nor an ear ever listened to, neither has it ever presented itself to the heart of a man."[17]

Do not allow your heart to be chained to the description of something that has never presented itself to the heart of a man. Many are the things that present themselves to the heart of a man but are hard to describe. How much harder, therefore, would be the description of something that has no chance of ever presenting itself to the heart, and that is not of the same world nor of the same category. And I do not mean by "heart" the body out of which the heart is constituted or the spirit contained in its ventricle, but rather the form of the spirit whose powers extend throughout the body. Now, each one of these three things might be called "heart," but it is impossible for this thing [ecstasy] to occur to any of these three. And yet there is no way of expressing anything beyond what occurs to these three. Therefore, he who seeks to express this state is seeking the impossible. He is like someone who wants to taste the dyed colors inasmuch as they are colors, and at the same time requests that black should taste, for example, sweet or [122] sour. However, in spite of all this, we will not let you go without some allusions by which we shall hint at the wonderful things Hayy saw when he was in that station. We will do this in the form of an allegory without knocking upon the door of the truth; for there is no other way to ascertain what is in that station without actually reaching it. So listen now with the ear of your heart to what I shall indicate to you and gaze at it with your mind's eye; perhaps you will find in it some form of guidance that may bring you to the highway. I demand that you not ask me at present for any oral explanation in addition to what I have entrusted to these pages. For my hands are tied, and it is dangerous to express arbitrarily something that cannot be expressed.

[Summary of the Tale—Continued]

Hayy, in spite of his superior intelligence and philosophic preparation, falls into the error of identifying himself with God. But with the help of divine mercy, he corrects his error. Furthermore, he comes to understand that the separate essences cannot be said to be one or multiple, since they are beyond the reach of any human logical classification and since the divine world can only be known through vision. Reason only observes the particulars and abstracts universal notions from them. Then the author describes in an allegorical form the descending hierarchy of the separate essences that Hayy perceives during his ecstasy, namely, the intelligences of the spheres, the fixed stars, and those of all the other spheres until one reaches the sublunary world. They are compared to a series of mirrors of diminishing perfection that reflect from the first to the last the image of the divine essence in a descending order of clarity. The mirror of the sublunary world is the last and least perfect of them all. The image of the divine essence seems to be reflected in it as in troubled waters and divided into a multitude of indefinite individual essences each of which is united to a body (this refers to human souls), some virtuous and happy, the others perverse and miserable. However, one should not think that these souls disappear when the body to which they are united disappears, as happens to the image reflected in a mirror once the mirror is destroyed. The comparison should not be taken literally since it is not the body that sustains the soul, but the soul the body. Likewise, since the sensible world is sustained by the divine, it necessarily follows the divine world just as the shadow necessarily follows the body [122–34].

[CONCLUSION]

This is as much as I could indicate to you now concerning what Hayy the son of Yaqzan intuitively beheld in that noble station. Do not expect any more than this through mere words. For this is almost impossible. As for the rest of his story, that I will tell you.

17. Cf. 1 Cor. 2:9.

After he had come back to the sensible world from the excursions he had undertaken, he became weary of the concerns of this life and he strongly yearned for the ultimate life. He sought to return to that station through the same means by which he had sought it at first, till he was able to attain it with less effort than before and also to stay there longer than he had stayed before. Then he returned to the sensible world, and [135] attempted later to attain his station once more and attained it with less effort than in both the first and the second preceding attempts, and his stay there was longer too. And so it grew easier and easier for him to attain that noble station and to continue in it longer and longer until he could attain it whenever he pleased and stay in it for as long as he pleased. He used to keep himself in that station and not turn away from it except when the necessities of his body, which he had cut down to the bare minimum, demanded it. In all this, he used to wish that it would please God, the Mighty and Majestic, to deliver him altogether from his body, which caused his separation from that station; so that [he might] give himself up perpetually to his [supreme] pleasure, and so that [he might] be relieved from the pain he suffered every time he had to retire from his station to attend to the necessities of the body. He continued in this state of affairs until he was past the seventh septenary of his birth, that is, he was fifty years old. Then he happened to come together with Asal; the story of what took place between them will be narrated—God willing—in what follows.

It is told that on an island close to [136] the one on which Hayy the son of Yaqzan was born—according to one of the two different accounts of the circumstances of his birth—there arrived one of the true religions received from one of the old prophets (upon whom be the blessings of God). It was a religion that imitated all the true beings through parables that present images of those things and establish their descriptions in the souls, as is customary in addressing the multitude. This religion continued to spread on the island and kept growing and gaining in power until the king adopted it himself and made the people embrace it.

Now there had grown in that island two young men of virtue and good will, called respectively Asal and Salaman, who embraced that religion and accepted it eagerly. They took it upon themselves to observe all its Laws and to follow regularly its practices; this formed the basis of their friendship. Sometimes they used to study the wording of that religious Law concerning the attributes of God, the Mighty and Majestic, and His angels, and also the character of resurrection, rewards, and punishments. Of the two, Asal delved more deeply into the esoteric meaning; he was more apt to find [137] spiritual notions, and was a more ambitious interpreter. As for Salaman, he was more apt to keep to the apparent meaning, to avoid interpretation, and to abstain from examination and reflection. However, both assiduously performed the external practices [of the religious Law], disciplined themselves, and controlled their passions.

Now there were in this religious Law certain arguments that favored seclusion and solitude, indicating that these led to salvation and [ultimate] success; and there were other arguments that favored sociability and adherence to the whole body of the community (*jamāʿa*). Asal devoted himself to the search for seclusion and favored the argument for it, because he was naturally inclined to continued meditation, to heeding the warnings [of the religious Law], and to penetrating deeply into the meanings [of the things mentioned in it]; and it was through solitude that he most frequently accomplished these objectives. In contrast, Salaman devoted himself to adhering to the whole body of the community and favored the argument for this position, because he was naturally timid as regards thought and examination. Following the majority, he thought, would lead to the suppression of evil thoughts and the removal of the promptings of the devil. Their differences on this issue caused [138] them to separate.

Asal had heard about the island on which it was said that Hayy the son of Yaqzan was formed. He knew also of its fertility, conveniences, and temperate climate, and that the one who seeks solitude can achieve it there. Resolved to move there and to retire from the company of men for the rest of his life, he gathered together what money he possessed; with a part of it he hired a ship to carry him to that island, and the rest he distributed among the poor. He bade farewell to his friend [Salaman] and went aboard. The mariners transported him to the island, set him ashore, and withdrew. Asal remained there worshiping God, the Mighty and Majestic, magnifying Him, sanctifying Him, and meditating upon His most beautiful names and exalted attributes without any interruption in the presence of his mind or disturbance in his thoughts. Whenever he felt the need for food, he took from the fruits or game of the island enough to satisfy his hunger. He remained in this state a while, enjoying the most complete felicity and the greatest delight through an intimate intercourse with his Lord, experiencing every day His kindness, the excellence of His gifts, and the ease with which He enabled him to satisfy his necessary needs and nourishment—all of which confirmed his belief in him and consoled Asal's heart. [139]

In the meantime, Hayy the son of Yaqzan was wholly immersed in his sublime stations. He never left his cave but once a week to take whatever nourishment was at hand. This is the reason why Asal did not discover his presence at first; he used to walk around the island and go over all its parts without seeing a human being or observing the traces of any footsteps. This swelled his joy and gladdened his heart as he was firmly resolved to lead the most retired and solitary life that was possible, until Hayy the son of Yaqzan happened to go out one day to seek his provisions at a place where Asal happened to be. They both spied one another. Asal did not entertain any doubt but that Hayy was a retired worshiper who must have come to that island in search of solitude as he himself had done, and feared that should he come up and make his acquaintance, this might disturb Hayy's state and disrupt the pursuit he was engaged in. Hayy the son of Yaqzan, however, did not know what Asal was; for of all the animals [140] he had seen, he had never seen anything with such a form. Now Asal had on a black coat made out of hair and wool, which Hayy the son of Yaqzan thought was a natural part of him and at which he stood wondering for quite a while. Asal turned and fled from fear that he might distract Hayy. But Hayy the son of Yaqzan ran after him out of his natural curiosity to look for the truth of things. When he saw that Asal began to run faster, he slowed down and hid himself from him, so that Asal thought he had left him and gone off far from the place where he was. Asal then proceeded with his prayer, recitation, invocation, supplication, and lamentation, until this made him forget everything else. Hayy the son of Yaqzan started to draw closer and closer, with Asal unaware of his presence, until he came so close as to hear his recitation and praise [of God], observing in him a sense of humility and that he was weeping. Hayy heard a pleasant voice and harmonious sounds such as he had never heard before in any kind of animal. Then he considered Asal's shape and lineaments and saw that he was of the same form as himself. He also found that the coat he had on was not a natural skin but an artificial attire like [141] his own. Upon watching the sincere humility of Asal, his supplication and weeping, he did not doubt but that he was one of those essences who know the True One. He felt himself seized by an affection toward him and a desire to know what was the matter with him, and what caused his weeping. He drew closer to him till Asal felt his presence and took to flight. Hayy the son of Yaqzan chased him energetically until he caught up with him—as the result of the vigor and the capacity, intellectual as well as physical, that God had bestowed upon him—seized him, held him fast, and would not let go of him. When Asal looked at him and saw that he was clothed with animal furs, his hair grown so long as to cover a great part of his body, and perceived his alertness and great strength; he trembled from fear and began to implore and entreat him with words, which Hayy the son of Yaqzan could not understand and did not know what they were meant to convey. [Hayy] could see the signs of alarm on Asal's face, however. Therefore, he endeavored to allay his fear with such voices as he had learned from some of the animals. He stroked his head and both sides of his neck, and caressed him, showing him a great joy and gladness, until Asal's agitation calmed and he understood that he meant him no harm.

Asal had formerly [142] studied most languages as a result of his love for the science of interpretation and had become an expert in them. So he began to speak to Hayy the son of Yaqzan in every language he knew, asking him about himself and trying to make himself understood, but without success. Hayy the son of Yaqzan wondered all the while at what he heard, not knowing what it was. Nevertheless, he showed gladness and good disposition; and they mutually wondered at each other. Asal had conserved some of the provisions he had brought along from the inhabited island. He offered it to Hayy the son of Yaqzan, who, having never seen such food before, did not know what it was. Asal ate a little of it and signaled Hayy to eat too. Hayy the son of Yaqzan remembered the dietary obligation he had resolved to abide by. Not knowing the constitution of the food he had been offered, nor whether or not he should permit himself to partake of it, he declined to eat. Asal, nonetheless, kept asking him and urging him beseechingly. As Hayy the son of Yaqzan had become fond of Asal and was afraid lest he might be vexed if he should continue to refuse, he went ahead and ate some of the food. As soon as [143] he had tasted it and liked it, Hayy realized that he had done wrong by violating the covenant he made with himself as regards diet. He repented what he did and wanted to separate from Asal and go back to his former condition, seeking to return to his sublime station. But he could not attain the vision quickly. Thereupon he decided to stay with Asal in the sensible world until he discovered what he really was and until he felt no more desire to be with him, after which he might apply himself to his station without any interruption. Thus he remained in the company of Asal. Now as Asal perceived Hayy's inability to speak, he felt secure since [Hayy's] company could pose no threat to his faith. He hoped to instruct him in speaking, in science, and in the faith, so that he [Asal] might obtain a great reward and be favored by God. Asal began to teach him how to speak, first, by pointing at particular beings and pronouncing their names, repeating them several times, and then making Hayy pronounce them. Hayy pronounced them at the same time as he in turn pointed to each being, until Asal taught him all the names. He helped him to improve gradually, until, in a very short time, Hayy could speak.

Then Asal began to ask him about his condition, and whence he came [144] to that island. Hayy the son of Yaqzan told him he knew nothing of his origin, nor of a father or a mother beyond the gazelle that reared him. Then Hayy described his experiences from beginning to end, and how he ascended in knowledge until he attained a degree of union [with God]. Asal heard him describe those truths and the essences separate from the sensible world, which know the essence of the Truth, the Mighty and Majestic. Then Hayy described the essence of the Truth, the Exalted and Majestic, with his beautiful qualities. And finally Hayy described, as far as he could, what he beheld when he attained union [with God], the joys of those who unite [with God], and the pains of those who are veiled from Him. After hearing all this, Asal had no doubt that all the things given in his own religious Law concerning God, the Mighty and Majestic, His angels, His books, His messengers, the last day, and His paradise and hell, are the similitudes of these things that Hayy the son of Yaqzan had beheld. The eye of his heart was thereby opened, the fire of his mind kindled. He found that reason and tradition agree, and he found a better access to the ways of interpretation. There remained not one difficulty in the religious Law that he did not now see clearly, nor anything locked up that was not opened, nor anything obscure that did not become plain. Thereupon he passed into the ranks of the *men of understanding* [12:111]. From that moment, Asal looked upon Hayy the son of [145] Yaqzan with veneration and respect, and he was convinced that Hayy was one of the saints of God who *need have no fear, neither shall they suffer* [2:38, 262, 274]. He took it upon himself to wait upon him, to follow in his steps, and to accept his directions with regard to the fulfillment of the religious-legal practices that his religion had taught him, but had seemed to be contradictory.

Hayy the son of Yaqzan, in his turn, began to inquire from him about himself and his present condition. Whereupon Asal proceeded to describe the island from which he came, the people who inhabit it, and their way of life before and after religion reached them. He described to him all the content of the religious Law concerning the divine world, paradise, hell, the quickening of the dead, the resurrection, the assembly for a final judgment, the balance, and the bridge.[18] Hayy the son of Yaqzan understood all this, not finding in it anything that disagreed with what he had intuitively seen in his sublime station. He recognized that the one who described these things and brought them forth was truthful in his description, veridical in his words, and a messenger from his Lord. He believed in him, accepted his truthfulness, and bore witness to his mission.

Then he began to find out from Asal what were the acts of worship that he [the messenger] ordained as duties. Asal described prayer, almsgiving, fasting, pilgrimage, and similar [146] external practices. Hayy accepted them, and he took it upon himself to carry them out in compliance with the command of whose author's veracity he had become convinced. There only remained two points that kept him wondering and whose wisdom he could not understand. One point was why this messenger, in the greatest part of his description of the divine world, used parables? Why he avoided the clear disclosure [of the truth] and thus led men to fall into the great error of

18. Or the "way," "path" (*sirāṭ*), which separates hell from paradise.

attributing corporeality to Him and believe certain things about the essence of the Truth from which He is completely exempt? And why he did the same concerning rewards and punishments? The other point was why he confined himself to those duties and acts of worship and permitted acquisition of wealth and excessive consumption of food so that people gave themselves up to vain occupations and turned away from the Truth. Hayy's own opinion was that nobody ought to eat anything more than necessary to keep body and soul together. As for riches, they meant nothing to him. He saw no point to the [147] rules of the religious Law with regard to wealth, such as almsgiving in its various forms, trading, and usury, and with regard to penalties and punishments. All this he found strange and considered it superfluous. He said that if people understood the truth of the matter they would avoid these vanities, turn toward the Truth, and dispense with all this. Nobody will then own private property for which alms would have to be paid, hands cut off for stealing it, or people die for robbing it. What misled Hayy was his belief that all men were endowed with excellent natures, clear-sighted sagacity, and resolute souls. He was not aware how stupid, deficient, ill-opinioned, and weak in resolution they were, *as the cattle; nay, they are further astray from the way* [25:44].

As his pity toward men increased and he entertained the ambition of becoming the instrument of their salvation, he made up his mind to reach them, and to lay bare the truth before them and make it clear for them. He discussed [148] his intention with Asal and asked him if a way could possibly be contrived to reach them. Asal informed him of their deficient nature and how they turn away from God. But Hayy could not comprehend that and still hoped to be able to pursue his intention. Asal, too, entertained the ambition that God might, through Hayy, lead into the right path some of his acquaintances, who were initiates and closer to salvation than the others: so he helped him to carry out his design. They resolved to keep close to the seashore without leaving it night or day, till God should please to offer them the opportunity to cross the sea. So they stayed by the shore supplicating and praying to God, the Mighty and Majestic, *that He may guide them to the right path in their design* [cf. 18:10].

It happened, by God's command, that a ship that had lost its course was driven [149] by the winds and the tumultuous waves upon the shore of that island. As the ship drew closer to the land, the people on board saw the two men on shore and made toward them. Asal spoke to them and asked that the two of them be taken along. The [mariners] responded favorably and took them aboard. God sent a fair wind, which in a short time brought the ship to the island they were seeking. There they landed and went into the city. Asal's friends met with him, and he told them the story of Hayy the son of Yaqzan. They flocked around Hayy, showed him great admiration, met with him, and esteemed and venerated him. Asal let Hayy know that this group was superior to all other men in understanding and sagacity; should he prove unable to instruct them, his chances of instructing the multitude were slim. Now the ruler [150] and chief of that island was Salaman, Asal's friend who believed in adhering to the whole body of the community and argued for prohibiting seclusion. Hayy the son of Yaqzan began to teach and to disclose the secrets of wisdom. But no sooner had he gone a little beyond the apparent, and started to describe what they had previously learned to be otherwise, than they began to feel ill at ease in his presence, to feel in their souls an abhorrence for what he told them; and they resented it in their hearts, although to his face they showed that they were pleased, out of respect for his being a stranger as well as for the sake of their friend Asal. Hayy the son of Yaqzan kept entreating them night and day, and kept explaining to them the truth both in private and in public. But this did not produce any effect except to increase their disdain and aversion, despite their love of goodness and their desire for the truth. Nonetheless, because of their deficient natures, they did not pursue the truth in the proper way, nor did they receive it in the proper manner nor [151] call for it at its own doors. On the contrary, they wanted to learn the truth on the authority of other men. So Hayy despaired of reforming them and lost hope about their ability to receive the truth.

Examining afterwards the different categories of men, he found that *each party was rejoicing in what it had* [cf. 23:53; 30:32], *taking their caprice to be their god* [cf. 25:43] and worshiping their desires. They were fighting desperately to collect the crumbs of this world, and *they were absorbed in amassing [wealth] until the day they reached their graves* [cf. 102:1–2]. All good advice is lost upon them, and kind words have no effect. Discussion only makes them more obstinate; and as for wisdom, there is no way they could acquire it, neither have they any portion of it. They were submerged in ignorance, and *what they were earning has rusted upon their hearts* [83:14]. *God has set a seal on their hearts and their hearing and on their eyes is a covering, and there awaits them a mighty chastisement* [2:7]. When he saw the pavilion of punishment surrounding them and the darkness of the veils covering them—all of them, except a few, do not take seriously anything but the worldly aspects of their religion; they disregard the observance of its practices [152] regardless of their easiness, and *they sold it for a small price* [cf. 3:187]; *commerce did divert them from the remembrance of God, the Exalted, and they had no fear of a day when hearts and eyes shall be turned about* [cf. 24:37]—it became clear to him, indeed he was absolutely sure: It was impossible to address them by way of unveiling [the pure truth]; and that to enjoin upon them any works beyond the measure [laid down by their messenger] was not expedient; and further, that the greatest benefit the multitude could get from the religious Law concerned their mundane life alone, so that they might live forthrightly and no man trespass the private property of the others. Only the exceptional and the rare among them would attain the happiness of the hereafter, namely, *the one who desires the tillage of the hereafter, and strives after it as he should—being a believer* [cf. 17:19]. As *for him who is impious, and prefers the life of this world, then surely hell is his abode* [79: 37–39]. What weariness can be greater, or what misery more overwhelming than that of the one who, if you examined his activities from the moment he wakes up till the time he goes to sleep, you would find does nothing but seek [153] after one or another of the vile sensible things: riches to collect, pleasures to partake of, lusts to satisfy, a rage for which he seeks relief, glory to obtain, or practice commended by the religious Law with which to make a vainglorious show or defend his own neck. All these things are *darkness upon darkness in a deep sea* [cf. 24:40], and *there is not one of you, but he shall go down to it, that for thy Lord is a thing decreed, determined* [19:71].

Upon comprehending that this is the condition of men and that the majority are like irrational animals, he knew that all wisdom, guidance to the right path, and good fortune reside in the utterances of the apostles of God and what is set forth by religious Law: nothing else is possible and nothing more could be added to it. Certain kinds of men are fit for certain kinds of work, and each man is more fit to do that for which he is made. *Such has been God's way with the ones who had passed away, and you shall find no change in God's way* [cf. 48:23]. Hence Hayy went back to Salaman and his friends, apologized for what he had said to them, and asked that he be forgiven for it. He informed them that he now shared their opinion and has been guided to the right path that they were following. He also exhorted them to keep firm in their observance of the prescriptions of the religious Law and the performance of the external [religious] practices and not to delve into what does not concern them. They should believe, furthermore, in the ambiguous [statements of the Law] and assent readily to them. They should avoid [154] innovations and private opinions and follow in the footsteps of their pious ancestors, forsaking all unprecedented novelties. He commanded them to avoid the indifference of the vulgar toward the religious Law, and their love of this world, and cautioned them with insistence against it. He and his friend Asal knew now that this is the only way in which this group, which has the desire but not the capacity for salvation, can achieve it. Should one try to raise them to the height of personal vision, this would upset their present order without enabling them to attain the grade of the happy ones. They will waver and suffer a relapse, ending in evil. However, if this same group should continue in this same condition till death overtook them, they would gain security and belong to the *Companions of the Right* [56:90, 91]. As for *the Outstrippers, they are the ones brought nigh [to God's Throne]* [56:10–11].

Asal and Hayy took their leave and separated from the group. They sought an opportunity to go back to their island, till it pleased God, the Mighty and Majestic, to help them and facilitate their passage back. Hayy sought his previous sublime station the same way he had sought it before, till he recovered it. Asal followed in Hayy's footsteps till he came close to him or almost did so. They both *worshiped God* [155] in that island *until death overtook them* [cf. 15:99].

This—may God assist you *through his inspiration* [cf. 58:22]—is the story of what happened to Hayy the son of Yaqzan, Asal, and Salaman. It contains certain statements that are not to be found in any book, nor heard in a common discourse. It is a part of that well-protected science which only those who know God accept and only those *deluded concerning God* ignore [cf. 31:33;

57:14; 82:6]. We have taken a road contrary to that of the pious ancestors who grudged its dissemination and parsimoniously guarded it. The reason that the disclosure of this secret and the tearing of its veil were made easy for us was the appearance, in our present time, of corrupt opinions aired and broached by some contemporaneous pretenders to philosophy, till they spread all over the countries, and the mischief caused by it has now become common. Fearing lest the weak ones who have rejected the authority of the prophets, and who would want to imitate the fools, should think that these opinions are the secrets guarded [156] against the ones unworthy of them, and so increase their inclination to, and love of, them; we decided to give them a glimpse of the secret of secrets in order to attract them to the side of self-fulfillment and avert them from this road. Nevertheless, we have not left whatever secrets we confided to these pages without a thin veil and a delicate curtain, which is easy to break by those worthy of doing so, but which turns thick for the ones unworthy of going beyond it so that they would be unable to go any further.

I ask my brothers who read this book to accept my apologies for my indulgence in explaining whatever I explained and for my liberality in writing it down. I did not do so except because I climbed heights that the eyes fail to see, and wished to simplify my discourse about them in order to attract others and make them desire to take to the way. I ask for God's indulgence and forgiveness, and that He may lead us unto the pure knowledge of Him. He is gracious and generous. Peace be with you, my brother whom it is my duty to help, and the mercy and blessing of God.

ELEVEN

AVERROES

The Decisive Treatise

Translated by Charles E. Butterworth

Averroes (Abū al-Walīd Muḥammad Ibn Aḥmad Ibn Rushd, 1126–1198) was born in Cordova to a distinguished family of jurists: both his grandfather and father occupied posts as jurists in that city. Little is known of his life and activities prior to 1168/9. He is reported to have studied jurisprudence, *kalām*, medicine, and the natural sciences; in 1153 he went to Marrakesh, where he was received by the founder of the Almohad dynasty, 'Abd al-Mu'min (r. 1132/3–1163), apparently in connection with the prince's plans to establish a school; and he composed a work on medicine. In 1168/9 he went to Marrakesh again, where he was introduced to 'Abd al-Mu'min's son and successor, Abū Ya'qūb (r. 1163–1184), by his aged vizier and chief physician, Ibn Tufayl. Shortly afterward, Ibn Tufayl reported to Averroes that the sovereign had complained to him about the lack of coherence in Aristotle's style, or rather in the style of his translators, and about the obscurity of Aristotle's aims. The sovereign hoped that someone would paraphrase Aristotle's works and make their aims more accessible. Ibn Tufayl himself was prevented from doing it because of his age and his occupation with government service (concentrating on what, he said, "I hold more important"), and he charged Averroes with this task. Subsequently, Averroes was named judge in Seville in 1169, where he started composing his commentaries (work that likely continued until 1195). At the same time, he returned to Cordova in 1171, probably as a judge. Later, he became chief justice of Cordova and must have traveled in Andalusia and Morocco. In 1182, upon the retirement of Ibn Tufayl as chief physician to Abū Ya'qūb, Averroes took his place in that role. He kept his favored position under Abū Ya'qūb's son and successor, Abū Yūsuf, from 1184 to 1195. He then fell temporarily out of favor; his works, except those that dealt with practical sciences, were ordered burned; and he was exiled to the little town of Lucena, near Cordova. But soon afterward the prince revoked his censure, and Averroes was called to Marrakesh, where he led a retired life until his death.

Although *The Decisive Treatise* was written probably shortly before 1180 (well before his public censure), it anticipates, and attempts to respond to, many of the conflicts that gave rise to his censure. Those conflicts stem from the status of philosophy in all times and places but especially in the Islamic world, and even more particularly among the Almohad dynasty in North Africa and Andalusia.

Although *The Decisive Treatise* is especially attuned to Averroes's own setting (which we will return to shortly), in certain respects it is also highly reminiscent of the most renowned defense of philosophy before the city, Plato's *Apology.* Although both works defend philosophy before the city and thus the laws (cf. Plato's *Crito*), neither offers a particularly philosophic defense of philosophy. Rather, both works adapt themselves to the legal setting. Indeed, in *The Decisive Treatise* Averroes addresses the legal circumstances even more specifically than does Socrates in the *Apology*—as one might expect of such a renowned jurist. The reader should be especially attuned to Averroes's (syllogistic) form of argumentation and consider in what ways it is philosophic and in what ways it takes on the character of a legal brief—making the best, if not always the most truthful, case for the defendant.

To return to Averroes's twelfth-century setting, the Almohad princes were interested in philosophy and patronized its study. They owed their rule, however, to the revival of a popular religion based on "the Qur'an and the sword." Thus they encouraged simultaneously the private study of the philosophic sciences and the public attachment to the letter of the divine Law. There were, however, many jurists and dialectical theologians who took the position that philosophic teachings were contrary to the revealed teaching and that philosophers were unbelievers. These jurists and theologians were able to arouse the multitude of believers to adopt their view, and they were thus able at times to exert pressure on the rulers to patronize them, rather than the philosophers, as the learned men of the community. Faced with popular indignation against philosophy at a time when he was in need of public support for his campaign in Spain, Abū Yūsuf quelled it with a temporary censure of Averroes, which he revoked as soon as he ended the campaign and returned to Marrakesh. Although *The Decisive Treatise* may not have been capable of preventing Averroes's censure in 1195, it attempts to put the alliance between the Almohad rulers and the philosophers against the antiphilosophic alliance of dialectical theologians and jurists on a firmer footing, by establishing an alliance between philosophy and the Law.

The Decisive Treatise was translated into Hebrew late in the thirteenth or early fourteenth century. The Arabic original was first edited by M. J. Müller: *Philosophie und Theologie von Averroes* (Munich, 1859). The page numbers in square brackets in the text of the translation below refer to the Müller edition. That edition was reedited and extensively revised by George F. Hourani in *Ibn Rushd (Averroes): Kitāb faṣl al-maqāl* (Leiden: E. J. Brill, 1959). Hourani published an English translation with a valuable introduction, summaries, and extensive notes in *Averroes on the Harmony of Religion and Philosophy,* E. J. W. Gibb Memorial Series, n.s. 21 (London: Luzac, 1961), which appeared in the first edition of the *Sourcebook.* The present translation by Charles E. Butterworth is based on Muhsin Mahdi's revisions of Hourani's 1959 edition. The complete edition by Butterworth, from which this translation is taken, also includes the following: a critical Arabic text, a biographical sketch of Averroes, an interpretive introduction (including an explanation of the editor's divisions of the text and this work), more extensive notes than could be included here, and the *Epistle Dedicatory.* Butterworth's edition is *Averroës: The Book of the Decisive Treatise Determining the Connection between the Law and Wisdom and Epistle Dedicatory* (Provo, UT: Brigham University Press, 2001).

In the name of God, the Merciful and the Compassionate.
May God be prayed to for Muḥammad and his family,
and may they be accorded peace.

[A. INTRODUCTION]

1. The jurist, imam, judge, and uniquely learned Abū al-Walīd Muḥammad Ibn Aḥmad Ibn Rushd (may God be pleased with him) said: Praise be to God with all praises, and a prayer for Muḥammad, His chosen servant and messenger. Now, the goal of this statement is for us to investigate, from the perspective of Law-based reflection,[1] whether reflection upon

1. The adjectival form of *sharīʿa*—that is, *sharʿī*—is rendered here as "Law-based." The term rendered "reflection" (*naẓar*) should be tracked closely throughout these opening sections. It should also be compared closely with the adjectival form of this root, usually rendered "theoretical," as below, sec. 15; see also note 19.

philosophy and the sciences of logic is permitted, prohibited, or commanded—and this as a recommendation or as an obligation—by the Law.[2]

[B. THAT PHILOSOPHY AND LOGIC ARE OBLIGATORY]

[1. That Philosophy Is Obligatory]

2. So we say: If the activity of philosophy is nothing more than reflection upon existing things and consideration of them insofar as they are an indication of the Artisan—I mean insofar as they are artifacts, for existing things indicate the Artisan only through cognizance[3] of the art in them, and the more complete cognizance of the art in them is, the more complete is cognizance of the Artisan—and if the Law has recommended and urged consideration of existing things, then it is evident that what this name indicates is either obligatory or recommended by the Law.

That the Law calls for consideration of existing things by means of the intellect and for pursuing cognizance of them by means of it is evident from various [2] verses in the Book of God (may He be blessed and exalted). There is His statement (may He be exalted): *Consider, you who have sight*[4] [59:2]; this is a text for the obligation of using both intellectual and Law-based syllogistic reasoning.[5] And there is His statement (may He be exalted): *Have they not reflected upon the kingdoms of the heavens and the earth and what things God has created?* [7:185]; this is a text urging reflection upon all existing things. And God (may He be exalted) has made it known that one of those whom He selected and venerated by means of this knowledge was Abraham (peace upon him); thus, He (may He be exalted) said: *And in this way we made Abraham see the kingdoms of the heavens and the earth, that he might be*... [and so on to the end of] the verse [6:75].[6] And He (may He be exalted) said: *Do they not reflect upon the camels, how they have been created, and upon the heaven, how it has been raised up?* [88:17]. And He said: *And they ponder the creation of the heavens and the earth* [3:191]—and so on, in innumerable other verses.

[2. The Case for Syllogistic Reasoning]

3. Since it has been determined that the Law makes it obligatory to reflect upon existing things by means of the intellect, and to consider them; and consideration is nothing more than inferring and drawing out the unknown from the known; and this is syllogistic reasoning or by means of syllogistic reasoning, therefore, it is obligatory that we go about reflecting upon the existing things by means of intellectual syllogistic reasoning. And it is evident that this manner of reflection the Law calls for and urges is the most complete kind of reflection by means of the most complete kind of syllogistic reasoning and is the one called "demonstration."

4. Since the Law has urged cognizance of God (may He be exalted) and of all of the things existing through Him by means of demonstration; and it is preferable—or even necessary—that anyone who wants to know God (may He be blessed and exalted) and all of the existing things by means

2. In his manual of law, Averroes explains that the jurists understand the judgments of the divine Law to fall into five categories: obligatory, recommended, prohibited, reprehensible, and permitted. Here, however, Averroes groups the first two under the more comprehensive category of "commanded" and—perhaps since it is not applicable to the present question—passes over "reprehensible" in silence. See *Bidāyat al-mujtahid wa nihāyat al-muqtaṣid* [The Legal Interpreter's Beginning and the Mediator's Ending], ed. 'Abd al-Ḥalīm Muḥammad 'Abd al-Ḥalīm and 'Abd al-Raḥmān Ḥasan Maḥmūd (Cairo: Dār al-Kutub al-Ḥadītha, 1975), 1:17–18.

3. Words derived from the Arabic root *'r.f* will be translated as "cognizant" or by related terms. Words derived from the Arabic root *'l.m.* will be translated as "knowledge" or "science" or by related terms. These Arabic terms seem to be used by Averroes to draw distinctions similar to those between *gignōskein* and *epistasthai* in Greek.

4. All Qur'anic translations in this selection are by Charles E. Butterworth.

5. The term translated by "syllogistic reasoning" is *qiyās*. Translators often render this term briefly as "syllogism" and at times even as "analogy." The latter translation reflects the fact that Law-based or legal reasoning primarily takes the form of analogical reasoning. The reader should attend to the many different forms of "syllogistic reasoning" Averroes enumerates.

6. The rest of the verse reads: *one of those who have certainty.*

of demonstration set out first to know the kinds of demonstrations, their conditions, and in what [way] demonstrative syllogistic reasoning differs from dialectical, rhetorical, and sophistical syllogistic reasoning; and that is not possible unless, prior to that, he sets out to become cognizant of what unqualified syllogistic reasoning is, how many kinds of it there are, and which of them is syllogistic reasoning and which not; and that is not possible either unless, prior to that, he sets out to become cognizant of the parts of which syllogistic reasoning is composed—I mean, the premises and their kinds—therefore, the one who has faith[7] in the Law and follows its command to reflect upon existing things perhaps coming under the obligation to set out, before reflecting, to become cognizant of these things whose status [3] with respect to reflection is that of tools to work.

For just as the jurist infers from the command to obtain juridical understanding of the statutes the obligation to become cognizant of the kinds of juridical syllogistic reasoning and which of them is syllogistic reasoning and which not, so, too, is it obligatory for the one cognizant [of God] to infer from the command to reflect upon the beings the obligation to become cognizant of intellectual syllogistic reasoning and its kinds. Nay, it is even more fitting that he do so; for if the jurist infers from His statement (may He be exalted): *Consider, you who have sight* [59:2], the obligation to become cognizant of juridical syllogistic reasoning, then how much more fitting is it that the one cognizant of God infer from that the obligation to become cognizant of intellectual syllogistic reasoning.

It is not for someone to say, "Now, this kind of reflection about intellectual syllogistic reasoning is a heretical innovation, since it did not exist in the earliest days [of Islam]." For reflection upon juridical syllogistic reasoning and its kinds is also something inferred after the earliest days, yet it is not opined to be a heretical innovation. So it is obligatory to believe the same about reflection upon intellectual syllogistic reasoning—and for this there is a reason, but this is not the place to mention it. Moreover, most of the adherents to this religion support intellectual syllogistic reasoning, except for a small group of strict literalists, and they are refuted by the texts [of the Qur'an].

5. Since it has been determined that the Law makes reflection upon intellectual syllogistic reasoning and its kinds obligatory, just as it makes reflection upon juridical syllogistic reasoning obligatory, therefore, it is evident that, if someone prior to us has not set out to investigate intellectual syllogistic reasoning and its kinds, it is obligatory for us to begin to investigate it and for the one who comes after to rely upon the one who preceded, so that cognizance of it might be perfected. For it is difficult or impossible for one person to grasp all that he needs of this by himself and from the beginning, just as it is difficult for one person to infer all he needs to be cognizant of concerning the kinds of juridical syllogistic reasoning. Nay, this is even more the case with being cognizant of intellectual syllogistic reasoning.

6. If someone other than us has already investigated that, it is evidently obligatory for us to rely on what the one who has preceded us says about what we are pursuing, regardless of whether that other person shares our religion or not. For when a valid sacrifice is performed by means of a tool, [4] no consideration is given, with respect to the validity of the sacrifice, as to whether the tool belongs to someone who shares in our religion or not, so long as it fulfills the conditions for validity. And by "not sharing [in our religion]," I mean those Ancients who reflected upon these things before the religion of Islam.

7. Since this is the case—and all that is needed with respect to reflection about the matter of intellectual syllogistic reasonings has been investigated by the Ancients in the most complete manner—therefore, we ought perhaps to seize their books in our hands and reflect upon what they have said about that. And if it is all correct, we will accept it from them; whereas, if there is anything not correct in it, we will alert [people] to it.

8. Since we have finished with this type of reflection and have acquired the tools by which we are able to consider existing things and the indication of artfulness in them—for one who is not cognizant of the artfulness is not cognizant of what has been artfully made, and one who is not cognizant of what has been artfully made is not cognizant of the Artisan—therefore, it is perhaps obligatory that we start investigating existing things according to the order and manner we have gained from the art of becoming cognizant about demonstrative syllogisms. It is evident, moreover, that this goal is completed for us with respect to existing things only when they

7. *Amana* (and terms from the same root) is translated throughout as "to have faith" (or by related phrases). *I'taqada* (and terms from the same root) is translated throughout as "to believe" (or by related phrases).

are investigated successively by one person after another and when, in doing so, the one coming after makes use of the one having preceded—along the lines of what occurs in the mathematical sciences.

For if we were to assume the art of geometry and, likewise, the art of astronomy to be nonexistent in this time of ours, and if a single man wished to discern on his own the sizes of the heavenly bodies, their shapes, and their distances from one another, that would not be possible for him—for example, to become cognizant of the size of the sun with respect to the earth and of other things about the sizes of the planets—not even if he were by nature the most intelligent person, unless it were by means of revelation or something resembling revelation. Indeed, if it were said to him that the sun is about 150 or 160 times greater than the earth, he would count this statement as madness on the part of the one who makes it. And this is something for which a demonstration has been brought forth in astronomy and which no one adept in that science doubts.

There is hardly any need to use an example from the art of mathematics, for reflection upon this art [5] of the roots of jurisprudence, and jurisprudence itself, has been perfected only over a long period of time. If someone today wished to grasp on his own all of the proofs inferred by those in the legal schools who reflect upon the controversial questions debated in most Islamic countries, even excepting the Maghrib,[8] he would deserve to be laughed at, because that would be impossible for him—in addition to having already been done. This is a self-evident matter, not only with respect to the scientific arts, but also with respect to the practical ones. For there is not an art among them that a single person can bring about on his own. So how can this be done with the art of arts—namely, wisdom?

9. Since this is so, if we find that our predecessors in former nations have reflected upon existing things and considered them according to what is required by the conditions of demonstration, it is perhaps obligatory for us to reflect upon what they say about that and upon what they establish in their books. Thus, we will accept, rejoice in, and thank them for whatever agrees with the truth; and we will alert to, warn against, and excuse them for whatever does not agree with the truth.

10. From this it has become evident that reflection upon the books of the Ancients is obligatory according to the Law, for their aim and intention in their books is the very intention to which the Law urges us. And [it has become evident] that whoever forbids reflection upon them by anyone suited to reflect upon them—namely, anyone who unites two qualities, the first being innate intelligence and the second Law-based justice and moral virtue—surely bars people from the door through which the Law calls them to cognizance of God—namely, the door of reflection leading to true cognizance of Him. That is extreme ignorance and estrangement from God (may He be exalted).

If someone goes astray in reflection and stumbles—due either to a deficiency in his innate disposition, poor ordering of his reflection, being overwhelmed by his passions, not finding a teacher to guide him to an understanding of what is in them, or because of a combination of all or more than one of these reasons—it does not follow that they[9] are to be forbidden to the one [6] who is suited to reflect upon them. For this manner of harm coming about due to them is something that attaches to them by accident, not by essence. It is not obligatory to renounce something useful in its nature and essence because of something harmful existing in it by accident. That is why he [that is, the Prophet] (peace upon him) said to the one who complained about having been ordered to give his brother honey to drink for his diarrhea—because the diarrhea increased when he was given the honey to drink—"God spoke the truth, whereas your brother's stomach lied."[10]

Indeed, we say that anyone who prevents someone suited to reflect upon the books of wisdom from doing so on the grounds that it is supposed some vicious people became perplexed due to reflecting upon them is like one who prevents thirsty people from drinking cool, fresh water until they die of thirst because some people choked on it and died. For dying by choking on water is an accidental matter, whereas [dying] by thirst is an essential, necessary matter. And what occurred through this art is something accidental, [occurring] through the rest of the arts. To how many jurists has jurisprudence been a cause of diminished devoutness and immersion in this world! Indeed, we find most jurists to be like this, yet what their art requires in essence is practical virtue.

8. Spain and North Africa.

9. That is, the books of the Ancients referred to above.

10. An allusion to Qur'an 16:69.

Therefore, it is not strange that there occurs, with respect to the art requiring scientific virtue, what occurs with respect to the art requiring practical virtue.

[C. THAT DEMONSTRATION ACCORDS WITH THE LAW]

[1. The Law Calls to Humans by Three Methods]

11. Since all of this has been determined and we, the Muslim community, believe that this divine Law of ours is true and is the one alerting to and calling for this happiness—which is cognizance of God (Mighty and Magnificent) and of His creation—therefore, that is determined for every Muslim in accordance with the method of assent his temperament and nature require.

That is because people's natures vary in excellence with respect to assent. Thus, some assent by means of demonstration; some assent by means of dialectical statements in the same way the one adhering to demonstration assents by means of demonstration, there being nothing greater in their natures; and some assent by means of rhetorical statements, just as the one adhering to demonstration assents by means of demonstrative statements.

That is because, when this divine Law of ours [7] called to people by means of these three methods, assent to it was extended to every human being—except to the one who denies it obstinately in speech or for whom no methods have been determined in it for summoning to God (may He be exalted) due to his own neglect of that. Therefore, he [that is, the Prophet] (peace upon him) was selected to be sent to "the red and the black"[11]—I mean, because of his Law containing [different] methods of calling to God (may He be exalted). And that is manifest in His statement: *Call to the path of your Lord by wisdom, fine preaching, and arguing with them by means of what is finest* [16:125].

[2. Demonstration Does Not Differ from the Law]

12. Since this Law is true and calls to the reflection leading to cognizance of the truth, we, the Muslim community, know firmly that demonstrative reflection does not lead to differing with what is set down in the Law. For truth does not oppose truth; rather, it agrees with and bears witness to it.

13. Since this is so, if demonstrative reflection leads to any manner of cognizance about any existing thing, that existing thing cannot escape either being passed over in silence in the Law or being made cognizable in it. If it is passed over in silence, there is no contradiction here; it has the status of the statutes passed over in silence that the jurist infers by means of Law-based syllogistic reasoning. If the Law does pronounce about it, the apparent sense of the pronouncement cannot escape either being in agreement with what demonstration leads to, or being different from it. If it is in agreement, there is no argument here. And, if it is different, that is where an interpretation is pursued. The meaning of interpretation is: drawing out the figurative significance of an utterance from its true significance[12] without violating the custom of the Arabic language with respect to figurative speech in doing so—such as calling a thing by what resembles it, its cause, its consequence, what compares to it, or another of the things enumerated in making the sorts of figurative discourse cognizable.

14. Since the jurist does this with respect to many of the Law-based statutes, how much more fitting is it for the one adhering to demonstrative science to do so. The jurist has only a syllogism based on supposition, whereas the one who is cognizant has a syllogism based on certainty. And we firmly affirm that, whenever demonstration leads to something differing from the apparent sense of the Law, [8] that apparent sense admits of interpretation according to the rule of interpretation in Arabic.

11. That is, to all human beings.

12. *Ikhrāj dalālat al-lafẓ min al-dalāla al-ḥaqīqiyya ilā al-dalāla al-mujāziyya.* The language here is somewhat ambiguous and reads, literally: "drawing the significance of an utterance out from its true significance to its figurative significance."

No Muslim doubts this proposition, nor is any faithful person suspicious of it. Its certainty has been greatly increased for anyone who has pursued this idea, tested it, and has as an intention this reconciling of what is intellected with what is transmitted. Indeed, we say that whenever the apparent sense of a pronouncement about something in the Law differs from what demonstration leads to, if the Law is considered and all of its parts scrutinized, there will invariably be found in the utterances of the Law something whose apparent sense bears witness, or comes close to bearing witness, to that interpretation.

Because of this idea, Muslims have formed a consensus[13] that it is not obligatory for all the utterances of the Law to be taken in their apparent sense, nor for all of them to be drawn out from their apparent sense by means of interpretation, though they disagree about which ones are to be interpreted and which not interpreted. The Ash'arites,[14] for example, interpret the verse about God's directing Himself [2:29] and the Tradition about His descent,[15] whereas the Ḥanbalites[16] take them in their apparent sense.

The reason an apparent and an inner sense are set down in the Law is the difference in people's innate dispositions and the variance in their innate capacities for assent. The reason contradictory apparent senses are set down in it is to alert "those well grounded in science" to the interpretation that reconciles them. This idea is pointed to in His statement (may He exalted): *He it is who has sent down to you the Book; in it, there are fixed verses*... on to His statement, *and those well grounded in science* [3:7].[17]

15. If someone were to say: "Muslims have formed a consensus that in the Law are things to be taken in their apparent sense and things to be interpreted, and there are things about which they disagree. So, is it permissible for demonstration to lead to interpreting what they have formed a consensus to take in its apparent sense, or to taking in its apparent sense what they have formed a consensus to interpret?" we would say: "If the consensus were established by a method of certainty, it would not be valid [to do so]; but if the consensus about them were suppositional, then it would be valid [to do so]." That is why Abū Ḥāmid [Alghazali], Abū al-Ma'ālī [al-Juwaynī],[18] and others from among the leading thinkers said that unbelief is to be affirmed of no one for going against consensus by interpreting things like these.

What may indicate to you that consensus is not to be determined with certainty about theoretical matters,[19] as it is possible for it to be determined about practical matters, is that it is not possible [9] for consensus to be determined about a particular question at a particular epoch unless: that epoch is delimited by us; all the learned men existing in that epoch are known to us, I mean, known as individuals and in their total number; the doctrine of each one of them on the question is transmitted to us by means of an uninterrupted transmission;[20] and, in addition to all this, it has been certified to us that the learned men existing at that time agreed that there is not an apparent and an inner sense to the Law, that it is obligatory that knowledge of every question be concealed from no one, and that there is only one method for people to know the Law.

It has been transmitted that many in the earliest days [of Islam] used to be of the opinion that the Law has both an apparent and an inner sense and that it is not obligatory for someone to know about the inner sense if he is not an adept in knowledge of it nor capable of understanding it. There is, for example, what al-Bukhāri relates about 'Alī Ibn Abū Ṭālib (may God be pleased with him), saying, "Speak to the people concerning what they are cognizant of. Do you want God and His messenger to be accused of lying?"[21] And there is, for

13. *Ajma'a:* From it is derived the noun "consensus" (*ijmā'*). Consensus is accepted in some schools of Islamic Law as a root or source of Law after the Qur'an and Tradition (*ḥadīth*).

14. Those who follow the theological teachings of Abū al-Ḥasan 'Alī al-Ash'arī (873–935).

15. The Tradition in question is, "God descends to the lower world."

16. Those who follow the juridical teachings of Aḥmad Ibn Ḥanbal (780–855), who was a strict literalist.

17. Following the reference to *fixed verses,* the Qur'an goes on to contrast them with verses that *resemble one another.* The former admit of no interpretation; the latter do admit of interpretation. Regarding the latter, the Qur'an goes on to say: *None knows their interpretation but God and those well grounded in science. They say, "We believe in it; everything is from our Lord."* Some interpreters believe the Qur'an insinuates divine guidance will somehow lead the interpreter; others, like Averroes, stress the role of "those well grounded in science."

18. See the historical introduction to the Alghazali selection (selection 8 above).

19. *Al-naẓariyyāt:* literally, "reflective matters." Unless otherwise noted, all future occurrences of the term "theoretical" translate this adjectival form of *naẓar.*

20. Uninterrupted transmission is one of the criteria for judging the soundness of Traditions about the Prophet.

21. Muḥammad Ibn Ismā'īl al-Bukhārī (810–870) is the author of one of the six canonical collections of Tradition. 'Alī Ibn Abū Ṭālib (d. 661) was the fourth orthodox caliph.

example, what is related of that about a group of the early followers [of Islam]. So how is it possible to conceive of consensus about a single theoretical question being transmitted to us when we firmly know that no single epoch has escaped having learned men who are of the opinion that there are things in the Law not all of the people ought to know in their true sense? That differs from what occurs with practical matters, for everybody is of the opinion that they are to be disclosed to all people alike; and, for consensus about them to be reached, we deem it sufficient that the question be widely diffused and that no difference [of opinion] about it be transmitted to us. Now, this is sufficient for reaching consensus about practical matters; but the case with scientific matters is different.

[3. Whether the Philosophers Are Guilty of Unbelief]

16. If you were to say: "If it is not obligatory to charge with unbelief one who goes against consensus with respect to interpretation, since consensus with respect to that is not conceivable, what do you say about the philosophers among the adherents of Islam like Abū Naṣr [Alfarabi] and Ibn Sīnā [Avicenna]? For in his book known as *The Incoherence [of the Philosophers]*, Abū Ḥāmid [Alghazali] has firmly charged both of them as unbelievers with respect to three questions: the argument about the eternity of the world, that the Exalted does not know particulars—may He be exalted above that—and [10] the interpretation of what is set forth about the resurrection of bodies and the way things are in the next life,"[22] we would say: "The apparent sense of what he says about that is that he does not firmly charge them with unbelief about that, for he has declared in the book *The Distinction* that charging someone with unbelief for going against consensus is tentative.[23] And it has become evident from our argument that it is not possible for consensus to be determined with respect to questions like these because of what is related about many of the first followers [of Islam], as well as others, holding that there are interpretations that it is not obligatory to expound except to those adept in interpretation."

These are *those well grounded in science*—for we choose to place the stop after His statement (may He be exalted): *and those well grounded in science* [3:7]. Now, if those adept in science did not know the interpretation, there would be nothing superior in their assent obliging them to a faith in Him not found among those not adept in science. Yet God has already described them as those who have faith in Him, and this refers only to faith coming about from demonstration. And it comes about only along with the science of interpretation.

Those faithful not adept in science are people whose faith in them[24] is not based on demonstration. So, if this faith by which God has described the learned is particular to them, then it is obligatory that it come about by means of demonstration. And if it is by means of demonstration, then it comes about only along with the science of interpretation. For God (may He be exalted) has already announced that there is an interpretation of them that is the truth, and demonstration is only of the truth. Since that is the case, it is not possible for an exhaustive consensus to be determined with respect to the interpretations by which God particularly characterized the learned. This is self-evident to anyone who is fair-minded.

17. In addition to all of this, we are of the opinion that Abū Ḥāmid [Alghazali] was mistaken about the Peripatetic sages when he accused them of saying that He (Holy and Exalted) does not know particulars at all. Rather, they are of the opinion that He knows them (may He be exalted) by means of a knowledge that is not of the same kind as our knowledge of them. That is because our knowledge of them is an effect of what is known, so that it is generated when the known thing is generated and changes when it changes. And the knowledge God (glorious is He) has of existence is the opposite of this: it is the cause of the thing known, which is the existing thing.

22. See *Tahāfut al-falāsifa*, ed. Maurice Bouyges (Beirut: Imprimerie Catholique, 1927) 376.2–10.

23. See *Fayṣal al-tafriqa* [Arbitrator of the Distinction] in *Al-quṣūr al-ʿawālī min rasāʾil al-Imām al-Ghazālī* (Cairo: al-Jundī, n.d.), 168–71.

24. That is, the verses of the Qur'an.

So, whoever likens [11] the two kinds of knowledge to one another sets down two opposite essences and their particular characteristics as being one, and that is the extreme of ignorance. If the name "knowledge" is said of knowledge that is generated and of knowledge that is eternal, it is said purely as a name that is shared, just as many names are said of opposite things—for example, *al-jalal,* said of great and small, and *al-ṣarīm,* said of light and darkness. Thus, there is no definition embracing both kinds of knowledge, as the dialectical theologians of our time fancy.

Prompted by one of our friends, we have devoted a statement to this question.[25] How is it to be fancied that the Peripatetics would say that He (glorious is He) does not know particulars with eternal knowledge, when they are of the opinion that true dream-visions contain premonitions of particular things that are to be generated in the future and that this premonitional knowledge reaches human beings in sleep due to the everlasting knowledge governing the whole and having mastery over it? Moreover, it is not only particulars that they are of the opinion He does not know in the way we know them, but universals as well. For, the universals known to us are also effects of the nature of the existing thing, whereas, with that knowledge [of His], it is the reverse. Therefore, that knowledge [of His] has been demonstrated to transcend description as "universal" or "particular." So there is no reason for disagreement about this question—I mean, about charging them with unbelief or not charging them with unbelief.

18. As for the question whether the world is eternal or has been generated, the disagreement between the Ash'arite dialectical theologians and the ancient sages almost comes back, in my view, to a disagreement about naming, especially with respect to some of the Ancients. That is because they agree that there are three sorts of existing things: two extremes and one intermediate between the extremes. And they agree about naming the two extremes but disagree about the intermediate.

One extreme is an existent thing that exists from something other than itself and by something—I mean, by an agent cause and from matter. And time precedes it—I mean, its existence. This is the case of bodies whose coming into being is apprehended [12] by sense perception—for example, the coming into being of water, air, earth, animals, plants, and so forth. The Ancients and the Ash'arites both agree in naming this sort of existing things "generated."

The extreme opposed to this is an existent thing that has not come into existence from something or by something and that time does not precede. About this, too, both factions agree in naming it "eternal." This existent thing is apprehended by demonstration: it is God (may He be blessed and exalted) who is the Agent of the whole, its Giver of Existence, and its Sustainer (glorious is He, and may His might be exalted).

The sort of being between these two extremes is an existent thing that has not come into existence from something and that time does not precede, but that does come into existence by something—I mean, by an agent. This is the world as a whole.

Now, all of them agree on the existence of these three attributes with respect to the world. For, the dialectical theologians admit that time does not precede it—or, rather, that is a consequence of their holding that time is something joined to motions and bodies. They also agree with the Ancients about future time being infinite and, likewise, future existence. And they disagree only about past time and past existence. For the dialectical theologians are of the opinion that it is limited, which is the doctrine of Plato and his sect, while Aristotle and his faction are of the opinion that it is infinite, as is the case with the future.

19. So it is evident that this latter existent thing has been taken as resembling the existing thing that truly comes into being and the eternally existing thing. Those overwhelmed by its resemblance to the eternal rather than to what is generated name it "eternal," and those overwhelmed by its resemblance to what is generated name it "generated." But, in truth, it is not truly generated, nor is it truly eternal. For what is truly generated is necessarily corruptible, and what is truly eternal has no cause. Among them are those who name it "everlastingly generated"—namely, Plato and his sect, because time according to them is finite with respect to the past.

25. See the introduction to the *Epistle Dedicatory* in Butterworth's complete edition of *The Decisive Treatise,* from which this translation has been taken, for his explanation of the relation between the *Epistle* and the rest of the *Treatise.* The complete edition includes the Arabic on facing pages, more extensive footnotes, and in-depth interpretation of the text. See the historical introduction to the present selection for bibliographical information.

20. Thus, the doctrines about the world are not all so far apart from one another that some of them should be charged as unbelief and others not. Indeed, for opinions [13] to be such that this should happen, it is obligatory that they be excessively far apart—I mean, that they be opposites of each other, as the dialectical theologians suppose they are with respect to this question—that is, that the name "eternity" and that of "generated" with respect to the world as a whole are opposites of each other. And it has already become evident from our statement that the matter is not like that.

21. In addition to all this, these opinions about the world do not conform to the apparent sense of the Law. For if the apparent sense of the Law is scrutinized, it will become apparent from the verses comprising a communication about the coming into existence of the world that, in truth, its form is generated, whereas being itself and time extend continuously at both extremes—I mean, without interruption. That is because His statement (may He be exalted): *And He is the one Who created the heavens and the earth in six days, and His throne was on the water* [11:7], requires, in its apparent sense, an existence before this existence—namely, the throne and water—and a time before this time, I mean, the one joined to the form of this existence, which is the number of the movement of the heavenly sphere. And His statement (may He be exalted): *On the day the earth shall be changed into other than earth, and the heavens also* [14:48], in its apparent sense also requires a second existence after this existence. And His statement (may He be exalted), *Then He directed Himself toward the heaven, and it was smoke* [41:11], requires in its apparent sense that the heavens were created from something.

22. Nor do the dialectical theologians conform to the apparent sense of the Law in what they say about the world, but interpret it. For it is not [said] in the Law that God was existing along with sheer nothingness; no text whatever to this effect is to be found. So how is it to be conceived that the dialectical theologians' interpretation of these verses would meet with consensus when the apparent sense of the Law with respect to the existence of the world, which we have stated, has already been stated by a faction among the sages?

23. It seems that those who disagree about the interpretation of these recondite questions have either hit the mark and are to be rewarded or have erred and are to be excused. For assent to something due to an indication arising in the soul is compulsory, not voluntary—I mean that it is not up to us not to assent or to assent as it is up to us to stand up or not to stand up.[26] Since a condition of responsibility is having choice, the one who assents to error because of vagueness occurring in it is excused if he is an adept of science. [14] Therefore, he (that is, the Prophet) said (peace upon him), "If the judge hits the mark after exerting himself, he will be rewarded twofold; and if he errs, he will have a single reward."

Now what judge is greater than the one who makes judgments about existence, as to whether it is thus or not thus? These judges are the learned ones whom God has selected for interpretation, and this error that is forgiven according to the Law is only the error occasioned by learned men when they reflect upon the recondite things that the Law makes them responsible for reflecting upon.

24. The error occasioned by any other sort of people is sheer sin, whether it is an error about theoretical or practical matters. Just as the judge who is ignorant of Tradition is not excused when he errs about a judgment, neither is the judge about existing things in whom the conditions for judgment do not exist excused; indeed, he is either a sinner or an unbeliever. And if it is stipulated, with respect to the judge about what is allowed and what is proscribed, that he combine within himself the reasons for exercising personal judgment[27]—namely, cognizance of the roots and cognizance of what is inferred from these roots by means of syllogistic reasoning—then how much more fitting is it for this to be stipulated with respect to the one who is to judge about existing things, I mean, that he be cognizant of the primary intellectual notions and how to infer from them.

25. In general, error with respect to the Law is of two types:

There is error that is excused for one who is adept in reflection about that thing concerning which error occurs, just as the skillful physician is excused if he errs with respect to the art of medicine and the skillful judge if he errs with respect to a judgment. But one who is not adept in that concern is not excused.

And there is error that is not excused for anyone whosoever. Rather, it is unbelief if it occurs with respect to the principles of the Law and

26. See Aristotle *On the Soul* 3.3 427b20.

27. *Ijtihād.*

heretical innovation if it occurs with respect to what is subordinate to the principles.

26. This error is the very one that comes about concerning the things that all the sorts of methods of indications lead to cognizance of. Thus, cognizance of that thing is, in this manner, possible for everyone. Such, for example, is affirmation of [the existence of] God (may He be blessed and exalted); of the prophetic missions; and of happiness in the hereafter and misery in the hereafter. That is because the three sorts of indications [15] due to which no one is exempted from assenting to what he is responsible for being cognizant of—I mean, the rhetorical, dialectical, and demonstrative indications—lead to these three roots.

So that one who denies things like these, when they are one of the roots of the Law, is an unbeliever who resists obstinately with his tongue but not his heart, or [who resists obstinately] due to his neglecting to expose himself to cognizance of what indicates them. For if he is an adept of demonstration, a path to assenting to them has been placed before him by demonstration; and if he is an adept of dialectic, then by dialectic; and if he is an adept of preaching, then by preaching. Therefore, he [the Prophet] (peace upon him) said, "I was ordered to combat people until they say, 'There is no god but God,' and have faith in me"—he means by whatever one of the three methods of bringing about faith that suits them.

27. Concerning the things that are known only by demonstration due to their being hidden, God has been gracious to His servants for whom there is no path by means of demonstration—either due to their innate dispositions, their habits, or their lack of means[28] for education—by coining for them likenesses and similarities of these [hidden things] and calling them to assent by means of those likenesses, since it is possible for assent to those likenesses to come about by means of the indications shared by all—I mean, the dialectical and the rhetorical. This is the reason for the Law being divided into an apparent sense and an inner sense. For the apparent sense is those likenesses coined for those meanings, and the inner sense is those meanings that reveal themselves only to those adept in demonstration. These [likenesses and meanings] are the four or five sorts of existing things that Abū Ḥāmid [Alghazali] mentioned in the book *The Distinction.*[29]

28. If it happens, as we have said, that we know something in itself by means of the three methods, there is no need for us to coin a likeness for it; and, as long as it is in its apparent sense, it does not admit of interpretation. If this manner of apparent sense refers to the roots [of the Law], the one who interprets it would be an unbeliever—like someone believing that there is no happiness or misery in the hereafter and that such a statement is intended only to safeguard people from one another in what pertains to their bodies and physical senses, that it is a stratagem, and that a human being has no end other than sensual existence.

29. If this has been determined for you, [16] then it is apparent to you from our statement that there is an apparent sense of the Law that it is not permissible to interpret. To interpret it is unbelief when it has to do with principles and heretical innovation when it has to do with what is subordinate to principles. There is also an apparent sense that it is obligatory for those adept in demonstration to interpret, it being unbelief for them to take it in its apparent sense. Yet for those not adept in demonstration to interpret it and draw it away from its apparent sense is unbelief or heretical innovation on their part.

30. Of this sort is the verse about God's directing Himself [2:29] and the Tradition about His descent.[30] Therefore, he [the Prophet] said (peace upon him) with respect to the black woman, when she announced that God was in heaven: "Set her free, for she is one of the faithful." For she was not one of those adept in demonstration. The reason for that is that for the sort of people who come to assent only due to the imagination—I mean, those who assent to something only insofar as they can imagine it—it is difficult to come to assent to an existing thing that is not linked with something imaginable.

This also applies to those who understand the link only as [God having] a place—they are the ones who in their reflection have moved somewhat beyond the rank of the first sort's belief in corporeality. Therefore, the answer to these people about verses and Traditions like these is that they pertain to the verses that resemble one another and that the stop is at His saying (may He be exalted), *None knows their interpretation but God* [3:7].[31] Even though there is consensus among the people of demonstration that this sort admits of

28. *Asbāb*, pl. of *sabab.*

29. See *Fayṣal al-tafriqa*, 150–56.

30. See above, sec. 14 and note 15.

31. See above, secs. 14 and 16.

interpretation, they disagree about its interpretation. And that is according to each one's rank with respect to cognizance of demonstration.

31. There is a third sort [of verses and Traditions] with respect to the Law, one wavering between these [other] two sorts and about which there is doubt. One group of those who occupy themselves with reflection attach this sort to the apparent sense that it is not permissible to interpret, and others attach it to the inner sense that it is not permissible for the learned to take according to its apparent sense. That is because this sort [of verses and Traditions] is recondite and abstruse. One who commits an error with respect to this is to be excused—I mean, one of the learned.

32. If it were said, "Since it has become evident that, in this respect, there are three ranks in the Law, then in which of these three ranks, according to you, belongs what is set forth with respect to descriptions of the next life and its conditions?" we would say, "With respect to this question, it is an evident matter that they belong to the sort about which there is disagreement." That is because we see [17] a group who pretend to demonstration, saying that it is obligatory to take these descriptions in their apparent sense since there is no demonstration rendering that apparent sense preposterous; and this is the method of the Ash'arites. Yet another group, who also occupy themselves with demonstration, interpret these descriptions; and they disagree greatly among themselves in their interpretation. Among this sort are to be counted Abū Ḥāmid [Alghazali] and many of the Sufis. And some combine both interpretations, as Abū Ḥāmid [Alghazali] does in some of his books.

33. It seems that the learned person who commits an error with respect to this question is to be excused and the one who hits the mark is to be thanked or rewarded—that is, if he acknowledges the existence [of the next life] and gives a manner of interpretation of it not leading to the disavowal of its existence. With respect to this [question], denying its existence is what is unbelief, because it is one of the roots of the Law and something to which assent comes about by the three methods shared by *the red and the black.*

34. For anyone not adept in science, it is obligatory to take them [the descriptions of the next life] in their apparent sense; for him, it is unbelief to interpret them because it leads to unbelief. That is why we are of the opinion that, for anyone among the people whose duty it is to have faith in the apparent sense, interpretation is unbelief because it leads to unbelief. Anyone adept in interpretation who divulges that to him calls him to unbelief; and the one who calls to unbelief is an unbeliever.

35. This is why it is obligatory that interpretations be established only in books using demonstrations. For if they are in books using demonstrations, no one but those adept in demonstration will get at them. Whereas, if they are established in other than demonstrative books with poetical and rhetorical or dialectical methods used in them, as Abū Ḥāmid [Alghazali] does, that is an error against the Law and against wisdom.

Yet the man intended only good. That is, he wished thereby to make those adept in science more numerous. But he actually made those adept in wickedness more numerous, yet not without some increase among those adept in science. In that way, one group came to slander wisdom, another group to slander the Law, and another group to reconcile the two. It seems that this was one of the intentions of [18] his books.

An indication that he wished thereby to alert people's minds is that he adhered to no single doctrine in his books. Rather, with the Ash'arites he was an Ash'arite, with the Sufis a Sufi, and with the philosophers a philosopher—so that he was, as it is said:

> One day a Yamanī, if I meet a man from Yaman,
> And if I meet a Ma'addī, then I'm of Adnān.[32]

36. What is obligatory for the imams of the Muslims is that they ban those of his books that contain science from all but those adept in science, just as it is obligatory upon them to ban demonstrative books from those not adept in them. Yet the harm befalling people from demonstrative books is lighter, because for the most part only those with superior innate dispositions take up demonstrative books. And this sort [of people] is misled only through a lack of practical virtue, reading in a disorderly manner, and turning to them without a teacher.

32. This verse is by 'Imrān Ibn Ḥiṭṭān al-Sadūsī, a poet who lived in the seventh century. South Arabian tribes were considered to be Yamanites; north Arabian tribes—among them the Ma'addī—were considered to be Adnānites.

Still, totally forbidding demonstrative books bars from what the Law calls to, because it is a wrong to the best sort of people and to the best sort of existing things. For justice with respect to the best sort of existing things is for them to be cognized to their utmost degree by those prepared to be cognizant of them to their utmost degree, and these are the best sort of people. Indeed, the greater the worth of the existing thing, the greater is the injustice with respect to it—namely, ignorance of it. Therefore, He said (may He be exalted): *Associating [other gods with God] is surely a major wrong* [31:13].[33]

[D. SUMMARY]

37. So this is what we were of the opinion we should establish with respect to this type of reflection—I mean, the discussion between the Law and wisdom and the statutes for interpreting the Law. If it were not for this being so widespread among people and these questions we have mentioned being so widespread, we would not have deemed it permissible to write a single letter about it; nor would we have to excuse ourselves to those adept in interpretation for doing so, because these questions are such as to be mentioned in demonstrative books. God is the Guide to and the Successful Giver of what is correct!

[E. ON WHAT IS INTENDED BY THE LAW AND ITS METHODS]

[1. What Is Intended by the Law]

38. You ought to know that what is intended by the Law is only to teach true science and true practice. True science is cognizance of God (may He be blessed and exalted) and of all the existing things as they are, especially the venerable ones among them; and cognizance of happiness in the hereafter and of misery in the hereafter. True practice is to follow the actions that promote happiness [19] and to avoid the actions that promote misery; and cognizance of these actions is what is called "practical science."

These [actions] are divided into two divisions. One is the apparent, bodily actions. The science of these is what is called "jurisprudence." The second division is actions of the soul—like gratitude, patience, and other moral habits that the Law calls to or bans. And the science of these is what is called "asceticism" and "the sciences of the hereafter."

Abū Ḥāmid [Alghazali] directed himself to this in his book. Since people had turned away from this type and become immersed in the other type—even though this type is more involved with piety, which is the cause of happiness—he called his book *The Revival of the Sciences of Religion.*

But we have digressed from the path we were on, so let us come back.

39. We say: Since what is intended by the Law is teaching true science and true practice; and teaching is of two sorts—forming a concept and bringing about assent—as those adept in dialectical theology have explained; and there are three methods of bringing about assent for people—demonstrative, dialectical, and rhetorical—and two methods of forming concepts, either by means of the thing itself or by means of a likeness of it; and not all people have natures such as to accept demonstrations or dialectical arguments, let alone demonstrative arguments, given the difficulty in teaching demonstrative arguments and the lengthy time needed by someone adept at learning them; and since what is intended by the Law is, indeed, to teach everyone, therefore, it is obligatory that the Law comprise all the manners of the methods of bringing about assent and all the manners of the methods of forming a concept.

33. In this Qur'anic passage, Luqman instructs his son to avoid associating other gods with God. Averroes uses the passage to illustrate how great the wrong can become when the learned, prohibited from reading demonstrative books, are led to ignorance of God, and thus to associationism or polytheism.

[2. The Methods in the Law for Assent and Concept]

40. Since some of the methods for bringing about assent—I mean, assent taking place because of them—are common to most people, namely, the rhetorical and the dialectical, the rhetorical being more common than the dialectical; and some of them are particular to fewer people, namely, the demonstrative; and what is primarily intended by the Law is taking care of the greater number without neglecting to alert the select [few], therefore, most of the methods declared in the Law are the methods shared [20] by the greater number with respect to concept or assent taking place.

41. There are four sorts of these methods in the Law.

One, even though it is shared, is particular[34] in both respects—I mean that, with respect to forming a concept and bringing about assent, it is certain, even though it is rhetorical or dialectical. These syllogisms are the ones whose premises happen to be certain, even though they are generally accepted or suppositional, and whose conclusions happen to be matters taken in themselves rather than as likenesses. For this sort of Law-based statements there is no interpretation, and the one who denies or interprets it is an unbeliever.

The premises in the second sort are certain, even though they are generally accepted or suppositional, and the conclusions are likenesses of the matters intended to be brought forth. This [sort of Law-based statements]—I mean, its conclusions—admits of interpretation.

The third is the reverse of this, namely, that the conclusions are the very matters intended to be brought forth, while the premises are generally accepted or suppositional without happening to be certain. For this [sort of Law-based statements]—I mean, its conclusions—interpretation is not admitted either, but its premises may admit of it.

The premises in the fourth are generally accepted or suppositional without happening to be certain, and its conclusions are likenesses of the matter intended to be brought forth. With respect to these [Law-based statements], the duty of the select is to interpret them, and the duty of the multitude is to let them stand in their apparent sense.

42. In general, with respect to everything in these [Law-based statements] admitting of an interpretation apprehended only by demonstration, the duty of the select is that interpretation, whereas the duty of the multitude is to take them in their apparent sense in both respects—I mean, with respect to concept and assent—for there is nothing more than that in their natures.

43. Interpretations may occur to those who reflect upon the Law due to the superiority some of these shared methods have over others with respect to bringing about assent—I mean, when the indication of the interpretation is more completely persuasive than the indication of the apparent sense. Interpretations such as these are for the multitude, and it is possible that they become a duty for those whose reflective powers reach that of dialectic. Into this type enter [21] some of the interpretations of the Ash'arites and the Mu'tazilites,[35] although for the most part the statements of the Mu'tazilites are more reliable. The duty of those within the multitude who are not capable of more than rhetorical statements is to let them stand in their apparent sense, and it is not permissible for them to know that interpretation at all.

[3. The Three Sorts of People and the Law's Provision for Them]

44. For people are of three sorts with respect to the Law.

One sort is in no way adept at interpretation. These are the rhetorical people, who are the overwhelming multitude. That is because no person of unimpaired intellect is exempted from this kind of assent.

Another sort is those adept in dialectical interpretation. These are those who are dialectical by nature alone, or by nature and by habit.

Another sort is those adept in certain [or demonstrative] interpretation. These are those who are demonstrative by nature and art—I mean, the art of wisdom. This interpretation ought not to be

34. That is, limited to fewer people.

35. See note 23 to Alghazali's *Deliverer from Error* (above, selection 8) on Mu'tazilites. Cf. note 14 above on Ash'arites.

declared to those adept in dialectic, not to mention the multitude.

45. When something pertaining to these interpretations is declared to someone not adept in them—especially demonstrative interpretations, due to their remoteness from things about which there is shared cognizance—both he who declares it and the one to whom it is declared are steered to unbelief. The reason is that interpretation includes two things: the rejection of the apparent sense and the establishing of the interpretation. Thus, if the apparent sense is rejected by someone who is an adept of the apparent sense without the interpretation being established for him, that leads him to unbelief if it is about the roots of the Law. So interpretations ought not to be declared to the multitude, nor established in rhetorical or dialectical books—I mean, books in which the statements posited are of these two sorts—as Abū Ḥāmid [Alghazali] did.[36]

46. For this kind [of people], it is obligatory to declare and to say, with respect to the apparent sense—when it is such that the doubt as to whether it is an apparent sense is in itself apparent to everyone, without cognizance of its interpretation being possible for them—that it is one of those [verses] that resemble one another [whose interpretation is] not known, except to God, and that it is obligatory for the stop in His saying (may He be exalted) to be placed here: *None knows their interpretation but God* [3:7].[37] In the same way is the answer to come forth with respect to a question about obscure matters for whose understanding no path exists for the multitude—as with His saying (may He be exalted): *And they will ask you about the spirit; say: "The spirit is by the command of my Lord; and of knowledge you have been given only a little"* [17:85].

47. Now, [22] anyone who declares these interpretations to those not adept in them is an unbeliever because of his calling people to unbelief. This is contrary to the call of the Lawgiver, especially when they are corrupt interpretations having to do with the roots of the Law—as has occurred with a group of people in our time. For we have witnessed some groups who suppose they are philosophizing and have, by means of their astounding wisdom, apprehended things that disagree with the Law in every manner—I mean, [things] not admitting of interpretation. And [they suppose] that it is obligatory to declare these things to the multitude. By declaring those corrupt beliefs to the multitude, they have become the reason for the multitude's and their own perdition in this world and in the hereafter.

48. Here is a likeness of these people's intention as contrasted to the intention of the Lawgiver: Someone is intent upon [going to] a skilled physician who is intent upon preserving the health of all of the people and removing sicknesses from them by setting down for them statements to which there is common assent[38] about the obligation of practicing the things that preserve their health and remove their sicknesses, as well as of avoiding the contrary things. He is not able to make them all become physicians, because the physician is the one who knows by demonstrative methods the things that preserve health and remove sickness. Then this one goes out to the people and says to them, "These methods this physician has set down for you are not true." And he sets about rejecting them until they have rejected them. Or he says, "They have interpretations." Yet they do not understand them and thus come to no assent as to what to do because of them.

Now are you of the opinion that people who are in this condition will do any of the things useful for preserving health and removing sickness? Or will this one who has declared that they should reject what they used to believe about those [things] be able to practice that with them—I mean, preserving health? No! Rather, he will not be able to practice these with them, nor will they be able to practice them; and perdition will encompass them all.

49. This is if he declares sound interpretations about those things to them, because of their not understanding that interpretation—not to mention his declaring corrupt interpretations to them. Because he will so interpret the matter to them that they will not be of the opinion that there is a health that must be preserved or a sickness that must be removed, not to mention [23] their being of the opinion that there are things such as to preserve health and remove sickness. And this is what happens with respect to the Law when anyone

36. Literally, "as Abū Ḥāmid [Alghazali] artfully did."

37. See above, sec. 14.

38. Literally, "statements of shared assent." Compare secs. 53–55 and 57 below.

declares an interpretation to the multitude or to someone not adept for it. He corrupts it and bars them from it; and the one who bars others from the Law is an unbeliever.

50. Now this illustration is certain and not poetical, as someone might say. It is a sound linking between the one and the other. That is because the link between the physician and the health of bodies is [the same as] the link between the Lawgiver and the health of souls—I mean, the physician is the one who seeks to preserve the health of bodies when it exists and to bring it back when it has disappeared, while the Lawgiver is the one who aspires to this with respect to the health of souls.

This health is what is called "piety." And the precious Book has declared in various verses that it is to be sought by means of Law-based actions. Thus, He (may He be exalted) said: *Fasting was prescribed for you, just as it was prescribed for those before you, so that you might come to be pious* [2:183). And He (may He be exalted) said: *Neither their flesh nor their blood will reach God, but piety on your part will reach Him* [22:37]. And He said: *Indeed, prayer puts an end to iniquity and to transgression* [29:45]; and so on in innumerable other verses to this effect contained in the precious Book.

Now the Lawgiver seeks this health only through Law-based knowledge and Law-based practice. And this health is the one from which happiness in the hereafter derives and misery in the hereafter from its contrary.

51. From this, it has become evident to you that sound interpretations—not to mention corrupt ones—must not be established in books for the multitude. Sound interpretation is the deposit mankind was charged with holding, and held, whereas all existing things shirked it—I mean the one mentioned in His statement (may He be exalted): *Indeed, we offered the deposit to the heavens, to the earth, and to the mountains,* [and so on to the end of] the verse [33:72].

[F. ON THE EMERGENCE OF FACTIONS WITHIN ISLAM]

[1. Different Opinions regarding Interpretation]

52. Because of the interpretations with respect to the Law—especially the corrupt ones—and the supposition that it is obligatory to declare them to everyone, factions emerged within Islam so that one charged the others with unbelief or with heretical innovation. Thus, the Muʿtatzilites interpreted many verses and many Traditions and declared their interpretations to the multitude, as did the Ashʿarites, although they resorted less to [23] interpretation. Because of that, they threw people into loathing, mutual hatred, and wars (*ḥurūb*); they tore the Law to shreds; and they split the people up into every sort of faction.

53. In addition to all this, in the methods they followed to establish their interpretations they were neither with the multitude nor with the select. They were not with the multitude because their methods were more obscure than the methods shared by the majority. And they were not with the select because, if their methods are examined, they are found to fall short of the conditions for demonstration—and that will be grasped after the slightest examination by anyone who is cognizant of the conditions for demonstration. Rather, many of the roots upon which the Ashʿarites base their cognizance are sophistical. For they deny many necessary things, such as the stability of accidents, the influence of some things upon others, the existence of necessary reasons for what is made to occur, substantial forms, and intermediates.

54. Those among them who reflect have wronged the Muslims in the sense that a group of Ashʿarites has charged with unbelief anyone who is not cognizant of the existence of the Creator (glorious is He) by the methods they have set down for cognizance of Him in their books. But, in truth, they are the ones who are the unbelievers and those who are misguided. From here on they disagreed, with one group saying, "The first obligation is reflection," and another group saying, "Faith is"—I mean, because they were not cognizant of which methods are the ones shared by everyone through whose doors the Law calls all the people and supposed that there is [only] one method. So they erred about the intention of the Lawgiver and were misguided and made others become misguided.

[2. How to Avoid the Evils Brought About by Factions]

55. If it were said, "If these methods followed by the Ash'arites and others adept in reflection are not the shared methods by which the Lawgiver intended to teach the multitude and by which alone it is possible to teach them, then which ones are these methods in this Law of ours?" we would say: "They are the methods that are established in the precious Book alone. For if the precious Book is examined, the three methods existing for all the people will be found in it; and these are the shared methods for teaching the majority of the people and [the method for teaching] the select. And if the matter is examined with respect to them, it will become apparent that no better shared methods for teaching the multitude are to be encountered than the methods mentioned in it."

56. So anyone who distorts these methods by making an interpretation that is not apparent in itself or that is more apparent to everyone than they are—and that is something nonexistent—rejects [25] their wisdom and rejects their intended action for procuring human happiness. That is very apparent from the condition of those in the earliest days [of Islam] and the condition of those who came after them. For those in the earliest days came to have perfect virtue and piety only by practicing[39] these statements, without making interpretations of them; and any one of them who grasped an interpretation did not think fit to declare it. When those who came after them practiced interpretation, their piety decreased, their disagreements became more numerous, their love for one another was removed, and they split up into factions.

57. It is obligatory for whoever wants to remove this heretical innovation from the Law to apply himself to the precious Book and pick from it the indications existing for every single thing we are responsible for believing. In his reflection he is to strive for their apparent sense as much as he can without interpreting anything, except insofar as the interpretation is apparent in itself—I mean, of an apparentness shared by everyone. For if the statements set down in the Law for teaching the people are examined, it seems that one reaches a point in defending them such that only someone who is an adept at demonstration pulls out of their apparent sense something that is not apparent in them. And this particular characteristic is not found in any other statements.

58. The statements of the Law declared to everyone in the precious Book have three particular characteristics that indicate their inimitability. The first is that nothing more completely persuasive and able to bring about assent for everyone is to be found than they. The second is that by their nature they admit of defense, ending up at a point where no one grasps an interpretation of them—if they are such as to have an interpretation—except those adept in demonstration. The third is that they contain a means of alerting those adept in the truth to the true interpretation. And this is not found in the doctrines of the Ash'arites, nor in the doctrines of the Mu'tazilites—I mean, their interpretation neither admits of defense, nor contains a means of alerting to the truth, nor is true. Therefore, innovative heresies have increased.

[G. CONCLUSION]

[1. The Need to Pursue the Task Set Forth Here]

59. We would love to devote ourselves to this intention and carry it out thoroughly; and if God prolongs our life, we shall establish as much of it as we can. That could possibly be a starting point for someone who comes afterwards. Now our soul is in [26] utmost sorrow and pain due to the corrupt dissensions and distorted beliefs that have permeated this Law, especially those that have occurred to it from among people linking themselves to wisdom. For injuries from a friend are graver than

39. Although "using" might be a less awkward rendering of *isti'māl,* Butterworth's rendering as "practicing" has been retained because it highlights the connection to the repeated usage of the same word in the next sentence in "practiced interpretation." Furthermore, it is unclear whether Averroes means to imply that it is the mere use of the relevant statements or their "implementation" in action that leads to "perfect virtue and piety"—though the latter seems more plausible.

injuries from an enemy—I mean that wisdom is the companion of the Law and its milk sister. So injuries from those linked to it are the gravest injuries apart from the enmity, hatred, and quarreling they bring about between both of them. These two are companions by nature and lovers by essence and instinct. It [the Law] has also been injured by many ignorant friends from among those who link themselves to it, namely, the factions existing within it. But God shows all people the right way, brings everyone to love Him, unites their hearts in pious fear of Him, and removes hatred and loathing from them through His grace and mercy.

[2. The Positive Role of the Present Rulership]

60. God has removed many of these evils, ignorant occurrences, and misguided paths by means of this triumphant rule.[40] By means of it, He has brought many good things closer, especially for that sort who follow the path of reflection and yearn for cognizance of the truth. That is, this rule calls the multitude to a middle method for being cognizant of God (glorious is He), raised above the low level of the traditionalists yet below the turbulence of the dialectical theologians, and alerts the select to the obligation for complete reflection on the root of the Law. By His grace, God is the Giver of success and the Guide.

40. The reference is to the rule of the Almohad sovereign Abū Yaʿqūb Yūsuf (r. 1163–1184).

BIBLIOGRAPHY AND FURTHER READING

Primary Sources in English

Bergh, Simon van den, ed. and trans. *Averroes: The Incoherence of the "Incoherence."* London: Luzac, 1954.

Butterworth, Charles E., ed. and trans. *Alfarabi: The Political Writings; "Selected Aphorisms" and Other Texts.* Ithaca, NY: Cornell University Press, 2001.

——. *Averroës: The Book of the Decisive Treatise Determining the Connection between the Law and Wisdom and Epistle Dedicatory.* Provo, UT: Brigham Young University Press, 2001.

——. *Averroes' Middle Commentary on Aristotle's "Poetics."* Princeton, NJ: Princeton University Press, 1986; reprint, South Bend, IN: St. Augustine's Press, 2000.

——. *Averroes' Three Short Commentaries on Aristotle's "Topics," "Rhetoric," and "Poetics."* Albany: SUNY Press, 1977; reprint, South Bend, IN: St. Augustine's Press, 1998.

——. "Al-Rāzī: The Book of the Philosophic Life." *Interpretation* 20.3 (1993): 227–36.

Goodman, Lenn E., trans. *Ibn Tufayl's "Hayy Ibn Yaqzān."* Updated ed. Chicago: University of Chicago Press, 2009.

Khadduri, Majid, trans. *The Islamic Law of Nations: Shaybani's "Sīyar."* Baltimore: Johns Hopkins University Press, 1966.

Khan, M. S., ed. and trans. *An Unpublished Treatise of Miskawaih on Justice.* Leiden: Brill, 1964.

Lerner, Ralph, trans. *Averroes on Plato's "Republic."* 1974. Reprint, Ithaca, NY: Cornell University Press, 2005.

Mahdi, Muhsin S., ed. and trans. *Alfarabi: The Political Writings; Philosophy of Plato and Aristotle.* New York: Free Press of Glencoe, 1962; revised editions, Ithaca, NY: Cornell University Press, 1969, 2002.

Marmura, Michael E., ed. and trans. *Al-Ghazālī: The Incoherence of the Philosophers.* 2nd ed. Provo, UT: Brigham Young University Press, 2002.

McCarthy, Richard J., SJ, trans. *Deliverance from Error and Other Works.* Boston: Twayne, 1980; 2nd ed., Louisville, KY: Fons Vitae, 2004.

Walzer, Richard, ed. and trans. *Al-Farabi on the Perfect State.* Oxford: Clarendon Press, 1985.

Zurayk, Constantine K., trans. *Miskawayh: The Refinement of Character.* Beirut: American University of Beirut, 1968.

Secondary Literature in English

Altmann, Alexander. "Ibn Bājja on Man's Ultimate Felicity." In *Harry Austryn Wolfson Jubilee Volume,* 47–87. Jerusalem: American Academy of Jewish Research, 1965. Reprinted in *Studies in Religious Philosophy and Mysticism,* 73–107. Ithaca, NY: Cornell University Press, 1969; London: Routledge and Kegan Paul, 1969.

Black, Deborah L. "Practical Wisdom, Moral Virtue, and Theoretical Knowledge: The Problem of the Autonomy of the Practical Realm in Arabic Philosophy." In *Moral and Political Philosophies in the Middle Ages,* edited by B. C. Bazáan, E. Andújar, and L. G. Sbrocchi, 1:451–65. Ottawa: LEGAS, 1995.

Blaustein, Michael. "The Scope and Methods of Rhetoric in Averroes' *Middle Commentary on Aristotle's 'Rhetoric.'*" In Butterworth, *The Political Aspects of Islamic Philosophy,* 262–303.

Butterworth, Charles E. "Averroes on Law and Political Well-Being." In *Enlightening Revolutions: Essays in Honor of Ralph Lerner,* edited by Svetozar Minkov, 23–30. Lanham, MD: Lexington Books, 2006.

——. "Averroes: Politics and Opinion." *American Political Science Review* 66 (1972): 894–901.

——. "Ethical and Political Philosophy." In *Cambridge Companion to Arabic Philosophy,* edited by Richard C. Taylor and Peter A. Adamson, 266–86. Cambridge: Cambridge University Press, 2005.

——. "Ethics in Medieval Islamic Philosophy." *Journal of Religious Ethics* 11 (1983): 224–39.

——. "Al-Fārābī's Statecraft: War and the Well-Ordered Regime." In *Cross, Crescent, and Sword,* edited by James T. Johnson and J. Kelsay, 79–100. New York: Greenwood Press, 1990.

——. "Al-Kindī and the Beginnings of Islamic Political Philosophy." In Butterworth, *The Political Aspects of Islamic Philosophy,* 11–60.

——. "Medieval Islamic Philosophy and the Virtue of Ethics." *Arabica* 34 (1987): 221–50.

——. "The Origins of Al-Rāzī's Political Philosophy." *Interpretation* 20.3 (1993): 237–57.

——. *Philosophy, Ethics, and Virtuous Rule: A Study of Averroes' Commentary on Plato's "Republic."* Cairo Papers in Social Science 9.1. Cairo: American University in Cairo Press, 1986.

——, ed. *The Political Aspects of Islamic Philosophy: Essays in Honor of Muhsin S. Mahdi.* Harvard Middle East Monographs 27. Cambridge, MA: Harvard University Press, 1992.

——. "The Political Teaching of Averroes." *Arabic Sciences and Philosophy* 2.2 (1992): 187–202.

——. "The Political Teaching of Avicenna." *Topoi* 19 (2000): 35–44.

——. "Rhetoric and Islamic Political Philosophy." *International Journal of Middle East Studies* 3 (1972): 187–98.

——. "The Rhetorician and His Relationship to the Community: Three Accounts of Aristotle's *Rhetoric*." In Marmura, *Islamic Theology and Philosophy,* 111–36.

Colmo, Christopher. "Alfarabi on the Prudence of Founders." *Review of Politics* 60.4 (1998): 719–41.

——. *Breaking with Athens: Alfarabi as Founder.* Lanham, MD: Lexington Books, 2005.

——. "Theory and Practice: Alfarabi's *Plato* Revisited." *American Political Science Review* 86.4 (1992): 966–76.

Conrad, Lawrence I., ed. *The World of Ibn Tufayl.* Leiden: Brill, 1996.

Daiber, Hans. "The Ruler as Philosopher: A New Interpretation of al-Fārābī's View." In *Medelingen der Koninklijke Nederlandse Akademie van Wetenschappen,* 133–49. Amsterdam, 1986.

Druart, Thérèse-Anne. "Al-Farabi and Emanationism." In *Studies in Medieval Philosophy,* edited by John F. Wippel, 28–43. Washington, DC: Catholic University of America Press, 1987.

Fakhry, Majid. *Ethical Theories in Islam.* 2nd ed. Leiden: Brill, 1994.

——. *A History of Islamic Philosophy.* 3rd ed. New York: Columbia University Press, 2004.

Firestone, Reuven. *Jihād: The Origin of Holy War in Islam.* New York: Oxford University Press, 1999.

Fradkin, Hillel. "The Political Thought of Ibn Ṭufayl." In Butterworth, *The Political Aspects of Islamic Philosophy,* 234–61.

Frank, Richard M. *Al-Ghazali and the Ash'arite School.* Durham, NC: Duke University Press, 1994.

——. "The Science of *Kalām*." *Arabic Sciences and Philosophy* 2 (1992): 7–37.

Galston, Miriam. *Politics and Excellence: The Political Philosophy of Alfarabi.* Princeton, NJ: Princeton University Press, 1990.

——. "Realism and Idealism in Avicenna's Political Philosophy." *Review of Politics* 41 (1979): 561–77.

——. "A Re-examination of al-Fārābī's Neoplatonism." *Journal of the History of Philosophy* 15.1 (1977): 13–32.

——. "The Theoretical and Practical Dimensions of Happiness as Portrayed in the Political Treatises of al-Fārābī." In Butterworth, *The Political Aspects of Islamic Philosophy,* 95–151.

Goodman, Lenn E. "Humanism and Islamic Ethics." Chap. 2 in *Islamic Humanism.* New York: Oxford University Press, 2003.

Harvey, Steven. "The Place of the Philosopher in the City according to Ibn Bājjah." In Butterworth, *The Political Aspects of Islamic Philosophy,* 199–233.

Hawi, Sami S. *Islamic Naturalism and Mysticism: A Philosophic Study of Ibn Ṭufayl's "Ḥayy Bin Yaqẓān."* Leiden: Brill, 1974.

Hourani, George F. "Introduction." In *Averroes: On the Harmony of Religion and Philosophy,* 1–42. London: Luzac & Co., 1967.

——. "The Principal Subject of *Ḥayy Ibn Yaqẓān*." *Journal of Near Eastern Studies* 15 (1956): 40–46.

Johnson, James Turner. *The Holy War Idea in Western and Islamic Traditions.* University Park: Pennsylvania State University Press, 1997.

Kelsay, John, and James Turner Johnson, eds. *Just War and Jihad.* New York: Greenwood Press, 1991.

Khadduri, Majid. *War and Peace in the Law of Islam.* Baltimore: Johns Hopkins University Press, 1955.

Kraemer, Joel L. *Humanism in the Renaissance of Islam: The Cultural Revival during the Buyid Age.* Leiden: Brill, 1986.

——. "The *Jihād* of the *Falāsifa*." *Jerusalem Studies in Arabic and Islam* 10 (1987): 288–324.

Lambton, Anne K. S. *State and Government in Medieval Islam.* Oxford: Oxford University Press, 1981.

Mahdi, Muhsin S. "Alfarabi against Philoponus." *Journal of Near Eastern Studies* 26.4 (1967): 233–60.

——. *Alfarabi and the Foundation of Islamic Political Philosophy.* Chicago: University of Chicago Press, 2001.

——. "Averroës on Divine Law and Human Wisdom." In *Ancients and Moderns: Essays on the Tradition of Political Philosophy in Honor of Leo Strauss,* edited by Joseph Cropsey, 114–31. New York: Basic Books, 1964.

——. "Al-Fārābī's Imperfect State." Review of *Al-Farabi on the Perfect State,* by Richard Walzer. *Journal of the American Oriental Society* 110.4 (1990): 691–726.

——. "Language and Logic in Classical Islam." In *Logic in Classical Islamic Culture,* edited by G. E. von Grunebaum, 51–83. Wiesbaden: Otto Harrassowitz, 1970.

——. "Man and His Universe in Medieval Arabic Philosophy." In *L'homme et son univers au moyen âge,* edited by Christian Wenin, 102–13. Louvain-la-Neuve: Éditions de l'Institut Supérieur de Philosophie, 1986.

——. "Philosophical Literature." Chap. 6 in *The Cambridge History of Arabic Literature: Religion, Learning and Science in the 'Abbasid Period,* edited by M. J. L. Young, J. D. Latham, and R. B. Serjeant, 76–105. Cambridge: Cambridge University Press, 1990.

——. "Remarks on Averroes' *Decisive Treatise.*" In Marmura, *Islamic Theology and Philosophy,* 188–202.

Marmura, Michael E. "Avicenna's Psychological Proof of Prophecy." *Journal of Near Eastern Studies* 22 (1963): 49–56.

——, ed. *Islamic Theology and Philosophy: Studies in Honor of George F. Hourani.* Albany: SUNY Press, 1984.

——. "The Philosopher and Society: Some Medieval Arabic Discussions." *Arab Studies Quarterly* 1 (1979): 309–23.

Morris, James B. "The Philosopher-Prophet in Avicenna's Political Philosophy." In Butterworth, *The Political Aspects of Islamic Philosophy,* 152–98.

Najjar, Fauzi M. "Al-Fārābī on Political Science." *Muslim World* 48.2 (1958): 94–103.

——. "Siyasa in Islamic Political Philosophy." In Marmura, *Islamic Theology and Philosophy,* 92–110.

Nasr, Seyyed Hossein, and Oliver Leaman, eds. *History of Islamic Philosophy.* 2 vols. London: Routledge Press, 1996.

Parens, Joshua. *An Islamic Philosophy of Virtuous Religions: Introducing Alfarabi.* Albany: SUNY Press, 2006.

——. *Metaphysics as Rhetoric: Alfarabi's "Summary of Plato's 'Laws.'"* Albany: SUNY Press, 1995.

Pines, Shlomo. "Aristotle's *Politics* in Arabic Philosophy." *Israel Oriental Studies* 5 (1975): 150–60.

Rosenthal, E. I. J. *Political Thought in Medieval Islam.* Cambridge: Cambridge University Press, 1962.

——. *Studia Semitica.* Vol. 2, *Islamic Themes.* Cambridge: Cambridge University Press, 1971. (Includes articles on Alfarabi, Ibn Bajja, and Averroes.)

Rosenthal, Franz. "On the Knowledge of Plato's Philosophy in the Islamic World." *Islamic Culture* 14 (1940): 387–422.

Sankari, F. A. "Plato and Al-Farabi: A Comparison of Some of Their Political Philosophies." *Muslim World* 60 (1970): 65–94.

Sherif, Mohamed A. *Ghazali's Theory of Virtue.* Albany: SUNY Press, 1975.

Shervani, H. K. "Al-Farabi's Political Theories." *Islamic Culture* 12 (1938): 288–305.

Strauss, Leo. "Farabi's *Plato.*" In *Louis Ginzberg Jubilee Volume,* edited by A. Marx, S. Lieberman, S. Spiegel, and S. Zeitlin, 357–93. New York: American Academy for Jewish Research, 1945.

——. "How Fārābī Read Plato's 'Laws.'" In *What Is Political Philosophy? And Other Studies,* 134–54. New York: Free Press of Glencoe, 1959; reprint, Chicago: University of Chicago Press, 1988.

——. *Philosophy and Law: Contributions to the Understanding of Maimonides and His Predecessors.* Translated by Eve Adler. Albany: SUNY Press, 1995. (Includes important discussions of Alfarabi, Averroes, and Avicenna.)

Walbridge, John. "The Political Thought of Quṭb al-Dīn al-Shīrāzī." In Butterworth, *The Political Aspects of Islamic Philosophy,* 345–78.

Walker, Paul E. "The Political Implications of al-Rāzī's Philosophy." In Butterworth, *The Political Aspects of Islamic Philosophy,* 61–94.

Walzer, Richard. *Greek into Arabic.* Cambridge, MA: Harvard University Press, 1962.

——. "The Rise of Islamic Philosophy." *Oriens* 3 (1950): 1–19.

Wolfson, Harry Austryn. *The Philosophy of Kalam.* Cambridge, MA: Harvard University Press, 1976.

Ziai, Hossein. "The Source and Nature of Authority: A Study of al-Suhrawardī's Illuminationist Political Doctrine." In Butterworth, *The Political Aspects of Islamic Philosophy,* 304–44.

Bibliographies

Daiber, Hans. *Bibliography of Islamic Philosophy.* 2 vols. Leiden: Brill, 1999.

Druart, Thérèse-Anne. "Brief Bibliographical Guide in Medieval and Islamic Philosophy and Theology (2002–2004)." http://philosophy.cua.edu/faculty/tad/biblio.cfm.

——. "Brief Bibliographical Guide in Medieval and Islamic Philosophy and Theology (2004–2006)." http://philosophy.cua.edu/faculty/tad/Bibliography%20 04-06.cfm.

PART II

POLITICAL PHILOSOPHY IN JUDAISM

Edited by Joshua Parens

INTRODUCTION

Jewish medieval political philosophy is deeply indebted to Islamic medieval political philosophy. This debt is evident in the similarity of central themes in the two traditions. Three of the four main themes of the Islamic part of this volume—the philosopher-king as prophet, the division of the sciences, and the solitary—carry over to the Jewish. The centrality of divine Law in the two traditions helps explain their similar themes. A prophet is required to reveal divine Law. Thus the philosopher-king is prominent in both Judaism and Islam. In the *Sourcebook*, we highlight the division of the sciences, especially in the Muslim and Jewish traditions, because the intimate connection between politics and theology, as well as the importance of jurisprudence (*fiqh/talmud*), is dictated by the centrality of divine Law in these traditions. Finally, the disjunction between the (solitary) philosopher and society is more obvious in a society ruled by a divine Law. In a society with a less comprehensive (or total) political life, this disjunction may not emerge at all.

Because Judaism is older than Islam, it requires some detective work to determine why medieval political philosophy emerged so much earlier and more boldly in the thought of Alfarabi than in the Jewish tradition. The most obvious reason is the Jewish people's loss of nationhood. The destruction of the Second Temple made continued reflection on politics seem irrelevant. It took a thinker with a Maimonidean ambition to reverse this trend. (By a Maimonidean ambition, I refer to Maimonides' aim, evident in his law code, the *Mishneh Torah*, to lead the Jews back to nationhood.) But there are less obvious reasons that political philosophy emerged later in Judaism. In *Guide of the Perplexed* 1.71, Maimonides offers a historical account of the emergence of *kalām* (dialectical theology), and less directly of political philosophy, in Judaism. Although there has been some debate about the accuracy of every detail of his account, the broad outlines appear to be accurate: *kalām* emerged first among Eastern Christian communities, as a means of defense against philosophy; second among Muslims; and third, and to a smaller extent, among Jews. Contact between Muslims and Eastern Christians contributed to the emergence of *kalām* within Islam. *Kalām* emerged first among Jews in Sephardic lands (Spain, North Africa, the Middle East), at least in part because of Muslim interest in *kalām* and Muslim rule over Jews in these lands.

Maimonides, like Alfarabi for the Islamic world,[1] argues that philosophy has existed within Judaism from the beginning—indeed, even before it was to be found among the Greeks (1.71). That such claims could be historically verified seems unlikely. There are a number of reasons to make such an argument. If philosophy had not existed all along, what would account for the (from Maimonides' point of view, relatively) recent emergence of *kalām* in Judaism? Does not philosophy precede *kalām*, since *kalām* is a defense against philosophy? However this may be, in the medieval period matters appear to be reversed: *kalām* appeared in Judaism before philosophy. Maimonides seeks to correct the mistaken impression of Jewish thinkers that *kalām*'s purpose is something other than the defense of religion against philosophy, an impression reinforced by the relatively late appearance or reappearance of philosophy.

The late emergence of dialectical theology within Judaism reflects the Torah's focus on Law or action. The Jewish focus on action is also evident

1. *Attainment of Happiness* 53 (in selection 4 above).

in the relatively hostile reaction to Maimonides' effort to codify the central beliefs of Judaism in his list of thirteen roots, which gave rise to great debate within Judaism.[2] In view of Judaism's stress on action, perhaps we should not be surprised at the relatively late emergence of political philosophy in Jewish thought. I mention in passing the obvious debt of Jewish medieval political philosophers to Islamic medieval political philosophers: Maimonides to Alfarabi, Ibn Bajja, and, to a lesser extent, Avicenna; Polgar to Alfarabi and Averroes. More important to our inquiry, however, than the debt of specific authors is the debt of Jewish authors to their Muslim counterparts regarding the key themes discussed in the introduction to the Islamic part of this volume. Again, three of the four themes discussed in the Islamic part are renewed here: the philosopher-king as prophet-legislator, the division of the sciences, and the solitary. (The fourth theme, Alghazali's attack on the philosophers, will also be treated, though in less detail than in part 1.)

Much as themes in the Islamic tradition taken over from ancient political philosophy entail substantial modifications of the original, so the themes that carry over from the Islamic to the Jewish tradition will often receive significantly different treatment. For example, the theme of the mystical solitary in Alghazali receives a very different treatment in Halevi, even though Halevi, like Alghazali for Islam, defends Judaism against the inroads of philosophy. Halevi departs from Alghazali by limiting rather than encouraging mystical solitude—no matter how large a role such solitude might have played from the beginning in Judaism.

The main novel theme in the Jewish part of the *Sourcebook* is the emergence of a variety of views on the character of law, especially whether there are laws that deserve to be called "rational" or "natural." In recent years a burgeoning secondary literature has attempted to show the wide prevalence of natural law theory in medieval Jewish thought. Because of length constraints, we have chosen to cut back certain vital chapters in this part of the *Sourcebook* (such as *Guide* 1.71 and much of the *Letter on Astrology*) to provide the teacher and student ready access to the material they will need at least to begin to enter the dispute over natural law in Judaism.

Let us take up the themes touched on in the introduction to part 1 and then turn to the additional theme of law, especially natural law. From Maimonides to Polgar and beyond, Jewish medieval political philosophers are emphatic in singling out Mosaic prophecy as unique. As followers of Alfarabi, they stress the philosophic and kingly virtues of the legislating prophet. At the same time, they are more specific than Alfarabi about who deserves this characterization—namely, Moses. It is not difficult to see why they would stress Moses so emphatically. Leaving aside the obvious traditional centrality of Moses in Judaism, it was an especially important task of Jewish medieval political philosophy, especially because it emerged after the rise of Islam and the development of Islamic medieval political philosophy, to emphasize the uniqueness of Mosaic prophecy. This was part and parcel of defending Judaism in a world dominated by Muslims in the Sephardic lands and by Christians in the Ashkenazic lands. In contrast, Alfarabi is deafeningly silent not only about Muhammad but also about all Islam-specific details of time and place. (Which is not to say that Alfarabi's accounts apply equally well to all the revealed religions. Rather, his avoidance of detail seems intended, among other things, to highlight the fact that his teaching is less about historical realities than about establishing a philosophic standard against which history might be measured.)[3]

Leaving aside Mosaic exceptionalism, Maimonides' prophetology is similar in its outlines to Alfarabi's. The question of whether prophecy is natural or revealed (that is, miraculous), which also emerged from our inquiry into Alfarabi, becomes only more intense in Maimonides. According to the latter, that prophecy occurs depends upon the prophet's possession of certain natural abilities and training. Aside from the highly naturalistic account of God's overflow of inspiration by way of the Active Intellect, the only "active" role God appears to play in prophecy is in withholding it (*Guide* 2.32; below, selection 15). Just how active that role really is can only begin to be settled on the

2. *Commentary on the Mishnah, Sanhedrin* 10, *Pereq Ḥeleq*, in *A Maimonides Reader*, ed. Isadore Twersky (Springfield, NJ: Behrman House, 1972), 401–23. On the subsequent debate, see Menachem Kellner, *Dogma in Medieval Jewish Thought* (1986; repr., Oxford: Littman Library of Jewish Civilization, 2004).

3. Cf. the freedom with which Avicenna refers to the historical realities of Islam in *Healing* (above, selection 7).

basis of the passages included in the *Sourcebook.* That being said, the reader must consider with great care Maimonides' examples from scripture of God's will withholding prophecy. Comparison with the *Letter on Astrology* is also very fruitful in this connection.[4]

One aspect of Maimonides' prophetology has drawn special scholarly attention in recent years, namely, the large role that he seems to afford imagination in prophecy. Both Alfarabi and Avicenna afford imagination a role in prophecy—the former a smaller role, and the latter a much larger, perhaps controlling, role. (Alfarabi seems to afford an even greater role to prudence than imagination, however.) The role of imagination is one of the features of Maimonides' prophetology that has led interpreters to view him as akin to modern political philosophers such as Spinoza. If Maimonides were to restrict the role of intellect to theoretical matters and reserve practical matters for the imagination, as some scholars suggest he does, then shocking possibilities would arise. Perhaps when Maimonides speaks of practical matters as generally accepted opinions, what he really means is that all practical matters are the product of a consensus of what most people imagine. If one ascribes a large enough role to imagination in Maimonides' prophetology, then one could accuse him of conventionalism and of a radical departure from Plato and Aristotle. Before leaping to conclusions about this, readers should consider that Maimonides is also regularly identified as a natural law theorist. This apparently minor theme, the status of the imagination in Maimonides' prophetology, then, has implications for the more pressing contemporary debate in political and legal philosophy between proponents of conventionalism and proponents of natural law. One thing is certain, the reader should not leap to judgment regarding Maimonides, considering the wide disagreement about his views on imagination (prudence) and law.[5]

I will digress for a moment to consider the significance of the opposition between conventionalism and natural law. The oldest and simplest expression of conventionalism is Thrasymachus's account of justice as the advantage of the stronger in Book 1 of Plato's *Republic.* Thrasymachus argues that in each city, whether it is a democracy, an aristocracy, or a tyranny, the rulers legislate for their own advantage (338D). Of course, according to such an account, any kind of regime is as just as any other. In one city, the many poor may be more powerful; in another city, the wealthy few may be more powerful. By the time the reader reaches Book 8 of the *Republic,* Socrates has shown at least one way of determining the superiority of certain regimes over others. In contrast, the main implication of Thrasymachus's conventionalism is that there is no natural standard of justice other than force or might.

The origin of natural law is a matter of debate, although most scholars agree that the first thinkers to propound such an idea were the Stoics. Of course, Thomas Aquinas is the most renowned medieval Christian proponent of natural law.[6] Matters are different in the Islamic and Jewish traditions. Saadya Gaon (882–942) set forth the first developed doctrine of natural law in Judaism—though the term used by Jews is "rational law." Saadya's argument, however, was not without precedent—indeed, it has been shown to have developed out of Mu'tazilite *kalām.*[7] Judah Halevi,[8] Isaac Abravanel, and Joseph Albo are also proponents of one or another version of rational or natural law. Leaving aside its genealogy, the natural law teaching is in many respects the opposite of conventionalism. The natural law teaching asserts not only that there is a natural standard of justice (or "natural right,"

4. For a more complete assessment of Maimonides' views, the reader would need to explore his extremely elusive usage of the word translated as "will" (*mashī'a*) throughout parts 1 and 2 of the *Guide.*

5. To make further progress in understanding the status of imagination and prudence, the interested reader should consider Maimonides' rare allusions to prudence in *Eight Chapters,* Chapter 1, in *The Ethical Writings of Maimonides,* ed. and trans. Raymond L. Weiss and Charles E. Butterworth (New York: New York University Press, 1975; repr., New York: Dover, 1983); *Guide* 1.54, 72, and 3.17, in *Guide of the Perplexed,* trans. Shlomo Pines (Chicago: University of Chicago Press, 1963), 2.40 (in the *Sourcebook*); and Joshua Parens, "Leaving the Garden: Maimonides and Spinoza on the Imagination and Practical Intellect Revisited," *Philosophy & Theology* 18.2 (2009): 219–46.

6. For a valuable introduction to the history of the concept of natural law, see Leo Strauss, "On Natural Law," in *Studies in Platonic Political Philosophy* (Chicago: University of Chicago Press, 1983), 137–46.

7. See Alexander Altmann, "Saadya's Conception of the Law," *Bulletin of the John Rylands Library* 28.2 (1944): 320–39; and Leo Strauss, "The Law of Reason in the *Kuzari,*" in *Persecution and the Art of Writing* (Glencoe, IL: Free Press, 1952; repr., Chicago: University of Chicago Press, 1988), 11, 97, 99.

8. Upon a first reading, it might appear that Halevi, by means of the Jewish sage, is rejecting rational laws. See the introduction to the Halevi selection for preliminary ideas about how to sort out the various senses of "intellectual *nomoi.*" Halevi's dialogue is one of the most difficult works in the *Sourcebook.*

dikaion phusei), as Plato and Aristotle argue, for example, but also that there are laws that capture that standard. In contrast, Aristotle is quite hazy about what is natural with respect to justice. The most straightforward claim he makes is that the best regime is the same everywhere (*Nicomachean Ethics* 1135a4–8)—implying the same potential for establishing a hierarchy among regime types as was established in the *Republic* (which he makes good on in the *Politics*)—although the rest of his political teaching implies that such a regime is rarely something one should strive for. Another feature of the natural right teaching in keeping with the focus on the best regime is that it privileges the philosophic way of life over other ways of life, including even the public devotion to the common good exemplified, for example, by Aristotle's great-souled man (see *Nicomachean Ethics* 10.7–8). Maimonides echoes this striking claim of the ancient philosophers by treating the ethically virtuous way of life as a means to or by-product of the best way of life—rather than as something sought for its own sake.[9] In contrast, natural law proponents such as Halevi privilege the life of action over the life of contemplation.

The most obvious and perhaps important departure of natural law from natural right is that it claims that certain laws possess comparable naturalness to Aristotle's extraordinarily high standard. On the one hand, the very inaccessibility of Aristotle's standard guarantees that human beings will continue to strive to know what this standard is or represents. On the other hand, natural law not only prohibits low things such as murder and theft, but also insinuates that all human beings possess *some* kind of innate grasp of such laws. Just what kind of innate grasp—that is, whether it is merely potentially present and whether all could arrive at it through the use of their own reason—is subject to dispute. The most sophisticated versions of this teaching, such as Thomas Aquinas's, explicitly resist the insinuation that such a grasp is so innate that it does not even need promulgation. The natural or rational law teaching of Saadya, however, is less clear on this matter. We will return to the issue of conventionalism and natural law shortly. For now, let us turn to the division of the sciences and the solitary.

Although we could not include as much material from Jewish as Muslim authors on the division of the sciences, the basic character of this division remains the same as in Islamic medieval political philosophy, especially Alfarabi. That is, Maimonides also affords a place of great importance to *fiqh* or *talmud* (jurisprudence)—as is evident in the enormous amount of energy he devoted to his *Commentary on the Mishnah* and, above all, his massive law code, the *Mishneh Torah.* Furthermore, Maimonides contrasts jurisprudence with *kalām,* alluding in the opening of the *Guide* to the distinction between *fiqh* and what he calls the "true science of the law." The affinities between this true science of the law and *kalām,* as well as between the former and political philosophy, make the *Guide* one of the most difficult of all medieval texts to interpret. If the relation between *kalām* and philosophy is one of hostility (see *Guide* 1.71), then how could Maimonides write a book containing elements of both?

Maimonides' *Guide* is first and foremost a work of *kalām;* it is only in some far more complicated sense a work of political philosophy.[10] (To a far greater extent than Maimonides, Alfarabi segregates the "kalamic" elements of his works from the more philosophic parts. Consider the concluding portion of the *Book of Religion,* selection 2, and the introductions to selections 2 and 3.) Leaving aside political philosophy, to approach the *Guide* initially as a work of "Jewish philosophy" is to ignore the depth of the dispute between philosophy and Judaism or religion—a dispute no less pointed than the one Alghazali (and, as we will see, Halevi) highlights between eternity and creation. Indeed, Maimonides also highlights the dispute between eternity and creation in part 2 of the *Guide.* Even if Maimonides develops a defense of Judaism less opposed to philosophy than that of some of his predecessors (such as Saadya and Halevi), his *Guide* will remain a closed book unless the reader attends first to its surface, the defense of Judaism.

9. Cf. Maimonides *Guide* 3.54, with Strauss, *Persecution and the Art of Writing,* 114.

10. See Strauss, *Persecution and the Art of Writing,* 40–41, 99–100. In the former passage, Strauss contrasts Maimonides' *kalām* as "intelligent, or enlightened *kalām*" with traditional *kalām* as "imaginative"; in the latter passage, he contrasts Halevi's *kalām* as not "typical" with the typical *kalām* of the Mu'tazilites—though he also stresses that Halevi embraces certain elements of the Mu'tazilite teaching. Both Maimonides and Halevi employ some form of *kalām,* but their relation to philosophy is very different. Presumably, then, their *kalām* is also quite different.

Let us turn from the complicated relation between jurisprudence and *kalām* in Maimonides' thought to consider the brief selection on the division of the sciences in the *Logic* included here. Perhaps Maimonides' most surprising departure from Alfarabi—a departure that is to be expected, however, if Maimonides is to do his job as defender of Judaism—is the doubt he creates about whether political science or political philosophy has any relevance to the revealed Law. (Indeed, the selection from the *Logic* has lent support to the claim that Maimonides is a conventionalist. As I will explain below, conventionalism could nicely complement radical dependence upon divine revelation.) Although Maimonides speaks disparagingly of the "regimes and *nomoi* [laws]" of "past religious communities" (*Logic*), and "the *nomoi* of the Greeks and the ravings of the Sabians" (*Guide* 2.39 end), one must ask whether Maimonides also implies thereby that the Law of Moses has made the "many books [of the philosophers . . . on all these things]" irrelevant? Might Maimonides distinguish the teachings of the political philosophers (for example, Plato's *Laws*) from, for example, the laws of Solon?[11] Is Maimonides indebted in matters not only of ethics but also of political philosophy to those he refers to as the "modern philosophers," such as Alfarabi, and even to the "ancient philosophers," such as Aristotle and Plato?[12] In the interest of the defense of Judaism, it would appear incumbent upon Maimonides to single out the Mosaic Law as in need of no supplement. Yet continued reflection on these passages, as well as on our later excerpts from the *Guide* (esp. 2.40 and 3.27 and 28), seems to suggest that philosophy or the perfection of one's rational faculty is the distinctive feature of truly divine law.

Maimonides' discussion of the "single" or "solitary" (*waḥid*) human being, who may be harmed by the Law (3.34), is an obvious continuation of Ibn Bajja and Ibn Tufayl's musings on the relation between philosopher, mystic, and Law. Even before Maimonides within the Jewish tradition, Halevi had begun to reflect on these types—but in a spirit closer to Alghazali. Together with Alghazali, Halevi offers the most searching criticism of the philosophic way of life in the *Sourcebook*. Halevi's *Kuzari* is as spirited as Alghazali's *Deliverer* and as enchanting as Ibn Tufayl's *Hayy*. It is a dialogue, based loosely on historical facts, about a Khazar king who attempts to determine what religion he should adopt, after discovering in a dream that his religious service is inadequate. The king engages in brief conversations with a philosopher, a Christian scholar, and a Muslim scholar, and much more extensive conversations with a Jewish scholar or sage. The final result of the conversation is a striking event in human history: the king and his counselors, and eventually his nation, convert to Judaism![13] Unlike many other authors of dialogues, Halevi follows Plato in what may be the key feature of the Platonic dialogue: the differentiation between the lead character (Socrates) and the author (Plato). Like Plato, Halevi signals the difference between himself and his lead character, the Jewish sage. On the opening page of his dialogue, Halevi notes: "Some of the arguments of the [Jewish] sage seemed persuasive to me and in agreement with my own belief." In other words, he agrees with some, but not all, of what the sage argues.[14]

Although Halevi (ca. 1080–1142) has obviously been influenced by Alghazali,[15] he is far more concerned than the latter about the threat mystical withdrawal might pose to society. The political frame of the *Kuzari* always brings the reader back to the question, How might a king, that is, a political leader, view this or that religious claim? In addition, two features of Jewish life and thought contribute to a modified reliance on mysticism. First, Jewish life in exile is lived in longing for a return to the Land of Israel. Second, Judaism is characterized by love of the People Israel. Jewish mysticism, unlike Alghazali's mysticism, is leavened by love of a place and of one's own. Leaving aside the *Kuzari*, Halevi was arguably the greatest medieval Jewish poet. His poetry, written for the most part before the *Kuzari*, includes numerous devotional poems about the Land of

11. For just such a distinction among different kinds of "pagan" *nomoi*, see the historical introduction to the selection from Halevi's *Kuzari* (selection 13).

12. See the introduction to Maimonides' *Eight Chapters* in Weiss and Butterworth, *The Ethical Writings of Maimonides*.

13. For information on the historical reality, see Kevin Alan Brook, *The Jews of Khazaria*, 2nd ed. (Lanham, MD: Rowman and Littlefield, 2006).

14. See Strauss, *Persecution and the Art of Writing*, 101 n. 17.

15. See Diana Lobel, *Between Mysticism and Philosophy* (Albany: SUNY Press, 2000), 4.

Israel. As we will note below, the *Kuzari* considers whether such love may even run the risk of being idolatrous. Be that as it may, these two features of Halevi's mysticism are powerful correctives to any tendency toward complete withdrawal into solitude. At the same time, these features seem to give rise to a highly ambiguous teaching on solitude. On the one hand, the Jewish sage (or scholar) appears to celebrate the ascetic withdrawal of prophets in the Bible (*Kuzari* 3.1). On the other hand, in an apparent, if confusing, echo of Plato, he argues as if the best human being of his own time is a "guardian of his city" (3.4). At a minimum, Halevi sees some deleterious effects of the solitary life in his own time. The loss of nationhood could only have intensified his awareness of this risk.

More than mystical withdrawal, Halevi's mystical love of the Land of Israel could be thought to run the risk of being characterized as what the Jewish scholar calls idolatry. It is worth recalling here the dialogic character of the *Kuzari*. The sage links the love of the dust and stones of the Land with the idolatrous worship of the golden calf (1.97, not included in the *Sourcebook*). The poet Halevi extols this love. Much as in the case of solitude and public-spiritedness, Halevi's own view here is very difficult to determine. The love of the Land may be necessary even if it runs the risk of being idolatry. Halevi seems to be willing to run the risk of idolatry in the name of the unification of the Jewish people. It would appear then that his mysticism is diametrically opposed to Alghazali's in its effects. It is not the mystic (in spite of prophetic solitude) but the philosopher who becomes the exemplar of the solitary in the *Kuzari*.

The *Kuzari* is an especially provocative counterpoint to Maimonides (as well as Polgar) because Halevi is such a staunch defender of the Hebrew Bible's greater stress on action than thought. As such, he criticizes the philosophers' apparent theoretical detachment from place. Here the tables are turned on the philosopher; like Socrates in Aristophanes' *Clouds*, the philosopher (not the mystic) appears to be an ascetic. Thus the theme of the solitary returns in a new light—offering opportunities to clarify or add to the insights we gained in the Islamic part of this volume. Like a pre-Socratic philosopher or Socrates before the second sailing in the *Phaedo*, Halevi's philosopher seems, at best, superficially concerned with practical affairs. More disturbingly, Halevi questions the sincerity of philosophers' attachment to any religion in particular. In doing so, he provides one of the most telling accounts of the options available to philosophers in relation to their own religious communities.[16]

Readers might want to consider the following questions surrounding the theme of the solitary in the Jewish part of this volume: Does Halevi portray philosophic solitude accurately? Does his reliance on mystical fuel for unification of a people and devotion to a land present any problems? Why is mysticism capable of running in both directions, toward solitude and toward public spirit? Can philosophy offer any guidance between these two extremes for the benefit of public life? Readers might also compare Maimonides' assessment of the roots of Jewish loss of national sovereignty in the *Letter on Astrology* (selection 17).

As we turn from the solitary to the theme of law, an obvious way of contrasting Maimonides and Halevi, previously alluded to, can serve as a bridge between these two themes. Although Halevi clearly privileges action over contemplation (or *theoria*), Maimonides just as clearly privileges the latter over the former. In privileging contemplation in this way, Maimonides loudly echoes the ancient Greek philosophers whose relevance for the Law he seems to call into question elsewhere.

Recent scholars of Maimonides' thought have disagreed vociferously about his views on Law. Some see Maimonides as a conventionalist, and others as a natural law theorist.[17] What accounts for these radically divergent interpretations? The main source of the difficulty, I believe, is two conflicting impressions left by Maimonides' thought as a whole. On the one hand, nearly every reader of

16. See Strauss, *Persecution and the Art of Writing*, 114–15.

17. For the conventionalist interpretation of Maimonides, see Marvin Fox, *Interpreting Maimonides* (Chicago: University of Chicago Press, 1990), chap. 6, "Maimonides and Aquinas on Natural Law," esp. 133; Kalman Bland, "Beauty, Maimonides, and Cultural Relativism in Medieval Jewish Thought," *Journal of Medieval and Early Modern Studies* 26.1 (1996): 85–112, esp. 90, 93. For the natural law interpretation of Maimonides, see David Novak, *Natural Law in Judaism* (Cambridge: Cambridge University Press, 1998), chap. 4, esp. 119–37. Although he does not use the term "natural law," by arguing for even deeper continuity between Saadya and Maimonides than does Novak, Lenn Goodman implies that Maimonides is a natural law theorist; see Lenn Goodman, "Rational Law/ Ritual Law," in *A People Apart*, ed. Daniel H. Frank (Albany: SUNY Press, 1993), 109–200; and Goodman, *God of Abraham* (New York: Oxford University Press, 1996), chap. 5, "Ethical Monism and Ethical Pluralism."

Maimonides' *Guide* can detect that, in that work, he is engaging in a radical demotion of action within Judaism. He seeks to elevate the pursuit of theoretical insight in an unprecedented manner. These complementary features of his thought lend weight to the view that he is a conventionalist of some kind—that is, he seems to have demoted action so far at times as to insinuate that it is shaped merely by convention. On the other hand, and in apparently flagrant contradiction of this initial impression, as has already been mentioned, Maimonides devoted many years of his life to improving and codifying Jewish jurisprudence. And the primary focus of that jurisprudence is legal and moral, not theoretical. At least to some, this devotion to guiding action within the Jewish community would suggest that his praise of theoretical insight is not intended to deny that reason can play an important role in reflection on action.

Yet conventionalist interpreters have argued that even the recognition that Maimonides devoted so much time and effort to the preservation and clarification of the Law can easily be reconciled with the view that he is a conventionalist. If good and evil are merely conventional, we are all the more dependent upon God for laying down clearly what is good and what evil—that is, we should be expected to be even more committed to the study of Torah and Talmud, as legal and moral works. Maimonides could seem to recommend this line of interpretation to his readers on at least two occasions, which I already mentioned while discussing Maimonides' views on the division of the sciences: the end of Chapter 14 of his *Treatise on the Art of Logic* and the end of *Guide* 2.39. On both occasions, he highlights the way in which revealed law has taken the place of pagan *nomoi*. In addition, in the former case, he notes that these *nomoi* were accompanied by philosophical treatises or rational reflection on laws—as if to say, now that we are the beneficiaries of revelation, we are excused from further rational reflection on law. One should wonder, however, whether Maimonides intends the description of the replacement of *nomoi* with revealed law as a description of the way things are when he arrives on the scene or as an extolling of this state of affairs.[18] If it is merely a description, it could be compatible with the view that Maimonides intends to change this state of affairs. Among other things, I hope to begin to show that he engages in rational reflection on law in a manner incompatible with conventionalism, as well as with natural law, though in a manner compatible with the natural right or justice teaching of Plato and Aristotle.

Eight Chapters, Chapter 6, and *Guide* 3.26, both now included in the *Sourcebook* for the first time, are central texts in the debate over whether Maimonides is a conventionalist or natural law theorist. In *Eight Chapters,* Maimonides characterizes most of the laws of the Second Table of the Decalogue as "generally accepted" (*mashhūr*). He contrasts these with "traditional laws" (*al-sharā'i' al-sam'iyya*): for example, mixing meat with milk. In *Guide* 3.26, he appeals to the same distinction with traditional Hebrew terms: *mishpatim* (judgments) for the former and *ḥuqqim* (statutes) for the latter. In *Eight Chapters,* Maimonides argues that the laws in the Second Table should not be characterized as "rational," as they have been by the dialectical theologians. And he claims that if "traditional laws" had not been forbidden by the Law, they would not be bad. Those who view Maimonides as a natural law theorist claim that he rejects "rational" as a description for the laws in the Second Table because he wants all of the Law to be viewed as rational. Those who view Maimonides as a conventionalist claim that the designation "generally accepted" means that the forbidden actions are bad merely because society has declared them so. There is a grain of truth in both interpretations. In keeping with the natural law view, Maimonides does hold that all of the Law aims at some good either for society or for the individual (*Guide* 3.27–28). In keeping with the conventionalist view, the designation "generally accepted" falls well short of the kind of universality that the "rational law" or "natural law" tradition intends. But the true sense of "generally accepted" is a delicate matter, indeed—and one often misunderstood, because it is not understood properly in the light of its Aristotelian origins.

As Leo Strauss has noted, "generally accepted opinion" in Maimonides' parlance is derived by way of Alfarabi from Aristotle. The Aristotelian

18. This interpretation of the role of the *Treatise on the Art of Logic* should be compared with a similar interpretation of Alfarabi's *Enumeration of the Sciences,* an obvious precursor to the *Art of Logic* (which, contrary to its title, is something of an enumeration of the sciences). For this interpretation of the *Enumeration,* see Muhsin Mahdi, *Alfarabi and the Foundation of Islamic Political Philosophy* (Chicago: University of Chicago Press, 2001), 82.

term is *endoxa*.[19] Unfortunately, Aristotle's treatment of *endoxa* can lend itself to a conventionalist reading. As he explains in the opening page of his *Topics*, there are different groupings of *endoxa:* at one extreme, the *endoxa* of the wise; at the other extreme, the *endoxa* of the multitude. The latter case could, at least in some instances, be interpreted as referring to wholly unexamined common opinion.[20] Where, then, would the Second Table of the Decalogue fall, toward the extreme of the unexamined or that of the wise?

To begin to answer this question, let us consider what Maimonides intends in his criticism of the dialectical theologians (practitioners of *kalām*), who view the laws of the Second Table as "rational laws." According to the Jewish inheritor of the Mu'tazilite *kalām*, Saadya Gaon, the designation "rational" means that these laws could either easily be deduced by reason or are intuitively obvious (see selection 12). Indeed, both Saadya and the Mu'tazila argue that laws such as those in the Second Table were revealed only because it might take reason some time to arrive at them. If so, then, in principle, reason alone is sufficient to propagate them, or in the parlance of Thomas, to promulgate them (*Summa Theologiae* 1–2.90.4). Yet one wonders whether by designating such laws as either rational or natural, these thinkers do not leave their traditions open to taking these laws for granted. At least, we may conclude that the designations "rational" and "natural" promulgate law in a manner far weaker than viewing them as divinely revealed.

In addition to these difficulties surrounding the origin of law in the natural or rational law tradition, the Mu'tazilite *kalām* and its Jewish proponents, such as Saadya and Halevi, stress God's just reward and punishment, or recompense.[21] The key problem in their account is that if law is inherently rational or natural, then should not its recompense be just as rational or natural or even necessary?

As Maimonides explains in both *Eight Chapters* (chap. 1) and the *Guide* (1.71 and 73), the dialectical theologians' main ailment was that they conflated that which can be imagined with the "nature of existence." That is, they thought that whatever can be imagined or is logically possible must also be possible in reality. They failed to measure the possible nature of existence against the limits placed upon it by necessity. This led to quite extreme results among the theological opponents of the Mu'tazila—that is, the Ash'ariyya—who, at times, developed fatalistic views that haunted medieval Islam, and which Maimonides is at great pains to oppose within Judaism. Although the Mu'tazila stressed human freedom, they were no more vigilant than the Ash'ariyya in distinguishing the merely logically possible from the "nature of existence." In addition and in general, the Mu'tazila argued for the compatibility of reason and revelation. And in particular, they argued that God's reasonableness must extend so far as to guarantee that for every evil or ill suffered in this life, some recompense would be offered in the next life. In effect, if the innocent suffer in this life, they suffer only so that God might reward them all the more in the next life (see *Guide* 3.17). What would appear harmless at first becomes more problematic upon closer inspection. Leaving aside the support this understanding might lend to fatalism, it would also lend itself to the view that God's recompense is a requirement of reason (or of nature). Now, Aquinas, at least, erects a bulwark against this by arguing that among the reasons *divine* law is needed in addition to natural law is that only God can understand the interior movements of the heart and only God can guarantee recompense supernaturally, especially beatitude (*Summa Theologiae* 1–2.91.4). In other words, not only is God the only being capable of knowing sinful intentions but God is also the only being who knows of crimes committed by human beings, unseen by other human beings. Furthermore, only God can rectify the residue of injustice resulting from crimes undetected and unpunished by human authorities.[22] Still, comparison of the Mu'tazila with Aquinas suggests that the very designation of a law as rational or natural might run the risk of leading one to expect recompense as somehow automatic. In other words, if certain laws such as the Second Table are designated as rational or natural, is there not some risk that one might come to take for granted the necessity (or rationality) of divine recompense, much as one runs the risk of taking

19. See Strauss, *Persecution and the Art of Writing*, 97.

20. Cf. Alfarabi *Attainment of Happiness* 40, 50; and Mahdi's note 5 to section 40 in his English translation of the *Philosophy of Plato and Aristotle* (Ithaca, NY: Cornell University Press, 1969, 2002).

21. Strauss, *Persecution and the Art of Writing*, 99–100 n. 14.

22. Cf. Plato *Republic* 613C ff.

for granted the giving (or promulgation) of the "natural law"—indeed, by nature.

My point is not that Aquinas falls into this trap but that talk of rational or natural law lends itself to taking law for granted. In addition, I believe that Maimonides' stress on the "generally accepted" character of such laws highlights their precariousness, both as to origin and as to recompense. This very precariousness stands as a constant reminder that the Law, even the features of it that we view as most obvious, rational, or natural, can be undermined all too easily. I believe that Maimonides' avoidance of the designation "rational," favored by the dialectical theologians, had in part to do with a desire to preserve in the minds of the adherents of the Law its dependence on God, as to both origin and recompense.

Perhaps the strongest support for my interpretation of Maimonides' reasons for opposing the appellation "rational law" is the drift of Western thought about "natural law," after Aquinas. On this decisive point, the modern natural law teaching is more or less opposed to that of Aquinas. Locke, in the opening parts of his *Essay concerning Human Understanding,* attacks the idea of innate principles of practical reason such as Thomas seems to imply in *Summa Theologiae* 1–2.94.2. Rather than rest natural law on the possession of a natural inclination toward the good of the community,[23] the modern account sets forth, in place of innate principles of practical reason, natural laws based upon the more trustworthy, because lower and more solid, "law of nature," which is that each man desires to preserve himself. How could Thomistic natural law with its high ends, including the desire to seek or know God, undergo such a fundamental transformation? To answer this question, we need to review briefly the character of the natural law in Thomas and to consider the historical circumstances of writers like Hobbes and Locke. The key feature in Thomas's account that lends itself to this transformation is his inclusion of the low end of the scale of natural goods in a way not countenanced by Aristotle (or Maimonides). Aquinas's lowest good is simply the good of self-preservation. Furthermore, by identifying the secondary precepts of the natural law with the Second Table of the Decalogue, he reinforces the view that what is natural determines the flooring beneath which man should be expected not to descend.[24] In contrast, Aristotle and Maimonides stress the high end of such goods. Although Maimonides does not appeal to what is *natural* in placing stress on the high end, he affirms that what makes the Law divine is that it aims at the cultivation of *knowledge* of the highest things (*Guide* 2.40, immediately following the apparent denigration of the pagan *nomoi*). Aristotle and Maimonides, in short, establish an almost impossibly high standard of what is natural. Of course, Aquinas admits comparable ends in his natural law, yet he does so in nearly the same breath as he admits the lowest of ends, self-preservation. Without intending it in the least, might Aquinas, as well as other natural law theorists, be said to set the stage for later, far lower conceptions of natural law? Perhaps all one might need to make the shift would be the judgment that the higher ends are just too dangerous to focus on anymore. Whether that judgment was correct, it seems to have been the judgment of thinkers like Hobbes and Locke.

Now we can return to the question of where the Second Table of the Decalogue fits within the range of meanings of generally accepted opinion or *endoxa.* That is, is it merely what is generally accepted by the multitude or by the wise? Although the Second Table lacks the universality of the truly natural or rational, I believe that Maimonides intends it to possess some of the reflected light of the opinions of the wise. I say this because in *Eight Chapters,* Chapter 6, Maimonides argues that things such as murder and theft that are generally accepted as bad are things that, according to the philosophers, it would be better not to desire rather than to desire and resist successfully. Contrary to those who attribute conventionalism to Maimonides, he implies that desiring some objects is naturally bad—though he studiously avoids reference to "rational law" to make his point. For conventionalist interpreters of Maimonides, the substitution of the Law for Aristotelian views of morality is so complete that there cannot be anything naturally better or worse.[25] Not so for Maimonides. In recent years he has acquired a reputation for conventionalism because he denigrates morality

23. It must be underlined that Aquinas counters this natural inclination toward the common good with the "tinder of (original) sin," which works at cross-purposes with that more desirable inclination (*Summa Theologiae* 1–2.91.6).

24. Cf. Strauss, "On Natural Law," 140–42.

25. See, for example, Fox, *Interpreting Maimonides,* 115–16.

profoundly (especially in *Guide* 1.2) and because interpreters have been tempted, by an apparent similarity between Maimonides' denigration of morality and that of early modern philosophers, to forget the differences between Maimonides and moderns such as Spinoza. As I have argued elsewhere, that appearance is deceiving. Above all, it must be remembered that in Maimonides' context, the only way for philosophy to receive a hearing was for him to engage in such a demotion of morality. Yet the reader must be careful not to confuse such a demotion with similar-looking arguments for conventionalism, relativism, or nihilism. Maimonides does not jettison an Aristotelian sense of what is naturally just—nor does he jettison that key faculty that is the remote ancestor of Aquinas's synderesis or conscience, namely, prudence. Rather, he is very cautious not to insinuate that the Law is the product of human reason alone—lest its divine origin and the promise of divine recompense be doubted. Indeed, without these, the Law possesses little more support than can be provided by the generally provident God of the philosophers.[26]

26. See Joshua Parens, "Prudence, Imagination, and Determination of Law in Alfarabi and Maimonides," in *Enlightening Revolutions*, ed. Svetozar Minkov (Lanham, MD: Lexington Books, 2006), 31–55, esp. 35.

TWELVE

SAADYA GAON

The Book of Doctrines and Beliefs

Translated by Alexander Altmann

Saadya Gaon (Sa'adya [also transliterated as Saadia and Saadiah] ben Joseph al-Fayyūmī, 892–942) was born in Abū Suweir in the district of Fayyūm (Upper Egypt). What little is known about his family or about his education is mostly conjectural. His opponents attacked him by attacking his father's apparent lack of education. What education Saadya received is inferred primarily from his having written his first two books, a Hebrew lexicon and rhyming dictionary and a Hebrew grammar, in his early twenties, and from his early correspondence with another leading light of his time, Isaac Israeli. In 915, Saadya emigrated from Egypt, for uncertain reasons, to Israel and eventually to Babylonia. According to the historian al-Mas'ūdi, Saadya studied under Abū Kathir Yaḥya al-Kātib during his stay in the Land of Israel. (Ibn Ḥazm, the extreme literalist in Qur'anic interpretation identifies this teacher and Saadya, among others, as Jewish *mutakallimūn.*) Some time before 921, Saadya left Israel, staying at least for a time in Aleppo. In 922, while still in Aleppo, Saadya entered into a dispute with Aaron ben Meir, the head of the Palestinian Talmudic academy in Jerusalem, about the dates for Passover and Rosh ha-Shanah—a technical point of great significance to Jewish life. Saadya sided with the Babylonian Talmudic academy in taking the more traditional approach to determining the date. His arguments against Ben Meir, presented in his *Book of the Festivals,* won him the attention of the Babylonian academies. Indeed, he was appointed to teach at the Pumbedita academy in 922. In 928, Saadya was appointed to the gaonate of the Sura academy. The gaon was not only the head of the academy but also the (or one of the leading) religious leader(s) of the Jewish people. His secular counterpart was the exilarch, who was afforded substantial political autonomy by the Babylonian authorities, that is, the caliphate in Baghdad. Much controversy surrounded Saadya's appointment. He seems to have been the first non-Babylonian Jew to be appointed to the gaonate; he was only thirty-six years old when appointed. Within two years of his appointment, a major falling-out took place between the gaon and the exilarch, David ben Zakkai. The exilarch had recently passed judgment in a case in which he was to profit by the decision. Saadya refused to give his signature to approve this judgment. Consequently, the exilarch appointed a gaon to replace Saadya, and Saadya appointed an exilarch to replace Ben Zakkai. For a brief period, two geonim and two exilarchs ruled at odds with one another. Eventually, the original exilarch bribed the new, usurper caliph, al-Qāhir, to certify his exilarchate and his counter-gaon.

This conflict, which began in 930, was brought to a more sustainable conclusion in 938 when Saadya was reinstalled as gaon, the position he held until his death in 942.

As gaon, Saadya produced a significant if dispersed body of *halakhic* (legal) writings. Scholars are still working to uncover all of his contributions. In addition to his philological writings, mentioned above, he produced other works in many areas, including an Arabic commentary on and translation of the entire Hebrew Bible, a commentary on the mystical *Book of Creation*, and a complete *Order [Siddur] of Prayers* for the Jewish year, including the introduction of new prayers. We are most interested in what happens to be his greatest work, the principal writing that would have justified Ibn Ḥazm's labeling Saadya a *mutakallim*,[1] his *Book of Doctrines and Beliefs*. Scholars sometimes identify this as the first work of medieval Jewish philosophy. For our purposes, however, it is crucial to highlight its *kalām* character. Recent scholars have shown that the *Book of Doctrines* follows a classic pattern established in Muʿtazila *kalām*. The two central doctrines of the Muʿtazila, God's justice and unity, are the central themes of the *Book of Doctrines*.[2] Leaving aside the introduction to the *Book of Doctrines*, which contains important inquiries into the bases of belief (*iʿtiqād*), the first two chapters argue for God's unity by first attempting to prove the world was created and that God is its creator. The last eight chapters all touch in one way or another on God's justice: Chapter 3 concerns God's laws and their prophetic origin; Chapter 4, the requirement of God's justice that human beings be free to obey; Chapter 5, the various moral human types; Chapter 6 concerns the nature and destiny of body and soul, refuting doctrines such as metempsychosis; Chapter 7, resurrection of the dead; Chapter 8, the redemption of the People Israel and why exile has for so long been the fate of the Jewish people; Chapter 9, the world to come; Chapter 10, the fitting, moral way of life.

Our selection is drawn from Chapter 3 of *The Book of Doctrines and Beliefs*. This reading contains what is perhaps the first discussion in the Jewish *kalām* tradition of the intellectual or rational law teaching—what came to be known in the West generally as the natural law teaching. It attempts to establish a divide between rational laws and revealed laws. Maimonides objects to this distinction and the very conception of a rational or intellectual law in our selection from *Eight Chapters*, Chapter 6 (below, selection 16).

S. Landauer published the Judeo-Arabic edition,[3] *Kitāb al-amānāt wa-al-iʿtiqādāt* (1880), based on one manuscript (Oxford) with a few corrections based on the other extant manuscript (Leningrad). Alexander Altmann based his abridged edition on these texts. His edition first appeared in *Three Jewish Philosophers* (Oxford: East and West Library, 1946; repr., New York: Jewish Publication Society, 1961). This abridged edition is now available by itself as *Saadya Gaon: The Book of Doctrines and Beliefs* (Indianapolis: Hackett, 2002), with a new introduction by Daniel H. Frank.

CHAPTER 3: COMMANDMENT AND PROHIBITION

Section 2. The Two Classes of Law: Laws of Reason and Laws of Revelation

After these introductory remarks, I now come to the subject proper. I declare that our Lord (be He exalted and glorified) has informed us through the words of His prophets that He wishes us to lead a religious life by following the religion (*dīn*) that He instituted for us. This religion contains laws (*sharīʿa*) that He has prescribed for us, and that it is our duty to keep and to fulfill in sincerity, as is said: *This day the Lord thy God commanded thee to do these statutes and judgments; thou shalt, therefore, observe and do them with all thy heart and with all thy soul* [Deut. 26:16]. His messengers established these laws for us by wondrous signs and miracles, and we commenced to keep and fulfill them forthwith. Later we found that speculation confirms the necessity of the Law for us. It would,

1. See Henry Malter, *Saadiah Gaon: His Life and Work* (New York: Hermon Press, 1969), 32–33.

2. Cf. Haggai Ben-Shammai, "Kalām in Medieval Jewish Philosophy," in *History of Jewish Philosophy*, ed. Daniel H. Frank and Oliver Leaman (London and New York: Routledge, 1997), 115–48, esp. 127–32.

3. Aside from some minor differences in grammar, Judeo-Arabic is Arabic written in Hebrew characters.

however, not have been appropriate to leave us to our own devices.[4]

It is desirable that I should explain which matters and aspects [of the divine Law] speculation confirms as necessary. (1) I maintain that reason bids us[5] respond to every benefactor either by returning his kindness if he is in need of it, or by offering thanks if he is not in need of recompense. Now since this is a dictate of reason itself, it would not have been fitting for the Creator (be He exalted and glorified) to waive this right in respect of Himself, but it was necessary that He should command his creatures to worship Him and to render thanks unto Him for having created them.[6] (2) Reason further lays down that the wise man should not permit himself to be vilified and treated with contempt. It is similarly necessary that the Creator should forbid his servants to treat Him in this way.[7] (3) Reason further prescribes that human beings should be forbidden to trespass upon one another's rights by any sort of aggression. It is likewise necessary that the wise should not permit them to act in such a way. (4) Reason, furthermore, permits[8] a wise man to employ a workman for any kind of work and pay him his wages for the sole purpose of allowing him to earn something; since this is a matter which results in benefit to the workman and causes no harm to the employer.[9]

If we put together these four points, their total is tantamount to a summary of the laws that our Lord has commanded us. That is to say, he imposed upon us the duty of knowing and serving Him with a sincere heart, as the prophet said: *And thou, Solomon, my son, know thou the God of thy father, and serve Him with a whole heart and with a willing mind* [1 Chron. 28:9]. Then he forbade us to hurl at Him insult and abuse although it causes Him no harm, seeing that it would not be consonant with wisdom to permit it. Thus it is said: *Whosoever curseth his God, shall bear his sin* [Lev. 24:15]. He did not permit us to trespass upon one another's rights nor to defraud one another, as is said: *Ye shall not steal; neither shall ye deal falsely, nor lie one to another* [Lev. 19:11]. These three groups of laws and their subdivisions form the first of the two classes of Law.[10] The first group of the three includes humbleness before God, worship, standing up in His presence, and so forth. All this is written in the Law.[11] The second group includes the prohibition of idolatry,[12] swearing falsely by His name, describing Him by derogatory attributes, and so forth. All this is written in the Law. To the third group belongs the practice of justice, truth-telling, equity, and impartiality, the avoidance of homicide, adultery, theft, tale-bearing, and trickery against one's fellow man; also the command that the believer should love his neighbor as he loves himself and whatever is involved in these precepts. All this is written in the Law.

In regard to all the things which He commands us to do, He has implanted approval of them in our reason; and in regard to all the things which He forbids us to do, He has implanted disapproval of them in our reason, as is said in the Book of Wisdom—wisdom being identical with reason—*For my mouth shall utter truth, and wickedness is an abomination to my lips* [Prov. 8:7].

The second class of Law[13] consists of matters regarding which reason passes no judgment in the way either of approval or disapproval so far as their essence is concerned. But our Lord has given us an abundance of such commandments and prohibitions in order to increase our reward and happiness through them, as is said: *The Lord was pleased, for His righteousness' sake, to make the Law great and glorious* [Isa. 42:21].[14] That which belongs to the things commanded by God assumes the character of "good," and that which belongs to the things forbidden by Him assumes the character of "evil" on account of the service thereby performed. Thus the second [class of Law] is in

4. Saadya echoes the Mu'tazilite view that the rational laws are discoverable by reason, but such a process takes considerable time. Consequently, God revealed His Law and thus enabled mankind to follow the right path immediately.

5. For an explanation of Saadya's usage of reason (*al-'aql*) here, and its Mu'tazilite background, the reader should consult the translator's article: Alexander Altmann, "Saadya's Conception of Law," *Bulletin of the John Rylands Library* 28.2 (1944): 320–39.

6. Gratitude is the classic example adduced by the Mu'tazila to demonstrate the existence of rational law.

7. This sentence refers to blasphemy and inappropriate attributes of God.

8. This fourth group of laws is not dictated, but only permitted by reason.

9. Cf. *Mishnah, Avot* 2:21.

10. A reference to the distinction between rational (*'aqliyya*) and revealed (literally, "heard," *sam'iyya*) law.

11. Literally, "is in the text" (*naṣṣ*) of the Torah.

12. Literally, "association" (*shirk*).

13. Revealed law. Cf. the final paragraph of this selection.

14. Here, Saadya alludes to an argument he offered in sec. 1 of this chapter, namely, that those who strain to obey the Law are more virtuous than those who obey with ease. Cf. the philosophic view as described in Maimonides *Eight Chapters,* Chapter 6 (below, selection 16).

fact joined to the first class.[15] In spite of this,[16] one cannot fail, upon closer examination, to find in it some slender moral benefits and rational basis to act against the greater moral benefits and firmer rational basis attached to the first class [of Law].

It is proper that I should first and foremost discuss the rational laws (*al-sharā'i' al-'aqliyya*). Wisdom lays down[17] that bloodshed must be prevented among human beings, for if it were allowed people would annihilate each other. That would mean, apart from the pain suffered, a frustration of the purpose that the Wise (God) intended to achieve through them. Homicide cuts them off from the attainment of any purpose He created and employs them for.

Wisdom further suggests the prohibition of adultery; for, otherwise, human beings would become similar to the animals. No person would be able to know and honor his father in return for the education he received at his hands. Nor would a father be able to bequeath to his son his means of livelihood though the son inherited his existence from him; nor would one know one's other relatives such as paternal and maternal uncles; nor would one be able to show them the kindness due to relatives.

Wisdom further imposes the prohibition of theft; for if it were permitted some people would rely on their ability to steal some other people's property, and would not do any productive work[18] nor amass wealth. But if everyone relied on this sort of subsistence, theft itself would be rendered impossible by the abolition of property since nothing at all would be found to steal.

Wisdom further lays down, and this is perhaps its first principle, that one should speak the truth and abstain from falsehood, for truth is a statement that accords with facts and actual conditions, whereas a lie is a statement that does not accord with facts and actual conditions. When the senses perceive an object in a certain state, and the soul ascribes to it another state, then the two statements conflict in the soul, and from their contradiction the soul knows that there is something wrong.[19]

I will furthermore say this: I have met certain people who think that our selection of these four things as objects of reprobation is wrong. In their opinion that is to be reprobated which causes them pain and grief, and the good, in their opinion, is that which causes them pleasure and rest. To this proposition I reply at length in chapter four on the subject of justice.[20] I will here mention only part of the reply. I say that one who holds this opinion has ignored all the arguments which I have adduced,[21] and one who ignores this is a fool with whom we need not trouble ourselves. Nevertheless, I shall not be content until I have compelled him to admit that his view is self-contradictory and impossible. I declare that the killing of an enemy while pleasing to the killer causes pain to the killed; that the seizure of any property or married woman while pleasing to the person who commits this act causes pain to the person who suffers it. According to the opinion of those who hold this theory, it would necessarily follow from their premise that each of these acts is both wisdom and folly at the same time; wisdom because it affords pleasure to the person who commits murder, robbery, and rape; and folly because it causes pain to his victim. But every theory that involves a self-contradiction is invalid. The contradictory qualities may also appear combined in relation to one person as in the case of honey into which poison has been dropped. In this case the same person eats something which affords pleasure and causes death at the same time. Surely, this compels them to admit that [according to their theory] wisdom and folly will exist together.

The second class of Law concerns such matters as are of a neutral character from the point of view of reason,[22] but which the Law has made the objects of commandment in some cases, and of prohibition in others, leaving the rest in their neutral state. Instances are the distinguishing from ordinary days of Sabbath and festivals; the selection of certain individuals to be prophets and leaders[23]; the prohibition to eat certain foodstuffs; the avoidance of sexual intercourse with certain

15. Because reason "permits" the fourth group of laws above, devoted to service to God; the second class of Law, based on service only, is reasonable, if to a lesser degree than the first class.

16. The second class's nonrational basis.

17. Cf. Altmann, "Saadya's Conception of Law," for evidence that this marks the beginning of a revised version of the argument so far. To start with, the translator notes the change from "Reason bids..." (see note 5 above) to "Wisdom (*ḥikma*) lays down..."

18. Literally, "cultivate the world."

19. Literally, "strange."

20. *Amānāt*, 149–50.

21. That is, the four dialectical arguments against homicide, adultery, theft, and falsehood.

22. Literally, "concerns that which is permissible [i.e., neither commanded nor prohibited] by reason."

23. *Imām*.

people; the abstention enforced during periods of impurity. The great motive for the observance of these principles and the laws derived and branching out from them is, of course, the command of our Lord and the promotion of our happiness resulting from it, but I find for most of them also some minor and partial motives of a useful character. I wish to point out and to discuss some of them, realizing as I do that God's wisdom (be He blessed and exalted) is above all this.

The distinction conferred upon certain times has these advantages: In the first place, it enables us to desist from our work at certain times and obtain a rest from our many travails; furthermore, to enjoy the pleasures of learned pursuits, and to have the benefit of additional prayer; there is also the advantage that people will be free to meet at gatherings and discuss matters concerning their religion and proclaim them in public, and so forth.

The distinction conferred upon a certain person has these advantages: It enables the public to receive reliable instruction from him, to ask his intercession; and it enables him to inspire people with a desire for godliness that they may attain something like his own rank, and to devote his efforts to promoting piety amongst men, since he is worthy of that; and similar activities.

The prohibition of eating certain animals has this advantage: It makes it impossible to liken any of the animals to the Creator, since it is unthinkable that one should permit oneself either to eat or to declare as impure what one likens to God; also it prevents people from worshiping any of the animals, since it is unthinkable that one should worship either what serves for food or what one declares as impure.

The prohibition of sexual intercourse with certain categories of women has this advantage: in the case of a married woman, I have already stated the reason before. As to one's mother, sister and daughter, the reason is this: the necessities of daily life foster intimacy between the members of a family. Consequently, if marriage between them were permitted, they would indulge in sexual license.[24] Another purpose is to prevent men from being attracted only by those women who are of beautiful appearance and rejecting those who are not, when they see that their own relatives do not desire them.

The laws of defilement and purity have this advantage: they teach men humility and reverence; they strengthen in them [the desire] to pray once more after a period of neglect;[25] they make people more conscious of the dignity of the Holy Place after they have abstained from entering it for a period; and they turn their minds to the fear of God.

If one examines most of these revealed laws (*al-sharā'i' al-sam'iyya*)[26] in the above fashion, one will find for them a great number of partial motives and reasons of usefulness. But the wisdom of the Creator and His knowledge is above everything human beings can attain, as is said: *For the heavens are higher than the earth, so are My ways higher than your ways* [Isa. 55:9].

24. Cf. Maimonides *Guide* 3.49. Saadya wrote a treatise on the subject, *Treatise on "Forbidden Marriages,"* a fragment of which has been edited with an English translation and introduction by H. Hirschfeld in *Jewish Quarterly Review* 17.4 (1905): 713–20.

25. Cf. *Babylonian Talmud, Berakhot* 20b ff.

26. Literally, "heard laws." Cf. *Eight Chapters,* Chapter 6 (below, selection 16); and Halevi *Kuzari* 2:48 (below, selection 13). Because Halevi uses so many different senses of law, Kogan has rendered the phrase, rendered here "revealed laws," as "traditional Laws" with the capitalization of "Law" to indicate Halevi's use of *sharī'a.*

THIRTEEN

JUDAH HALEVI

The Book of Refutation and Proof on Behalf of the Despised Religion, or, The Kuzari

Translated by Barry Kogan (and Lawrence Berman)

Judah Halevi (Yehuda ben Shmuel ha-Levi, ca. 1075–1141) was likely born in Tudela on the Muslim side of the border with Castile. Until the beginning of the twentieth century he was thought to have been born in Toledo, the capital of the Christian kingdom of Castile. Indeed, he is sometimes referred to as "the Castilian" and did spend significant periods of his life in Christian territory. His life was shaped for better or for worse by living at the crossroads of the Spanish Reconquista and the Almoravid invasion of the late 1090s, and his life came to an end shortly after the Almohad invasion of the 1130s. One thing is certain: the events of Halevi's lifetime brought home to him the special precariousness of Jewish life at this time in exile. He may have spent some of his childhood in Castile, the child of wealthy and educated Jews. In one way or another, he received a good education in Hebrew and Arabic, including all of the biblical, Talmudic, philosophic, and *kalām* learning that would serve him so well later. (His Hebrew poetry, for which he is most famous, displays the Arabic styles and conventions of the time.) Halevi traveled to the Muslim south at a relatively early age, intending to study in the Jewish center of learning in Granada. He was befriended by the famous poet Moses Ibn Ezra, after winning a competition based on a poem by Ibn Ezra. Along the way to Granada, he spent some time in Cordova and Lucena. He may have studied with Joseph Ibn Migash in Lucena—but certainly was in contact with him. He left Granada with the Almoravid invasion (ca. 1090s). For the next twenty years, Halevi traveled, spending some time in Toledo. His renown as a poet, at a relatively early age, spread throughout Muslim and Christian Spain. In Toledo, however, he practiced medicine (and engaged in trade) and at some point married. He fathered one daughter, who is believed to have married Isaac Ibn Ezra, the son of the famous poet and biblical exegete Abraham Ibn Ezra, with whom Halevi was good friends. In 1108, Halevi's patron Solomon Ibn Ferrizuel, a nobleman in the court of Alfonso VI of Castile, was murdered. Halevi set out on his travels, again. Over the next thirty years, he made the decision gradually to immigrate to the Land of Israel. In 1140, he traveled to Alexandria, and in 1141 to Cairo—to which his renown had spread. From Cairo, he set sail for Ashkelon or Acre. He died, under suspicious circumstances, after approximately a month in the Land of Israel, about which he had written so much poetry.

The vast majority of Halevi's oeuvre is poetry. He is widely viewed as the greatest Hebrew poet of the medieval period, and perhaps of all time, leaving aside the Psalms. He wrote approximately 80 love poems, 180 poems of eulogy and lamentation, 350 liturgical poems, and, perhaps his most important works, 35 poems called *Songs of Zion* and *Songs of the Sea*—the latter about the journey to Zion.

In addition to this large body of poetry, Halevi wrote one of the most important defenses of Judaism in its history. Widely known simply as the *Kuzari,* this large work is titled the *Book of Refutation and Proof on Behalf of the Despised Religion.* It is the surprising story of the conversion of the king of the Khazars (*Khazari* in Arabic, thus *Kuzari* in Hebrew) and his followers to Judaism.[1] (The Khazars formed a Turkic nation—or empire, as some would have it—straddling present-day Ukraine, southern Russia, and Kazakhstan.) The *Kuzari* is a dialogue between the king, a philosopher, and a sage or scholar of Judaism, a scholar of Christianity, and a scholar of Islam. Besides one of the most powerful defenses of Judaism, it contains one of the most searching critiques of philosophy in medieval literature. It also adds greater depth and complexity to the *kalām* distinction set forth by Saadya. Like Saadya, Halevi distinguishes between intellectual (or rational) and revealed laws; however, his account of intellectual laws (or *nomoi*) alludes to at least three different types of law:[2] (1) the intellectual laws of the philosophers, (2) those of the pagans or Sabians (e.g., 1:81), and (3) those of the *mutakallimūn* (e.g., 2:48, 3:7, 3:11). Type 1 can also be subdivided into (a) the governance of the solitary (e.g., 1:1) and (b) the laws established by philosophers such as Plato in his *Laws* (cf. 1:81 below). And because Halevi refers primarily to pagan philosophers, there can be overlap between type 1b and type 2. The reader should attend to Halevi's obvious rejection of type 1a, and his almost equally obvious embrace of type 3. He reveals his allegiance to the rational law tradition of Saadya in expressing and attempting to justify these preferences.

The *Kuzari* is a dialogue in five parts. As a dialogue rather than a treatise, its contents are difficult to summarize. Treatise[3] 1 presents the Khazar king's search for the way of life containing fitting (religious) actions. (It is one of the author's conceits that the king has already been assured through a prophetic dream that his intentions are good; it is his actions that are wanting.) The bulk of the conversation consists in the Jewish scholar or sage's efforts to defend the despised religion. Treatise 2 opens with the king eager to convert to Judaism. It contains discussions of the names of God, the election of the Land of Israel and of the People Israel, in opposition to the king's penchant for more ascetic, otherworldly actions. Treatise 3 develops the portrait of the exemplary Jew, at least of the day, as the "guardian of the city." At once, the scholar opposes the asceticism of the Qaraites (a sect that rejected the Oral Law or Talmud and adopted literalism in the interpretation of the Bible), as well as of the other monotheistic religions, and defends the value of the rabbinic tradition. Treatise 4 takes up the names of God once more and attempts to plumb the depths of the link between the mysterious God of Abraham and the prophets (as opposed to the God of the philosophers) with the aid of the mystical work the *Book of Creation* (on which Saadya wrote a commentary). Treatise 5 is devoted to *kalām* arguments in defense of the religion, against the philosophers.

The first modern edition of the *Kuzari* was Hartwig Hirschfeld's *Das Buch al-Chazari, im arabischen Urtext, sowie in der hebräischen Übersetzung* (Leipzig, 1887). Barry Kogan (and the late Lawrence V. Berman) have translated the *Kuzari* from the critical Judeo-Arabic[4] edition by D. H. Baneth and H. Ben-Shammai: *Kitāb al-radd wa-al-dalīl fī al-dīn al-dhalīl* (Jerusalem: Magnes Press, 1977). The following are excerpts from their translation, which is forthcoming in the Yale Judaica Series. The page numbers in brackets refer to the Hirschfeld edition.

1. For information on the historical reality of the Jewish Khazars, the interested reader should see Kevin Alan Brook, *The Jews of Khazaria,* 2nd ed. (Lanham, MD: Rowman and Littlefield, 2006).

2. For a detailed tracking of these types of law, the reader should see Leo Strauss, "The Law of Reason in the *Kuzari,*" in *Persecution of the Art of Writing* (1952; repr., Chicago: University of Chicago Press, 1988), 95–141.

3. The term "Treatise" (*ma'amar*) for the parts of the *Kuzari* was inserted by the editors, Baneth and Ben-Shammai. It is a standard term, like "book" and "chapter," that has no bearing on the character of the *Kuzari* as a dialogue rather than a treatise.

4. Aside from some minor differences in grammar, Judeo-Arabic is Arabic written in Hebrew characters.

TREATISE ONE

(1:1) I was asked about whatever argumentation I had against those who differ with us, such as the philosophers and the adherents of the religions, as well as the dissenters[5] who differ with the multitude [of Jews]; and I recalled what I had heard of the arguments of the sage, who was with the king of the Khazars when the latter adopted the religion of the Jews some 400 years ago today according to the testimony mentioned in the "Book of Histories."

A dream came to him repeatedly as though an angel were addressing him, saying, "Your intention is pleasing to God, but your actions are not." Now he used to be very diligent with regard to the worship prescribed by the Khazar religion to the extent that he himself used to officiate at the temple-service and the sacrifices with pure and sincere intent. Nevertheless, each time he exerted himself diligently with regard to those acts, the angel came to him at night, telling him, "Your intention is pleasing, but your actions are not." This prompted him to investigate the various religions and sects, and ultimately both he and the multitude of the Khazars became Jews. Some of the arguments of the sage seemed persuasive to me and in agreement with my own belief. Accordingly, I thought that I should record [2] this argumentation just as it took place, *and the intelligent will understand* [Dan. 12:10].

It has been reported that when the king of the Khazars realized in his dream that his intention was pleasing to God but his actions were not pleasing, and [when he further realized] in his sleep that He was commanding him to seek out those actions that are pleasing to God, he asked a philosopher about the latter's belief.

The philosopher said to him: Not so! There is no "being pleased" and no "feeling hatred" on the part of God, because He, may He be exalted, is beyond desires and aims. The reason is that [having] an aim indicates there is a deficiency in the one who has it, while achieving one's aim is a perfection for him [who does so]; but as long as it remains unfulfilled, it is a deficiency. Likewise, according to the philosophers, He is beyond [4] the knowledge of particulars because they change with the times, whereas there is no change in God's knowledge. Therefore, He is not aware of you, let alone of your intentions and your actions, nor does He hear your prayers or observe your movements.

Indeed, even though the philosophers say that He created you, this is meant only metaphorically because He is the cause of [all the] causes involved in the creation of every created thing, not because this [creation] was intended on His part. In fact, He did not create man at all because the world is eternal; and man has never ceased coming into being out of a man before him. Combined within him there are forms, natural dispositions, and character traits coming from his father, his mother, and his relatives, as well as qualities deriving from the different climates, lands, foods, and waters, interacting with the influences of the celestial spheres, the planets, and the signs of the zodiac, through the various relations that come about because of them.[6] Everything goes back to the First Cause, not because of an aim that it has, but rather [because of] an emanation from which a second cause emanated, then a third, and then a fourth set of causes. These causes and their effects are necessarily connected to one another and have become part of a [continuous] chain, just as you see them. Their necessary connection is eternal, just as the First Cause is eternal, it has no beginning.

Now every single individual in this world has causes by means of which it can be made complete. Thus, an individual whose causes are perfect becomes perfect, while an individual whose causes are deficient becomes deficient, like the Ethiopian who is capable of receiving no more than the form of a man and whose reasoning capacity is at the most deficient level possible. But the philosopher is someone who is provided with dispositions by means of which he receives the natural, moral, intellectual, and practical virtues, and does not lack anything pertaining to perfection. These perfections, however, are [at first only] potential, and they need both instruction and training in order to bring them to actuality. Only then will the individual aptitudes with which he was provided become manifest as, for instance, a perfection, a deficiency, or as [one of] an infinite variety of intermediate states.

Accordingly, a light belonging to the divine hierarchy, called the Active Intellect will attach itself

5. The Qaraites.

6. Cf. Alfarabi *Political Regime* secs. 65–67 (above, selection 3).

to the perfect individual, and his passive intellect will attach itself to that light with such a unifying attachment that the individual will think that he is that Active Intellect, with there being no difference between the two of them. His organs, I mean, the limbs of that individual, will be used only in performing the most perfect actions, at the most appropriate times, and in accordance with the very best conditions, as if they were organs of the Active Intellect itself and not of the material, passive intellect, which used to employ them before, sometimes rightly, but more often wrongly. The former always does so in the right way.

This degree is the ultimate end for which the perfect individual hopes after his soul has been purified of doubts and acquired mastery [6] of the sciences according to their true character, so that it may come to be like an angel. It thus attains the lowest level of the divine kingdom, which is separate from bodies. This is the level of the Active Intellect, an angel whose rank is just below that of the angel which is in charge of the sphere of the moon. They are both intellects devoid of the various kinds of matter and coeternal with the First Cause. They do not fear extinction—ever. Thus, the soul of the perfect man and that [Active] Intellect become one and the same thing. He is not concerned about the extinction of his body and his organs because he and that [Active Intellect] have become one and the same thing. His soul delights in life because he becomes a part of the group consisting of Hermes, Asclepius, Socrates, Plato, and Aristotle. In fact, he and they, and everyone who is at their level [of perfection], and the Active Intellect are one and the same thing. This, then, is what is called "God's being pleased," speaking symbolically or by way of approximation.[7]

Pursue it, therefore, and pursue knowledge of the true realities of things so that your intellect may become active and not passive. Keep to the way that is most just with regard to both character traits and actions because it helps one to conceive that which is true, to persevere in study, and to resemble that same Active Intellect. Contentment, modesty, and submissiveness, and every virtuous character trait will follow this, together with reverence for the First Cause, not in order to have it grant you its favor or to spare you its wrath, but in order for you to resemble the Active Intellect by preferring truth [over falsehood], describing every thing as it should be described, and believing it to be as it really is.

These are some of the attributes of the intellect. Once you can be described by this kind of belief, you will (1) not be concerned about what kind of Law you observe or profess or revere, or what kind of speech, language, or actions [you employ to do so]; or else, (2) create a religion for yourself for the sake of [cultivating] submissiveness, reverence, and praise, and also for governing your character traits, your home, and your city, if you are accepted by them; or, finally, (3) adopt the intellectual nomoi composed by the philosophers as your religion. Make the purification of your soul your purpose and your aim, and, in general, seek out the purification of your heart in any way that is possible for you, after first acquiring knowledge of the universals belonging to the sciences in accordance with their true character. Then you will achieve your goal, I mean, attachment to that spiritual entity, that is, the Active Intellect. Perhaps it will inform you and also command you through knowledge of hidden things conveyed by way of veridical dreams and images that are "right on the mark."

(1:2) The Khazar said to him: Your statement is certainly persuasive, but it's not in keeping with my request because I know by myself that I am pure [in my] soul and direct [my] actions [8] towards pleasing the Lord. Nevertheless, I was told that these actions are not pleasing, even though the intention is pleasing. Undoubtedly, therefore, there are certain actions that are pleasing in themselves and not dependent on mere opinions. Otherwise, [consider the fact] that the Christian and the Muslim, who have divided up the whole world between themselves, wage war against one another, although each of them has already directed his intention sincerely towards [pleasing] God. Each has taken up the monastic life; each has practiced asceticism; and each has fasted and prayed. Yet each has gone off determined to kill his counterpart, believing that the greatest good and [the best way to achieve] closeness to God lies in killing the other. And so, they are both killed, while each of them believes that his journey leads to the Garden [of Eden] and Paradise. But it is rationally impossible for both of them to be right.

(1:3) The philosopher said: There is no [call to] kill [either] one of these people according to the

7. Cf. Alfarabi, *Political Regime* sec. 85 (above, selection 3).

religion of the philosophers, since they follow the intellect.

(1:4) The Khazar said: What source of confusion could be greater, according to the philosophers, than the [Christian's and the Muslim's] belief in complete innovation—that the world was created in six days and that the First Cause speaks to individual human beings? Not only that, [there is the problem of God's] being beyond the knowledge of particulars, which the philosophers have declared regarding Him. Nevertheless, on the strength of the philosophers' actions, their [knowledge of the] sciences, their investigation [of the truth], and their personal efforts [to attain it], prophecy should have been well-known and widespread among them, owing to their attachment to spiritual things; and they should be described as having performed extraordinary feats, miracles, and wonders as well. But, in fact, we sometimes see veridical dreams come to someone who has not been concerned with science nor with the purification of his soul, while we find the very opposite of this in the case of those who have sought it. This proves that the divine order [of things] as well as the souls [of certain human beings] have a secret character other than what you have mentioned, O philosopher.

Then the Khazar said to himself: I will ask the Christians and the Muslims, for undoubtedly one of the two types of [religious] practice [they follow] is the one that is pleasing. As for the Jews, well, what is obvious from their despicable condition, paltry numbers, and everyone's loathing for them is quite sufficient [for me to ignore them]. Therefore, he invited a certain Christian scholar and asked him about his knowledge and his actions.

(1:10) The Khazar said: Yes, of course. It seems that I am forced to ask the Jews because they are the remnant of the children of Israel. For I now realize that they themselves are the proof that God has a Law on earth. He then summoned one of the sages of the Jews and asked him about his belief.

(1:11) Accordingly, [the Jewish sage] said to him: I have faith in the God of Abraham, Isaac, and Israel, who brought the children of Israel out of Egypt with signs and miracles, provided for them in the wilderness, and gave them the land of [Canaan] after they had crossed the sea and the Jordan miraculously. He sent Moses with His Law, and then thousands of prophets after him to support His Law by means of promises [of reward] to whoever observed it and threats [of punishment] to whoever disobeyed it. Our faith pertains to all that was included in the Torah, but the story is long.

(1:12) The Khazar said: I had originally decided not to ask a Jew because I knew about the destruction of their traditions and the inferiority of their opinions, since their misfortune has not left them anything worth praising. Why, then, didn't you say, O Jew, that you have faith in the Creator of the world, who orders it and governs it, and in Him who created you and provided for you, and [use] similar such descriptions, which constitute proof for everyone who has a religion? Because of descriptions like these, people pursue truth and justice in order to imitate the Creator with reference to His wisdom and justice. [16]

(1:13) The [Jewish] sage said: What you are referring to is the syllogistic, governmental religion to which speculation leads, but it contains many doubtful points. Ask the philosophers about it, and you will not find them agreeing on a single action or a single belief because they are [merely] claims. Some of them, they can demonstrate. Some of them, they can support persuasively; but some of them they cannot even support persuasively, let alone establish by demonstration.

(1:14) The Khazar said: I think your speech now, O Jew, is more likely [to persuade me] than the opening part of it was before, and I would like additional proof.

(1:15) The sage said: On the contrary, the opening part of my speech is the demonstration. What is more, it is [based on] direct observation (*al-'iyān*)[8] and doesn't need proof and demonstration.

(1:31) The [Jewish] sage said: [It is] by virtue of the natural order, [that] nourishment, growth, procreation, as well as their various powers and all the conditions pertaining to them, become necessary. In that respect, plants and animals are distinguished from earth, stones, minerals, and elements.

8. Literally, "eyewitness." Compare 2:48 below: "direct experience" for *al-'iyān al-mushāhada.*

(1:32) The Khazar said: This is a generalization which needs to be worked out in detail, but it is true. [20]
(1:33) The sage said: [It is] by means of the psychic order [that] all animals are distinguished; and movements, volitions, character traits, external and internal senses, and so forth necessarily follow from it.
(1:34) The Khazar said: This, too, cannot be rejected.
(1:35) The sage said: [It is] by means of the intellectual order [that] the rational [animal] is distinguished from all of the [other] animals. Moreover, the improvement of [people's] character traits, and then the improvement of the household, and then, finally the improvement of the city necessarily follows from it. And, [thus,] political regimes and political nomoi come into being.
(1:36) The Khazar said: This too is true.
(1:37) The sage said: Then what level is above this one?
(1:38) The Khazar said: The level of the great men of knowledge.
(1:39) [The sage said]: I had in mind [here] nothing other than a level that distinguishes its representatives by means of an essential difference, in the same way that plants are distinguished from inanimate things, and man is distinguished from beasts. However, differences of more and less are infinite, since they are merely accidental differences and are not really [different] levels.
(1:40) The Khazar said: In that case, then, there is no level beyond man among the various beings that can be perceived by the senses.
(1:41) The sage said: Well, then, if we should find a man who enters fire without its harming him, who goes without food for a long period without feeling hunger, whose face has a radiance that [people's] eyes cannot bear [to gaze upon], who does not fall ill or become senile and worn out, so that when he has reached his [allotted] life span, he dies a death freely chosen like someone who climbs into his bed to sleep on a certain day and at a certain hour, in addition to knowing hidden things about what has been and what will be, wouldn't this be the level that is essentially different from the level of ordinary people?
(1:42) The Khazar said: Even more! This level would be characteristic of the divine kingdom, if it exists; and this [kind of] person would come under the dominion of the divine order and not of the intellectual, the psychic, or the natural order.

(1:80) The Khazar said: Let's go back to our original aim. Tell me how your religion developed and then how it spread and came to be viewed, how concord emerged after discord, and how much time it took for your religion to become well established and built-up, until it was [fully] constructed and complete. For undoubtedly the beginnings of religious communities are to be found in individuals who help one another in supporting the opinion that God wishes to prevail. And so they keep on growing in numbers and [eventually] achieve victory by themselves or a victorious king arises on their behalf, who forces the multitude to accept that opinion.
(1:81) The sage said: Only the intellectual nomoi, which have their origin in man, arise and develop in this way. When [a man who frames such laws] appears on the scene and meets with success, it is said that he is "supported by God," "inspired," and other things of this kind. But the nomos that has its origin in God arises only suddenly. It was told: "Be!" and it came into being, just like the creation of the world.
(1:82) The Khazar said: Truly, you have left us awestruck, O sage!

[68] TREATISE TWO

(2:1) Subsequently, all that is reported in the history of the Khazars about the matter of the Khazar king took place: In the mountains of Warsan, he revealed the secret of his dream to his vizier, the very dream that came to him repeatedly, to the effect that he should seek out those actions that are pleasing to God, exalted be He. So, both of them, the king and his vizier, set out on foot together for the uninhabited mountains by the sea. [It then tells of] how they happened upon a certain cave during the night in which a group of Jews used to rest every Sabbath, how they disclosed themselves to them, converted to their religion, and were circumcised in that very cave. The two of them then returned to their country, resolute in the religion of the Jews, yet concealing the secret of their belief until they cautiously revealed the secret little by little to several groups among their upper classes. Eventually, they grew numerous and made public what they had kept secret. Moreover, they prevailed over the rest of the Khazars, and converted them to the religion of the Jews as well. They sent for scholars and books from various countries, and they studied the Torah.

[Next, we learn about] their noble conduct as well as their triumph over their enemies, their conquest of the countries [adjacent to them], the treasures that were disclosed to them, how their troops ultimately came to be a great multitude, amounting to hundreds of thousands, in conjunction with their love for the religion and their longing for the Temple—to the extent that they set up a replica of the Tabernacle that Moses (peace be upon him) had set up, how they honored those who were native-born members of the children of Israel, and asked to be blessed [by them], in keeping with all that has been mentioned in their history. Now when the king studied the Torah and the books of the prophets, he took that same sage as his teacher and began to ask him Hebraic questions. The first thing he asked him about was the names and attributes that are ascribed to God and what appears to be implied by some of them with respect to corporeality, despite the absurdity of that [notion] according to the intellect. Similarly, the Law also dismisses it in the clearest terms. [70]

❧

(2:46) The [Jewish] sage said: Sometimes, your forgetfulness about the roots [of faith] that I set out for you and which you yourself granted really pains me. Didn't we agree that one draws near to God only by means of actions commanded by God? Do you think that such drawing near is simply a matter of being submissive and abasing oneself and whatever else follows along the same lines?

(2:47) The Khazar said: Yes, with justice, that is exactly what I think. I have read it in your books, just as it was taught: *What does the Lord (YHVH), your God demand of you? Only this: To revere the Lord your God,* and so on [Deut. 10:12], and *what the Lord requires of you* [Micah 6:8], and there are many other passages besides those.

(2:48) The sage said: These and similar such things are the intellectual nomoi (*al-nawāmīs al-ʿaqliyya*). They are the preparation and preamble to the divine Law (*al-sharīʿa al-ilāhiyya*) and precede it both in nature and in time. They are indispensable for governing any group of human beings, no matter what it might be, so that even a band of robbers cannot avoid adhering to justice in what is between them. Otherwise, their association would not last. Now when Israel's rebelliousness got to [108] the point that they disregarded even the intellectual [and] governmental Laws (*al-sharāʾiʿ al-ʿaqliyya wa-al-siyāsiyya*), which are as indispensable [for every group as certain natural things are indispensable] for every individual, such as eating and drinking, moving and resting, and sleeping and being awake, but nevertheless held fast to the acts of worship pertaining to the sacrifices and the other divine and traditional Laws (*al-sharāʾiʿ al-ilāhiyya wa-al-samʿiyya*), He became satisfied with less from them. Hence, they were told: If only you kept the Laws that even the least and lowest groups accept as obligatory, such as adhering to justice and the good and also acknowledging God's bounty! For the divine Law can be fulfilled completely only after perfect adherence to the governmental and intellectual Law [has been achieved]; and included within the intellectual Law is both adhering to justice and acknowledging God's bounty.

Accordingly, how is it [acceptable] for someone who neglects this to offer sacrifices and to observe the Sabbath, circumcision, and other things of that sort that the intellect neither requires nor rejects? They are the Laws by means of which *Israel* was singled out, [constituting] an addition to the intellectual ones, and by means of which the bounty of the divine order reached them. But they did not know how these Laws became obligatory, just as they did not know how it happened that the *glory of the Lord (YHVH)* descended among them, how the *fire of the Lord* consumes their sacrifices, how they heard the Lord's address to them, and how everything that happened to them took place with respect to those things that [people's] intellects can[not] concede as possible"—were it not for direct experience (*al-ʿiyān al-mushāhada*) and the personally attested spectacle [they saw], which cannot be rejected. Thus, it was because of a situation like this that they were told: *what the Lord requires of you* [Micah 6:8], and *Add your burnt offerings to your other sacrifices* [Jer. 7:21], and other things like these. Is it possible for the Israelite [addressed in this way] to confine himself to *doing justice* and *loving mercy* [Micah 6:8], while treating *circumcision,* the Sabbath, and the rest of the commandments as superfluous, and then prosper?

(2:49) The Khazar said: Not according to what you set forth earlier. He only becomes a virtuous man, according to the opinion of the philosophers, and he doesn't care about which way he takes to draw near [to God], whether by becoming a Jew, a Christian, or something else, or by [following] whatever he invents for himself. But now we've gone back to using intellectual speculation, syllogistic reasoning, and independent judgment, whereby all men get into situations in which they strive to be in accord with the Law because their own reasoning has led them to it; and this is absurd.

(2:50) The sage said: The divine Law does not make us worship through asceticism, but rather through moderation and giving each of the faculties of the soul and the body its due with justice, without giving in to excess, because giving in to excess with regard to one faculty is tantamount to taking away from another. Thus, whoever inclines toward the faculty of lust becomes deficient with regard to the faculty of thought, and vice versa.[9] Again, whoever inclines toward gaining mastery over others becomes deficient with regard to some other faculty. Therefore, prolonged fasting is not [an act of] worship for someone whose appetites are weak, [110] who discards them and is therefore physically feeble. On the contrary, here, living in ease and comfort, would be an appropriate counterpoise and precaution [against this]. Neither is being excessively frugal with money [an act of] worship, if it happened to be acquired lawfully, easily, and without distracting one from learning and good works, especially for someone who has a family and children and is well-disposed to making charitable contributions that would please God. On the contrary, increasing [his contributions] is more appropriate for him. In general, our Law is divided [equally] between *fear, love,* and *joy.* You may draw near to your Lord through each of them. Accordingly, your submission on fast days [brings you] no closer to God than your joy on *Sabbaths and festivals,* if your joy arises from thought and intention.

Now, just as the *prayers of supplication* require thought and intention, so, too, does joy in His order and His Law require thought and intention, so that you may rejoice in the Law itself out of love for its Giver. Moreover, you will see how He has shown [His] preference for you by means of it. It is as though you were one of His guests, invited to enjoy His table and His favors, for which you give thanks both inwardly and outwardly. If emotion wells up within you to the point of singing and dancing because of your joy, especially [joy] in the Law, then that singing and dancing are [expressions of genuine] worship and a bond between you and the divine order. Moreover, our Law has not left these matters unaddressed, either. On the contrary, they are regulated precisely, since it is not within the capacity of human beings to determine exactly those things that benefit the faculties of [people's] souls and bodies, nor to establish what [proportion of] rest and exercise is right for us, nor to calculate what the land will produce so that it may be left fallow during the *seventh year* and the *jubilee year,* while still contributing the obligatory tithe, and other things besides that from it.[10] Therefore, He ordained the idleness that pertains to the Sabbath, the festivals, and the land. All of this is *a remembrance of the Exodus from Egypt* and a *remembrance of the Work of Creation,* for these two things are linked to each other by the divine will alone [and] not by chance or by nature, just as He, exalted be He, said: *You have but to inquire about bygone ages…,* and so on [Deut. 4:32]; *Has any people ever heard the voice of God…,* and so on [Deut. 4:33]; *Or has any God ventured…,* and so on [Deut. 4:34].

Thus, observance of the Sabbath is in itself the [ultimate] acknowledgment of divine sovereignty. However, it is an acknowledgment, as it were, in the language of deeds because whoever believes that there was rest on the Sabbath from the *Work of Creation* has already acknowledged the [world's having come into being as a] complete innovation without any doubt. And if he acknowledges the [world's having come into being as a] complete innovation, he also acknowledges the One who brings about this complete innovation, the Artisan, exalted be He. But, whoever does not believe it has fallen into doubts [associated with belief in the] eternity of the world, and his belief with regard to the Creator of the world, exalted be He, is also not pure. Hence, observance of the obligations of the Sabbath is closer to God than worship [in general], asceticism, and pious isolation.

Consider how the divine order, which was connected with Abraham, and then with a multitude of his choicest [offspring], [112] and then with the Holy Land, began to lead the nation step by step, to preserve its progeny so that no one would

9. Cf. Saadya Gaon *The Book of Doctrines and Beliefs* chap. 10.

10. Cf. Maimonides *Guide* 3.26 (below, selection 15).

be left abandoned, and to place them in the most secure, the most agreeable, and the most fertile place, causing them to grow miraculously until He moved them and planted them in the soil that was most suitable for the choicest [offspring of Adam] [Jer. 2:4–7, 22]. Accordingly, it was called *the God of Abraham* [Ps. 47:10; 2 Kings 17:26–27; Gen. 24:3; Zeph. 2:11] and *the God of the land* [2 Kings 17:26–27], just as it was called *[He who is] enthroned on the cherubim* [1 Sam. 4:4], *He who dwells in Zion* [Ps. 123:1], and *He who dwells in Jerusalem* [Ps. 135:21], making these places analogous to the heavens, as it is said: *Enthroned in heaven* [Ps. 123:1]. Now because the strength of His light in these places is just like the manifestation of His light in the heavens, but is mediated by [a people] worthy of receiving that light, He causes it to pour forth over them, and that which comes from Him is called *love*. This is what has been set down in writing for us and also enjoined upon us to believe, to praise, and to be thankful for in [the prayer that begins] "With everlasting love You have loved us . . ."[11] so that we might think of the beginning [of these things as being] from Him, not from ourselves, just as we say with respect to the creation of animals, for example, that they did not create themselves. Rather, God fashioned them and brought them to perfection because He saw matter well suited to that form. Similarly, He, exalted be He, is the One who promptly set out and began bringing us out of Egypt in order for us to become His army and for Him to become our King, just as He said: *I the Lord am your God who brought you out of the land of Egypt to be your God* [Num. 15:41; Lev. 22:33]. Even more, He spoke also of *Israel, in whom I glory* [Isa. 49:3].

TREATISE THREE

(3:1) The sage said: Among us, the distinguishing mark of the worshiper does not consist in being detached from this world, lest he become a burden to it and it become a burden to him; for he would hate his life, which is one of God's favors to him. By means of it, He bestows benefits upon him, just as it says: *I will let you enjoy the full count of your days* [Exod. 23:26]; *And you will have a long life* [Deut. 22:7]. Rather, he loves this world and long life too because they enable him to earn the hereafter; and everything which increases goodness contributes to [reaching] a higher level in the hereafter. Of course, he would love to be at the level of *Enoch*, of whom it was said: *Enoch walked [with God]* [Gen. 5:24], or at the level of *Elijah* [2 Kings 2:11], to be free enough to seclude himself for the company of the angels; for he would not feel lonely during solitude and seclusion. On the contrary, they would be his companions, while in the crowd he would feel lonely due to his being deprived of witnessing the kingdom of heaven, [the experience of] which enables him to dispense with food and drink. For people such as these, complete seclusion is appropriate. Indeed, they desire death because they have reached the ultimate limit, beyond which there is no additional level one could hope for.

Now, the learned who philosophize also desire seclusion so that their thoughts might become clear in order to draw sound conclusions from their syllogistic reasonings, to achieve certainty for themselves regarding whatever doubts they might still have. Along with this, they want to meet students who will urge them on to investigation and recollection, just like someone with a burning desire to amass wealth, who loathes being engaged otherwise than with someone who will do business with him so that he might reap a profit together with him. This is the level of Socrates and those who are like him. But these are singular individuals. There is no hope of attaining their level today.

Of course, in the presence of the *Divine Presence*, within the Holy Land, among that nation which is naturally disposed towards prophecy, there were people who would engage in ascetic practices and live in uninhabited regions, joining with those like them, and, in general, not

11. Cf. *Babylonian Talmud, Berakhot* 11b and the second benediction of the *Shema* and its blessings for the morning service, Daily Prayer Book.

isolating themselves. On the contrary, they would assist one another in [studying] the sciences of the Law and its actions, which bring one closer to that [142] level *in holiness and purity.* They were *the prophetic bands.* However, at this time, in this place, and amidst this people, when *prophecy is not widespread* [1 Sam. 3:1], given the scarcity of that knowledge which is acquired and the absence of that knowledge which is innate, whoever makes himself live in a state of isolation by means of ascetic practices has put himself through both psychological and physical pain and illness. The humbling effects characteristic of those illnesses are evident in him, though it is thought that he has humbled himself through his submissiveness and obedience. He becomes a prisoner, denying life, weary of both his prison and his pains, and finding no pleasure in his seclusion. And how could this be otherwise, when he has neither come into contact with divine light, which would keep him company, like the prophets, nor acquired sciences that would suffice to occupy and delight him for the rest of his life, like the philosophers?

Grant that he is pious [and] superior, a person who loves confiding in his Lord in seclusion, rising, praying, and supplicating through whatever he may remember of *supplications* and *petitions.* However, these innovations are satisfying only on the days when they are fresh. The more they are recited over and over by the tongue, the less the soul is affected by them; nor does it experience grief or mercy because of them. Thus, night and day pass by and his soul makes its demands on him through its natural faculties of seeing, hearing, speaking, moving about at will, eating, drinking, copulating, making a profit, caring for family, sharing with those who are weak, and supporting the Law when he sees it wanting. Will he not remain caught and entangled, regretting all that he has tied his soul to, and by his very regretfulness, increasing his distance from the divine order to which he [originally] wished to come close?

(3:2) The Khazar said: Then describe for me the actions of a superior person among you today.

(3:3) The sage said: The superior person is the guardian of his city, acting justly and assigning its people their daily provisions and everything they need. He treats them fairly inasmuch as he does not cheat any of them nor give anyone more than he deserves. Subsequently, when he needs them, he will find them obedient and immediately responsive to his call. He commands them, and they carry out the command. He forbids them, and they desist.

(3:4) The Khazar said: I asked you about a superior person, not about a ruler.

(3:5) The sage said: The superior person is someone who is a ruler, someone obeyed by his senses as well as his psychic and bodily faculties. He governs them by a political governance, just as it is said: *And [it is better] to have self-control than to conquer a city* [Prov. 16:32]. He is the one who is [truly] fit for rule because if [144] he were to lead a city, he would deal justly with it, in the same way that he deals justly with his body and his soul. For he has subdued his appetitive faculties and prevented them from becoming excessive after giving them their rightful share and providing them with whatever will remedy their deficiencies, through food in moderation, drink in moderation, bathing, and pursuing a livelihood in moderation too. He has also subdued his spirited faculties, which demand a show of victory, after giving them their rightful portion and providing them with a stake in that victory which is useful, such as debates about the sciences and ideas, and also in rebuking malicious people.

Moreover, he has also given his senses their rightful share in whatever redounds to his benefit, so that he directs his hands, feet, and tongue towards that which is necessary and the most useful choice—likewise for hearing and seeing and the common sense, which follow them; then, for imagination, estimation, cogitation, and memory; and then the faculty of volition which gives directions to all of these. Moreover, it also takes direction, being subservient to the free choice of the intellect.

Now, he does not neglect even one of these limbs and faculties with regard to whatever concerns it alone, lest it damage the rest. When he has satisfied the need that each of them has and given them a sufficient amount of rest and sleep, and also given the vital faculties all that sustains them with respect to wakefulness and movement in regard to the activities of this world, he then calls upon his "community." Just as the ruler who is obeyed calls upon his troops, who are obedient to whatever he has in mind, to attach themselves to that level which is above them [all], I mean, the divine level, which is above the intellectual level.

Thus, he arranges his "community" hierarchically and organizes it, imitating the way in which *Moses, our Master, peace be upon him,* arranged his community hierarchically around *Mount Sinai.* He commands the faculty of volition to be receptive and obedient to whatever order comes from him so that it will follow him immediately and thus employ the other faculties and limbs in accordance with whatever he orders without disagreement. He also commands it not to pay attention to the demons of the estimative and imaginative [faculties], and neither to accept them nor assent to them until it consults with the intellect. If it approves of what they both think, [the voluntary faculty] accepts it; but if not, it rebels against them both. Thus, the voluntary [faculty] accepts that [judgment] by [the intellect] and resolves to follow it. Then it guides the organs of cogitation and frees it from all prior mundane thoughts. It assigns the imaginative [faculty] the task of presenting the most splendid representations of existing things that it has, with the aid of memory, so that it may thereby imitate the divine order, which is being sought, such as, for example, the *gathering of Mount Sinai* [Exod. 19–20; Deut. 4:9–5:28], and the *gathering of Abraham and Isaac at Mount Moriah* [Gen. 22:11–18], and also *the Tabernacle of Moses (peace be upon him) the order of the service* [Exod. 25:1–9], the indwelling of the *glory* within the *Temple*, and [146] much else besides. He orders the retentive [faculty] to hold that in trust and not to forget it. Moreover, he prevents the estimative [faculty] and its demons from making the truth seem unclear and doubtful. He also prevents the spirited and appetitive [faculties] from prejudicing and corrupting the voluntary [faculty] and causing it to be preoccupied with whatever anger and desire lie within themselves.

After this preliminary step, the voluntary faculty rouses all of the limbs that are employed by it with ardor, eagerness, and joy, so that they stand when it is time to stand, without becoming sluggish; they prostrate themselves when it orders them to prostrate themselves; and they sit down when it is time to be seated. Eyes are fixed, like those of a servant, on his master [Ps. 123:2]. Both hands stop their fidgeting, and the one does not touch the other. Both feet become straight for the purpose of standing up, and all of his limbs are at attention, as though amazed and anxious, to obey their ruler. It does not concern them that pain or fatigue may be involved in doing so. The tongue fully conforms to the thought so as not to go beyond it. But neither does he speak during prayer in a rote or mechanical way, like the starling and the parrot. On the contrary, there is both thought and reflection in every word so that his hour [at prayer] becomes the choicest part of his time as well as its "fruit," while the rest of his hours become like pathways that lead to that one. He longs for its approach because during that time he resembles those beings that are spiritual and is remote from those that are bestial. Thus, the fruit of his day and his night becomes those three times of prayer, and their fruit is the Sabbath day because it is reserved for entering into contact with the divine order [Gen. 2:3] and worshiping it with *joy*, not with submissiveness, as has been explained.

The regular provision of this in relation to the soul is like the regular provision of nourishment in relation to the body. Thus, one prays for the sake of one's soul and takes nourishment for the sake of one's body. Moreover, the blessing of prayer remains with him until the time arises for another prayer, just as the strength received from breakfast remains until one eats dinner. Even so, the soul remains troubled whenever the time of prayer is far off, by reason of whatever mundane concerns beset it, particularly if necessity calls for the company of boys, women, and evil people. For he will hear something that disturbs the serenity of his soul, such as obscene words and songs to which the soul is drawn, that he will be unable to control. But at the time of prayer, he purifies his soul of what is past and prepares it for the future. Then, too, not a week goes by in accordance with this regular arrangement without the soul and the body becoming weary. Disturbing residues accumulate over the course of the week, which he is unable to purify and cleanse away except by linking a whole day of worship with rest for the body. Thus, the body receives in full [148] on the Sabbath what it missed during the six workdays and is prepared for the future. The soul also recollects what it missed by being preoccupied with the body. It is as if it were treated and cured of a prior illness on that day and provided with whatever will ward off that illness in the future, much like what *Job* used to do every week with regard to his children, as it says: *Perhaps my children have sinned* [Job 1:5].

Then, he initiates the monthly medical treatment, which is a *time of atonement for all their generations,*[12] meaning, *the generations of the*

12. Daily Prayer Book, Additional Service, New Moon.

months, the new events [arising with the succession] of days, as when it says: *For you do not know what the day will bring* [Prov. 27:1]. Then, he initiates the *three pilgrimage festivals,* and then the day of the revered fast on which there is forgiveness for past sins. On that day, he will seek to redress all that he omitted during the days of the weeks and months [of the preceding year], while the soul frees itself from the evil promptings of the estimative, spirited, and appetitive [faculties] and completely turns away from helping them, whether by thought or deed.

Now even if it is not possible to repent for thinking—because thoughts associated with what took place in the past overpower the soul through the remembrance of things it heard from childhood, like poems and stories and other such things—it may nonetheless free itself with respect to actions and excuse itself for those thoughts as well. Moreover, it will undertake not to speak of them with the tongue, let alone to act them out, as it was said: *I have determined that my mouth should not transgress* [Ps. 17:3]. His fasting on that day is the kind of fasting by which he comes close to resembling the angels, because he spends it in submissiveness, obedience, standing at attention, bending the knee, giving praise, and singing exultantly. All of his bodily faculties abstain from natural concerns and concentrate on the Law, as though there were no bestial nature within him. The fast of a virtuous man, when he fasts, is also like this, namely, that seeing and hearing as well as the tongue "fast" too, so that nothing preoccupies them other than what brings one close to God, exalted be He. The same is true of the internal faculties, such as imagination, cogitation, and the others; and worthy actions will also be linked with that.

(3:6) The Khazar said: Those actions are known.

(3:7) The sage said: The governmental actions and the intellectual nomoi are the things that are known. But the divine ones, which are added to these in order to be realized within the religious community of a *living God* [Josh. 3:10] who governs it, are not known until they come from Him in an explicated and detailed manner. Indeed, even if the essential characteristics of those governmental and intellectual nomoi were known, their precise determination is not known; for we know that giving charity and sharing [150] are obligatory and that training the soul through fasting and obedience is obligatory. Moreover, deceit is disgraceful, and promiscuous behavior with women is disgraceful too, as is having intercourse with certain relatives, whereas honoring parents and whatever else resembles that are obligatory. However, defining and determining that so that it is appropriate for everyone belongs only to God, exalted be He.[13] As for the divine actions, they are outside the scope of our intellects [but not] rejected by the intellect. Rather, the intellect will follow them unquestioningly, just as a person who is sick will follow the physician unquestioningly with regard to his medicines and prescriptions. Don't you see how far *circumcision* is from syllogistic reasoning and how it has no connection with governance? Still, *Abraham* submitted himself to it, despite the difficulty of the command from the standpoint of nature, when he was one hundred years old, for his own sake and for the sake of his child. It became a *sign of the covenant* so that the divine order might attach itself to him and to his progeny, as it says: *I will establish My covenant between Me and you, and your offspring to come, as an everlasting covenant throughout the ages to be God to you,* and so on [Gen 17:7].

(3:11) The sage said: The superior person among us respectfully heeds these divine Laws (*al-sharā'i' al-ilāhiyya*), I mean, *circumcision,* the Sabbaths and festivals and their concomitants, which are legislated by God, and also [the obligation] to be mindful of the *forbidden sexual relations,* the *mixed kinds* in relation to plants, clothes, and animals, the *seventh year* and the *jubilee year,* being on guard against *idolatry* and all that pertains to it, such as seeking knowledge of what is hidden without prophecy, the *Urim* and the *Thummim,* or *dreams.* Therefore, he will not listen to an augur, or an astrologer, or someone who casts lots, or someone who finds either good or evil omens in the flight of birds. [He will also] be on guard against *bodily discharges, menstruating women,* eating and touching unclean animals, and *leprosy* too. [He will also] be mindful of the blood and the fat of sacrificial animals because they are part and parcel of *the fires of the Lord (YHVH).* He respectfully complies with whatever is incumbent upon him for every transgression, be it unintentional or intentional, by [offering] a *sacrifice,* aside from

13. Cf. Maimonides *Guide* 3.26 (below, selection 15).

all that is incumbent upon him with respect to *redemption of the first born,* the *first fruits,* and the *first born* [animals], and also a *sacrifice* for every mother who gives birth within his domain, as well as the *sacrifice* and *gift offering* to purify himself of *discharges* and *leprosy,* aside from what is incumbent upon him with respect to the *first* and *second tithes,* the *poor tithe, appearing three times a year, Passover* and its concomitant requirements, which [in each case] is a *sacrifice of the Lord* incumbent on *every citizen of Israel.* [There is also] the *sukkah* [Lev. 23:42] and the *lulav* [Lev. 23:40] and the *shofar,* and whatever sanctified and purified implements and utensils are needed for these various *gift-offerings* and sacrifices, as well as whatever purification and sanctification he needs, and, finally, observance of *peah* and *orlah* and [fruits designated as] *qodesh hilulim* [Lev. 19:9–10, 23, 24].

In general, he will observe whatever he possibly can of the divine ordinances, so as to be truthful when he says: *I have neither transgressed nor neglected any of Your commandments* [Deut. 26:13], quite apart from the *votive offerings, freewill offerings,*[14] *sacred gifts of greeting* [Lev. 3:6 ff.], and whatever he may take upon himself with respect to *becoming a Nazirite* [Num. 6:1–21]. These things and others like them are the divine Laws, [154] and the complete fulfillment of most of them comes about through the *service of the priests* [in the Temple].

Now the governmental Laws (*al-sharā'i' al-siyāsiyya*), for example, consist of: *You shall not murder; You shall not commit adultery; You shall not steal; You shall not bear [false witness] against your neighbor* [Exod. 20:13–16]; *Honor [your] father and mother* [Exod. 20:12]; *Love your neighbor [as yourself]* [Lev. 19:18]; *You too must befriend the stranger* [Deut 10:19]; *You shall not deal deceitfully or falsely* [Lev. 19:11]; having nothing to do with *usury* and *interest* [Lev. 25:36]; striving to have *honest scales, honest weights,* an *honest ephah,* and an *honest hin* [Lev. 19:36]; leaving behind the *gleanings, the fallen fruit,* and the *corners* [of one's fields] [Lev. 19:9–10; Deut. 24:20], and whatever resembles this.

The psychic Laws (*al-sharā'i' al-nafsāniyya*) are: *I, the Lord (YHVH), am your God; You shall have no [other gods before Me];* and *You shall not take [the Lord's name in vain]* (Exod. 20:2–7), with the addition of whatever has proved to be true within this Law, [for example,] that He, exalted be He, observes and is acquainted with the inner thoughts of mankind, not to mention their actions and their words; that He repays their good as well as their evil, and that *the eyes of the Lord range over the whole earth* [Zech. 4:10; 2 Chron. 16:9]. Therefore, the superior person should neither act, speak, nor think, without believing that there are eyes in his presence, which see him, observe him, reward him, punish him, and also criticize him for every deviation [from what is proper] with respect to his words as well as his deeds. Thus, he will walk and also sit down like someone afraid and ashamed, embarrassed by his activities at times; just as he will be joyful, happy, and feel good about himself, when he has done a good deed. It is as though he is acting graciously toward his Lord, when he undergoes some hardship in obeying Him.

TREATISE FOUR

(4:13) The sage said: The difference between the adherent of a revealed Law and the adherent of philosophy is far-reaching because the adherent of a revealed Law seeks out the Lord for the sake of great benefits, quite apart from the benefit of knowing Him. But the person who devotes himself to philosophy seeks Him out only for the purpose of describing Him according to His true character, just as he seeks to describe the earth [by asserting], for example, that it is at the center of the largest sphere, but not at the center of the sphere of the zodiac, as well as other things that are known besides this. Being ignorant about God is detrimental to him only in the way that being ignorant about the earth is to someone who has said that it is flat. The benefit, in his view, consists only in knowing things according to their true character, [thus] becoming like the Active Intellect so that he may come to be identical with it. Whether he is a true believer or a freethinker is of no concern, if he philosophizes. One of the fundamental principles of his belief is that, *[the Lord will do] nothing*

14. *Mishnah, Qinnim* 1:1.

[good] and nothing bad [Zeph. 1:12]. He also believes in the past eternity of this world; therefore, he does not think that it was ever non-existent up to the point at which it was created. On the contrary, it has not ceased [to exist in the past], and it will never cease [to exist in the future]. Moreover, God, exalted be He, is its "Creator" [only] in a metaphorical sense, not according to [254] what is understood by the expression [literally]. By "Creator" [and] "Artisan," he means only that He is its cause and ground, whereby the effect [namely, the world] has not ceased to co-exist with the cause [namely, God]. If the cause is potential, then the effect is potential; but if it is actual, then the effect is actual. Now God, exalted be He, is an actual cause. Therefore, His effect is actual as long as He is a cause of it. However, even though [the philosophers] have gone this far, they may nonetheless be excused because they were not in a position [to grasp] divine science except by way of reason, and this is what their reasoning has brought them to. Those among them who are fair-minded say to those who follow a revealed Law what Socrates said: "O people, I do not deny this divine wisdom of yours. Rather, I say that I don't comprehend it. I am wise only in human wisdom."[15]

❧

(4:15) ...Now the name of *YHVH*[16] is identical with what is designated by Him as [His] *"face,"* when it says: *My face will go [in the lead]...* [Exod. 33:14], and *If Your face does not go [in the lead]...* [Exod. 33:15]. It [was] also the object of [Moses'] request when it says: *Let YHVH go in our midst* [Exod. 34:9]. The meaning of *Elohim* may be grasped by reasoning because the intellect leads to [the conclusion] that the world has a Ruler and Source of order. People differ about it in accordance with their ways of reasoning, but the most important of the opinions about Him is that of the philosophers. As for the meaning of *YHVH*, it cannot be grasped by reasoning, but rather by being witnessed in that prophetic [kind of] seeing by which man is almost able to separate himself from his species and attach himself to an angelic species, so that a *different spirit* [Num. 14:24] arises within him, just as it says: *You will become another man* [1 Sam. 10:6]; *God gave him another heart* [1 Sam. 10:9]; *Then the spirit seized Amasai* (1 Chron. 12:19); *The hand of YHVH came upon me* [Ezek. 37:1, 40:1]; and, *Let a vigorous spirit sustain me* [Ps. 51:14]. [These expressions] are allusions to the *holy spirit,* which enwraps the prophet at the time of [his] prophecy, the *Nazirite* [Judg. 13:7, 25], and whoever *is anointed,* whether for the *priesthood* [Exod. 40:13–16] or for the kingdom, at the time that the prophet anoints him, or at the time that God supports him and shows him the right way toward some thing, or at the time that the *priest* is inspired with knowledge of what is hidden, when he has inquired of the *Urim* and the *Thummim.* Then, the previous doubts which used to fill him with misgivings about *Elohim* will be resolved for man, and he will make light of those syllogistic arguments that are used to acquire knowledge of [His] lordship and unity. Moreover, at that time, man becomes an [exemplary] worshiper, passionately in love with the One he worships, consumed with loving Him even to the point of dying because of the great enjoyment he finds in being attached to Him [260] and the hurt and loss [he experiences] in being far from Him. [This is] in direct contrast to those who devote themselves to philosophy, who see in the worship of God [only] good manners and saying what is true with regard to exalting Him above other things that exist, just as the sun ought to be exalted above other things that are visible, and [who suppose] that there is nothing more involved in the denial of God than a [certain] baseness characteristic of the soul that is content to accept falsehood.

(4:16) The Khazar said: The difference between *Elohim* and *YHVH* has become clear to me, and I have also understood the difference between the *God of Abraham* and the *God of Aristotle.* One longs for *YHVH, exalted be He,* by tasting[17] and witnessing for oneself, while one inclines towards *Elohim* by reasoning. Moreover, that very tasting invites the one who has experienced it to be consumed with loving Him even to the point of dying and [to prefer] death [to living] without Him, whereas this very reasoning makes one see that exalting Him is obligatory as long as one is not harmed and one does not undergo hardship because of it. Therefore, Aristotle should be excused for attaching no importance to the actions

15. Cf. Plato *Apology* 20D–E.

16. Up to this moment, we have followed the Jewish practice of substituting "Lord" for "YHVH," by writing "the Lord (YHVH)." We do not do so here because Halevi has made the contrast between the God of philosophy and the God of Judaism as identified by the unprounceable name (YHVH) the theme of his discussion.

17. See the introduction to Alghazali *Deliverer* (above, selection 8).

belonging to the nomos, since he doubts whether God has any knowledge of that.

(4:17) [The sage said:] Well, [then, by that standard] it was right for *Abraham* to have undergone all that he did in *Ur of the Chaldees* [Gen. 15:7], and then in departing from [his] homeland [Gen. 12:1 [ff.], and also in [accepting] *circumcision* [Gen. 17:24], and again in expelling *Ishmael* [Gen. 21:14], and even further in [his] anxiety about slaughtering *Isaac* [Gen. 22: 1–19], since all that he experienced with respect to the divine order he experienced by savoring, not by reasoning. Moreover, he saw that nothing relating to his particular circumstances was hidden from Him. He saw too, that [God] rewarded him for his goodness moment by moment and also guided him towards His righteous paths, so that Abraham would neither go forwards nor backwards unless it was with His authorization. How, then, could he not look down upon his earlier syllogistic arguments? Thus, it was just as the *Sages, of blessed memory,* explained homiletically with regard to: *He took him outside* [Gen. 15:5] [namely,] "He said to him: Abandon your astronomy."[18] It means that He ordered him to abstain from his scientific studies based on reasoning, such as astronomy and other such things, and to take upon himself the duty of obeying the One he had experienced by tasting, just as it says: *Taste and see how good YHVH is* [Ps. 34:9].

Thus, *YHVH* is rightly called the *God of Israel* [Exod. 5:1] because this outlook [on God] is entirely lacking among other [peoples] beside themselves. He is [likewise] called the *God of the land* (2 Kings 17:26) because it has [a special character] that belongs to its air, its soil, and its skies, which helps [to promote] that [kind of intense experience], in conjunction with those [other] factors that are like cultivation and preparation [because they are designed] to produce this kind [of individual].

Thus, everyone who follows the divine nomos is only following those endowed with this [kind of] vision. Their souls are content with accepting their traditions on faith, despite the simplicity of their speech and the coarseness of their parables, whereas they are not content with accepting the traditions of the philosophers on faith, despite the refined character of their stories, the beautiful organization of their compositions, and whatever flashes forth because of them with respect to demonstration. Yet, the multitudes do not [262] follow them, as if the truth had already been revealed to people's souls, just as it is said, "Words of truth are recognized."[19]

(4:18) The Khazar said: I see that you are attacking the philosophers and ascribing to them the very opposite of what is generally known about them, so that someone who has withdrawn from society and practiced asceticism is said to have devoted himself to philosophy and also to have adopted the viewpoint of the philosophers. Yet you are robbing them of every worthy action.

(4:19) The sage said: Not at all. What I said is the very foundation of their belief that the ultimate happiness available to man consists only in [having] theoretical knowledge and obtaining a grasp of the existents as things that are intelligible by means of the potential intellect, [which] then becomes an actual intellect, and then an acquired intellect, approaching the Active Intellect, so that one does not fear extinction. Now this can be completed only by spending one's lifetime in investigation and continuous reflection. It cannot be completed simultaneously with [having] worldly preoccupations. That is why they thought ascetic renunciation was the proper course of action with regard to wealth, honor, pleasure, and children, so that these things would not distract one from [the pursuit of] knowledge. But, then, when man becomes cognizant of that end which is desired from knowledge, he is not concerned about what he does; for, in fact, [the philosophers] are not concerned about receiving a reward for that God-fearing behavior [they display], nor do they think that if they were to steal forbidden property or to commit murder that they would be punished [hereafter] for it. However, they have commanded what is good and forbidden what is reprehensible in the most appropriate and most excellent way, and [they have also commanded people] to imitate the Creator, who has established things in the best way. Accordingly, they produced the nomoi, namely, rules of political governance [which are] not legally binding, but to which exceptions can be made, unless there is some [overriding] necessity [not to make exceptions]. However, the Law is not like that except in its governmental parts, [and] it has already been explained in jurisprudence what is subject to exception and what is not subject to it.

18. *Babylonian Talmud, Shabbat* 156a; *Nedarim* 32b. Cf. Maimonides *Letter on Astrology* (below, selection 17).

19. *Babylonian Talmud, Sotah* 9b.

TREATISE FIVE

(5:1) The Khazar said: I can't help imposing on you to give me a clear, accessible account of the roots and articles of faith, using the method of the dialectical theologians. Surely, it's permissible for me to hear them, just as it was permissible for you to learn about them, either to believe them or to refute them [as the case may be,] since the exalted level of pure belief without investigation is simply beyond me. Besides, doubts and opinions and discussions of philosophers and adherents of various religious communities and faiths have already been presented to me. Thus, the most appropriate thing for me is knowledge and proficiency in refuting corrupt opinions that arise from ignorance. Adhering to tradition on faith is appropriate only in connection with a willing soul, but with a recalcitrant one, investigation is better, especially when investigation leads to confirming that very adherence to tradition on faith. For then both levels [of attainment] will come together for people, I mean, knowledge and adherence to tradition at the same time.

(5:2) The sage said: But who among us has a steadfast soul that is not misled by the opinions that pass through it, such as those of natural scientists, astronomers, believers in talismans, magicians, materialists, those who devote themselves to philosophy, and others? One arrives at faith only after having come through many ranks of unbelievers. But "life is short, and the art is long."[20] [By contrast, having] faith by nature happens only to unique individuals. To them, all of these opinions are repugnant, and the points at which [such opinions] are in error occur to them at once. I hope that you may be one of those unique individuals.

But if there is no way to avoid [complying with your request,] I will not take you down the path of the Qaraites,[21] who made it all the way to divine science without [taking the intervening] steps. [Rather,] I will summarize the essential points for you, which should help you in forming a concept of prime matter, which is common [to all material objects], and then in sequence the elements, nature, the soul, the intellect, [296] and finally [divine science]. After that, I will offer convincing arguments for the rational soul's ability to dispense with the body, then for the rewards of the afterlife, and then for the decree and destiny [that God ordains,] as succinctly and briefly as possible.

(5:22) Subsequently, it came about, owing to the concern of this sage, that he decided to leave the land of the Khazars in order to go directly to *Jerusalem, may it be rebuilt and made secure.* But then parting from him proved to be difficult for the Khazar, and so he spoke to him about that, saying, "What would one seek in the Syro-Palestine today, when the Divine Presence is no longer there and drawing close to God is something one can attain in any place by means of pure intention and fervent desire? Why should you burden yourself with danger on land and sea and among different peoples?"

(5:23) The sage said: But, actually, it is the Divine Presence that is visible to the eye that has disappeared, since it reveals itself only to a prophet or a multitude that is pleasing [to God] in that special place. It is also the one that is eagerly awaited on the basis of its saying: *For every eye shall behold the Lord's (YHVH's) return to Zion* [Isa. 52:8], and also because of what we say in our prayer, "May our eyes behold when You return to your dwelling-place, to Zion."[22] The hidden, spiritual, Divine Presence, however, is with any native-born Israelite who is blameless [in his] actions, pure of heart, and sincere in his intention toward the Lord of Israel.

Again, the land of Syro-Palestine is special to the Lord of Israel, and actions become complete only within it. Moreover, many Israelite Laws are not incumbent on those who do not dwell in Syro-Palestine. And, [finally,] intention is sincere, and the heart is pure only in those places that are believed to be special to God. [This would be true] even if that were a fantasy and a metaphor. How much the more so, then, when that is the reality, as explained previously. Therefore, the desire for [the Land] is powerfully aroused, and intention becomes sincere within it, especially for someone who has come to it from afar, [and more] especially for someone who has sinned in the past and wants to ask for forgiveness at a time when there

20. Hippocrates, Aphorism 1.

21. For the Qaraites, see the historical introduction to the *Kuzari.*

22. Daily Prayer Book, seventeenth benediction of the *Amidah.*

is no access to the *sacrifices* that were ordained by God for each sin, *intentional as well as unintentional.* Thus, he will be familiar with the saying [358] of the Sages: "Exile atones for sin,"[23] especially if he were to immigrate to a place that is pleasing [to God].

As for risking danger on land and sea, such a risk does not come under [the prohibition], *Do not try the Lord* [Deut. 6:16]. Rather, it would be like the risk one takes if one had an article of merchandise from which one hoped to realize a profit. If one were to take even greater risks than this in connection with one's desire and hope for forgiveness, he would certainly be excused for exposing himself to dangerous situations after he had made a [final] accounting of his soul, given thanks for all that took place during his lifetime, become content with it, and set aside the rest of his days for the purpose of pleasing his Lord. [Thus, he enters into danger; and if his God rescues him,] he will give praise and thanks. But if He causes him to die on account of his sins, he is satisfied, bears it calmly, and is certain that he had obtained forgiveness for most of his sins through his death. Besides, my opinion is more likely to be correct than the opinion of those who expose themselves to danger in wars in order to be remembered for [their] bravery and preeminence in battle [or] to receive a great reward. The fact is that it is less dangerous than [what is risked by] those who go into battle for the sake of a reward in a holy war.

(5:24) The Khazar said: I used to think that you loved freedom, but now I see that you are adding to your servitude by [taking on] obligations that would be incumbent upon you to fulfill [only] if you lived in Syro-Palestine—Laws that are not incumbent upon you to fulfill here.

(5:25) The sage said: I seek only freedom from servitude to the many whom I try to please but cannot. If I were to strive for it throughout my life, and even if I were to attain it, it would not benefit me. I mean, of course, servitude to human beings and seeking to please them. Rather, I seek to serve One whom it is possible to please with the slightest effort, and it is beneficial both in this world and in the hereafter. That is what pleases God, exalted be He; for serving Him is [true] freedom, and humbling oneself for His sake is true exaltation.

(5:26) The Khazar said: If you believe everything that you've mentioned, then God, exalted be He, already knows your intention, and the intention is sufficient for God, who knows intentions and reveals the things that are hidden.

(5:27) The sage said: This is true, if the action is impossible [to carry out]. But man is given a free hand in what he hopes for and what he does, and so man is blameworthy if he does not wrest a clearly recognizable reward for a clearly recognizable action. That is why it was said: *You shall sound short blasts on the trumpets, that you may be remembered before the Lord, your God.... They shall be a reminder to you* [before your God] [Num. 10:9–10]... [a sacred occasion] *commemorated with loud blasts.* [Lev. 23:24]. It is not that God needs to be reminded and notified, but rather because [360] actions need to be made perfect, and [only] then do they deserve their reward, just as the ideas [that are part] of prayer need to be articulated with the most perfect [expression of] supplication and submissiveness there can be. When the intention and the action have each been made as perfect as required, there is a reward for them. But then, that [way of perfecting an intention by performing the corresponding action] comes to be seen by people as if it were a reminder, inasmuch as, "The Torah spoke in accordance with the language of human beings."[24] If the action occurs without [the intention or the intention without] the action, the endeavor [to make one's actions perfect] fails, unless—by God!—it pertains to something that was impossible [to fulfill]. In that case, however, presenting the intention [by itself] and offering an excuse for the action [not being performed] is of some benefit, as, for example, when we offer an excuse [for not appearing in person three times each year to worship at the Temple by saying] in our prayers, "And because of our sins, we were exiled from our land"[25] and the like. Moreover, there is a reward for rousing people and moving them to love that holy place and giving [them] assurance of that order which is still awaited, as it says: *You will surely arise and take pity on Zion, for it is time*

23. *Babylonian Talmud, Berakhot* 56a; *Sanhedrin* 37b. Cf. Maimonides *Guide* 2.32 and *Letter on Astrology* (below, selections 15 and 17).

24. *Babylonian Talmud, Berakhot* 31b; cf. *Nedarim* 3a.

25. *Maḥzor,* Additional Service, *Amidah.* See *Maḥzor Matleh Levi* 230.

to be gracious to her; the appointed time has come. Your servants take delight in its stones and cherish its dust [Ps. 102:14–15]. This means that *Jerusalem* will be rebuilt only when *Israel* desires it so completely that they will feel compassion even for its stones and its dust.

(5:28) The Khazar said: If this is so, then hindering you would be a sin and helping you a good deed. May God help you and be both your defender and friend! And may He be pleased with you in His grace as well! Now, [go in] *peace.*

This book has been completed with the help and excellent assistance of God, exalted be He. To the Giver of help, praise without end!

FOURTEEN

MAIMONIDES

Logic

Translated by Muhsin Mahdi

Moses Maimonides (Moshe ben Maimon, 1137/38–1204) was born in Cordova. He received his early training in Jewish studies from his father, who was a scholar of some note. In addition, he was instructed in philosophy and the natural sciences by local Muslim scholars, among them students of Ibn Bajja. With the fall of Cordova to the Almohads in 1148, his father fled with his family and wandered about Spain for over a decade. Ca. 1160 the family settled in Fez, where Maimonides continued studying with Muslim scholars. But, again, the pressure of religious persecution forced the family to leave, ca. 1165. After passing through Acre and Jerusalem in 1165, Maimonides settled in al-Fusṭāṭ (Old Cairo) in 1166. Here he entered into a medical career (supplemented by trade in precious gems and pharmaceuticals from abroad) as a means of livelihood, finally serving as physician to Saladin's court. Maimonides was a communal leader (although scholars continue to debate how long he was officially Ra'īs al-yuhūd [Head of the Jews], he appears to have risen to the highest positions of communal, judicial, and religious authority possible for a Jew at this time in Egypt, with religious authority well beyond the confines of Egypt), and much of his time was occupied in answering legal and doctrinal questions addressed to him by Jews in all lands. He died in Cairo and was buried at Tiberias.[1] Maimonides' work comes close to being encyclopedic. He was the author of works on logic, astronomy, and medicine. His *Commentary on the Mishnah* (1168) and the *Mishneh Torah* (Code) (1180) are comprehensive attempts to represent the immense complexities of Talmudic legislation in a clear and systematic fashion. In the *Guide of the Perplexed* (1185–1190), Maimonides addressed himself to the challenge posed by Greek philosophy to the believer in a revealed Law.

The *Treatise on the Art of Logic* [*Maqāla fī ṣināʿat al-manṭiq; Millot ha-higgayon*] may have been written by Maimonides as early as the age of sixteen.[2] It is addressed to a man who is described

1. For the first critical biography of Maimonides, see Joel L. Kraemer, *Maimonides: The Life and World of One of Civilization's Greatest Minds* (New York: Doubleday, 2008).

2. Herbert Davidson has raised some doubts not only about when Maimonides likely composed this work, but also about whether it was even composed by him (see Herbert A. Davidson, *Moses Maimonides: The Man and His Work* [New York: Oxford University Press, 2004], 318). As Davidson had already raised these objections elsewhere, prior to the publication of Davidson's book Ahmad Hasnawi responded to them in his "Réflexions sur la terminologie logique de Maïmonide et son contexte farabien: "*Le guide de perplexes* et *La traité de logique*," in *Maïmonide: Philosophe et savant*, ed. Tony Lévy and Roshdi Rashed (Leuven: Peeters, 2004), 39–78.

as being an authority on the sciences based on the Law and an authority on Arabic eloquence. This man has asked one who has studied the art of logic (that is, Maimonides) to explain to him the various technical terms used in logic, briefly, without going into details, and without necessarily being exhaustive. The following statement on political science occurs in the fourteenth (final) chapter of the treatise.[3] It is preceded in this chapter by a classification of the sciences. Philosophy or science is divided into (1) theoretical philosophy, and (2) what is variously called practical philosophy, human philosophy, political philosophy, or political science. Theoretical philosophy is divided into (a) mathematics, (b) physics, and (c) theology.[4] Mathematics, in turn, is divided into (i) arithmetic, (ii) geometry, (iii) astronomy, and (iv) music. Theology is divided into (i) speech about God and the angels, and (ii) divine science or metaphysics. Practical philosophy[5] is divided into (a) ethics, (b) household management, (c) governance of the city, or politics in the strict sense, and (d) governance of the large nation.

Two complete Arabic manuscripts were edited, with a Turkish translation, by Mubahat Türker in *Ankara Üniversitesi Dil ve Tarih-Coğrafya Fakültesi Dergisi* 18 (1960): 40–64. (The passage below corresponds to p. 63 of the Arabic text in the Türker edition.) An earlier critical edition, containing the Arabic text of the first half of the *Logic* (all that had hitherto been available), medieval Hebrew translations of the whole work by Moses Ibn Tibbon, Ahitub, and Vivas, and an English translation, was edited by Israel Efros under the title *Maimonides' Treatise on Logic* (New York: American Academy for Jewish Research, 1938).

CHAPTER 14

[Political Science]

Political science falls into four parts: first, the individual man's governance of himself; second, the governance of the household; third, the governance of the city; and fourth, the governance of the large nation or of the nations.

Man's governance of his self consists in his making it acquire the virtuous moral habits and removing from it the vile moral habits if these are already present. Moral habits are the settled states that form in the soul until they become habitual dispositions from which the actions originate. The philosophers characterize moral habit as being a virtue or a vice; they call the noble moral habits "moral virtues" and they call the base moral habits "moral vices." The actions stemming from the virtuous moral habits, they call good (*khairāt*); and the actions stemming from the base moral habits, they call evil (*shurūr*). Similarly, they characterize intellecting, too—that is, conceiving the intelligibles—as being a virtue or a vice. Thus they speak of intellectual virtues and of intellectual vices. The philosophers have many books on morals. They call every governance by which a man governs another "a regime."

The governance of the household consists in knowing[6] how they [that is, the members of the household] help each other, and what is sufficient for them, so that their conditions may be well ordered, as far as this is possible in view of the requisites of that particular time and place.

The governance of the city is a science that imparts to its citizens knowledge of true happiness and imparts to them the [way of] striving to achieve it; and knowledge of true misery, imparting to them the [way of] striving to guard against it, and training their moral habits to abandon what are only presumed to be happiness so that they not take pleasure in them and doggedly pursue them. It explains to them what are only presumed to be miseries so that they not suffer pain over them and dread them. Moreover, it prescribes for them rules of justice that order their associations properly. The learned men of past religious communities (*milal*) used

3. For an analysis of this selection, the reader should consult Leo Strauss's "Maimonides' Statement on Political Science," in *What Is Political Philosophy? And Other Studies* (New York: Free Press of Glencoe, 1959; repr., Chicago: University of Chicago Press, 1988), 155–69. Also see Joshua Parens, "Strauss on Maimonides' Secretive Political Science," *Perspectives on Political Science* 39.2 (2010): 82–86.

4. Cf. Aristotle's similar division of theoretical philosophy at *Metaphysics* 1026a5–23.

5. Cf. Aristotle's similar division of prudence, which he compares with the "political art," *Nicomachean Ethics* 1141b23–35.

6. Reading *ya'lam* for *ta'allam* with Ibn Tibbon (*yīda'*).

to formulate,[7] each of them according to his perfection, regimens and rules through which their princes governed the subjects; they called them nomoi; and the nations used to be governed by those nomoi. On all these things, the philosophers have many books that have been translated into Arabic, and the ones that have not been translated are perhaps even more numerous. In these times, all this—I mean the regimes and the nomoi—has been dispensed with, and men are being governed by divine commands (*al-awāmir al-ilāhiyya*).

7. Reading *taṣna'* with the printed text and Vivas, or perhaps *ṭaḍa'* (lay down) with Ibn Tibbon and Ahitub.

FIFTEEN

MAIMONIDES

The Guide of the Perplexed

Translated by Ralph Lerner, Muhsin Mahdi (and Joshua Parens)

The Guide of the Perplexed (*Dalālat al-ḥā'irin; Moreh Nevukhim*) is addressed to a certain young man and to those like him who are troubled by the disparity that exists between the teaching of the Law, literally understood, and the teaching of the philosophers. To help such men—believers who have some acquaintance with the writings of the philosophers—in their perplexity, Maimonides has composed this work. The *Guide* is not addressed to the ordinary run of mankind or to those who have not engaged in any study beyond the jurisprudence based on the Law. Maimonides is speaking to individuals who have attained a certain measure of theoretical understanding and who have developed certain habits of reading. In his instructions for studying this work, he pointedly remarks that the diction used by him in the *Guide* has been chosen "with great exactness and exceeding precision." The chapters translated here from Part 2 are all taken from that section of the *Guide* whose theme is prophecy; special attention is given to the prophet's legislative function. The last group of chapters (from Part 3) concerns the determination of laws, the relation between action and opinion or belief, and the relation between the solitary and the Law.

The *Guide* was written in Judeo-Arabic.[1] It was twice translated into Hebrew and was available to readers of Latin within fifty years of Maimonides' death. The critical edition of the Judeo-Arabic text, together with a French translation, was published by S. Munk in three volumes under the title *Le guide des égarés* (Paris, 1856–66). This text was revised and reissued by Issachar Joel (Jerusalem, 1931). The present translation is based on the Shlomo Pines translation (Chicago: University of Chicago Press, 1963). The numbers in brackets in the body of the text refer to the pagination of Munk's edition.

1. Aside from some minor differences in grammar, Judeo-Arabic is Arabic written in Hebrew characters.

PART 2

Chapter 32

The opinions of people concerning prophecy are like their opinions concerning the eternity of the world or its creation. I mean by this that just as the people to whose mind the existence of the deity is firmly established, have, as we have explained, three opinions concerning the eternity of the world or its creation, so are there also three opinions concerning prophecy. I shall not pay attention to the opinion of Epicurus, for he does not believe in the existence of a deity, let alone believe in a prophecy. I only aim to state the opinions of those who believe in the deity.

The first opinion—that of the multitude of the ignorant communities who accept prophecy and also believed by some of the vulgar among the followers of our Law—is that God, the Exalted, chooses whom He wishes from among men, turns him into a prophet, and sends him with a mission. According to them it makes no difference whether this individual is a man of knowledge or [73a] ignorant, aged or young. However, they also posit as a condition his having a certain goodness and sound morality. For up to now people have not gone so far as to say that God sometimes turns a wicked man into a prophet unless He has first, according to this opinion, turned him into a good man.

The second opinion—that of the philosophers—is that prophecy is a certain perfection in the nature of man. This perfection is not achieved in any individual from among men except after a training that makes that which exists in the potentiality of the species pass into actuality, provided an impediment due to temperament or to some external cause does not impede this, as is the case with regard to every perfection whose existence is possible in a certain species. For the existence of that perfection in its extreme and ultimate form in every individual of that species is not possible. It must, however, exist necessarily in at least one particular individual; if, in order to be achieved, this perfection requires something that actualizes it, that something necessarily exists. According to this opinion it is not possible that an ignoramus should turn into a prophet; nor can a man who is not a prophet become a prophet overnight, as though one has made a find. Things are rather as follows: a virtuous individual who is perfect with respect to his rational and moral qualities, when his imaginative faculty is in its most perfect state and when he has been prepared in the way that you will hear, he will necessarily become a prophet, inasmuch as this is a perfection that belongs to us by nature. According to this opinion an individual cannot be fit for prophecy and prepared for it and not become a prophet, any more than an individual having a healthy temperament can be nourished with excellent food without sound blood and similar things being generated from that food.

The third opinion—the opinion of our Law and the foundation of our doctrine—is identical with the [73b] philosophic opinion except in one thing. For we believe that it may happen that one who is fit for prophecy and prepared for it should not become a prophet, namely, on account of the divine will. To my mind this is like all the miracles and takes the same course as they. For the natural thing is that everyone who is fit by his natural disposition and who trains himself in his education and study will become a prophet. He who is prevented from it is like him who has been prevented (like Jeroboam) from moving his hand or (like the King of Aram's army going out to seek Elisha) from seeing.[2] As for preparation and perfection in the moral and rational qualities being basic for us, this is their saying: "Prophecy only rests upon a wise, strong, and rich man."[3] We have explained this in the *Commentary on the Mishnah* and in the great compilation [namely, the *Code* or *Mishneh Torah*], and we have narrated that the disciples of the prophets were always engaged in preparation. As for the fact that one who prepares is sometimes prevented from becoming a prophet, you may know it from the history of Baruch, son of Neriah. For he followed Jeremiah, who trained, taught, and prepared him. And he aspired to become a prophet but was prevented. As he says: *I am weary with my groanings and I find no rest* [Jer. 45:3]. Thereupon he was told through Jeremiah: *Thus shalt thou say unto him: Thus saith the Lord,* and so on. *And seekest thou great things for thyself? Seek*

2. Cf. 1 Kings 13:4; 2 Kings 6:18.

3. *Babylonian Talmud, Shabbat* 92a.

them not [Jer. 45:4–5]. It is possible to say that this is a clear statement that prophecy is too great a thing for Baruch. Similarly it may be said, as we shall explain, that in the passage: *Yea, her prophets find no vision from the Lord* [Lam. 2:9], this was the case because they were in Exile.[4] However we find many texts, some of them scriptural and some of them dicta of the sages, all of which follow this fundamental: that God turns whom He wills, whenever He wills it, into a prophet—but only someone perfect and virtuous to the utmost degree. But as regards one of the ignorant among the vulgar, [74a] this is not possible according to us—I mean that He should turn one of them into a prophet—except as it is possible that He should turn an ass or a frog into a prophet. It is our fundamental that there must be training and perfection, whereupon the possibility arises to which the power of the deity becomes attached. You should not be led astray by His saying: *Before I formed thee in the belly I knew thee, and before thou camest forth from the womb I sanctified thee* [Jer. 1:5]. For this is the state of every prophet: he must have a natural preparedness in his original natural disposition, as shall be explained. As for his saying: *For I am young* [Jer. 1:6], you know that in the Hebrew language Joseph the righteous was called *young* [cf. Gen. 41:12] though he was thirty years old, and that Joshua was called *young* though he was near his sixtieth year. For it says with reference to the time of the doings concerning the calf: *But his servant Joshua, son of Nun, a young man, departed not,* and so on [Exod. 33:11]. Now Moses our Master was at that time eighty-one years old, and his whole life lasted one hundred and twenty years. Joshua lived after him fourteen years, and the life of Joshua lasted one hundred and ten years. Accordingly it is clear that Joshua was at that time at least fifty-seven years old, and was nevertheless called young. Again you should not be led astray by His dictum figuring in the promises: *I will pour out My spirit upon all flesh, and your sons and your daughters shall prophesy* [Joel 3:1]; for He interprets this and lets us know what kind of prophecy is meant, for He says: *Your old men shall dream dreams, your young men shall see visions* [Joel 3:1]. For everyone who tells of the unseen, whether this be by way of soothsaying and divination or by way of a true dream, is likewise called a prophet. For this reason prophets of Baal and prophets of Asherah are called prophets. Do you not see that He, the Exalted, says: *If there arise among you a prophet or a dreamer of dreams* [Deut. 13: 2]? As for the Presence at Mount Sinai, though through a miracle all the people saw the great fire and heard the frightening and terrifying voices, [74b] only those who were fit for it achieved the rank of prophecy, and even those in varying degrees. Do you not see that He says: *Come up unto the Lord, thou and Aaron, Nadab and Abihu, and seventy of the elders of Israel* [Exod. 24:1]? He (peace be upon him) had the highest rank, as He said: *And Moses alone shall come near unto the Lord; but they shall not come near* [Exod. 24:2]. Aaron was below him; Nadab and Abihu below Aaron; the seventy elders below Nadab and Abihu; and the other people below the latter according to their degrees of perfection. A text of the sages (may their memory be a blessing) reads: "Moses is an enclosure apart, and Aaron an enclosure apart."[5]

As we have come to speak of the Presence at Mount Sinai, in a separate chapter we shall give indications as to what becomes clear regarding that Presence as it was—from the scriptural texts, if they are well examined, and from the dicta of the sages.

Chapter 36

Know that the truth and essence of prophecy consist in its being an emanation from God, the Mighty and Majestic, through the mediation of the active intellect to the rational faculty in the first place and thereafter to the imaginative faculty. This is the highest degree of man and the ultimate perfection that [78a] can exist for his species; and this state is the ultimate perfection of the imaginative faculty. This is something that can in no way exist in every man. And it is not something that may be attained through perfection in the theoretical sciences and through improvement of moral habits (to the end that all of them become as fine and beautiful as can be) without there being in

4. Compare the *Letter on Astrology* and *Eight Chapters,* chap. 7.

5. *Mekhilta,* Commentary on Exod. 19:24.

addition the highest possible degree of perfection of the imaginative faculty in respect of its original natural disposition. Now you already know that the perfection of these bodily faculties to which the imaginative faculty belongs follows from the best possible temperament, the best possible size, and the purest possible matter, of the part of the body that is the substratum for the faculty in question. It is not a thing whose lack could be made good or whose deficiency could be remedied in any way by means of a regimen. For with regard to a part of the body whose temperament was bad in the original natural disposition, the utmost that the corrective regimen can achieve is to keep it in some sort of health; it cannot restore it to its best possible condition. If, however, its defect derives from its size, position, or substance (I mean the substance of the matter from which it is generated), there is no device that can help. You know all this; it is therefore useless to explain it at length.

You already know also the actions of this imaginative faculty that are in its nature, such as retaining sense perceptions, combining them, and imitation, and that its greatest and noblest action takes place only when the senses rest and are not performing their actions. It is then that a certain emanation flows to this faculty according to its preparation, and it is the cause of the true dreams. This same emanation is the cause of prophecy. There is only a difference in degree, not in kind. You already know that [the sages] have said time and again: "A dream is the sixtieth part of prophecy."[6] [78b] No proportion, however, can be established between two things differing in kind. One is not justified in saying, for instance, that the perfection of a man is a certain number of times greater than the perfection of a horse. They reiterated this point in Bereshit Rabbah, saying: "Dream is the unripe fruit of prophecy."[7] This is an extraordinary comparison. For unripe fruit is the individual fruit itself, but one that has fallen before it was perfect and before it had matured. Similarly, the action of the imaginative faculty in the state of sleep is also its action in the state of prophecy; there is, however, a deficiency in it and it does not reach its ultimate term. Why should we teach you by means of the dicta of [the sages] (may their memory be a blessing) and leave aside the texts of the Torah? *If there be a prophet among you, I the Lord do make Myself known unto him in a vision, I do speak with him in a dream* [Num. 12:6]. Thus He, the Exalted, has informed us of the truth and essence of prophecy and has let us know that it is a perfection that comes in a dream or in a vision (*mar'eh*). The word *mar'eh* (vision) derives from the verb *ra'oh* (to see). This signifies that the imaginative faculty achieves so great a perfection of action that it sees the thing as if it were outside, and that the thing whose origin is due to it appears to have come to it by way of external sensation. In those two groups, I mean vision and dream, all the degrees of prophecy are included, as shall be explained. It is already known that a matter that occupies a man greatly—he being bent upon it and desirous of it—while he is awake and while his senses function, is the one with regard to which the imaginative faculty acts while he is asleep when the [active] intellect emanates to it in accordance with its [that is, the imagination's] preparation. It would be superfluous to cite examples of this and to expatiate on it as this is a manifest matter that everyone already knows. It is similar to the apprehension of the senses with regard to which no one with sound natural disposition would disagree.

After these premises, you should know that if[8] a [79a] human individual the substance of whose brain at the origin of his natural disposition is extremely well-proportioned as regards the purity of its matter and the particular temperament of each of its [that is, the brain's] parts and as regards its size and position, and is not affected by impediments due to temperament that derive from another part of the body; then that individual obtains knowledge and wisdom until he passes from potentiality to actuality and acquires a perfect and complete human intellect and pure and well-tempered human moral habits. All his desires are directed to acquiring the science of the secrets of this existence and knowledge of its causes, and his thought always goes toward noble matters, and he is interested only in the knowledge of the deity and in reflection on His works and on what ought to be believed with regard to that. His thought is detached from, and his desire abolished for, bestial things. (I mean the preference for the pleasures of eating, drinking, copulation, and, in general, of the sense of touch, which Aristotle explained in

6. *Babylonian Talmud, Berakhot* 57b.

7. *Genesis Rabbah* 17 and 44.

8. The apodosis of this conditional sentence begins with the words "there is no doubt," on p. 79b.

the *Ethics,* saying that this sense is a disgrace for us.[9] How fine is what he said, and how true it is that it is a disgrace! For we have it only insofar as we are animals like the other beasts, and nothing that belongs to the notion of humanity pertains to it. As for the other sensual pleasures—those, for instance, that derive from the sense of smell, from hearing, and from seeing—there may be found in them sometimes, though they are bodily, pleasure for man as man, as Aristotle has explained. We have been led to speak of things that are not to the purpose, but there was need for it. For most of the thoughts of those who are outstanding among men of science are preoccupied with the pleasures of this sense and are desirous of them. And then they wonder how it is that they do not become prophets, if prophecy is something natural.) It is [79b] likewise necessary that the thought of that individual be detached from the spurious kinds of rulership and that his desire for them should be abolished—I mean the wish to dominate or to be held great by the vulgar and to obtain from them honor and obedience for its own sake. Rather, [he should] regard all people according to their various states with respect to which they are undoubtedly either like domestic animals or like beasts of prey. (Concerning these, the perfect man who lives in solitude, if he thinks of them at all, does so only with a view to saving himself from the harm coming from those among them who are harmful if he happens to associate with them, or to obtaining an advantage that may be obtained from them if he is forced to it by some of his needs.) There is no doubt that whenever—in an individual of this description—his imaginative faculty, which is as perfect as possible, acts and receives from the [active] intellect an emanation corresponding to his theoretical perfection; this individual will apprehend only divine and most extraordinary matters, will see only God and His angels, and will only be aware, and achieve knowledge of, matters that constitute true opinions and general directives for the well-being of men in their relations with one another. It is known that with regard to these three aims that we have given—namely, the perfection of the rational faculty through study, the perfection of the imaginative faculty through natural disposition, and the perfection of moral habit through turning thought away from all bodily pleasures and putting an end to the desire for the various kinds of ignorant and evil glorification—there are among those who are perfect very many differences in rank; and on the differences in rank with regard to these three aims depend the differences in rank that subsist among the degrees of all the prophets.

You know that every bodily faculty sometimes grows tired, is weakened, and is corrupted, [80a] and at other times is in a sound state. Now this imaginative faculty is undoubtedly a bodily faculty. Accordingly you will find that the prophecy of the prophets ceased when they were sad or angry or the like. You know their saying that "prophecy does not descend during sadness or languor";[10] that revelation did not come to Jacob our Father as long as he was mourning because of the fact that his imaginative faculty was preoccupied with the loss of Joseph;[11] and that, after the disastrous incident of the spies and until the whole generation of the desert had perished, revelation did not come to Moses (peace be upon him) in the way that it had come before,[12] because—seeing the enormity of their crime—he suffered greatly because of this matter. This was so even though the imaginative faculty did not enter into his prophecy (peace be upon him); rather the [active] intellect emanated to him without its mediation. For, as we have mentioned several times, he did not prophesy like the other prophets by means of parables. This will be made clear later on, for it is not the purpose of this chapter. Similarly, you will find that several prophets prophesied during a certain time and that afterwards prophecy departed from them and did not continue because of an accident that had supervened. This is undoubtedly the essential proximate cause of the departure of prophecy during the time of the Exile. For what languor or sadness can befall a man in any state that would be stronger than that due to his being a thrall slave in bondage to the ignorant immoral communities who combine the privation

9. Cf. *Nicomachean Ethics* 1118b2 ff.: "Hence the sense to which profligacy is related is the most universal of the senses; and there appears (*doxeien*) to be good ground for the disrepute in which it is held, because it belongs to us not as human beings but as animals" (Rackham). Cf. *The Guide of the Perplexed* 1.46, 47.

10. *Babylonian Talmud, Shabbat* 30b. Also cf. Maimonides *Eight Chapters,* chaps. 4, 7.

11. Cf. *Chapters of Rabbi Eliezer* 38.

12. *Babylonian Talmud, Ta'anit* 30b. Also cf. Maimonides *Eight Chapters,* chap. 4; and *Guide* 2.35 and esp. 45, below (pp. 196–97).

of true reason with the perfection of the lusts of the beasts? *And there shall be no might in thine hand* [Deut. 28:32]. This was what we have been threatened with. And this was what he meant by saying: *They shall run to and fro to seek the word of the Lord, and shall not find it* [Amos 8:12]. And it also says: *Her king and her princes are among the nations, the Law is no more; yea, her prophets find no vision from the Lord* [Lam. 2:9]. This is true and the cause thereof is clear. For the instrument has ceased to function. This also will be the cause for the return of prophecy [80b] to us in its customary form, as has been promised in the days of the Messiah, may he be revealed soon.

Chapter 37

You ought to turn your attention to the nature of that which is in this divine emanation coming to us, through which we perceive intellectually and because of which our intellects vary in excellence. For sometimes something comes from it to a certain individual, the measure of that something being such that it renders him perfect and nothing more. Sometimes, in contrast, the measure of what comes to the individual, beyond rendering him perfect, emanates to render others perfect. This is what happens to all beings: Some of them achieve perfection to an extent that enables them to govern others, whereas others achieve perfection only in a measure that enables them to be governed by others, as we have explained.

After this, you should know that when this intellectual emanation flows only to the rational faculty and none of it overflows to the imaginative faculty—either because of the scantiness of what flows or because of some deficiency existing in the imaginative faculty in its natural disposition that makes it impossible for it to receive the emanation of the [active] intellect—then this is the class of men of science, theoretical men. If, in contrast, this emanation is to both faculties—I mean both the rational and the imaginative (as we and others among the philosophers have explained)—and if the imaginative faculty is in its ultimate perfection as regards the natural disposition, then this is the class of prophets. If, again, the emanation is only to the imaginative faculty, the defect of the rational faculty deriving either from its original natural disposition or from insufficiency of training, then this class are those who govern cities [81a] and are the legislators, the soothsayers, the augurs, and those who have true dreams. Likewise, all those who do extraordinary things by means of strange devices and secret arts, although they are not men of science, belong to this third class. One of the things that you must ascertain is that some of those belonging to this third class have extraordinary imaginings, dreams, and amazed states while they are awake, similar to the vision of prophecy, so that they think of themselves as prophets. And they greatly marvel at what they apprehend of those imaginings and think that they acquired sciences without instruction; and they bring great confusion into theoretical matters of great import; true notions and imaginary ones are strangely confused for them. All this is due to the power of the imaginative faculty and the weakness of the rational faculty, and to [the latter's] not having obtained anything—I mean thereby that it has not passed into actuality.

It is known that in each of these three classes there are very many differences of degree and that each of the first two classes is divided into two parts, as we have explained. For the measure of the emanation reaching each of these two is either such as only to render the individual who receives it perfect and nothing more, or such that from that individual's perfection there is something left over that renders others perfect. As regards the first class—that of the men of science—that which emanates to the rational faculty of an individual [among them] is sometimes such that it makes him into a man who inquires and is endowed with understanding, who knows and discerns, but is not moved to teach others or to compose works, neither finding in himself a desire for this nor having the ability to do it. And sometimes that which emanates to him is such that it moves him of necessity to compose works and to teach. The same holds good for the second class. Sometimes the revelation that comes to him only renders that prophet perfect and nothing more. And sometimes what comes to him [81b] of it compels him to address a call to the people, teach them, and let his own perfection flow to them.

It has already become clear to you that, were it not for this additional perfection, sciences would not be set forth in books and prophets would not call upon people to know the truth. For a man of science does not compose anything for himself in order to teach himself what he already knows. Rather the nature of this [active] intellect is such that it always flows and extends from the one who receives that emanation to another one who receives it after him, until it reaches an individual beyond whom that emanation cannot go, but only renders him perfect, as we have stated in a parable in one of the chapters of this Treatise.[13] The nature of this matter makes it necessary for someone to whom this additional measure of emanation has come, to address a call to people, regardless of whether that call is listened to or not, and even if it leads to his being harmed in his body. We even find that prophets addressed a call to people until they were killed; this divine emanation moves them and does not leave them to rest and be quiet in any way, even if they meet with great misfortunes. For this reason you will find that Jeremiah (peace be upon him) explicitly stated that because of the contempt he received from those disobedient ones and unbelievers who lived in his time, he wished to conceal his prophecy and not to call them to the truth that they rejected but he was not able to do it. He says: *Because the word of the Lord is made a reproach unto me, and a derision, all the day. And if I say: I will not make mention of Him, nor speak any more in His name; then there is in my heart as it were a burning fire shut up in my bones, and I weary myself to hold it in, but cannot* [Jer. 20:8–9]. This is the meaning of the words of the other prophet: *The Lord God hath spoken, who shall not prophesy?* [Amos 3:8]. Know this. [82a]

Chapter 38

Know that in every man there is necessarily the power of boldness (*qūwa iqdām*).[14] Were this not so, he would not be moved in his thought to ward off what harms him. Among the powers of the soul, this power is, according to me, similar to the power of repulsion among the natural powers. This power of boldness varies as to strength and weakness, as do other powers, so that you find among people some who will advance upon a lion, but others flee from a mouse. You find someone who advances against an army and fights it, and find another who trembles and fears if a woman shouts at him. There also must be a kind of temperamental preparation in the original natural disposition, which in turn increases and applies itself to bringing out what is potential [into actuality] and in accordance with a certain opinion. It may also diminish through a deficiency of application and in accordance with a certain opinion. The abundance or the weakness of this power in the young is made clear to you from their infancy.

Similarly this power of divination exists in all men, but varies in degree. It exists especially with regard to things with which a man is greatly concerned and about which his thought turns, so that you find in your soul that so and so spoke or acted in such and such a manner in such and such an episode, and the thing is really so. You find among men one whose conjecturing and divination are very strong and habitually hit the mark, so that he hardly imagines that a thing comes to pass without its happening wholly or in part as he imagined it. The causes of this are many—they are various anterior, posterior, and present circumstances. [82b] But in virtue of the strength of this divination, the mind goes over all these premises and draws from

13. Cf. *Guide* 1.72 and 2.11.

14. Although Pines renders this as the "faculty of courage," this seems misleading. (N.B., over the course of the chapter, I have allowed the translation to shift to "faculty," when used in connection with imagination and intellect.) First, the virtue courage is not a faculty. Second, elsewhere Maimonides uses the Arabic word one would expect for the virtue courage—*shajā'a*—in *Eight Chapters,* chap. 4, following Alfarabi *Selected Aphorisms,* no. 8. Third, leaving aside the choice of the word *iqdām,* the first clue that Maimonides is not discussing a virtue is his reference to it as a "power" (*qūwa*). (Cf. Aristotle's discussion of the differences among virtues [as *hexeis*], feelings [*pathē*], and predispositions or powers [*dunameis*] [*Nicomachean Ethics* 1105b21–1106a14]. Although *pathos* and *dunamis* are very close in meaning, *hexis* concerns the rational side of the soul more than do those terms.) Note that Maimonides uses the same word, *qūwa,* again in connection with Moses in 2.45, below, which Pines renders, as we do, as "power," rather than "faculty."

Aristotle's account of "courage" (*andreia*) is complicated by the fact that he identifies it as a mean with respect to two opposing things, fear and boldness (*tharros*) (*Nicomachean Ethics* 1107b1–5, 1115a7–10, 1116a1–17). (To complicate matters, fear is obviously a feeling [*pathos*], but boldness seems to be a power [*dunamis*].) "Boldness" seems to be what is intended here, in the *Guide,* because it lacks the fixity of a virtue. Furthermore, boldness, though itself a source of courage, is also often linked to mere feelings, such as hope (1117a10–15).

them conclusions in the shortest time, so that it is thought to happen in no time. In virtue of this power, certain people give warnings concerning great future events.

These two powers must necessarily be very strong in prophets, I mean the power of boldness and that of divination. And when the [active] intellect emanates to them, these two powers become very greatly strengthened so that this may finally reach the point you know: namely, the lone individual, having only his staff, went boldly to the great king in order to save a religious community from the burden of slavery, and had no fear or dread because it was said to him: *I will be with thee* [Exod. 3:12]. This too is a state that varies in them [that is, the prophets] but it is indispensable. Thus it was said to Jeremiah: *Be not afraid of them,* and so on. *Be not dismayed at them,* and so on. *For, behold, I have made thee this day a fortified city,* and so on [Jer. 1:8, 17, 18]. And it was said to Ezekiel: *Be not afraid of them or of their words* [Ezek. 2:6]. Similarly you will find all of them (peace be upon them) to be endowed with great boldness. Also, because of the abundance of the power of divination in them, they give information as regards future events in the shortest time. This power likewise varies in them as you already know.

Know that the true prophets obtain theoretical apprehensions without doubt. By theory [or speculation] alone, man is unable to grasp the causes from which that known thing necessarily follows. This has a counterpart in their giving information as regards matters about which man, using only common conjecture and divination, is unable to give information. For the very emanation that flowed to the imaginative power [or faculty] (so as to render it perfect so that its act brings about its giving information as to what will happen and its apprehending such matters as though they had been perceived by the senses and had reached this imaginative faculty from the senses) [83a] also perfects the act of the rational power [or faculty], so that its act brings about its knowing things that are true; and it achieves this apprehension as if it had apprehended it by starting from theoretical premises. This is the truth that is believed by whoever chooses to be equitable toward himself. For all things bear witness to one another and indicate one another. It is even more fitting that this should pertain to the rational faculty. For the active intellect truly emanates only to it [that is, to the rational faculty], and that is what brings it into actuality. It is from the rational faculty that the emanation comes to the imaginative faculty. How then could the perfection of the imaginative faculty reach this measure [that is] the apprehension of what has not reached it from the senses, without the rational faculty being affected in a similar way [that is] apprehending without having apprehended by way of premises, inference, and reflection?

This is the true meaning of prophecy, and those are the opinions that are peculiar to the prophetic teaching. I have stipulated in my saying, "the true prophets," in order not to involve myself with the people belonging to the third class, who are utterly devoid of rational [notions] and knowledge, but have mere imaginings and thoughts. Perhaps they—I mean what these people apprehend—are merely opinions that they once had had and of which traces have remained impressed upon their imaginings together with everything else that is in their imaginative faculty. But after they voided and annulled many of their imaginings, the traces of these opinions remained alone and reappeared to them; and they thought them to be something that had unexpectedly occurred to them and something that had come from outside. According to me, they are comparable to a man who had with him in his house thousands of individual animals. Then all of them except one individual, which was one of those that were there, went out of that house. When the man remained alone with that individual, [83b] he thought that it had just now come to his house, whereas that was not the case; rather he was one of those who did not leave. This is one of the positions that are sophistical and destructive. How many among those who have aspired to obtain discernment have perished through this! Because of this you will find that certain groups of people establish the truth of their opinions by means of dreams that they have seen, thinking that what they have seen in sleep is something else than the opinion that they believed in or heard while awake. Therefore one ought not to pay attention to one whose rational faculty has not become perfect and who has not attained utmost theoretical perfection. For only one who achieves theoretical perfection is able to apprehend other objects of knowledge when the divine intellect emanates to him. It is he who is truly a prophet. This is explicitly stated: *And the prophet [possesseth] a heart of wisdom* [Ps. 90:12]. It says here that one who is truly a prophet has *a heart of wisdom.* This too ought to be known.

Chapter 39

Having spoken of the essence of prophecy and made known its truth and explained that the prophecy of Moses our Master is different from the prophecy of the others, we shall say that the call to the Law followed necessarily from that apprehension alone. That is because this call addressed to us by Moses our Master was not preceded by a similar call by any one of those we know who lived from the time of Adam to him; nor was a call similar to that one made by one of our prophets after him. Such is the fundamental of our Law: that there will never be another Law. Hence, according to our opinion, there never has been any Law and there never will be any other than the one Law, which is the [84a] Law of Moses our Master. The explanation of this, as stated in the texts of the prophetic books and as is found in the traditions, is as follows. Not one of the prophets—such as the Patriarchs, Shem, Eber, Noah, Methuselah, and Enoch—who came before Moses our Master has ever said to a class of people: "God has sent me to you and has commanded me to say to you such and such things; He has forbidden you to do such and such things and has commanded you to do such and such things." This is a thing that is not attested to by any text of the Torah and does not figure in any true tradition. These men only received revelation (*waḥy*)[15] from God, as we have explained. He who received an emanation of great magnitude, as for instance Abraham, assembled the people and called upon them by way of teaching and instruction to a truth that he had apprehended. In this manner Abraham taught the people and explained to them by means of theoretical proofs that the world has but one deity, that He has created all other things, and that these forms[16] ought not to be worshiped nor any of the created things. This is what he enjoined the people to do, attracting them by means of beautiful speeches and by means of the benefits he conferred upon them. But he never said: "God has sent me to you and has given me commandments and prohibitions." Even when the commandment of circumcision was laid upon him, his sons, and his servants, he circumcised them and did not call upon men to do so in the form of prophetic call. Do you not see the text of the Torah referring to him that reads: *For I have known him,* and so on [Gen. 18:19]?[17] Thus it is made clear that he acted only through injunction. Isaac, Jacob, Levi, Kohat, and Amram also addressed their call to the people in this form. You will find likewise that the sages say with reference to the prophets who came before him: "the court of justice of Eber, the court of justice of Methuselah, the school of Methuselah."[18] All of them (peace be upon them) were prophets who merely taught the people as instructors, teachers, [84b] and guides, rather than saying; "The Lord said to me: 'Speak to the sons of so and so.' " Things were like that before Moses our Master. As for Moses, you know what was said to him, what he said, and what all the people said to him: *This day we have seen that God doth speak,* and so on [Deut. 5:21]. As for all the prophets from among us who came after Moses our Master, you know the text of all their stories and the fact that they had the same position as preachers calling men to the Law of Moses, threatening those who turn away from it, and holding our promises to those who are forthright in following it. We likewise believe that things will always be this way. As it says: *It is not in heaven,* and so on [Deut. 30:12]; *for us and for our children for ever* [Deut. 29:28]. And that is as it ought to be. For when a thing is as perfect as it is possible to be within the species, it is impossible that within that species there should be found another thing that does not fall short of that perfection either because of excess or deficiency. Thus in comparison with the balanced temperament that has the highest degree of balance in a particular species, every other temperament that deviates from that degree of balance will have either deficiency or excess. Things are similar with regard to this Law, as is clear from its balance. For it says: *Just statutes and judgments* [Deut. 4:8]; now you know that the meaning of *just* is balanced. For these are manners of worship in which there is no burden and excess—such as

15. Compare Alfarabi *Book of Religion* 1 (in selection 2) and *Political Regime* 80 (in selection 3).

16. I.e., the forms of the stars, etc.

17. The verse continues: *to the end that he may command his sons and his house after him, that they may keep the way of the Lord, to do righteousness and judgment.*

18. *Genesis Rabbah* 43.

monastic life and pilgrimage and similar things—nor a deficiency necessarily leading to greed and being engrossed in indulgence, so that the perfection of man is diminished with respect to his moral habits and to his speculation—this being the case with regard to all the other nomoi of past religious communities. When we speak in this Treatise about the reasons of the Laws, their balance and wisdom will be made clear to you insofar as this is necessary. For this reason it is said with reference to them: *The Law of the Lord is perfect* [Ps. 19:8]. As for those who deem that its burdens are hard, heavy, and difficult to bear—all of this is due to an error in considering them. I shall explain later on [85a] how easy they truly are in the eyes of the perfect ones. For this reason it says: *What doth the Lord thy God require of thee,* and so on [Deut. 10:12]. And it says: *Have I been a wilderness unto Israel,* and so on [Jer. 2:31]. However all this refers to the virtuous; whereas in the eyes of those who are unjust, violent, and tyrannical, the existence of a judge who renders tyranny impossible is a most harmful and hard thing. Similarly for the greedy and the vile, the hardest thing in their eyes is that which hinders their abandoning themselves to debauchery and which punishes those who indulge in it. Similarly everyone who is deficient in any respect considers that a hindrance in the way of the evil that he prefers because of his moral viciousness is a great burden. Accordingly, the ease or difficulty of the Law should not be measured on the basis of the passion of every wicked, vile, and morally corrupt man, but should be considered with reference to the man who is perfect among the people, for it is the aim of this Law that everyone should be such a man. Only this Law is called by us divine Law; whereas the other political governances—such as the nomoi of the Greeks and the ravings of the Sabians and of others—are all due to the activity of certain rulers, rather than prophets, as I have explained several times.

Chapter 40

It has been explained with utmost clarity that man is political by nature and that it is his nature to associate with others. He is not like the other animals for whom association is not a necessity. Because of the manifold composition of this species—for, as you know, it is the last one to have been composed—there are many differences between the individuals belonging to it, so that you can hardly find two individuals who are alike in [85b] any one of the species of moral habits, any more than their visible forms are alike. The cause of this is the difference of the temperaments: the material [constituents] differ, and so do the accidents that adhere to the form—for every natural form has certain accidents adhering specifically to it, other than those that adhere to the material. Nothing like this great individual difference is found among any other animal species. Rather the differences between the individuals of every species are slight, except for man. For you find among us two individuals who seem to belong to two different species with regard to each moral habit: You find in one individual cruelty that reaches a point at which he kills the youngest of his sons in his great anger; another individual is full of pity at the killing of a bug or any other insect—his soul being too tender for this. The same holds good for most accidents.

Now as the nature of the human species requires that there be those differences among the individuals belonging to it and as, in addition, association is a necessity for this nature, it is by no means possible that his association should be accomplished except—and this is necessarily so—through a ruler who gauges the actions of the individuals, perfecting that which is deficient and reducing that which is excessive, and who lays down actions and moral habits for all of them to practice always in the same way, until the natural diversity is hidden through the multiple points of conventional accord, and so the society becomes well-ordered. Therefore I say that the Law, although it is not natural, has a basis in what is natural.[19] It was a part of the wisdom of the deity with regard to the continuance of this species, that He put it into its nature (when He willed its existence), that individuals belonging to it should have the faculty of ruling. Among them there is

19. Cf. Aristotle *Nicomachean Ethics* 1103a24–6.

one to whom that governance has been revealed by prophecy directly; he is the prophet or the one who lays down the nomos. Among them there are also those who have the faculty to compel people to accomplish, observe, [86a] and actualize that which has been laid down by those two. They are the sovereign who adopts that nomos and the one who claims to be a prophet and who adopts the Law of the prophet—either the whole of it or a portion. His adopting a portion and abandoning another portion may be due either to this being easier for him or, out of jealousy, to make people think that those matters came to him through revelation and that with regard to them he does not follow somebody else. For among the people there are men who admire a certain perfection, take pleasure in it, have a passion for it, and wish that people should imagine that they have this perfection, though they know that they possess no perfection. Thus you see that there are many who lay claim to, and give out as their own, the poetry of someone else. This has also been done with regard to certain works of men of science and to particular points of many sciences. An envious and lazy individual comes upon a thing invented by somebody else and claims that it was he who invented it. This has also happened with regard to this prophetic perfection. For we find people who laid a claim to prophecy and said things with regard to which there had never been at any time a revelation coming from God—such as Zedekiah, son of Chenaanah.[20] And we find other people who laid a claim to prophecy and said things that God has undoubtedly said—I mean things that had come through a revelation, but a revelation addressed to other people; thus, for instance, Hananiah, son of Azzur.[21] Accordingly they adopted them as their own and adorned themselves with them. The knowledge and discernment of all this are very clear. I shall explain this to you in order that the matter should not be obscure to you and that you should have a distinction by which you can separate the governances of nomoi that have been laid down, the governances of the divine Law, and the governances of those who took over something from the dicta of the prophets, raised a claim to it, and gave it out as their own.

As regards the nomoi with respect to which those who have laid them down have stated explicitly that these are nomoi that they have laid down by following their own thoughts, there is no need to adduce proofs for this; for, with its being recognized by the adversary, no further evidence is needed. I only want to make known to you the governances [86b] that are claimed to be prophetic; some of them are truly prophetic—I mean divine—others are [established on the basis of a human] nomos, and still others are plagiarisms.

Accordingly, if you find a Law the whole end of which and the whole purpose of the chief thereof, who determined the actions required by it, are exclusively the ordering of the city and of its circumstances and the removal of injustice and oppression from it; and if in that Law attention is not at all directed toward theoretical matters, no heed is given to perfecting the rational faculty, and no regard is accorded to opinions being correct or faulty—the whole purpose of that Law being, on the contrary, the arrangement, in whatever way this may be brought about, of the circumstances of people in their relations with one another and their obtaining, in accordance with the opinion of that chief, some presumed happiness—you will then know that that Law [has the character of] a nomos and that its promulgator belongs, as we have mentioned, to the third class, I mean to those who are perfect only in their imaginative faculty.

And if you find a Law all of whose governances attend to the aforementioned soundness of the bodily states and also to the soundness of belief—a Law that takes pains to give correct opinions regarding God, the Exalted, in the first place, and with regard to the angels, and that desires to make man wise, to give him understanding, and to awaken his attention, so that he knows the whole of existence as it truly is—you must know that this governance comes from Him, the Exalted, and that this Law is divine.

It remains for you to know whether he who lays claim to such a governance is a perfect man to whom a revelation of that governance has been made, or whether he is an individual who lays claim to these dicta, having plagiarized them. The way of putting this to a test is to consider the perfection of the individual, carefully to examine his actions, and to study his way of life. The strongest of the indications you should attend to is his renunciation of, and contempt for, the bodily pleasures, for this is the first of the degrees of the people of science and, all the more, of the

20. Cf. 1 Kings 22:11, 24.

21. Cf. Jer. 28:1 ff.

prophets. In particular this holds good with regard to the sense [87a] that is a disgrace for us—as Aristotle has stated—and especially in what belongs to it with regard to the foulness of copulation. For this reason, God has stigmatized with it everyone who lays claim to prophecy, so that the truth should be made clear to those who seek it and they should not go astray and fall into error. Do you not see how Zedekiah, son of Maaseiah, and Ahab, son of Kolaiah, claimed prophecy, were followed by the people, and gave forth dicta deriving from a revelation that had come to others; and how they plunged themselves into the vileness of the pleasure of copulation so that they fornicated with the wives of their companions and followers so that God made them notorious, just as He disgraced others, and the King of Babylon burned them? As Jeremiah has explained, saying: *And of them shall be taken up a curse by all the exiles of Judah that are in Babylon, saying: The Lord make thee like Zedekiah and like Ahab, whom the King of Babylon roasted in the fire; because they have wrought vile deeds in Israel, and have committed adultery with their neighbors' wives, and have spoken words in My name falsely, which I commanded them not; but I am He who knoweth and am witness, saith the Lord* [Jer. 29:22–23]. Understand this intention.

Chapter 45

After the preceding explanation of the truth of prophecy according to the requirements of theory together with the explanation supplied by our Law, I ought to mention to you the degrees of prophecy according to these two roots. Now not everybody who is found in one of the degrees, which I call degrees of prophecy, is a prophet. For the first and second degree are steppingstones toward prophecy, and he who has attained one of them is not to be considered among the prophets discussed previously. And even though he may sometimes be called a prophet, this term is applied to him in a general sort of way, because he is very close to the prophets. You should not be misled with regard to these degrees by the fact that sometimes you find in the books [93a] of prophecy that a revelation came to a prophet in the form characteristic of one of their degrees and then it is explained with regard to the very same prophet that a revelation came to him in the form characteristic of another degree. For as regards the degrees I shall mention, it sometimes happens that some of the revelation of one particular prophet comes to him in a form characteristic of a certain degree, whereas another revelation, which comes to him at another time, corresponds to a degree inferior to that of the first revelation. For just as a prophet may not prophesy continuously the whole of his life, but prophesies at a certain moment and is abandoned by prophecy at other moments, so may he also prophesy at a certain moment in a form characteristic of a high degree and at another moment in a form characteristic of an inferior degree. Sometimes perhaps he may not attain this high degree more than once in his lifetime and then is deprived of it and perhaps remains fixed in a degree inferior to this until the cessation of his prophesying. For there is no doubt that the prophesying of all the prophets comes to an end before their death, either shortly or a long time before, as was explained with regard to Jeremiah by the saying: *At the termination of the word of the Lord by the mouth of Jeremiah* [Ezra 1:11], and as was explained with regard to David by the saying: *Now these are the last words of David* [2 Sam. 23:1]. From this, one must draw an inference to all the prophets. After having made this introduction and explained it, I shall begin to set forth the degrees that have been alluded to, and shall say:

The First Degree: The first of the degrees of prophecy is that an individual is accompanied by divine help, which moves and activates him to a righteous, great, and important action—such as the deliverance of a community of virtuous people from a community of wicked people, or the deliverance of a virtuous and great man, or the conferring of benefits on numerous people. The individual in question finds in himself something [93b] that moves and incites him to the action, and this is called "the spirit of the Lord." And it is said of the individual who is accompanied by this state that *the spirit of the Lord came upon him*,[22] or that *the*

22. Cf. Judg. 14:6, 19; 1 Sam. 10:6, 16:13.

spirit of the Lord clothed him,[23] or that *the spirit of the Lord rested upon him,*[24] or that *the Lord was with him;*[25] or other similar expressions are applied to him. This is the grade of all the judges of Israel of whom it is said in general: *And when the Lord raised them up judges, then the Lord was the judge, and delivered them* [Judg. 2:18]. This is also the grade of all the virtuous messiahs[26] of Israel. This is explained especially as regards some judges and kings: *Then the spirit of the Lord came upon Jephthah* [Judg. 11:29]. And it is said of Samson: *And the spirit of the Lord came upon him* [Judg. 14:19]. And it is said: *And the spirit of God came upon Saul when he heard [those] tidings* [1 Sam. 11:6). Similarly it is said of Amasai when the Holy Spirit moved him to help David: *Then the spirit clothed Amasai who was chief of the captains: Thine are we, David, and on thy side, thou son of Jesse; peace,* and so on [1 Chron. 12:19]. Know that such a power (*qūwa*) did not abandon Moses our Master from the moment he reached manhood. It was because of this that he was moved to slay the Egyptian and to reprove the one who was in the wrong among the two men that struggled.[27] The strength of this power in him shows in the fact that when—after having been filled with fear and having fled—he came to Midian as a stranger full of fear and saw some wrong that was done, he could not refrain from putting an end to it and was incapable of patience with regard to it, as it says: *But Moses stood up and helped them* [Exod. 2:17]. David likewise was accompanied by such a power from the time that he was anointed with the oil of anointment, as is found in the text: *And the spirit of the Lord came upon David from that day forward* [1 Sam. 16:13]. And it was for this reason that he attacked the lion, the bear, and the Philistine. Such a spirit of the Lord by no means caused one of these to speak of anything; rather the end of this power was to move the one strengthened by it to a certain action: not to any [94a] chance action, but only to the defense of the wronged—whether one great man or a community—or to what leads to that result. And just as not everyone who has seen a true dream is a prophet, not everyone who is accompanied by [divine] help in some matter—whatever it may be, such as the acquisition of property or the achievement of an end that concerns him alone—is said to have been accompanied by the spirit of the Lord, or to have the Lord with him, or to have done what he has done through the Holy Spirit. We say this only about one who has performed a very great good or what leads to that result—as, for instance, the success of Joseph in the house of the Egyptian,[28] which was, as is clear, the first cause for great things that occurred afterwards.

The Second Degree: It consists in an individual's finding that a certain thing has descended upon him and that another power has come upon him and has made him speak; so that he talks wise sayings or in words of praise or in useful admonitory dicta, or concerning governmental or divine matters—and all this while he is awake and his senses function as usual. This is the one of whom it is said that he "speaks through the Holy Spirit." It is through this kind of Holy Spirit that David composed "Psalms," and Solomon "Proverbs," "Ecclesiastes," and "Song of Songs." "Daniel" and "Job" and "Chronicles" and all the other Writings[29] have likewise been composed through this kind of Holy Spirit. For this reason people call them Writings, meaning thereby that they are written through the Holy Spirit. The sages have stated explicitly that "the Scroll of Esther was spoken through the Holy Spirit."[30] It is of this kind of Holy Spirit that David has said: *The spirit of the Lord spoke by me and His word was upon my tongue* [2 Sam. 23:2]; he meant that it caused him to speak the words in question. [94b] It was to this group that the seventy elders belonged, of whom it is said: *And it came to pass, that, when the spirit rested upon them, they prophesied, but they did so no more* [Num. 11:25]. Eldad and Medad and every High Priest who was questioned through the Urim and Thummim also belong to this class, I mean that as the sages have mentioned: "The divine Presence rests upon him, and he speaks through the Holy Spirit."[31] Yahaziel, son of Zechariah, likewise belongs to this class, as it is he of whom it is said in Chronicles: *The spirit of the Lord came upon him in the midst of the congregation; and he said: Hearken ye, all Judah,*

23. Cf. Judg. 6:34; 1 Chron. 12:19; 2 Chron. 24:20.
24. Cf. Num. 11:25–26; Isa. 11:2.
25. Cf. Judg. 2:18; 1 Sam. 3:19, 18:12.
26. Or "anointed ones."
27. Cf. Exod. 2:11–13.
28. Cf. Gen. 39:2.
29. The Hebrew Bible is divided into three parts: the Torah (Pentateuch), the Prophets, and the Writings (Hagiographa).
30. *Babylonian Talmud, Megillah* 7a.
31. *Babylonian Talmud, Yoma* 73b.

and ye inhabitants of Jerusalem, and thou king Jehoshaphat. Thus saith the Lord unto you, and so on [2 Chron. 20:14–15]. So does Zechariah, the son of Jehoiada the priest, belong to this group, for it is said of him: *And the spirit of God clothed Zechariah, the son of Jehoiada the priest; and he stood above the people, and said unto them: Thus saith God* [2 Chron. 24:20]. Similarly Azariah, son of Oded, of whom it is said: *And the spirit of God came upon Azariah, son of Oded; and he went out to meet Asa,* and so on [2 Chron. 15:1–2]. The same applies to all those of whom something similar is said. Know too that Balaam, when he was righteous, also belonged to this kind. This is the meaning that it intends to convey in the dictum: *And the Lord put a word in Balaam's mouth* [Num. 23:5]. It is as if it said that he spoke through the Holy Spirit. It is for this reason that [Balaam] says of himself, *who heareth the words of God* [Num. 24:4]. One of the things to which we must draw attention is that David and Solomon and Daniel belong to this class and not to that of Isaiah and Jeremiah and Nathan the prophet and Ahijah the Shilonite and men similar to them. For they—I mean David and Solomon and Daniel—spoke and said what they said through the Holy Spirit. As for David's saying: *The God of Israel said, the Rock of Israel spoke to me* [2 Sam. 23:3], it means that [God] gave him a promise through a prophet, either through Nathan or somebody else; as: *And the Lord said unto her* [Gen. 25:23]; and as: *Wherefore the Lord said* [95a] *unto Solomon: Forasmuch as this is done of thee, and thou hast not kept My covenant* [1 Kings 11:11]—a saying that undoubtedly is a threat to him made through the prophet Ahijah the Shilonite or somebody else. Similarly the saying concerning Solomon: *In Gibeon the Lord appeared to Solomon in a dream by night; and God said,* and so on [1 Kings 3:5], is not pure prophecy like: *The word of the Lord came unto Abram in a vision, saying* [Gen. 15:1], nor is it like: *And God spoke unto Israel in the visions of the night* [Gen. 46:2], nor is it like the prophecy of Isaiah and Jeremiah. For even if revelation came to each of these in a dream, that revelation informs him that it is a prophecy and that revelation has come to him; whereas in this story about Solomon it says at the end: *And Solomon awoke, and, behold, it was a dream* [1 Kings 3:15]; and similarly in the second story it says: *The Lord appeared to Solomon the second time, as He had appeared unto him at Gibeon* [1 Kings 9:2], which has been explained to be a dream. This grade is below the one of which it is said: *I will speak unto him in a dream* [Num. 12:6]. For those who prophesy in a dream, by no means call this state a dream after prophecy has come to them in a dream, but state decidedly that it was a revelation. Just as Jacob our Father said; for when he awoke from that prophetic dream, he did not say that this is a dream, but stated decidedly and said: *Surely the Lord is in this place,* and so on [Gen. 28:16]. And he said: *God Almighty appeared unto me as Luz in the land of Canaan* [Gen. 48:3]; he thus decided that that was a revelation. Whereas with regard to Solomon, it says: *And Solomon awoke, and, behold, it was a dream.* Similarly you will find that Daniel applies the expression "dreams" to them, even though he saw an angel in those dreams and heard words spoken in them. He calls them dreams even after having learned what he did through them. Thus it says: *Then was the secret revealed unto Daniel in a vision of the night* [Dan. 2:19]. It also says: *Then he wrote the dream,* and so on [Dan. 7:1]; *I saw in my vision by night,* and so on [Dan. 7:2]; *And the visions* [95b] *of my head affrighted me* [Dan. 7:15]. And he says: *And I was appalled at the vision, but understood it not* [Dan. 8:27]. There is no doubt that this degree is below the degree of those of whom it is said: *I will speak unto him in a dream* [Num. 12:6]. For this reason the religious community has reached a consensus to classify the Book of Daniel among the Writings, and not among the Prophets. For this reason I called your attention to the fact that in this kind of prophecy that came to Daniel and Solomon—even though an angel was seen in a dream—as long as they did not find in themselves that that was a pure prophecy, but rather that it was a dream prophesying the truth of certain matters, it is like those who speak through the Holy Spirit. This is the second degree. Similarly when arranging the Holy Scriptures, they[32] made no difference between "Proverbs" and "Ecclesiastes" and "Daniel" and "Psalms," on the one hand, and the "Scroll of Ruth" or the "Scroll of Esther," on the other; all of them have been written through the Holy Spirit. Also all these are called, in a general way, prophets.

The Third Degree: This is the first of the degrees of those who say: "The word of the Lord came to

32. The ones who did this.

me," or expressions having a similar sense. That is, a prophet sees a parable in a dream according to all the conditions set forth before with regard to the truth of prophecy. And it is in this very dream of prophecy that the meaning of that parable—what was intended thereby—is made manifest to him, as in most of the parables of Zechariah.

The Fourth Degree consists in his hearing articulate and clear speech in the dream of prophecy, but without seeing the speaker—as has happened to Samuel in the first revelation that came to him, as we have explained with regard to him. [96a]

The Fifth Degree: This consists in his being addressed by a man in a dream—as it says in one of Ezekiel's prophecies: *And the man said unto me: Son of man,* and so on [Ezek. 40:4].

The Sixth Degree consists in his being addressed by an angel in a dream. This is the state of the majority of the prophets. Thus it says: *And the angel of God said unto me in the dream,* and so on [Gen. 31:11].

The Seventh Degree consists in his seeing in the dream of prophecy, as it were, that He, the Exalted, addresses him. Thus Isaiah says: *I saw*[33] *the Lord,* and so on [Isa. 6:1]. *And He said:*[34] *Whom shall I send,* and so on [Isa. 6:8]. Thus Micaiah, son of Imla, says: *I saw the Lord,* and so on [1 Kings 22:19; 2 Chron. 18:18].

The Eighth Degree consists in revelation coming to him in a vision of prophecy and his seeing parables—as Abraham in the vision between the pieces,[35] since these parables came in a vision during the day, as has been explained.

The Ninth Degree consists in his hearing speech in a vision—as is said with regard to Abraham: *And, behold, the word of the Lord came unto him, saying: This shall not be thine heir* [Gen. 15:4]. [96b]

The Tenth Degree consists in his seeing a man who addresses him in a vision of prophecy—as Abraham again by the terebinths of Mamre and as Joshua in Jericho.

The Eleventh Degree consists in his seeing an angel who addresses him in a vision—as Abraham at the time of the binding. According to me, this is the highest of the degrees of the prophets whose states are attested by the books, assuming what has been determined concerning the perfection of the rational faculties of the individual according to the requirements of theory, and assuming that one exempts Moses our Master. As regards the question whether it is possible that a prophet would also see in a vision of prophecy that God, as it were, addressed him—this, according to me, is improbable; the power of the act of the imagination does not reach this point, and we have not found this state in the other prophets. For this reason it is clearly said in the Torah: *I will make Myself known unto him (elav etvada) in a vision, and will speak unto him in a dream* [Num. 12:6]. Thus it assigns speech to dreams only, assigning to visions the union and emanation of the [active] intellect, this being signified by its saying: *elav etvada.* For [*etvada*] is a reflexive form of the verb *yado'a* (to know). Thus it is not explicitly stated that speech coming from God can be heard in a vision.

Inasmuch as I found scriptural texts attesting that prophets heard speech—it having been made clear that this was in a vision—I said by way of conjecture that it is possible that, in this speech that is heard in a dream and the like of which may not occur in a vision, it is God who is making him imagine that He is addressing him; all this is based on the external meaning. One could also say that every vision in which you find the hearing of an address, was in its beginning a [97a] vision, but ended in a state of submersion [in sleep] and became a dream, as we have explained with regard to the saying: *And a deep sleep fell upon Abram* [Gen. 15:12]. [The sages] have said: "This is the deep sleep of prophecy."[36] Therefore all speech that is heard, whatever the way may be in which it is heard, was heard only in a dream as the text has it: *I will speak unto him in a dream* [Num. 12:6]. In contrast, in a vision of prophecy only parables or intellectual unions[37] are apprehended, which lead to the attainment of scientific matters similar to those attained through speculation, as we have explained. This is the meaning of its saying: *I will make Myself known unto him in a vision* [Num. 12:6]. Consequently, according to this last interpretation, there are eight degrees of prophecy; the highest and most perfect among them being the one in which [the prophet] prophesies in a vision—taking this in a general way—even though, as has been mentioned, he is merely addressed by a man.

33. The verb has a different tense in the Bible.

34. The verb has a different form in the Bible.

35. Cf. Gen. 15:9–10.

36. *Genesis Rabbah* 17 and 44.

37. I.e., the union of the active intellect with the intellect of the prophet.

Perhaps you will raise the objection against me, saying: "You have counted among the degrees of prophecy the prophet's hearing an address from God who addresses him, as in the cases of Isaiah and Micaiah. How can this be when our fundamental is that all prophets hear an address only through the intermediary of an angel, with the exception of Moses our Master, of whom it is said: *With him do I speak mouth to mouth* [Num. 12:8]?" Know then that this is in fact so, and that the intermediary here is the imaginative faculty. For he hears only in a dream of prophecy that God has spoken to him. Moses our Master, in contrast, heard Him *from above the ark-cover, from between the two cherubim* [Exod. 25:22], without action on the part of the imaginative faculty. We have already explained in *Mishneh Torah* the differentia of that prophecy and have commented on the meaning of *mouth to mouth* [Num. 12:8], and: *As a man speaketh unto his friend* [Exod. 33:11], and others. Understand it from there, for there is no need to repeat what has already been said.

PART 3

Chapter 26

Just as there is disagreement among the theoretical men of the adherents of Law whether His works, may He be exalted, follow from wisdom or from nothing but will and without being aimed at an end at all; so they have the very same disagreement about our laws, which He has revealed to us. Thus some do not seek for them any cause at all and say that all laws follow from nothing but His will. And others say that every command and prohibition among them follows from wisdom and seeks some end, and that all the laws have causes and were revealed for the sake of some advantage. But all of them have a cause, though we ignore causes of some of them and we do not know in what respect they partake of wisdom—that is the doctrine of all of us, both the many and the few. The texts of the Book on that are clear: *just statutes (ḥuqqim) and judgments (mishpatim)* [Deut. 4:8]; *The judgments of the Lord are true, they are altogether just* [Ps. 19:10].

About those called *statutes* (*ḥuqqim*) such as *mixed fabric, meat with milk, and the scapegoat,* the sages, peace be upon them, said, "[Statutes] that I legislated for you, you do not have permission to inquire into them.[38] Satan criticizes them and the nations of the world argue against them." The multitude of the sages do not believe they are things that do not have any cause and for which one must not seek an end. For this, according to what we have explained, would amount to the actions being in vain. The multitude of the sages, however, believe that they definitely have a cause, I mean, a useful end, but that it is concealed from us either due to the insufficiency of our intellects or to a deficiency of our knowledge. Thus, in their view, there is a cause for every *commandment* (*mizṿot*), I mean, for any particular command or prohibition there is an advantageous end. In some, it is clear in what respect they are useful, for example, the prohibition of killing and stealing. In others, their usefulness is not clear, for example, the prohibition of *first fruits* and of [sowing] *the vineyard with diverse seeds* [Deut. 22:9]. Those whose usefulness is clear in the eyes of the multitude are called *judgments* (*mishpatim*), and those whose usefulness is not clear in the eyes of the multitude are called *statutes* (*ḥuqqim*).... What everyone of sound intellect ought to believe about this matter is what I will set forth: The generalities of the *commandments* (*mizṿot*) necessarily have a cause and have been revealed for the sake of some advantage. As for the particulars, it was them about which it was said that they were given to command something. For example, the killing of animals because of the need for good nourishment is clearly advantageous, as we will explain; however, that they should have their throat slit well above the chest and that their esophagus and windpipe should be cut at a particular location, this is...for "purifying the people."[39]...The true reality of the particulars [of the *commandments*] is illustrated by the sacrifices. The offering of sacrifices is [that is, the generalities of the sacrifices are] for a great and manifest advantage, as I shall

38. *Babylonian Talmud, Yoma* 67b.

39. *Genesis Rabbah* 44.

make clear.[40] However, that this sacrifice is a *lamb* and that sacrifice is a *ram* and that the number of sacrifices should be a particular number, for these things no cause will ever be found.[41] Everyone who occupies himself in seeking causes for one of these particulars succumbs to an enduring madness in the course of which they do not put an end to an incongruity, but only increase the number of incongruities. One who imagines that a cause can be found for these is as far from the truth as one who imagines that the generalities of the *commandments* (*mizvot*) do not seek any real advantage.

Know that wisdom made it necessary or, if you will, say that the necessary determined that there should be particulars whose cause could not be found, such that it was an impossibility with respect to the Law that there not be in it anything of this sort. In such a case the impossibility results from your saying why in a given case a *lamb* rather than a *ram,* the similar question would then need to be asked why a *ram* rather than a *lamb.* It is necessary that a particular species [be determined]. The same would apply should you ask why there are *seven lambs* and not *eight.* It could be asked whether one should say *eight* or *ten* or *twenty.* It is necessary, however, that a particular number be determined. This resembles the nature of the possible, for it is necessary that one of the possibilities come into being. The question should not be raised why this possibility and not another came to pass because this question would inevitably occur for any other possibility that might come into being. Know this issue and grasp it. The constant statements [of the sages] about finding the causes and about Solomon knowing the causes refer to the advantage of that *commandment* found in a general way, not in its particularities....

Chapter 27

The Law as a whole aims at two things: the well-being of the soul and the well-being of the body. As for the well-being of the soul, it consists in the multitude acquiring correct opinions corresponding to their respective capacity. Therefore some of them [namely, the opinions] are set forth explicitly and some of them are set forth in parables. For it is not within the nature of the common multitude[42] that its capacity should suffice for apprehending that subject matter as it is. As for the well-being of the body, it comes about by the improvement of their ways of living one with another. This matter is achieved through two things: One of them is the removal of reciprocal wrongdoing from among them. This consists in not allowing any human individual to act according to his will and up to the limits of his power, but compelling him to do that which is useful to all. The second consists in the acquisition by every human individual of moral qualities that are useful for social intercourse so that the affair (*amr*) of the city may be well ordered. Know that as between these two aims, one is undoubtedly greater in nobility, namely, the well-being of the soul, I mean the giving of correct opinions. The second aim, I mean the well-being of the body, is prior in nature and time. The latter aim consists in the governance of the city and the well-being of the states of all its people according to their capacity. This second is the more urgent one, and it is the one regarding which every effort has been made to expound it and to expound all its particulars. For the first aim can be achieved only after achieving this second one. For it has already been demonstrated that man has two perfections: a first perfection, which is the perfection of the body, and an ultimate perfection, which is the perfection of the soul. His first perfection [60a] consists in his being healthy and in the very best bodily state, and this is only possible through his finding the things necessary for him whenever he seeks them. These are his food and the rest of the things needed for the governance of his body, such as shelter, bathing, and so forth. This cannot be achieved in any way by one isolated individual. An individual can attain all this only through a political association, it being already known that man is political by nature. His ultimate perfection is to become rational in actuality, I mean to have an intellect in actuality; and that is to know everything concerning all the beings that it is within the capacity of man to know in accordance with his ultimate perfection.

40. Cf. *Guide* 3.29, 32.

41. Cf. Aristotle *Nicomachean Ethics* 1134b23.

42. Or "within the common nature of the multitude."

It is clear that this ultimate perfection does not comprise either actions or moral habits and that it consists only of opinions arrived at through speculation and made necessary by investigation. It is also clear that this noble ultimate perfection can be achieved only after the first perfection has been achieved. For a man cannot cognize an intelligible even when made to comprehend it, and still less become aware of it of his own accord, while in pain or very hungry or thirsty or hot or very cold. But once the first perfection has been achieved it is possible to achieve the ultimate perfection, which is undoubtedly more noble and is the only cause of lasting life.

As for the truth-telling Law, of which, as we have already explained, there is only one and no other, namely, the Law of Moses our Master, it has come to give us both perfections—I mean the well-being of the states of people in their relations with one another through the removal of reciprocal wrongdoing and through the adoption of noble and excellent moral character, to make possible the preservation of the population of the country and the perpetuation of their being under a single order, so that [60b] every one of them achieves his first perfection; and the soundness of the beliefs and the giving of correct opinions through which ultimate perfection is achieved. The text of the Torah has spoken of both perfections and has informed us that the end of this Law in its entirety is the achievement of these two perfections. He, the Exalted, said: *And the Lord commanded us to do all these statutes (ḥuqqim), to fear the Lord our God, for our good always, that He might preserve us alive, as it is at this day* [Deut. 6:24]. Here He puts the ultimate perfection first on account of its nobility, just as we have explained that it is the ultimate end. Hence His saying here: *For our good always.* You know already what [the sages] (may their memory be a blessing) have said in commenting on the saying of the Exalted: *That it may be well with thee, and that thou mayest prolong thy days* [Deut. 22:7]. They said: "That it may be well with thee in a world in which everything is well and that thou mayest prolong thy days in a world the whole of which is long."[43] Similarly the intention of His saying here, *For our good always,* is this same notion: I mean the attainment of "a world in which everything is well and [the whole of which is] long." And this is lasting life. However, His saying, *That He might preserve us alive, as it is at this day,* refers to this first and bodily life, which lasts for a certain duration and which can only be well ordered through political association, as we have explained.

Chapter 28

Among the things to which your attention must be directed is that you should know that as regards the correct opinions through which the ultimate perfection is obtained, the Law has given only their end and has called to believe in them in a summary way—namely, in the existence of the deity, the Exalted, His unity, His knowledge, His power, His will, and His eternity. All these are ultimate ends that do not become evident [61a] in detail and with precision except after knowing many opinions.[44] In the same way the Law has called to adopt certain beliefs, the belief in which is necessary for the sake of the well-being of political conditions—like our belief that the Exalted becomes violently angry with those who disobey him and that it is therefore necessary to fear Him and to dread Him and to take care not to disobey. As regards all the other correct opinions concerning the whole of this existence—opinions that constitute all the theoretical sciences in their many kinds through which those opinions forming the ultimate end are validated—the Law, although it does not call to them explicitly as it does with regard to the former, does do this in summary fashion by saying: *To love the Lord* [Deut. 11:13, 22; 19:9; 30:6, 12, 20]. You already know what is found regarding the expression "love": *With all thy heart, and with all thy soul, and with all thy might* [Deut. 6:5]. We have already explained in *Mishneh Torah* that this love becomes valid only through the apprehension of the whole of existence as it is and through the consideration of His wisdom in it. We have also mentioned there that the sages (may their memory be a blessing) call attention to this notion.

43. *Babylonian Talmud, Qiddushin* 39b.

44. Cf. *Guide* 3.51 (124b).

What results from all that we have now stated as a premise regarding this subject is that whenever a commandment, be it a prescription or a prohibition, requires removing reciprocal wrongdoing, or urging to a noble moral habit leading to a good social relationship, or giving a correct opinion that ought to be believed either on account of itself or because it is necessary for the removal of reciprocal wrongdoing or for the acquisition of a noble moral habit, such a commandment has a clear cause and is of manifest utility. No question as to the end need be posed with regard to such commandments. For at no time at all was anyone perplexed or asked why we were commanded by the Law that God is one, or why we were forbidden to [61b] kill and to steal or why we were forbidden to exercise vengeance and retaliation, or why we were ordered to love one another. Rather the things about which people were perplexed and opinions differed—so that some said that they are completely useless except as mere commands, whereas others said that they are useful, but their utility is hidden from us—are the commandments from whose external meaning it does not appear that they are useful according to one of the three notions we have mentioned; I mean that they neither give one of the opinions nor instill a noble moral habit nor remove a reciprocal wrongdoing. Apparently these commandments are not related to the well-being of the soul, as they do not give a belief, or to the well-being of the body, as they do not give rules useful for the governance of the city or for the governance of the household—the prohibition of the mingled stuff, of the mingling [of diverse species], and of meat in milk,[45] and the commandment concerning the covering of blood, the heifer whose neck was broken, and the firstling of an ass,[46] and others of the same kind. You will hear my explanation for all of them and the exposition of their correct and demonstrated causes, with the sole exception—as I have mentioned to you—of certain details and a few commandments. I shall explain that all these and others of the same kind have to be related to one of the three notions—either to the soundness of a belief or to the well-being of the circumstances of the city, which is achieved through two things: removal of reciprocal wrongdoing and acquisition of excellent moral habit.

Sum up what we have said concerning beliefs as follows. In some cases a commandment gives a correct belief, which is the one and only thing aimed at—like the belief in the unity and eternity of the deity and in His not being a body. In other cases the belief is necessary for the removal of reciprocal wrongdoing or for the acquisition of a noble moral habit—like the belief that He, the Exalted, has a violent anger against those who do injustice, according to what is said: *And My wrath shall wax hot, and I will kill,* and so on [Exod. 22:23], and as the belief that He, the Exalted, [62a] responds instantaneously to the prayer of someone wronged or deceived: *And it shall come to pass, when he crieth unto Me, that I will hear; for I am gracious* [Exod. 22:26].

Chapter 34

Among the things that you likewise ought to know is that the Law does not pay attention to the exceptional, and legislation is not made with a view to things that are rare. Rather, in everything that it wishes to bring about, be it an opinion or a moral habit or a useful work, it is directed only toward the things that occur in the majority of cases and pays no attention to what happens rarely or to the harm occurring to a single human being resulting from this determination and governance of the Law.[47] For the Law is a divine thing. It is your business to reflect on the natural things in which those general advantages, which are in them, comprise and necessarily lead to harms that befall certain individuals, as became clear from our discourse and the discourse of others. In view of this consideration also, do not wonder that the purpose of the Law is not perfectly achieved in each individual and that, on the contrary, it necessarily follows that there should be individuals whom this governance of the Law does not make perfect. For not everything that derives necessarily from the natural specific forms is actualized in each and every individual. Indeed, all things proceed from one deity and

45. Cf. Deut. 22:11; Lev. 19:19; Exod. 23:19. Cf. *Eight Chapters,* chap. 6 (below, selection 16).

46. Cf. Lev. 17:13; Deut. 21:1–9; Exod. 13:13.

47. Cf. *Guide* 1.34 (39a).

one agent and *have been given from one shepherd* [Eccles. 12:11]. The contrary of this is impossible, and we have already explained that the impossible has a permanent nature that never changes.[48] In view of this consideration it also will not be possible that the Laws be dependent on changes in the circumstances of the individuals and of the times, as is the case with regard to medical treatment, which is particularized for every individual in conformity with his present temperament. Rather, the governance of the Law ought to be unqualified and common for the generality, [75a] even if that is required only for certain individuals and not required for others; for if it were made to fit individuals, corruption would befall the generality, and "you would make out of it something that varies."[49] For this reason, matters that are primarily intended in the Law, ought to be dependent on neither time nor place; rather, the decrees ought to be unqualified and common, in accord with what He, the Exalted, says: *As for the congregation, there shall be one statute (ḥuqqah) for you* [Num. 15:15]. However, only the common interests, those of the majority, are considered in them, as we have explained.

After I have set forth these premises, I shall begin to explain what I have intended to explain.

48. Cf. *Guide* 1.71, 73, tenth premise; 3.17, opinion of the Ash'arites; and *Eight Chapters*, chap. 1.

49. A Talmudic expression; cf., e.g., *Babylonian Talmud, Shabbat* 35b.

SIXTEEN

MAIMONIDES

Eight Chapters

Translated by Joshua Parens

The *Eight Chapters* is the introduction to Maimonides' commentary on the Tractate Avot from his *Commentary on the Mishnah.* The Talmud is composed of the Mishnah, compiled by Rabbi Judah ha-Nasi in the third century, and various commentaries on the Mishnah. One of the most renowned sections of the Mishnah is the chapters of Avot or Pirqei Avot (the Chapters of the Fathers), which are often studied by Jews in isolation from the rest of the Talmud. This section contains a collection of sundry ethical sayings of the rabbinic sages. Maimonides includes a commentary on those sayings in his *Commentary on the Mishnah* but also presents a more systematic account of ethics in his introduction to that commentary. That introduction is today called the *Eight Chapters.*

The *Eight Chapters* is deeply indebted both to ancient philosophy (especially Aristotle's *Nicomachean Ethics*) and to what Maimonides refers to as "modern" philosophers (by which he means Alfarabi, especially his *Selected Aphorisms*).[1]

The *Eight Chapters* consists of a brief introduction and eight chapters. The introduction promises the reader that, in keeping with the Talmudic claim that "piety brings about...the holy spirit,"[2] this work or the tractate it comments on serves as training in prophecy. (Cf. *Guide* 2.32.) Chapter 1 offers an account of the soul based on the Aristotelian account presented in *On the Soul* and more summarily at the end of the first book of the *Nicomachean Ethics.* Chapter 2 outlines the differences between the biblical and the philosophic accounts of the origin of transgression. Chapter 3 explains moral vice in medical terms and recommends to the reader that he consult the "wise men" (*'ulamā'*) or "physicians of the soul." Chapter 4 offers an inventory of a group of virtues, which resemble in many, though not all, respects those of the *Nicomachean Ethics* (bk. 4). It also recommends a medical treatment of the soul modeled on the *Ethics,* Book 2. Along the way, Maimonides draws a crucial contrast between the "wise" and the "virtuous." The virtuous are those who go to the opposite extreme from that embraced by most human beings. When the ignorant see the ascetic extreme of the virtuous they mistake this way of life for the best way of

1. See the *Selected Aphorisms* in *Alfarabi: The Political Writings; "Selected Aphorisms" and Other Texts,* ed. and trans. Charles E. Butterworth (Ithaca, NY: Cornell University Press, 2001), 1–67. On the link between the *Eight Chapters* and the *Aphorisms,* see Herbert A. Davidson, "Maimonides' *Shemonah Peraqim* and Alfarabi's *Fuṣūl al-Madanī,*" *Proceedings of the American Academy for Jewish Research* 31 (1963): 33–50.

2. *Babylonian Talmud, 'Avodah Zarah* 20b.

life. Although Maimonides commends the pursuit of the mean rather than this extreme, he acknowledges that, according to the philosophers, it would be very difficult to find anyone possessing all of the virtues. Chapter 5 explains the goal of the training in prophecy or the best life, namely, knowledge of God—while conceding that one cannot study all of the time. Chapter 6 is the text that follows, which contains one of Maimonides' most important discussions of the status and character of the various kinds of law, by relating them to Aristotle's distinction between self-restraint and virtue (*aretē*). This selection should be compared especially with selections 12, 13, and 14 from Saadya, Halevi, and *Guide* 3.26. Chapter 7 explains the various kinds of veils, a metaphor borrowed from Sufi lore, that prevent the potential prophet from attaining prophecy, including vices such as irascibility (cf. chap. 4). Chapter 8 concludes with discussions of human freedom and repentance in which Maimonides highlights the agreement between the philosophers and the Law regarding freedom. He establishes an alliance between philosophy and Law against astral determinism or fatalism. This should be compared with the *Letter on Astrology.*

This translation is based on the Judeo-Arabic text edited by Joseph Kafiḥ,[3] *Mishnah 'im Perush Rabbeinu Mosheh ben Maimon* (Jerusalem: Mossad ha-Rav Kook, 1963–68). I have followed the emendations (due to typesetter errors) derived by Charles E. Butterworth and Raymond L. Weiss from M. Wolff's *Acht Capitel* (Leipzig: H. Hunger, 1863). My translation is indebted to Butterworth's and Weiss's translation in *Ethical Writings of Maimonides* (New York: New York University Press, 1975; repr., New York: Dover, 1983).

CHAPTER SIX: ON THE DIFFERENCE BETWEEN THE VIRTUOUS AND THE SELF-RESTRAINED

The philosophers said that though the self-restrained person does virtuous deeds, he does good things while longing and yearning to do evil deeds. He contends with his longing and opposes by his action what his power, his longing, and the states [of his soul] urge upon him. He does good things while being troubled by doing them. As for the virtuous person, he follows in his deed what his longing and the states [of his soul] urge upon him. He does good things while longing and yearning for them. The philosophers are unanimous that the virtuous person is more virtuous and more perfect than the self-restrained. They said, however, that the self-restrained can stand in for the virtuous in most matters, though he is necessarily lower in rank because he craves doing evil—even though he does not do it. His yearning is a bad state of the soul.

Solomon had said something like this. He said: *The soul of the wicked desires evil* [Prov. 21:10]. He told about the delight of the virtuous person in doing good things and the pain of the vicious in doing them. This is the saying: *A delight to the just is doing justice, but distress to evil-doers* [Prov. 21:15]. This is what is manifest in the *kalām*[4] of the Law that agrees with what the philosophers have mentioned.

When we examined the *kalām* of the sages about this issue, we found that, for them, one who longs and yearns for prohibited things is more virtuous and more perfect than one who does not long for them and is not pained at refraining from them. They even said that the more virtuous and the more perfect an individual is the more he yearns for prohibited things and is pained [at refraining from them].[5] They related tales about that. And they said, "Whoever is greater than his friend has a greater [evil] impulse than he."[6] As if this were not enough, they said that the recompense of the self-restrained is according to his pain in restraining himself.[7] They said, "The recompense is according to the pain."[8] Even further

3. Aside from some minor differences in grammar, Judeo-Arabic is Arabic written in Hebrew characters.

4. *Kalām,* like the Greek term *logos,* primarily means "discourse, speech, or reasoning." Of course, I retain *kalām* here because, though its primary meaning is likely "discourse," the present discussion at least alludes to *kalām* as dialectical theology. Maimonides alludes to a dispute between the sages and the philosophers, while appearing to resolve the dispute.

5. This is the location of the printer's error present in the Kafiḥ edition, noted by Butterworth and Weiss by comparison with Wolff.

6. *Babylonian Talmud, Sukkah* 52a.

7. Compare Saadya Gaon, *The Book of Doctrines and Beliefs,* trans. Alexander Altmann (Indianapolis: Hackett, 2002) 3.1.

8. *Mishnah, Avot* 5:26.

than that, they commanded that a person be self-restrained and they forbid that he should say, "I would not naturally crave this disobedience, if it were not forbidden by the Law." This is their statement, "Rabban Shimon ben Gamliel says, 'Let a man not say, "I do not want to eat meat with milk, I do not want to wear mixed fabric, I do not want to have illicit sexual relations," rather "I want to, but what shall I do—my Father in heaven has forbidden me." ' "[9]

If the external sense of the two *kalāms* are understood superficially, the speeches are contradictory. The matter is not thus. Rather both *kalāms* are correct, and there is not any opposition between them at all. The evils that in the view of the philosophers are evils are those about which they said that the one who would not long for them is more virtuous than the one who longs for them and restrains himself; they are the things generally accepted by all the people as bad, such as murder, theft, robbery, hurting one who has not done harm, repaying a benefactor with harm, belittling parents, and things like this. They are the laws about which the sages, peace be upon them, said, "If they were not written down, they would deserve to be written down."[10] Some of our modern scholars who suffer from the disease of the *mutakallimūn* call them intellectual [or rational] laws (*al-sharā'i' al-'aqliyya*).[11] There is no doubt that the soul that longs and yearns for any of these things is deficient and that the virtuous soul neither craves any of these evils at all nor is pained by being denied them.

As for the things the sages said about the self-restrained being more virtuous and his compensation being greater, they concern the traditional laws (*al-sharā'i' al-sam'iyya*).[12] This is correct because if it were not for the Law they would not be evils at all. For this reason, they said that a person needs to allow his soul to continue to love them and to not place any impediment to them other than the Law. Consider their wisdom, peace be upon them, and the examples they used. For [Rabban Shimon ben Gamliel] did not say, "Let a man not say, 'I do not want to kill, I do not want to steal, I do not want to lie, but I want to—but what shall I do.' " Rather, he mentioned only traditional matters: meat with milk, wearing mixed fabric, and illicit sexual relations. These laws and ones similar to them are what God calls *My statutes* (*ḥuqqoti*). They said, "Statutes (*ḥuqqim*) that I legislated for you, you do not have permission to inquire into them. The nations of the world argue against them and Satan criticizes them, such as the red heifer and the scapegoat, etc."[13] Those called intellectual [or rational] by the moderns [*mutakallimūn*] are called *commandments* according to the sages' elucidation.

Thus, from all that we have said it has become clear what the disobediences are which it is more virtuous for him to not long for than to long for but restrain himself from, and which are the converse. This is a marvelous point and an extraordinary accommodation between these claims. The text of these claims implies the correctness of what we have elucidated. The purpose of this chapter has been achieved.

9. Cf. *Sifra* to Lev. 20:26.

10. *Babylonian Talmud, Yoma* 67b. The original passage includes in its list of such unwritten laws illicit sexual relations.

11. An obvious reference to Saadya, other Jewish *mutakallimūn,* such as Halevi, as well as Muslim *mutakallimūn.* Cf. the disease reference to Chapter 1 of *Eight Chapters* and *Guide* 1.73. These modern scholars, the *mutakallimūn,* conflate the imaginable with the possible—thus undermining the "nature of existence" (*Guide* 1.71).

12. Cf. the closing paragraphs of the *Book of Doctrines and Beliefs* in selection 12 above, where this is translated "revealed laws."

13. *Babylonian Talmud, Yoma* 67b.

SEVENTEEN

MAIMONIDES

Letter on Astrology

Translated by Ralph Lerner

This letter (also known as the "Letter to Marseilles") by and large explains the circumstances attending its composition. A long and detailed series of questions relating to astrology has been sent to Maimonides by a group of Provençal rabbis. Maimonides is, as it were, compelled to answer, even though he has already discussed the problems posed by astrology in the *Mishneh Torah* (*Code*) and in the *Guide of the Perplexed*. The rabbis have to be informed of the difference between the pseudoscience of astrology and the genuine science of the stars. This leads to an account of the controversy between the philosophers and the Jews concerning the origin of the universe and, further, to the controversy between philosophers, astrologers, and Jews with respect to the workings of providence. Maimonides' discussion of the fall of the Jewish commonwealth attributes the political disaster of defeat and consequent worldwide dispersion of the people to the ancient Jews' preoccupation with astrology. It is noteworthy that astrology is here regarded less as a transgression of the second commandment than as a witless diversion from the activities that help preserve political communities.

The Hebrew text of this letter, together with variant readings, has been edited by Alexander Marx in *Hebrew Union College Annual* 3 (1926): 349–58. Numbers in brackets refer to this edition. A translation of the complete letter can be found in Ralph Lerner, *Maimonides' Empire of Light: Popular Enlightenment in an Age of Belief* (Chicago: University of Chicago Press, 2000), 178–87.

[350]. ... Know, my masters, that it is not proper for a man to accept as trustworthy anything other than one of these three things. The first is a thing for which there is a clear proof deriving from man's reasoning—such as arithmetic, geometry, and astronomy. The second is a thing that a man perceives through one of the five senses—such as when he knows with certainty that this is red and this is black and the like through the sight of his eye; or as when he tastes that this is bitter and this is sweet; or as when he feels that this is hot and this is cold or as when he hears that this sound is clear[1] and this sound is indistinct; or as when he smells that this is a pleasing smell and this is a displeasing smell and the like. The third is a thing that a man receives from the prophets or from the

1. Reading *ṣalul*, as two MSS have it. If one reads *ṣarud* with Marx, the phrase would be as follows: "that this sound is harsh and this sound is indistinct."

righteous. Every reasonable man ought to distinguish in his mind and thought all the things that he accepts as trustworthy, and say: "This I accept as trustworthy because of tradition, and this because of sense-perception, and this on grounds of reason." Anyone who accepts as trustworthy anything that is not of these three species, of him it is said: *The simple believeth everything* [Prov. 14:15]. Thus you ought to know that fools have composed thousands of books of nothingness and emptiness. Any number of men, great in years but not in wisdom, wasted all their days in studying these books and imagined that these follies are science. They came to think of themselves as wise men because they knew that science. The thing about which most of the world errs, or all of it—save for a few individuals, *the remnant whom the Lord shall call* [cf. Joel 3:5]—is that thing of which I am apprising you. The great sickness and the *grievous evil* [cf. Eccles. 5:12, 15] consist in this: that all the things that man finds written in books, he presumes to think of as true—and all the more so if the books are old. And since many individuals have busied themselves with those books and have engaged in discussions concerning them, the rash fellow's mind at once leaps to the conclusion that these are words of wisdom, and he says to himself: *Has the pen of the scribes wrought in vain* [cf. Jer. 8:8], and have they vainly engaged in these things? This is why our kingdom was lost and our Temple was destroyed and we were brought to this: for our fathers sinned and are no more because they found many books dealing with these themes of the stargazers, these things being the root of idolatry, as we have made clear in "Laws Concerning Idolatry."[2] They erred and were drawn after them, imagining them to be glorious science and to be of great utility. They did not busy themselves with the art of war or with the conquest of lands, but imagined that those studies would help them. Therefore the prophets called them *fools* and *dolts* [cf. Jer. 4:22]. And truly fools they were, for they walked after confused things that do not profit [cf. 1 Sam. 12:21 and Jer. 2:8]....

2. See *Mishneh Torah, Book of Knowledge.* Cf. *Guide* 3.29.

EIGHTEEN

ISAAC POLGAR

The Support of Religion

Translated by Charles H. Manekin

Little is known about Isaac Polgar (Yitzḥaq ben Joseph Ibn Polgar, also known as Pulgar or Policar, ca. first half of the fourteenth century) except the role he played in attempting to refute the anti-Jewish polemics of his former teacher, Abner of Burgos (who was renamed, upon conversion to Christianity, Alfonso of Valladolid or Alfonso Burgensis). We know that Abner lived ca. 1270–1340. He was a physician who, due to the suffering of the Jews of Castile of his time and to experiencing visions, which he could not explain, decided at approximately the age of fifty to convert to Christianity. In addition, he was committed to a blend of astrology, mysticism, deterministic *kalām,* and certain versions of Christian doctrines of predestination. Abner and Polgar exchanged a series of epistles, culminating on Polgar's side in his *Support of Religion,* a combination of a defense of Judaism and an attack on Abner's determinism. Polgar combines elements from the teachings of Alfarabi, Averroes, and Maimonides, though he is most widely recognized as theoretically informed by Averroes.

The *Support of Religion* is composed of five parts: (1) a defense of Judaism, including its main tenets regarding Moses, the Torah, the world to come, and the Messiah; (2) a dialogue between a philosophic youth and an old man, the voice of religion, in which Polgar foreshadows the radical claim of Spinoza that the imagination is solely responsible for prophecy; (3) an attack on astral determinism, revisiting many of Maimonides' arguments against determinism; (4) an attack on magic and the expectation of everyday miracles; and (5) a dialogue between a dead man and a living one on the soul and its destiny. In the following selection from Part 1, Polgar returns to the connection between the philosopher-king and the Law so crucial to Alfarabi, and subsequently Maimonides and Averroes. Indeed, in the third gate, Polgar shows even more clearly than Maimonides the dependence of Jewish medieval political philosophy on the Platonic tradition of political philosophy by listing the virtues of the philosophic ruler—a list found with some variation not only in Alfarabi,[1] but also in Averroes' commentary on Plato's *Republic* and of course in the *Republic* itself, bk. 6 485A–487A. Finally, Polgar displays the profound influence of Averroes on Jewish medieval political philosophy.[2]

1. See *Attainment of Happiness* 60; and *Virtuous City* 15.13 (Walzer ed.).

2. See Abraham Melamed, *The Philosopher-King in Medieval and Renaissance Jewish Political Thought,* ed. Lenn E. Goodman (Albany: SUNY Press, 2003).

The translation is of the critical Hebrew edition *'Ezer ha-Dat* by Jacob Levinger (Tel Aviv: Chaim Rosenberg School of Jewish Studies, 1984), 31–56.

PART ONE

The First Gate

[3a] It is well known to the sages that the rational faculty, the essential difference through which man is particularized and distinguished, and on account of which man is man, is divided into two types.

The first is the theoretical intellect through which the generalities of things are known. Using his intellect man abstracts the form of things from their matters, combines some intelligibles[3] with others, and separates some from others. Neither representation[4] nor sensation is capable of performing these activities. This type of intellect is not required or necessary for maintaining man's livelihood or for fulfilling his needs. Its usefulness lies in its being the instrument through which man apprehends the truth of things solely insofar as they are true. Then the human soul cleaves to the soul of the first intelligence[5] and they become one. Now since these intelligibles are also perpetually and immutably existing intelligences, the soul that apprehends them and cleaves to the eternal first intelligence also exists permanently through their existence, and therein consist the soul's felicity and salvation from annihilation. By means of this faculty man acquires the scholarly disciplines and endeavors to learn them.

The second of the rational faculty's types is the intellect through which man distinguishes and recognizes the fair from the ugly. The end to which it aspires is solely practical, that is, what is required to sustain one's living.[6] For one cannot survive without the wondrous actions and the marvelous tools that the various occupations provide, such as the mill, the grape-press, the ship, etc.

It has also been demonstrated that man possesses another faculty required for his living, which he shares with some other animals, and which he calls the faculty of desire. Through this faculty man desires or abhors an object, draws near to the pleasant and avoids the harmful. The faculty serves as the basis for the activities of will, courage, anger, fear, mercy, cruelty, love, hate, and other occurrences of the soul. By means of it man generally acquires the virtues, which are the [Divine] commandments and the true qualities of righteousness. Since, as I mentioned, these three faculties are absolutely indispensable for man—the one for maintaining his soul, the other two for his living and his conduct—the species of man was required to awake and rise up from its youthful sleep of ignorance, and to be guided and instructed in its application and use of each of these three faculties[7] according to the proper order. This is called [3b] Law (*Torah*), which means "to teach," that is, to teach men the proper order of their activities and the path they should take. Hence, it contains some of the true and right beliefs that are incumbent upon us by virtue of our possessing wisdom and a rational soul.

Now most of men's business and concerns consist in pursuing their living, and most men cannot devote their entire life to directing their mind and preparing their intellect to know and to apprehend these beliefs from their origins and principles, which are the true sciences. So, of necessity, one who particularizes[8] the heavenly-emanated religion was required in order to establish as part of Law most of the true principles of belief, namely, those that are indispensable for man's completion and perfection. He recorded them as traditional beliefs in order that a man not die bereft of them, as do the ignorant nations *who came in darkness and whose name will be concealed in darkness* [cf. Eccles. 6.4].

3. *Muskalot,* i.e., accurate concepts and true propositions.

4. *Ziyyur;* from the context it is clear that Polgar is not referring to an intellectual representation, although the term often carries that sense.

5. *Ha-maskil ha-rishon.* A more accurate translation of *maskil* would be "intellecter" or "intelligizer," but these words don't exist in English. It would appear that Polgar refers thereby to the Agent Intellect. Below, when referring to a philosopher or sage, *maskil* is translated as "thinker."

6. *Miḥyah:* "living," "sustenance," "livelihood."

7. Literally, "to walk and to endeavor in each of these three faculties."

8. Reading *meyaḥed* with most of the MSS; Levinger suggests *meyuḥad,* but neither reading works entirely well. On this reading the "particularizer" is Moses.

Also placed within Law were the orders and regimens pertaining to each of the other two psychic faculties. This was required for man's livelihood and because he is political by nature. That is to say, his nature and vitality render it impossible for him to exist unless he is connected to the rest of mankind. For the slice of bread that is a man's provision for half of a day cannot be produced or made without the assistance and participation of a number of men and a number of trades that emanate from the practical intellect. The same applies for the rest of man's needs. Inasmuch as men's natures, temperaments, and dispositions differ, they require of absolute necessity a religion and law that will regulate their conduct in a proper and right manner.[9] Otherwise, the intrepid will harass the weak, the rich the poor, and the important the insignificant.

Now the books of the sages teach us that a great nation and an absolutely virtuous people is the nation that has no need of judge or physician.[10] For since its people conduct themselves in the best manner, and their actions are completely flawless, equitable, and moral, and performed entirely without destructive evils like jealousy, hatred, envy, anger, etc., there is no need for a judge that compels, or an arbiter that punishes, as the sage says, "Were all of Israel righteous, there would be no need for *Seder Nezikin.*" And since they are wise and understanding, knowing how to avoid bad food and other things that corrupt the body, and accustoming themselves [4a] to things that preserve the body and maintain its proper constitution, they will have no need of a physician that preserves health and gets rid of illness. For someone who refrains from eating mushrooms and cumin has no need to be cured of the choking sickness that they cause.

We also learn from these books that an acclaimed people is the people that is governed by the most perfect master and officer possible—namely, the natural king. He instructs and guides them in the ways that are the essence and substance of the Law.

We have demonstrated truly the necessity of the existence of the essence of Law and belief for every thinker.[11]

The Second Gate

Man possesses corporeal faculties (that is, faculties that need, in order to achieve their perfection, various corporeal instruments that perform and complete all the requisite activities), namely, the faculties of sense perception, imagination, and cogitation, as well as another spiritual and holy faculty, that is, the intellect. When this [latter] faculty is completely perfected it does not need any instrument or body, for its end is nothing but the perfect apprehension of knowledge and true beliefs, as I will explain in this chapter. Hence, if a man is perfect with respect to both these kinds of faculties it follows that his actions and behavior will be moderate, correct, and equitable to the utmost, and that he will know and believe and apprehend the intelligibles of things as they really are.

Now when a scholar examines our acclaimed Law he will find therein most of the true and necessary matters that men must know at the outset. These are the ones whose subjects are weighty, and whose demonstrations are clearly cogent.[12] He will also find right qualities, good and correct actions, and righteous statutes and laws that are moderate, correct, and equitable to the utmost.

I shall first relate and arrange for you some of the worthy, true beliefs found therein:

All peoples believe that the first principle and ultimate end of all the knowledge that man acquires via his theoretical intellect is twofold: first, man's knowledge and apprehension, to the best of his ability, of the Governor of everything and His Attributes; second, man's knowledge of himself and his ultimate end. Each of these matters is explained and established via tradition in our religion.

The first is to make known to all peoples God's existence (may He be blessed), through whose

9. Cf. Maimonides *Guide* 2.40 (above, selection 15).

10. Cf. Ibn Bajja *Governance of the Solitary* chap. 1 (above, selection 9).

11. Reading *hekhreaḥ* for *ve-hekreaḥ*. For the term "thinker," see note 3 above.

12. *Ḥazaqim bi-meqomoteihem:* literally, "strong in their *topoi.*" The term *meqomot* in its technical sense refers to the rules of inferences discussed by Aristotle in the *Topics.*

[4b] force is moved the encompassing sphere.[13] This is first evident in our religion from the verse: *I am the Lord your God* [Exod. 20:2]; His unity, evident in the verse: *You shall have no other gods before Me* [Exod. 20:3]; and in the verse: *Hear O Israel, the Lord our God the Lord is one* [Deut. 6:4]; that He is not a body, which is known and explicit in the verse: *Take therefore good heed to yourselves: for you saw no manner of form* [Deut. 4:15]; nor a force within a body, in the sense that nothing that happens to dark bodies can be verified of Him. This is known and evident from the verse: *I the Lord have not changed* [Mal. 3:6], that is, I do not undergo change according to any kind of change, whereas every body or force within a body undergoes change, as is known elsewhere. Hence, according to our belief, there is an existent that is First, One, and neither a body nor a force within a body.

The second is the worthy principle that is the end of man, namely, to love his Creator, to desire Him, and to cleave unto Him, in order to return his spirit to God, its giver. This is explicit in many places in the Law, such as the verses: *And you shall love the Lord your God* [Deut. 6:5], and *You shall cleave to Him* [Deut. 10:20], and *To love the Lord your God, to heed His voice, and to cleave unto Him* [Deut. 30:20]. And in order to plant firmly this love alone in the hearts of men, the Law emphatically cautioned them to flee idolatry and to distance themselves greatly from it and from similar things; and not to stray and wander after their hearts' pondering and their eyes' craving. It also wrote down many of the true beliefs that are established within our religion. Now every thinker who has applied himself to understanding Aristotle's physical and metaphysical treatises will know that these beliefs are made evident through powerful demonstrations and comprehensive proofs therein. Only one who rejects primary intelligibles will deny and refute these beliefs.

After I have informed you of some of the worthy beliefs written in Law, I will inform you of some of its equitable statutes, righteous judgments, and right dispositions:

The kind of human action that is unavoidable, as I noted above, can be divided into three classes: how a man acts toward himself; how he acts toward his household; and how he acts toward the men of his city. When the thinker looks at what actions the Law mandates, examining them one after another, he will find them [5a] to contain the most superior actions and excellent practices.

In the first class one finds that the Law mandates bodily cleanliness and the avoidance of impurities, such as contact with a carcass, unclean reptile, or a dead body, and the preparation of a latrine and a spade.[14] We are also admonished not to enter a leprous and moldy house, or to wear leprous garments, for mold darkens and removes the radiance of the vital spirit that serves in our hearts as the matter and seat of our souls. It also rots our body and renders it ill. In order to accustom our souls to accept those beliefs that constitute our ultimate felicity, we are admonished to perform and to carry out everything that we have undertaken, as it is written: *That which has gone out of your lips you shall keep and perform* [Deut. 23:24]. And in order to sanctify and to benefit us further, all of the coarse and thick foods that corrupt the body and render it ill are forbidden to us: foods that dim the bright light of the intellect, through whose perfection and purity the soul cleaves to its Creator, and returns to the place from which it was taken. There is no need to mention these foods here for they are well known in the medical arts.

Anyone who examines our Law in the second class, that is, how a man acts toward his household, will find mandated therein equitable rules of conduct, as well as righteous and pure statutes, such as our separation from women during their entire menstrual period. This practice is the cause of cleanliness and purity, as well as the preparation of the semen for generation; it is also the cause of our being saved from the tremendous illness of leprosy, despite its being quite prevalent among the peoples around us. The Law also admonished us to respect our father and mother, who are God's partners (blessed be He) in producing man. This practice is the cause of a household's welfare and well-ordered living. The Law also commanded us to act mercifully and generously toward servants and maids and family members, as it is written: *If a man smite the eye of his servant, or the eye of his maid, and destroy it; he shall let him go free for his eye's sake*

13. Compare this paragraph with the opening paragraphs of Maimonides' *Mishneh Torah* and with his *Commentary on the Mishnah, Sanhedrin* 10, *Pereq Ḥeleq,* in *A Maimonides Reader,* ed. Isadore Twersky (Springfield, NJ: Behrman House, 1972), 401–23.

14. See Deut. 3:13–14.

[Exod. 21:27]. For it is beneficent and generous to free a servant and to annul his servitude following the loss of his limb, as it is to bestow gifts on the servant who has fulfilled his period of servitude,[15] as it is written: *You surely bestow on him [out of your flock and out of your threshing-floor and out of your winepress;] as the Lord has blessed you, so you will bless him* [Deut. 15:14]; and not to bring back a servant who has fled.

The third class is how a man acts toward the men of his city. Here our religion contains equitable statutes and good practices *which if a man do he shall live on account of them* [Lev. 18:5]. These are divided into five categories: The first is to love [5b] one's fellow men. For a man is loved by those he loves, and this is a cause of peace. This category is evident from the verse: *Love thy neighbor as thyself* [Lev. 19:18]. The second is to distance oneself from envy and jealousy, which is a cause of theft, robbery, and quarrel, as it is written: *Do not envy* [Exod. 20:14]. The third is to be forgiving of others' transgressions, for this leads to humility, as it is written: *Do not avenge or bear a grudge* [Lev. 19:18]; also, to prepare cities of refuge for the unintentional killer. The fourth is to act generously and beneficently, a cause for the preservation of men and the sustaining of the life of the poor among the rich. We are admonished to give alms to the poor, to loan them money, to return their pledge; to leave them the gleanings, the corner produce, and the forgotten sheave of the field, as well as the cluster and single grapes of the vineyard; to unload the yoke of a man and his beast; not to take usury from one's brother, and not to take for a pledge the vessels he uses to cook his food—and, indeed, all the commandments that teach a man beneficence. The fifth comprises the judgments and laws that regulate the dealings of men with each other. When the thinker examines the judgments of our religion, and weighs them thoughtfully, he will find them conforming to the most superior edicts and the most excellent practices in both capital and monetary law. I do not think that any man will abandon and leave the ways of our Law for another religion because of some deficiency in the equity of its judgments.[16]

Thus we have demonstrated for you how pristine and sacred our Law is in all three of the aforementioned classes, and that all its commandments and the admonitions have been mandated for our benefit and our good. As Solomon (peace be upon him) said: *He that keeps the commandment keeps his own soul; but he that despises his way shall die* [Prov. 19:16]. Now if the commandments were not mandated for our benefit and good, as I just mentioned, but rather were royal decrees that expressed the will of the Lord, blessed be He, as is the opinion of some of our vulgar fools, then we would not be permitted to change anything about them, nor could our sages (of blessed memory) say, "One who is in distress is exempt from the requirement of sitting in the Festival Booth"; or "One desecrates the Sabbath for somebody who is not dangerously ill";[17] nor would we compensate monetarily the loss of a limb, and many other examples.

I find the following comprehensive proof and complete demonstration sufficient to show that our Law is correct and flawless with respect to both perfections, that is, belief in what is true and acts of justice and equity: Let one examine and contemplate intellectually the ten dicta written on the Tablets [6a] of the Convenant, which God's angel brought down from heaven to us, ordering and arranging them. For the first five are not required necessarily for maintaining man and his subsistence in this world. They are required necessarily for belief in what is true solely insofar as it is true, as I mentioned with respect to this type of knowledge in the previous gate. This is not the case with the five last dicta: they are required necessarily for man's life and survival in this world alone since he cannot exist without them. For this reason the dicta were written on two tablets, five facing five. The first five on the first table are arranged as follows:

The first, *I am the Lord Your God* [Exod. 20:2], teaches the existence of the Creator, blessed be He, which is the fundamental principle of knowledge and the root of scientific disciplines, as I mentioned. Next to it is the second, *You shall have no other gods besides me* [Exod. 20:3], which means that the aforementioned God is one. Now

15. These two laws apply to two different categories of servants: the former to a non-Jewish servant, the latter to a Jewish servant.

16. This is doubtlessly directed against Polgar's former teacher, Abner. See the historical introduction to this selection.

17. As Levinger points out, this is surprising, since the general view is that one does not desecrate the Sabbath for one who is not seriously ill. His proposed reading is not very convincing.

this is also a worthy and superior thing to know, but it is less useful than the utility of the first, for a believer in dualism is not as wicked and deficient as one who believes that the world does not have a governor. The third is *You shall not take the name of the Lord in vain* [Exod. 20:7], which means not to swear falsely. He who swears to a falsehood denies the true reality of God (may He be exalted). For whoever swears sets on the same level the truth of what he swears to His truth. Now if he swears to a falsehood, he denies His truth (may He be exalted), which is unique among all the truths, since only He is the necessary of existence by virtue of Himself, as is known. Hence whoever denies God's truth (may He be exalted), which is one of his attributes, sins grievously, but not like the sin of the believer in dualism, nor like the sin of the denier of God's existence (may He be blessed). The fourth is *Observe the Sabbath Day to keep it holy* [Deut. 5:12]. The main point of this precept is to teach the honor of the essence of the human soul and to contemplate its rank above the other lower creatures, as can be seen from an examination of the commentaries on Genesis. This, too, is a glorious precept, though the sin of denying it is less grievous than the sin of denying God's truth, or than the sin involved with denying the first two. The fifth is *Honor your father and mother* [Exod. 20:12]. Now although this precept has some benefit for establishing one's living in this world, it is placed here solely in the manner of correct belief. [6b] For since the father, through giving the form, and the mother, through giving the matter, are partners with the Holy One, blessed be He, with respect to offspring, man is obligated to honor them in the same manner that he honors God. If he disparages them he sins, but his sin is not like the sins of the first four.

The first of the five commandments on the second tablet is *You shall not murder* [Exod. 20:13]. For of all the crimes and harm that a man can do to his fellow, nothing compares with murder. The second is *You shall not commit adultery* [Exod. 20:13]. For one who commits adultery with his fellow's wife sins against him, but not as grievously as were he to murder him. The third is *You shall not steal* [Exod. 20:13]. For the thief sins against the money of his fellow, but not as grievously as were he to commit adultery with his wife, even less were he to murder him. The fourth is *You shall not bear false witness against your neighbor* [Exod. 20:13], which is also a sin, though not like the sin of the thief, because he has not yet performed a deed. The fifth is *You shall not envy* [Exod. 20:14], because the Law has admonished against innermost thoughts. Yet in this there is not even the speaking out loud that occurs in bearing false witness; consequently, its sin is not as great.

See, I have taught you that every one of the five divinely-ordained dicta written on the first tablet (those that follow from the requirements of true belief alone) as well as the five written on the second tablet (those that follow from the requirements of worldly livelihood) are arranged hierarchically in such a manner that their order cannot possibly be changed, nor their rank and degree altered. *Happy is the people whose god is the Lord* [Prov. 144:15]. *Happy are the innocent wayfarers who walk in the Law of the Lord* [Prov. 119:1].

After this preamble, I shall compose for you a demonstrative syllogism according to logical method, constructed from true and valid premises and formally sound. Based on what has been revealed in these chapters, I shall show with this syllogism that our religious law is the true one, and that all other religious laws are the contrary of truth and the ways of sound order: *so that all the peoples of the earth will see that the name of the Lord is proclaimed on us* [Deut. 28:10]. *The wise man hearing them will increase wisdom, and the discerning man will acquire stratagems* [Prov. 1:5]. *Take him and pay attention to him* [Jer. 39:12].

Inasmuch as every religious law is composed and made up of different beliefs and patterns of activities, the more the beliefs of such a law are true and manifest, and its activities proper and well founded, the more that law will be sound and true. Now, the beliefs of our religious law are so true and valid that nobody denies them. Its activities also [7a] display the utmost order and correctness, as I explained. The conclusion to be drawn is that the religion of the Jews is the most correct and valid of all the religions. How goodly is our portion, and how pleasant our fate!

Through my explanation it becomes known that any religion whose customs and beliefs have become removed from the ways of our Law, or altered in the slightest, will have its distance from the truth commensurate with its specific distance and alteration [from the ways of our Law]. This is what we wished to explain.

The Third Gate

The philosophical sages have explained that the man who is worthy of being appointed ruler and sovereign over the admirable and virtuous city must fulfill ten conditions.[18] (1) He should be fit of body and whole of limbs that are appropriate and necessary for his actions. (2) He should by nature be capable of understanding whatever he considers, of apprehending things as they really are and whatever he hears according to the intention of the speaker. (3) He should always remember whatever he knows, understands, and hears without forgetting a thing. (4) He should understand, apprehend, and sense hidden matters from the hints and "chapter headings" that have been transmitted to him, so that he is able to infer them from their places of concealment. This is "the one who discerns something on the basis of something else."[19] (5) He should possess a *skilled tongue* [Isa. 50:4] to express in straightforward speech the correct interpretation, and clear examination, of everything in his mind; [and this,] in order to instruct and educate other people. (6) He should be eager and desirous to teach and benefit others with his wisdom, rather than lazy, envious, or pained by the toil of teaching. (7) He should by nature love truth and its possessors, and hate falsehood and those that believe in it. (8) He should not be immersed in bodily pleasures that are of no benefit, such as eating meat or drinking wine to excess, lewdness, witnessing all sorts of frivolity, listening to music and idle stories. (9) He should be proud and esteem himself, possessing a soul that does not defile or degrade itself with ugly and base things. Rather it rises by its nature and transcends anything besides it. (10) Wealth and fortune should be contemptible in his eyes; likewise all the bodily accidents like power, taking vengeance, etc. (11) He should by nature love justice [7b] and law, hate injustice and oppression, and intend to rescue the poor from the stronger party—not from cruelty and wickedness, but from his love and passion for justice. (12) His actions should proceed from strength and resoluteness, greatness of soul and firmness, not from fear or anxiety.

I say that in order to bring the aforementioned man to perfection so that he may attain his final goal, [i.e.,] to raise him to the topmost level, he must possess an additional trait. This will bring the sum total of [qualities] by which the perfect man is identified[20] to thirteen. The trait is (13) that all his actions should proceed from his human rather than from his bestial aspect. Now the explanation of this [quality] is as follows: A man seeks and moves to perform activities as a result of some passions that arise in his soul, for example, lust, anger, envy, jealousy, love of vengeance, and so on. These passions proceed from the vital, bestial aspect within him, for he does not perform these actions by virtue of his human aspect but rather by virtue of his being an animal. Only the actions that he performs through choice and intellectual thought, to achieve a certain goal or utility, are considered human. Sometimes bestial activities are human, namely, when they are performed through human intellectual thought. For example, when a man eats something not because of his appetite or desire for it, but with the intention of improving his body's health through strengthening an organ, or expelling waste, or changing a bodily humor, then his action is human. Occasionally an action will be a composite of the human and the bestial, as when its initial cause is a passion arising in the soul, as I just mentioned, but when its object is also considered by intellectual thought to be beneficial and goal-oriented.

When you consider the aforementioned matters, you will know and understand that an agent whose activities proceed from the passions of his soul, who follows the arbitrariness of his heart and strays after his desires, and whose intellect is incapable of showing him the impropriety of his actions: *He is like the beasts that perish* [Ps. 49:13]. If, in addition to his evil deeds, he is convinced by his sick, despicable, and disgusting intellect that he acts well and walks in an upright path, then he is the lowest of the low. A beast is better off than he is, for a beast is not commanded [by God], whereas he is—and yet he does the opposite of the commander's[21] intentions.

When a man makes all his activities [8a] human, that is, not the result of any passion arising in his soul or bestial activity, even though he desires very much to perform it, he is the perfect man. However, if there exists a man whose soul is moved towards an action, or who desires something, solely because his intellect considers it to

18. Cf. note 1 above.

19. Cf. *Babylonian Talmud, Ḥagigah* 14a.

20. Literally, "is sought."

21. Or "the commandment's."

be appropriate for the pursuit of a certain end or a known benefit; then it is not fitting to call him merely perfect, but rather *divine* and the *angel of the Lord of Hosts.*

Now the man who possesses such precious virtues is fit and prepared to achieve the ultimate human rank, for the sake of which he went out into this world, that is, that his rational power, which is a natural power[22] in matter, becomes the substratum for the hylic intellect to such an extent that they become one thing, possessing matter and form. That hylic intellect becomes perfected and completed when all the intelligibles that were in it potentially are now actualized. The intelligibles themselves are the forms of this intellect: they have conjoined together and become one essence because of the identity of the intellect and the intelligible. When the latter are actualized they become Actual Intellect.

Since the intelligibles that exist in the hylic intellect in act are the same as those that had previously existed in it potentially, and since they now connect with each other and become one; they are considered and understood to be one existing thing in itself, counted, with respect to its content, as among the spiritual entities. For the agent intellect that they cognize intellectually is not approached with respect to those intelligibles existing at one time potentially, but rather with respect to their being at that time completely in act. Then this intellect is called "acquired intellect."

When this acquired intellect is considered as something like matter with respect to the agent intellect, and all the intelligibles collected together become one thing, namely, the agent intellect itself; then man becomes [truly] man and something else, namely, separate intellect, and all is united. I will further comment upon this matter in its proper place.[23] When such a man, who is the end and first intention of the human species, is found to have had an emanation from that glorious intellect received by his rational faculty, he is a sage and a philosopher; when by his imaginative faculty, he is a prophet.

Now when considered from his own viewpoint this divine man (who possesses complete felicity and true perfection) ought to live separate and apart, solitary and isolated, from the rest of man—for no one is like him or comparable to him.[24] From the viewpoint of the general divine providence of the human species, and with respect to his own trait of generosity and excessive goodness that continues unceasingly to overflow upon others, however, it is necessary that, like a shepherd over his flock, he dwell and be immersed in their midst and bear their troubles [cf. Deut. 1:12]; so that he may govern them [8b] and rectify their ways, each one according to his rank and his potential—to such an extent that the city in which he dwells will have no need for any other judge or physician, as I mentioned. It is also necessary with respect to his overflow of generosity that, when he becomes advanced in years and elderly, he will write for them a book in order to teach and to guide those who come after him and who never knew him personally the way in which they should walk, as well as his commandments and statutes according to which they should conduct their lives, *so they will live by them.* This writ should stand before them in place of his own form and shape, so that they fear him as if they saw him with their own eyes. That is the true essence of the sanctified Law. *Happy is the people who has it so!* [Ps. 144:15].

After I have recounted for you the qualities of the man that render him fit to be appointed ruler and sovereign over the pure and worthy city, and the measure of his [intellectual] apprehension, I shall inform you truly that Moses our Master was the one who possessed these qualities, and that he also ascended to God, that is, to the most supreme rank possible. I shall inform you first that the aforementioned thirteen conditions found their fulfillment in him in the most correct and equitable manner.

With respect to the first condition, that he should be healthy and strong in body, I say that the matter of his strength is well-known from his killing of the Egyptian who was beating [the Israelite],[25] from his saving the daughters of Jethro from the shepherds and removing the well-stone [to water their flock], and from his being 120 years old and *his eyes undimmed and his vigor unabated* [Deut. 34:7].[26]

22. If we emend *tiv'it* to *tevu'ah,* then the phrase reads: "which is a power embedded in matter," which makes better sense.

23. That is, in the Fifth Gate.

24. Cf. this paragraph with Ibn Bajja *Governance of the Solitary* (above, selection 9), Ibn Tufayl *Hayy the Son of Yaqzan* (above, selection 10), and Maimonides *Guide* 2.37 (above, selection 15).

25. Contrast Maimonides' more ambiguous interpretation of this event in *Guide* 2.45, first degree of prophecy (above, selection 15).

26. Actually, there is no scriptural indication that Moses removed the well-stone in order to water the flock of Jethro's daughters.

Also with respect to the second condition, the greatness of Moses' knowledge and the completeness of his perfection are renowned among all the nations. The Law testifies of him: *Never again did there arise in Israel a prophet like Moses* [Deut. 34:10].

With respect to the third condition, Moses was well known for remembering to relate in Deuteronomy all the stories and details that happened to him, not forgetting anything, even with all the hardships he encountered in his dealings with the community.

That he fulfilled the fourth condition is testified to by two trustworthy pieces of evidence: the first is that when he saw the burning bush that was not consumed, he considered the matter carefully, then cognized and apprehended that it was an angel of God in the blazing fire out of the bush. The second is that when he asked of God, saying: *When I come to the Israelites and say to them, "The God of your fathers has sent me to you," and they ask of me, "What is His name?" what shall I say to them?* [Exod. 3:13]; and God answered him: *Thus shall you speak to the Israelites: "A-H-Y-H sent me to you"* [Exod. 3:14]. He understood from that word, "the worthy essence of God" (blessed be He); and he knew thereby that He was the essence of being, and the cause of everything that comes into being, and also that his existence and being are not anything superadded to His essence, and the other lofty and awesome matters that are understood from this word. [9a] Now in order to conceal, hide, and store them away, he switched and exchanged the letters that are customarily exchanged in the language, such as *alef* for *yod* and *yod* for *vav*, and that became the sanctified name.[27]

As for the fifth condition, consider his vigorous language and charming expressions in the Song by the Sea [Exod. 15] and in the portion *Give ear, O heavens* [Deut. 32], and in the threats and admonitions [of the Law].

That he fulfills the sixth condition is known and ascertained in his failure to envy the prophesying Eldad and Medad: *Would that all the Lord's people were prophets* [Num. 11:29]; and in his instructing the elders and Joshua, and making his spirit emanate upon them, and also on Aaron and Hur.

His fulfillment of the seventh and eleventh conditions is well known and familiar to one who looks at the equity of his judgments and the correctness of his statutes and his laws, as well what is said of him, *He is trusted throughout my house.*

His fulfillment of the eighth and tenth conditions is well known from his leaving behind all earthly pleasure and choosing spiritual ones. For he divorced his wife and sent her away from the moment that he began to prophesy, and he also survived forty days without eating, which is not a natural power.[28]

The ninth condition, that he exalt and esteem himself, is difficult to find in Moses, about whom the verse testifies: *The man Moses was exceedingly humble* [Num. 12:7]. It is well-known that humility is intermediate between pride and meekness, and that Moses inclined in his qualities towards the side of meekness, since he had been chosen [by God], as the sages have said, "Be exceedingly meek."[29] Still, it is impossible for a man like him, who had been appointed king and ruler over a numerous people, not to possess, on occasion, somewhat of a hard heart and anger so that he may instill fear and dread in those who scoff at morality.[30] Accordingly, the twelfth condition also is found among his qualities.

As for the thirteenth trait, it is fitting and obligatory for us to believe that Moses possessed the perfection and the completeness to reach the aforementioned final end. For his soul, which isolated and separated itself from his matter, which it despised, changed the customs of nature and produced the well-known miracles (just as the separate forms change the material objects, and do what they will with them) and was able to prophesy at any time that it wished, as is written: *Stand by, and let me hear what instructions the Lord gives about you* [Num. 9:8]. All this resulted from his always being attached to the spiritual entities and his becoming divine

27. The author's point may be as follows: When Moses asks God for his name so that he can transmit it to the Israelites, God gives the name *AHYH.* In order to conceal its philosophical secrets from the multitude, Moses, on his own initiative, switched letters and changed the name to *YHVH,* the Ineffable Name.

28. Or perhaps "which is not within the power of something which is born." The phrase *be-koaḥ ha-toledet* here does not refer to astrological power, since Polgar denies any such powers in the Third Part of the work.

29. *Avot* 4:4.

30. Contrast Maimonides' more ambiguous interpretations of Moses' anger and meekness in *Eight Chapters* chap. 4 and *Mishneh Torah, Book of Knowledge,* "Laws concerning Character Traits," chap. 2, both in *The Ethical Writings of Maimonides,* ed. Raymond L. Weiss and Charles E. Butterworth (New York: New York University Press, 1975; repr., New York: Dover, 1983).

and perfect, for [9b] the corporeal accidents neither hindered, or thwarted, or obstructed him. Nor was his rational power at that time in any corporeal faculty. Indeed, how can the activity of a physical power be attributed to someone who sat forty days and forty nights without eating and drinking?

So I have proved to you, as I intended, that Moses our King was most apt and fitting to be the officer and head of the holy people....

The Fifth Gate

[11b] There is no need for the thinker to view our long exile and troubled daily existence, so abhorrent to our souls, as proof that the justification for our Law is deficient and that the truth of our beliefs is nonexistent. On the contrary, he should believe that this is a mark and sign of the truth of our religion, the equity of our Law, and the justness of our regulations. You should know, if you are discerning, that the more subtle, refined, and marvelous a religious belief is (as attested by the intellect's true nature, which is the correct judge), the less likely it is to be accepted by the majority of the multitude. Women and the ignorant, because of the inaction of their theoretical intellect, incline and tend to believe all sorts of exaggerated and inflated wonders having to do with corporeal matters, whose existence is impossible—this, because they think that they honor and magnify the rank of God, may He be blessed. For by virtue of their corrupt representation and weak intelligence, they say that if God were only able to act within [the realm of] possible things, then how would people view his marvels and miracles? And what would be the difference between his actions and our actions, with respect to doing things that are impossible? In fact, they believe this not only in His case, but also in the case of those savants whom they consider wise, that is, that their wisdom is for naught if they cannot alter nature and perform marvels and impossibilities. Some of these simpletons testify to others that they saw a certain man (whom they consider wise) to perform miracles and marvels by reciting the name of a heavenly prince or angel or demon; they tell ludicrous stories that properly provoke derision.

Now *the inclination of man's heart is evil from his youth* [Gen. 8:21]. Unless he educates and exerts himself in the ways of the intellect, and the various true sciences, he will direct and incline himself to admire and give credence to these corrupt beliefs and vain exaggerations. For, as I mentioned above, he has no intellect *in actu* that serves as a judge to distinguish for him the true from the false, the plausible from the far-fetched. He simply determines his mind to believe everything that leaves the preacher's lips, especially when he sees it written—for the fools think that you cannot write or affirm anything in a book unless it is the truth!

You see, therefore, that the weirder and more intellectually absurd [12a] the notions of a given religion are, the longer it will last, the more it will succeed, and the greater the number of its adherents will become. For when a religious leader who is considered wise by the multitude represents these popular and beloved marvels and exaggerations in his comments and expositions, the multitude hurries to believe them as if they had witnessed them with their own eyes—especially when that prattler testifies and swears to them that he saw them himself. The people will then conceive and think that they have magnified God by doing this, as I mentioned above.

I have also heard mentioned in connection with some of the "believers" that they preach to the multitude and say to them, "Know that a man is considered good in God's eyes when he believes what his eyes have not seen. For one who believes what he has been shown deserves no reward for that."[31] In short, there is no limit to the folly of fools.

Now I am not referring here to the miracles and marvels that were performed by our prophets (of blessed memory), which were publicized and well known to all. For the possibility of the occurrence of miracles at the hands of the prophets is a matter known to thinkers, as is the manner in which prophets act through their souls, and sometimes change the course of nature, as is explained in its proper place.

31. "Believers" is presumably a reference to Christians, and the doctrines associated with faith here appear to be Christian in origin. Again, Abner may be the source.

Do you not see that our Master Moses was obliged to make a heavenly voice speak with them, as it is written: *The Lord said to Moses, "I will come to you in a thick cloud, so that the people may hear when I speak with you and so believe in you ever after"* [Exod. 19:9]. He promised them all sorts of bodily delights for the performance of commandments, and threatened them with misfortunes and illnesses for their transgressions. Nowhere did he speak to them of the subject of the world to come, where truly lies the reward for the commandments and the true punishment for transgressions. For if he had thought that their intellect was perfect he would have explained to them that man achieves perpetual life, that is, the world to come; through the performance of the commandments, wherein lies man's benefit; and through distancing himself from transgression, wherein lies his evil. This would have been a more appropriate reason for them always to believe in the Lord and his servant Moses. But on that occasion[32] he admonished them saying that they should not think, because of the voice that they had heard, that the Creator is corporeal: *You should be very careful, for your own sake, since you saw no shape* [Deut. 4:15]; so that they may not stumble and fall into that most wicked of opinions. And when they saw that Moses tarried in descending from the mountain, they requested and pressured Aaron to make a corporeal god so that finally he made for them the golden calf. See, also, what troubles David was in with his foolish neighbors, who would ask him to show them his god so that they [12b] may see him with their own eyes: *My tears have been my bread day and night; I am asked all the day, "Where is your God?"* [Ps. 42:4].

When you have examined and contemplated these matters, you will not find it difficult to explain the plethora of troubles and misfortunes that beset the nation of the virtuous, as well as the paucity of their members. For that nation's beliefs are wondrous, sacred, remarkable, and distinct from those of the other nations, since they are derived and follow from reason, which is remote and despised by them; also since they contain prohibitions and restrictions with respect to bodily delights, for example, various sorts of food and sexual intercourse. Hence, most of the ignorant will avoid them and despise the commandments. This is indeed a clear proof of the truth of their belief, because fools only choose folly, as we see from the dictum of King Solomon: *How long will you simpletons love simplicity, you scoffers be easy to scoff, you fools hate knowledge?* [Prov. 1:21].

Now throughout history the boors have mocked and cursed the thinkers for failing to accept their vanities, as it is written, *There is a certain people scattered and dispersed among the peoples and all the provinces of your kingdom, and their laws are different from those of every other people, and the royal laws they do not observe* [Esther 3:8]. There are so few of these people that they are scarcely worth being called a nation. Do not be astonished at this. For the thinkers are never more than a small number at any time, as our blessed sages have said, "One in a generation." Still, because of the great amount of pity that God shows us, and the individual providence within us, He will not abandon or deliver us into the hands of our enemies, though we live amidst those who seek our harm. For when you ask all individuals of the nations surrounding us, "Do you desire to destroy this nation that dwells among you?" Some will say that they would give or contribute the choice portion of their wealth to this end, and some others would [even] dismember themselves. Nevertheless, God does not allow them to dominate us unto destruction, nor does He permit the Destroyer to bring about our annihilation, as it is written: *Yet, even then, when they are in the land of their enemies, I will not reject them nor despise them so as to annihilate them, breaking my covenant with them* [Lev. 26:44]. See, I have revealed and explained to you the reason why we have endured travails regularly in the present time and throughout our history, although we hold true beliefs.

I will also explain the Exile by means of another thesis: I already told you that peoples' conflicting customs and opinions make it an absolutely necessity and a complete requirement to establish religious laws. [13a] This is what I demonstrated already in the First Gate. For most despise what some prize. The trait of envy is also found and contained within all[33] or most of the people, as the sage[34] has said: *I have seen that all labor and all skillful work comes from mutual envy* [Eccles. 4:4]. It is the worst of all qualities, as the sage has said: *There is the cruelty to fury and anger, but who can*

32. The Gathering of the People at Mount Sinai.

33. Reading *be-kol* for *be-rov.*

34. King Solomon, considered by tradition to be the author of Ecclesiastes, Song of Songs, and Proverbs.

stand before envy? [Prov. 27:4]. Envy is the cause of robbery, injustice, and oppression of the poor man. Accordingly, the more a nation is impressed with the awe of the Lord, and its people fearful of the chastisements of religion in order to avoid sin, the more they will keep and preserve themselves from oppression, theft, and from performing evil. By contrast, the more a religion permits its adherents, through its commandments and statutes, to indulge in various bodily pleasures, or does not completely forbid the aforementioned vice, that is, envy, the more the believers of that religion will be cruel and wicked, the spillers of innocent bold.

Now inasmuch as our perfect Law forbids us from, and admonishes us against, walking in these worthless ways, and prevents us from acquiring the evil of the aforementioned despicable trait; it follows that we shall belong to the ranks of the oppressed, rather than the oppressor; the offended, rather than the offender. However, inasmuch as bodily desires are not forbidden to the other nations, including this trait [envy], it follows that they will be the oppressors and the offenders. For the evil inclination of their heart, which is the cause of desire, does not allow them to guard against committing evil. They do not apprehend that evil is indeed evil.

After I have prefaced for you these premises, I shall return and explain the topic under consideration:

When we were in our own country, rooted in our own lands, we were separated and elevated above all the surrounding nations. We observed the commandments of our praiseworthy Law that forbid and prevent us from all sorts of bodily desires. We smashed the yoke of the [evil] inclination around our necks. Then we ceased from oppressing others. Moreover, we were obligated and compelled and commanded to exert and occupy ourselves with the Law, and with various sorts of sciences, day and night. Now this weakened and sapped our strength. Moreover, the trait of mercy [13b] and tenderheartedness was implanted within us, and we became occupied with the sacrificial rites, and the Temple service.

As a result of all this, [the waging of] wars was forgotten by us, and weapons were abolished. The Israelites and the Judaeans forgot what they had learned of the bow, and they beat their swords into plowshares and their swords into pruning hooks [cf. Isa. 2:4]. For their intention was to turn away from evil and to do good, to seek peace and to pursue it [cf. Prov. 34:15]. Now the trait belonging to the nations that surrounded us was the opposite of the trait of justice and of our other traits. Their heart was full of hardness and cruelty because of their overwhelming desire and jealousy of what we possessed,[35] as David (of blessed memory) said: *I am [a man of] peace; but when I speak, they are for war* [Ps. 120:7]. Also *they all handle the sword and are proficient in the ways of war* [Song of Sol. 3:8], for their manner is to attack like beasts, bears, and lions. They did not talk of peace with us, but rather grit their teeth and gathered in force against us, laid waste our cities, destroyed our temple, and carried off our captives. The tiny few of us that survived were scattered and dispersed among all the lands. Nevertheless, because we recognize for certain that the truth was with us, and that desire for this material world and its pleasures is vanity and an evil wind, we shall shoulder its sorrows, and we shall trust in the God of our salvation, who will gaze at us from above and will save us to such an extent that we are able to live among our enemies, and to dwell in the tents of those who seek our ill.

I have now explained for you by means of a demonstration and an argument based on nature why we are immersed in sorrow and exile, although we accepted the true belief in God, and we are sanctified above all other nations. As for those who are envious of me, let them not suspect that I have deviated from the strict line of faith by composing an argument based on nature. For, indeed, I only composed it in order to "know what to respond to the heretic." I believe to make known that our cities were destroyed because of our sins, that our temple was laid waste because of our abundance of transgressions, and that we were exiled from our land because of our offenses. God in his mercy will atone for our many acts of atonement and will gather together our dispersed. He will save us and lead us upright to our land.

35. Literally, "jealousy of us."

NINETEEN

ABRAVANEL

Commentary on the Bible

Translated by Robert Sacks

Isaac Abravanel (or Abarbanel, 1437–1508) was born in Lisbon of a family that for generations had enjoyed political and social prominence in Spain and Portugal. Abravanel received both a traditional Jewish and a humanistic education; he also studied and drew upon the work of Christian exegetes. Early in life, he entered into the service of King Alfonso V of Portugal as treasurer. Alfonso V's trust and admiration for Abravanel lasted until the monarch's death in 1481. The new king, John II, was not so well disposed toward Abravanel. Finding himself accused of collaboration with the duke of Braganca, he escaped to Castile under threat of execution. The banished Abravanel, all his possessions confiscated, then began his great commentaries on the Bible. Soon, however, he managed to find himself back in the sphere of practical politics—first in Spain, then in Italy. When the Jews were forced to leave Spain in 1492, he moved to Naples, but it was not long before that city was taken by the French. He was again forced south. After holding several other positions, he was employed by the Venetian republic to conclude a commercial treaty with his native land of Portugal. He died in Venice and was buried at Padua. In addition to his extensive exegetic writings (covering all of the Bible except for the Hagiographa), Abravanel produced a number of messianological and apologetic works, as well as a commentary on Maimonides' *Guide of the Perplexed.*

The following brief selections are intended to give the reader some notion of Abravanel's political teaching and of the foundations on which it rests. At bottom, there is a general concept of nature (explicit in the discussion of the origin of the arts, but implicit in other passages as well) that serves as a measure of Abravanel's dissatisfaction with the classical view of politics. A question runs throughout these selections: What kind of political life did the Creator intend human beings to lead? In attempting to answer this question by way of determining how the ancient Jews were governed, Abravanel reaches a position markedly closer to Aquinas than to Maimonides' teaching. Abravanel is practically unique among medieval Jewish commentators in denying that the Bible positively commanded the Jews to establish a monarchy. His denial of that institution's necessity appears to be, however, less an expression of humanistic republicanism than a part of his broader disparagement of political life as such. He preserves the monarchical principle to the extent that he sees human organization culminating in a single head. But that head is a prophet-king like Moses—a man so preoccupied with divine matters that he must be instructed by a Gentile in matters pertaining to the administration of justice. Such "low things" are no concern of the prophet. Accordingly, the transpolitical prophet is not to be understood within the confines of political philosophy.

Abravanel's commentaries on the Bible were held in particularly high regard by Christian scholars of the seventeenth and eighteenth centuries. More than thirty Latin editions were published. The following selections were, at the time of the original publication of the *Sourcebook* (1963), believed to be translated here for the first time in a modern language. At that time, no critical edition of the Hebrew text of Abravanel's commentaries existed. The following passages may be found in his *Commentary on the Pentateuch* (Hanau, 1710) and in his *Commentary on the Prior Prophets* (Frankfurt, 1736). (In recent years, a project has been under way at Bar Ilan University to produce a critical Hebrew edition of all of the traditional commentaries on the Hebrew Bible, including Abravanel's. Michael Carasik has been engaged in a partial English translation of these commentaries, including Abravanel's questions, for the Jewish Publication Society.) The numbers in brackets in the body of the translation refer to page and column in the 1710 and 1736 editions.

COMMENTARY ON THE PENTATEUCH

And the whole earth was of one language and of one speech. And it came to pass, as they journeyed east, that they found a plain in the land of Shinar; and they dwelt there. And they said one to another: "Come, let us make brick and burn them thoroughly." And they had brick for stone, and slime had they for mortar. And they said: "Come, let us build us a town, and a tower, with its top in heaven, and let us make us a name; lest we be scattered abroad upon the face of the whole earth." And the Lord came down to see the town and the tower, which the children of men built. And the Lord said: "Behold, they are one people, and they have all one language; and this is what they begin to do; and now nothing will be withheld from them, which they purpose to do. Come, let us go down, and there confound their language, that they may not understand one another's speech." So the Lord scattered them abroad from thence upon the face of all the earth; and they left off to build the town. Therefore was the name of it called Babel; because the Lord did there confound the language of all the earth; and from thence did the Lord scatter them abroad upon the face of all the earth [Gen. 11:1–9].

[41a1] I say that according to me it is more proper and fitting to say regarding the sin of the generation of the Tower of Babel and their transgression, that they stumbled and sinned in the same way that our First Father and his son Cain sinned, and his seed as well. Now man[1] was created by the Holy One (blessed be He) in His image, possessing an intellecting soul, so that he might perfect his soul by cognizing his Creator and knowing His actions. Before him were placed all the things that were necessary for the maintenance of his life—food and drink, like the fruits of the trees of the Garden [of Eden] and the waters of its rivers. All this existed by nature, without any need at all for human art, so that he did not have to busy himself with seeking them—except for divine knowledge, since it was for this that he was created. Man sinned in that he was not satisfied with the natural things that He had placed before him, but was attracted to the things of the appetite and the generally accepted actions. Because of his sin, he was driven out of the Garden of Eden, place of rest, toward the East, filled with disgrace; and the ground was cursed on his account. The natural things did not satisfy him, and since he chose what was superfluous, he found it necessary to do hard work, as the Master wrote. Cain also chose to engage in artful things and therefore became a tiller of the ground. All day he ploughed the thicket in order to plant, broke and harrowed his ground. But his intellect [41a2] gave way to his bestial part and served it. Therefore he was a tiller of the ground. Abel, in contrast, who became a shepherd, was attracted to the natural things and satisfied himself with them; for there is neither work nor art in shepherding a flock, apart from governing them according to the way of nature. Hence all the Holy Fathers—Abraham, Isaac, and Jacob—and the tribes and Moses and David our

1. Literally, "Adam."

Fathers were shepherds; they were not tillers of the ground. And Noah too, though he sinned in his being attracted to wine, is not called "a tiller of the ground" by scripture, but rather a *man of the ground* [Gen. 9:20]—that is to say, a lord and ruler over it. But Cain, because his intellect had given way to his bestial part [by engaging] in the arts, was called *a tiller of the ground* [Gen. 4:2]. Thus he built a town and called its name Enoch,[2] because he educated and instructed his sons in practicing the arts that are related to the building[3] of a town and the founding of a city. Similarly all the sons of Cain took up the work of their fathers and were attracted to the superfluous arts. So Jubal was *the father of all such as handle the harp and pipe.* And Tubal-cain was the father of all such as forge *brass and iron.* And Jabal, too, in making an effort to purchase sheep, mixed art with the work of God, something that had not previously been done. Thus it is said of him that he was *the father of all such as dwell in tents and have cattle* [cf. Gen. 4:20–22]. All the sons of Cain pursued the superfluous things; violence and destruction increased among their people until they were punished on account of it in the days of the Flood and were wiped off the earth.

Similarly, the sins of the generation of the Tower of Babel were like the sin of Adam and Cain and his sons since—having a multiplicity of the natural things necessary for their existence by God from heaven, freed of [any need for] art and all labor, and prepared to busy themselves with the perfection of their souls—their thoughts were not set at rest by the great natural gift that their Creator had prepared for them. Rather, they sought and put all their thoughts to finding the arts by which a town might be built, one comprehending all the arts and having a tower in its midst, in order to come together there and to make themselves political instead of being rustics. For they thought that the end particular to them was the political association, so that joining and company might arise among them; and that this was the highest of the human ends, together with the things that would follow from it, namely, fame, office, rule, imaginary honors, the delight of gathering possessions, and the violence and robbery and bloodshed that follow—none of which was to be found while they were in the fields, each one by himself. As Solomon said: *God made man upright; but they have sought out many inventions* [Eccles. 7:29]. All of this unnatural superfluity hinders and frustrates man in attaining his true perfection of the soul. Thus, these sinning people were punished in their souls, in that He confounded their language and scattered them over the face of the entire earth; just as He had driven the first man out of the Garden of Eden, and had driven Cain out of the land in which he dwelt, and had driven his sons out of the world by means of the waters of the Flood. For their sin was the same insofar as they placed the Tree of Knowledge as their final end and abandoned the Tree of Life, which is the true end. Thus, it was fitting that their punishment too be alike.

[41b1] You ought not to say: "If these superfluous arts and the association into a city or town were evil in the eyes of the Lord, why was it that he did not forbid them to Israel afterwards?" For the answer to this is clear. When He (blessed be He) saw that Adam and all his progeny had already sunk into an appetite for the superfluous arts and were drowned in them, He did not forbid them to His people; for He watched and saw that they could not be removed from him *inasmuch as he is also flesh* [Gen. 6:3]. However, He admonished[4] the Children of Israel to conduct themselves in those artful things justly and in a becoming manner, not disgracefully. This is like the matter of having a king, which was loathsome in His eyes; but when He saw that they were going to choose one in any case, He commanded that the choice be made by His prophets, and that it be made from among their brethren, and several other commandments that stem from the matter of having a king, as will become clear in its place. Indeed, you see that in all the days during which the Children of Israel were traveling in the desert, under divine governance, He (blessed be He) never satisfied their need with anything other than natural divine things—from the manna, the quails, and the well, even to clothing and shoes and clouds of glory[5]—but never with anything of art. As it is written: *Thy raiment waxed not old upon thee, neither did thy foot swell* [Deut. 8:4]. But when they had come into an inhabited land,

2. This name means "education" or "initiation"; cf. Gen. 4:17.
3. Reading *be-binyan* rather than *be-ʾinyan.*
4. Reading *hizhir* rather than *zaru.*
5. Cf. Exod. 16:15 ff., 16:13; Num. 21:16 ff.; Exod. 13:21 and passim.

He left them to their nature in all the uses of their generally accepted arts.

The human arts are arranged in accordance with nature in three ways: (1) Some of them help nature to do its work—like tilling the ground and the art of medicine and the like. Of these it is said that they used to say, "Let us arise and dwell in heaven";[6] that is to say, they would take part in the heavenly causes, which are the natural agents, and help them and be like them by means of their arts. Of these it is said: *And from thence did the Lord scatter them abroad* [Gen. 11:9]; for, by His will, the things of nature are sufficient unto themselves and have no need of the help of art, as was the case at the beginning of the Creation. (2) There are arts that differ from, and are alien to, nature, for they make things in which nature plays no role—like most of the productive arts, such as the making of clothing, house-building, ship-making, and others. Concerning this sect of those possessing sciences alien to nature, the sage says that they used to say, "Let us go up into heaven and perform worship of idols."[7] For just as the heavens perform natural acts upon this matter, so they would perform acts alien [to the acts of heaven] without following them [that is, without using the same means as heaven]. Of these it is said: *Because the Lord did there confound the language of all the earth* [Gen. 11:9]; for it was because of these alien arts that they had need of alien words and alien terms, and that was the confounding of their language, as I have explained. (3) The third way of the arts is opposed to and against nature—like throwing a stone upward or causing fire to go downward. Also like this, among men, is the attempt of some to domineer over others and to subjugate some to others, though nature has made men free and equal at their birth. Concerning this sect [it is said that] they used to say, "Let us arise and make war upon heaven";[8] that is to say, their arts were opposed to, and made war upon, the natural custom.[9]

[42a2] Now in the early days, until the Generation of the Flood, the whole of mankind were influenced and overseen by Him (blessed be He) in all their affairs, without any intermediary either for good or for evil. Therefore there could always be found among them wise men who had understanding of the true divine science, like Adam and Seth and Eber and Methuselah, Lemach, Noah, and their like. Among them there was to be found pure natural custom[10] without any quest for the superfluities and the imaginary arts. And withal, they had a single language, that which the Holy One (blessed be He) had taught to the first man. However, in departing from the Ancient of Days and leaving natural custom to pursue the arts, which hinder perfection, in the building of the town and the tower, *the Lord came down to see* [Gen. 11:5] their doings, for up until then He had truly been their overseer. He said: "Since these [men] were not satisfied with being one people having one language, and have begun to do the works of the imaginary arts, *I will hide My face from them* [Deut. 32:20] and from their governance, and I shall commit them to the princes on high [that is, the angels]." Thus His saying to these princes, *Come, let us go down* [Gen. 11:7]; that is to say, "Come with Me to oversee the nations of the human species, for each one of us shall oversee a single nation. And just as My divine providence has been removed from them, so shall the divine holy language be wrested from them in such a manner that they will be divided into fragmented and conventional languages, each of them related and particular to the governance of the princes on high," just as the holy language is particular to His governance (blessed be He).

And it came to pass on the morrow, that Moses sat to judge the people; and the people stood about Moses from the morning unto the evening. And when Moses' father-in-law [Jethro] *saw all that he did to the people, he said: "What is this thing that thou doest to the people? Why sittest thou thyself alone, and all the people stand about thee from morning unto even?" And Moses said unto his father-in-law: "Because the people come unto me to inquire of God; when they have a matter it cometh unto me; and I judge between a man and his neighbor, and I make*

6. Cf. *Genesis Rabbah* 38:6.

7. Cf. *Genesis Rabbah* 38:6.

8. Cf. *Genesis Rabbah* 38:6.

9. Cf. Abravanel's use of "natural custom," here and in the following, with Saadya's (above, selection 12) and Halevi's (above, selection 13) uses of "rational law," as well as Maimonides' critique of "rational law" (above, selection 16).

10. See note 9.

them know the statutes of God, and His Laws." And Moses' father-in-law said unto him: "The thing that thou doest is not good. Thou wilt surely wear away, both thou, and this people that is with thee; for the thing is too heavy for thee; thou art not able to perform it thyself alone. Hearken now unto my voice, I will give thee counsel, and God be with thee: be thou for the people before God, and bring thou the causes unto God. And thou shalt teach them the statutes and the Laws, and shalt show them the way wherein they must walk, and the work that they must do. Moreover thou shalt provide out of all the people able men, such as fear God, men of truth, hating unjust gain; and place such over them to be captains of thousands, captains of hundreds, captains of fifties, and captains of tens. And let them judge the people at all seasons; and it shall be, that every great matter they shall bring unto thee, but every small matter they shall judge themselves; so shall they make it easier for thee and bear the burden with thee. If thou shalt do this thing, and God command thee so, then thou shalt be able to endure, and all this people also shall go to their place in peace." So Moses hearkened to the voice of his father-in-law, and did all that he had said. And Moses chose able men out of all Israel, and made them heads over the people, captains of thousands, captains of hundreds, captains of fifties, and captains of tens. And they judged the people at all seasons: the hard causes they brought unto Moses, but every small matter they judged themselves. And Moses let his father-in-law depart; and he went his way into his own land [Exod. 18:13–27].

[134a2] Concerning the multitude of judges that Jethro advised and that Moses appointed—captains of thousands and captains of hundreds, captains of fifties and captains of tens—their number being over 71,600, as the sages (may their memory be a blessing) have mentioned. Rabbi Abraham ben Ezra [applied the verse:] *For the transgression of a land many are the captains thereof* [Prov. 28:2]. There is no doubt that this is a hard and shocking thing. For his understanding was that the captains of thousands were captains who had a thousand men in their houses serving them. And similarly, the captains of hundreds were those each one of whom had a hundred men in his house serving him, and similarly for the rest. But to me that is a worthless opinion because the Israelites in Egypt were not dukes or kings that any of them might have a thousand servants, or even a hundred. Even in the case of Moses, the scripture only mentions that he had one servant: *And his servant Joshua, the son of Nun, a young man* [Exod. 33:11]. How could it be that any one of a people who only yesterday were humbled before mortar and bricks should have a thousand servants, or a hundred or fifty or even ten? If all of the congregation were holy, and He was in their midst, why should some of them be slaves and hirelings to others, and why should these be in subjugation to the others? If it was to find food for his life, each one could partake of the manna, *each man according to his eating* [Exod. 16:16]. And even the verse, *For the transgression of a land many are the captains thereof* [Prov. 28:2], indicates rather that they are all on one level, not that some of them are captains humbling others.

As for the captains, with each increase in their number, the governance of the people is better arranged, provided only that they are ordered one under another, all culminating in a single head, as Abū Naṣr [Alfarabi] has made clear in the *Principles of Beings*.[11] This analogy may be found in the organs of a man and in the relation that the beings have to one another within the order of the world until one reaches the First Cause (blessed be He). What stands in the way of the same occurring in this matter, that is, the captains of tens under the captains of fifties, and the latter under the captains of hundreds, and the latter under the captains of thousands? It is possible to interpret it as meaning that, because Israel's camp was great and numerous, Jethro's advice was that Moses should appoint leaders and judges. And, in order that everyone should be subject to them, he gave to each captain of those leaders, men under his control to serve him, that they might follow him as the need arises, to go out in the army, or to move camp, or to castigate and punish those who were judged.[12] Among those leaders was one whose rank was so high that he had a thousand men who would preserve his headship and give heed to his bidding. And for such as was not so elevated there were a hundred men, and for another fifty, and thus for each of the others according to his rank and perfection. But those leaders [134b1] were few, and they would judge the people at all times. What is correct in my eyes is that with regard to the matter of judgment

11. This was the title of the Hebrew translation of Alfarabi's *Political Regime.* See the historical introduction to selection 3 above.

12. Reading *ha-nishpatim* rather than *ha-shofetim.*

and the matter of wars—which are the most comprehensive things affecting the people—Jethro, in his wisdom, and Moses our lord too, saw that each time an appointment became more encompassing, it became less ordered. Therefore they did not assign captains over tens of thousands or over hundreds of thousands or the like, since surrounding oneself with great numbers of men would confuse governance. It is sufficient that the most general appointment should be over one thousand men. For with regard to the matter of judgment, it is sufficient that one man judge a thousand individuals. (In the case of wars, it is even clearer that only rarely can a single man of might be found who is able to lead and order a thousand men so that they would go and come in a proper fashion.) However the captains who are under them—that is, captains of hundreds and captains of fifties and captains of tens—are needed in addition to the captains of thousands with regard to the matter of judgment. They differ in their governance and appointment in three ways: The first way is that they [the judges] will differ with regard to kind and [type of] governance. For some of them will judge cases of criminal law, and some cases of civil law. And of these, in each tribe some will judge matters of real estate, and others matters of goods, and such various things, in such a way that it is necessary that there be many judges.

When thou art come unto the land that the Lord thy God giveth thee, and shalt possess it, and shalt dwell therein; and shalt say: "I will set a king over me, like all the nations that are round about me"; thou shalt in any wise set him king over thee, whom the Lord thy God shall choose; one from among thy brethren shalt thou set king over thee; thou mayest not put a foreigner over thee, who is not thy brother. Only he shall not multiply horses to himself, nor cause the people to return to Egypt, to the end that he should multiply horses; forasmuch as the Lord hath said unto you: "Ye shall henceforth return no more that way." Neither shall he multiply wives to himself, that his heart turn not away; neither shall he greatly multiply to himself silver and gold. And it shall be, when he sitteth upon the throne of his kingdom, that he shall write him a copy of this Law in a book, out of that which is before the priests the Levites. And it shall be with him, and he shall read therein all the days of his life; that he may learn to fear the Lord his God, to keep all the words of this Law and these statutes, to do them; that his heart be not lifted up above his brethren, and that he turn not aside from the commandment, to the right hand, or to the left; to the end that he may prolong his days in his kingdom, he and his children, in the midst of Israel [Deut. 17:14–20].

[295b2] Even though it be admitted that the existence of a king is useful and necessary for a people to improve the political association and maintain it—a proposition that is contrary to the truth—it is not so for the people of Israel, because for them it is neither needful nor necessary. The explanation of this is that the need that a people has for kings can be grouped under three headings: The first concerns the subject of wars, [namely,] saving the people from their enemies and fighting for their land. The second is to order the nomoi and set down the Laws that are necessary for maintaining them. The third is to administer extralegal stripes and punishments occasionally, according to the need of the hour, as is proper to the absolute divine power that he has.

But the nation of Israel has no need for any of these three things. This is not [necessary] as regards wars and saving them from their enemies, because Israel is saved by the Lord, and it is He who fights for them. As it is written: *Happy art thou, O Israel, who is like unto thee? A people saved by the Lord, the shield of thy help, and who is the sword of thy excellency! And thine enemies shall dwindle away before thee; and thou shalt tread upon their high places* [Deut. 33:29]. Also, this judge would go out and come before them in wars, as we found in the cases of Joshua and Gideon and Samuel and the rest of the judges. Nor did they have need for a king to establish Laws and nomoi, for *Moses commanded us a Law,* and so on [Deut. 33:4]. And He (blessed be He) commanded: *Ye shall not add unto the word,* and so on [Deut. 4:2]. *Behold, I have taught you statutes and judgments, even as the Lord my God has commanded me* [Deut. 4:5]. *And what great nation is there that hath God so nigh,* and so on [cf. Deut. 4:7]. *And what great nation is there that hath statutes and judgments so righteous,* and so on [Deut. 4:8]. And the king of Israel did not have it in his power to innovate anything in the Law, or to subtract from it—as it is written of him: *And that he turn not aside from the commandment, to the right hand, or to the left* [Deut. 17:20]. Nor was a king necessary in Israel to administer stripes and punishments occasionally, according to the need of the hour, for the Holy One (blessed be He) delegated that to the Great Court of Law—that is, the Sanhedrin—as I have explained in commenting [on Deut. 17:8]. And aside from that, He (blessed be He) announced to us that if a judge, relying upon a righteously-ordered judgment, should declare a wicked man to be innocent, He (blessed be He) would punish the evildoer by His great law, as it is written: *Keep thee far from a false matter; and the innocent and righteous slay thou not; for I will not justify the wicked* [Exod. 23:7]. That is, whatever you are not able to punish by the law, I Myself will punish it.

Thus it has been made clear that these three matters—saving [the people in times of] war, setting down the Law and the commandments, and [the administration of] occasional extralegal punishments and stripes—are all done by Him (blessed be He) for His people. Thus He (blessed be He) was their king, and there was nothing whatever for which they needed a king of flesh and blood. This matter had already been written in the Law, and was repeated in the Prophets, and was repeated yet again in the Hagiographa.[13] For Moses our Master (peace be upon him) said: *The Lord shall reign for ever and ever. For the horses of Pharaoh went [with his chariots and with his horsemen into the sea,]* and so on [Exod. 15:18–19]. That is, the Holy One (blessed be He) waged war upon [296a1] the sea for Israel against Egypt and caused their enemies to be drowned. Thus, He *shall reign for ever and ever,* and they have no need for any other king. In the Prophets, Isaiah said: *For the Lord is our Judge, the Lord is our Legislator, the Lord is our King and He will save us* [cf. Isa. 33:2]. In this passage he alludes to the three reasons for which a king is made. With regard to the judgment made according to the need of the hour, he says: *The Lord is our Judge.* And with regard to the ordering of statutes and nomoi, all of which are called "statute," he says: *The Lord is our Legislator;* that is, He orders statutes for us. Concerning wars, he says: *The Lord is our King and He will save us.* In the Hagiographa it is said: *Lift up your heads, O ye gates; and be ye lifted up, ye everlasting doors; that the King of glory shall come in. Who is the King of glory? The Lord strong and mighty, the Lord mighty in battle* [Ps. 24:7–8]. That is, it is not proper to call a corporeal man "King of glory," but only Him (blessed be He) for it is He who is strong and mighty in battle, waging war for His people.

Thus it is clear from all this that although it be admitted that a king is necessary for the [other] nations, that does not justify it for the Israelite nation, especially since experience has already shown of the kings of Israel and the kings of Judah that *they are of them that rebel against the light* [Job 24:13]. They turned the hearts of the Children of Israel backward—as you know in the case of Jeroboam, the son of Nebat, and all the rest of the kings of Israel and most of the kings of Judah—so that on account of them, *Judah is gone into exile because of affliction, and because of great idolatry.*[14] We do not see this among the judges of Israel or their prophets. All of them were god-fearing men of valor, and men of truth. Not one of the prophets turned his heart from the Lord to worship other gods, in contradistinction to the kings, which of whom was saved from idolatry? All of this testifies to the fact that the governance of the judges was good, but that the governance of the kings was bad, harmful, and very dangerous.

Now hear the interpretation of the portion [of the scripture] concerning the king, and the commandment as it is in truth! It says: *When thou art come unto the land that the Lord thy God giveth thee, and shalt possess it, and shalt dwell therein, and shalt say: I will set a king over me, like all the nations that are round about me* [Deut. 17:14]. This is by no means a commandment, for He (blessed be He) did not command them to say that and to ask for a king. It is only a statement regarding the future, telling what will be said after you will already have been in the chosen land, after the conquests and all the wars are over, and after the partition [of the conquered territory among the people has been completed]. That is what it means when it says: *Thou shalt possess it and shalt dwell therein.* I Myself know that you shall be ungrateful when, of yourselves, you shall say, *I will set a king over me,* not from the necessity of having to wage war against the nations [inhabiting Canaan] or of conquering the land—for it has already been conquered before you—but only to make yourselves like the other nations that set kings over themselves. This is somewhat foolish, because you should have asked for a king upon first entering the land, in order to wage your wars, since that was the time when he was most properly needed,

13. See above, selection 15, note 29.

14. Literally, "worship of stars and constellations." Cf. Lam. 1:3, where the last phrase quoted by Abravanel reads: *and because of great servitude.*

not after the conquest and the partition and when you have been dwelling securely alone in the land. This is why it says: *And thou shalt say: I will set a king over me, like all the nations that are round about me;* that is, not by necessity, nor from any need, but only that you might act according to the deeds of the [other] nations. It mentions that when this shall happen, they shall not cause that king to reign whom they wish, but rather that one whom the Lord shall choose from among their brethren. This is the essence of the commandment and its true import: *Then thou shalt set him king over thee...from among thy brethren* [Deut. 17:15].[15] Not that they are commanded to ask for one, but only that when they should ask for one out of their own wish, they should not choose him by themselves, but rather that one whom the Lord shall choose from among their brethren. Accordingly, the matter of having a king was a positive commandment stemming from a permission—as if to say, when you wish to do it, even though it is not proper, thou shalt do it in no other way than this.

COMMENTARY ON THE PRIOR PROPHETS

Then all the elders of Israel gathered themselves together, and came to Samuel unto Ramah. And they said unto him: "Behold, thou art old, and thy sons walk not in thy ways; now make us a king to judge us like all the nations." But the thing displeased Samuel, when they said: "Give us a king to judge us." And Samuel prayed unto the Lord. And the Lord said unto Samuel: "Hearken unto the voice of the people in all that they say unto thee; for they have not rejected thee, but they have rejected Me, that I should not be king over them" [1 Sam. 8:4–7].

[92a2] I myself *in my straits have prepared* [1 Chron. 22:14] three speeches that consolidate the truth of this homiletic discourse: The first speech is to investigate whether a king is necessary for the political association. The second speech—[accepting for the moment] the argument that it is necessary—is whether a king is necessary for the people of Israel as it is for the rest of the nations. The third speech is an interpretation of the portion [of the scripture] concerning the king, and an understanding of the commandment and its truth. Now I think that all this confusion, which I have noted, befell the above-mentioned sages[16] *because, even because* [Ezek. 13:10] they did not plumb the truth of the commandment and its root. All of them accepted the notion that there was a positive commandment laid upon Israel to ask for a king. But I am not of this opinion. After presenting these three speeches by way of preface, I shall resolve the above-mentioned question in accord with what I think.

The first speech maintains that we ought to know first whether the existence of a king among a people is a necessary thing, required in itself, and without which nothing is possible. Those who have investigated it (Aristotle and his companions),[17] think that this is so, and that the relation of the king to the political association is like the relation of the heart to the body of an animal possessing a heart, and like the relation of what is to the First Cause (blessed be He). They believe that kingship entails three things: the first is unity and the absence of partnership; the second is continuity and the absence of change; the third is absolute power. But in truth, their thought concerning the obligation to have a king and his necessity is false, since it is not destructive that a people have many leaders who come together and unite and agree on a single plan, and that governance and judgment be according to their decision. Why should their governance not be temporary, changing from year to year, more or less? When the term comes for other judges and officers, they would take their place and look to see whether the preceding ones had transgressed in exercising their art. Whatever their wrongdoing, God would set aright any wrongdoing they had committed. And why could their power not be limited and ordered in accord with the Laws and judgments? The law is that [if there is a dispute between] an individual and a majority, the rule goes according to the majority. It is more likely that an individual man would transgress and sin in the office of king (either through his

15. This translation of the verse follows Abravanel's interpretation.

16. Maimonides, David Kimchi, Naḥmanides, Gersonides, Rav Nissim, and Paulus Burgensis.

17. This appears to be a gloss.

stupidity or his lust or his anger—as it is said: *The wrath of a king is as messengers of death*[18] [Prov. 16:14]), [92b1] than that a large number of men would sin *while they took counsel together against him* [cf. Ps. 31:14]. For if any one of them should sin, his companions would restrain him from doing so. And since judgment is due to be given shortly, the terror of flesh and blood will be upon them, and *they shall come trembling unto the Lord and to His goodness* [Hos. 3:5], and to the punishment of the judges succeeding them who will punish them, *and their wickedness shall be revealed before the congregation* [cf. Prov. 26:26]. The divine one (Aristotle),[19] says in the beginning of the *Metaphysics* that the truth is easy when considered in relation to the knowledge that many men have and the attainment thereof by all of them together, but very hard for the individual by himself.[20] This shows that ignorance is more apt to be found in an individual, while understanding together with the comprehension of the truth are more apt to be found among the many. With the power of those who understand being limited, they will not expose themselves by doing what is not proper.

What reasonable arguments do we have to bring to bear upon this point? The wise one (Aristotle)[21] has already taught us that experience prevails over the syllogism. *Behold, and see* [Lam. 1:12] the lands whose governance has been in the hands of kings. You will see their abominations and their idols; each of them *does what is right in his own eyes* [cf. Judg. 17:6], and *the land is filled with violence because of them* [cf. Gen. 6:13], *and who may say unto him* [the king], *What doest thou?* [Eccles. 8:4].

Today we see many lands whose governance is in the hands of judges and temporary rulers chosen from among them every three months, and *a king against whom there is no rising up* [cf. Prov. 30:31]. *Let us choose for them a judgment* [cf. Job 34:4] of a defined order, and they shall have dominion over the people as they practice the art of war; *not a man shall stand against them* [cf. Josh. 21:42], *whether it be for correction, or for their land, or for mercy* [cf. Job 37:13]. But if any one of them should sin in some matter, he would receive his fitting punishment from those who are soon to replace them, and in such a way that no one would presume to do so again. *Hast thou not known? hast thou not heard* [Isa. 40:28] that *the fourth dreadful beast* [Dan. 7:7], wicked Rome, ruled the entire world *and devoured the whole earth and trod it down and broke it in pieces* [cf. Dan. 7:23]? While her governance was in the hands of consuls, *they were in full strength, and likewise many* [Nah. 1:12], but after Caesar attained sole power, *she became tributary* [Lam. 1:1]. And even today the government of Venice is a mistress *that is great among the nations, and princess among the provinces* [Lam. 1:1]; and the government of Florence *is the beauty of all lands* [Ezek. 20:6]; and the government of Genoa *is dreadful and strong* [cf. Dan. 7:7]. But Lucca, Siena, and Bologna and the other lands that are without a king, but are governed by leaders who are chosen for a limited time, are, as I have mentioned, just governments *in which there is nothing perverse or crooked* [Prov. 8:8], where *no man lifts up his hand or his foot* [Gen. 41:44] *for every matter of trespass* [Exod. 22:8]. They conquer lands that are not their own by wisdom, understanding, and knowledge. All of this shows that the existence of a king is neither necessary nor obligatory for a people. Rather, it is very harmful and involves tremendous danger—both to his people and to his servants—for him to have in his hand the power to annihilate, kill, and destroy according to his whim.

[93a1] The third speech is an interpretation of the portion [of scripture] concerning the king that occurs in the Law, and the understanding of the truth of the commandment.

I say that the scripture relates, according to my opinion, that in the latter days—after Israel will have been in the land, have inherited it, and, by God's compassion for them, have dwelt therein—without any need, ungratefully they shall request permission to set a king over themselves, not out of necessity, but only in order to make themselves like the other nations that set kings over themselves. Thus it is written: *When thou art come unto the land that the Lord thy God giveth thee, and shalt possess it, and shalt dwell therein* [Deut. 17:14]. That is to say, out of foolishness you will not ask for a king at a time when wars are being waged to conquer the land—which would be the most suitable time to need him—but only after you will have

18. Abravanel suppresses part of this verse.

19. This appears to be a gloss.

20. Aristotle *Metaphysics* 2.1 993a30 ff.

21. This appears to be a gloss.

inherited the land and have divided it up [93a2] and have dwelt therein securely. (And all of this was under the providence of Him, blessed be He, and without a king, who thus was not necessary and for whom there was no need whatever.) Then shalt thou say: *I will set a king over me;* and that is being *like all the nations that are round about me*—that is to say, not by necessity nor for some other end. But when this should happen, He (blessed be He) commanded that they should not cause that king to reign whom they wish, but rather that one whom the Lord their God should choose from among their brethren. This is the commandment in essence and in truth: *Then thou shalt set him king over thee, whom the Lord thy God shall choose; one from among thy brethren* [Deut. 17:15].[22] That is to say, the king for whom they shall ask should be chosen by Him (blessed be He) and from among their brethren—not that they were thereby commanded to ask for one.

According to this, the commandment depends on something that was a matter of permission. It is as if it is said: If you wish to do this (even though it is not proper), you must not do it in any other way than this. It is like the verse: *When thou goest forth to war against thine enemies and the Lord thy God hath delivered them,* and so on, *and thou seest among the captives a woman of goodly form, and thou hast a desire unto her [and wouldest take her to thee to wife; then thou shalt bring her into thy home, and she shall shave her head],* and so on [Deut. 21:10 ff.]. For it is not commanded that he desire her or take her or have intercourse with her in her impurity, but it is only a matter of permission, though an act of the evil desire. It is only commanded that after that first intercourse, *then thou shalt bring her into thy house,* and so on, as the sages (may their memory be a blessing) have said.[23] It is also like the verse: *When thou shalt beget children and children's children, and ye shall have been long in the land, and shall deal corruptly, and make a graven image, even the likeness of any thing, [and shall do that which is evil in the sight of the Lord thy God to provoke Him to anger]* [Deut. 4:25]. This is not a commandment, but only a matter of permission, though an act of sin. But the end of the passage, *And thou wilt return unto the Lord thy God* [Deut. 4:30], is a positive commandment to return in penitence [for having done that] which was dependent upon a matter of permission. Thus the matter of kingship, similarly, is to be understood in the same way. The request for one was not commanded, but only permitted, though an act of the evil desire; while the stipulation was added that they should only set up that king whom God (blessed be He) had chosen from among their brethren, and in no other way.

And the speech pleased the Lord, that Solomon had asked this thing. And God said unto him: "Because thou hast asked this thing, and hast not asked for thyself long life; neither hast asked riches for thyself, nor hast asked the life of thine enemies; but hast asked for thyself understanding to discern justice; behold, I have done according to thy word: lo, I have given thee a wise and an understanding heart; so that there hath been none like thee before thee, neither after thee shall any arise like unto thee" [1 Kings 3:10–12].

[211a1] Even though it be admitted that the wisdom of the prophets varies according to the rank of their prophecy, it would not be proper to understand thereby those [kinds of] knowledge in which Solomon perfected himself—that is to say, the knowledge of governing a household or a city—for all that is far from the concern of prophecy. You see that Jethro guided Moses in the matter of the administration of justice, until he had taught him the way to appoint captains and how to govern the people. That was because Moses and the rest of the prophets neither busied themselves nor troubled their souls with these low things. Nor did they bother about the knowledge of the things that come-into-being and pass-away, nor about grasping their forms and their essences. For these are not the things that a prophet needs as prophet: neither the knowledge of the natures of the spheres and the stars, nor their number, nor their movements, nor their powers over the things below and how they act upon them, nor the making of talismans—all of which were embraced by Solomon's wisdom. For the knowledge of these things does not lie within the realm of prophecy, nor is it connected with it. Nor [need the prophet] have knowledge of the separate [substances[24]] in

22. This translation of the verse follows Abravanel's interpretation.

23. Cf. *Babylonian Talmud, Qiddushin* 21b.

24. According to the medieval Aristotelians, the heavens were moved by a series of intellects that were separated from the body and subsisted in themselves.

the same way in which Solomon grasped them; for he, as I have mentioned, apprehended the changes in their actions, and their officiating over the nations and over other things, and the ways in which each of them rules, and the way in which he should serve and labor in order to cause the [divine] emanation[25] to descend from it upon his nation. Now none of these things are matters the knowledge of which is needed by the prophet. For his knowledge is only of those things that are peculiar to Him (blessed be He), and the way in which He governs His creatures and, in particular, the Israelite nation, and the way in which the emanation is made to descend from Him (blessed be He) upon the nation by means of the holy sefirot.[26] The knowledge of the separate [substances] that is fitting [for a prophet to know extends] only insofar as they are emissaries of [211a2] providence and are connected with the affairs of the Israelite nation and are the means by which prophecy and miracles occur. In all of this, the wisdom of the prophets was according to the rank of their prophecies.

Therefore, with regard to the wisdom of divine things and the wisdom of the Law, it is proper that we say that the preeminence of the prophets was greater than the rank of Solomon, in proportion as their rank in prophecy was greater than his rank. However, in the remaining kinds of science and understanding, Solomon's wisdom was greater than theirs. It was this knowledge that the sages (may their memory be a blessing) had in mind when they said in the Midrash: "He was wiser than any other man, than the first man, than Abraham, than Moses, than Joseph, than the Generation of the Desert, which was a generation of knowledge. Since of this knowledge it was said to him [Solomon]: *Lo, I have given thee a wise and an understanding heart; so that there hath been none like thee before thee, neither after thee shall any arise like unto thee*" [1 Kings 3:12].[27]

25. Correcting a misprint in the text to read *ha-shefa'*.

26. According to the teaching of the Kabbalah, *sefirot* were the ranks or steps through which the Infinite and Inscrutable made himself manifest in the world.

27. *Tanḥuma*, chap. *Ḥuqqat*.

BIBLIOGRAPHY AND FURTHER READING

Primary Sources in English

Altmann, Alexander, trans. *Saadya Gaon: The Book of Doctrines and Beliefs.* Edited by Daniel H. Frank. Indianapolis: Hackett, 2002. (This translation is abridged; cf. Rosenblatt below.)

Feldman, Seymour, trans. *Gersonides: Wars of the Lord.* 4 vols. Philadelphia: Jewish Publication Society, 1984–87.

Geffen, M. David, trans. "Elijah del Medigo: Examination of Religion." PhD diss., Columbia University, 1971.

Goodman, Lenn E., trans. *Rambam: Readings in the Philosophy of Moses Maimonides.* New York: Viking, 1976.

Harvey, Steven, trans. *Falaquera's "Epistle of the Debate": An Introduction to Jewish Philosophy.* Harvard Judaic Texts and Studies 8. Cambridge, MA: Harvard University Press, 1987.

Hershman, Abraham M., trans. [Maimonides' *Mishneh Torah,* vol. 14.] *The Book of Judges.* Yale Judaica Series 3. New Haven, CT: Yale University Press, 1949.

Hirschfeld, Hartwig, trans. *Judah Halevi: The Kuzari; An Argument for the Faith of Israel.* London: George Routledge and Sons, Ltd., 1905; reprint, New York: Schocken Books, 1964. (A translation by Barry Kogan is forthcoming in the Yale Judaica Series.)

Husik, Isaac, ed. and trans. *Joseph Albo: Sefer ha-Ikkarim [Book of Roots].* 4 vols. Philadelphia: Jewish Publication Society of America, 1929–30.

Hyamson, Moses, trans. [Maimonides' *Mishneh Torah,* vol. 1.] *The Book of Knowledge.* Jerusalem and New York: Feldheim, 1981.

Lerner, Ralph. *Maimonides' Empire of Light: Popular Enlightenment in an Age of Belief.* Chicago: University of Chicago Press, 2000. (Includes the opening four chapters of the *Book of Knowledge,* the *Treatise on Resurrection,* and the complete *Letter on Astrology.*)

Pines, Shlomo, trans. *The Guide of the Perplexed.* 2 vols. Chicago: University of Chicago Press, 1963. (Includes an extensive "Translator's Introduction" by Pines, and Leo Strauss's "How to Begin to Study *The Guide of the Perplexed.*")

Rosenblatt, Samuel, trans. *Saadia Gaon: The Book of Beliefs and Opinions.* Yale Judaica Series 1. 1948. Reprint, New Haven, CT: Yale University Press, 1976.

Twersky, Isadore, ed. *A Maimonides Reader.* Springfield, NJ: Behrman House, 1972.

Walzer, Michael, and Menachem Loberbaum and Noam J. Zohar. *The Jewish Political Tradition.* 2 vols. (4 vols. projected). New Haven, CT: Yale University Press, 2001–3.

Weiss, Raymond L., and Charles E. Butterworth, eds. and trans. *The Ethical Writings of Maimonides.* New York: New York University Press, 1975; reprint, New York: Dover, 1983.

Secondary Literature in English and Hebrew

Altmann, Alexander. "Maimonides' 'Four Perfections.'" *Israel Oriental Society* 2 (1972): 15–24.

——. "Saadya's Conception of the Law." *Bulletin of the John Rylands Library* 28.2 (1944): 320–39.

Berman, Lawrence V. "The Fall of Man." *Association for Jewish Studies Review* 5 (1980): 1–15.

——. "Ibn Bajjah and Maimonides: A Chapter in the History of Political Philosophy" [in Hebrew with English summary]. PhD diss., Hebrew University, 1959.

——."The Ideal State of the Philosophers and Prophetic Laws." In *A Straight Path: Studies in Medieval Philosophy and Culture,* edited by Ruth Link-Salinger, 10–22. Washington, DC: Catholic University of America Press, 1988.

——. "Maimonides, the Disciple of Alfarabi." *Israel Oriental Studies* 4 (1974): 154–78.

——. "The Political Interpretation of the Maxim: The Purpose of Philosophy Is the Imitation of God." *Studia Islamica* 15 (1961): 53–61.

——. "A Reexamination of Maimonides' Statement on Political Science." *Journal of the American Oriental Society* 89 (1969): 106–11.

——. "The Structure of the Commandments of the Torah in the Thought of Maimonides." In *Studies in Jewish Religious and Intellectual History,* edited by Siegfried Stein and Raphael Loewe, 51–66. University, AL: Alabama University Press, 1979.

Blumberg, Harry Z. "Al-Farabi, Ibn Bajjah, and Maimonides on the Governance of the Solitary: Sources and Influences" [in Hebrew]. *Sinai* 78 (1976): 135–45.

Davidson, Herbert A. "Maimonides on Metaphysical Knowledge." In *Maimonidean Studies,* edited by Arthur Hyman, 3:49–103. New York: Yeshiva University Press, 1992–93.

——. "Maimonides' *Shemonah Peraqim* [Eight Chapters] and Alfarabi's *Fuṣūl al-Madanī* [Aphorisms of the Statesman]." *Proceedings of the American Academy for Jewish Research* 31 (1963): 33–50.

——. *Moses Maimonides: The Man and His Work.* New York: Oxford University Press, 2004.

Frank, Daniel H., ed. *Maimonides* issue of the *American Catholic Philosophical Quarterly* 76.1 (2002). (Includes some articles on Maimonides' ethics.)

Frank, Daniel H., and Oliver Leaman, eds. *A History of Jewish Philosophy.* London: Routledge, 1987.

Galston, Miriam. "Philosopher-King *v.* Prophet." *Israel Oriental Studies* 8 (1978): 204–18.

——. "The Purpose of the Law according to Maimonides." *Jewish Quarterly Review* 69 (1978): 27–51.

Goodman, Lenn E. "Ethical Monism and Ethical Pluralism." Chap. 5 of *God of Abraham.* New York: Oxford University Press, 1996.

——. "Rational Law/ Ritual Law." In *A People Apart,* edited by Daniel H. Frank, 109–200. Albany: SUNY Press, 1993.

Guttman, Julius. *Philosophies of Judaism.* New York: Schocken, 1964.

Harvey, Steven. "Falaquera's Alfarabi: An Example of the Judaization of the Islamic Falasifa." *Terumah* 12 (2002): 211–47.

——. "Maimonides in the Sultan's Palace." In *Perspectives on Maimonides,* 47–75. Oxford: Oxford University Press, 1991; reprint, Littman Library of Jewish Civilization, 2007.

Harvey, Warren Zev. "Ethics and Meta-Ethics, Aesthetics and Meta-Aesthetics in Maimonides." In *Maimonides and Philosophy,* edited by S. Pines and Y. Yovel, 131–38. Dordrecht: Martinus Nijhoff, 1986.

——. "Maimonides and Spinoza on the Knowledge of Good and Evil." Translated by Yoel Lerner. In *Studies in Jewish Thought,* edited by Joseph Dan, 131–46. Binah series 2. Westport, CT: Praeger, 1989.

——. "Political Philosophy and Halakhah in Maimonides." Translated by Sam Friedman. In *Jewish Intellectual History in the Middle Ages,* edited by Joseph Dan, 47–64. Binah series 3. Westport, CT: Praeger, 1994.

Havlin, Shlomo Zalman. "*Ḥuqqim* and *Mishpatim* in the Bible, Talmudic literature, and Maimonides" [in Hebrew]. *Annual of Bar-Ilan University: Studies in Judaica and Humanities,* edited by Z. A. Steinfeld, 26–27 (1995): 135–66.

Hayoun, Maurice-Ruben. *Moshe Narboni* [in French]. Tübingen: J. C. B. Mohr, 1986.

Husik, Isaac. *A History of Mediaeval Jewish Philosophy.* Philadelphia: Jewish Publication Society of America, 1941; reprint (with new preface by Steven Harvey), Mineola, NY: Dover, 2002.

Ivry, Alfred L. "The Logical and Scientific Premises of Maimonides' Thought." In *Perspectives on Jewish Thought and Mysticism,* edited by Alfred Ivry, Elliott R. Wolfson, and Allan Arkush, 63–97. Amsterdam: Harwood, 1998.

Kaplan, Lawrence. "Maimonides on the Singularity of the Jewish People." *Da'at* 15 (1985): v–xxvi.

Kasher, Hannah. "Hitmaqdut be-yaḥid o be-yaḥad iyyun mashveh bein R. Yehuda ha-Levi u-bein ha-Rambam" [Focusing on Aloneness and Togetherness: A Comparative Study of Rabbi Yehuda ha-Levi and the Rambam]. *Iyyun* 37 (1988): 238–46.

——. "The Myth of 'God's Anger' in the *Guide of the Perplexed*" [in Hebrew]. *Eshel Beer Sheva* 4 (1996): 95–111.

Kellner, Menachem. *Dogma in Medieval Jewish Thought: From Maimonides to Abravanel.* 1986. Reprint, Oxford: Littman Library of Jewish Civilization, 2004.

——. "Gersonides on Miracles, the Messiah, and Resurrection" [in Hebrew]. *Da'at* 4 (1980): 5–34.

——. *Maimonides on Judaism and the Jewish People.* Albany: SUNY Press, 1991.

Klein-Braslavy, Sara. *Maimonides' Interpretation of the Adam Stories in Genesis* [in Hebrew]. Jerusalem: Reuven Mass, 1986.

——. *Maimonides' Interpretation of the Story of Creation* [in Hebrew]. Jerusalem: Reuven Mass, 1987.

Kleven, Terence. "A Study of Part I, Chapters 1–7 of Maimonides' *The Guide of the Perplexed.*" *Interpretation* 20.1 (1992): 3–16.

Kraemer, Joel L. "Alfarabi's *Opinions of the Virtuous City* and Maimonides' *Foundations of the Law.*" In *Studia Orientalia: Memoriae E. H. Baneth Dedicata,* 107–53. Jerusalem: Magnes Press, 1979.

——. "How (Not) to Read *The Guide of the Perplexed.*" *Jerusalem Studies in Arabic and Islam* 32 (2006): 350–409.

——. *Maimonides: The Life and World of One of Civilization's Greatest Minds.* New York: Doubleday, 2008.

——, ed. *Perspectives on Maimonides.* Oxford: Oxford University Press, 1991; reprint, Littman Library of Jewish Civilization, 2007.

——. "*Shari'a* and *Namus* in the Philosophic Thought of Maimonides" [in Hebrew]. *Te'udah* 4 (1986): 183–202.

Kreisel, Howard. *Maimonides' Political Thought: Studies in Ethics, Law, and the Human Ideal.* Albany: SUNY Press, 1999.

——. *Prophecy: The History of an Idea in Medieval Jewish Philosophy.* Dordrecht: Kluwer, 2001.

Lawee, Eric. *Isaac Abarbanel's Stance toward Tradition: Defense, Dissent, and Dialogue.* Albany: SUNY Press, 2001.

Lerner, Ralph. *Maimonides' Empire of Light.* Chicago: University of Chicago Press, 2000.

——. "Maimonides' Governance of the Solitary." In *Perspectives on Maimonides,* edited by Joel Kraemer, 33–46. Oxford: Oxford University Press, 1991; reprint, Littman Library of Jewish Civilization, 2007.

——. "Maimonides' *Letter on Astrology.*" *History of Religions* 8 (1968): 143–58.

——. "Natural Law in Albo's *Book of Roots.*" In *Ancients and Moderns: Essays on the Tradition of Political Philosophy in Honor of Leo Strauss,* edited by Joseph Cropsey, 132–47. New York: Basic Books, 1964.

Levinger, Jacob. *Maimonides as Philosopher and Codifier* [in Hebrew]. Jerusalem: Bialik Institute, 1989.

Lobel, Diana. *Between Mysticism and Philosophy: Sufi Language of Religious Experience in Judah Ha-Levi's "Kuzari."* Albany: SUNY Press, 2000.

Macy, Jeffrey. "The Theological-Political Teaching of *Shemonah Peraqim* [Eight Chapters]: A Reappraisal of the Text and of Its Arabic Sources." *Proceedings of the Eighth World Congress of Jewish Studies,* Jerusalem, Division C, August 16–21, 1981.

Melamed, Abraham. "Isaac Abravanel and Aristotle's *Politics:* A Drama of Errors." *Jewish Political Studies Review* 5 (1993): 55–73.

——. "Medieval and Renaissance Jewish Political Philosophy." In *A History of Jewish Philosophy,* edited by Daniel H. Frank and Oliver Leaman, 415–49. London: Routledge, 1987.

——. *The Philosopher-King in Medieval and Renaissance Jewish Political Thought.* Edited by Lenn E. Goodman. Albany: SUNY Press, 2003.

Motzkin, Aryeh L. "On Halevi's *Kuzari* as a Platonic Dialogue." *Interpretation* 9 (1980–81): 111–24.

Novak, David. *Natural Law in Judaism.* Cambridge: Cambridge University Press, 1998.

Ormsby, Eric, ed. *Moses Maimonides and His Time.* Washington, DC: Catholic University of America Press, 1989. (Contains useful responses to S. Pines's influential "Limitations" article.)

Parens, Joshua S. "Leaving the Garden: Maimonides and Spinoza on the Imagination and Practical Intellect Revisited." *Philosophy & Theology* 18.2 (2009): 219–46.

——. "Maimonidean Ethics Revisited: Development and Asceticism in Maimonides?" *Journal of Jewish Thought and Philosophy* 12.3 (2003): 33–61.

——. "Prudence, Imagination, and Determination of Law in Alfarabi and Maimonides." In *Enlightening Revolutions: Essays in Honor of Ralph Lerner,* edited by Svetozar Minkov with Stéphane Douard, 31–55. Lanham, MD: Lexington Books, 2006.

——. "Strauss on Maimonides' Secretive Political Science." *Perspectives on Political Science* 39.2 (2010): 82–86.

Pines, Shlomo. "Limitations of Human Knowledge according to al-Fārābī, Ibn Bājja, and Maimonides." In *Studies in Medieval Jewish History and Literature,* edited by I. Twersky, 82–109. Cambridge, MA: Harvard University Press, 1979. Reprinted in *Collected Works of Shlomo Pines,* edited by W. Z. Harvey and Moshe Idel, 5:404–31. Jerusalem: Magnes Press, 1997.

——. "The Resurrection of the Jewish State according to Ibn Caspi and Spinoza" [in Hebrew]. *Iyyun* 14 (1963): 289–317.

——. "Some Topics Dealt with in Pulgar's Treatise *Ezer ha-dat* and Parallels in Spinoza" [in Hebrew]. In *Studies in Jewish Mysticism, Philosophy, and Ethical Literature, Presented to Isaiah Tishby,* edited by Joseph Dan, 395–457. Jerusalem: Magnes Press, 1986.

——. "Truth and Falsehood versus Good and Evil: A Study in Jewish and General Philosophy in Connection with the *Guide of the Perplexed,* I, 2." In *Studies in Maimonides,* edited by Isadore Twersky, 95–157. Cambridge, MA: Harvard University Press, 1990.

Pines, Shlomo, and Yirmiyahu Yovel, eds. *Maimonides and Philosophy: Papers Presented at the Sixth Jerusalem Philosophical Encounter.* Dordrecht: Martinus Nijhoff, 1986.

Ravitzky, Aviezer. "Kings and Laws in Late Medieval Jewish Thought (Nissim of Gerona vs. Isaac Abravanel)." In *Scholars and Scholarship: The Interaction between Judaism and Other Cultures,* edited by Leo Landman, 67–90. New York: Michael Scharf Trust of the Yeshiva University Press, 1990.

Reines, A. J. "Abravanel on Prophecy in the 'Moreh Nebukhim.'" *Hebrew Union College Annual* 31 (1960): 107–35.

——. "Maimonides' Concept of Mosaic Prophecy." *Hebrew Union College Annual* 40 (1970): 352–62.

Rosenthal, Erwin I. J. "Political Ideas in Moshe Narboni's *Commentary on Ibn Tufail's 'Hayy ben Yaqzan.'*" In *Hommage à Georges Vajda,* edited by Gérard Nahon and Charles Touati, 227–34. Louvain: Peeters, 1980.

——. *Studia Semitica.* Vol. 1, *Jewish Themes.* Cambridge: Cambridge University Press, 1971. (Includes articles on Maimonides and on law.)

Samuelson, Norbert. "Comments on Maimonides' Concept of Mosaic Prophecy." *Central Conference of American Rabbis* 18 (1971): 9–25.

Schwarzchild, Steven S. "Moral Radicalism and 'Middlingness' in the Ethics of Maimonides." *Jewish Quarterly Review* 52 (1977): 297–365. Reprinted

in *The Pursuit of the Ideal: The Jewish Writings of Steven Schwarzchild,* edited by Menachem Kellner, 137–60. Albany: SUNY Press, 1990.
Schweid, Eliezer. "Joseph Albo's System of Dogmas as Distinct from Maimonides'" [in Hebrew]. *Tarbiz* 33 (1964): 74–84.
——. "Omanut ha-dialoge *ha-Sefer ha-Kuzari* u-mashma'uta ha-iyyunit" [The Dialogical Art of the Kuzari and Its Theoretical Significance]. In *Ta'am ve-Hakahah.* Ramat Gan: Masada Press, 1970.
Seeskin, Kenneth, ed. *Cambridge Companion to Maimonides.* Cambridge: Cambridge University Press, 2005.
Silman, Yochanan. *Philosopher and Prophet: Judah Halevi, the "Kuzari," and the Evolution of His Thought.* Albany: SUNY Press, 1995.
Sirat, Colette. *A History of Jewish Philosophy in the Middle Ages.* Cambridge: Cambridge University Press, 1990. (Translation of 1985 French edition.)
Stern, Josef. *Problems and Parables of Law: Maimonides and Nahmanides on Reasons for the Commandments (Ta'amei Ha-Mitzvot).* Albany: SUNY Press, 1998.
Strauss, Leo. "The Law of Reason in the *Kuzari.*" In *Persecution and the Art of Writing,* 95–141. Glencoe, IL: Free Press, 1952; reprint, Chicago: University of Chicago, 1988.
——. "Literary Character of the *Guide for the Perplexed.*" In *Persecution and the Art of Writing,* 22–37.
——. "Maimonides' Statement on Political Science." In *What Is Political Philosophy? And Other Studies,* 155–69. New York: Free Press of Glencoe, 1959; reprint, Chicago: University of Chicago Press, 1988.
——. "On Abravanel's Philosophical Tendency and Political Teaching." In *Isaac Abravanel: Six Lectures,* edited by J. B. Trend and H. Loewe, 95–129. Cambridge: Cambridge University Press, 1937.
——. *Philosophy and Law: Contributions to the Understanding of Maimonides and His Predecessors.* Translated by Eve Adler. Albany: SUNY Press, 1995. (This entry and the next are translations of *Philosophie und Gesetz* [1935].)
——. *Philosophy and Law: Essays toward the Understanding of Maimonides and His Predecessors.* Translated by Fred Baumann. New York: Jewish Publication Society, 1987.
——. "The Place of the Doctrine of Providence according to Maimonides." *Review of Metaphysics* 57 (March 2004): 537–49.
——. "Some Remarks on the Political Science of Maimonides and Farabi." *Interpretation* 18.1 (1990): 3–30. (Translation by Robert Bartlett of "Quelques remarques sur la science politique de Maïmonide et de Farabi," *Revue des Études Juives* 100 [1936]: 1–37.)
Stroumsa, Sarah. *Maimonides in His World: Portrait of a Mediterranean Thinker.* Princeton, NJ: Princeton University Press, 2009.
Weiss, Raymond. *Maimonides' Ethics: The Encounter of Philosophy and Religious Morality.* Chicago: University of Chicago Press, 1991.
Wolfson, Harry Austryn. "Halevi and Maimonides on Prophecy." *Jewish Quarterly Review* 32 (1941–42): 345–70; 33 (1942): 49–82.

Bibliographies

For Jewish medieval political philosophy in general, also see the bibliographies in Melamed (1987 and 2003) and Sirat (1990) above. For Maimonides in particular, see Kreisel (1999) and Seeskin (2005) above and the following:

Ben-Shammai, Batyah. "Twenty-Five Years of Research on the Rambam: A Bibliography, 1965–1990" [in Hebrew]. In *Maimonidean Studies,* edited by Arthur Hyman, 2:17–42. New York: Yeshiva University Press, 1991.
Lachterman, David R. "Maimonidean Studies 1950–1986: A Bibliography." In *Maimonidean Studies,* edited by Arthur Hyman, 1:197–216. New York: Yeshiva University Press, 1990.

PART III

POLITICAL PHILOSOPHY IN CHRISTIANITY

Edited by Joseph C. Macfarland

INTRODUCTION

The phrase "political philosophy" is liable to a dual interpretation, as noted in the general introduction to this volume. Does it refer narrowly to a philosophical study of politics as a branch of philosophy more generally? Or is political philosophy a comprehensive and authoritative pursuit that is directive of other sciences, including the religious sciences? This ambiguity in the meaning of political philosophy—between its narrow, subordinate sense and its comprehensive, authoritative sense—is itself the object of our study. Within the medieval Christian tradition the narrower understanding of political philosophy was prevalent, in part, because these authors took their bearings from Aristotle's *Nicomachean Ethics* and *Politics* rather than from Plato's *Republic* and *Laws.* In the schema laid out by Aristotle, practical philosophy is distinguished from the theoretical; the theoretical sciences are more honorable and serious than the practical, and the most honorable of the theoretical sciences is first philosophy, occasionally called "theology" by Aristotle and generally called "metaphysics" by Christian readers.[1] Practical philosophy as a whole is referred to as "politics" or "political philosophy."[2] But "politics" can also be construed more narrowly: to know politics is the same disposition as having prudence, and prudence may involve knowing the good of the individual (prudence proper), of the household (domestic prudence), or of the city (political prudence; *Ethics* 6.8 1141b30–35). "Politics"—thus viewed as pertaining especially or exclusively to the city—becomes a subdivision of practical philosophy. This narrower sense of "politics" was strengthened by the convention among many Christian authors of referring to practical philosophy broadly understood as "moral philosophy."[3] This relative demotion of politics vis-à-vis ethics in Christianity conformed to the distinctive character of its sacred scripture as teaching ethical counsels rather than promulgating a law. Politics, as a branch of practical philosophy or moral philosophy, is subordinate to the more honorable theoretical sciences, especially to the most honorable science, metaphysics; for Christian readers, moreover, metaphysics in turn served sacred theology.[4]

Political philosophy, thus understood as a subordinate branch of philosophy, may nevertheless enjoy a considerable, if limited, autonomy. It attempts to discover and articulate the human good as it is known by nature and achieved through human action (referred to sometimes by Christian authors as earthly or political happiness). It subsequently discovers how political communities assist in bringing individuals to this earthly end. This form of political philosophy might pay little regard to natural philosophy or metaphysics, insofar as human communities operate without regard to the orderliness or the rule of the natural whole. It may be practiced without reference to the end of man, insofar as this end lies beyond nature (eternal happiness) or insofar as the surest

1. Aristotle *Nicomachean Ethics* 6.7 1141a20–23; *Metaphysics* 6.1 1026a7–23.

2. Aristotle *Ethics* 1.2 1094a28–1094b5, 7.11 1152b1; *Politics* 3.12 1282b14–23.

3. Roger Bacon, *Opus Maius: Moral Philosophy,* pt. 1 [Proemium], sec. 11; Thomas Aquinas *Commentary on the Nicomachean Ethics* 1.1.1–6; Dante *Il Convivio* 2.14.14–18. Janet Coleman traces this convention back to the sixth-century authors Anicius Manlius Severinus Boethius and Isidore of Seville ("The Science of Politics and Late Medieval Academic Debate," in *Criticism and Dissent in the Middle Ages,* ed. R. Copeland [Cambridge: Cambridge University Press, 1996], 185; see Isidore of Seville *Etymologies* 2.24.3–6, 11, 16).

4. Consider Thomas Aquinas *Commentary on the Ethics* 1.2.31; *Summa Theologiae* 1.1.5.

means to achieve our natural end (contemplative happiness) lies beyond nature. This circumscribed political philosophy may be pursued, therefore, without any immediate or overt direction from metaphysics or sacred theology.

This narrowly defined conception of "politics" or "political philosophy" does not, however, conform to Aristotle's assertion that politics is the most authoritative or architectonic discipline. The understanding of politics as authoritative or architectonic requires that ethics, as knowledge of the good of the individual, be put to work in the context of knowledge of the good for the political whole, which is "nobler and more divine" (*Ethics* 1.2 1094a28–1094b11, also 6.8 1142a9–11). Political philosophy in its authoritative mode directs which sciences are to be pursued, by whom, and to what purpose. Other subjects of inquiry, such as the orderliness of the whole and the nature of its governance, appear to be investigated with the conduct of politics in mind (*Metaphysics* 12.8 1074b1–14, 12.9 1075a12–1076a4). This second possibility for political philosophy, its authoritative form, puts us in mind of the political philosophy of Alfarabi, Averroes, or perhaps Maimonides, as each came to understand it from studying not Aristotle's *Politics*, but Plato's *Republic* and *Laws*. In its authoritative form, political philosophy might encompass inquiries otherwise pertaining to divine science, such as the nature of prophecy or providence. As noted above, we aim to study precisely this ambiguity in the meaning of political philosophy, between its narrow, subordinate sense and its comprehensive, authoritative sense. Secular as well as ecclesiastical authors, theologians as much as masters of the faculty of arts, practiced political philosophy as a branch of moral philosophy. In some cases there is little or no evident subordination to theology; in others the subordination may be evident and thoroughgoing. We come thus to the fundamental question: Was political philosophy also practiced by any Christian authors in its authoritative and comprehensive mode, implying the subordination of metaphysics or theology to its own ends? How did the practice of political philosophy among the Christian authors resemble, take after, or differ from its practice among their predecessors in the Islamic and Jewish traditions?

Inasmuch as political philosophy in its comprehensive and authoritative sense guides religious sciences such as theology, one might first ask whether Christian authors taught the superiority of philosophy over theology. This brings us to the vexed question of whether in the thirteenth and fourteenth centuries there existed "Latin Averroists": writers who, under the influence of Averroes's commentaries on Aristotle, advanced conclusions in philosophy that contradicted sacred doctrine. The medieval university consisted of four faculties: theology, medicine, law, and the arts. Study in the faculty of arts was a prerequisite for study in the other three faculties, and it originally focused on the arts of grammar, logic, and rhetoric. In the course of the thirteenth century, however, as the works of Aristotle were gradually translated and incorporated into the university curricula, the faculty of arts became, in effect, a faculty of philosophy. Prompted by the study of Aristotle's *Physics, Metaphysics,* and *De Anima,* as well as the commentaries on those works, masters (i.e., teachers) in the arts faculties often investigated questions such as whether it was demonstrable that the world was created in time, and whether the intellect of human beings is distinct in different persons.[5] Some masters drew conclusions on natural grounds that contradicted sacred doctrine—for example, that the world is eternal or that there is a single intellect for all human beings (since natural reasoning on the soul conceived of the intellect as the only part or power of soul that could be separate from the body and thus immortal [*De Anima* 2.2 413b26–29], a single intellect for humanity implicitly denied the immortality of individual human souls). These and other heterodox inquiries were enveloped within a general tendency of certain masters of the arts, under the influence of Aristotle's *Ethics* and the commentaries on it, to exalt the contemplative life and the pursuit of philosophy with an exuberance that

5. Aristotle distinguishes an active from a potential intellect (*De Anima* 3.4 429a19–29, 3.5 430a10–26). Hellenistic and medieval commentators frequently understood the active intellect to be a single entity, separate from body, and so separate from any individual human; by some it was identified with God. Averroes, drawing on Themistius, maintained in addition that the "possible" or "material" intellect, which is given form by the active or agent intellect, is similarly separate from body and common to all humankind. The latter doctrine was more controversial than the former, as it denied to the individual human soul the proper possession of any part of the intellect and, thus, removed any Aristotelian ground for inferring the immortality of the soul. Such arguments are reviewed and rebutted in Thomas Aquinas's *Summa contra Gentiles* 2.55–79.

appeared at times to dispense with the further aid of divine salvation through Christ.[6] Names associated with this putative movement included Boethius of Dacia and Siger of Brabant in the 1260s and 1270s and Jean of Jandun in the early fourteenth century. That these and similar heterodox conclusions were taught at the University of Paris appears to be corroborated by the actions of the bishop of Paris, Etienne Tempier, who, in 1270, forbade masters of the arts to teach doctrines belonging to theology and, in 1277, condemned 219 suspect propositions and forbade them to be taught in the university. These disciplinary actions indicate that the philosophizing masters in the faculty of arts had at least disturbed the conventional primacy of theology over philosophy.

This picture of "Latin Averroism" in the thirteenth century, however, has been subject to severe scrutiny in recent decades and, for a variety of reasons, has yielded to a common suspicion that the phrase is inaccurate, or even a "historiographical myth."[7] Three reasons will be noted here. First, the name "Averroism" is misleading, inasmuch as the medieval authors often identified as Averroists typically did not cite Averroes's commentaries on Aristotle as being authoritative but overtly drew their conclusions from their own reading of Aristotle's texts.[8] Averroes's commentaries were certainly influential, yet suspect teachings could be gleaned from other non-Christian sources, such as Maimonides' *Guide*, Avicenna's *Metaphysics*, and the occasional work of Alfarabi translated into Latin, or directly from Aristotle's works.[9] Second, the heterodox masters of the arts seem not to have imitated Averroes in the most important respect: whereas the *Decisive Treatise* teaches explicitly the superiority of philosophy to dialectical theology in discerning the intention of divine law, when the alleged Averroists encountered a contradiction between a philosophical conclusion and a point of sacred doctrine, they did not affirm the truth of philosophy but invariably affirmed the truth of scripture.[10] Of course, reading these works today, we may in some cases suspect the sincerity of these affirmations—the bishop of Paris evidently thought such affirmations disingenuous—but the intentions of these writers have remained sufficiently uncertain to bring the designation "Averroism" into question.

The third reason for questioning the aptness of the term "Averroism" is the least recognized and most important for our purposes: the masters of the arts seem not to have practiced *political* philosophy in the mode of Averroes or his predecessors. In the medieval university the study of politics received relatively little attention: if politics was studied as a discipline anywhere in the university, it was in the faculty of law, where the fundamental texts were Roman civil law and Gratian's *Decretum* (the original systematic presentation of canon law).[11] Even when Aristotle's works were

6. De Libera emphasizes as the signature issue for Averroism not the unicity of the intellect, but the tendency of masters in the faculty of arts, such as Boethius, to regard contemplation as the primary means to happiness; De Libera traces this tendency to Albert's *Commentary on the Ethics* and ultimately to Alfarabi, preferring the adjective "Farabian" to "Averroist" (Alain de Libera and Maurice-Reuben Hayoun, *Averroès and l'Averroïsme* [Paris: Presses Universitaires de France, 1991]). Others have argued that the substitution of "Farabian" for "Averroist" does not avoid the misleading character of these historiographical categories; the heterodox views cannot be accounted for by tracing those views to any one source (Luca Bianchi, "Felicità intellettuale, ascetismo, e arabismo: Nota sul *De summo bono* di Boezio di Dacia," in *Le felicità nel medioevo*, ed. Maria Bettetini and Francesco D. Paparella [Louvain-La-Neuve, 2005]).

7. The works that first prompted an interest in Latin Averroism were E. Renan, *Averroès et l'Averroïsme: Essai historique* (Paris: Michel Lévy Frères, 1861; Paris: Calmann-Lévy, 1882); also *Œuvres complètes de Ernest Renan* (Paris: Calmann-Lévy, 1947); and P. Mandonnet, *Siger de Brabant et l'Averroïsme latin au XIIIme siècle* (Louvain: Institut Supérieur de Philosophie de l'Université, 1908, 1911; Geneva: Slatkine Reprints, 1976). On Averroism as a "historiographical myth," see Libera and Hayoun, *Averroès and l'Averroïsme*; and Gregorio Piaia, "Averroïsme politique: Anatomie d'une myth historigraphique," in *Orientalische Kultur und europäisches Mittelalter: Miscellanea mediaevalia*, ed. Albert Zimmermann et al. (Berlin: Walter de Gruyter, 1985).

8. Thus Fernand Van Steenberghen (*Thomas Aquinas and Radical Aristotelianism* [Washington, DC: The Catholic University of America Press, 1980]) prefers the term "heterodox Aristotelianism," which has the advantage of more accurately representing the practice of masters of the faculty of arts in Paris in the 1270s. "Averroist" has the advantage of being a term of abuse at least occasionally used in the thirteenth century and more frequently in the fourteenth and fifteenth centuries (D. N. Hasse, "Averroica secta: Notes on the Formation of Averroist Movements in Fourteenth-Century Bologna and Renaissance Italy," in *Averroes et les Averroïsmes juif et latin*, ed. J.-B. Brenet [Turnhout: Brepols, 2007]).

9. *The Errors of the Philosophers*, attributed to Giles of Rome, ca. 1270, enumerates heretical teachings by Aristotle, Averroes, Avicenna, and Maimonides (in *Medieval Philosophy*, ed. Herman Shapiro [New York: Modern Library, 1964], 392–95).

10. *The Decisive Treatise* had not been translated into Latin in this period; occasional glimpses into Averroes's view of the relationship of philosophy and theology were available from scattered passages in his commentaries (for a summary of the import of these passages, see M. Grignaschi, "Indagine sui passi del 'commento' suscettibili di avere promosso la formazione di un averroismo politico," in *Il pensiero politico del basso medioevo*, ed. Carlo Dolcini [Bologna: Patron Editore, 1983]).

11. Jürgen Miethke, *De potestate papae: Die päpstliche Amtskompetenz im Widerstreit der politischen Theorie von Thomas von Aquin bis Wilhelm von Ockham* (Tübingen: Mohr Siebeck, 2000), 6–22.

introduced, the *Politics* was relatively neglected: it was not translated in its entirety until two decades after the *Ethics*. Furthermore, whereas the *Ethics* was an established part of the curriculum and the subject of a very large number of commentaries in the thirteenth century, the *Politics* had no fixed place in the curriculum (at the University of Paris, for example), and few commentaries were written on it.[12] These trends are confirmed in the activity of the philosophizing masters: while the propositions condemned by the bishop of Paris addressed heterodox readings of Aristotle's *Ethics, De Anima, Physics,* and *Metaphysics,* not one proposition addressed the interpretation of the *Politics.*[13] In the arts faculty in Paris there were two exceptions to this relative neglect of the *Politics:* Siger of Brabant reportedly gave a public disputation on the *Politics* (although no written record of the disputation survives), and Peter of Auvergne produced a commentary, excerpts of which appear in this volume.[14] Several of the propositions condemned in 1277 do address topics fundamental to a comprehensive political philosophy, such as the nature of divine providence (e.g., Props. 13–26) and of prophecy (Props. 176–78), yet such notions—arising in commentaries on Aristotle's *Physics* or *On Dreams*—appear to have belonged to natural philosophy rather than political philosophy.

This relative neglect of the *Politics* need not imply the total neglect of political philosophy, since the *Ethics,* too, is a work of political philosophy. The masters of the arts, as noted above, exhibited a profound interest in ethics and the highest human good, exemplified in Boethius's *On the Supreme Good.* This short work argues that the supreme good for man lies in the exercise of the speculative intellect, such that all genuinely virtuous actions tend in some way to that end. Yet this work neither openly acknowledges the political ramifications of this provocative opinion nor reflects upon the political conditions that would permit this opinion to be safely taught and acted upon. In the ethical teaching of the so-called Averroists the highest human good, the life of contemplation, appears to be pursued by the individual without reference to the political society to which he belongs: philosophy is a solitary pursuit.

Recalling our original question—was political philosophy practiced by Christian authors as an authoritative or comprehensive discipline that would imply a subordination of metaphysics or theology?—at this stage we may answer: If certain philosophizing masters of the arts tacitly adhered to their philosophical conclusions, even when these conclusions contradicted sacred doctrine, then indeed they privately upheld the primacy of philosophy over theology, but without conceiving of this philosophizing as an inherently political activity. Although the political import of such radical inquiry in the natural sciences seems not to have been well understood by the masters of the arts, it was rather well understood by the bishop of Paris, Etienne Tempier, when he forbade members of the university to teach—or even to listen to—the 219 suspect propositions. This political act sought to ensure that masters of the arts pursued philosophical inquiry within a framework laid down by the masters of theology, and to ensure that even the theologians employed philosophical arguments within the limits prescribed by the edict.[15] Tempier's central concern appears to have been that the contradiction of Christian doctrine by philosophical argument implied that there were "fables and falsehoods" in the "Christian law" (Prop. 181), in other words, that the community of the faithful—the most comprehensive community, directed to the highest end—lacked a true foundation. If the necessarily political import of such radical inquiries had not been sufficiently manifest prior to the condemnations, it became wholly manifest in the wake of them. Although Tempier's condemnation

12. Christoph Flüeler, *Rezeption und Interpretation der aristotelischen Politica im späten Mittelalter* (Amsterdam and Philadelphia: B. R. Grüner, 1992), 33.

13. For this reason some have wondered why the first English translation of the 219 Propositions appeared in a sourcebook of *political* philosophy (Luca Bianchi, *Il vescovo e i filosofi: La condanna parigina del 1277 e l'evoluzione dell'aristotelismo scolastico* [Bergamo: Lubrina, 1990], 43); also Cary J. Nederman, "Aristotelianism and the Origins of 'Political Science' in the Twelfth Century," *Journal of the History of Ideas* 52 [1991]: 194).

14. Peter, it should be noted, did not earn the same notoriety as Siger or Boethius of Dacia. Siger's disputation was reported by Pierre Dubois in his *Recovery of the Holy Land* [ca. 1305–7], trans. Walter I. Brandt (New York: Columbia University Press, 1956), sec. 132 [lxxx], pp. 189–90. The lack of interest in politics on the part of masters of the faculty of arts is discussed by E. L. Fortin, *Dissent and Philosophy in the Middle Ages: Dante and His Precursors* (Lanham, MD: Lexington Books, 2002), 46–50. In the same period, Albert the Great and Thomas Aquinas composed commentaries on the *Politics,* though not in the faculties of the arts or theology.

15. The condemnation was intended not only to suppress heterodox philosophical teaching among certain masters of the arts, but also, and perhaps primarily, to establish the institutional preeminence of a neo-Augustinian theology over Thomas's practice of theology (David Piché, *La condemnation parisienne de 1277* [Paris: J. Vrin, 1999], 8, 170 ff.).

was valid only in the environs of Paris, a similar edict was promulgated in Oxford, and lists of the condemned propositions were widely circulated. The extant writings and the events of the 1260s and 1270s may not bear witness to the existence of political philosophy in the comprehensive sense, but they at least indicate a need for it. Political thinkers from the following generations, such as Dante and Marsilius of Padua, were indeed sometimes identified as Averroists, in their own times or in modern scholarship.[16] It should be clear, however, that our intention is not to vindicate or question these identifications: we have touched on the controversy concerning "Latin Averroism" as a means of clarifying what would be expected of the practice of political philosophy in the comprehensive sense within medieval Christianity.

Political philosophy as a subordinate branch of practical philosophy was clearly practiced by a variety of Christian authors; it is incumbent upon us to investigate and determine whether a given author practiced political philosophy in the comprehensive sense. We should attend to the narrowness or breadth of the competence of his political philosophy, its explicit or implicit relationship to theology, as well as its principles, sources, and ultimate ends. Philosophy begins from the study of nature; political philosophy practiced even as a subordinate branch of philosophy enjoys a provisional independence from other disciplines, inasmuch as, within its own domain, its takes only nature and reason as its foundation and measure. Our question about the character and scope of the political philosophy in each case, including its relation to theology, may be answered by attending to what exactly is thought to be natural within political life. In the remainder of this introduction we will touch on three ways in which nature becomes a measure or a standard within politics: the naturalness of the city, the natural law, and the naturalness of kingly rule. Reviewing these three intersections of nature and politics will also give us the occasion to state reasons for several changes in the present edition of the *Sourcebook*. Although each of the three intersections will be discussed separately, the first two can be fully understood only in the light of the third.

Aristotle's *Politics* is perhaps most famous for its argument that a human being is by nature a political animal (1.2 1253a3 ff.). This assertion rests on the observation that man alone has speech with which he can indicate not only what is pleasurable and painful, but what is advantageous and harmful as well as just and unjust. The argument does not merely state that man is a *social* animal by nature, as if no one form of association had priority over the others. Man is a political animal because the city (*polis*) is the self-sufficient end toward which the other, non-self-sufficient communities (e.g., families, villages) tend. The argument does not imply a broader fellowship with all human beings (as one finds in Cicero's *De Officiis* 1.16.50). Man naturally belongs to one kind of community that comprehends the other communities, is complete in itself, and is limited in scope and scale. Finally, one conclusion of this teaching (relevant to what follows) is that one who by nature does not belong to a city is less than or greater than a human being, a beast or a god. Aristotle's account of the naturalness of the city is not perfectly congruent with sacred doctrine, especially as it was articulated by Augustine. Augustine had argued that human beings, even in their original state, sought fellowship (*societas*) with all other humans, and only in consequence of original sin did humans seek mastery or lordship (*dominium*) over one another.[17] If the original fellowship of human beings did not include coercion, then politics—what Aristotle meant by the word and what we commonly mean by it—seems to correspond to a mixture of this original fellowship with the mastery that pertains to our fallen nature. This connection of politics specifically to fallen nature does not prevent the city from securing a genuine advantage for its citizens: a well-governed city obtains an ordered concord among citizens resulting in temporal peace (*City of God* 19.13, 14). But the principal advantage of the temporal peace of the earthly city is that it permits each citizen to attend to the strife

16. For the accusation against Dante by Guido Vernani in the early fourteenth century, see Anthony K. Cassell, *The Monarchia Controversy* (Washington, DC: The Catholic University of America Press, 2004), 178–79; also John Marenbon, "Dante's Averroism," in *Poetry and Philosophy in the Middle Ages*, ed. John Marenbon (Leiden: Brill, 2001), 349–74. The classic treatment is Bruno Nardi, "Il concetto dell'Impero nello svolgimento del pensiero dantesco," in *Saggi di filosofia dantesca* (Milan and Genoa, 1930; repr., Florence: La Nuova Italia, 1967), 215–75. Marsilius is also frequently spoken of as an Averroist (Etienne Gilson, *History of Christian Philosophy in the Middle Ages* [New York: Random House, 1955], 524–27; Alan Gewirth, *Marsilius of Padua, The Defender of the Peace*, [New York: Columbia University Press, 1951], 1:39–44).

17. *City of God* 19.12, 15; 12.21. A student new to the subject might also read 2.21–22; 4.4; 14.11–15, 28; 15. 1–8; and 19.6–17.

within his soul and to seek the still higher end of eternal peace in the city of God. By this argument, the *polis* is not the natural end or goal of other communities, it is not a complete community, and its end serves the higher end of a more universal community.

The magnitude of the difference between Augustine and Aristotle on this question has long been disputed by serious readers of these authors; rather than attempt to establish a particular reading of them, let it suffice to note that the authors included in the *Sourcebook* likewise had to grapple with this question. This question concerning the naturalness of the city (the political community) became a critical point of contention in the debate concerning whether secular polities were independent of or subordinate to the church as the kingdom of God on its earthly pilgrimage. Augustine did not seek to subordinate secular polities to ecclesiastical rule, yet arguments akin to his that diminished the status of politics were eventually put to this use. While the city in Augustine's view has a partly natural basis and strives to obtain a limited advantage for its citizens, the city is finally judged in the context of ends that exceed our fallen nature, and in the light of wisdom that exceeds our reasoning faculties. For the authors in the *Sourcebook,* Aristotle's argument on the naturalness of the city served as an invitation to examine politics as a branch of philosophy taking only nature and our own reasoning powers as measures. The naturalness of the city appears to shield secular polities from ecclesiastical claims to rule. Every medieval Christian author had to reconcile in some degree what he had learned from Aristotle and Augustine; it is neither accurate nor useful merely to label an author as Aristotelian or Augustinian in respect to this question. But for each author it will prove useful to ask: What is the fundamental human community? The city? The nation? Humanity? What are the grounds of its natural character? What does this imply about the sufficiency of human wisdom to guide this community? This opposition of Aristotle and Augustine invites a comparison with the opposition of philosophy and theology, as if the general relation of philosophy to theology could be read in the way a medieval author draws on or respects these two authorities. Caution, however, is warranted, inasmuch as Aristotle's position on the naturalness of the city may not be the definitive philosophical statement on the subject, just as Augustine's may not be the definitive statement of the intention of scripture. For example, despite the vigorous secularism of the First Discourse of the *Defender of the Peace,* Marsilius does not follow Aristotle in asserting that man is a political animal by nature. The difficulties in negotiating this question are highlighted by new selections by Giles of Rome and Ptolemy of Lucca, as these two authors, more than others, exhibit a simultaneous dependence on Augustine and Aristotle.

The second intersection of nature and politics is the notion of natural law. Aristotle's *Ethics* and *Politics* present no natural law teaching. In the *Ethics,* Aristotle contrasts "political right according to nature" with political right "according to law" or convention: thus nature and law offer mutually exclusive types of political right (5.7 1134b18 ff.). What exactly is meant by right by nature remains elusive, as Aristotle says that among human beings it is everywhere variable. The *Politics* advances the notion that the lawfulness of the law lies in its rationality or intelligibility: it is argued that because the law does not have passion or desire, when one wishes to be ruled by the law rather than by any human being, one wishes to be ruled by God and by the intellect (3.16 1287a29). While this passage puts forth a kind of a rational law teaching, Aristotle appears to disown this argument on behalf of law when he later concludes that the rule of the best man is superior to the rule of law (3.18 1288a33, discussed below).[18] It is important to remember that, for Aristotle, the laws in every city fundamentally depend on the specific character of the regime in that city (3.12 1282b1–13, 4.1 1298a15–25). Since the regime is always limited in scope to the city, there can be no universally valid law.

Thus, although Aristotle's works prompted inquiry into the naturalness of political life, the tradition of natural law thinking in Christianity did not arise from but rather predated the translation of Aristotle's works, having already been established through a confusing variety of sources. The provenance for natural law thinking in classical political philosophy lies in Cicero's works and in

18. In the *Rhetoric* Aristotle also mentions a "common law" that is "according to nature" and "divined" by men, although they nevertheless do not agree about it (1.13 1373b).

the Stoics whose arguments he appropriated: early Stoics had argued that one achieves moral goodness by living in accord with nature; when Cicero presented Stoic teachings, often in dialogue form, he spoke of a "true law" or an "eternal law" that is "right reason in agreement with nature."[19] These diverse articulations of natural law thinking (very broadly understood) were subsequently invoked from time to time by fathers of the church such as Ambrose and Augustine, often in explicit or tacit reference to Cicero and the Stoics, but without any systematic theoretical development.[20] These varied articulations of natural law thinking evidently found sanction in Paul's letter to the Romans ("When Gentiles do by nature the things contained in the law... [they] are a law unto themselves" [Rom. 2:14–15]). Parallel to these developments, the Stoic teaching also left traces in Roman civil law; this source established the explicit distinction between the *ius civile,* the *ius naturale,* and the *ius gentium* (the civil law, the natural law, and the law of nations). This distinction was transmitted to many medieval thinkers through a brief restatement by the sixth-century scholar Isidore of Seville. The most important texts on the natural law were the restatements and compilations of these sources in medieval commentaries on Roman civil law and, still more significantly, in the *Decretum* of Gratian and later elaborations on the canon law.[21]

Our authors drew upon Aristotle's brief account of political right by nature, often reformulating it to harmonize with the prior natural law tradition. What follows from denying natural right was apparent in certain documents from the canon law tradition, which maintained that polities instituted under nature—especially man's fallen nature—are unjust; justice is then obtained only through the spiritual power of the church.[22] A recovery of natural right could thus have political implications in the recurring contests between secular and ecclesiastical powers. Thomas understood that without natural right or natural law, what is just would be determined solely through instituted laws, which inevitably vary. In highlighting the contrast between natural justice and legal justice, he mitigated the perplexity of Aristotle's statement that natural justice is variable, arguing that human nature is immutable and that the precepts reasoned from this nature are likewise immutable and everywhere valid. This sharpened distinction between natural (immutable) justice and legal (variable) justice reveals their connection: positive laws are an extension or determination of natural justice with respect to those things that are indifferent and variable. Variable legal justice therefore originates in immutable natural justice: written law may instantiate precepts of natural law, just as the moral precepts of Mosaic law belong to the law of nature (*Summa Theologiae* 1.2.100). Natural justice also includes the law of nations (*ius gentium*), laws that are separately established among different peoples but coincidentally stand everywhere in agreement.[23] This elaboration of the natural law tends to give law in general a cosmopolitan rather than political or civic character. Thomas's reading of Aristotle dispels somewhat the elusive character of natural right and magnifies its significance for social life.

Could Thomas's expanded account of the connection between natural right and right by law obscure the significance of the initial distinction between them? In this vein, and in contrast to Thomas, Marsilius of Padua states that precepts commonly enacted everywhere must nevertheless not be understood as "natural" in the strict sense, since they require this legal enactment (2.12.7). Even the "common dictate of reason," which is

19. *De Republica* 3.5.8, 3.22.33; *De Legibus* 1.5.18–19, 1.13.39. In the dialogues the Stoic arguments are often opposed by members of the New Academy, the school of philosophy to which Cicero himself subscribes (see Seth Benardete, "Cicero's *de legibus* I: Its Plan and Intention," *American Journal of Philology* 108 [1987]: 295–309). *De Republica* and *De Legibus* were known in the patristic era but were not available in the medieval period; in that period related passages on natural law were found in *De Officiis* and *De Inventione* (2.22.65–67).

20. For citations of specific passages in various authors, see Michael Bertram Crowe, *The Changing Profile of the Natural Law* (The Hague: Martinus Nijhoff, 1977), 61–67.

21. *The Digest of Justinian,* ed. Theodor Mommsen and trans. Alan Watson (Philadelphia: University of Pennsylvania Press, 1985) 1.1.1, 6, 9; *The Etymologies of Isidore of Seville,* trans. Stephen Barney et al. (Cambridge: Cambridge University Press, 2006) 5.1–6; Gratian, *The Treatise on the Laws (Decretum DD. 1–20), with the Ordinary Gloss,* trans. A. Thompson and J. Gordley (Washington, DC: The Catholic University of America Press, 1993). The various ancient and medieval sources are summarized by Paul Sigmund, *The Natural Law in Political Thought* (Cambridge, MA: Winthrop Publishers, 1971).

22. Within this volume, this opinion is represented in *On Ecclesiastical Power* by Giles of Rome, though it did not originate with Giles. In Giles's other political work, *On the Government of Princes,* his account of natural law hews closer to that of Thomas.

23. The *ius gentium* has an ambiguous status: it is a positive law (*Summa Theologiae* 1–2.95.4 co.) that follows rationally from the premises of the natural law and is therefore a part of natural justice (1–2.95.4 ad 1; 2–2.57.3 ad 3).

free from legal enactment and accords with equity, he calls only a "quasi-natural law" (1.3.4, 1.19.13). He radically reduces the profile of natural law: civil law does not originate in natural law; the sole source of law is the "legislator," that is, "the whole body of citizens, or the weightier part thereof" (1.12.3, discussed below). For Marsilius, the law remains fundamentally an artifact of the city. As each practices political philosophy in a Christian context, neither Thomas nor Marsilius simply reproduces Aristotle's account of natural right. Whereas Thomas removes some of the elusiveness from natural right and lends it greater definition, Marsilius's comments are so restrictive as to make us wonder: Has he restored to natural right its elusiveness, or does he intend to question its existence altogether?

Our purpose in surveying accounts of the intersection of nature and law has been to ask: Are the traditional ways of speaking about natural law subordinated to a philosophical elucidation of natural right, or are the philosophical ways of speaking about this matter put in the service of some traditional account? Answering this question is difficult because Aristotle's understanding of natural right is elusive, and the possible significations of "natural law" so varied. If one is disposed to favor Aristotle's account over Thomas's, a disjunction appears to open up between what natural right is, and what can be said about it in such a way that it can benefit society. This difficulty is also evident in the brief but complex account given by William of Ockham, who distinguishes three ways that natural law is spoken of in the Christian tradition. Natural law is, first, what follows from natural reason that "in no case fails"; second, what accords with equity and accords with the state of nature prior to original sin; and third, what is known from reason on the supposition of established law, often on the supposition of the law of nations (*ius gentium*). The first two are prior to positive law, while the third is consequent upon it; thus the first two seem to merit the name "natural" more than the third, although Ockham does not say so. Moreover, the second and the third can contradict one another: there is no private property by the second mode of natural law (as there would have been no private property in the original state of nature), whereas property is regulated under the third mode. Natural law refers equally to what is accepted in a society that is rarely established (e.g., the absence of property), and what is commonly accepted in all societies (e.g., deposits must be returned). Natural laws may be known both from reason and from scripture, as natural laws are explicitly or implicitly contained in scripture.[24] Ockham distinguishes the modes without ranking or evaluating them; one is left to contemplate and negotiate the tension between them. To facilitate inquiry into the ways of speaking about natural law, discussions of the natural law in the first edition of the *Sourcebook* (Marsilius's *Defender of the Peace* and Ockham's *Dialogue*) have been supplemented by new passages from Aquinas's *Commentary on the Nicomachean Ethics* and Giles of Rome's *On Ecclesiastical Power.*[25]

The third intersection of nature and politics, the naturalness of kingly rule as the best regime, complicates the assertion of the naturalness of politics in multiple ways. In Aristotle's discussion of slavery, the account of "rule" is briefly moved to a more comprehensive level involving all natural beings. In every composite being, something is ruling and something is ruled: in a living being, the soul has a despotic rule over the body; in a human being, the intelligence has a kingly and political rule over the desires (*Politics* 1.5 1254a22–b5). Within the city, kingship is said to be the best form of rule; insofar as kingship is rule of one part exclusively over another, it appears more akin to rule as it is found in other natural beings.[26] Several medieval authors develop this argument further than Aristotle, for they observe that God's governance of the whole, even his governance by means of nature, is kingly, and that this divine rule is a paradigm for rule within the city.[27] Aristotle himself says that kingship is best

24. Is it known from scripture, from reason, or from both that a society in the original state of nature would have had no private property? Many medieval authors were familiar with Aristotle's report, in Book 2 of the *Politics*, that there was no private property in the city of Plato's *Republic* (e.g., Ockham *A Short Discourse on Tyrannical Government* 3.7; also Ptolemy of Lucca *On the Government of Rulers* 4.4). The question did not have merely theoretical interest: Ockham alienated himself from the papacy by vociferously defending the practice of apostolic poverty within the Franciscan order.

25. The reader will also want to consult the questions concerning law in Aquinas's *Summa Theologiae* 1–2.90–97, 100.

26. Aristotle *Politics* 4.2 1289a40; cf. *Nicomachean Ethics* 5.7 1160a35.

27. Peter of Auvergne *Commentary on the Politics* 3.12.14, 3.16.5; Ptolemy of Lucca *On the Government of Rulers* 3.1, 3; Dante *Monarchy* 1.7–10.

and *divine* (*Politics* 4.2 1289a40); yet, in saying it is divine, does he put its naturalness into doubt? Within his discussion of kingship he poses the question: Is it better to be ruled by the best man or by the best laws? When men are ruled by laws, citizens share in ruling and being ruled; this arrangement of sharing rule characterizes political rule (3.16 1287a13–19). To say that man is a political animal by nature seems to imply that sharing rule under law is natural. But in the purest form of kingship, "total kingship" (*pambasileia*), the best man rules without taking turns and without submitting to law: thus, although kingship is one of the six types of polity, total kingship seems to be nonpolitical (3.14 1285b30–33); perhaps for this reason, Aristotle remarks that some men think it is not natural (3.16 1287a12). Faced with these ambiguities, Thomas Aquinas understands Aristotle as saying that there are fundamentally two forms of rule, kingly and political. This same opposition guides the organization of Ptolemy's portion of *On the Government of Rulers* and is fundamental to medieval political thought.[28]

This opposition, however, between kingly and political rule remains puzzling: How is it that humans are by nature political animals, but the rule that seems best and most natural also seems nonpolitical? Which is better, kingly rule without law or political rule under law? The gap opened up between kingship and law has repercussions for our prior two subjects. First, if kingship without law is most natural and yet not political, then the assertion that man is a political animal by nature seems to have been qualified. What belongs to a human being by nature as a citizen might be overridden by his membership in a larger, more divine community. Second, the gap opened up between kingship and law appears to put into question the possibility of a natural law: if the most natural rule is rule of the greatest wisdom without any law, what place is there for an established natural law? Conversely, if one maintains the existence of a natural law, one is maintaining that rule in accord with the highest wisdom somehow has the character of lawfulness (perhaps a rational lawfulness), and the opposition of kingship and law is thereby implicitly rejected.

This problem of kingship and law was sometimes understood by our authors simply as a question concerning the choice of regime: For a given city or people, is kingship preferable to polity? Furthermore, in a given kingdom, how far ought the king's authority to extend over the law?[29] The nature of the problem, however, presses beyond the choice of regime in a narrowly political sense because the criterion for meriting this kingship is formulated in such an extraordinary manner: one who rules as a king without law would have to differ from his subjects in virtue and political ability as a god differs from human beings (*Politics* 3.13 1284a4–14). What sort of excellence Aristotle had in mind, he does not say: Is practical wisdom understood, which a king would surely need, or is theoretical wisdom understood (*Ethics* 10.7 1177b27–35), which alone seems to render human life divine? Perhaps Aristotle's reticence on this subject was intended to shield political rule from radically monarchic or tyrannical claims to rule, but this original ambiguity could also be exploited. Might total kingship be exemplified in the kingship of Christ, since his actions seemed, on occasion, to void the Mosaic law, which he claimed to fulfill, and since his own kingship—when fully realized—would obviate the need for the Roman law, to which he had remained obedient? Aristotle adduces examples of every type of kingship except total kingship; one might therefore surmise that this peculiar kingship has never existed. Or one might think that it can have existed only in the most extraordinary of circumstances, only in the kingdom of Christ and perhaps in the rule of the Roman pontiff as the vicar of Christ.

It is important to note that the *Politics* played no part in the historical development of the "plenitude of power," the doctrine that the pope had the authority to act both in accord with law and beyond law. This doctrine (as well as reservations about it) had been developed in canon law decades prior to the translation of the *Politics*.[30] Moreover, the canonists, when contemplating a monarchic rule not limited by law, had before them passages in Roman civil law stating that what pleases the emperor has the force of law, and that the emperor

28. Ptolemy of Lucca *On the Government of Rulers* 2.8, 9; Thomas Aquinas *Commentary on the Politics* 1.1.6.

29. Peter of Auvergne *Commentary on the Politics* 3.9.1, 3.11.1, 3.16.5; Ptolemy of Lucca *On the Government of Rulers* 2.9.4–5, 3.11.9; Jean Dunabin, "Aristotle in the Schools," in *Trends in Medieval Political Thought*, ed. Beryl Smalley and P. R. L. Brown (New York: Barnes & Noble, 1965), 65–85; Thomas Renna, "Aristotle and the French Monarchy, 1260–1303," *Viator* 9 (1978): 309–24.

30. John A. Watt, *The Theory of Papal Monarchy in the Thirteenth Century: The Contribution of the Canonists* (New York: Fordham University Press, 1965), esp. 75–105.

is not bound by law.[31] The question before us is not the source of the doctrine of plenitude of power, but rather: What did medieval readers think when they found the Philosopher discussing the complete kingship of a man of the highest virtue?

Aristotle's ambiguous statements on total kingship appeared, at least to some readers, to justify prior papal or imperial claims to an authority that transcended local, particular polities.[32] Thus Ockham engaged Aristotle's *Politics* at greatest length in those parts of the *Dialogue* that address the papal claims to plenitude of power. In a preliminary assessment of the impact of the *Politics,* we might have been tempted to conclude that Aristotle's account of the naturalness of the city provided an antidote to a vulgar Augustinism that demoted politics and subordinated secular polities to the supervisory and comprehensive care of the church. But this preliminary view fails to take into account how Aristotle's thinking, in its full complexity, could be employed to expand a monarchic ecclesiastical power as well as to limit it. Those who philosophized about politics in the tracks of Aristotle, and who wished to curtail the claims of the church to temporal power, found it necessary to examine, rethink, and in some cases tacitly alter or censure Aristotle's account of total kingship. Dante created an image of Aristotle's total kingship in his description of the "temporal Monarchy," thereby raising the Roman emperor to a status parallel to the pope's. Yet, in doing so, he distorted Aristotle's account of total kingship by asserting the real existence of such a monarchy. Marsilius, by contrast, in order to destroy the papal plenitude of power, attacks the grounds of Aristotle's total kingship and makes political rule the necessary condition for every lawmaking community (thus, as noted above, the source of law is the "whole body of citizens, or the weightier part thereof"). Ockham accepted Aristotle's arguments on behalf of total kingship—neither appropriating them to his own purposes nor attacking them—but he denied that such authority belonged to any secular or ecclesiastical ruler. He emphasized instead the conventional or legal component inherent in all existing forms of rule. (The interaction of our medieval authors with Aristotle's thought is sketched here roughly and only in the first moment of a complex dialogue.) However highly each author regarded Aristotle as *the* Philosopher, when that author reckoned with the tension between kingship and law in the *Politics,* he had to come to a decision about its meaning and substitute some element of clarity for its original ambiguity, thus giving to this highly ambiguous fulcrum point in Aristotle's political thought a novel shape and significance. Such innovations needed no apologies, since political philosophy for these authors was neither a theoretical inquiry, in which the changeable is suspect, nor a historical inquiry, in which fidelity to the source is paramount, but a practical science to be revived and put to work.

Aristotle's account of the tension between kingship and law holds interest for us not because it was employed in the rhetorical contests between the papacy and its multiple secular opponents, but precisely the reverse: the rhetorical contests hold interest for us as the arena in which the opposition of kingship and law was examined and rethought. The opposition of kingship and law is the place in Aristotle's works in which he takes up and discusses Plato's account of the philosopher-king. In the second book of the *Politics,* Aristotle explicitly criticizes at length the community of property and of family as described in the *Republic* (2.2 1261a10–2.5 1264b25). However, he fails to mention Socrates' third proposal, the kingship of the philosopher. Aristotle's discussion of this subject appears to have been postponed until the third book of the *Politics.* We observed in the general introduction to this volume that Plato's *Republic* and *Laws* served as the primary guides to political philosophy in Islam and Judaism, that the *Republic* and the *Laws* provided the models of the philosopher-king and prophet-legislator, and that these books were not known in medieval Christianity. In this community, Aristotle's ambiguous account of total kingship was the primary window through which the idea of the philosopher-king could be glimpsed and contemplated; it was the vexing question that might prompt Christian readers at least to consider propositions analogous to Alfarabi's, that the ideas of the philosopher and the supreme ruler, the legislator and the prophet,

31. *The Digest of Justinian* 1.3.21, 1.4.1, 32.1.23.

32. Harvey C. Mansfield, *Taming the Prince: The Ambivalence of Modern Executive Power* (Baltimore: Johns Hopkins University Press, 1989), 86, 115.

are the same (*Attainment of Happiness* 58), or Maimonides' statement that perfection in the theoretical sciences is a necessary, though not sufficient, condition for prophecy (*Guide* 2.36). Reflection on the ambiguities of total kingship was therefore the context in which one might encounter and consider Averroism. What sort man is altogether beyond law? Such rule could belong to Christ alone, who, though he obeyed Roman law and fulfilled Mosaic law, described a kingdom whose promise exceeded either. Yet if the teaching of Jesus is *itself* deemed a "law"—as the Christian authors sometimes adopted the practice of referring to religion in general as "law"—then one might consider whether the unnamed excellence intended by Aristotle is some other wisdom that exceeds all forms of law. The possibility of such an authoritative excellence places in a new light Aristotle's assertion that, among all the arts and sciences, the discipline of politics is architectonic. Therefore, in considering each author here as a reader of Aristotle, it should prove useful to ask: What sort of human being, if any, has virtue such that he differs from others, as gods from men? What role does this human have in relation to his city, its regime and laws? These questions may serve as a means to discover whether a particular author, while practicing political philosophy in the narrow sense, sought to practice what we have designated political philosophy in its comprehensive form.

In rethinking what they found in Aristotle's *Ethics* and *Politics,* our authors, as we noted, did not leave political philosophy as they found it. Medieval political thinkers are often studied in order to elucidate the ways in which they anticipated modern political thought: the doctrine of natural law, as briefly but powerfully elucidated by Thomas, received still more attention and weight in the early modern period; the simple separation of church and state is given an emphasis in Dante's *Monarchy* that easily evokes modern political thought, even if the teleological grounds of Dante's separation are very different from the modern grounds for it; readers find intimations of popular sovereignty in Marsilius of Padua, and of natural rights in William of Ockham. Reading these authors for the sake of discovering such "anticipations" can have the defect of emphasizing indirectly what the medievals might have learned from our contemporaries, rather than what we still might learn from the medievals. Such anticipations, however, do prompt a final question: Is there anything in the practice of political philosophy in Christianity that might account for the more stubborn persistence of political philosophy in this setting than in the Islamic and Jewish worlds? Initially one might look to the proliferation of universities throughout Europe, in which philosophy was sustained in an institutional setting. That this answer is not sufficient is clear from the observations made above: the ecclesiastical support of the universities affected the range and character of thinking within these institutions, and however much philosophy in general was enriched through sanctioned university studies, political philosophy was practiced in large part outside of the university curricula. The same cause that prompted the elevation of theology over philosophy—the fundamental character of this sacred text as a teaching rather than a law—also entailed a distinction of priest and ruler that, although endlessly disputed, was in diverse measures taken for granted by very nearly all. This distinction in fact between priesthood and rulership (however much it was obscured in debate) meant that the precariousness of philosophy in the domain of one could be somewhat remedied by appeal to the other. Whereas, in the case of Socrates, the philosopher was censured for impiety by the ruling part of the city, philosophers in this setting, if accused of impiety by the church on the one side, might ally themselves with rulers on the other. Whether in this economy of freedom and constraint the activity of philosophizing as such was improved must be left to the reader to decide.

TWENTY

ROGER BACON

Opus Maius: Moral Philosophy

Translated by Richard McKeon, Donald McCarthy, and Ernest Fortin

The details of Roger Bacon's life (ca. 1214/20–1292) have been the subject of much discussion.[1] The place and the exact date of his birth are in doubt. He received his early education at Oxford, at which time he might have come to know Robert Grosseteste, for whom he always professed the greatest admiration. Bacon came to Paris ca. 1240, where he was one of the first to lecture on the natural treatises and the *Metaphysics* of Aristotle. Upon his return to Oxford ca. 1247 he attended the lectures of Adam Marsh. A considerable change appears to have taken place in his intellectual life at this time. For the next ten years he devoted himself wholeheartedly to the study of various disciplines, including mathematics, languages, and experimental science. In 1257 or thereabouts, he entered the Franciscan order but was never ordained to the priesthood. His new duties as a friar seem to have necessitated some curtailment of his scientific work. Bacon seems to have returned to Paris in the early 1260s, although not as a teacher in the university. A new milestone in his career was reached when, through his own overtures, his work was brought to the attention of Cardinal Guy de Foulques, later Pope Clement IV (1265). The latter asked to be supplied with a copy of Bacon's philosophic writings. Bacon, who had as yet composed no major treatise on philosophy, conceived the ambitious project of an encyclopedic work (the *Scriptum Principale*) embracing the whole of knowledge but was forced to abandon the idea in favor of a work of more modest dimensions, since known as the *Opus Maius*. This was followed by the *Opus Minus* and the *Opus Tertium,* which summarize and complement the teachings of his major work. All three books were written within a period of eighteen months and dispatched to Clement IV. Clement's death in 1268 deprived the author once and for all of the papal approval and financial support on which he relied for his projected reform of learning in the church. Bacon was not overtly entangled in the condemnations in Paris and Oxford in 1277, and he had denounced the Averroist teaching on the unicity of the intellect. Yet his writings evidence interest in the issues central to the condemnations, and sometime between 1277 and 1279, when he was again in England, he was condemned and confined

1. A good overview of the difficulties in determining the details of Bacon's life may be found in David C. Lindberg, *Roger Bacon's Philosophy of Nature* (Oxford: Clarendon Press, 1983), xv–xxvi.

to house arrest by his superiors in his order, perhaps because of suspected novelties related to his astrological studies, and perhaps particularly with regard to whether celestial conjunctions had some influence on the incarnation of Christ.[2] Neither his convictions nor his combativeness was affected by these disciplinary measures. Traces of his bitterness at the vexatious treatment meted out by his superiors and of the sharp invectives against the vices and ignorance of the clergy, with which his *Compendium Philosophiae* and other earlier writings abound, are still apparent in his last (unfinished) work, the *Compendium Studii Theologiae* (1292).

The *Opus Maius,* on which Bacon's fame chiefly rests, is a long plea (*persuasio*) designed to win Clement IV over to Bacon's views concerning the necessity of a vast educational reform. By the author's own repeated admission, it is written for, and uses methods and arguments suited to, "wise men," as opposed to the vulgar or the herd, for whom a simple and crude presentation of the truth is all that is needed or possible. The whole work is divided into seven parts: (1) the causes of error, especially custom; (2) wisdom, that is, the sacred scriptures and theology, as served in turn by philosophy and canon law; (3) the study of languages, especially Hebrew, Greek, and Latin; (4) mathematics, including geometry, astronomy, and geography; (5) optics; (6) experimental science; and (7) moral philosophy. Implicit in the structure of the *Opus Maius* (and explicit in the *Opus Minus*) is a critique of the medieval university of the time.[3] Bacon advocated the study of Hebrew and Greek in order to improve understanding of the Bible and, in the case of Greek, understanding of the classical philosophers. He strongly advocated the study of mathematics, especially astronomy, first, in order to attain greater accuracy in geographical and chronological knowledge, although ultimately in order to bring greater certainty to theology. Moreover, Bacon was the first Latin author to master the works of Alhacen (Ibn al-Haytham) on perspective, thus influencing John Pecham; the works of Bacon, Pecham, and Witelo on optics were dominant in Europe until Kepler. Bacon argued that the superiority of Christianity could be made evident to followers of other sects only in the field of philosophy, as it is common to all sects, and for this reason the sciences ought to receive more attention in the university.

The last part of the *Opus Maius,* on moral philosophy (1267), is itself made up of six parts, the contents of which are grouped by the author under two general heads described as the "speculative part" and the "practical part" of moral philosophy. Accordingly, the first half of the *Opus Maius* deals with the broad principles of morality within the traditional framework of man's relation to God (Part 1), to his neighbor (Part 2), and to himself (Part 3). The second half treats the belief in, or acceptance of, the true religion (Part 4), the love and practice of that religion (Part 5), and, in a cursory manner, the question of forensic oratory (Part 6).

Bacon makes extensive use of Arabic materials in translation—such as Alfarabi's *Enumeration of the Sciences*—and he openly reads Aristotle in the light of commentaries by Avicenna or Averroes; Bacon provides a link therefore between Islam and Christendom in the thirteenth century. Yet he is not one of the authors suspected by modern scholars of being a "Latin Averroist" or "heterodox Aristotelian." Aristotle's works play a less prominent role in Bacon's practical philosophy than is true for his later contemporaries: he admires the *Nicomachean Ethics* and cites the *Rhetoric* but seems not to have read the *Politics.* His moral philosophy is strongly influenced by the Latin Stoic tradition: Part 3 of his moral philosophy quotes at great length the works of Seneca that were not then readily available. Also notable is the influence of Augustine's *City of God* and *On Christian Doctrine.*

The translation of Parts 1 through 3, and a portion of Part 4 (through the Second Distinction, 1.22) were taken from Richard McKeon, *Selections from Medieval Philosophers* (New York: Charles Scribner's Sons, 1930), 2:81–106; this translation was revised by the original editors in the light of a subsequent edition of the Latin text by F. Delorme and E. Massa, *Rogeri Baconis Moralis Philosophia* (Turin: Thesaurus Mundi, 1953). The remaining selections from Part 4 (Second Distinction, 3.16–5.3 and 6.1–6) were translated by Ernest Fortin from the Delorme-Massa edition, and the selections from Parts 5 and 6, by Donald McCarthy. The Delorme-Massa edition, to which the italic numbers refer, is based largely

2. Paul L. Sidelko, "The Condemnation of Roger Bacon," *Journal of Medieval History* 22 (1996): 69–81.

3. Jeremiah Hackett, "Roger Bacon on the Classification of the Sciences," in *Roger Bacon and the Sciences,* ed. J. Hackett (Leiden: Brill, 1997).

on Bacon's own manuscript (Vat. Lat. 4295), discovered by A. Pelzer in 1919, and represents a substantial improvement over earlier editions of the *Moral Philosophy.*

MORAL PHILOSOPHY

Part One

[Proemium]

1. I have shown in the preceding parts that the knowledge of languages, and mathematics, and perspective as well as experimental science are extremely useful and particularly necessary in the pursuit of wisdom. Without them no one can advance as he should in wisdom, taken not only absolutely but relatively to the Church of God and to the other three sciences described above. 2. Now I wish likewise to go over the roots of the fifth science, which is better and more noble than all those previously mentioned; and it is the practical one among them all, that is, the operative one, and it deals with our actions in this life and in the other life. In fact, all other sciences are called speculative. For although certain of them are active and operative, nevertheless, they are concerned with artificial and natural actions, and they consider the truths of things and of scientific activities that have reference to the speculative intellect, and they are not related to things pertaining to the practical intellect. which is called practical because it directs *praxis,* that is, the operation of good and evil. 3. Whence the term "practical" is taken here in a restricted sense as applying to the activities of morality in accordance with which we become good or evil; although if "practical" is taken in a broad sense for all operative science, many other sciences are practical; but this one is called practical by antonomasia because of the chief operations of man, which are related to virtues and vices and to the happiness and misery of the other life. [4]

4. This practical science, then, is called moral and civil science, which places man in his proper order to God and to his neighbor and to himself, and proves these orders and invites and moves us to them efficaciously. For this science is concerned with the salvation of man, which must be accomplished through virtue and happiness; and this science aspires to that salvation so far as philosophy can. From these things, it appears in general that this science is more noble than all the other parts of philosophy. For since it is the inward end of human wisdom and since the end is what is most noble in anything, this science must of necessity be the most noble. 5. Besides, this science alone or in the highest degree treats of the same questions as theology, because theology considers nothing other than the five subjects mentioned above, although in another manner, namely, in the faith of Christ. However, this science, too, contains many outstanding testimonies for the same faith; and it scents from afar the principal articles for the great aid of the Christian faith, as what follows will declare. But theology is the most noble of the sciences; therefore, this one, which agrees in the highest degree with it, is more noble than the others. In order that the very great utility of this science may be apparent, its parts must be investigated to the end that what we wish may be drawn from the parts and from the whole.

6. Moreover, since moral philosophy is the end of all the parts of philosophy, the conclusions of the other sciences must be the principles in it in accordance with the relation of preceding sciences to those that follow, because the conclusions of the preceding are naturally assumed in those that follow. And therefore, it is fitting that they be carefully proved and certified in the preceding sciences, that they may be worthy of acceptance in the sciences that follow, as is evident from metaphysics. 7. Therefore, the principles of moral philosophy are certified in the preceding sciences; and for that reason these principles should [5] be drawn from the other sciences, not because they belong to those sciences, but because these sciences have prepared them for their mistress. Whence, wheresoever they may be found they must be ascribed to moral philosophy, since in substance they are moral. And, although they may be repeated in the other sciences, it is by the grace of moral philosophy. Wherefore, all things of this sort must be reckoned as moral philosophy and ascribed to it. Therefore, if we wish to use them according to their right, they must be brought together in moral science from all the other sciences.

8. Nor is it strange if philosophers have spread moral philosophy through all speculative philosophy: because they knew that it is of the salvation of man; and therefore, they have mixed beautiful doctrines in all the sciences, that men might always be moved to the good of salvation, and that all might know that the other sciences are to be sought after only for this one science, which is the mistress of human wisdom. 9. Therefore, if I adduce authorities from other places than those that are contained in the books on morals, it must be considered that they should properly be placed in this science; nor can we say that they have not been written in the books of this science, since we do not have except in part in Latin the philosophy of Aristotle, Avicenna, and Averroes, who are the principal authors in this science. 10. For just as theology understands that salvation-bringing truths belong to it, wheresoever they be found, as was stated in the beginning and touched on later, so too moral philosophy vindicates as its own whatever it finds written elsewhere on things of this sort.

11. Moreover, this moral science is called by Aristotle and [6] by others civil science, because it shows the rights of citizens and of cities. And since it was common for cities to dominate regions as Rome ruled the world, for that reason this science is called civil from the city (*civitas*), although it is formed to construct the laws of the kingdom and the empire.

12. This science, moreover, teaches in the first place to draw up the laws and the rights of living; secondly, it teaches that these rights are to be believed and approved and that men are to be stimulated to act and live according to these laws. The first part is divided into three sections; for first comes naturally the relation of man to God and in respect to the angelic substances; secondly, his relation to his neighbor; thirdly, to himself, as the Scripture states. 13. For in the first place in the books of Moses are the commands and laws concerning God and divine worship; in the second place, concerning the relation of man to his neighbor in the same books and those that follow; in the third place, there are instructions concerning customs, as in the books of Solomon. In the same way in the New Testament, these three alone are contained. For man cannot assume other relations.

14. Not only because of the first but because of all those that follow, it is necessary that the principles of this science, by which the others are verified, be set forth in the beginning. Of these principles, however, there are some that are purely principles and are capable of being stated only metaphysically. 15. Others, although they are principles with respect to the sciences that follow, are nevertheless either first conclusions of this science [that is, morals], or else, although they enjoy some of the privilege of a principle, still because of their extreme difficulty, and because they are highly controversial, and because of their excellent utility in respect to the sciences that follow, they should be sufficiently established; just as Aristotle in the beginning of his *Natural Philosophy* proves the first [7] principle of that science, namely, that there is motion, against those who suppose only the one immovable being.[4] 16. It should be noted, however, that metaphysics and moral philosophy agree with each other to the highest degree; for both have to do with God and angels and eternal life and with many subjects of this sort, although in different ways. For metaphysics investigates metaphysically the things that are proper to it by means of what is common to all the sciences, and it inquires into spiritual things by way of the corporeal, and through created things it finds the Creator, and through the present life it treats of the future life, and it sets forth many preambles to moral philosophy. 17. Hence, lest I should confuse different sciences with each other by trying to prove here what is proper to metaphysics, I shall repeat here only the things that metaphysics investigates for the sake of civil science, so that, as is proper, I may join this science with metaphysics, in so far as what is assumed here is explained in metaphysics.

1

1. I state, therefore, that God must be, just as He must be shown to be in metaphysics. Second, that all men know naturally that God is. Third, that God is of infinite power and of infinite goodness, and together with that, that He is of infinite essence and substance, so that it follows thus that He is best, wisest, and most powerful. Fourth, that God is one in essence and not many. Fifth, that not only is He one in essence but three in another manner, which has to be explained in general by

4. Cf. Aristotle *Physics* 1.2 185a12 ff.

metaphysicians, but here it must be explained in its proper discipline. 2. Sixth, that He has created all things and governs them in the being of nature. Seventh, that besides corporeal things He has formed [*8*] spiritual substances, which we call intelligences and angels; for intelligence is the name of a nature, and angel is the name of a function; and how many they are and what their operations are, as it pertains to metaphysics, as far as it is possible for them to be known by human reason. Eighth, that besides angels He made other spiritual substances, which are the rational souls in men. Ninth, that He has made them immortal. 3. Tenth, that there exists the happiness of another life, that is, the highest good. Eleventh, that man is capable of this happiness. Twelfth, that God governs the human race in the way of morals just as He governs other things in the being of nature. Thirteenth, that God promises future felicity to those who live rightly in accordance with the governance of God, as Avicenna teaches in Book 10 of the *Metaphysics,*[5] and that a horrible future infelicity is due those who live evilly. 4. Fourteenth, that worship is due God with all reverence and devotion. Fifteenth, that as man is ordered naturally to God through the reverence due Him, so he is ordered to his neighbor by justice and peace, and to himself by honorableness of life. Sixteenth, that man cannot know by his own effort how to please God with the worship due Him, nor how he should stand in relation to his neighbor nor to himself, but he needs the revelation of truth in these things. 5. Seventeenth, that the revelation must be made to one only; that he must be the mediator of God and men and the vicar of God on earth, to whom is subjected the whole human race, and in whom one must believe without contradiction when it has been proved with certitude that he is such as I have just described him; and he is the lawgiver and the high priest who in spiritual and in temporal things has the plenitude of power, as a "human God," as [9] Avicenna says in Book 10 of the *Metaphysics,* "whom it is permissible to adore after God."[6]

6. By these principles metaphysics is continuous with moral philosophy and comes down to it as its end; thus Avicenna joins them beautifully at the end of his *Metaphysics.* The other principles, however, are peculiar to this science and are not to be explained in metaphysics, although Avicenna adds a number of them. But in the beginning of his volume he gives the reason for this: that he had not constructed a moral philosophy and he did not know whether he would complete one; and therefore he mixed with these metaphysical principles many that are nevertheless proper to moral philosophy, as is evident to the inquirer. 7. And once these have been considered, the legislator should then at the beginning take up the properties of God in particular, and of angels, and the happiness and the misery of the other life, and the immortality of bodies, and things of this sort to which the metaphysician could not aspire. For the metaphysician treats in all these principally of the question of whether the thing is; because it is proper for him to take up that question in regard to all things, in that he considers that which is and being in their common properties. 8. But the other sciences take up other questions involved in things, namely, what each one is, and of what kind, and how much, and other questions of this sort, in accordance with the ten categories. The moral philosopher, however, has to explain, not all the secrets of God and of the angels and of others, but those that are necessary to the multitude, on which all men should agree, lest they fall into doubts and heresies, as Avicenna teaches in the "Roots of Moral Philosophy."[7]

2

1. I say, therefore, that moral philosophy explains first the Trinity in relation to God, which truth the legislator has by revelation [*10*] rather than by reason. The reason, indeed, why philosophers have said a great deal concerning divine things in particular, which exceed human reason and fall under revelation, was touched on before. For it was shown how they could have many noble truths concerning God that were had through a revelation made to them, as the Apostle says, *for God revealed* [these things] *to them* [Rom. 1:19], but more completely to the patriarchs and the prophets who, it is known, had revelation and from whom the philosophers learned all things, as was proved clearly above. 2. For the patriarchs and the prophets not only treated divine things

5. Avicenna *Metaphysics* 10.2 (442). (Numbers in parentheses after Avicenna's *[Healing:] Metaphysics* 10 refer to the pages of the Arabic text translated in part 1 of this volume, selection 7. Bacon quotes the Latin translation.)

6. Avicenna *Metaphysics* 10.5 (455).

7. Ibid. 10.2 (442–43).

theologically and prophetically but also philosophically, because they devised and taught all philosophy, as was proved in the second part of this work. The metaphysician, however, was able to teach sufficiently that God is, and that He is known naturally, and that He is of infinite power, and that He is one, and that He is three. But how the Trinity is, he could not there explain to the full; and, therefore, that must be shown here.

3. There is, then, the blessed Trinity, the Father and the Son and the Holy Spirit. For Claudianus, one of the expositors of the sacred Scripture, in the book in which he combats the following heresy, that "God feels nothing with a sense of passion but with the affect of one who has compassion," brings forward this argument: Plato "with praiseworthy daring, admirable genius, unchangeable purpose, sought, found, and proclaimed three persons in the divinity: God the Father, also the paternal mind, art, or counsel, and the love of the two for each other. He taught thus not only that we must believe in one supreme equitrinal undivided divinity, but he demonstrated that He must be thus."[8] These things are clear from his book on divine things. [*11*] 4. Porphyry, too, as Augustine says in Book 10 of the *City of God,* spoke of "the Father and his Son," whom he called the "paternal intellect and mind," and "the medium of them, by whom," as Augustine says, "we think he meant the Holy Spirit";[9] and following our manner he called each one God, where, although he "uses words loosely," he sees nevertheless what should be maintained. And Augustine, in the same book, recounts that a certain philosopher, whose name he does not give, repeated the beginning of the Gospel according to John as far as the incarnation of Christ, in which the distinction of the divine persons is stated clearly.[10] Augustine, also in Book 10 of the *City of God,* insists that Porphyry says that sins cannot be purged except by the Son of God.[11]

5. And Aristotle says in the beginning of the treatise *On the Heaven and the World* that in divine worship we exercise ourselves to magnify the one God by the number three,[12] which is prominent in the properties of the things that were created. And therefore, since every creature, as is evident from the part on metaphysics, is a trace and imprint of the Trinity, there must be a Trinity in the Creator. And in the beginning of his treatise *On the Heaven and the World* he argues that there is a trinity inherent in all things because it exists in the Creator. And since Aristotle completed the philosophy of his predecessors to the limit of the possibility of his times, he had to feel far more certainly concerning the blessed Trinity of persons that he might confess the Father and the Son and the Holy Spirit.

6. For this reason there were three sacrifices in the law of Aristotle and three prayers, as [*12*] Averroes says in his commentary on the beginning of the treatise *On the Heaven and the World;*[13] and this is manifest from the *Politics* of Aristotle, which is a book of laws. Avicenna, moreover, the most outstanding expositor of Aristotle, assumes the Holy Spirit in the "Roots of Moral Philosophy."[14]

7. But he [that is, Aristotle] could perceive the truth concerning the Father and the Son far better, because it is more difficult to understand the procession of the Holy Spirit from two distinct persons than the generation of one of them from the other. For this reason philosophers failed more in the comprehension of the Holy Spirit than in the knowledge of the Father and the Son. And therefore those who were able to have a knowledge of the Holy Spirit had far more knowledge of the other persons. 8. The philosopher Ethicus in his book on divine and human and natural things, which he wrote in the Hebrew, the Greek, and the Latin language, because of the greatness of the secrets, places in God the Father, the Word of the Father, and the Holy Spirit, and maintains that there are three persons, namely, the Father and the Son and the Holy Spirit.[15] This must also be held by reason. This reasoning, nevertheless, could not have been given before the things that have to be expressed of God in particular nor before the authorities of the moral philosophers, which are introduced to this same end in this science as in the place appropriate to them.

9. I say, therefore, that God is of infinite power; and infinite power is capable of infinite operation; therefore, something infinite can come from God, but not something different by its essence, because then there could be several gods, the contrary of which has been shown in the part on metaphysics.

8. Claudianus Mamertus *De Statu Animae* 2.7.
9. Augustine *City of God* 10.29; cf. 10.23.
10. Ibid. 10.29.
11. Ibid. 10.28.
12. Aristotle *De Caelo* 1.1 268a14–15.
13. Averroes *In De Caelo* 1.2.
14. Avicenna *Metaphysics* 10.2 (442).
15. Ethicus (or Aethicus) *Cosmographia* 1.12. Little is known of the author of the *Cosmographia,* who was probably active in northern Europe in the seventh century.

Therefore, that which is begotten of God must be God since it has the essence of its progenitor; but it is different in person. 10. And this which is begotten has infinite power, [*13*] since it is infinite good. Hence it can bring forth something infinite; hence it is able to bring forth another person. Either, then, the Father brings forth the same person and then the Holy Spirit will proceed from both of them; or He will be brought forth from the Son only, and in that case He will not be equal to the Father nor will there be a perfect kinship and proportion among the divine persons, which is contrary to reason. 11. Further, there cannot be parity of love according to this view, because the Father would love the Son more than the Holy Spirit, because He begets the Son and does not bring forth the Holy Spirit. But since the Holy Spirit is God, because He has the divine essence, an infinite love must be due Him; and therefore, the Father will love Him with an infinite love as He does the Son. And likewise because the love of the Father cannot be other than infinite, because His love is in accordance with His power, it remains, therefore, that the love of the Father for the Holy Spirit will be as great as the love of the Son for the Holy Spirit. Wherefore, the Holy Spirit as well as the Son must be brought forth from the Father.

12. That, however, there are not and cannot be more persons cannot and should not be explained here, but must be assumed until it is proved in the fourth part of this science [of morals], to which the full measure of the demonstration is assigned. But it was necessary that the Trinity of persons, namely, of the Father and the Son and the Holy Spirit, be proved and expounded here because it is the radical foundation in this science for establishing divine worship and for many other things. 13. Nor should it be alleged in opposition that no science has to prove its principles. For how that is to be understood has been shown above. But other things that can be inquired concerning God and in [*14*] which there should be probable doubt, are conclusions of the fourth part and, therefore, will be determined there.

Part Two

1

1. The second part treats of the laws and statutes governing the relations of men among themselves. In the first place, the welfare of the human species is considered in the line of propagation, to bind people by laws in their increase. Therefore laws of marriage are given, and they determine how marriages must be made and how impediments are to be removed, and most of all, that fornicators and sodomites should be excluded from cities, for "they are inimical to the construction of the city," since "they draw men away from that which is better in cities, namely, marriage," as Avicenna and others maintain.[16]

2. Next, laws are given in accordance with which subjects are ordered to prelates and princes, and contrariwise, and servants to masters, according to every type of dominion and servitude; and laws are given in accordance with which the father of the family must live in guiding his offspring and family, and the master is ordered in respect to his disciples. Next, the doctors and the skilled in each of the sciences and arts are appointed; and those best suited to engage in studies and duties of this sort are chosen, according to the advice of wise men, from the youths who are to be instructed; and the rest are deputed to the military service to execute justice and to check malefactors. 3. And "it is necessary," as Avicenna says, "that this be the first intention in instituting the law, namely, to order the city in three parts, that is, into disposers, ministers, and those learned in the law, and that in each of them someone in charge be appointed. After him, other officials inferior to him should be appointed, and after these still others, until few remain; to the end that [*40*] no one should be useless in the city and not have some praiseworthy function, and that some utility to the city may be derived from each one."[17] 4. Whence, in Plato, that city is said to be most justly ordered in which each disregards his own proper desires. Therefore, as Avicenna says, the prince of the city should prohibit "idleness and disoccupation." "As for those who cannot be curbed, they should be

16. Avicenna *Metaphysics* 10.4 (448).

17. Ibid. 10.4 (447).

expelled from the city, unless the cause is infirmity or old age; and then a place should be set apart in which people of that sort should remain and have a procurator allotted to them."

5. "It is necessary, moreover, that there be in the city a certain place for the moneys of the commonwealth, which should be derived partly from the law governing contracts, partly from fines that are inflicted for punishment, partly from the estates and spoil of rebels, partly from other sources; and to the end that this public fund be available partly for those who cannot earn money for themselves because of infirmity and old age, and partly for teachers of the law and partly for public uses."[18]

6. And then, the legislator instructs men to make patrimonies and inheritances and testaments, because Avicenna says that the substance "necessary for life is partly the branch and is partly the root. But the root is the patrimony and anything bequeathed and given by testament, of which three roots the most secure is patrimony."[19] The branch of substance, however, comes from gains derived from kinds of business.

7. Then laws should be published concerning contracts in every kind of business, in buying, selling, leasing, hiring, borrowing, lending, paying, saving, and the like, "that whatever can do harm in contracts may be removed," as Avicenna says.[20]

Then, laws must be framed in accordance with which it may be shown in all lawsuits [*41*] and in all cases what is right or wrong, and by means of which legal processes may be terminated, that peace and justice may be fostered among the citizens.

8. Then, as Avicenna says, activities "by which inheritances and fortunes are lost" and by which the peace and concord of citizens are disturbed, must be prohibited; and the practitioners of these activities are "the people who wish to win for the sake of some gain, such as the wrestler, the gambler," and others of this sort. "In the same way, activities should be prohibited that lead to things contrary to the utilities," as, for instance, "teaching how to steal and plunder,"[21] and other things of this sort.

9. And further ordinances should be made, as Avicenna says, "that men aid and defend each other, and that they be unanimous in fighting against the enemies of the law." "If, however, there be another city or kingdom of good constitutions and laws, this is not opposed to it, unless the time should come when there must be no other law than this one, the establishment of which, since it is the best, must then be extended throughout the whole world." And in this statement the Christian law is hinted at, as will be explained below. "If, however, there should be some among them who are at variance with the law, they should first be corrected that they may return to their senses; but if they do not wish to do that, let them be put to death."[22]

2

1. The last point that is required here is that the legislator "set up a successor to himself." This is done, according to Avicenna, in the following manner. He should do it "with the consensus of the nobles and of the people; and he should choose such a one as can rule well and be prudent and be of good morals, brave, kind, skilled [*42*] in governing and learned in the law, than whom none is more learned, and this should be manifest to all.

2. "But if thereafter they should so disagree that they wish to choose another, they have in that denied God; and therefore the legislator should interpose in his law enactments to the effect that the entire city should fall unanimously upon anyone who should wish to intrude himself by power or money and should kill him. But if they shall be able to do this and shall not have done it, they have in that contradicted God, and he is not guilty of blood who kills one of this sort, provided, however, it is previously known to the people."[23] If, on the other hand, he who is to be made successor is not worthy and has been so proved, another should be appointed.

3. And so in a summary way the design of the roots [or fundamentals] of this second part [of moral philosophy] and of those matters that proceed from such fundamentals are brought to a close. In this part is comprehended the civil law, which is now in use among the Latins, as is manifest from the roots of this part. Moreover, it is certain that the Latins have derived their rights and laws from the Greeks, that is, from the books of Aristotle and Theophrastus, his successor, as well as the laws of the twelve tables, which were taken first from the laws of Solon the Athenian.

18. Ibid.
19. Ibid. 10.4 (449).
20. Ibid. 10.5 (452).
21. Ibid. 10.4 (448).
22. Ibid. 10.5 (453).
23. Ibid. 10.5 (451–52).

Part Three

[Proemium]

1. The third part of moral and civil science is concerned with the conduct of each person relative to himself; that everyone may have honorableness of life and may abandon the foulness of vices because of future happiness and the horror of eternal punishment. That this should be the third part appears clearly, since it is plain that that part which contains the worship of God is first, as has been declared. The common good, moreover, is set before the private good, as Aristotle says in Book 7 of the *Metaphysics.* But the preceding part has to do with the common good, whereas this part advances the private good. For charity is the greatest virtue, and it is ordered to the common good, and concord and peace and justice attend it, which virtues go beyond the morals of individual persons. For man is a social animal and it is one of his properties, as Avicenna says in Book 5 of his treatise *On the Soul* and in the "Roots of Moral Philosophy," that he should not live alone like the brute animal which in its life suffices to itself alone.[24] Therefore, the laws that order men to their neighbor are the more important.

2. According to the same Aristotle and to Averroes, [46] in Book 10 of the *Metaphysics,* the hermit, who is not part of the city but is concerned with himself alone, is neither good nor evil.[25] And Cicero, in his book *On Duties,* quoting the words of Plato, says that Plato wrote very truly: "We are not born for ourselves alone; our native land claims part of our origin, our friends part, and, as the Stoics are pleased to believe, all things are created for the use of men, and men are generated for the sake of men, that they may be able to aid one another."[26] As Cicero himself, in Book 5 of the *Academics,* says, "Nothing is so noble as the communication of benefits."[27] It is, in fact, innate in man "that he have something of the civil and the popular, which something the Greeks call *politikon.*"[28] Hence, in the book *On the Happy Life,* Seneca says, "This word is required of man that he aid men; if he is able to, many; if he is less able, a few; if still less, his neighbors; if less, himself."[29]

3. Wherefore, the second principal part of moral philosophy must be concerned with common laws, as has been stated; and the third will be on the life and the honesty that each one should pursue. This, moreover, is true according to the order of the dignity of nature and absolutely speaking, although Aristotle does not adopt this manner in his books, for he proceeds according to the way of investigation and hence from the things that are better known to us and not from those better known to nature. But since we have already made certain through him and others what the power of this science requires, we can arrange its parts according to the order that the dignity of nature demands.

4. And here the philosophers have said wondrous things concerning virtues and vices; so that every Christian may be confounded when we conceive that unbelievers had such sublimities of virtues, [47] whereas we seem to fall ignominiously from the glory of virtues. For the rest, we should be greatly encouraged to aspire to the apex of virtue, and, stirred by noble examples, we should give forth more noble fruits of virtues, since we have greater aid in life than those philosophers, and since we are assured we shall receive greater aids beyond comparison by the grace of God. I shall first repeat certain things relating to virtues and vices in general; secondly, I shall pass on to particulars.

Part Four

First Distinction

[Proemium]

1. I have dwelt at length on this third part of moral philosophy because of the beauty and utility of moral teachings and because the books from which I have gathered these roots, flowers, and fruits of morals are rarely found. Now, however, I wish to go on to the fourth part of this science, which, although it is not so copious and so pregnant as the third, is nevertheless more wonderful

24. Avicenna *De Anima* 5.1; *Metaphysics* 10.2 (441).
25. Aristotle *Metaphysics* 9.4 1055b21.
26. Cicero *De Officiis* 1.7.22.
27. Cf. rather Cicero *De Finibus* 5.23.65.
28. Cicero *De Finibus* 5.23.66.
29. Seneca *De Vita Beata* 30.5.

and more worthy, not only than that part, but than all the preceding parts, since it consists in establishing that the true religion, which the human race should accept, is worthy of belief and approval.
2. Nor is there any branch of philosophy more necessary for man or of so great utility or dignity as the fifth part of this science, which teaches to love and acknowledge by works the religion to which we have already assented. For it is especially on account of these parts that all sciences are subordinated to moral philosophy. In fact, all wisdom is ordered with a view to knowing the salvation of the human race; and this salvation consists in the perception of the things that lead man to the happiness of the other life. Avicenna says of this happiness that it is such "as eye has not seen nor [*188*] ear heard,"[30] as has been touched on above. 3. And since Parts Four and Five of moral philosophy purpose to investigate this salvation and to attract men to it, all the sciences, arts, and functions, and whatever falls under the consideration of man, are bound to this part of the noble consideration of civil science. 4. For this reason it is most useful to consider the intention of these parts, and it belongs to every Christian to do so for the confirmation of his profession and that he may have wherewith to correct those who have wandered astray. Assuredly, God can never deny to the human race a knowledge of the way of salvation, since according to the Apostle He wishes all men to be saved.[31] And His goodness is infinite; wherefore He has always left men means by which they may be enlightened to know the way of truth.

Second Distinction

[Proemium]

1. Having set forth these principal religions in respect to the use of peoples as well as in respect to the ways of astronomy and in respect to the diversities of their ends, the consideration proceeds to the means of persuading men of the truth of religion.

1

1. It was said earlier in the part on mathematics, in relation to the conversion of unbelievers, that the persuasion of the true religion, which is the Christian religion alone, is brought about in a twofold manner: either by miracles, which are beyond us and beyond unbelievers, and concerning this way no man can presume; or else by a way common to unbelievers and to us, which is in our power and which they cannot deny, because it proceeds by the ways of human reasoning and by the ways of philosophy. Philosophy is indeed proper to unbelievers, since we have derived the whole of philosophy from them, and not without the greatest reason, that we may have confirmation of our faith for ourselves and that we may pray efficaciously for the salvation of unbelievers. [*196*] 2. Nor should the statement of Gregory be urged in objection, that "faith has no merit where human reason lends proof."[32] For this statement must be understood of the Christian man who would lean only or principally on human reason. But this should not be done; on the contrary, he must believe in the Church and the Scripture and the saints and the Catholic doctors, and that he should do principally. 3. But for the solace of human frailty, that it may avoid temptations and errors, it is useful for the Christian to have effective reasons for the things that he believes, and he should have a reason for his faith ready for everyone who requires it of him, as the blessed Peter teaches in his first Epistle, saying, *But sanctify in your hearts Christ as Lord; being ready always to give answer to every man that asketh you a reason concerning the faith and hope that is in you* [1 Pet. 3:15]. 4. But we cannot argue here by quoting our law nor the authorities of the saints, because unbelievers deny the Lord Christ and His law and saints. Wherefore it is necessary to seek reasons in another way, and this way is common to us and to unbelievers, namely, philosophy. But the power of philosophy in this part accords with the wisdom of God; indeed, it is the trace of the divine wisdom given by God to man, that by this trace man may be moved to divine truths. 5. Nor are these things proper to philosophy, but are common to philosophy and theology and to believers and unbelievers, given by God and revealed to philosophers, to the end that the human race might be prepared for special divine truths. And hence the reasons of which I speak are not unrelated to faith nor outside the principles of faith, but are dug from its roots, as will be manifest from what we have to say.

30. Avicenna *Metaphysics* 10.2 (443).
31. Cf. Tim. 2:4.
32. Gregory the Great *Homiliae xl in Evangelia* 2.26.1 (Patrologia Latina, ed. J.-P. Migne [hereafter PL], 76:1197).

6. I could, of course, set forth the simple and crude methods suited to the common run of unbelievers, but that is not worthwhile. For the vulgar is too [*197*] imperfect, and therefore the argument of faith that the vulgar must have is crude and confused and unworthy of wise men. I wish, therefore, to go higher and give an argument of which wise men must judge. For in every nation there are some men who are assiduous and apt to wisdom, who are open to rational arguments, so that once they have been informed, persuasion through them of the vulgar is made easier.

7. I assume in the beginning, of course, that there are three kinds of knowledge: one is in the effort of personal discovery through experience; another is through teaching; the third precedes these, and is the way to them, and is called natural knowledge because it is common to all. 8. That, in fact, is natural which is common to all individuals of the same species, as burning is natural to fire, according to the example of Aristotle himself in Book 5 of the *Ethics;*[33] and Cicero says this same thing in Book 1 of the *Tusculan Questions,*[34] and we see it in an infinite number of examples. For we say the cries of brutes signify naturally because they are common to the individuals of their species; and things are known naturally by us of the sort in which we all agree, as that "every whole is greater than its part," and others of this sort, both simple and complex. 9. We know likewise that the rational soul is formed to know the truth and to love it, and the proof of this love is the exhibition of action, according to Gregory[35] and all the saints and philosophers. There are some, however, who think that there are two parts in the soul, or two powers, so that there is one by which the soul knows the truth, another by which it wills to love the truth known. 10. Others, on the other hand, believe that the substance [*198*] of the soul is one and that it performs both functions, because these acts are ordered to each other, in that the knowledge of truth exists on account of the love for it; for one and the same power, according to them, first apprehends the truth and then loves it and is completed in action. 11. Hence Aristotle holds, in Book 3 of the treatise *On the Soul,* that the speculative intellect becomes practical by the extension of knowledge of truth to the love of it.[36] Nor does he ever make a specific difference between the speculative intellect and the practical as he does between the intellect and the senses and the vegetative soul. 12. For he argues, in Book 2 of the treatise *On the Soul,* that these three are diverse in species, because their operations are diverse in species, that is, understanding, perceiving, and vegetating; nor are they ordered in relation to one another.[37] But the knowledge of truth is ordered toward the love of it, and it is formed because of it; and therefore the power, or nature, or substance of the rational soul that knows the truth and loves it is one. 13. Hence in Book 3 of the treatise *On the Soul,* Aristotle begins thus: "However, concerning the part of the soul with which it knows and judges, I must now speak,"[38] meaning that it is the same part that has both functions, just as in the sensitive part, because it is the same power that knows and desires, as is evident in every sense; for the sense of touch knows the hot and desires it, and the sense of taste knows flavors and desires them, and so with the others. But it is not of great moment how we speak of these [that is, the senses]; for we know that the rational soul is formed to know and to love the truth.

14. But the truth of religion is perceived only so far as the knowledge of God abounds in one, for every religion is referred to God; and therefore he who wishes to arrive at certain knowledge of religion must begin with God. But the knowledge of God, so far as concerns the question of whether He is, is known to all naturally, as [*199*] Cicero teaches in his book on the immortality of the soul; and he proves this by saying, "No nation is so savage and monstrous that its mind has not been imbued with an opinion of God, nor is there a people that does not show some form of divine worship."[39] 15. But if Avicenna says in Book 1 of the *Metaphysics* that "this science seeks to establish the being of God by demonstration,"[40] it must be said that this is true as regards full certitude. For the natural knowledge that anyone has of God is weak, and it is weakened

33. Aristotle *Nicomachean Ethics* 5.7 1134b25–27.

34. Cicero *Tusculan Disputations* 1.13.29–30.

35. Gregory the Great *Homiliae xl in Evangelia* 2.30.1 (PL 76:1220).

36. Cf. Aristotle *De Anima* 3.10 433a9–27. Aristotle does not state that the speculative intellect is practical "by extension"; this phrase, common in medieval philosophy, arose from an early mistranslation of *De Anima* (L. Minio-Paluello, *Opuscula: The Latin Aristotle* [Amsterdam: Adolf M. Hakkert, 1972], 277–85).

37. Aristotle *De Anima* 2.2 413b24–33.

38. Ibid. 3.4 429a10–13. This text occurs at the beginning of Book 3 in Averroes and in the older Latin versions.

39. Cicero *Tusculan Disputations* 1.13.30.

40. Avicenna *Metaphysics* 1.1.

by sins, which are numerous in anyone, for sin obscures the soul especially as regards divine things. Therefore, it is necessary that this knowledge be aided by argument and faith.

16. But the knowledge of the unity of God, and of what God is, and how, and of what sort, is not possessed naturally. For in these matters men are always in disaccord, some maintaining several gods, others considering that the stars are gods, others, things here below, as do even now the pure pagans and the idolaters. And so they must err in religion. All others who say that there is one God do not understand other points that are true of God. 17. And therefore one who advances a religion must know at the outset how to present the attributes that are required of God in general. However, it is not necessary that he go into all the particular truths in the beginning, rather he should proceed little by little and he should begin with the easier questions in this way. For as the geometer sets down his definitions, that the things he deals with may be known in respect to what they are and what they are called, so one must proceed here, because unless one knows what it is that is meant by a name, there will be no demonstration.

18. Let us then call God the first cause, antecedent to which there is no other, which did not emerge into being, and will not be capable of ceasing to exist, of infinite power, wisdom, and goodness, creator of everything and director of everything, according to the natural capacity of each individual thing. And in this definition Tartars, Saracens, [*200*] Jews, and Christians agree. The wise men also among the idolaters and the pagans, when they have been given the reason for this, cannot contradict it; nor consequently can the multitude, over whom the wise men stand as directors and leaders. 19. For two ways of arguing to this end will be presented for them: one by the consensus of all other nations and religions. But the lesser should conform itself to the greater part, and the part that does not accord with its whole is disgraceful. It is clear that there are wiser men in the other religions; and the pagans and the idolaters are not ignorant of this. 20. For when a meeting is arranged with them, they are convinced easily, and they perceive their own ignorance clearly, as appeared in the case of the emperor of the Tartars who summoned before him Christians, Saracens, and idolaters to confer on the truth of religion, and forthwith the idolaters were confounded and convinced. This fact is evident from the book *On the Practices of the Tartars* addressed to our Lord the present King of France. 21. And when Christians confer with pagans, like the Pruceni and the other nations, they yield easily; and once they have been convinced, they believe and see that they are held by errors. The proof of this is that they are most willing to become Christians if the Church were willing to permit them to retain their freedom and to enjoy their goods in peace. 22. But the Christian princes who labor for their conversion, and most of all the brothers of the Teutonic house, wish to reduce them to servitude, as is known to the Preachers and the Friars Minor [that is, the Dominicans and the Franciscans] and other good men throughout Germany and Poland; and, therefore, they offer opposition. Hence they stand against oppression, not against the arguments of a better religion.

3

16. Besides, the power to know in man does not suffice for the bodies of this world and sensible objects, as is evident to anyone. For no one knows truly and adequately the nature of a single thing, however small, as, for example, one small plant or fly or some other object, and we observe an infinite discord among wise men in regard to the natures of corporeal beings. Much more, then, will man err in regard to insensible things, such as the spiritual substances and the state of the other life, and especially in relation to the things that pertain to God and to God's will. 17. For this reason it is necessary that he have revelation. Aristotle says to this effect in Book 2 of the *Metaphysics* that in relation to things such as these, which are most manifest in themselves, our intellect is like the eye of a bat or an owl in relation to the sun.[41] 18. And Avicenna says in Book 5 of the *Metaphysics* that in relation to the things that belong to the Lord of the ages in His kingdom, man is like a person deaf from birth in relation to pleasurable harmonies and like a paralytic in relation to tasty food.[42] Hence man will not be able to arrive at certitude concerning these things, any more than the bat, the owl, and the paralytic concerning the things mentioned.

41. Aristotle *Metaphysics* 2.1 993b9–10.

42. Cf. Avicenna *Metaphysics* 9.7.

19. Furthermore, Alfarabi says in the "Morals" on this subject that "in relation to the divine truths a wise man is like an untaught child in relation to a man most wise by human wisdom; and so he will not be able to advance except through teaching and revelation." And he adds that "if man could attain by himself the truths of divine religion, then the world would not need [*210*] revelation and prophecy; but these," as he says, "have been granted to the world and are necessary."[43] Hence man cannot know these truths by himself. 20. This is also clearly taught by Avicenna in the "Roots of Moral Philosophy" when he states that "the revelation of religion must necessarily be made by God" and that "mortal man cannot rise to these immortal things,"[44] in accordance with what Seneca says in his book *On the Tranquillity of the Soul,* namely, that man is too mortal for immortal things.[45]

21. Then just as man cannot attain to these things by himself, so he must not presume to prove these things by himself without revelation and instruction; rather he should believe for three reasons. One reason consists in this, that the things that belong to the other world, and especially God's will and what pertains to God, are of infinite dignity; hence they are not commensurate with human misery. 22. Nor is man worthy of striving to explore them by his own power so as to understand them; that is why it suffices for him to believe the one who instructs him. Indeed, he is not even worthy to believe these things because of his sins and his wretchedness; let him rejoice then that he is taught by another, but not unless it is by God or by angels on God's authority. It is evident, therefore, that man should not attempt to inquire into these divine truths before he is taught and believes. 23. Moreover, God Himself knows infinitely better and with greater certitude the things that belong to Him than a creature could ever know them; and the authority and wisdom of God are infinite, and no human authority or wisdom can compare with them, especially with respect to the things that belong to God. It remains, therefore, that the authority of God alone should be sought, since His goodness is infinite and by it He wills to reveal to the human race what is necessary for salvation.

24. And beyond doubt we see this realized in the religions, namely, that all men believe that they possess their religions through revelation. [*211*] This is indeed plainly the case with Christians and Jews. The Saracens, too, believe that Muhammad received a revelation, and he himself claimed as much, for otherwise he would not have been believed; and if he did not receive this revelation from God, he received it from the demons. 25. The Tartars likewise maintain that God revealed their religion, as is written in the book already mentioned and as is certain. In like manner, the idolaters and the pagans believe that God should reveal what pertains to those religions, for otherwise man would not believe man in this matter; for every man who propounds a religion ascribes his authority to God so that he may more easily be believed.

4

1. Since then such is the case, we must further argue that revelation should be made to only one perfect lawgiver and that a single perfect law should be given by God. And this is apparent because of divisions and heresies. For if there were several heads, the human race could not be united, since everyone strives to uphold his own view. 2. Moreover, since there is one God and one human race, which must be regulated by the wisdom of God, this wisdom must receive its unity from the twofold unity just mentioned, or otherwise it would not be conformed either to one God or to one human race. If, indeed, there were several gods and several worlds, and, so to speak, several human races, then there could be several divine wisdoms; but it is impossible that there be many gods and many worlds; and hence it is impossible that the wisdom of God should be multiple. 3. Moreover, since the perfect religion should make known to man whatever he has to know about God and whatever is useful to man, it follows that another religion either will be superfluous if it teaches the same things, or will be erroneous if it promulgates contrary teachings. For this reason there can be only one perfect and trustworthy religion and, likewise, [*212*] only one lawgiver who receives it from God; for, if religion is one, the lawgiver is also one and vice versa. This

43. Alfarabi, *Enumeration of the Sciences,* chap. 5, p. 109. (Page numbers refer to the Arabic text translated above in part 1, selection 1. Bacon quotes the Latin translation.)

44. Avicenna *Metaphysics* 10.2 (442).

45. Cf. rather Seneca *De Otio* 5.7.

is what Avicenna teaches in his "Roots of Moral Philosophy" as well as Alfarabi in his "Morals."[46] 4. For, as Avicenna says, there must be a single mediator of God and man, the vicar of God on earth, who receives the law from God and promulgates it, and of whom Alfarabi says that he cannot be a liar, once it is established that he comes by an inspiration from God. Once we have ascertained this truth, his word must remain unquestioned; nor should his statements be subjected to any further examination or consideration; rather he should be fully believed.

5

1. Now that this has been established, we must ask who should be proclaimed as the lawgiver and which religion should be propagated throughout the world. The principal rites, as we have said, are six. The first is that of the pagans, who live by custom alone and have no priests, but each man is his own teacher. 2. The second rite is that of the idolaters, who have priests and agree on certain regulations and assemble in one place at proper hours to perform their solemn rites; for they have large bells, like the Christians, as we have already learned. The idolaters also differ from the pagans in that they worship man-made objects, whereas the pagans worship natural things such as groves, rivers, and the like in endless number. 3. The third rite is that of the Tartars, who cultivate philosophy and the magic arts; the fourth is that of the Saracens; the fifth, that of the Jews; the sixth, that of the Christians. There are no other major religions in this world, nor will there be any others until the religion of the antichrist.

6

1. Now one can establish that the Christian law should be preferred in the following ways. First, by means of the teachings of the philosophers indicated above in the application of mathematics to the Church and in the first part of the *Moral Philosophy.* For there noble testimonies are given concerning the articles of the Christian faith, namely, the Trinity, Christ, the Blessed Virgin, the creation of the world, angels, souls and the judgment to come, eternal life, the resurrection of bodies, the pains of purgatory, the pains of hell, and the like, which are found in the Christian religion. 2. Philosophy, however, does not agree in this manner with the religion of the Jews and of the Saracens, nor do the philosophers provide testimonies in their favor. Hence it is evident that, since philosophy is a preamble to religion and disposes men to it, the religion of the Christians is the only one that should be held. [*215*]

3. Moreover, the philosophers not only pave the way for the Christian religion, but destroy the two other religions; for Seneca, in the book that he composed against the religion of the Jews, shows in many ways that it is most irrational and erroneous in that it is bound by the letter alone, in accordance with the belief of the carnal Jews who thought that it suffices for salvation.[47] 4. The Saracen philosophers also find fault with their own law and calculate that it will quickly come to an end. Avicenna, in Book 9 of the *Metaphysics,* takes issue with Muhammad because he spoke only of corporal pleasures and not of spiritual pleasures.[48] 5. Albumazar, too, in Book 1 of the *Conjunctions,* teaches that that religion will not last longer than 693 years;[49] and 665 years have already elapsed; and he asserts that it can come to an end in less time, as we mentioned earlier in the part on mathematics. It is also clear that the Tartars have nearly obliterated the entire dominion of the Saracens from the north, the east, and the west as far as Egypt and Africa, in such a way that the Caliph, who occupies the position of the Pope among them, was destroyed thirteen years ago, and Baghdad, the city of this Caliph, was captured along with an infinite multitude of Saracens.

6. But we can see this same thing in another way through the Sibyls. For, as we have made clear earlier, these Sibyls were proclaiming that Christ is God, and they set forth all the main articles of the Christian religion; but they offer no testimony in favor of the others; on the contrary, they stated that this religion alone is conducive to salvation.

46. Avicenna *Metaphysics* 10.5 (452–53); Alfarabi, *Enumeration of the Sciences,* chap. 5, p. 110.

47. Cf. Augustine *City of God* 6.11, in which Augustine cites a now lost work of Seneca.

48. Avicenna *Metaphysics* 9.7.

49. Albumazar (Abu Ma'shar al-Balkhi, d. 886) *De Magnis Conjunctionibus et Annorum Revolutionibus ac Eorum Perfectionibus* (Augsburg, 1489) 2.7.

Part Five

[Proemium]

1. The articles of the fourth part of moral philosophy or civil science have now been treated, which part consists in persuading men to believe and receive the true religion.[50] Now follows the fifth part, which tries to persuade believers to love that religion, and to acknowledge it by appropriate works in the observance of laws and the goodness of morals, accompanied by the desire of future happiness; also, to shrink from, hate, and vigorously detest whatever is contrary to laws, virtues, and beatitude, and to turn away from them in action.

1

1. Now our feeble intellect has great difficulty with regard to these operables; for operables are more difficult to know than are the objects of speculative knowledge. Also our corrupt will finds them exceedingly hard to bear, and does not take pleasure in them. Further, our irascible power, to which the execution of these operations is due, fails to perform better than moderately well. 2. Nor is this surprising, since these are the highest truths concerning God and divine worship, eternal life, the laws of justice and the glory of peace, and the sublimeness of virtues. Thus our intellect is related to them as a person deaf from birth is related to the pleasure of harmony, as Avicenna pointed out in Book 9 of his *Metaphysics,*[51] or as the eye of a bat is related to the light of the sun, according to Aristotle in Book 1 of his *Metaphysics.*[52] 3. Further, our will, according to Avicenna, in the same place,[53] is related to them in the same way as a paralyzed person is related to tasty food, which, although presented to him, he still is not able to sense. Such is our condition with respect to the things now being treated; for we have been corrupted by sins and impeded by the grossness of our body and blinded by the sensible and temporal world, whereas these matters are eternal and beyond sensation. [*248*]

4. And this is true not only of this part of moral philosophy, but also of the fourth and sixth parts. For there are three speculative parts of moral philosophy, which teach one to speculate on the nature and number of the things one should know concerning God and divine worship, eternal life, civil laws, and morals; those are the first three parts of the present work, which are concerned with the composition of the religion of the faithful. 5. There are, moreover, three practical parts as well, which teach one how and in what way a man ought to be swayed to believe the things that are required in that religion [Part Four], how he ought to be swayed to the love and fulfillment of the law once he has believed and received it [Part Five], and, thirdly, how to sway either a judge or an adversary to consent to justice in the causes that arise between fellow citizens because of the complexity of legal cases [Part Six]. 6. Hence this practical half is related to the first half as the curing of the sick and the conserving of health, which are treated in the practical part of medicine, are related to that part of medicine which teaches what health is, and what are the various illnesses, and how many there are, and what are their symptoms, causes, medicines and other remedies, and their number. For even though a man knows all these things from books, that does not mean that he also knows how to practice. 7. For there are many physicians who know these matters quite well enough to lecture on them, and to discuss and explain them, but who still do not know the precautions and ways of practice; they therefore have a speculative knowledge of medicine, but not a practical one. This distinction is also true in the cure of the soul from sin and in the preservation of spiritual health, which consists in the devout worship of God, an ardent desire of future happiness, and in a love of and zeal for laws, justice, peace, and the goodness of virtues.

8. Now it should not be a matter of surprise that within this civil science two parts are distinguished, namely the speculative and the practical, even though the science as a whole is called practical in relation to all the other sciences; for in every science there are somehow these two parts, as Avicenna teaches in [*249*] the beginning of his *Art of Medicine;*[54] likewise the man who translated Aristotle's *Ethics* from Greek into Arabic explicitly teaches that moral science has the parts we have

50. *Secta* (literally, "sect"), which has been translated as "religion" throughout this selection.

51. Avicenna *Metaphysics* 9.7.

52. Aristotle *Metaphysics* 2.1 993b9.

53. Avicenna *Metaphysics* 9.7.

54. Avicenna *Codex Totius Medicinae* 1.1.1.

explained. 9. For when the phrase "practical science" is predicated absolutely and most properly, it refers exclusively to the science of our moral operations, as moral; for the Greek word *praxis* is the same as the Latin word "operation." And in this case every other science is called speculative, since every other science speculates about the truth that has been stripped of the good. For truth is the end of the speculative, while good is the end of the practical, as Aristotle says in Book 2 of his *Metaphysics.*[55] 10. Therefore every science that does not teach us to be good is absolutely and properly speculative, and this applies to every other science except moral science. And only that science which teaches us to become good is absolutely and most properly practical; this applies, within the various parts of philosophy, to moral science, although the complete science about these matters is to be found in Sacred Scripture.

11. Still, the words "practical" and "speculative" are also used in another way, namely relatively and less properly. And so within moral science itself, that part is called "speculative" which considers the nature and number of the truths of that science; and since these truths are concerned with our operations, that part does not lose the name "practical" taken in its absolute sense; rather, it is called "speculative" because it does not itself extend to inducing men to act morally, nor does it designate the ways or precautions of action; rather, the practical part does this. 12. Now here I speak of three kinds of moral works: the first is to sway the mind to believe and receive the truths of religion; the principles of this work have already been laid down. The second is to sway the mind to the love and fulfillment of what is good, and to the hatred and avoidance of what is evil; the fifth part will treat of these matters. The third is to sway the mind of a judge or adversary to consent to justice when cases are pleaded; this work remains to be treated in the sixth part. [*250*]

2

1. Since, however, in our mortal corruption practical matters are far better, more difficult, less pleasant, and less operable [than are speculative matters], they require stronger remedies and inducements than do the speculative. Now the first remedy that can be humanly produced is some discourse that is able to incline the mind; and this discourse is an argument taken from a group of veracious arguments, and lacks fraud or sophistry. 2. Now because of well-known works of Aristotle on these matters, we are familiar with two kinds of arguments, namely dialectical and demonstrative. A dialectical argument moves the speculative intellect to a feeble knowledge of truth, namely, to opinion, not to science; "for a demonstration is a syllogism that produces science," as Aristotle says,[56] and therefore perfects the speculative intellect in the knowledge of truth. 3. But moral philosophy "is not for the sake of speculation, but for the sake of becoming good," as he says in the beginning of Book 2 of his *Ethics;*[57] and in the same place he says that "science contributes little or nothing to virtue." Hence these scientific arguments do not suffice in moral philosophy; and this is true precisely of the practical part of this science. 4. Hence Aristotle, in Book 1 of his *Ethics,*[58] resolves that moral science does not have to use demonstration, but rhetorical argument. For it is equally erroneous, he says there, for moral science to use demonstration as it is for a mathematical science to attempt a rhetorical argument. For a demonstration does not sway the practical intellect to its operations; rather, it is essentially related to the speculative intellect, since it does not proceed beyond a knowledge of truth. And therefore dialectical arguments are likewise invalid in matters of morals and persuasion, since if there is no room in these matters for demonstration, then neither is there room for dialectical argument. For the end of it is demonstration, in that a dialectical argument prepares the way to demonstration; for we are aroused by an opinion of the truth in order that we may more easily [*251*] arrive at the science of it. Therefore these two kinds of argument are unable to sway the mind to good, but only to a knowledge of what is true.

5. Yet it is necessary that we be swayed to what is good; in fact, it is far more necessary that we be so swayed than that we be moved to the speculation of bare truth, since virtue and happiness are better and more necessary than mere science. Therefore it is necessary that we have stronger inducements [in practical matters]. Further, the practical intellect is more noble than the speculative. 6. Further, the practical intellect is related to what is good

55. Aristotle *Metaphysics* 2.1 993b20–21.

56. Aristotle *Posterior Analytics* 1.4 73a24.

57. Aristotle *Nicomachean Ethics* 2.2 1103b26–28.

58. Ibid. 1.1 1094b19–27.

in a more difficult and less delightful way than the speculative intellect is related to truth; and therefore it is necessary that we have better and stronger inducements to sway us to assent to the truths concerned with the good of the soul, to perform them, and so that we might be inclined to justice in cases that are pleaded. But a rhetorical argument is effective in these matters; hence it is the sort of argument that we must choose. 7. This argument, however, is not known to the ordinary run of arts students among the Latins, because the books of Aristotle and of his commentators have only recently been translated and are not yet used by students. Now Ciceronian rhetoric does not teach this argument, except in terms of cases to be pleaded, in order that an orator might persuade a judge to agree with the orator's case and be unfavorable to that of the adversary. But as I have pointed out, there are three kinds of swaying, and therefore this argument as taught by Cicero is inadequate; rather, we need the complete doctrine, found in Aristotle and his commentators.

8. Now this rhetorical persuasion to three moral works, namely to believe, to do, and to judge rightly, follows the general principles of eloquence, which are to render the hearer docile, well disposed, and eager. Therefore it is necessary to hold the hearer by pleasure so that he will become diligent and eager; for he who takes delight in moral matters, greatly benefits his fellow citizens. [*252*] 9. Likewise it is necessary to explain truth clearly, distinctly, briefly, and plausibly, and to untie the knotty questions and difficulties that occur, so that the hearer may be rendered docile and grasp with ease a truth that is proposed to him. And it is necessary, if he is to become well-disposed to believing, to doing, and to judging correctly, to propose useful things. For that discourse which takes away tediousness, leaves out difficulty, and promises usefulness, is the one that lays hold of the mind and sways it to the works we have been speaking of. 10. Hence, in the book *On the Condition of the World,* Cicero gives us the beautiful aphorism: "The ideal orator is the one who, when speaking, instructs the mind, gives it pleasure, and moves it deeply. To teach is obligatory, to please is voluntary, to move is indispensable,"[59] since, as Augustine explains, teaching and pleasure do not sway.

11. Hence Augustine, in Book 4 of his treatise *On Christian Doctrine,*[60] gives an excellent explanation of this aphorism of Cicero when he says: the duty of an orator is "to teach, to delight, and to sway; 'to teach is a necessity, to delight is a sweetness, to sway is a victory.'"[61] 12. Now to teach is a matter of necessity because "perhaps once the things to be taught are learned, the hearers will be so moved by them that greater powers of eloquence will be unnecessary for them to be swayed; but persuasion should be brought in when the hearers know what is to be believed,"[62] done, and thought, and yet do not so believe, do, or judge as they should. "And therefore to sway is not necessary, since it does not always have to be performed."[63] But to sway is the victory, "since it is possible that hearers be taught and delighted,"[64] and still not believe, do, or be swayed to justice. 13. But just as the hearer understands if you speak clearly and distinctly and untie his doubts, "and is delighted if you speak sweetly, so also he is swayed if he believes what you exhort, loves what you promise, fears what you threaten, hates what you censure, embraces what you command, sorrows at what you hold to be sorrowful, rejoices when you preach something joyful, [*253*] commiserates with those you present as in misery, flees the things that, by inspiring fear, you propose as to be avoided,"[65] sympathizes and agrees with your case, if he is a judge, and looks down on your opponent's, "and whatever else ought to be done through the grand style of eloquence in order to move the minds of the hearers."[66]

14. For there are three styles: the humble or simple style, the moderate style, and the grand style. The humble style is content with simple eloquence; the moderate style enjoys every rhetorical ornament; but the grand style leans heavily upon words that move one affectively. For teaching, the humble or plain style is required; to please requires the moderate style, and to sway, the grand.

15. Hence Cicero says: "An eloquent man is one who can speak simply about matters of little importance, temperately about matters of moderate importance, and grandly about great things."[67] "The word 'moderate' (*modicis*) is taken from

59. Cicero *De Optimo Genere Oratorum* 1.3.
60. Augustine *De Doctrina Christiana* 4.12.27.
61. Cicero *Orator* 21.69.
62. Augustine *De Doctrina Christiana* 4.12.28.
63. Ibid.
64. Ibid.
65. Ibid. 4.12.27.
66. Ibid.
67. Cicero *Orator* 29.101.

the word 'measure' (*modus*); for we are speaking improperly when we use the word 'moderate' for what is small";[68] hence moderate things are in the middle. Therefore, of these three, teaching is the least, to delight is in the middle, and to sway is the greatest. 16. And therefore not only does the simple style consist in speaking of small things, the moderate style in pleading about moderate matters, and the grand style in persuading with regard to great things, but also teaching should be done in the humble style, delighting should be provided by a moderate style, and swaying stands in need of a magnificent eloquence; for teaching holds the lowest level, delighting the intermediate, and persuading the highest of all. 17. And therefore whatever is proposed for understanding, is presented in the humble style, which consists in a simple eloquence and which stands mainly upon obvious teachings, all complicated questions having been eliminated. But whatever is presented to be loved or hated needs a moderate style: a pleasurable one for objects to be loved, a dreadful one for what is to be hated. And whatever is proposed for action, needs words that move one affectively, whereby an affection is in a wonderful way turned into a fulfillment; and these affective words pertain rather to the grand style.

3

1. Now these conditions of rhetorical argument are common to all three parts of the practical half of moral philosophy, since each uses these [*254*] common principles. In moral matters this argument so surpasses all demonstration that in this half of moral philosophy one rhetorical argument has more strength than a thousand demonstrations; for a demonstration either does not move the practical intellect, or moves it only in a very incidental way, whereas a rhetorical argument moves it directly and absolutely, and is able to sway the mind—something that a demonstration cannot do. 2. This fifth part, however, uses rhetorical argument more effectively than do the other two parts, since it teaches how to sway a mind to things more difficult and less pleasurable to human corruption than do the other parts. For believing is easy compared with doing, and doing the things that pertain to divine worship, civil laws, and virtues is more difficult than to be inclined to justice in cases that are pleaded. 3. For far more and greater things are found in the works of the fifth part than in the fourth or sixth parts, since the perfection of life consists in the works of this fifth part; for the fourth part teaches us to believe and to consent, the sixth to have compassion and to commiserate, whereas this part teaches us to acknowledge in actions the things that we perceive are to be believed, and that we judge are to be commiserated, so that we might fulfill all the works of mercy. 4. Many believe that assistance should be given to the needy, fewer feel compassion, and very few actually put their hand to the task. This is because it is good to believe that assistance should be given, but it is better to have compassion, and to give actual assistance is the best of all; but with regard to what is best we are very unmanageable and lacking in ability. 5. But no wonder, in view of the fact that the better things and even the good ones, being placed as they are on a positive level, are in many ways irksome and a cause of dread for human frailty. And therefore this fifth part teaches one to make arguments in behalf of beauty, in order to carry the mind to consent suddenly and before it has had time to foresee the opposite position, as Alfarabi teaches in his book *On the Sciences*.[69]

6. And because that is the case, the rhetorical argument is divided into [*255*] three species. The first species is concerned with the things that pertain to the faith and the proof of the true religion. Now among believers there are six principles in which that proof is rooted: the Church, Sacred Scripture, the witness of the saints, the abundance of miracles, the power of reasons, and the consensus of all Catholic teachers. As for persuading nonbelievers, attention is paid to many of these principles as well as to others, as was pointed out previously. The second species of rhetorical argument is concerned with the things that sway one to compassion for justice; these are dealt with in Cicero's rhetorical works. The third species is concerned with the things that sway us to action as regards divine worship, laws, and virtues. 7. The first two species are simply called "rhetorical,"

68. Augustine *De Doctrina Christiana* 4.18.35.

69. Alfarabi, *Enumeration of the Sciences,* chap. 2 (see the Latin translation by Gerard of Cremona in *Catálogo de las ciencias,* ed. G. Palencia [Madrid, 1932; 2nd ed., 1953], p. 140, lines 15–26, also in *Al-Fārābi: Über die Wissenschaften,* ed. Franz Schupp [Hamburg: Felix Meiner Verlag, 2005], p. 52, lines 10–12; cf. the abbreviated Latin translation of Domenicus Gundissalinus in *Al-Fārābi: Über die Wissenschaften,* ed. Jakob H. J. Schneider [Freiburg: Herder, 2006], p. 134, lines 9–17).

and they do not change this name. But the third species, which is persuasive in those matters considered by the present fifth part, while it is "rhetorical," is also called by its proper name "poetic" by Aristotle[70] and the other philosophers, since veracious poets use it in swaying men to the honesty of virtues; for,

> Poets wish to be useful or to give pleasure.[71]
> He who mixes the useful with the pleasant, wins all the votes.[72]

8. Hence good poets, such as Horace and those like him, desire to be beneficial and to delight in order to sway men, but vain and gossipy poets, such as Ovid and his like, wish to delight without caring to be beneficial, and hence do injury to the honesty of morals.

9. But the unlearned are ignorant of the way of putting this argument together, since we do not have a Latin translation of Aristotle's book on the subject. Still, diligent ones can gather much of the sense of this argument through Averroes' commentary, and through the book of Aristotle that has been translated into Latin, although it is not in common use; in the beginning of this commentary, Hermannus, the translator, says that Aristotle's text was too difficult for him to translate.

10. Likewise, Horace's *Art of Poetry* is much [*256*] concerned with this argument, as also are Alfarabi in his work *On Science,*[73] Avicenna in the beginning of his *Logic,*[74] which the Latins possess, and Algazel in his *Treatise on Logic.*[75]

4

1. But since the usefulness of philosophy is clear only when it is drawn to what is divine, this part of philosophy can very beautifully be of service in divine matters, according to what is beautifully and magnificently taught by the saints, and especially Saint Augustine in Book 4 of his treatise *On Christian Doctrine.* For the whole of Book 4 is concerned with the present subject matter, and almost everything that I have said here is found in that book, in a philosophical mode. 2. And no wonder, since Augustine was an author and teacher of rhetoric before [*259*] he became a Christian, and he taught this science publicly, as is written in his life.[76] Whence neither Cicero nor Seneca nor any philosopher was able to attain to the dignity of eloquence that, according to Augustine, is found in sacred doctrine. 3. He says, therefore, that the humble and moderate styles have a place in temporal matters, but not in divine things, since they are the highest, except to the extent that the grand style of speaking requires the intermixture of the other two, for the reasons previously stated.[77] "When," as he says, "the ecclesiastical orator urges something to be done, it is necessary that he not only teach in order to instruct and delight in order to hold one's attention, but also that he persuade in order to achieve the victory."[78] "Now this orator of ours, when he speaks of what is just, good, and holy, so acts that he will be heard with understanding, freely, and obediently."[79]

4. Hence, he says: "Since both what is false and what is true can be urged by the art of rhetoric, who dares to say that the defenders of truth ought to be unarmed against falsity, in such a way that those who urge falsity shall know how to render their hearers well disposed, eager, and docile, while this is not known"[80] by those who propose the truth? 5. "Should those who teach what is false teach briefly, aptly, and plausibly, while the teachers of truth speak so as to be boring to hear, hard to understand, and unpleasant to believe? Should those who lead the minds of their hearers into error frighten, sadden, exhilarate, and exhort with ardor, while the defenders of truth are sleepy, phlegmatic, and cold,"[81] using discourse that is diffuse like a child's, disconnected like a woman's, made ugly by an asinine crudeness, and which gives birth to hearers that are languid and lazy—a birth that is accompanied with dread?

70. Cf. Aristotle *Poetics* chap. 2 1148b24–27.

71. Horace *Ars Poetica* 333.

72. Ibid. 343.

73. Alfarabi, *Enumeration of the Sciences,* chap. 2 (*Catálogo de las ciencias,* 139–40; *Al-Fārābi Über die Wissenschaften,* trans. Gerhard of Cremona, 50–52; *Al-Fārābi: Über die Wissenschaften,* trans. Dominicus Gundissalinus, 140).

74. Avicenna *Logic* (Venice, 1508) fol. 2.

75. Algazel *Liber Logicae* (ed. P. Liechtenstein, 1506) fol. b4.

76. Cf. Possidius *Vita Sancti Augustini* 1.

77. According to the omitted passages, styles are mixed for the sake of variety and because whatever must be done by virtue of the grand style must be taught by means of the humble style (chap. 3, secs. 11–13).

78. Augustine *De Doctrina Christiana* 4.13.29.

79. Ibid. 4.15.32.

80. Ibid. 4.2.3.

81. Ibid.

6. And he says further: "What is better than a nourishing sweetness or a sweet nourishment?"[82] And, "Wherever I understand the authors of the Canonical Scriptures, not only does it seem impossible to be wiser than they, but also to be more eloquent. . . . Nor should they speak in any other fashion. For just as there is one eloquence that is more in keeping with a youthful speaker, [*260*] and another one with age (for that should not be called eloquence which does not fit the speaker), 7. so also there is an eloquence that is in keeping with men who are most worthy of the highest authority, and plainly, divine. It is with this eloquence that the authors of the Canon spoke, an eloquence that alone is fitted to them, and they to it. For the more humble it seems, the loftier it is, and it reaches its heights, not by its windiness but by its solidity. But wherever I do not understand them, their eloquence is not so obvious to me; still I have no doubts but that even there it is the same as where I do understand them."[83] 8. And, "What surprises and amazes me more is that they have so used this eloquence of ours that it is neither absent from them nor conspicuous in them. For it is necessary for them neither to reject it nor to make a display of it; and the first would be the case if they avoided that eloquence completely, the second, if it were easily discernible."[84] "For these works were not composed by human industry; rather, they were poured forth by the divine mind."[85]

Part Six

1. The sixth part of moral philosophy, which is also the third and final part of that half which is called "practical," consists in the pleading of cases before a judge in order to sway the judge so well that as a result he is compassionate and favorable to the just party, and displeased with its adversary. But I hold myself to be excused both because of the great length of the present work and because of the greatness of your wisdom, which, even if it should abound in others, is here superior by reason of experience.

2. But this part is treated in its principles in Aristotle's book *On the Rhetorical Argument* and in Alfarabi's commentary on that book, both of which are to be found among the Latins, although almost no one takes them into consideration. Also the rhetorical treatises of Cicero and Seneca teach in a particular way and in the proper discipline how to compose this sort of argument. 3. Also many have the habit of this argument, for example, jurists. But the first and original art has not up to the present been found among the Latins, except what was recently and poorly translated in the book of Aristotle and the commentary on it; for the fontal art concerning this argument is given only in logic, to which belongs the task of assigning the differences and conditions of arguments.

4. We do not, however, have the full mind of Aristotle in Latin; for Aristotle's book and the commentary on it were first translated from Greek into Arabic, and then from Arabic into Latin; and, besides, the translator told me that he did not know logic, and hence he waited a long time before translating the book, and finally omitted to translate into Latin the book *On the Poetic Argument,* the reason being that he did not understand that book, as he himself confesses in the prologue to his translation of Averroes' commentary. Still, a studious person can catch a faint scent of his views, even though he cannot taste them; for a wine that is decanted from a third vase retains little of its vigor.

82. Ibid. 4.5.8.
83. Ibid. 4.6.9.
84. Ibid. 4.6.10.
85. Ibid. 4.7.21.

TWENTY-ONE

THOMAS AQUINAS

Commentary on the Nicomachean Ethics

Translated by Charles I. Litzinger

Thomas Aquinas (1225–1274), born at Roccasecca, was the youngest son of Landulf of Aquino, a knight of minor nobility, though related to prominent figures in the kingdom of Sicily and the court of Emperor Frederick II.[1] Thomas received his first education as an oblate at the neighboring Benedictine monastery of Monte Cassino. In 1239 he proceeded to the university in Naples (established by Frederick in 1224), where he completed his training in the faculty of arts and first came into contact with the writings of Aristotle. In 1244 he decided to enter the newly founded (1216) Dominican order, but his family vehemently opposed his decision, and a brother, then in the service of the emperor, abducted Thomas and brought him home, where his family confined him for fifteen months in a vain effort to dissuade him. He later pursued his studies under Albert the Great, whose pupil he became perhaps at Paris before 1248 and certainly at Cologne from 1248 to 1252. He returned to Paris in 1252 and embarked upon a teaching and writing career that was to occupy the remaining twenty-two years of his life. From 1252 to 1259 he received his degree in theology, lectured at the Dominican convent of St. Jacques, and composed his early works. In 1259 he was sent to Italy and taught successively at Anagni (1259–1261), Orvieto (1261–1264), Rome (1265–1267), and Viterbo (1268). It was in Italy that he met his confrere William of Moerbeke and undertook with him a series of commentaries on Aristotle. Thomas resumed his teaching in Paris at the beginning of 1269 during the most theologically and philosophically turbulent period of the thirteenth century. At that time he became engaged in the controversy with the so-called Latin Averroists within the faculty of arts, he defended the mendicant orders against the attacks of the secular clergy in the schools, and he upheld his own doctrinal positions against the more traditional views of the bishop, Etienne Tempier, the Franciscan John Peckham, and other contemporary theologians. In 1272 he was recalled to Naples to found a new *studium generale* at the university and directed the teaching of theology there until the following year. He died on March 7, 1274, at the Cistercian Abbey of Fossanova, between Naples and Rome, on his way to the Ecumenical Council of Lyons. At the time of his canonization

1. Modifications in biographical details from the first edition of the *Sourcebook* are taken from James A. Weisheipl, OP, *Friar Thomas d'Aquino: His Life, Thought, and Work* (Garden City, NY: Doubleday, 1974).

by John XXII in 1323, the bishop of Paris, Etienne de Bourret, praised his teaching and withdrew the condemnation of propositions by Etienne Tempier, to the extent to which the condemnation was aimed at Aquinas's doctrines. Aquinas was declared "Doctor of the Church" by Pius V in 1567. After a period of eclipse, he again came into his own in the nineteenth century. Leo XIII's bull, *Aeterni Patris* (1879), enjoined his study on all students of theology.

Aquinas's enormous literary output falls roughly into the following categories: (1) philosophic commentaries on Aristotle (*Peri Hermeneias, Posterior Analytics, Physics, De Caelo, De Generatione et Corruptione, Metereologica, De Anima, De Sensu et Sensato, De Memoria et Reminiscentia, Metaphysics, Nicomachean Ethics, Politics*) and on the *Liber de Causis;* (2) scriptural commentaries on Job, the Psalms, the Canticle of Canticles, Isaiah, Jeremiah, the Lamentations, Matthew, John, and the Epistles of St. Paul; (3) theological commentaries on Peter Lombard (*Liber Sententiarum*), Boethius (*De Trinitate, De Hebdomadibus*), and the pseudo-Dionysius (*De Divinis Nominibus*); (4) theological syntheses (*Summa contra Gentiles, Summa Theologiae*); (5) scholastic disputations (*Quaestiones Disputatae, Quaestiones Quodlibetales*); and, finally, various lesser theological and philosophic works.

Aquinas's teachings on political philosophy are to be found especially in his commentaries on the *Ethics* and the *Politics,* in his short treatise *On Kingship, to the King of Cyprus,* and in various articles of his *Summa Theologiae.* Of particular importance are the questions on law and justice in the latter work (Ia IIae, Questions 90–108; and IIa IIae, Questions 57–60) as well as the articles on equality and mastery in the state of original nature (Ia, Question 96, articles 3 and 4). Aquinas's fullest discussion of Averroism occurs in his *Summa contra Gentiles* (especially Book 1, Chapters 63–71; Book 2, Chapters 31–38, 59–61, 68–81; Book 3, Chapters 41–45, 69–75, 84–87, 92–100); on the subject of the relation between faith and reason, consult Book 1, Chapters 1–9.

Aquinas's commentary on the *Ethics* was written ca. 1270–1272 and is one of the many commentaries on that work in the thirteenth century. Unlike the natural treatises and *Metaphysics* of Aristotle, the *Ethics* was never debarred from the schools by ecclesiastical authority. The first part of Aristotle's work—the so-called *Ethica Vetus* (Books 2–3) and *Ethica Nova* (Book 1)—had been known and used in the West since the beginning of the century. In 1240, Herman the German translated the entire *Nicomachean Ethics* from the Arabic, as well as Averroes's middle commentary on that work. Shortly afterward, ca. 1240–1243, Robert Grosseteste provided the first complete translation from the Greek. The procedure observed by Aquinas in the present work is typical of all his commentaries on Aristotle. It is characterized, among other things, by its literalness (as opposed to the more or less free paraphrases of other commentators, such as Albert the Great), and by the extreme care with which it scrutinizes the text. The divisions with which each new section begins, and which form an integral part of the commentary, are calculated to bring out the overall design of the *Ethics,* as well as the particular structure of each part in its minutest detail. Each section is thus related to the whole and explained briefly or, if necessary, at greater length. The first and most apparent aim of the commentary is to clarify the meaning of Aristotle's text, not to add to it or develop from it an original philosophic teaching. Whether or not Aquinas's interpretation remains faithful in each case to Aristotle's intention is a matter of controversy. Whatever the answer to this question, he was, and is still, regarded as one of Aristotle's greatest commentators.

The following passages are taken from the first complete English translation by Father Charles I. Litzinger, OP: St. Thomas Aquinas, *Commentary on the Nicomachean Ethics of Aristotle,* Library of Living Catholic Thought (Chicago: Henry Regenery Co., 1964; Notre Dame, IN: Dumb Ox Books, 1993). This translation is based on the edition of R. Spiazzi, OP: S. Thomae Aquinatis, *In Decem Libros Ethicorum Aristotelis Expositio* (Turin, 1949). The translation, slightly modified by the editors of the first edition of the *Sourcebook,* has been further modified in order to conform to the Leonine edition that has since appeared (*Sententia Libri Ethicorum, Sancti Thomae de Aquino Opera Omnia,* t. XLVII, 2 vols. [Rome, 1969]) and to lend clarity to several political terms; the footnotes have also been augmented. The numbered paragraph divisions of the Spiazzi edition and Litzinger translation, though not present in the Leonine edition, have been retained for ease of reference; the page numbers of the Leonine edition are indicated by italicized numbers within the text. For reasons of space, the text of Aristotle, which precedes each lesson in the commentary, has been omitted, as have the words of Aristotle that Aquinas repeats in the text of the commentary itself in order to identify the precise passage to which he is referring. In the place of these quotations, bracketed references to numbered paragraphs have been inserted so that the reader may more easily follow Aquinas's analysis of the structure of Aristotle's argument. The references to Aristotle at the beginning of each lesson should suffice to enable the reader to locate the passages in question. Aquinas's commentary is divided into books and lessons. The first three lessons of Book 1 deal with the subject of moral philosophy, the relationship of politics as an architectonic science to other sciences, and the proper mode of moral philosophy. The three lessons taken from Books 5 and 6 deal with natural justice and legal justice, equity as a corrective to legal justice, and the virtue of prudence, including legislative, "architectonic" prudence.

BOOK ONE

Lesson One

[1.1 1094a1–18]

1. As the Philosopher says in the beginning of the *Metaphysics,* it is the business of the wise man to order.[2] The reason for this is that wisdom is the highest perfection of reason, whose characteristic is to know order. Even if the sensitive powers know some things absolutely, nevertheless it belongs to the intellect or reason alone to know the order of one thing to another. Now a twofold order is found in things. One, of parts of a whole or of a multitude among themselves, as the parts of a house are mutually ordered to one another. The second order is that of things [*4*] to an end. This order is of greater importance than the first. For, as the Philosopher says in Book 11 of the *Metaphysics,* the order of the parts of an army among themselves exists because of the order of the whole army to the commander.[3] Now order is related to reason in a fourfold way. There is one order that reason does not establish but only considers; such is the order of things in nature. There is a second order that reason, in considering, establishes in its own act; for example, when it arranges its concepts among themselves and the signs of concepts, since they are sounds that signify something. There is a third order that reason, in considering, establishes in the operations of the will. There is a fourth order that reason, in considering, establishes in the external things that it produces, like a chest and a house.

2. Because reason's consideration is perfected through the habit (*habitus*) of science, there are different sciences according to the different orders that reason properly considers. It pertains to natural philosophy to consider the order of things that human reason considers but does not establish—taken in such a way that with natural philosophy we also include mathematics and metaphysics. The order that reason makes in its own act, by considering, pertains to rational philosophy [that is, logic], which properly considers the order of the parts of speech to one another and the order of principles to conclusions. The order of voluntary actions pertains to the consideration of moral philosophy. The order that reason, in considering, establishes in the external things produced by human reason pertains to the mechanical arts. Accordingly it is proper to moral philosophy, to which our attention is at present directed, to consider human operations in so far as they are ordered to one another and to an end.

3. I call human operations those that spring from man's will following the order of reason. For if some operations are found in man that are not subject to the will and reason, they are not properly called human but natural, as clearly appears in the operations of the vegetative soul. These in no way fall under the consideration of moral philosophy. As the subject of natural philosophy is motion, or mobile being, so the subject of moral philosophy is human action ordered to an end, or even man, as he is an agent voluntarily acting for an end.

4. It must be known that, because man is by nature a social animal, needing many things to live that he cannot get for himself if alone, it follows that man naturally is a part of a multitude, which furnishes him help to live well. He needs

2. Aristotle *Metaphysics* 1.2 982a18.

3. Ibid. 12.10 1075a14.

this help for two reasons. First, to have what is necessary for life, without which he cannot live the present life; and for this, man is helped by the domestic multitude of which he is a part. For every man is the recipient of generation and nourishment and instruction from his parents. Likewise individuals, who are members of the family, help one another to procure the necessities of life. In another way, man receives help from the multitude of which he is a part to have a perfect sufficiency for life; namely, that man may not only live but live well, having everything that suffices him for living; and in this way man is helped by the civil multitude of which he is a member, not only in regard to bodily needs—as certainly in the city there are many crafts that a single household cannot provide—but also in regard to right conduct, inasmuch as public authority restrains with fear of punishment insolent young men whom paternal admonition is not able to correct.

5. It must be known, moreover, that the whole that the political multitude or the family constitutes has only a unity of order, by reason of which it is not something absolutely one. Therefore, a part of this whole can have an operation that is not the operation of the whole, as a soldier in an army has an activity that does not belong to the whole army. However, this whole does have an operation that is not proper to its parts but to the whole, for example, a battle of the entire army. Likewise the movement of a boat is an operation of the crew rowing the boat. There is also a whole that has a unity, not of order alone, but of composition or of conjunction or even of continuity, according to which unity a thing is one absolutely; and therefore there is no operation of the part that does not belong to the whole. For in continuous things the motion of the whole and of the part is the same. Similarly in composites and in conjoined things, the operation of a part is principally that of the whole. For this reason it is necessary that such consideration of both the whole and its parts should belong to the same science. It does not, however, pertain to the same science to consider the whole that has unity only of order and the parts of this whole.

6. Thus it is that moral philosophy is divided into three parts. The first of these, which is called monastic, considers an individual's operations as ordered to an end. The second, called economics, considers the operations of the domestic group. The third, called politics, considers the operations of the civil group.

7. Aristotle, therefore, beginning the treatment of moral philosophy in the first part of this book called [5] *Ethics* or *Morals,* first gives an introduction in which he does three things. First, he shows what he intends to do. Secondly, he determines the manner of treatment [§ 32]. Thirdly, he explains what manner of person the student of this science ought to be [§ 37]. In regard to the initial point he does two things. First, he presents in advance certain things necessary to show his intention. Secondly, he makes known his intention [§ 19]. In regard to the first he does two things. First, he lays down the necessity of the end. Then he compares habits and acts with the end [§ 15]. Concerning the first point he does three things. He states in the beginning that all things human are ordered to an end. Next, he mentions the different ends [§ 12]. Lastly, he establishes a comparison among ends [§ 14]. In regard to the first point he does two things. He states what he intends, and then he explains his purpose [§ 9].

8. In regard to the first we should consider that there are two principles of human acts, namely, the intellect or reason and the appetite, which are active principles, as is said in Book 3 of *On the Soul.*[4] In the intellect or reason, the speculative and the practical are considered. In the rational appetite, choice and execution are considered. Now all these are ordered to some good as to an end; for truth is the end of speculation. Therefore, as regards the speculative intellect, he lists teaching, by which science is conveyed from teacher to student. In regard to the practical intellect, he lists art, which is right reason applied to things to be made, as is stated in Book 6 of this work.[5] In respect to the act of the appetitive intellect, he lists choice, and as regards execution, he lists the act. He does not mention prudence, which is in the practical reason as art is, because choice is properly directed by prudence. He says, therefore, that each of these obviously seeks a certain good as an end.

9. Then he manifests his intention through the definition of the good. In regard to this we should take into account that good is reckoned among primary things, to such a degree that, according to the Platonists, the good is prior to being. But, in reality, the good is convertible with being. Now

4. Aristotle *De Anima* 3.10 433a9 ff.

5. Aristotle *Nicomachean Ethics* 6.4 1140a9.

primary things cannot be understood by anything prior, but by something posterior, as causes are understood through proper effects. And since the good is properly the moving principle of the appetite, the good is described by the movement of the appetitive faculty, just as a motive power is usually manifested through motion. For this reason he says that the philosophers have rightly declared that the good is what all things desire.

10. Nor is there a difficulty about those who desire evil. For they do not desire evil except under the aspect of good, that is, in so far as they think it is a good. In this way their intention primarily aims at the good and only incidentally touches on evil.

11. The expression "what all things desire" is to be understood not only of beings having knowledge, which apprehend the good, but also of beings lacking knowledge. These things by a natural desire tend toward the good, not as knowing the good, but because they are moved to the good by some knowing being, that is, by the direction of the divine intellect, in the same way that an arrow speeds toward a target by the aim of the archer. The very tending toward the good is the desiring of the good. Hence, he says all things desire the good in so far as they tend toward the good. But there is not one good to which all tend, as will be said later. Therefore a particular good is not meant here, but rather the good in general. However, because nothing is good except in so far as it is a likeness and participation of the highest good, the highest good itself is in some way desired in every good. Thus it can be said that the true good is what all things desire.

12. Then he shows the diversity of ends. In this we must keep in mind that the final good, to which the inclination [6] of each thing tends, is its ultimate perfection. Now the first perfection is had after the manner of a form, but the second perfection in the manner of an operation. Therefore there must be this diversity of ends, namely, that some ends are the operations and other ends are the works themselves, that is, certain products, which are outside the operations.

13. For evidence of this we must consider that operation is of two kinds, as is said in Book 9 of the *Metaphysics*.[6] One, which remains in the agent himself, as seeing, wishing, and understanding, is an operation of the type properly called action. The other is an operation going out into external matter and is properly called making. This as well is of two kinds: sometimes a person accepts external matter only for use, as a horse for riding and a zither for playing, and at other times he takes external matter to change it into some other form, as when a carpenter constructs a house or a bed. Accordingly, the first and second of these operations do not have any product that is their end, but each of them is an end. The first, however, is more noble than the second, inasmuch as it remains in the agent himself. But the third operation is a kind of generation whose end is a thing generated. So in operations of the third type, the works themselves are the ends.

14. Then he presents the third point, saying that whenever the products, which are outside the operations, are ends, the products necessarily are better than the operations, just as the thing generated is better than the generative action. The end is more important than the means—in fact the means have goodness from their relation to the end.

15. Then he compares habits and acts with the end. Concerning this he does four things. First, he shows that different things are ordered to different ends. He says first that, since there are many operations and arts and sciences, they must have different ends, for ends and means are proportional. This he shows by saying that the end of medical art is health; of shipbuilding, navigation; of strategy, victory; and of domestic economy or the management of a household, riches. The last is said according to a common opinion. He himself proves in the first book of the *Politics* that riches are not the end of domestic economy but the instruments.[7]

16. Secondly, he sets down the order of habits among themselves. It happens that one operative habit, which he calls a faculty (*virtus*), is subordinated to another—as the art of bridle-making is subordinated to the art of riding because the rider tells the bridle-maker how he should make the bridle.[8] In this way the rider is the designer (*architector*), that is, the chief producer of the thing itself. The same argument holds for the other arts that make additional equipment needed for riding, such as saddles or the like. The equestrian art is again subordinated to the military, for in ancient

6. Aristotle *Metaphysics* 9.8 1050a23.

7. Aristotle *Politics* 1.9 1257b34 ff.

8. The Latin *virtus* translates the Greek *dunamis,* "power or potentiality," rather than *aretē,* "virtue."

times the army included not only mounted soldiers but everyone who fought for victory. Hence under military art there is not only the equestrian but every art or faculty ordered to war, namely, archery, gunnery, and everything else of this kind. In this same way other arts are subordinated to still others.

17. Thirdly, he lays down the order of ends according to the order of habits. He says that in all arts or faculties it is commonly true that the ends of the architectonic arts or virtues are absolutely more desirable to everyone than the ends of the arts or virtues that are subordinated to the chief ends. He proves this from the fact that men follow or seek the ends of the inferior arts or faculties for the sake of the ends of the superior. The text, however, is suspensive, and should be read as follows: "In all such faculties a subordination of one to another is found..., in all these the architectonic ends," and so forth.

18. Fourthly, he shows that it makes no difference in the order of ends whether the end is a product or an operation. He says that it makes no difference as regards the order that these ends be operations or some product other than the operations, as appears from the doctrine given above. The end of bridle-making is a finished bridle; but the end of horsemanship, which is of greater importance, is an operation, that is, riding. The contrary is true in medicine and gymnastics, for the end of medicine is something produced, namely, health; whereas the end of gymnastics, which is comprised under medicine, is an operation, namely, exercise. [*7*]

Lesson Two

[1.2 1094a19–b11]

19. Having finished the things that are necessary for manifesting his intention, the Philosopher begins now to make known that intention, that is, to show what the principal purpose of this science is. Concerning this he does three things. First, he shows from what was said before that there is some supreme (*optimus*) end of human affairs. Secondly, he shows that it is necessary to know this end [§ 23]. Thirdly, he shows to which science this knowledge belongs [§ 25]. He proves the first by three reasons. The principal one is this. Whatever end is such that we wish other things because of it, and we wish it for itself and not because of something else, then that end is not only a good, but the supreme good. This is apparent from the fact that an end for the sake of which other ends are sought is always of greater importance, as is evident from what was said before. But it is necessary that there be some such end. Therefore, in human affairs there is an end that is good and best.

20. He proves the minor by a second argument, one leading to an impossible conclusion. It is evident from what we have said that one end is desired on account of another. Therefore, either we arrive at some end that is not desired on account of another, or we do not. If we do, the proposition is proved. If, however, we do not find some such end, it follows that every end will be desired on account of another end. In this case we must [8] proceed to infinity. But it is impossible in ends to proceed to infinity. Therefore there must be some end that is not desired on account of another.

21. That it is impossible in ends to proceed to infinity is proved by a third argument that also leads to an impossibility. If we should proceed to infinity in desiring ends, so that one end should always be desired on account of another to infinity, we will never arrive at the point where a man may attain the ends desired. But a man desires in vain what he cannot get; therefore, the end he desires would be useless and vain. But this desire is natural, for it was said above that the good is what all things naturally desire. Hence it follows that a natural desire would be useless and vain. But this is impossible. The reason is that a natural desire is nothing else but an inclination belonging to things by the disposition of the first mover, which disposition cannot be in vain. Therefore, it is impossible that in ends we should proceed to infinity.

22. Therefore, there must be some ultimate end on account of which all other things are desired, while this end itself is not desired on account of anything else. So there must be some supreme end of human affairs.

23. Then he shows that the knowledge of this end is necessary for man. In regard to this he does two things. First, he shows that it is necessary for man to know such an end. Secondly, he shows what man should know about it. He concludes then from what has been said that it is necessary

for man to know that there is a supreme end of human affairs because this has great importance for life, that is, it is of great help in all phases of human living. This is apparent for the following reason. Nothing that is directed to another can be directly attained by man unless he knows that other to which it is to be directed. This is obvious from the example of the archer who shoots straight by keeping his eye on the target at which he is aiming. Now man's whole life ought to be ordered to the supreme and ultimate end of human life. For living a human life correctly it is necessary, therefore, to have a knowledge of the ultimate and supreme end of human life. The explanation is that the reason for the means must always be found in the end itself, as also is proved in Book 2 of the *Physics.*[9]

24. Then he shows what ought to be known about that end. He says that, since it is true that the knowledge of the supreme end is necessary for human life, we must determine what is the supreme end, and to which speculative or practical science its consideration belongs. By "disciplines" he understands the speculative sciences, and by "faculties" (*virtutes*) the practical sciences, since they are principles of some operations. And he says that we must "try" to determine in order to suggest the difficulty there is in grasping the ultimate end of human life, as in considering all highest causes. On the other hand, he says that we should understand this in outline (*figuraliter*), that is, with probability, because such a manner of understanding is suitable for human things, as will be said later on. Now the first of these two belongs to the treatise on this science because such a consideration is about the matter of this science, while the second belongs to the introduction, where the purpose of this science is explained.

25. Therefore, immediately after, he shows to which science the consideration of this end belongs. In regard to this he does two things. First, he gives a reason to prove what he proposes. Secondly, he proves something that he has taken for granted. First then he states the reason for what he proposes, which is this: the supreme end belongs to the most important and most truly architectonic science. This is clear from what was said above, for it was pointed out that the sciences or arts that treat of the means to the end are contained under the science or art treating of the end. So it is necessary that the ultimate end should belong to the most important science as concerned with the primary and most important end, and to the truly architectonic science as telling the others what they should do.[10] But political science appears to be such, namely, the most important and the most architectonic. Therefore, it belongs to it to consider the supreme end.

26. Then he proves what he has taken for granted: that political science is such a science. First, he proves that it is the most truly architectonic, and secondly, that it is the most important [§ 30]. In regard to the first he does two things. First, he ascribes to political or civil science the things that belong to an architectonic science.[11] Secondly, from this he infers what he intended [§ 29]. There are two characteristics of an architectonic science. One is that it dictates what is to be done by the art or science subject to it, as the equestrian art dictates to bridle-making. The other is that it uses [9] it for its own ends. Now the first of these is applicable to politics or political science both in regard to the speculative and in regard to the practical sciences, in different ways, however. Political science dictates to a practical science both concerning its use—whether or not it should operate—and concerning the specification of its act. It dictates to the smith not only that he use his art but also that he use it in such a fashion as to make knives of a particular kind. Both are ordered to the end of human living.

27. But political science dictates to a speculative science only concerning its use and not concerning the specification of its work. Political science orders that some teach or learn geometry; and actions of this kind, in so far as they are voluntary, belong to the matter of ethics and can be ordered to the goal of human living. But the political ruler does not dictate to geometry what conclusions it should draw about a triangle, for this is not subject to the human will nor can it be ordered to human living, but it depends on the very nature (*ratio*) of things. Therefore he says that political science ordains which disciplines, both practical and speculative, should be studied in a city, who should study them, and for how long.

9. Aristotle *Physics* 2.9 200a7 ff.

10. "Primary and most important" translates the superlative of *principalis;* the latter translates the Greek *kuriōtatē,* often rendered in English as "most authoritative."

11. Literally, "he ascribes to *politica* or *civilis* the things..." Both adjectives, *politica* and *civilis,* seem to modify the implied noun *scientia* (the explicit form, *politica scientia,* appears at 1.2 § 31; *civilis scientia* at 1.2 § 26). Cf. *Commentary on the Nicomachean Ethics* 6.7 § 1196.

28. The other characteristic of an architectonic science, the use of subordinate sciences, belongs to political science only in reference to the practical sciences. Hence, he adds, we see that the most highly esteemed, that is, the noblest, skills or operative arts fall under political science, namely, strategy, domestic economy, and rhetoric, which political science uses for its own end, that is, for the common good of the city.

29. Then he draws a conclusion from these two premises. He says that since political science, which is practical, uses the other practical disciplines, as was said above, and since it legislates what is to be done and what is not to be done, as previously stated, it follows that the end of this science as architectonic embraces or contains under itself the ends of the other practical sciences. Hence he concludes that the end of political science is the good of man, that is, the supreme end of human things.

30. Then he shows that political science is the most important science, from the very nature (*ratio*) of its proper end. It is evident that in so far as a cause is more powerful, it extends to more effects. Hence in so far as the good, which has the nature of a final cause, is more powerful, it extends to more effects. So even though the good be the same for one man and for a whole city, it seems much better and more perfect to attain, that is, to procure, and to save, that is, to preserve, the good of a whole city than the good of one man. Certainly it is a part of that love which should exist among men that a man seek and preserve the good even of a single human being. But it is much better and more divine that this be done for a whole nation and for cities. Or it is sometimes desirable that this be done for one city only, but it is much more divine that it be done for a whole nation, which includes many cities. This is said to be more divine because it shows greater likeness to God, who is the universal cause of all goods. But this good that is common to one or to several cities, is the object of our inquiry, that is, of the particular art called political science. Hence to it, as the most important science, belongs most of all the consideration of the ultimate end of human life.

31. But we should note that he says political science is the most important, not simply, but in the genus of the practical sciences, which are concerned with human things, the ultimate end of which political science considers. The ultimate end of the whole universe is considered in divine science, which is the most important without qualification.[12] He says that it belongs to political science to treat of the ultimate end of human life. This, however, he discusses here since the teaching of this book covers the first elements of political science. [*11*]

Lesson Three

[1.3 1094b12–1095a13]

32. After the Philosopher has shown what is the good principally intended in this science, he now determines the method proper to this science. He does this first on the part of the teacher and next on the part of the student [§ 37]. In regard to the first he lays down this argument. The method of manifesting the truth in any science ought to be suitable to the subject matter of that science. He shows this from the fact that certitude cannot be found, nor should it be sought, in the same degree in all discussions where we reason about anything. Likewise, the same method is not used in all products that are made by art; but each craftsman works with the material in a way suited to that material, in one way with wax, in another with clay, in still another with metal. Now the matter of moral study is of such a nature that perfect certitude is not suitable to it. He shows this from two classes of things that seem to belong to the material with which moral study is concerned.

33. In the matter of morals the first and foremost place is held by virtuous works, which he calls here just works and which are the chief concern of political science. Regarding them there is no certain opinion among men; rather a great difference is found in what men judge about them. In this matter a variety of errors occurs, for certain actions, considered just and good by some, are looked upon as unjust and bad by others according to different times and places and persons. For a deed is

12. Regarding "divine science" (i.e., theology, metaphysics, or first philosophy) as the mistress of all other sciences, consult Aquinas's prologue to his *Commentary on the Metaphysics.*

considered vicious at one time and in one country, but at a different time and in a different country it is not considered to be so. Because of this difference, it happens that some people are of the opinion that nothing is just or good by nature, but only on account of legislation. We shall treat more fully of this opinion in Book 5 of this work.[13]

34. Secondly, the external goods that are used by men for a purpose have a moral consideration. In regard to them also it happens that we find the error just mentioned, because these material goods are not always used in the same way by everyone. Some men are helped by them, while others are harmed by them. Many have been ruined by having riches; for instance, those who were murdered by robbers. Others, by reason of their physical strength on which they rely, have carelessly exposed themselves to dangers. Thus it is evident that moral matters are variable and divergent and do not possess complete certitude.

35. Because, in the art of demonstrative science, principles must conform to conclusions, it is desirable and preferable, when treating subjects so variable, and when proceeding from premises of a like nature, to bring out the truth first in a rough way by applying universal principles and simples to singulars and composites, in which the action consists. For it is necessary in every practical science to proceed in the manner of composition, whereas in a speculative science it is necessary to proceed in an analytical manner, by resolving the composites into simple principles. Secondly, we should present the truth in outline, that is, in an approximate way. This is to proceed from the proper principles of this science. Moral science treats of voluntary acts, and what moves the will is not only the good but the apparent good. Thirdly, we are going to speak of events as they happen in the majority of cases, that is, of voluntary acts, which proceed from the will, inclined perhaps to one alternative rather than another but not operating under compulsion. In these, too, we must proceed in such a way that principles are conformable to conclusions.

36. Then he shows that the student must accept this limitation in moral matters. He says that it is proper that each one should take whatever is said to him by another in the same way, that is, as the matter warrants. The reason is that a well-educated or well-instructed man should look for as much certitude in any matter as the nature of the subject admits. There cannot be as much certainty in variable and contingent matter as in necessary matter, [*12*] which is always the same. Therefore, the well-educated man ought not to look for greater nor be satisfied with less certitude than is appropriate to the subject under discussion. It seems an equal fault to allow a mathematician to use rhetorical arguments and to demand from the rhetorician conclusive demonstrations such as a mathematician should give. Both of these things happen because the method appropriate to the matter is not considered. Mathematics is concerned with matter in which complete certitude is found, whereas rhetoric deals with political matter, where manifold variation occurs.

37. Then he shows what sort of person the student of this science ought to be. First, he shows who is an unsuitable student, and secondly, who is an unprofitable student [§ 39]. Thirdly, he shows who is a proper student [§ 41]. In respect to the first he does two things. First, he introduces certain things necessary to explain his proposition. He states that each man can judge well only the things he knows. Thus a man educated in one particular subject can judge well what belongs to that subject. But the man who is well educated in all subjects can judge well about all without restriction to a particular subject.

38. Secondly, he draws his conclusion, namely, that a young man is not a proper student of political science nor of any part of moral science, which is comprised under political science, because, as was said, a man can judge well only the things he knows. Now every student should make good judgments about what he studies, so that he may accept what is well said but not what is badly said. Therefore, no one can be a proper hearer unless he has some knowledge of what he ought to study. But a young man does not have a knowledge of things belonging to moral science, for, these are known mostly through experience, and a young man is inexperienced in the ways of life because of the very brevity of his life. And yet the arguments of moral science proceed from, and are also about, things that pertain to the actions of human life. For instance, if it be said that the generous man keeps the cheaper things for himself and makes a

13. *Commentary on the Ethics* 5.12 § 1025; Aristotle *Nicomachean Ethics* 5.7 1134b24–28.

present of the more expensive to others, a young man will perhaps judge this not to be true because of his inexperience. It is the same with other civil matters. Hence it is evident that a young man is not a proper student of political science.

39. Then he shows who is an unprofitable student of this science. Here we must consider that moral science teaches men to follow reason and to refrain from the things to which the passions of the soul incline, such as concupiscence, anger, and the like. Toward these, men are inclined in two ways. In one way by choice, for instance, when a man of set purpose intends to satisfy his concupiscence. Such a one he calls a follower of passions. The other way is when a man resolves to abstain from harmful pleasures but is sometimes overcome by the urge of passions, so that contrary to his resolution he follows the promptings of passion. A man of this type is said to be incontinent.

40. He affirms, then, that the follower of the passions will study this science in vain, that is, without any result and uselessly, that is, without attaining its proper end. The end of this science is not knowledge alone, which the followers of passion can perhaps gain; rather the end of this science, as of all practical sciences, is human action. Now those who follow the passions do not attain virtuous acts. So in regard to this it makes no difference whether the student of this science is immature in age or immature in character, that is, a follower of the passions. The reason is that, as the immature in age fails to achieve the end of this science which is knowledge, so the immature in character fails to achieve the end which is action. His deficiency is not due to time but to the fact that he lives according to his passions, seeking the particulars to which the passions incline. Now, for such men the knowledge of this science is useless; the same may be said of the incontinent who do not act in accord with their knowledge of moral matters.

41. Then he shows who is a proper student of this science. He says that it is very useful to have a knowledge of moral matters for those who satisfy all their desires and act in externals according to the order of reason.

42. Lastly, in the conclusion he sums up what has been discussed in this introduction, stating that this much has been said in a preliminary manner about the student—this was treated last; stating also what is the method of demonstrating—this was treated in the middle of the introduction; and lastly what our purpose is, namely, what the principal aim of this science is—this was treated first.

BOOK FIVE

Lesson Twelve

[5.7 1134b18–1135a15]

1016. After the Philosopher has shown what sort of thing political justice is, i.e., unqualified justice, now he makes a division of it. First he divides political justice into species. Second, he touches upon the division of this justice into individual parts [§ 1031]. He discusses the first point from three aspects. First he proposes the division. Next he explains it [§ 1018]. Last he rejects an error opposed to that division [§ 1025]. He says first that there is a twofold division of political justice: natural justice (*iustum naturale*), and legal justice (*iustum legale*). This is the same as the division that the jurists make, namely, that one kind of right is natural and the other positive. They call right (*ius*) the very thing that Aristotle calls the just object (*iustum*). Isidore too says in *The Books of Etymologies* that right is as it were what is just.[14] But there seems to be inconsistency in that political is the same as civil. In this way what the Philosopher considers the whole division seems to be considered by the jurists as part of the division for they make civil law a part of positive law.[15]

14. Isidore of Seville *Etymologies* 5.3.1 (*The Etymologies of Isidore of Seville,* ed. Stephen A. Barney [Cambridge: Cambridge University Press, 2006]).

15. Because the words *political* and *civil* (*politicus* and *civilis*) are taken as synonymous, Aristotle's "political justice," *iustum politicum,* appears equivalent to the jurists' "civil law," *ius civile.* For Aristotle, however, political justice is a whole that is divided into parts, natural and legal, while for the jurists, civil right is not the whole, but a part of positive right. For the jurists, right as a whole is divided into natural law, civil law, and the law of nations (*ius naturale, ius civile,* and *ius gentium*); the latter two appear to be positive. See *The Digest of Justinian,* ed. T. Mommsen and P. Krueger, trans. A. Watson (Philadelphia: University of Pennsylvania Press, 1985), vol. 1, 1.1.1, 1.1.9.

1017. But we must take into account that political or civil is taken here in one way by the Philosopher and in another way by the jurists. The Philosopher here calls justice political or civil from the usage the citizens are accustomed to, but the jurists call right political or civil from the cause, viz., that some city has established it for itself. For this reason the Philosopher appropriately designates legal or posited by law that which they call positive. Political justice then is properly divided by means of these two, for the citizens use justice to the extent that it is imparted to the human mind by nature and to the extent that it is posited by law.

1018. Then he indicates the parts of the preceding division. First he explains natural justice in two ways: in one way according to its effect or power (*virtus*), saying that justice is natural which everywhere has the same capacity, that is, power, to induce good and prevent evil. This happens because nature, the cause of this justice, is the same everywhere among all men. But justice by the decree of some city or prince has force only among those who are subject to the jurisdiction of that city or prince. In the other way he explains this justice according to its cause, when he says that natural justice does not consist in what seems or does not seem to be, i.e., it does not arise from human conjecture but from nature. [*305*] In speculative matters there are [first] some things naturally known, like indemonstrable principles and [second] things closely connected with them; [third] there are other things discovered by human ingenuity. Likewise in practical matters there are [first] some principles naturally known, indemonstrable principles as it were, and [second] things related to them, as evil must be avoided, no one is to be unjustly injured, theft must not be committed and so on; [third] others are devised by human diligence which are here called just legal enactments.

1019. We must consider that that justice is natural to which nature inclines men. But a twofold nature is observed in man. One, by which he is an animal, is that which is common to him and other animals. The other nature belongs to man properly inasmuch as he is man, as he distinguishes the disgraceful from the honorable by reason. However, jurists call only that right natural which follows the inclination of nature common to man and other animals, as the union of male and female, the education of offspring, and so forth. But the right which follows the inclination proper to the nature of man, i.e., precisely as he is a rational animal, the jurists call the right of the peoples (*ius gentium*) because all peoples are accustomed to follow it, for example, that agreements are to be kept, legates are safe among enemies, and so on.[16] Both of these, though, are included under natural justice as it is here taken by the Philosopher.

1020. Next he explains legal justice and seems to give three differences in justice of this kind. The first is this: when something is universally or commonly imposed by law. Regarding this he says that justice is called legal which in the beginning, i.e., before it becomes law, is indifferent whether something is done in this way or that, but when it is laid down, i.e., enacted into law, then a difference arises because observing it is just, disregarding it is unjust. Thus in some city it is enacted that a prisoner may be redeemed for a *mina*, that is at a fixed price, and that a goat should be offered in sacrifice but that two sheep are not to be sacrificed.

1021. The second difference in legal justice is that something is stated by law in a particular case, for instance, when a city or a prince grants some privilege—called a private law—to an individual person. Touching this point he says there are also legal enactments, not those that are enacted in a general way but whatever are prescribed by men as law in individual cases. It was enacted, for example, in a particular city that sacrifice should be offered to a woman named Brasidas who rendered great service to the city.[17]

1022. The third difference in legal justice is that sentences passed by judges are called a kind of legal justice. In regard to this he adds that the decrees of judges are also legal enactments.

1023. But here we must take into consideration that legal or positive justice always has its origin in natural justice, as Cicero says in his *Rhetoric*.[18] Origin from natural right can occur in two ways: in one way, as a conclusion from principles, and in such a manner positive or legal right cannot originate from natural right. For once the premises

16. *The Digest of Justinian* 1.1.1.3–4.

17. Brasidas, a Spartan general, was worshipped as a hero by the citizens of Amphipolis in whose defense he fell in 422 BC (Thucydides *The Peloponnesian War* 5.8–11).

18. Cicero *De Inventione* 2.21.65, 2.53.160.

are stated, the conclusion necessarily follows. But since natural justice exists always and everywhere, as has been pointed out, this is not applicable to legal or positive justice. On this account it is necessary that whatever follows from natural justice, a conclusion as it were, will be natural justice. Thus, from the fact that no one should be unjustly injured [*306*] it follows that theft must not be committed—this belongs to natural right. In another way, something can originate from natural justice after the manner of a determination, and thus all positive or legal justice arises from natural justice. For example, that a thief be punished is natural justice but that he be punished by such and such a penalty is posited by law.

1024. Also we must consider here that legal justice has its origin in two ways from natural justice in the preceding manner. In one way it exists with an admixture of some human error, and in the other without such error. Aristotle explains this by examples. It is natural justice that a citizen who is oppressed without any fault on his part should be aided, and consequently that a prisoner should be ransomed, but the fixing of the price, which pertains to legal justice, proceeds from natural justice without any error. Likewise it is natural justice that honor be bestowed on a benefactor, but that divine honor be given to a human—that Brasidas be offered a sacrifice—arises from human error. But the just decrees of judges are applications of legal justice to particular cases.

1025. He then rejects an error opposed to this division. On this point he does three things. First he proposes the error together with the reason for it. Second, he refutes it [§ 1026]. Third, he asks a question occasioned by the refutation [§ 1027]. He says first that some were of the opinion that all just things are of the sort that is established by law, and there is then no natural justice. This was the opinion of the Cyrenaics, the followers of the Socratic philosopher Aristippus.[19] They were influenced by this reason: that which is according to nature is invariable, and wherever it is it has the same force, as is obvious fire burns in Greece as well as in Persia. Apparently this is not true of justice because all just things seem to be changed at times. Nothing seems to be more just than that a deposit should be returned to the owner. Nevertheless the return must not be made to a madman demanding his sword or to a traitor to his country demanding money for arms. So then it seems that there is nothing just by nature.

1026. Then he provides a refutation, saying that the statement that natural things are unchangeable is not so universally, but is true in some respect. The reason is that the nature of divine things never changes, for example, the nature of separated substances and of the heavenly bodies, which the ancients called gods. But with us humans, who are counted among the perishable things, there is something according to nature and yet whatever is in us is changeable either intrinsically or extrinsically (*per se* or *per accidens*). Moreover, there is in us something natural like having two feet, and something not natural like having a coat. Although all the things that are just among us are somehow variable, nevertheless some of them are naturally just.

1027. Next he raises a doubt occasioned by the preceding refutation. He handles the first point in a twofold manner. First he asks the question; then he answers it. First he proposes this question. If all just human things are changeable the question remains: of the things that change, what kind is just by nature, and what kind is just not by nature but by the laying down of the law and agreement among men, if both are changeable in a similar way?

1028. He then answers the question just asked. He considers this point in a twofold manner. First he shows how things just by nature are changeable. Then he shows how things just by law are changeable [§ 1030]. He says it is obvious that the arrangement found in other natural things among us, likewise applies to things just by nature. Those things that are natural with us occur in the same way in the greater number of cases but fail in a few. Thus it is natural that the right hand is stronger than the left, and this is so in the greater number of instances, although it happens occasionally that some men are ambidextrous since their left hand is as strong as their right. So also the things that are just by nature, for example, that a deposit ought to be returned, must be observed in the majority of cases but is changed in the minority.

1029. However, we must keep in mind that the essences (*rationes*) of changeable things are

19. Aristippus (ca. 435–350 BC) held that pleasure is the rational end of life (Cicero *De Officiis* 3.33.116). The Cyrenaics neglected the study of natural things on account of their uncertainty and held that nothing is just or noble by nature (Diogenes Laertius *The Lives of Eminent Philosophers* 2.87–93).

immutable; hence whatever is [*307*] natural to us, belonging as it were to the essence of man, is not changeable in any way, for instance that man is an animal. But things that follow nature, like dispositions, actions, and movement, are variable in the fewer instances. Likewise those actions belonging to the essence itself of justice cannot be changed in any way, for example, theft must not be committed because it is an injustice. But those actions that follow are changeable in a few cases.

1030. Then he shows how the legally just are changeable indifferently. He says that the things that are just according to arrangement and advantage, i.e., by what is agreed among men for some utility, are similar to measures of salable commodities, wine and wheat. For the measures of wine and wheat are not everywhere equal, but they are greater where products are bought wholesale and smaller where products are sold retail. So also things that are not naturally just but fixed by men are not the same everywhere, thus the same punishment is not inflicted everywhere for theft. The reason is that the civil life or the regime is not the same everywhere. All laws are framed as they are suited to the end of the regime, although only one regime is everywhere best according to nature.

1031. Next he treats the division of justice in regard to the individual parts. He says that each particular just and legal thing is related to human affairs as a universal to singulars. The reason is that actions which are done according to justice are many but each just thing is one, as it were a kind of universal. Thus, that a deposit must be returned is one which has a reference to many persons and many cases.

1032. He then shows what just action and unjust action are. First, what unjust action is; then what just action is. He says that unjust action and unjust thing differ, for an unjust thing is something that is contrary to justice either by nature or by human decree, as theft. But the doing of an action by someone, for instance, stealing is called unjust action, the execution of injustice so to speak. However, before this is done by anyone it is not called an unjust action but an unjust thing.

1033. Then he says that in a similar way just action is present when a person does a thing which is just by nature or by regulation of law. But with the Greeks the doing of a just thing in general is rather called *dikaiopragēma* or doing of what is just, but every doing of a just thing does not seem to be called justifying action, i.e., by restoring what is unjust to justice.[20]

1034. Finally, he says that we must discuss later, in the *Politics*, the character, the number, and the species of each type of justice, viz., natural and legal.

BOOK FIVE

Lesson Sixteen

[5.10 1137a31–1138a3]

1078. After the Philosopher has finished the consideration of justice in general, he now begins to consider equity which is a general directive of justice. First he indicates his intention. Then he proceeds with his proposition [§ 1079]. He says first that following what has been said, we should discuss equity, that designates a certain habit, and the equitable thing that is its object. In the discussion we should declare how equity is related to justice and how its object, which is called the equitable thing, is related to the just thing, the object of justice. In Greek *epiiches* is understood as what is reasonable or becoming; it is derived from *epy* meaning "above" and *ykos* meaning "obedient," because by equity a person is obedient in a higher way when he follows the intention of the legislator where the words of the law are discordant.[21]

1079. Then he proceeds with his proposition. He discusses it under three headings. First he determines the object of equity. Second, the subject of it [§ 1089]. Last, he determines the habit [§ 1090]. He considers the initial point in a twofold manner.

20. *Iniustificatio* refers to every "unjust action," but *iustificatio* refers narrowly to those "just actions" that correct an unjust action; *dikaiopragēma* refers to any just action in general. The transliterations of Greek words have been modernized, with the exception of *epieikēs* (5.16 § 1078]).

21. The etymology of *epiikēs* (in a modern transliteration) is partially incorrect: the second part of the word comes from *eikos*, meaning "likely, probable." Thomas's etymology seems more suitable for *epēkoos*, "to give ear to."

First he raises a doubt; then he solves it [§ 1081]. He says first that if we look closely, it does not seem that the equitable thing is absolutely the same as the just, because the equitable sometimes departs from what is legally just; nor does it seem to be altogether different in species from what is just. He assigns a reason for these things: sometimes we praise what is equitable and declare that it is well done. Likewise we praise the kind of man who does it—we even call him a manly and perfect individual. So it is evident that, when we transfer praise to what is equitable, or to a person [*323*] as if to a greater good, we show what is equitable as something better than what is just. Hence the equitable does not seem to be the same absolutely as the just thing.

1080. On the other hand (if we wish to follow reason) it seems inappropriate if what is equitable is praiseworthy and something over and above the just. It seems necessary that either the just thing is not morally upright,[22] i.e., good, or that if what is equitable is different from the just, [the equitable] is not good because good is achieved in one way, as was pointed out in the second book;[23] or it is necessary that if both are good, they are identical. So he infers that a doubt arises about what is equitable on account of the things just stated. On the one hand it seems that it is not the same inasmuch as it is praised as better than the just thing, on the other it seems that it is the same as the just thing, for what is beyond the just apparently is not good and praiseworthy.

1081. Next he solves the question raised. He handles this point in two ways. First he sets forth the truth. Then he assigns the reason [§ 1082]. He says first that everything that has been said for either side of the doubt is in some way right, and if correctly understood no opposition lies hidden there. It is true that what is equitable is one kind of just thing and is better than another just thing because, as was noted before, justice which citizens practice is divided into natural and legal. For what is equitable is better than what is legally just but is contained under the naturally just. Consequently it is not said to be better than the just thing as if it were some other genus distinct from the genus of just things. Thus, it is clear that the just and the equitable are the same, because [the equitable] is contained in the genus of the just and, while both are good, that is, the legally just and the equitable, the equitable is better.

1082. Then he assigns the reason, treating it in a threefold manner. First he assigns the reason for doubt. Second, he indicates the reason for the truth proposed [§ 1083]. Third, he infers the truth intended [§ 1087]. He says first that this is what raised the doubt: that the equitable is something just, yet it is not the legally just, but a certain directing of legal justice. For we said that it was contained under natural justice from which legal justice has its origin, for whatever is born must be directed by the principle from which it originates.

1083. Then he assigns the reason for the truth proposed, i.e., why legal justice has need of direction. He discusses this point from three aspects. First he points out a defect in legal justice. Next he shows that this defect does not destroy the rectitude of legal justice [§ 1085]. Last he infers the necessity for direction [§ 1086]. He says first that the reason why legal justice has need of direction is that every law is proposed universally. Since particulars are infinite, the human understanding cannot embrace them to make a law that applies to every individual case. Therefore a law must be framed in a universal way, for example, whoever commits murder will be put to death.

1084. It is evident that our intellect can predicate something universally true about some things, as in the case of what is necessary where no defect can occur. But about other things it is not possible that something true be predicated universally, in the case of what is contingent. Here even though something is true in most instances, nevertheless it errs in a few instances. And such are the human acts about which laws are framed. In these things the legislator necessarily speaks in a universal way on account of the impossibility of comprehending particulars; however, he cannot be correct in all the situations for which he legislates since error arises in some few cases. For this reason the legislator accepts what happens in most cases, and nevertheless he is not ignorant that a fault (*peccatum*) is possible in some cases. Thus the anatomist says that man has five fingers, although he knows that by a mistake of nature it happens that man has more or less in rarer cases.

22. "Morally upright" translates *studiosus,* the Latin rendering of the Greek *spoudaios;* see *Nicomachean Ethics* 5.2 1130b3–5, 9.8 1169a18–33; and Aristotle *Categories* 1.8 10b5–8.

23. Thomas Aquinas *Commentary on the Ethics* 2.7 § § 319–321; *Nicomachean Ethics* 2.6 1106b28.

1085. Next he shows that the previously mentioned defect does not destroy the rectitude of law or of legal justice. He says that, although a fault may be committed in some cases by the observance of the law, nevertheless the law is correct because that fault is not on the part of the law (since it was made according to reason) nor on the part of the legislator (who legislated according to the condition of the material), but the fault is in the nature of the thing. Such is the material of human actions that they are not done always in the same way but are done otherwise in certain infrequent instances. For example, the return [*324*] of a deposit is in itself just, and it is good in most cases, but in a particular situation it can be bad, for instance, if a sword is returned to a madman.

1086. He then infers the necessity for directing legal justice. He says that when the law proposes something in a universal way, and the observance is not beneficial in a special instance, rightly it is held that a person should correct what is deficient in the law. Where the legislator evidently left indeterminate a particular case (in which the law falls short) he is at fault, i.e., he proposed a defective proposition in speaking absolutely or universally. The reason is that even the legislator himself, had he been present where such a case happened, would have determined that it be corrected in this way. Moreover, had he foreseen this from the beginning he would have put it in the law. But he could not comprehend all particulars; in a certain city it was decreed under penalty of death that strangers were not to climb the walls of the city for fear they would usurp the civil government. But during an enemy invasion some strangers by climbing the walls defended the city from invaders. They do not deserve to be punished by death; it would be against the natural law to reward benefactors with punishment. Therefore in this case legal justice must be directed by natural justice.

1087. Then he infers the truth intended, affirming that by reason of what has been said it is clear what the equitable is. It is a just thing and it is better than one kind of justice: not better than the naturally just that must be observed absolutely, that is, universally, but better than the legally just, in which a fault occurs because it is laid down absolutely, i.e., universally. Hence the nature of the equitable is that it be directive of the law where the law is deficient for some particular case. Indeed the law does fail in particular cases. The reason why not everything can be determined according to the law is that the law cannot possibly be framed to meet some rare particular incidents, since all cases of this kind cannot be foreseen by man. On account of this, after the enactment of the law, a decision of the judges is required by which the universal statement of the law is applied to a particular matter. Because the material of human acts is indeterminate, it follows that their norm, which is the law, must be indeterminate, as if it did not always exist in the same condition.

1088. He offers an example of a norm for building in Lesbos. In this island there are certain hard stones that cannot easily be dressed by chisel so they may be arranged in an entirely correct position. Therefore the builders there use a leaden rule (*regula*). Just as this leaden rule conforms to the shape of the stone and does not stay in the same form, so the sentence of the judge must be adapted to the things according to their suitableness. In this way then he ends by way of summary that it is clear from the premises what the equitable thing is, that it is something just which is better than one kind of just thing, viz., the legally just.

1089. Next he determines the subject of equity. He affirms that it is evident from what has been proposed who the equitable man is: he who chooses and does the things which have been discussed. He lays down a certain characteristic of this kind of virtuous person. He says that such a one is not *akribodikaios*, i.e., a zealous enforcer of justice in the worse sense, for vengeance, like those who are severe in punishing, [*325*] but rather like those who mitigate the penalties although they may have the law on their side in punishing.[24] The legislator does not intend punishments in themselves but as a kind of medicine for offenses (*peccatum*). Therefore the equitable person does not add more punishment than is sufficient to prevent offenses.

1090. He then determines the habit of the virtue. He says that this habit, called equity, is a particular species of justice and is not a habit different from legal justice; we said the same about its object, for habits are known by reason of their objects.

24. *Akribodikaios* is a compound of *dikaios*, "just," and *akribēs*, "exact, precise" (which in Book 1, Lesson 3 is translated as *certum*, "certain").

BOOK SIX

Lesson Seven

[6.8 1141b2–1142a31]

1195. After the Philosopher has shown what is absolutely primary among all the intellectual virtues, he now shows what is primary in human affairs.[25] First he explains his proposition. Then he makes known something that he had stated above [§ 1208]. On the initial point he does three things. First he proposes his objective. Next he makes known his proposition [§ 1196]. Finally he rejects an error [§ 1203]. He says first that although wisdom, which is absolutely primary (*principalis*) among all others, does not consist in the knowledge of human things, nevertheless there is a certain architectonic (i.e., ruling and dominating) reason or knowledge here, viz., in the order of human affairs.

1196. Then he makes known his proposition, distinguishing the things which pertain to a knowledge of human affairs. First he distinguishes political prudence from prudence as such.[26] Next he defines political prudence [§ 1197]. Last he defines prudence [§ 1199]. He says then that prudence and political prudence are substantially the same habit because each is a right plan (*recta ratio*) of things to be done about what is good or bad for man. But they differ specifically (*secundum rationem*), for prudence as such is the right plan of things to be done in the light of what is good or bad for one man, that is, oneself. Political prudence, however, deals with things good or bad for the whole civic multitude. Consequently, political prudence is to prudence simply as legal justice to the virtue [of justice], as was indicated heretofore in the fifth book.[27] When the extremes have been stated, we see the median, i.e., the prudence of the household, which holds a middle place between that regulating one man and the city.

1197. Next he defines political prudence. He divides it into two parts, noting that one part of the habit dealing with the whole city is, so to speak, architectonic or legislative prudence. An architectonic art derives its name from its role, to determine for others what is to be done. Hence rulers imposing a law on subjects are in civic matters as architects are regarding things to be built. Because of this, the legislative (that is, right reason according to which rulers frame correct laws) is called architectonic prudence. But the other part of political prudence, namely, that which is concerned with individual operable things, goes by the general name, political prudence. In fact, the laws are compared to the works of man [*357*] as universals to particulars, as the fifth book stated about legally just things.[28] Likewise, as legislative prudence gives the precept, so also political prudence puts it in effect and conserves the norms stated in the law.

1198. Obviously it belongs to executive political prudence to frame a decree that is simply the application of universal reason to a particular practicable, for it is called a decree only in regard to some practicable. Moreover, since every practicable is individual, it follows that a decree concerns some singular ultimate, i.e., an individual—it is called an ultimate because our knowledge begins from it, proceeding to universals, and terminates at the ultimate itself by way of descent. Likewise the decree itself can be called ultimate because it is the application of a law, universally stated, to an individual practicable. Because the prudence that executes the positive law retains for itself the general name of political prudence, it follows that only those who see to the execution of the enacted laws are said to be politically engaged since they alone are working in civil affairs, like *cheirotechnai,* i.e., manual workers in things to be built; and legislators bear the same relation to them as do architects to those who execute their plans.

1199. Then he treats prudence. First he shows what should be called prudence. Then he infers a corollary from what has been said [§ 1202]. He

25. Book 6, Lesson 6 relates how wisdom is the primary intellectual virtue on grounds that it treats the most honorable and divine things.

26. Literally, "he distinguishes *politica* from prudence." In this context *politica* modifies the implied noun *prudence;* thus it is translated "political prudence" (*prudentia politica* appears at 6.7 § 1200). In Book 1, Lesson 2 *politica* was translated "political science" (cf. 1.2 § § 25–26). Prudence, however, is not a science (*Nicomachean Ethics* 6.5 1140b2; *Commentary on the Ethics* 6.4 § 1164, also 6.7 § 1200).

27. *Commentary on the Ethics* 5.16 § § 1083–1084; *Nicomachean Ethics* 5.10 1137b13–17.

28. *Commentary on the Ethics* 5.16 § § 1083–1084; *Nicomachean Ethics* 5.10 1137b13.

says first that although political prudence, both legislative and executive, is prudence, nevertheless, that which is concerned with one person only, oneself, seems to be especially prudence. And reason of this type directive of oneself retains the general name prudence, since the other parts of prudence are qualified by particular names. One of these is called domestic, that is, the prudence that administers a household. Another is called legislative, that is, the prudence in making laws. Still another is political, that is, the prudence in executing the laws. Each of these is divided into consultative and judicial; for in things to be done we must first investigate something by the inquiry of counsel, then judge the thing investigated.

1200. As has been noted previously, we must consider that prudence is not only in the reason but has a function likewise in the appetitive faculty.[29] Therefore, the things mentioned here are all species of prudence, to the extent that they do not reside in the reason alone but have ramifications in the appetitive faculty. Inasmuch as they are exclusively in the reason they are called certain kinds of practical science, viz., ethical, domestic, and political science.

1201. Likewise we must consider that, because the whole is more important than the part, and consequently the city than the household and the household than one man, political prudence must be more important than domestic and the latter more important than personal prudence. Moreover, legislative prudence has greater importance among the parts of political prudence, and without qualification is absolutely principal about actions which man must perform.

1202. Then he infers a corollary from what has been discussed. He says that, because individual prudence is a part of general prudence, it follows that to know the things good for oneself—which belongs to this prudence—is a particular kind of human knowledge unlike others by reason of the diverse things pertaining to one man.

1203. Next he rejects an error. First he presents it. Then, he gives a proof for it [§ 1204]. Last, he excludes the error by disproving it [§ 1206]. He says first that, to some people, only that man seems prudent who knows and diligently cultivates the things having to do with himself. However, those who are public officials do not seem to be prudent but rather *polupragmones*, i.e., busy with a variety of affairs pertaining to the multitude.

1204. Then he gives a proof of the foregoing error. He does this first by a statement of Euripides the poet who has one of his characters, a soldier fighting for his country, say: "How could I be prudent when I have neglected to take care of [*358*] myself, i.e., I did not attend to my own affairs but, one of many, I am sharing military service equally with them."

1205. Then he proposes a reason for this notion. He says that some people affirm that public officials are not prudent, since they are intent on superfluous or vain things and are doing something more than their individual concern. Because of the inordinateness of their hidden self-love, men seek only what is good for themselves; and they deem that each one must do only what is good for himself. From this opinion of theirs it follows that, for some men, only those are prudent who are intent on their own affairs.

1206. Next he rejects this error. He says that the particular good of each individual person cannot be attained without domestic prudence, i.e., without the proper administration of the household, nor without civic virtue (*urbanitas*), i.e., without the proper administration of the city, just as the good of the part cannot be attained without the good of the whole. Hence it is evident that statesmen and household stewards are not intent on anything superfluous but on what pertains to themselves.

1207. Nevertheless, political and domestic prudence are not sufficient without personal prudence. The reason is that when the city and the household have been properly arranged, it is still not evident how one's own personal affairs must be disposed. Therefore, it is necessary to attend to this by the prudence of dealing with an individual's good.

1208. Then he clarifies a previous assertion: that prudence is not only concerned with universals but also with particulars.[30] On this point he does two things. First he explains his proposition. Next he compares prudence with science and understanding [§ 1213]. For the initial point he offers two reasons. In regard to the first he does two things. First, he gives a confirmation of the proposition. Then he brings up a particular question on

29. *Commentary on the Ethics* 6.4 § 1174; *Nicomachean Ethics* 6.5 1140b25–30.

30. *Commentary on the Ethics* 6.6 § 1194; *Nicomachean Ethics* 6.7 1141b15–23.

this heading [§ 1209]. He states first that a sign of the previous assertion, that prudence is concerned not only with universals but also particulars, is that youths become geometricians and *disciplinati,* i.e., instructed in the exact sciences or mathematics, and are "erudite in studies of this kind," i.e., they attain perfection at the limit of these sciences.[31] However, it does not seem that a youth can become prudent. The reason is that prudence deals with particulars which are made known to us by experience. But a lad does not have experience because much time is needed to get experience.

1209. Then he raises a question about why a boy can become a mathematician but cannot become "wise," i.e., a metaphysician, or *physicus,* i.e., a natural philosopher. As regards natural philosophy, he answers that the principles of mathematics are known by abstraction from sensible objects (of which one has experience); for this reason little time is needed to grasp them. But the principles of nature, which are not separated from sensible objects, are studied via experience. For this much time is needed.

1210. As to wisdom, he adds that youths do not believe, i.e., grasp with the mind, although they mouth, things pertaining to wisdom or metaphysics. But the mathematical objects are not obscure to them because mathematical proofs concern sensibly conceivable objects while things pertaining to wisdom are purely rational. Youths can easily understand whatever falls under imagination, but they do not grasp things exceeding sense and imagination; for they lack understanding strong enough or trained to such considerations both because of the shortness of their lives and the many physical changes they are undergoing.

1211. Therefore, the proper order of learning [*359*] is that boys first be instructed in things pertaining to logic because logic teaches the method of the whole of philosophy. Next, they should be instructed in mathematics, which does not need experience and does not exceed the imagination. Third, in natural sciences, which, even though not exceeding sense and imagination, nevertheless require experience. Fourth, in the moral sciences, which require experience and a soul free from passions, as was noted in the first book.[32] Fifth, in the sapiential and divine sciences, which exceed imagination and require a vigorous understanding.

1212. He then gives the second reason. It was said that the work of prudence is to deliberate well.[33] But in deliberating a twofold error can happen. One concerns the universal, e.g., whether it is true that all sluggish waters are unhealthy. The other concerns the particular, e.g., whether this water is sluggish. Therefore, prudence must give direction to both universals and particulars.

1213. Then he compares prudence with the things mentioned above: first, with science and next, with understanding. He says first, it is evident from the premises that prudence is not science, for science has to do with universals, as was stated before.[34] But prudence deals with a singular ultimate, viz., the particular, since the practicable is something particular. So it is clear that prudence is not science.

1214. Next he compares prudence with understanding (*intellectus*).[35] First he shows the agreement. Second he shows the difference [§ 1216]. He says first that both science and prudence are receptive of, or in contact with (according to another text), understanding, i.e., have some agreement with understanding as a habit of principles. It was previously pointed out that understanding concerns certain principles or ultimates, that is, indemonstrable principles for which there is no proof, because they cannot be established by reason but immediately become known by themselves. But prudence is concerned with an ultimate, i.e., a singular practicable that must be taken as a principle in things to be done. Yet there is no scientific knowledge of the singular ultimate, for it is not proved by reason; there is, though, sensitive knowledge of it because this ultimate is perceived by one of the senses. However, it is not apprehended by that sense which perceives the species of proper sensibles (for instance, color, sound, and so on—this is the proper sense) but by the inner sense which perceives things sensibly conceivable. Similarly, in mathematics we know

31. The *scientiae disciplinales* comprise mathematics in the broad sense: geometry, arithmetic, astronomy, music, and associated sciences such as optics or mechanics. Cf. the Latin translation of Alfarabi's *Enumeration of the Sciences: Al-Farabi: De Scientiis,* ed. Jakob H. J. Schneider (Freiburg: Herder, 2006).

32. *Commentary on the Ethics* 1.3 § § 38–40; *Nicomachean Ethics* 1.3 1095a2–12.

33. *Commentary on the Ethics* 6.4 § § 1162–1163; *Nicomachean Ethics* 6.5 1140a25–32.

34. *Commentary on the Ethics* 6.4 § § 1144–1152, 6.5 § 1175; *Nicomachean Ethics* 6.3 1139b25–36, 6.6 1140b31.

35. Understanding is one of the five intellectual virtues, together with art, science, prudence, and wisdom. Cf. *Commentary on the Ethics* 6.5 § § 1175–1179; *Nicomachean Ethics* 6.6 1140b31–1141a8.

the ultimate triangle, or the triangle conceived as singular, because there we also conform to a sensibly conceivable singular, as in the natural sciences we conform to a sensible singular.[36]

1215. Prudence, which perfects particular reason rightly to judge singular practicable relations, pertains rather to this, i.e., the inner sense. Hence even dumb animals who are endowed with an excellent natural estimative power are said to be prudent. But that sense which is concerned with proper sensibles has a certain other perfecting quality, viz., a skill in discerning shades of color or taste and the like. So prudence agrees with understanding in this that it deals with an ultimate.

1216. Then he shows the difference between prudence and understanding. Understanding is not given to inquiring, but prudence is, because it is deliberative. To deliberate and to inquire differ as proper and common, for deliberation is a kind of inquiry—as was said in the third book.[37]

36. Thomas distinguishes the "sensibly conceivable" (*imaginabile*) from the "sensible" (*sensibile*).

37. *Commentary on the Ethics* 3.8 § 476; *Nicomachean Ethics* 3.3 1112b20–25.

TWENTY-TWO

THOMAS AQUINAS AND PETER OF AUVERGNE

Commentary on the Politics

Translated by Ernest L. Fortin, Peter D. O'Neill, and Joseph C. Macfarland

The *Politics* was among the last of Aristotle's major works to be translated and studied in the schools (followed only by the *Poetics*). There is no mention of the *Politics* in the new statutes concerning the curriculum in the arts faculty in Paris in 1255. Although the division of moral philosophy into ethics, economics, and politics was already known, prior to that time no use was made of any part of the *Politics*. The canon and civil laws, and works such as Cicero's *De Officiis*, constituted the standard texts on politics in the schools. A first, incomplete Latin translation of the *Politics* (Books 1 through 2.11) was made in the early 1260s, probably by William of Moerbeke; it is certain that William revised this translation and provided the first complete translation of the work ca. 1265. As soon as the *Politics* became available, it exercised a wide influence and was cited in theological works as well as political tracts. Unlike Aristotle's other major works, however, the *Politics* did not find a place within the ordinary curriculum of the faculty of arts in Paris; in Oxford its place in the curriculum was equivalent to that of minor works of natural philosophy. Thomas Aquinas and Albert the Great wrote commentaries and gave lectures on the *Politics* not in the faculty of arts, where the study of other Aristotelian works was required, but in the schools of their monastic order. Thomas's commentary, which extends only to Book 3, Chapter 8 (1280a7), was written between 1270 and 1272. It is not known at what time Albert wrote his commentary, but it is plausible that his commentary was known to Thomas. The first master to lecture on the *Politics* within the faculty of arts—as part of a philosophical education—appears to have been Siger of Brabant (as briefly reported in Pierre Dubois's *Recovery of the Holy Land* [*De Recuperatione Terrae Sanctae*, ca. 1305–7]); Siger's lectures, however, have not been preserved in any known manuscript.[1] The best-known commentary from a master of the faculty of arts was written by Peter of Auvergne. Peter not only completed Thomas's literal commentary, *Scriptum super Libros III–VIII Politicorum Aristotelis*, but also composed a separate question commentary, *Quaestiones super Libros Politicorum Aristotelis* (in the latter form the commentator exercises more latitude in framing and resolving questions). Commentaries on the

1. Pierre Dubois, *The Recovery of the Holy Land*, trans. Walter I. Brandt (New York: Columbia University Press, 1956), sec. 132 [lxxx], 189–90. Some library catalogues also testify to a commentary by Giles of Rome, but no manuscript has been found.

Politics were later written by Guido Vernani (1324–1330, who paraphrased Thomas and Albert extensively), Walter Burley (1342, who paraphrased Peter), Nicholas Oresme (1371–1374), and Nicholas de Vaudémont (1379–1387, whose commentary was formerly attributed to John Buridan). For a thorough list of the extant commentaries, consult Christoph Flüeler, *Rezeption und Interpretation der aristotelischen Politica im späten Mittelalter* (Amsterdam and Philadelphia: B. R. Grüner, 1992).[2]

Peter of Auvergne came from Crocq in the diocese of Clermont; the date of his birth is not known. It is likely that he studied at the University of Paris as a secular cleric (i.e., not as a member of any monastic order). He presumably heard Aquinas lecture during the latter's second stay in Paris (1269–1272). In 1275, Peter, by then a master in the faculty of arts, was appointed rector of the university by the papal legate, Simon de Brion, after an extended vacancy of the office caused by severe dissensions between the regional divisions of students (the dissensions in question seem not to have had any doctrinal origin).[3] Peter was appointed a master of theology in 1296 and bishop of Clermont in 1302; he died in 1304. Peter was respected in his own time, and his works include the completion of Thomas's literal commentary on *De Caelo et Mundo,* additional literal commentaries on the *Parva Naturalia,* question commentaries on the *Metaphysics* and the *Nicomachean Ethics* (Books 1 and 2), and six theological *Quodlibeta* that he delivered as a master of theology. Peter was called, by Ptolemy of Lucca, "the most faithful student" (*fidelissimus discipulus*) of Aquinas, and Aquinas's influence has been discerned especially in Peter's commentaries on the *Ethics* and *Metaphysics.* Peter, however, often staked out positions that distinguished him from Aquinas in crucial respects (e.g., on the distinction of essence and existence). Peter's congruence with Aquinas's thinking cannot be assumed.

In extant manuscripts from the thirteenth and fourteenth centuries, Aquinas's literal commentary on the *Politics* is generally followed immediately by Peter's. At present it is not possible to say when Peter's commentary was written, except that it was begun no earlier than Thomas's death in 1274 and no later than Peter's departure from the university in 1302. As Peter began his literal commentary at the start of Book 3, and Thomas left off in the middle of the same book, some manuscripts furnish commentaries by both men for the first six lessons in that book. Although several manuscripts indicate that the commentary, beginning with either 3.1 or 3.7, was written by Peter, other manuscripts neglect to report Peter's authorship. Furthermore, an early and influential printed edition (Rome, 1492) included Peter's commentary without attribution and so tacitly attributed the entire work to Thomas; this practice continued into the twentieth century. For the publication history, consult the Leonine edition of Thomas's commentary: *Sententia Libri Politicorum, Sancti Thomae de Aquino Opera Omnia,* vol. 58, ed. H.-F. Dondaine and L.-J. Bataillon (Rome, 1971). Critical editions of both Peter's literal commentary on the *Politics* and his question commentary on the same are due to appear in print, edited by L. Lanza and M. Toste, respectively.

The translation of Thomas's commentary (Proemium; Book 1, Lesson 1) was made by Ernest L. Fortin and Peter D. O'Neill; it was based on the edition of R. Spiazzi, OP: S. Thomae Aquinatis, *In Libros Politicorum Aristotelis Expositio* (Turin, 1951) but has been corrected in accord with the Leonine edition. The translation of Peter's commentary on the *Politics* (selections from Book 3, Lessons 8, 9, and 12–16), by Joseph C. Macfarland, was made from a draft of the forthcoming critical edition very generously provided by Lidia Lanza. To conserve space, the text of Aristotle, which often precedes each lesson in the published editions of the commentaries, has been omitted. Also omitted are the words of Aristotle that Aquinas and Peter repeat in the commentary itself in order to identify the precise passage to which they are referring. In place of these quotations, we have inserted bracketed references to subsequent paragraphs or lessons so that the reader may follow the commentators' analysis of the structure of Aristotle's argument. The numbered paragraphs correspond to the unnumbered paragraph divisions found in the respective critical editions. Aquinas's Proemium discusses the nature and necessity of political science. Book 1, Lesson 1 in his commentary establishes the subject of that science.

2. The details on the reception of the *Politics* given here are largely taken from Flüeler's work; important information has also been provided by L. Lanza and M. Toste.

3. R.-A. Gauthier, "II: Siger en 1272–1275, Aubry de Reims et la scission des Normands," *Revue des sciences philosophiques et theologiques* 68 (1984): 3–49.

In the selections from Lessons 8, 9, 11, and 12 in Book 3, Peter, in reviewing the question of who ought to rule, presents opposing arguments for the rule of the multitude and for the rule of the best man. In the selections from Lessons 13–16, Peter investigates kingship as the best regime. Two principal justifications for kingship emerge (the excellence of the best man and the baseness of the multitude), as well as the circumstances in which political rule is preferable to kingly rule.

PROEMIUM

1. As the Philosopher teaches in Book 2 of the *Physics,* art imitates nature.[4] The reason for this is that operations and effects stand proportionately in the same relation to one another as their principles among themselves. Now the principle of those things that come about through art is the human intellect, and the human intellect derives according to a certain resemblance from the divine intellect, which is the principle of natural things. Hence the operations of art must imitate the operations of nature and the things that exist through art must imitate the things that are in nature. For if an instructor of some art were to produce a work of art, the disciple who receives his art from him would have to observe that work so that he himself might act in like manner. And so in the things that it makes, the human intellect, which derives the light of intelligence from the divine intellect, must be informed by the examination of the things that come about through nature so that it may operate in the same way. And that is why the Philosopher says that if art were to make the works of nature, it would operate in the same way as nature; and, conversely, if nature were to make the works of art, it would make them the same way art does.[5]

2. But nature, of course, does not achieve works of art; it only prepares certain principles and in some way supplies artists with a model according to which they may operate. Art, on the other hand, can examine the works of nature and use them to perfect its own work; it cannot, however, perfect the works of nature. From this it is clear that human reason can only know the things that exist according to nature, whereas it both knows and makes the things that exist according to art. The human sciences that deal with natural things are necessarily speculative, therefore, while those that deal with things made by man are practical or operative according to the imitation of nature.

3. Now nature in its operation proceeds from the simple to the complex, so that in the things that come about through the operation of nature, that which is most complex is perfect and whole and constitutes the end of the other things, as is apparent in the case of every whole with respect to its parts. Hence human reason also, operating from the simple to the complex, proceeds as it were from the imperfect to the perfect.

4. Now since human reason has to order not only the things that are used by man but also men themselves, who are ruled by reason, it proceeds in either case from the simple to the complex: in the case of the things used by man when, for example, it builds a ship out of wood and a house out of wood and stones; in the case of men themselves when, for example, it orders many men so as to form a certain society. And since among these societies there are various degrees and orders, the highest is that of the city, which is ordered to the satisfaction of all the needs of human life. Hence of all the human societies this one is the most perfect. And because the things used by man are ordered to man as to their end, which is superior to the means, that whole which is the city is therefore necessarily superior to all the other wholes that may be known and constituted by human reason.

5. From what we have said then concerning political doctrine, with which Aristotle deals in this book, four things may be gathered. First, the necessity of this science. For in order to arrive at the perfection of human wisdom, which is called philosophy, it is necessary to teach something about all that can be known by reason. Since then that whole which is the city is subject to a certain judgment of reason, it is necessary, so that philosophy may be complete, to institute a discipline that deals with the city; and this discipline is called politics or civil science.

4. Aristotle *Physics* 2.2 194a21.

5. Ibid. 2.8 199a13.

6. Secondly, we can infer the genus of this science. For since the practical sciences are distinguished from the speculative sciences in that the speculative sciences are ordered exclusively to the knowledge of the truth, whereas the practical sciences are ordered to some work, this science must be comprised under practical philosophy, inasmuch as the city is a certain whole that human reason not only knows but also acts upon. Furthermore, since reason acts upon certain things by way of making, in which case its operation goes out into external matter—this pertains properly to the arts that are called mechanical, such as that of the smith and the shipwright and the like—and other things by way of action, in which case the operation remains within the agent, as when one deliberates, chooses, wills, and performs other similar acts pertaining to moral science, it is obvious that political science, which is concerned with the ordering of men, is not comprised under the sciences that pertain to making or mechanical arts, but under the sciences that pertain to action, which are the moral sciences.

7. Thirdly, we can infer the dignity and the order of political science with reference to all the other practical sciences. The city is indeed the most important of the things that can be constituted by human reason, for all the other human societies are related to it. Furthermore, all the wholes constituted by the mechanical arts out of the things that are used by men are ordered to man as to their end. If the more important science, then, is the one that deals with what is more noble and perfect, of all the practical sciences political science must necessarily be architectonic and more important than all the others, inasmuch as it is concerned with the highest and perfect good in human affairs. And that is why the Philosopher says at the end of Book 10 of the *Ethics* that the philosophy that deals with human affairs finds its perfection in politics.[6]

8. Fourthly, from what has already been said we can deduce the mode and the order of this science. For just as the speculative sciences, which treat of some whole, from an examination of the parts and principles arrive at a knowledge of the whole by manifesting its properties and operations, so too this science examines the parts and the principles of the city and gives us a knowledge of it by manifesting its parts, its properties, and its operations. And because it is a practical science, it manifests in addition how each thing may be realized, as is necessary in every practical science.

BOOK ONE

Lesson One

[1.1 1252a1–1.2 1253a38]

1. After these preliminary remarks, then, it should be noted that in this book Aristotle begins with a preamble of some kind in which he manifests the aim of this science; then he proceeds to manifest what he has proposed. Concerning the first point, he does two things. First, he shows the dignity of the city, with which politics is concerned, from its end; secondly, he compares the city to the other societies [§ 5]. Concerning the first point, he intends to prove two things: first, that the city is ordered to some good as to its end [§ 2]; secondly, that the good to which the city is ordered is the highest human good [§ 3].

2. Concerning the first point, he sets down the following argument. Every society is established for the sake of some good. But every city is a society of some kind, as we see clearly. Therefore, every city is established for the sake of some good. Since then the minor premise is evident, he proves the major as follows. All men perform everything they do for the sake of that which is seen as a good, whether it is truly good or not. But every society is established through the work of someone. Therefore, all societies seek some good, that is to say, they aim at some good as an end.

3. Then he shows that that good to which the city is ordered is the highest among human goods by means of the following argument. If every society is ordered to a good, that society which is the highest necessarily seeks the good that is the highest among all human goods. For the relation among the means to an end is determined according to the relation among the ends. Now he makes clear which society is the highest by what he adds.

6. Aristotle *Nicomachean Ethics* 10.9 1181b14.

4. For a society is indeed a certain whole. But in all wholes is found an order such that that whole which includes another whole within itself is the higher; a wall, for example, is a whole, and because it is included in that whole which is the house, it is clear that the house is the higher of the two wholes; and likewise, the society that includes other societies is the higher. Now it is clear that the city includes all the other societies, for households and villages are both comprised under the city; and so political society itself is the highest society. Therefore, it seeks the highest among all human goods, for it aims at the common good, which is better and more divine than the good of one individual, as is stated in the beginning of the *Ethics*.[7]

5. Then he compares the city to the other societies, and in this connection he does three things. First, he states the false opinion of certain persons. Secondly, he shows how the falsity of the stated opinion can be made known [§ 10]. Thirdly, in accordance with the method indicated, he sets down the true relationship of the city to the other societies [§ 12]. Concerning the first point, he does two things. First, he states the false opinion. Secondly, he produces their reason [§ 7].

6. Concerning the first point, it should be noted that there is a twofold society that is obvious to all, namely, the city and the household. The city is governed by a twofold rule (*regimen*), namely, the political and the kingly. There is kingly rule when he who is set over the city has full power, whereas there is political rule when he who is set over the city exercises a power restricted by certain laws of the city. Similarly, the household has a twofold rule, namely, the domestic and the despotic. Everyone who possesses slaves is called a despot, whereas the procurator or superintendent of a family is called the domestic head.[8] Hence despotic rule is that by which a master commands slaves, while domestic rule is that by which one dispenses the things that pertain to the entire family, in which are contained not only slaves but many free people as well. Some persons have maintained then, but not rightly, that these two rules do not differ but are entirely the same.

7. Then he sets forth their reason, which is as follows. Things that differ solely by reason of larger and smaller numbers do not differ specifically, because a difference according to more and less does not diversify a species. But the rules just mentioned differ solely by reason of larger or smaller numbers; this they manifested as follows.

8. If the society that is ruled is made up of a small number of people, as in the case of some small household, he who is set over them is called the father of the family and he possesses despotic rule. If the society is made up of a larger number of people, in such a way as to contain not only slaves but a number of free men as well, he who is set over them is called the domestic head. And if the society is made up of a still larger number of people, for example, not only of those who belong to one household but of those who belong to one city, then the rule is said to be political or kingly. The falsity of what certain persons used to say to the effect that the household and the city differ only by reason of their magnitude and smallness, in such a way that a large household is a small city and vice versa, will become apparent from what follows.

9. Likewise they used to assert also that political rule and kingly rule differed solely by reason of larger and smaller numbers. For, when a man himself rules absolutely and in all ways, the rule is said to be kingly. When, however, he commands in part, in accordance with scientific arguments, that is, in accordance with the laws set down by political teaching, the rule is said to be political, as though he were in part a ruler, namely, as regards the things that come under his power, and in part a subject, namely, as he regards the things in which he is subjected to the law. From all this they inferred that all the previously mentioned rules, some of which pertain to the city and others to the household, do not differ in species.

10. Then he shows the means by which the falsity of this opinion can be manifested. He states that what has been said is not true, and that this will become evident to those who examine the matter according to the mode indicated, that is, according to the art of studying such things as will be set down below. Now the mode of this art is the following. Just as, in other things, in order to arrive at a knowledge of the whole, it is necessary to

7. Ibid. 1.1 1094b9. Throughout this argument, "highest" renders the superlative of *principalis,* which is translated "important" both in the Proemium above (§ 7) and in the *Commentary on the Ethics* 1.2 §§ 26–31. *Principalis* is cognate with *principans,* "ruler," and *principium,* "principle."

8. The expression "domestic head" is used here to render the Latin *oeconomus* (*oikonomos,* "steward or administrator of the household"), for which there seems to be no exact equivalent in the English language.

divide the compound into its elements, that is, into the indivisibles, which are the smallest parts of the whole (for instance, to understand a sentence it is necessary to divide it into its letters, and to understand a natural mixed body it is necessary to divide it into its elements), in the same manner if we examine those things out of which the city is compounded, we shall be able to see better what each one of the previously mentioned rules is in itself, and how they differ from one another, and whether in each case something can be studied in an artful way. For in all things we see that if someone examines things as they arise from their principles, he will best be able to contemplate the truth in them. And just as this is true of other things, so also is it true of those things to which we are directing our attention.

11. Now in these words of the Philosopher it should be noted that, in order to arrive at a knowledge of compounds, it is necessary to use the way of analysis, namely, so that we may divide the compound into its elements. Afterwards, however, the way of composition is necessary, so that from the indivisible principles already known we may judge of the things that proceed from these principles.

12. Then, in accordance with the mode just indicated, he sets down the true relationship of the other societies to the city; and in connection with this, he does two things. First, he treats of the other societies that are ordered to the city. Secondly, he treats of civil society [§ 31]. Concerning the first point, he does three things. First, he sets forth the society of one person to another person [§ 13]. Secondly, he sets down the domestic society, which comprises different associations of persons [§ 24]. Thirdly, he sets down the village society, which is made up of several groups [§ 26]. Concerning the first point, he does two things. First, he sets down two personal associations. Secondly, he compares them to each other [§ 17].

13. Now the first of these two personal associations that he sets down is that of male and female; and he says that, since we have to divide the city into its smallest parts, it is necessary to say that the first union is that of persons who cannot be without each other, namely, the male and the female. For this union is for the sake of generation through which are produced both males and females. From this it is clear that they cannot be without each other.

14. He shows how this union is the first by adding that it is "not by choice." Here it should be noted that in man there is something that is proper to him, namely, reason, according to which it belongs to him to act from counsel and choice. There is also found in man something that is common to him and to others; such is the ability to generate. This then does not belong to him as a result of choice, that is, in so far as he has a reason that chooses; rather it belongs to him in accord with the form (*ratio*) common to him and to animals and even to plants. For there is in all these a natural appetite to leave after them another being like themselves, so that in this manner, through generation, what cannot be preserved numerically the same is preserved according to its species.[9]

15. There is, accordingly, a natural appetite of this kind in all other natural corruptible beings. But because living beings, namely, plants and animals, have a special way of generating in that they generate from themselves, he makes special mention of plants and animals. For even in plants a masculine and a feminine power is found, but they are joined in the same individual, even though there is a greater abundance of one or the other in this or that individual, in such a way that we can imagine a plant to be at all times such as are male and female at the time of intercourse.

16. Then he sets down the second association of persons, namely, that of ruler and subject. This association too stems from nature for the sake of preservation, for nature aims not only at generation but also at the preservation of the things generated. That among men this indeed comes about through the association of ruler and subject he shows by the fact that he who by his intellect can foresee the things that are conducive to preservation, for instance, by providing what is advantageous and repelling what is harmful, naturally rules and dominates, whereas he who by reason of bodily strength is able to carry out in deed what the wise man has foreseen mentally is naturally a subject and a slave. From this it clearly appears that the same thing is profitable to both in view of their preservation, namely, that the former should rule and the latter be ruled. For he who by reason of his wisdom can foresee mentally would not be able to survive at times because of a deficiency of bodily strength if he did not have a slave to carry out his ideas, nor would he who abounds in bodily

9. Cf. Aristotle *De Anima* 2.4 415b7.

strength be able to survive if he were not ruled by the prudence of another.

17. Then he compares the associations just mentioned to each other; first, according to the truth; secondly, he rules out an error [§ 19]. He infers then, first of all, from what has been said that there is a natural distinction between woman and slave. For a woman has a natural disposition to beget from another, but she is not robust in body, which is what is required in a slave. And so the two associations just mentioned differ from each other. Now he establishes the cause for this distinction from the fact that nature does not make things in the same way as those who manufacture Delphic knives out of brass, that is to say, out of metal, for some poor people. For among the Delphians certain knives were made that were designed to serve several purposes, as for example, if a single knife were to be used to cut, to file, and to perform other similar duties. This was done for the benefit of the poor who could not afford several instruments. Nature, however, does not act in such a way as to order one thing to different functions; rather it assigns one thing to one function. For this reason woman is not assigned by nature to serve but to beget. Thus all things will best come about when an instrument is not used for many functions but for one only.

18. This is to be understood, however, of cases in which an obstacle would be encountered in one or both of the two functions to which the same instrument were to be assigned, for instance, if it were often necessary to exercise both functions simultaneously. But if the different functions are exercised one after the other, the adaptation of a single instrument to several functions does not give rise to any obstacle. Hence the tongue is suited for two functions of nature, namely, taste and speech, as is said in Book 3 of *De Anima.*[10] For these two functions do not coincide with each other in time.

19. Then he rules out the contrary error. First, he states the error. Secondly, he shows the cause of the error [§ 23]. He says then, first of all, that among the barbarians, woman and slave are considered as belonging to the same order; for they use women as slaves.

20. There can be a doubt here, however, as to who are called barbarians. Some people say that everyone is a barbarian to the man who does not understand his tongue. Hence the Apostle says, *If I know not the power of the voice, I shall be to him, to whom I speak, a barbarian, and he that speaketh, a barbarian to me* [1 Cor. 14:11]. To others it seems that those men are called barbarians who have no written language in their own vernacular. Hence Bede is said to have translated the liberal arts into the English language, lest the English be reputed barbarians. And to others it seems that the barbarians are those who are not ruled by any civil laws. And in fact all these things come close to the truth in some way.

21. For by the name "barbarian" something foreign is understood. Now a man can be said to be foreign either absolutely or in relation to someone. He who is lacking in reason, according to which one is said to be a man, seems to be foreign to the human race absolutely speaking; and so the men who are called barbarians absolutely are the ones who are lacking in reason, either because they happen to live in an exceedingly intemperate region of the sky, so that by the very disposition of the region they are found to be dull for the most part, or else because of some evil custom prevailing in certain lands from which it comes about that men are rendered irrational and almost brutal. Now it is evident that it is from the power of reason that men are ruled by reasonable laws and that they are practiced in writing. Hence barbarism is appropriately manifested by this sign, that men either do not live under laws or live under irrational ones, and likewise that among certain peoples there is no training in writing.

22. But a man is said to be foreign in relation to someone if he cannot communicate with him. Men are born to communicate with one another above all by means of speech, and because of this, people who cannot understand one another's speech can be called barbarians with reference to one another. The Philosopher, however, is speaking here of those who are barbarians absolutely.

23. Then he establishes the cause of the error just mentioned. Its cause, he says, is that among barbarians there is no rule according to nature. For it was stated above that the man who rules according to nature is the one who is able to foresee with the mind, whereas the slave is the one who is able to carry things out with the body. Now barbarians

10. Aristotle *De Anima* 2.8 420b17; cf. *The Parts of Animals* 2.17 660a15 ff., 4.6 683a20 ff.

for the most part are found to be robust in body and deficient in mind. Hence the natural order of rule and subjection cannot exist among them. But there arises among them a certain association of female and male slave, that is to say, they commonly make use of a female slave, namely, a woman, and of a male slave. And because there is no natural rule among barbarians but only among those who abound in reason, the poets say that it is fitting that the Greeks, who were endowed with wisdom, should rule over the barbarians, as if to say that it is the same thing by nature to be a barbarian and to be a slave. But when the converse takes place, there ensues a perversion and a lack of order in the world, according to the words of Solomon, *I have seen servants upon horses and princes walking on the ground as servants* [Eccles. 10:7].

24. Then he treats of the domestic society, which is made up of several personal associations. In this connection he does three things. First, he shows what this society consists of. Secondly, he shows its purpose [§ 25]. Thirdly, he shows how those who live in this society are designated [§ 25]. He says then, first of all, that out of the two previously mentioned personal associations, one of which is ordered to generation and the other to preservation, the first household is constituted. For in a household there have to be a man and a woman, and a master and a slave. Now it is called the first household because there is also another personal association that is found in the household, namely, that of father and son, which arises out of the first. Hence the first two associations are primordial. To show this he adduces a saying of the poet Hesiod, who stated that a household has these three things: a master who rules, a woman, and an ox for plowing. For in a poor household the ox takes the place of a servant; man uses an ox, just as he uses a servant, to carry out some work.

25. Then he shows to what the domestic society is ordered. Here it should be noted that every human association is an association according to certain acts. Now among human acts some are performed every day: such as eating, warming oneself at the fire, and others like these, whereas other things are not performed every day, such as buying, fighting, and others like these. Now it is natural for men to communicate among themselves by helping one another in each of these two kinds of work. Thus he says that a household is nothing other than a certain society set up according to nature for everyday life, that is, for the acts that have to be performed daily. And he goes on to show this by means of names. For a certain Charondas by name calls those who communicate in a household *homositios*, or men of one fare, because they communicate in food; and a certain other named Epimenides, a Cretan by nationality, calls them *homokapnos*, or men of one smoke, because they sit at the same fire.

26. Then he sets down the third society, namely, the village. First, he shows of what this society is made up and what its purpose is. Secondly, he shows that it is natural [§ 27]. He says then, first of all, that the first association made up of several households is called a village; and it is called the first as distinguished from the second, which is the city. Now this society is not established for everyday life, as he says of the household; rather it is instituted for the sake of nondaily uses. For those who are fellow-villagers do not communicate with one another in the daily acts in which those who are members of one household communicate, such as eating, sitting at the fire, and things of this sort; rather they communicate with one another in certain external acts that are not performed daily.

27. Then he shows that the village society is natural. First, he establishes his thesis by means of a reason. Secondly, by means of certain signs [§ 28]. He says then, first of all, that the proximity of households, which constitutes the village (*vicus*), seems to be according to nature in the highest degree. For nothing is more natural than the propagation of many from one in animals; and this brings about a proximity of households. Indeed, some people call those who have neighboring (*vicinus*) households foster brothers and children, that is, sons and children of children, that is, grandsons, so that we may understand that such a proximity of households originally springs from the fact that sons and grandsons, having multiplied, founded different households and lived close to one another. Hence, since the multiplication of offspring is natural, it follows that the village society is natural.

28. Then he manifests the same thing by means of signs. First, according to what we see among men. Secondly, according to what used to be said about the gods [§ 30]. He says then, first of all, that, since the neighborhood was established as a result of the multiplication of offspring, from this it came about that at first any city was ruled by a king, and some nations have kings up to this time, even if individual cities do not have their own kings. This is so because cities and nations are established out of those who were subject to a king.

29. And he shows how this sign corresponds to what has already been said by what he adds, namely, that every household is ruled by some very old member, just as sons are ruled by the father of the family. Hence it comes about that the entire neighborhood too, which was formed of blood relations, was ruled on account of this kinship by someone who was first in the order of kinship, just as a city is ruled by a king. That is why Homer has said that each one lays down laws for his wife and children, like the king in a city. Now this rule passed from households and villages to cities, because different villages are like a city spread out into different parts; and thus in former times men used to dwell dispersed through villages and not gathered in one city. So it is clear then that the rule of the king over a city or a nation derived from the rule of an older member in a household or a village.

30. Then he sets down another sign from what used to be said about the gods. He states that because of what has just been indicated, all the pagans used to say that their gods were ruled by some king and claimed that Jupiter was the king of the gods, and this because some men are still ruled by kings; but in former times almost all men were ruled by kings. This was the first regime (*regimen*), as will be said later.[11] Now just as men liken the outward appearance of the gods, that is to say, their forms, to themselves, thinking the gods to be in the image of certain men, so also they liken the lives of the gods, that is to say, their behavior, to their own, thinking them to behave the way they see men behave. Aristotle is here referring, after the manner of the Platonists, to the substances separated from matter and created by only one supreme god, to whom the pagans erroneously attributed both human forms and human habits, as the Philosopher says here.[12]

31.[13] After having treated of the societies ordered to the city, the Philosopher treats here of civil society itself. This treatise is divided into three parts. First, he shows what kind of society the city is. Secondly, he shows that it is natural [§ 34]. Thirdly, he treats of the foundation of the city [§ 46]. Concerning the first point, he shows the condition of the city with reference to three things. First, he shows of what things the city is made up. For, just as a village is made up of several households, so a city is made up of several villages.

32. Secondly, he says that the city is a perfect society; and this he proves from the fact that, since every association among all men is ordered to something necessary for life, that society will be perfect which is ordered to this: that man have sufficiently whatever is necessary for life. Such a society is the city. For it is of the nature (*ratio*) of the city that in it should be found all the things that are sufficient for human life; and so it is. And for this reason it is made up of several villages, in one of which the art of the smith is practiced, in another the art of the weaver, and so of the others. Hence it is evident that the city is a perfect society.

33. Thirdly, he shows to what the city is ordered. It is originally made for the sake of living, namely, that men might find sufficiently that from which they might be able to live; but from its existence it comes about that men not only live but that they live well, in so far as by the laws of the city the life of men is ordered to the virtues.

34. Then he shows that civil society is natural. In this connection he does three things. First, he shows that the city is natural. Secondly, that man is by nature a political animal [§ 37]. Thirdly, he shows what is prior according to nature, whether it is one man, the household, or the city [§ 43]. Concerning the first point, he sets down two arguments, the first of which is as follows. The end of natural things is their nature. But the city is the end of the previously mentioned societies, which were shown to be natural. Therefore, the city is natural.

35. Now, that nature is the end of natural things he proves by the following argument. We call the nature of each thing that which belongs to it when its generation is perfect; for example, the nature of man is that which he possesses once his generation is perfect, and the same holds for a horse and for a house, in such a way, however, that by the nature of a house is understood its form. But the disposition that a thing has by reason of its perfect generation is the end of all the things that precede its generation. Therefore, that which is the end of the natural principles from which something is generated is the nature of a thing. And thus, since the city is generated from the previously mentioned societies, which are natural, it will itself be natural.

11. Aristotle *Politics* 3.15 1286b8–10; cf. 3.14 1285a30–b19.
12. Cf. Aristotle *Metaphysics* 12.8 1074b1–8.
13. In the Leonine edition the first lesson is divided into 1/a and 1/b; 1/b begins here.

36. Then he sets down the second argument, which is as follows. That which is best in each thing is the end and that for the sake of which something comes about. But to have what is sufficient is best. Therefore, it has the nature (*ratio*) of an end. And thus, since the city is a society that has of itself what is sufficient for life, it is itself the end of the previously mentioned societies. Hence it is clear that this second argument is presented as a proof of the minor of the preceding one.

37. Then he shows that man is by nature a political animal. First, he infers this from the naturalness of the city. Secondly, he proves this from man's proper operation [§ 40]. Concerning the first point, he does two things. First, he establishes his thesis. Secondly, he rules out a doubt [§ 38]. He infers then, first of all, from what has already been said that a city is made up of things that are according to nature. And since a city is nothing other than a congregation of men, it follows that man is a naturally political animal.

38. However, there could be a doubt in someone's mind concerning this, due to the fact that the things that are according to nature are found in all men. But not all men are found to be city dwellers. And so, in order to eliminate this doubt, he goes on to say that some men are not political on account of fortune, for instance, because they have been expelled from the city, or because poverty compels them to till fields or tend animals. And it is clear that this is not contrary to what has been said to the effect that man is naturally political, because other natural things too are sometimes lacking on account of fortune, for example, when someone loses a hand through amputation or when he is deprived of an eye. But if a man is such that he is not political on account of nature, it is necessary either that he is bad, as when this happens as a result of the corruption of human nature, or that he is better than man, namely, in so far as he has a nature more perfect than that generally found in other men, in such a way that by himself he can be self-sufficient without the company of men, as was the case with John the Baptist and Blessed Anthony the hermit.

39. In support of this he adduces a saying of Homer cursing someone who was not political because of depravity. For he says of him that he was "companionless" because he could not be contained by the bond of friendship, "lawless" because he could not be contained under the yoke of the law, and "vicious" because he could not be contained under the rule of reason. Now he who is such by nature, being quarrelsome and living without yoke, is at the same time necessarily inclined to be "avid for war," just as we see that asocial birds are rapacious.[14]

40. Then he proves from his proper operation that man is a political animal, more so even than the bee and any gregarious animal, by the following argument. We say that nature does nothing in vain because it always works for a determinate end. Hence, if nature gives to a being something that of itself is ordered to some end, it follows that this end is given to this being by nature. For we see that, whereas certain other animals have a voice, man alone above the other animals has speech. Indeed, although certain animals produce human speech, they do not properly speak, because they do not understand what they are saying but produce such sounds out of a certain habit.

41. Now there is a difference between language and mere voice.[15] Voice is a sign of pain and pleasure and consequently of the other passions, such as anger and fear, which are all ordered to pleasure and pain, as is said in Book 2 of the *Ethics*.[16] Thus voice is given to the other animals, whose nature attains the level where they sense their pleasures and pains, and they signify this to one another by means of certain natural sounds of the voice, as a lion by his roar and a dog by his bark, in the place of which we use interjections. Human speech, on the other hand, signifies what is useful and what is harmful. It follows from this that it signifies the just and the unjust. For justice and injustice consist in this, that some people are treated equally or unequally as regards useful and harmful things. Thus speech is proper to men, because it is proper to them, as compared to the other animals, to have a knowledge of the good and the bad, the just and the unjust, and other such things that can be signified by speech.

42. Since language is given to man by nature, therefore, and since language is ordered to this,

14. Aristotle compares the asocial man to an isolated piece in "draughts," which appears to have been mistranslated as a "flying animal."

15. The distinction between sound, voice, and speech is discussed at greater length by Aristotle in *De Anima* 2.8 419b3 ff.

16. Aristotle *Nicomachean Ethics* 2.5 1105b23.

that men communicate with one another as regards the useful and the harmful, the just and the unjust, and other such things, it follows, from the fact that nature does nothing in vain, that men naturally communicate with one another in reference to these things. But communication in reference to these things is what makes a household and a city. Therefore, man is naturally a domestic and political animal.

43. Then he shows from what has been said that the city is by nature prior to the household and to one individual man by the following argument. The whole is necessarily prior to the part, namely, in the order of nature and perfection. This is to be understood, however, of the part of matter, not of the part of the species, as is shown in Book 7 of the *Metaphysics.*[17] And he proves this as follows: if the whole man is destroyed, neither the foot nor the hand remains, except equivocally, in the manner in which a hand made out of stone can be called a hand. This because such a part is corrupted when the whole is corrupted. Now that which is corrupted does not retain its species, from which it receives its definition. Hence it is clear that the name does not retain the same meaning, and so it is predicated in an equivocal sense.

44. That the part is corrupted when the whole is corrupted he shows by the fact that every part is defined by its operation and by the power by which it operates. For example, the definition of a foot is that it is an organic member having the power to walk. And thus, from the fact that it no longer has this power and this operation, it is not the same according to its species but is equivocally called a foot. The same reasoning holds for other similar parts, which are called parts of matter, in whose definition the whole is included, just as circle is included in the definition of a semicircle, for a semicircle is a half circle. Not so, however, with the parts of the species, which are included in the definition of the whole, as, for example, lines are included in the definition of a triangle.

45. So it is clear then that the whole is naturally prior to the parts of matter, even though the parts are prior in the order of generation. But individual men are related to the whole city as are the parts of man to man. For, just as a hand or a foot cannot exist without a man, so too one man cannot live self-sufficiently by himself when separated from the city. Now if it should happen that someone is unable to participate in civil society because of his depravity, he is worse than a man and is, as it were, a beast. If, on the other hand, he does not need anyone and is self-sufficient as it were, so that he is not part of a city, he is better than a man, for he is, as it were, a god. It remains true, therefore, from what has been said, that the city is by nature prior to one man.

46. Then he treats of the foundation of the city and infers from what has been said that there is in all men a certain natural impulse toward civil society, as also toward the virtues. But nevertheless, just as the virtues are acquired through human exercise, as is stated in Book 2 of the *Ethics,*[18] in the same way cities are founded by human industry. Now the man who first founded a city was the cause of the greatest goods for men.

47. For man is the best of the animals if virtue, to which he has a natural inclination, is perfected in him. But if he is without law and justice, man is the worst of all the animals. This he proves as follows. Injustice is all the more cruel in proportion as it has a greater number of arms, that is, instruments for doing evil. Now prudence and virtue, which of themselves are ordered to the good, belong to man according to his nature. But when a man is evil, he makes use of these as certain arms to do evil; for example, by his shrewdness he thinks up different frauds, and through abstinence he becomes capable of bearing hunger and thirst, so that he might be more persevering in his malice, and so of the other virtues. Hence it is that a man without virtue is most vicious and savage as regards the corruption of his irascible appetite, being as he is cruel and without affection; and as regards the corruption of his concupiscible appetite, he is most evil in relation to sexual matters and greediness for food.

48. But man is reduced to justice by means of the political order. This is clear from the fact that among the Greeks the order of political society and the judgment of justice are called by the same name, to wit, *dikē*. Hence it is evident that the man who founded the city kept men from being most evil and brought them to a state of excellence in accordance with justice and the virtues.

17. Aristotle *Metaphysics* 7.10 1035b3 ff.

18. Aristotle *Nicomachean Ethics* 2.1 1103a14 ff.

BOOK THREE

Lesson Eight

1. [1281a11] After the Philosopher distinguished the regimes according to a difference in ruling offices and made clear the end for which the city is established, in this part he investigates who ought to rule in the city.[19] And since a ruling office (*principatus*) should be assigned according to an excess of some good, he searches for the sort of superiority according to which the offices should be assigned. This is divided into two parts: in the first he asks who ought to rule in the city [Lessons 8 and 9]; in the second he seeks the superiority according to which rule ought to be assigned [Lessons 10 and 11]. The first also has two parts: first he raises a problem, as if reaching a solution; second, he argues against the solution [§ 2]. First, after determining that the regimes ought to be distinguished according to the difference in their rulership (*principatus*), he says that a problem follows: Who in the city ought to have lordship? Since someone must have lordship, either the multitude will dominate, as in a democratic regime, or the wealthy, as in an oligarchy, or the virtuous, as in an aristocracy, or the best one, as in a kingdom, or one worst one, as in a tyranny.[20]

2. He argues against each of these, at least against several. This is divided into two parts: first, he does what was said; second, he investigates in particular whether it is more advantageous for the multitude or a few virtuous men to have lordship [§ 10]. The first in two parts: he shows, first, that it is not advantageous for the multitude or the wealthy to have lordship and, second, also not for one who is morally good [§ 7]...[21]

6. [1281a28] He shows that it is not just for the virtuous, whether few or many, to have lordship.[22] For someone might say that it is true that it is not advantageous for the wealthy few or the multitude to have lordship, but it is advantageous and just for the virtuous to rule and to be lords among all men. But this appears to be false since, if only the virtuous rule, all others will not be honored, as they will not attain the honor of ruling, since the ruling offices are honors. For such offices are a reward for virtue, and honor is [a reward for virtue], as is said in the first and fourth books of the *Ethics*.[23] Therefore, who does not attain a ruling office does not achieve honor. The others would remain without honor from the virtuous rulers, but this is insupportable. For this is a cause of dissension, as all men naturally desire honor and they desire to be honored by the good and the wise who are able to judge better and more correctly. If therefore honor is given to the [virtuous] men, dissension and many evils follow in the city. Hence, it is not just for the virtuous to have lordship.

7. He shows that it is not just for a virtuous one to have lordship. It is divided into two parts: first, he does what is said; second, since someone could say that it is not advantageous for a human being to rule, but rather for the human to be ruled by the law, he shows the contrary [§ 8]. First he says that it is not advantageous for one greatly virtuous to rule, since if one greatly virtuous has lordship, many will lack the honor of the ruling office. But this is insupportable, since from this follows dissensions and tumults in the city, as was said. Moreover, this regime will seem worse than an oligarchy, since in an oligarchic rulership [honors] are given to several men, but in this rulership they are given to one alone. This seems to be worse because, the more an evil is shared, the less it stands out and the more tolerable it is. Clearly, then, it is not advantageous for one virtuous man to have lordship.

8. Since someone could say that the law ought to dominate rather than a human being, he argues against this. And first he sets forth an argument by which it seems that the law ought to have lordship; second, he argues the contrary [§ 9]. First he says it is unjust and vicious for a human being to rule and not the law, since passions are joined to a human. Passions distract the will and make it deviate from the correct end, thus perverting the judgment of reason. The law has no passions; hence, by means

19. The first section in the Spiazzi edition is § 414; the critical edition has the same section divisions as the Spiazzi edition.

20. Throughout both "have lordship" and "dominate" translate forms of *dominari*.

21. Arguments against the claims to rule by the many poor and the wealthy few have been omitted. "Morally good" translates *studiosus*, the Latin rendering of the Greek *spoudaios*; see *Nicomachean Ethics* 5.2 1130b3–5, 9.8 1169a18–33; and Aristotle *Categories* 1.8 10b5–8.

22. This paragraph is keyed to Aristotle's word *epieikēs*, the "good" or "equitable" men (*Politics* 3.6 1281a29).

23. Cf. Aristotle *Nicomachean Ethics* 1.5 1095b27–31, 4.3 1123b35–1124a1.

of law no deviation from the correct judgment of reason comes about. Since it would be better and more just for that to rule which cannot deviate from the correct end than for that to rule which can, and a human can deviate from the correct end, while law truly cannot, it is clear that is just for law to have lordship, not a human being.

9. He argues the contrary. He says that it does not appear to be true that it is just for the law to dominate universally since the laws turn out to be oligarchic and democratic, and such laws are established and ordered for the sake of their end. In these laws the absolutely correct end is not presupposed, as was said before;[24] therefore these laws are not absolutely just. Hence it is clear that it does not matter whether one says that the law rules, or anything else from the [regime] rules, since it always comes to the same unsuitable result, just as was shown before about all of them.

10. [1281a39] Other things having been left aside, he gets down to investigating especially whether it would be more advantageous for the multitude or for a few virtuous men to have lordship...

11. First he shows that it would be more advantageous for the multitude to have lordship than the virtuous few; second, he solves the problem, and another annexed to it [Lesson 9]. The first in two parts: first he states a proposition; second, he argues for it [§ 13]. The first is in two parts: first he makes clear the proposition; second, he sets out a distinction among some things that were mentioned [§ 12]. In the first part, he says that if many men are not simply virtuous, when they come together into some unity they make a particular morally good unity—not in such a way that anyone would do something morally good by himself, and [another] something better—but all of them together would make a particular morally good whole, and they are [together] something better than anyone taken separately. And this he makes clear by a comparison. He says, just as men prepare a supper at the common expense of the city, each one bringing a small amount, but what is gathered from everything brought is a great quantity, so in the matter set out, if there are many, and anyone has some virtue and prudence, when they come together as one they will make something great and virtuous. For in whatever respect one is deficient, another happens to have plenty of it, so that if one is not inclined to fortitude, another will be so inclined, and if one is not inclined to temperance, another will be so inclined, and where one will not be able to foresee things well, another will be able. And if they have thus come together, they will make, as it were, one virtuous and perfect human being. I say a human being having a multitude of senses with which he can discern [things], and a multitude of hands and feet with which he can get to work and be at work. The situation is similar for morals and for the intellect. For when they have come together, from all will be produced, as it were, one human being perfect in intellect as regards the intellectual virtues and perfect in desire as regards the moral virtues. He adduces another comparison, saying that because many joined together are in some degree better than anyone of them, musical and poetic works happen to be better composed and brought to perfection by several than by one. For the arts and sciences were discovered in this way, first one man discovered something and handed it down, perhaps confusedly, and then later another man took it up and added to it and handed down the whole in a more orderly way, and so on in succession until the arts were perfected and the sciences discovered.[25] Clearly some men discover some things, but all together discover all things; and clearly what all have discovered is greater and more perfect than what anyone has done by himself.

12. He makes a distinction between one man who is morally good absolutely and anyone of them out of whom—when they come together as one—something morally good is made.[26] And he says that the morally good men, or the virtuous, differ from anyone of those many (of whom, when they come together into one, something virtuous is made), just as a good person differs from one not good, since virtuous men are simply good, but anyone of those taken by himself is not good, since he is not perfectly virtuous. Moreover, morally good men differ from those taken separately just as pictures made by art differ from true things. It must be understood that the painter who wishes through his art to paint something, such as the image of a human being, carefully looks at the

24. Aristotle *Politics* 3.9 1280a8–1281a11.

25. Cf. Aristotle *Nicomachean Ethics* 1.7 1098a21–26; *Metaphysics* 2.1 993b2.

26. In this paragraph "man" translates *vir* (man as opposed to woman); this is distinguished from "human being" (*homo*) and the frequent masculine demonstrative pronouns, from which "man" is elsewhere interpolated.

good arrangement of the eyes in this person, setting aside the bad arrangement of other parts; in another person he looks at the good arrangement of the hands, setting aside the bad arrangement of other parts; and so he regards the better arrangements of other parts in diverse persons and sets aside the ugly. Out of all these things gathered together he then makes an image more beautiful than anyone of those persons from whom he took something. And clearly anyone of those from whom he has taken a feature has something beautiful, but not the beautiful simply. But whatever is taken from them is beautiful absolutely. So it is likewise in the matter proposed. Anyone of the many has something of virtue but is not simply virtuous: that which is taken from these men absolutely is virtuous absolutely. And this is what he means when he says "Artistic pictures differ from true things, from those from which they are taken," in that the true things taken separately are gathered into one, and the image—composed from the well-arranged parts existing in different persons—is more beautiful than anyone of them, one of whom had beautiful eyes, and another beautiful hands. For he may happen to discover one apart from the rest who has more beautiful eyes than the ones pictured, however much he is deficient in other things; likewise someone may have hands more beautiful than the ones pictured, however much he is deficient in other things; and similarly with other particulars. Likewise, to the purpose, the morally good man differs from anyone of them spoken of before because he has all the good dispositions of soul combined and in one subject. Anyone of them could have one disposition in which he will be able to surpass the virtuous [man], but in absolute terms he would be surpassed by him.

13. Reasoning from the stated proposition, he says it is not clear whether a distinction of this sort would happen to apply to the multitude, and to the whole people with respect to the virtuous few, namely, that the whole multitude would be better than those few virtuous men. Nevertheless, it is impossible for some persons to be better with respect to virtue, for there is a certain bestial multitude in which humans are inclined to bestial acts and have little reason. And in such a multitude it is not true that, if those humans should convene into one, from them something virtuous could be made. This differs from the multitude in which each one has some virtue and prudence, and they are inclined to virtuous action, and in such a multitude it is true that, when they convene into one, something virtuous is made from them. And this is what the Philosopher says, that, by Jove, in one multitude it is not true that the multitude could make something virtuous, but concerning another multitude it can be true. On account of which the argument can be fashioned thus: it is better to be ruled by what is better and more morally good, but it does happen that a particular multitude is better and more morally good than a few virtuous men, as was proven, therefore, etc.

Lesson Nine

1. [1281b21] After the Philosopher has raised the problem of whether it would be more advantageous for the multitude to have lordship than the virtuous, in this part he solves it and annexes to it a certain problem.[27] It has two parts: first, from the things that have been determined he introduces a solution to the question and he poses a connected question; second, he solves the connected question [§ 2]. First he says that because of the things that were said, the problem which was investigated can be solved, whether it is more advantageous for the multitude to dominate than the virtuous few. For from the things said it appears that the multitude is twofold. One is bestial, in which no one has reason or [only] a little, but is inclined to bestial acts. Clearly it is in no way advantageous for this multitude to have lordship since it is without reason both jointly and taken separately. There is another multitude where all have some reason, are inclined to prudence, and are quite persuadable by reason; it is more advantageous for this sort of multitude to have lordship than for the virtuous few. For however much each one is not virtuous, nevertheless what is made from all when they come together is virtuous. And thus appears the solution to the question since, where there is such a multitude, it is more advantageous for it to have lordship than

27. The first section corresponds to Spiazzi edition § 427.

for the virtuous, and where the multitude is not of this sort, but is bestial, in no way is it advantageous. Another question related to this one could be solved by this as a result, namely, whether the multitude and the free men ought to choose their lords and to correct them, and for whom is it advantageous for there to be lords, if it is advantageous. He identifies those about whom this question is raised: they are the sort who do not have some merit or the good of virtue.[28]

Lesson Eleven

11. [1283b27] He solves the problem.[29] First he gives the solution; second, he introduces something for explaining things that were said [Lesson 12, § 1]. First, the Philosopher appears to put together a solution from the arguments that were treated on either side. For it is the custom of the Philosopher that he argues on either side of a particular problem (since arguments on either side arrive at some truth) and puts his solution together from all the arguments. He says therefore that all these things that are argued make it clear that not one of them taken by itself is that upon which the dignity of the ruling office ought to be assigned—neither wealth, nor freedom, nor virtue, and so on with the others—since the multitude, wishing to rule, would argue against those who want to rule because of wealth and virtue. The multitude argues this justly and reasonably, since the better and the wealthier ought to rule in the city, but the multitude happens to be better and wealthier than the few, not because any one person of the multitude is better or wealthier, but all taken together happen to be better and wealthier. For it is possible that some prudent and wise men (*viri*) will be in the multitude, and others very wealthy, and that both these and the other popular sort will be well-persuadable by reason and obedient. For this sort of multitude to rule is better than for a few to do so because two things are required for ruling: knowledge for ruling correctly and power. But in such a multitude these two things are found: since it has wise men and prudent ones, it knows how to rule; since it is a multitude, it has the power of coercion and repelling enemies. Hence the multitude argues rationally against those men because it is better for it to rule. For the multitude gathers the wealthy and the noble, the virtuous and the power of the people; thus, for the whole multitude to rule appears to be more rational wherever it will be possible to find such a multitude. But a base multitude is not persuadable. And because of this one must look to several things, and not only one, in choosing the rulership. This the Philosopher said before.

Lesson Twelve

1. [1283b35] After the Philosopher has explained how, in assigning the ruling office, one ought to look not to one thing, but to many, he introduces something to explain what was said.[30] It is divided into two parts: first, he sets forth a certain problem; second, he declares something that seems to be opposed to certain speeches [§ 3]. The first has two parts: first he states the problem; then he solves it [§ 2]. First he says: it was said that it is more advantageous for a certain multitude to rule than for a few or for one; and that in assigning the rulership, consideration should not be given to one thing, but to many. In this way he is able to solve or confront a problem that some have inquired into and left unsolved: for they have questioned whether the lawgiver who wants to establish correct laws ought to establish them in order to promote the good of the whole multitude, or those who are better in respect of wealth or in virtue (on the assumption that this multitude would have wise and rich men, and others persuadable by and obedient to reason).

28. The remainder of Lesson 9 is omitted.

29. This lesson investigates the problem of "whether the ruling office ought to be assigned according to a superiority in some one of these things," e.g., wealth, birth, virtue, or the worth of the multitude (3.11.3, in reference to *Politics* 1283a26–29). In the prior sections, arguments are given for and against the items in the list; the problem is solved in this section.

30. This section corresponds to Spiazzi § 460.

2. He solves the problem. He says one must accept what is correct and better. But it is better and more correct that the laws should be given for the good of the entire city, the community, and the citizens. For laws are made about whatever promotes the goal of the city; the goal of the city is in truth the good it promotes in common; therefore, the laws should be ordered to the common good of the entire city and the citizens. He is called a citizen who has the virtue by which he can rightly rule and be ruled at different times; but the one and the other follows the presupposition and the form [of the regime], even in different regimes. In a democracy the people choose to dominate for the sake of their freedom, in the oligarchy, for the sake of wealth, but in the best regime, he is called a citizen who chooses to and can be ruled and rule for the sake of a virtuous life.

3. [1284a3] He makes manifest something which appears contrary to certain prior speeches. For it was said that it is more advantageous for a multitude to exercise lordship than for one or more. He means to inquire whether, if one or more are found in the city who surpass all others in virtue, it would be advantageous for that one or those several to have lordship. For if it be advantageous, what was just now determined is not true. Concerning this he does two things: first, he shows that this one would not be a citizen; second, he shows how this one should be disposed to the city, and the city to him [§ 14]. The first in two parts: first, he states his conclusion; second, he argues for it [§ 4]. First he says: if in some city one is found who surpasses all others in virtue, or more virtuous men are found surpassing the others (although not so many that from them a city could be filled or made), and [if] he or they were to surpass the others so much that the virtue of all the others and the civil power (*potentia*) itself could not be equal to the virtue and power of those several, nor to the virtue and power of that one, if he should be but one alone, such a person will not be part of the city, nor those several if more are virtuous.[31]

4. He proves what was said. First, he argues that he or they are not part of the city; second, he responds to an objection that could be made [§ 12]; third, he corrects a certain saying [§ 13]. The first also has three parts, since he proves that this one is not part of the city, first, for political reasons; second, by the actions and speeches of others [§ 6]; third, by a comparison [§ 11]. The first also has two parts, since he proves it by two arguments. The first argument consists in this: it is absolutely just that those who are equal in virtue receive and attain the ruling office equally, and those who are unequal receive it unequally.[32] But this man[33] surpasses or they surpass all others in virtue; consequently this one or those several ought to receive more than all the others. But all the others, because of their number, believe that they ought to receive more than him or those few; hence, if those surpassing in virtue and power should receive more than all the others, they will appear to wrong the others; dissension and tumults will then follow in the city and the proportion in the city will be destroyed. This is insupportable. Wherefore neither he nor they—if there are several outstanding men in the city—will be citizens because such a person surpassing all others in virtue is likely to be almost a god. Regarding this it must be understood that someone can attain to perfect virtue and act for himself in two ways: either through the common condition of human beings, or beyond the common manner or condition of human beings. This comes about through heroic virtue. Virtue is heroic when someone, by means of moral and intellectual virtue, attains the operation of any virtue that is above the common human condition. This is something divine because it comes to exist in a human by means of something divine, which is the intellect; so the Philosopher here says.[34] Such a human, so surpassing all others, he says, exists "as a god."

5. He supplies a second argument, which is: the law which is given in a city is necessary for citizens who are equal in power and birth. This is evident since the law concerns the things that promote the goal of the regime. But in these things not all are adequate to guiding themselves by themselves, and thus they need a law to guide them in the things they do; or the law is given to those who are equal in power and birth in this way because they do not suffice to guide themselves in actions, and such men are called citizens. But to those who so surpass the others in virtue no law is given: for

31. On why a human is "part" of the city, and who is not part of the city, see *Politics* 1.1 1253a26; cf. Thomas Aquinas *Commentary on the Politics* 1.35, 39.

32. On what is "just absolutely," *Politics* 3.9 1280a8–1281a11; Peter *Commentary on the Politics* (*Scriptum super Libros III–VIII Politicorum*) 3.7.

33. Peter uses pronouns here; the word "man" (*vir*) does not appear in the selections from this lesson.

34. On "heroic" virtue, Aristotle *Nicomachean Ethics* 7.1 1145a20; on the intellect as the most divine part, *Nicomachean Ethics* 10.7 1177a13.

they are a law to themselves. And this is evident because the law is a particular ordering according to reason concerning the things that promote the goal of the regime.[35] For these men have this order in themselves and thus are they laws for themselves. Therefore, whoever wanted to give a law to those virtuous men would be ridiculous, since in them the cause for which law is given does not exist. Therefore, such preeminent men will not be citizens.

6. That he who so surpasses all others would not be a citizen, he proves by the deeds of others. It is divided into five parts, as he proves it five times....[36]

10. [1284a38] He gives a fifth argument declaring the same. He says that in some cities particular men having lordship and power over the cities have done the same: for example, when the Athenians, having subjected to themselves the Samians, Chians, and Lesbians by means of treaties between them, surpassed them and ruled them, how much more they then humbled them, oppressing them and neglecting the previously valid treaties. The king of the Persians acted in the same manner when, having subjugated to himself the Medes and Babylonians, he often scattered the prudent and more shrewd among them. Because the king saw that these men were prudent and shrewd, had been in ruling offices, and had lived political lives, and because he feared that if they remained together, they would be able to discover in their wisdom the way to shake themselves free of his yoke, he scattered them, and so these preeminent men were transported to other provinces because of their wisdom. Therefore, this sort of predicament exists universally for all regimes, namely, because those who surpass others in power and virtue are not citizens. This is observed in deviant regimes as men ruling there seek their own proper good, so they banish from the city those who surpass others in power and virtue; and not only those who seek their own good do this, but also those doing the common good....[37]

13. [1284b15] He shows how to correct something said before. For it was said and explained that those surpassing all others ought to be banished from the city, and this appears very harsh. Thus, the Philosopher, wanting to correct this, says that the talk about banishing the man who surpasses all others in power and virtue is somewhat just, but not absolutely just. It would have been better to order the regime from the beginning so that it would not be necessary to make use of banishment, since banishment is dangerous: as they would not be banished if they were not powerful, these men can harm the city. And thus it would have been better to have arranged the city so that banishment would not have to be used, so that from the beginning the city would have been ordered so that it would not have been permitted for someone to surpass a fixed degree of wealth, nor to surpass others in whatever degree, nor for outstanding men to be taken in, but [only] equals; and if someone happened to surpass [the others], he would be corrected and guided somehow. And if there were a "second sailing," that is, if the arrangement were to fall to second-rate, it would be corrected by such banishment, for then banishment would have to be used. But this was not done in certain cities, since those banishing the outstanding men did not look to the common good of the regime, but only to their own proper good, and wickedly and seditiously, and on account of a wicked passion which they had towards those men.

14. He shows how he who surpasses the others in the city with respect to power and virtue should be disposed to the city, and the city to him. And he says that in regimes not correctly arranged, but deviating greatly, it is advantageous to banish such an outstanding man from the city, and it is just—not absolutely—but just on the basis of a supposition, as in a democracy. For in this regime the equality of the citizens is sought, and such superiority is contrary to the goal of this regime, on account of which banishment is just in it. In an oligarchy as well it is not advantageous for such a man to be a citizen since through his power he would turn the regime around to his will. Nor is it advantageous for such a man to exist in a tyranny, since such a man would want very much to tyrannize. Wherefore, clearly in deviant regimes to banish such a man is just, not absolutely just, but just on a supposition, since in these regimes there is no absolute justice, but only justice on a supposition, as was said before.[38] But in the best regime the great problem is

35. Aristotle *Politics* 3.16 1287a18.

36. Discussion of the first four examples is omitted.

37. The argument by comparison and the response to an objection are omitted.

38. Aristotle *Politics* 3.9 1280a8–1281a11; Peter *Commentary on the Politics* (*Scriptum super Libros III–VIII Politicorum*) 3.7.

how it should be disposed to such a man: there is no problem about the man who surpasses all others in fortitude, or in wealth, or in number of friends, but concerning that man who would stand out from all others in virtue or in the goods for the soul, what ought the city do about him? For it must not be said that he should be driven out of the city, or transported elsewhere: for this is against reason, because he is the best. Hence, in no way is he to be driven out. Nor should he be appointed to the ruling office as others are, so that he would rule at one time and not at another. It would be as if we wanted Jove to rule at one time and not at another, and this is ridiculous. And thus what is left, when such a man is the best, what is just and worthy, is for all to obey him joyfully so that he would be king; or, if there were several, that they would be kings and rulers, not sometimes so and sometimes not, but always.

It must be recognized that the Philosopher appears to contradict himself. For he said before that [a] it is better for a certain multitude to rule than for a few to do so. He even said that [b] if one were to rule, the others would be dishonored, which is insupportable. In this part he says that [c] he who surpasses all others is not a citizen; but he who is not a citizen ought not to rule; hence, this man ought not to rule—the contrary of which he says here. To this it must be said that if one should be found who surpasses all others in virtue, he ought to rule. And the reason for this is that he ought more to rule who comes nearer to natural rulership (*principatus naturalis*) and to the rulership of the whole. But he who so surpasses all others in virtue is of this sort: therefore it is advantageous that he alone rule. The major proposition is apparent in animals: for the part that rules is the heart; but the heart is *one* thing and it is the authoritative thing (*principale*) from which virtue is drawn to the individual parts of the body. Furthermore, in the whole world there is one ruler, but the rulership of the whole world is one and the best. Wherefore, in the city, he who is better and who is more one comes nearer to resembling the rulership that is natural and of the whole. Consequently, that rulership will be better in which there is one ruler, and it will be more advantageous for him to rule who, being one, is best. Such is he who surpasses all others in virtue: therefore, it is clear that it is more advantageous for him to rule than another.

The first objection [a] stated above, that it is more advantageous for the multitude to rule, is not valid, since that argument has to be understood [to apply] wherever the regime is made of men equal and similar, and the virtue of one does not surpass the virtue of all the others, which does not apply in the present proposition. Nor is the second objection [b] valid, that if one or several were to rule, all others would be dishonored, because in the correctly ordered regime whoever cares a great deal about status and rank, both his own and another's, wants for himself the honor befitting his rank, wants for another the honor befitting that one's rank, and does not want the honor of another for himself. And if there is one who is preeminent before all others in virtue, everyone wants for him the honor owed to him, and thus they are not dishonored because each and every one has the honor owed to him. Nor is the third objection [c] valid, about which it is said that this man is not a citizen. Indeed, it is true that he who rules by being preeminent in virtue is not a citizen, but is above the citizen, for someone is a citizen in the same way as he is related to the law. But although it is assumed that he should not rule unless he is a citizen, this is not true in the kingly and absolutely best regime, the regime in which he who was said holds lordship.

Lesson Thirteen

1. [1284b35] After the Philosopher has distinguished the regimes according to differences in the ruling offices, he follows up with each one of them. This has two parts: first, he defines each one of the regimes; second, he shows the things by which they are ruined and preserved, at the beginning of the fifth book. The first part is divided into two: first, he determines the best regime, namely, kingship; second, he defines the others, at the beginning of the fourth book. The first part again has two parts: first, he sets forth his aim; secondly, he follows it [§ 2]. He says first that, after the foregoing investigations about the regimes, perhaps it is well to pass on to the consideration of kingship. The reason for this is because, among the correct regimes, kingship is the best and the most correct of the regimes; and thus it is the rule (*regula*) and the measure of all others. For in each and every

genus the best, the most perfect [of that kind] is the measure of the others, on account of which it is necessary first to speak about kingship. Regarding kingship it must be considered whether it is advantageous for a city or province (that must be inhabited) to be ruled by a king or not, but more advantageous for the city or province to be ruled by a certain multitude or by a few particular men (*viri*). First it must be seen whether there are several modes of kingly monarchy and differences [between them], or is there one mode only.

2. He pursues his intention. This has two parts: first, he distinguishes the modes of kingly monarchy; second, he follows up with the principal mode [Lesson 14]. The first in two parts: first, he establishes the different modes of this monarchy; second, he reduces these to two modes [§ 14]. The first again has two parts: first, he establishes the four modes; second, in reviewing them he adds a fifth which is the principal mode [§ 12]. The first in four parts, following the four modes he establishes...[39]

4. [1285a16] He sets forth the second kind of monarchy. This is divided into two parts: first, he establishes the species; second, he reveals its characteristics. First he says, in addition to the kind of monarchy just spoken of, there is another kind by which certain men reign among the barbarians. But those men are called barbarians who are deficient in reason: for "barbarian" almost means foreigner, and because a human being uses reason, those who fall short in reasoning are called barbarians, as was apparent in the first book.[40]

5. He reveals its characteristics. First, that it is voluntary; second, that it is secure. First he says that this sort of kingship, by which certain men rule barbarians, is like a monarchic tyranny, and whoever rules in them rules in accord with both law and ancestral laws. For the customs handed down from parents to children are called ancestral laws, and these men rule according to such laws. And since barbarians are naturally more servile than Greeks, and those in Asia are more servile than those in Europe, because Europe is in the middle between Africa and Asia,[41] and just as it is a mean with respect to location, so the human beings occupy a mean as regards other dispositions. In addition, these barbarians endure despotic rulership without sorrow because they have an inclination to endure it. But what follows natural inclination is voluntary. Hence, it is clear that such men voluntarily endure this sort of despotic rulership, which is that of lord to slave. Hence, it is clear why rulers in this sort of kingdom are likened to tyrants.

6. He says that this sort of monarchy is a secure type. And the reason for this is that the ruler in this sort of kingdom rules on account of his birth and by custom. On account of his birth he holds lordship over the willing, both because it is by ancestral laws and customs that are handed down from the parents, and because it is by birth: for when a father is reigning, they become accustomed to being subject in a way to the son, and when the son reigns later, they submit willingly to him because they are used to it. Moreover, the [father and son] rule in accord with custom and laws, but whatever exists by custom is pleasurable, and so the subjects hate the rulers less. A sign that it is secure is that these barbarians guard their king, since they love him and freely submit to him. But a tyrant is guarded by foreigners, while citizens guard their own kings with their arms since they submit to them willingly and in accord with law. Tyrants rule subjects against their will, and because of this tyrants keep a guard over the citizens, being distrustful of their subjects. It therefore appears that these are two kinds of kingly monarchy...

12. [1285b20] He first summarizes the four modes; then he adds a fifth [§ 13]. First, he says that the kinds of kingly monarchy are four in number. One kind [was] that in which certain men ruled by heroic virtue, in accord with the times. In this monarchy the prince ruled over willing subjects. He was lord in certain defined matters, not in all things. For the king was leader of the army, handed down judgments, and was lord over those things that belonged to divine worship, such as the selection of priests, their punishment, and other such things, although not their possessions.[42] The

39. Discussion of the first, third, and fourth modes of kingship is omitted.

40. Thomas's *Commentary on the Politics* 1.1.20–22, in reference to Aristotle *Politics* 1.1 1252b5–8; cf. 1.6 1255a28–33.

41. Cf. *Politics* 7.7 1327b18 ff.

42. According to Aristotle, the heroic kings presided over those sacrifices that did not belong to the priests (*Politics* 3.14 1285b10–17). Because the Latin translation (*Aristotelis Politica*, ed. F. Susemihl [Leipzig: B. G. Teubner, 1894]) substitutes "possessions" (*substantia*) for "sacrifices" (perhaps the Greek word *ousia* was read in place of *thusia*), the priestly "sacrifices" denied to kings were understood instead as priestly "possessions" denied to kings. Cf. the omitted paragraphs of Peter *Commentary on the Politics* 3.13.10–11, Spiazzi ed. §§ 483–484. Note, however, that it is impossible to know whether the modern Susemihl edition of Moerbeke's translation agrees in these and other details with the particular manuscript translation used by Peter.

second kind is that by which certain men ruled barbarians; in this rulership the king ruled by familial succession and according to law, and it is a despotic rulership. The third kind is called "Aesymneta," and this monarchy is said to be a tyranny by election. The fourth kind is the Laconic, in which a ruler exercises lordship in accord with law. This sort of monarchy was said to be "leadership of the army" in battle, "to put it simply": this he says because the king was not lord of all things, but of those that pertain to battle. This leadership was by familial succession and perpetual. The four kinds differ from one another in this way.

13. He says that there is a fifth kind of kingly monarchy in which the lord rules all things. Thus each nation and city are ordered in the way that household rulership is ordered—in household rulership one rules for the utility of those under him, and he is the lord of all things which are in the household[43]—and so it is in kingship, one rules for the utility of those under him. The rule within the household is a sort of kingdom, and the kingdom is a sort of household rulership over the city and the nation, either one city or one nation, or several cities and nations.

14. He reduces these modes to fewer, namely, to two. First, he does this; second, he shows what must now be said about them [§ 15]. First he says that there are roughly two kinds, "so to speak," of kingly monarchy, to which the others are in some way reduced. He says "so to speak" because distinguishing them by their own articulable forms (*rationes*) they are several, but considering them inasmuch as they are reduced to two, they are two. One is the Laconic, in which someone rules according to law. The other is kingship. The Laconic falls short of kingship because in the Laconic the king rules according to law—he is not lord of all things—but in kingship he rules in accord with his virtue and he is lord of all things. The others are means between these [two], or privations of them, since in some the rulers have lordship over more matters than in the Laconic monarchy, but of fewer than in kingship, such as the monarchy in which someone rules by heroic virtue and even that monarchy which is called elected tyranny. Therefore, clearly from these matters two things remain to be considered. First, concerning leadership of the army, whether it is more advantageous for the leader of the army to be perpetual or not, and whether it is more advantageous that he assume office through familial succession or by election. Concerning kingship, it remains to be considered whether it is advantageous that one be the ruler of all things, or that it be not one, but rather more.

15. He shows what must be said about them. He says that, thinking about the leadership of the army belongs more to the legislator than to the statesman. For leadership of the army exists in all regimes, and so reflection upon it can be dismissed for the present. But kingly monarchy is a kind of regime, on account of which it is necessary to consider and run through the problems that can arise concerning it.

Lesson Fourteen

1. [1286a7] After the Philosopher has distinguished kingly monarchy and established its five modes, he follows up with the first mode and the mode principally spoken of, that is, with kingship.[44] And first he proceeds with certain problems from which the nature of kingship becomes apparent. Second, he shows that the virtue of the best king and the best man is the same, at the end of this, the third book.[45] The first in two parts: first he investigates whether it is more advantageous for the city to be ruled[46] by the best laws or by the best human beings [Lesson 14]; second, whether by one best man (*optimus vir*) or by several [Lesson 15]. The first again has two parts: first he investigates whether it is better for the city to be ruled by the best laws or by the best men; second, he raises other problems [§ 16]. The first once again in two parts: first, he sets forth the problem; second, he pursues it [§ 2]. In the first, therefore, he says the first thing about kingship that must be

43. *Dominus*, "lord," also means "owner" and is etymologically related to *domus*, "household."

44. Does kingship in the "first mode" refer to heroic kingship, since this type appears first in the summary list in the commentary above (3.13.12)? Or does it refer to absolute kingship (*rex simpliciter*, 3.15.1; *Politics* 1287a9), which is called the "principal mode" at 3.13.2 but is the "fifth mode" in the list at 3.13.12? This section corresponds to Spiazzi edition § 489.

45. Peter *Commentary on the Politics* 3.16.8, Spiazzi ed. § 528; cf. Aristotle *Politics* 3.18.1288a39.

46. Until this lesson the word "rule" has translated *principari*; in this lesson it usually translates *regere*.

investigated is whether it is more advantageous for the city to be ruled by the best man or by the best laws.

2. First, he argues that a kingdom is better ruled by the best man; second, he argues the contrary [§ 3]. That a kingdom is better ruled by the best man than by the best laws, he shows by reason and by example. And he says that, in the opinion of some, it is more advantageous for the city to be ruled by the best man because the city is better ruled by him who can make a conclusive determination about all emerging events. But law cannot do this since law speaks only universally, [and says] nothing about particulars. But particulars are infinite and cannot be apprehended; moreover, law does not ordain what it says to emerging matters. But this the best man can do through his prudence, for he judges correctly about what can be done and his desire is upright because of his moral virtue. He then inserts an example before coming to a conclusion: he says that we see this in other arts, that it is not always good to act in keeping with an art as it is written down, because some things are written that, if one were to act in accord with them, it could be harmful to someone, as is apparent in medicine. For a doctor does not in all cases consider what is written in medicine since many things are dismissed by the prudence of the doctor. So among the Egyptians it was written that after the third day the doctor was permitted to stir, that is, to take action to drive out the disease with medicine, since before the third day the nature of the disease could not easily be seen, and if he acted before the third day he was at his own peril. But to observe this in all things was not good: for in some cases to act quickly is advantageous, in others delay is better, according to differences in the disease and the medicine. Likewise in a polity it is not always advantageous to be ruled by what is written or by the law, since sometimes the law is lacking in some particular, and then it needs someone to guide it. Therefore, it is clear that it is better for the kingdom to be ruled by the best man than by the best laws.

3. He argues that it is better for the city to be ruled by the best laws. First he does this; second, he raises an objection in favor of the contrary position [§ 4]. First, he says that it is necessary that this universal speech belong to the men who are ruling because it is better for the city to be ruled by him who does not have conjoined passions than by him who naturally has them, since passions overturn rational judgment. For passion is the movement of the appetite from the imagination of good or evil. But the law does not have passions attached as a human being does; thus, the city is better ruled by the best laws than by the best man.

4. He argues the contrary. First, he raises an objection; second, he removes it [§ 5]. First he says that someone might say, as if in opposition, that however much a human being naturally has passions joined to himself, nevertheless a good human being will deliberate about particulars, and he himself will judge correctly through his capacity for deliberation. Whence it is better that the city be ruled by the best man than by the best law.

5. He removes the objection, leading to another problem out of whose solution appears the solution of this objection. There are two parts: first, he does what was said; second, he infers a corollary [§ 10]. The first again has two parts: first, he sets down the problem; second, he solves it by proving another part [§ 6]. He says first that it is clear that a man ruling in a city must know the laws and make laws. Nevertheless, he need not be the lord of all things: for given that he exercises lordship according to law, he need not exercise lordship in all things, but he must exercise lordship in those things that cannot be brought to a conclusion by law, either not well or simply not at all. And then the problem is whether, in this case, when judging about the particulars that the law cannot well determine, ought one to rule, or many?

6. [1286a26] He solves [the problem] by proving another part. This is divided into three parts, since he proves in this case it is better for several men to pass judgment, by three arguments [§§ 6–8]. He says first that when a particular case emerges which cannot be brought to a conclusion by means of the law, then several men come together and dispute with one another about it, investigating and deliberating about it, and after deliberating, making a judgment. All such things are judgments about particulars regarding which the law cannot come to a conclusion. Several men can do this, and not one, because several deliberating about something can see more than one. Therefore it is clear that one is weaker than several in judging, and his judgment is inferior to the judgment of several. Just as the city is more splendid [made] out of many than out of few, and better is the judgment of many than of one, so also a supper prepared from many dishes (i.e., a supper in which there are many dishes) is more splendid than a simple supper in which there is but one dish. Because of this it is therefore clear that a great crowd,

or several men, will judge better and with greater certainty than any one at all from the crowd. And the reasoning of the Philosopher briefly consists in this: in a case that cannot be determined by the law, judgment ought to be made by him who can judge better and with more certainty. But in such a case several can judge better and more certainly than one; therefore in such a case judgment ought to be made by several men. He explains the minor premise of this argument.

7. He gives a second argument for the same. He says that it is clear that several men are more indifferent than is one or a few with respect to passions that are tumultuous and overturn upright judgment, just as a greater and broader body of water is more indifferent as it flows to more places than a small one. For a little water flows quickly to one place, and likewise one man can be more preoccupied by passions than several. For when one has been preoccupied by some other passion, it corrupts his judgment. Where there are several men, it is difficult for judgment to be corrupted by the impulse of the passion since, if some are impassioned, their passions will nevertheless be restrained by the reason of the others, and thus it will be difficult for them to sin, and most of all if the multitude be not base. But should the multitude consist of those who are free by means of virtue, such men do nothing against the law unless the law is deficient. Let us suppose that the multitude under consideration is this sort. The argument of the Philosopher consists in this: in the case that is not concluded by the law, judgment ought to be made by him who is more indifferent in respect of the passions. But several are more indifferent in respect of the passions than one. Hence, judgment is more appropriately rendered by several than by one...

10. [1286b3] He draws two corollaries. There are two parts, from the two corollaries. First he deduces the preeminence of aristocracy over kingship. He says, if it is so—as was shown—that it would be better for several good [men] to judge than for one, and that the regime in which several wise men rule is an aristocracy, while that in which one wise man rules alone is a kingship, then it is clear that aristocracy is better than kingship, given that both would either have the power or not have it, to this point is aristocracy better than kingship....[47]

16. [1286b22] He brings in other problems. It is divided into two parts, as he poses two problems.[48] First he says that if anyone should say that it is best for the city to be directed by one, there will be a problem concerning how he should be appointed, whether by election or by familial succession. He shows that [the king] ought not be appointed by familial succession because there is a doubt about the succeeding sons, what sort of men are they going to be. And it can happen that the son is wicked: if that one would be appointed by familial succession, a wicked man will assume the ruling office. But this is insupportable; therefore, he must not be appointed by succession. But because someone might perhaps say that a good father, who sees that his son is wicked, will hand over the kingdom not to his son but to someone else, [the Philosopher] refutes the objection and says that this is difficult to believe, a father dismissing a son and handing the ruling office to another. For this is above the common capacity of human beings. He must leave the ruling office to him whom he loves more, and what is nearer by nature is loved more by nature. But a son is like another father, and thus just as the father loves himself more than any other, so after himself he naturally loves his natural son more than any one else. Hence, he more readily leaves the kingdom to him than to any other.

And it must be understood that by its essence (*per se*) it is always better to be appointed to the throne by election than by succession. But succession is better in fact (*per accidens*). The first statement is apparent: it is better for the ruler to be appointed in whatever mode it comes to pass that, by its essence, the better man is obtained; but it so happens that the better man is appointed by election than by familial succession, since he who is discovered from among several within the entire multitude is better than one alone. And election *per se* is appetite determined by reason.[49] Nevertheless, *per accidens* it is better to appoint a ruler by familial succession because in an election there often comes to be dissension among those voting. Moreover, when the voters are wicked, they come to elect a wicked man. Both of these are bad for the city. Furthermore, being accustomed to one person exercising lordship does much to render him

47. The second corollary, on how each regime devolves from another, is omitted.

48. Peter's discussion of the second problem is omitted.

49. Peter alludes to Aristotle's definition of choice (*electio*); cf. *Nicomachean Ethics* 6.2 1139b6.

subject to the other, and because the subjects become accustomed to the son's father while he is reigning, they are inclined to be subjects of the son. Besides, it is rather harsh and strange that someone who is your equal today will be your lord and ruler tomorrow. And, thus, *per accidens* it is better that the ruler be appointed by familial succession than by election.[50]

Lesson Fifteen

1. [1287a1] After the Philosopher has investigated whether it would be more advantageous for the city to be ruled by the best laws or the best man, in this part he investigates whether it would be more advantageous for it to be ruled by one best man or by several.[51] It is divided into two parts: first he gives his intention and the reason for it; second he follows up on it [§ 2]. First he says that, after what was said before, it remains to speak about the absolute king (*rex simpliciter*) who in all things acts and rules according to his will and not according to law, and not following what is set in motion by another. This must be considered. The reason for this is that he who rules according to law is not a king absolutely, nor is his rulership a species of kingship, as was said above. And that it is not a distinct species of kingship is apparent since the ruling office which leads the army is found in all regimes, such as democracies and aristocracies...[52]

2. It is divided into three parts: first, he poses a problem; second, he lays out the argument for it [§ 3]; third, he determines the truth [Lesson 16]. First, resuming his intention, he says that we must now speak about absolute kingship in which someone exercises lordship in all things according to his will and not according to law. It appears from certain matters that it is neither according to nature, nor from a natural inclination, nor consonant with reason for one to be lord over all things according to his will where the city consists of those similar in virtue, that is, similar in natural disposition.

3. He shows that it is not natural for one to exercise lordship over several who are similar to him in virtue and natural disposition. It is divided into four parts, following the four arguments he adduces for this problem.[53] The first in two parts: first, he sets out the argument; second, he infers from this that it is better that the city be ruled by the law than by a man (*vir*) [§ 4]. First he says that justice is the same and virtue is the same among men similar in natural disposition and in virtue. For we say that justice is equality.[54] Therefore, for those having the same virtue and natural disposition, justice and standing are the same, since their virtue is the same, and since their standing follows upon their virtue; and for those not having the same virtue, neither their standing nor their justice is the same. If we therefore posit that some are similar in virtue, their standing will be the same and what is just for them will be the same; thus, it is not advantageous for a particular one to lord over these according to his will, since their standing would not be the same. And just as we see in natural things that it is not advantageous for unequal [animals] to have equal provisions because what is beneficial for one is harmful for another (for some are hot, others cold, and it is manifest that these need different victuals), it is the same way with honors. For if unequals in virtue should receive what is equal, it is unjust, and if equals what is unequal, it is likewise unjust. But if some should be similar in virtue and natural disposition, and one rules the others according to his will, clearly equals are receiving what is unequal. This is unequal and unjust. Therefore clearly it is not advantageous for one to lord over those equal in virtue and natural disposition.

4. [1287a16] From what was said [that it is better for several men to rule than for one man to rule] he infers that it is better for the best law to rule than for the best man (*optimus vir*) to do so. First, he makes the inference; second, he adduces an argument in proof of it [§ 6]. The first in two parts: first, he does what was said; second, he infers from the same that it is better for the law to rule than [even] for several best [men] to do so [§ 5]. First, as noted, he says it is just that men equal in virtue

50. Peter's discussion of the second problem is omitted.

51. The first section corresponds to Spiazzi ed. § 507.

52. Peter *Commentary on the Politics* 3.12.15. The remainder of the section is omitted.

53. The arguments begin in paragraphs 3, 11, 12, 14; only the first and last are included here.

54. Aristotle *Politics* 3.12 1282b18–28.

and natural disposition have what is equal, because of which it is clear that, if several are equal or similar in virtue and natural disposition, one is not more born to rule or be subject than another, and thus one ought no more to rule another. And since it is necessary that someone rule, it is just for all to rule in the same way, in turn and according to a certain arrangement (*ordo*). But ruling according to an arrangement and in turn is a particular law, for law is a certain arrangement. Therefore clearly it is better and more desirable for the law to rule than for some one citizen.

5. From the same he infers that it is better for the law to rule than several men, although few. And he says that according to the same argument, if it is better that several rule than one, it is nevertheless better for them to rule according to law than by their own wills, and it is better for them to be appointed to serve and to minister to the law. For just as was said before, equal honor and standing are owed to those equal in virtue; therefore, if the city is made from those equal in virtue, equal honor is owed to them. Therefore, it is not advantageous for some of them to always rule, but it is necessary there exist various ruling offices so that certain men rule [in one] way, and others in others in accord with a particular arrangement. Therefore, they must rule according to a certain arrangement, but this is a certain law. Therefore, if it is better for several men to rule than for one, clearly it is better for several to rule in accord with the law than by their own wills.

6. He advances an argument for proving that it is better for the law to rule, or for a human being in accord with the law, than for a good man (*vir bonus*) to rule according to his own will. It is divided into two parts: first, he does what is said; second, he refutes an argument by comparison, advanced before, that had proved it would be better for a human being to rule than for the law [§ 8; cf. 3.14.2]. The first again has two parts: first, he shows the matters about which the law speaks, and those which ought to be left to the ruler; second, he poses an argument for proving it is better for the law to rule than for a human being [§ 7]. In the first he says that whatever cannot be determined by the law, neither can a human being on his own make known and manifest except by prudence and by great and long experience. Truly law by itself ordains nothing about particulars, but only generalities. For law is a general declaration, as it is said, thus it is necessarily lacking in some particular, and particulars of this sort left to the ruler ought to be managed and judged by him in accord with a correct decision. Moreover, if something were found to be better according to reason than what the established law (*lex posita*) would determine, it must be left to the ruler so that he himself ordains [it] on behalf of the law. So two things are discharged to the ruler: the first is to judge and correctly manage particulars through the law, where it is possible for this to be done by law; the second is that, where the written law is deficient in some particular case, he should guide [matters], and this is done through the virtue called *epieikēs* [equity]. Or if the established law is not arranged well in accord with reason, it should be suspended by the ruler so that, the law suspended, he may discover a better law—either the ruler by himself or with the consent of the multitude—and ordain it through law.

7. He advances an argument for proving that it is better for the law to rule than the best man according to his own will. And it must be understood that anything whatever is most of all called "that" or named after that which is most authoritative (*principale*) in it, as is said in the tenth book of the *Ethics*.[55] In a human being the intellect is truly authoritative. And thus a human being is most of all called an intellect or [called a human being] on account of the intellect, and thus a human is said to be at work most of all when he is working with the intellect.[56] It happens that sometimes a human being is working with the intellect such that he is not impeded by sensation at all, nor does he use sensation except inasmuch as is necessary to him, and then a human is said to be absolutely (*simpliciter*) at work, since he is working in conformity with what is more simple in him. But because he needs sensation, sometimes the sensitive appetite comes to be joined to the working of the intellect, and then he is called a composite human. And when a human is working in conformity with the intellect and is not impeded by sense at all, then he is working most of all in conformity with intellect and reason, and with something divine existing within, both because the intellect is something

55. Aristotle *Nicomachean Ethics* 10.7 1178a2–4; Thomas Aquinas *Commentary on the Ethics* 10.11.12 [§ 2109]. Cf. *Nicomachean Ethics* 9.4 1166a23; Thomas Aquinas *Commentary on the Ethics* 9.4.11 [§ 1807].

56. Aristotle *Nicomachean Ethics* 10.7 1177a13–16; Thomas Aquinas *Commentary on the Ethics* 10.10.1–5 [§§ 2080–2085].

divine in him, and because his work is above the common mode of humans. Therefore he says, whoever instructs that the intellect rule—or a human being [rule] in conformity with the intellect, so that sensitive appetite (somehow withdrawing) is not joined to it—wishes or instructs God [to rule], that is, that a human being rule in conformity with something divine and that the law rule. He who wishes a human being to rule accompanied by the sensitive appetite, appoints a beast, that is, he appoints something through which a human is similar to beasts, sensitive appetite. But for something divine to rule is better than what is connected to a beast; for if a human being with sensitive appetite rules in conformity with intellect, when there are passions in the appetite that subvert [the intellect] and so subvert the judgment of reason, it will happen at last that the ruler, falling into concupiscence and rage, will kill good and virtuous men (*viri*). But this is insupportable. Therefore it is better for a human being to rule absolutely (*absolute*) through the intellect than by means of an intellect connected to sensitive appetite. Therefore, when the law is without passion and is in conformity with reason, what remains is that the law itself is intellect without sensitive appetite. Hence, it is better that the law rule than a human being.

8. [1287a32] He refutes an argument advanced before based on a comparison with the productive arts, for the sake of proving that it would be better for a human to rule than the law, first, by the destruction of the premise [that it is not good to work by art, §§ 8 and 9]; second, by disproving the similarity [of art to politics, § 10]. The first in two parts, because he proves twice that what was assumed is not true...

9. Second, he declares that the premise is false. He says that it is better to work by that through which [one] can work more correctly and assuredly. But one can work more correctly and assuredly by art than by reason, since one working by reason comes to have passions that subvert judgment. And because of this doctors who are ill send for other doctors so that they themselves can be cured because of this, namely, that however much ability they have in the art, they are in suffering (*passione*), and men disturbed by passion cannot make correct judgments. Likewise those who are coaches of young people, when exercising, call in other coaches so that they may see if they are performing well themselves, as they are not able to rightly judge about their own affairs, since in many things they do not judge well nor truly about themselves. Therefore clearly the judgment of reason is disturbed by passions. But one working by art does not have passions in this manner, wherefore he is able to judge better and more assuredly [by art] than by reason. And then [the Philosopher] infers a certain conclusion that follows not immediately from what was just said, but from what was said before, and it follows thus: it was said that it is not just for a man (*vir*) to rule anyone similar and equal in virtue and in natural disposition, but it is just that they rule in turn and by an arrangement. And this is to rule according to law; therefore, it is just to rule and to work in accord with law. Therefore, since the law is a mean, plainly those seeking justice seek the mean.

10. He refutes the argument by destroying the similarity. He says that the argument for this falls short in another way, for there is no resemblance between the arts and politics. And this is apparent since the laws of regimes—which are made firm by custom because humans have become used to living according to custom—are more authoritative and concern more authoritative things than the laws of productive arts. For the laws of regimes concern possible actions ordered to the goal of the regime and the things by which the soul is perfected, whereas the laws of an art (or the things which belong to an art) concern the things by which the body is perfected, such as medicine. Thus, just as the soul is better than the body and more authoritative,[57] so the laws concerning the things by which the soul is perfected are more authoritative and better than those things concerning the dispositions of and benefits to the body. It is therefore clear that however much a human being following an art judges assuredly and with certitude, nevertheless not with more certitude than [he judges] by the laws which follow custom since these, and not the ones by art, are more authoritative....

14. [1287b26] He gives a fourth argument.[58] He says that it is insupportable to say that one would perceive with two eyes and two ears better than many [men] with many ears and many eyes. And it is absurd to say that one would work with two hands and two feet better than many men with many hands and many feet. It is likewise absurd

57. Cf. Aristotle *Politics* 1.5 1254b5–6.

58. The fourth argument is that it is not natural for one to rule over several who are similar in virtue; see above 3.15.3.

that one would judge better by his own prudence than would many. And we see that rulers make for themselves many eyes and many hands and feet because they make for themselves many co-rulers: for he summons these feet and hands and eyes because he discerns and works by means of them. Yet they make co-princes of men who are friends to him *and* to the principality because, if they were not friends of one, but friends of the other, such as friends of the principality, they would care for the good not of the prince, but of the principality.[59] Furthermore, if they did not love the principality, but loved the prince, they would not care for the good of the principality. But co-princes ought to have a care for the good of the prince and of the principality. And thus they make co-princes friends to themselves and to the principality, because friends do nothing except what is correct and respectable, and if they are friends to the prince and the principality, they attend to the good of each. It is in this way that friends ought to be similar. Therefore, if these men ought to be co-princes with him, clearly men similar and equal in virtue ought to rule in a similar fashion. Therefore, it is not natural for one to rule according to his will over anyone similar and equal to him in regard to virtue.

And he appends a recapitulation saying, these are the things that cause doubt about kingship. And it must be understood about what was said that the prince takes for himself co-princes that are friends to him and to the principality, because the form (*ratio*) of the prince is taken from the form of the principality, and the good of the prince is ordered towards the good of the principality. And thus he who loves the prince in accord with what a prince is, loves the principality. But he who rules can be considered in two ways, either as a prince or as this sort of human being. And thus someone can love him either as a prince or as such a human being. If he should love him as the prince, he loves the principality, and procuring the good of one, he would procure the good of the other. If he should love him as this sort of man or that, he need not love the principality, and then he would procure his good inasmuch as he is this sort of man or that, not having a care for the good of the principality.

Lesson Sixteen

1. [1287b36] After the Philosopher has given arguments for showing that it is not natural for one, on the basis of virtue, to rule over many, in this part he determines the truth.[60] It has two parts: first, he puts forward his intention with a certain distinction; second, he makes it clear [§ 2]. In the first part he says: it was said that it is not advantageous for one to lord over many men who are similar. But perhaps it is advantageous for certain men, but not advantageous for others. It must be understood that one thing is just and beneficial according to its nature when ordered to a despotic [nature], another is just and expedient when ordered to a political [nature].[61] And it is clear that these are not one and the same. This is apparent because a rulership is despotic in which someone rules another who was born to be subject, as a slave is, and he rules firstly and principally for his own good. A rulership is political in which someone rules men free and equal in respect of virtue, and for the good of the subjects. Therefore, just as these rulerships are different, so also what is just in the arrangement for one rulership is not just in the arrangement for the other. Clearly, then, despotic justice and political justice are not the same. In a tyranny and in other deviant regimes there is no justice absolutely because there is no justice absolutely in regimes in which the end is contrary to nature. But in deviant regimes the end is contrary to nature: for regimes of this sort are contrary to nature; consequently, in these regimes there is no justice absolutely or according to nature.

2. He gives the solution in detail. First he states that among men similar in nature and equally well-disposed to virtue, it is not just for one to be the lord except in a certain manner; second, he explains what is this manner [§ 3].[62] He says in the first part that, clearly from what is stated

59. "Prince" and "principality," like "ruler" and "rulership" elsewhere, translate *princeps* and *principatus*.

60. This section corresponds to Spiazzi ed. § 521.

61. Aristotle's three possibilities (despotic, kingly, and political) in the Latin translation (ed. Susemihl) are here reduced to two (despotic and political).

62. The explanation that begins in § 3 concludes in § 5.

above, it is neither according to nature, nor advantageous, nor just, for one to rule men similar and equal with respect to virtue, whether he rules not according to law but according to his will (as if he himself were the law), or he rules not according to his own will, but according to law, [and] whether the prince is good and the subjects are good, or he is bad and they are bad, or he is better and has preeminence over all others in virtue, unless [he is better] in a certain manner. This is apparent from the things said. For those similar in virtue, as was said, it is just that [their] standing be the same; but if one were to rule those similar in virtue, their standing would not be the same. Moreover, it was said before that several can see more things and judge more correctly than one. From these things it is clear that, for those who are similar in regard to virtue, it is not just that one from among them rule...

5. [1288a15] He explains what is that manner by which it is advantageous for one to rule many, and how. First he does it; second, he recapitulates it [§ 6]. In the first he says that if it should happen that one entire family, or one among others in a certain family, so differs from the others with respect to virtue that its virtue surpasses the virtue of all the others, it is just that this family be royal, or, if he be one, that this man[63] be [king], and that there be one kingship and lordship of all. For what is according to nature is that he who surpasses in respect of virtue should be lord of the others. Therefore, if the virtue of someone should surpass the virtue of the others, it is natural that this man be king and lord. Not only because of this is it just that he is king—because he absolutely surpasses [the others], [but] as it was said before, all those who have established regimes, such as aristocrats, oligarchs, and democrats, have said that it is just for him who surpasses [others] to rule. For all those thinking about this superiority have said that he who surpasses the others ought to rule, although they have not specified the same [kind of] superiority (these in virtue, those in wealth, others in freedom). But it is advantageous for him who surpasses the others in virtue to rule; nor is it advantageous to kill, banish, or chase him out: for this would remove the measuring rule (*regula*) for living from the city or province. Moreover, it is not advantageous for this man to rule not partially (rather than over all things) and for the sake of some certain time (rather than always) on the grounds that the part is not born to surpass its whole. But he surpasses all others in virtue; therefore, the others are a part with regard to him. Consequently, they are not born to surpass him, but he, always surpassing more in respect of virtue, ought to rule. Hence it remains that he ought to rule all men and always, he ought to be the lord, and all these ought to obey such a man just as if from natural inclination.

But it must be understood that, however many may be appropriate in virtue and education, nevertheless sometimes one must rule in a kingly rulership. For there exists a particular multitude of virtuous men, and because of this it has standing and is called a "political" multitude. The other [multitude] which is greatly deficient in reason is called "despotic." For either multitude it is advantageous to be ruled by a kingly rulership: the first, insofar as there exists *one* who surpasses all others in virtue; for the other it is advantageous to be ruled by one inasmuch as there is *anyone* who surpasses all others in virtue. But they differ since rulership in the first differs greatly from the despotic kind, but rulership in the second is very near [to the despotic] because the multitude is deficient in reason, whereas in the first it is not. They also differ in that the second kingship lasts longer than the first because less virtue suffices for the second than for the first, and thus one who surpasses the others can easily be found [in the second], not in the first. For because all attain reason in the first multitude, it happens that some are able to discover various ways and means of driving out the prince. Not so in the second, since there they are deficient in reason and thus unable to discover means or precautions against the ruler. Thus, the second is more durable than the first.[64]

63. Neither the word for "man" (*vir*) nor the word for human (*homo*) appears in this section; "this man" translates the masculine demonstrative pronoun (*ille*).

64. The last paragraphs are omitted. They conclude a question addressed in the opening of Book 3, whether the virtue of the best man and that of the best citizen are the same.

TWENTY-THREE

BOETHIUS OF DACIA

On the Supreme Good

Translated by John F. Wippel

Often very little information has come down to us about the lives of our authors, but our ignorance is especially acute in the case of Boethius. We know that he came from Denmark and that he was a master in the faculty of arts in Paris ca. 1270, probably as a secular cleric. He appears to have been embroiled in the controversies surrounding the so-called Latin Averroists in the 1270s: several manuscripts of the propositions condemned in 1277 mention Boethius, together with Siger of Brabant, as the masters principally connected with the condemned propositions.[1] Boethius, however, was not summoned before the inquisitor, as Siger was in 1276: from this it is inferred that he had ceased teaching in Paris prior to 1276. A bibliographical catalogue for the Dominican order, written in 1315, gives the name of Boethius together with his works; it therefore appears that he became a Dominican sometime after his active period as a master of arts in Paris. Nothing is known of the time or place of his death.

After enjoying some notoriety in the 1270s, Boethius fell into obscurity; *On the Supreme Good* was discovered only in 1924. Several of the manuscripts of this short treatise are anonymous; in three manuscripts the treatise is attributed to Thomas Aquinas. It is not certain when it was composed. On the one hand, because several manuscripts of the treatise refer to Book Lambda of the *Metaphysics* as Book 11 rather than 12, it is inferred that the treatise was written before 1270—that is, before the revision of the Latin translation of the *Metaphysics* by William of Moerbeke. On the other hand, because Boethius says very little about how the happiness he describes is related to the supernatural end of man and salvation through Christ, some have inferred that the discourse was likely written after 1272, at which time the masters and bachelors of arts in Paris had been explicitly forbidden to discuss questions of theology. As the treatise argues that the supreme good for man is the exercise of the speculative intellect, and that virtuous actions are those that tend in some way to this end, the treatise is sometimes thought to be the source of the proposition condemned by the bishop of Paris in 1277 "that there is no more excellent state than to study philosophy" (Prop. 1). The treatise may also be the target of Proposition 171—that Aristotle's intellectual and moral virtues suffice to dispose one for eternal happiness—although it does not

1. John F. Wippel, *Boethius of Dacia* (Toronto: Pontifical Institute of Medieval Studies, 1987), 3 n. 10.

explicitly take the controversial step of extending the necessary conditions of happiness in this life to the next.[2] Yet, whatever bearing the condemnation of 1277 has on the treatise, Boethius remains notable for arguing more emphatically than any Christian author represented here that the life of the philosopher is the best and highest human life, and that actions must be weighed with regard to whether they foster that way of life.

Several propositions condemned in 1277 have been associated with another work by Boethius, *On the Eternity of the World.* This treatise argues that everything graspable by human reason should be disputed by the philosopher; that the natural philosopher, on the basis of the principles of his science, is unable to consider a motion that is first in time; that the natural philosopher, as natural philosopher, should deny anything (such as the creation of the world in time) that is contrary to the principles of his science and thus destroys his science; and, finally, that it is nevertheless true on the basis of faith that the world was created in time by God. It is likely that the condemned Proposition 6 was directed at this treatise, and several other propositions are thought to be directed at it (Props. 2, 191, 214–216).[3] It is disputed, of course, whether the condemned propositions, as stated, reflect a correct understanding of the intention of Boethius. Boethius is also noted for his commentaries on logic and grammar (*Quaestiones super Librum Topicorum,* ed. N. J. Green-Pedersen and J. Pinborg, Corpus Philosophorum Danicorum Medii Aevi 6.1 [Copenhagen, 1976] and *Quaestiones super Priscianum Maiorum,* ed. J. Pinborg and H. Roos, Corpus Philosophorum Danicorum Medii Aevi 4 [Copenhagen, 1969]). He is noted especially for his role in the development of "modistic" grammar, according to which the various ways (modes) of being determine the various modes of conceiving (the subject of logic), and the modes of conception in turn determine the modes of signification (e.g, parts of speech, case, gender).[4] By this account the modes of signification are the same across all languages (although the assigned sounds differ, of course, for each language), and grammar, therefore, has universals as its subject and is raised to the status of a science.

The translation of *On the Supreme Good,* by John F. Wippel, is taken from *Boethius of Dacia: On the Supreme Good, On the Eternity of the World, On Dreams* (Toronto: Pontifical Institute of Mediaeval Studies, 1987). We are also greatly indebted to Wippel's introduction for much of the information given above. In the various manuscripts this short work is given other titles, including "The Proper Life for Philosophers," "On the Human Good," and "The Life of the Philosopher." The translation is made from the critical edition, *Boethii Daci Opera: Opuscula De Aeternitate Mundi, De Summo Bono, De Somniis,* ed. N. G. Green-Pedersen, Corpus Philosophorum Danicorum Medii Aevi 6.2 (Copenhagen, 1976), 368–77. Bracketed, indented numbers within the text indicate the page numbers of this edition.

ON THE SUPREME GOOD

Since in every kind of being there is a supreme possible good, and since man too is a certain kind (*species*) of being, there must be a supreme possible good for man. I do not speak of a good which is supreme in the absolute sense, but of one that is supreme for man; for the goods which are accessible to man are limited and do not extend to infinity. By reason let us seek to determine what the supreme good is which is accessible to man.

The supreme good for man should be his in terms of his highest power, and not according to the vegetative soul, which is [also] found in plants,

2. David Piché, with Claude LaFleur, *La condamnation parisienne de 1277* (Paris: J. Vrin, 1999), 243 ff.; Luca Bianchi, "Felicità terrena e beatitudine ultraterrena: Boezio di Dacia e l'articolo 157 censurato da Tempier," in *Chemins de la pensée médiévale: Études offertes à Zénon Kaluza,* ed. Paul J. J. M. Bakker (Brepols: Fédération Internationale des Instituts d'Études Médiévales, 2002).

3. Wippel, *Boethius of Dacia,* 11, 18; Wippel cites Roland Hissette, *Enquête sur les 219 articles condamnés à Paris le 7 Mars 1277* (Louvain: Publ. Universitaires; and Paris: Vander-Oyez, 1977), 284–85, 307–9.

4. Sten Ebbesen, "The Paris Arts Faculty: Siger of Brabant, Boethius of Dacia, Radulphus Brito," in *Medieval Philosophy,* ed. John Marenbon, vol. 3 of *Routledge History of Philosophy,* (London: Routledge, 1998), 269–90, esp. 273–78; see also "Speculative Grammar," in *The Cambridge History of Later Medieval Philosophy,* ed. N. Kretzmann, A. Kenny, and J. Pinborg (Cambridge: Cambridge University Press, 1982), 254–69. For an example of Boethius's thinking on logic, see "The Sophisma 'Every Man Is of Necessity an Animal,'" in *The Cambridge Translations of Medieval Philosophical Texts,* vol. 1, *Logic and Philosophy of Language,* ed. N. Kretzmann and E. Stump (Cambridge: Cambridge University Press, 1988), 480–510.

nor according to the sensitive soul, which is [also] found in animals and from which their sensual pleasures arise. But man's highest power is his reason and intellect. For this is the supreme director of human life both in the order of speculation and in the order of action. Therefore, the supreme good attainable by man must be his by means of his intellect. Therefore, men who are so weighed down by sense pleasures that they lose intellectual goods should grieve. For they never attain their supreme good. They are so given to the senses that they do not seek that which is the good of the intellect itself. Against these the Philosopher protests, saying: "Woe to you men who are [*370*] numbered among beasts and who do not attend to that which is divine within you!"[5] He calls the intellect that which is divine in man. For if there is anything divine in man, it is right for it to be the intellect.[6] Just as that which is best among all beings is the divine, so also that which is best in man we call divine.

Moreover, one power of the human intellect is speculative and the other practical. This is clear from this fact, that man theorizes about certain objects which he does not actively cause, e.g., eternal things, and actively causes others under the intellect's direction whereby he realizes a means which can be chosen in human acts. From this, then, we know in general that these two intellectual powers are present in man.[7] But the supreme good accessible to man in terms of the speculative power of his intellect is knowledge of what is true and delight in the same. Knowledge of what is true gives delight. An intelligible object gives delight to the one who knows it. And the more wondrous and noble the intelligible object and the greater the power of the apprehending intellect to comprehend perfectly, the greater the intellectual delight. One who has tasted such delight spurns every lesser pleasure, such as that of sense. The latter is, in truth, less, and is more base. And the man who chooses such pleasure is, because of that pleasure, more base than one who chooses the former.

It is because of this, because the object known gives delight to the one who knows, that the Philosopher [Aristotle] in Book 12 of the *Metaphysics* maintains that the first intellect enjoys the most pleasurable life.[8] [*371*] For since the first intellect is the most powerful in understanding and the object which it knows is the noblest, its essence itself—for what nobler object can the divine intellect have than the divine essence?—therefore, it has the life of greatest delight. No greater good can befall man in terms of his speculative intellect than knowledge of the totality of beings which come from the first principle and, by means of this, knowledge of the first principle insofar as such is possible, and delight in it. Therefore, our conclusion above follows: that the supreme good available to man by means of his speculative intellect is knowledge of what is true in individual cases, and delight in the same.

Likewise, the supreme good available to man in terms of his practical intellect is the doing of good, and delight in the same. For what greater good can befall man in terms of his practical intellect than to realize a fitting means in human action and to delight therein?

No man is just save him who takes delight in acts of justice. The same must be said of the acts of the other moral virtues. From what has been said one can evidently conclude that the supreme good open to man is to know the true, to do the good, and to delight in both.

And because the highest good possible for man is happiness (*beatitudo*), it follows that human happiness consists in knowing the true, doing the good, and taking delight in both. The military profession is prescribed in a state by the lawmaker for this reason, that when enemies have been expelled, citizens may devote themselves to intellectual virtues in contemplating the true, and to moral virtues in doing good, and thus live a happy life; for the happy life consists in these two.[9] [*372*] This then is a greater good, which man can receive from God and which God can give to man in this life. With reason does a man desire a long

5. Neither the editors of the treatise, Grabmann and Green-Pedersen, nor the translator has succeeded in finding the quoted passage in Aristotle.

6. Cf. *Nicomachean Ethics* 10.7 1177a14–18.

7. Cf. Aristotle *Metaphysics* 6.1 1025b18–28 for the distinction between theoretical, productive, and practical thought and, corresponding to this, sciences. As used there and as Boethius here uses the term "speculative," it is captured in English by contemplation that is sought for its own sake.

8. Aristotle *Metaphysics* 12.7 1072b24. Note that Green-Pedersen follows another manuscript tradition and reads this as Book 11 of the *Metaphysics* (p. 370 n. 42). If this is indeed the original reading, it would suggest a date prior to 1270, the widely accepted date for William of Moerbeke's revision of the Latin translation of Aristotle's *Metaphysics*, which included his translation of Book 11. This means, of course, that Book 12, by our numbering, had until then been known as Book 11. On this, see J. Weisheipl, *Friar Thomas d'Aquino: His Life, Thought, and Works, with Corrigenda and Addenda* (Washington, DC: The Catholic University of America Press, 1983), 235, 474.

9. Cf. Aristotle *Nicomachean Ethics* 10.7 1177b4–1178a8; Thomas Aquinas *Commentary on the Nicomachean Ethics* 10.11 (Leonine ed., 47.2: 586–88).

life who desires it for this, to become more perfect in this good. He who shares more perfectly in that happiness which reason tells us is possible for man in this life draws closer to that happiness which we expect in the life to come on the authority of faith.[10]

And since so great a good is possible for man, as has been said, it is right (*dignus*) for all human actions to be directed toward that good, so as to attain it. All actions regarding a certain law are right and proper when they tend toward the end of the law, and better the more closely they approach the end of the law. Actions which are opposed to the end of the law or which are weak (and not perfect according to the precepts of the law) or even indifferent (without either being opposed to the end of the law or in accord with its precepts), all such actions are sin against that law to a greater or lesser degree as is clear from what has been said. The same is true in man himself. All designs and deliberations, all actions and desires of man which tend to this supreme good which is available to man according to the above, these are right (*rectus*) and proper. When man so acts, he acts in accord with nature. For he acts for the sake of the supreme good, to which he is ordered by nature. And when he so acts he is properly ordered, for then he is ordered to his best and his ultimate end. But all actions of man which are not ordered to this good, or which are not such as to render man stronger and better disposed for actions which are ordered to this good, all such actions in man are sin.

Wherefore the happy man never does anything except works of happiness (*felicitas*), or works by means of which he becomes stronger and better fitted for works of happiness. Therefore, whether the happy man sleeps or is awake or is eating, he lives in happiness so long as he does those things in order to be rendered stronger for the works of happiness. [*373*] Therefore, all acts of man which are not directed to this supreme good of man which has been described, whether they are opposed to it or whether they are indifferent, all such acts constitute sin in man to a greater or lesser degree, as is clear.[11] The cause of all such acts is inordinate desire. It is also the cause of all moral evil. Moreover, inordinate desire in man is the cause which most greatly prevents him from attaining that which is desired naturally. For all men naturally desire to know.[12] But only the smallest number of men, sad to say, devote themselves to the pursuit of wisdom. Inordinate desire bars the others from such a good. Thus we find certain men pursuing a life of laziness, others detestable sense pleasures, and others giving themselves to the desire for riches. So it is that all today are prevented by inordinate desire from attaining to their supreme good, with the exception of a very small number of men, men who should be honored.

I say they are to be honored because they despise sense desire and pursue the delight of reason and intellectual desire, laboring after[13] knowledge of the truth of things. Again I say they are to be honored because they live according to the natural order. All lower powers (*virtutes*) found in man naturally are for the sake of the highest power. Thus the nutritive power is there for the sake of the sensitive. For the sensitive power is a perfection of an animated body, and an animated body cannot live without food. But it is the nutritive power which changes and assimilates food. Therefore, it follows that the nutritive power exists in man for the sake of the sensitive. And the sensitive power is for the sake of the intellective since, in us, intelligibles are derived from things imagined. Wherefore, we understand with greater difficulty things which of themselves cannot be imagined by us. [*374*] But imagination presupposes the senses. The proof of this is that one who imagines is also affected on the level of sense. Wherefore, according to the Philosopher, imagination or *phantasia* is a movement arising from an actual exercise of sense.[14] [Just as all lower powers in man are for the sake of the highest], so too the operations of all man's lower powers are for the sake of the operations of his highest power, the intellect. And if, among the operations of the intellective power, there is one which is best and most perfect, all others naturally exist for its sake. When a man performs such an operation, he enjoys the highest state possible for man.

Such men are the philosophers, who spend their lives in the pursuit of wisdom. Wherefore, all powers found in the philosopher operate

10. This is the single reference in this work to religious belief in a greater happiness in the life to come.

11. Here, as in the preceding paragraph, Boethius rejects the possibility that human actions, i.e., those for which man is responsible, might be regarded as morally indifferent.

12. Aristotle *Metaphysics* 1.1 980a21.

13. Literally, "sweating after."

14. Cf. Aristotle *De Anima* 3.3 429a1–2. On imagination as distinct both from perception (by the external senses) and from thinking, see earlier in this same chapter (427b14–428b30).

according to the natural order, the prior for the sake of the posterior, the lower for the sake of the higher and more perfect. But all other men, who live according to lower powers and choose their operations and the pleasures found in such operations, are not ordered in accord with nature. They sin against the natural order. For man to turn away from the natural order is sin in man. Because the philosopher does not turn away from this order, for this reason he does not sin against the natural order.

Morally speaking, the philosopher is virtuous for three reasons. *First,* because he recognizes the baseness of action in which vice consists and the nobility of action in which virtue consists. Therefore, he can more easily choose the one and avoid the other and always act according to right reason. He who so acts never sins. But such is not true of the ignorant man. It is difficult for him to act rightly. *Secondly,* because he who has tasted a greater delight despises every lesser delight. But the philosopher has tasted intellectual delight in theoretical consideration of the truths of beings. This delight is greater than that of sense. Therefore, he despises sense pleasures. [*375*] But many sins and vices consist in excessive sense pleasure. *Thirdly,* because there is no sin in understanding and theorizing. There is no possibility of excess and of sin in the order of absolute goods. But the action of the philosopher is such a contemplation of truth. Therefore, it is easier for the philosopher to be virtuous than for another.

So it is that the philosopher lives as man was born to live, and according to the natural order. Since in man all lower powers and their operations are for the sake of higher powers and their operations, and all taken together for the highest power and that highest action, which is contemplation of truth and delight in the same, above all, the first truth, the desire to know will never be satisfied until the uncreated being is known. As the Commentator says, all men naturally desire to know about the divine intellect.[15]

Desire for any knowable object is a kind of desire for the first knowable object. This is the proof. The closer beings are to the first knowable being, the more we desire to know them and the more we delight in thinking of them. Therefore, by studying the caused beings which are in the world and their natures and relationships to one another, the philosopher is led to consider the highest causes of things. For a knowledge of effects leads to a knowledge of the cause. And in noting that higher causes and their natures are such that they must have another cause, he is led to a knowledge of the first cause. And because there is pleasure in speculative knowledge, and all the more so [*376*] the nobler the objects known, the philosopher leads a life of very great pleasure.

The philosopher also knows and observes that it is necessary for this cause to be its own cause of being, that is to say, not to have another cause. If there were nothing in the universe which was not caused by another, then there would be nothing at all. He also notes that this cause must be eternal and unchangeable, always remaining the same. For if it were not eternal, then nothing whatsoever would be eternal. And again, since certain things in the world have begun to be, and since one being which begins to be cannot be a sufficient cause of another being which begins to be, as is evident, it clearly follows that all things in this world which begin to be must derive from an eternal cause. This cause is also unchangeable and always remains the same, for change is possible only in imperfect things. And if there is some most perfect being in the universe, it is right (*dignus*) for this to be the first cause.

The philosopher also notes that the entire being of the universe, with the exception of this first cause itself, must come from it and thus, just as this first cause is the cause which produces beings, so it orders them to one another and maintains them in existence—certain ones in terms of their individual identity and without any kind of change (as the separated substances); certain ones according to their individual identity, but as subject to change (as the heavenly bodies); and certain ones in terms of their species alone (as those which are below the sphere of [the moon] such as the lowest levels of beings).[16]

He also notes that just as all things derive from this first cause, so too, all things are ordered to it. For that being in which the principle from which all things [come] is joined to the end to which all things [return], that is the first being

15. Averroes *In XII Metaphysicam,* com. 51, in *Aristotelis Opera cum Averrois Commentariis* (Venice, 1562), vol. 8, fol. 335r.

16. For Boethius the first cause is not merely an unmoved mover but that which both produces and conserves its effects in terms of their being. According to the prevailing view of his time, Boethius would not admit that heavenly bodies are subject to corruption, but that they do undergo change by way of circular motion. Bodies that fall below the lunar sphere—earthly bodies—are subject to generation and corruption.

[*377*] according to the philosophers and God the Blessed according to the holy men. Nevertheless, in this order there is great range. Those beings which are closest to the first principle are nobler and more perfect. Those things which are farther removed from the first principle are lower and less perfect.

This first principle is to this world as the father of a family is to his household, as a commander is to his army, and as the common good is to the state (*civitas*). Just as the army is one because of the unity of its commander, and just as the good of the army is in the commander essentially and in others according to their relationship to him,[17] so too, from the unity of this first principle derives the unity of the world, and the good of this world is in this first principle essentially, and in other beings of this world insofar as they participate in the first principle and are ordered to it. So it is that there is no good in any being in this world which is not participated from the first principle.

Considering all these things, the philosopher is moved to wonder at this first principle and to love it. For we love that from which our goods derive, and we love that to the greatest degree from which our greatest goods derive.

Therefore, the philosopher, noting that all goods come to him from this first principle and are preserved for him insofar as they are preserved by this first principle, is moved to the greatest love for this first principle. This is in accord with the right order of nature[18] and with right reason from the side of the intellect. And since everyone takes delight in that which he loves and maximum delight in that which he loves to the maximum degree, and since the philosopher has the greatest love for this first principle, as has been indicated, it follows that the philosopher takes maximum delight in this first principle and in contemplating its goodness, and that this alone is right pleasure. This is the life of the philosopher. Whoever does not lead such a life does not live rightly. However, I call "philosopher" any man who lives according to the right order of nature and who has acquired the best and ultimate end of human life. And the first principle of whom we have spoken is the glorious and most high God, who is blessed forever and ever. Amen.

17. Cf. Aristotle *Metaphysics* 12.10 1075a12–16.

18. Reading "right order" of nature with manuscript G (Paris, Bibliothèque Nationale 15.819), which contains a very early abbreviation of this treatise and which was part of the library belonging to Godfrey of Fontaines. Godfrey was a student at Paris during part of Boethius's regency there, quite likely in the arts faculty for some of that time, and interested in the thought of Siger and Boethius. See John F. Wippel, *The Metaphysical Thought of Godfrey of Fontaines: A Study in Late Thirteenth-Century Philosophy* (Washington, DC: The Catholic University of America Press, 1981), xvi–xix.

TWENTY-FOUR

CONDEMNATION OF 219 PROPOSITIONS

Translated by Ernest L. Fortin and Peter D. O'Neill

The condemnation of 219 propositions by Etienne Tempier on March 7, 1277, was the most dramatic event in the history of the University of Paris during the second half of the thirteenth century. As bishop of Paris, Tempier had been requested by Pope John XXI to investigate and report on the teachings of certain masters of the faculty of arts. With the help of sixteen theologians, among them Henry of Ghent, Tempier drew up a list of propositions culled from various contemporary works, condemned them, threatened the promoters of these doctrines with excommunication unless they presented themselves to the bishop or his chancellor within a specified period of time, and reserved the right to impose further sanctions on them.

Tempier's sentence was only one in a series of actions designed to cope with the situation created by the rise of Aristotelianism at the University of Paris during the course of the thirteenth century and with the latent threat that this movement presented for the Christian faith. Earlier ecclesiastical decrees in 1210 and 1215, provoked by the teachings of Almaric of Bene and David of Dinant, had cautioned against the new dangers and forbidden, under pain of excommunication, the public or private "reading" (that is, teaching) in Paris of the *libri naturales* of Aristotle—that is, the *Physics*, *Metaphysics*, *De Anima*, and other minor works. Also included in the ban were certain commentaries on these works, presumably those of Avicenna and perhaps those of Alfarabi. The same general policy was maintained by Gregory IX in 1231, at least until the works in question could be examined and "purged of every suspicion of error." Ten propositions held by a Dominican were condemned by a synod of masters of theology in 1241, and three years later the condemnation was repeated by the bishop, William of Auvergne. However, the absence of any reaction to these measures in the following years seems to indicate that they were never enforced strictly. Roger Bacon, as a master in the faculty of arts in Paris, taught Aristotle's natural treatises between 1241 and 1247, and evidence suggests that the prohibitions were disregarded and became a dead letter. In 1255, a new statute was promulgated, reorganizing the curriculum of the faculty of arts and legalizing the study of all the known works of Aristotle, along with three Aristotelian pseudepigrapha, the *Liber de Causis*, the *De Plantis*, and the *De Differentia Spiritus et Animae*. The stage was thus set for the crisis that erupted a few years later, ca. 1265.

In 1270, Tempier condemned a series of thirteen errors dealing with the eternity of the world, divine providence, free will, and the unity of the intellectual soul and likewise threatened to excommunicate all those who taught these errors knowingly. Tempier evidently acted on his own authority, since there is no record of formal participation by the masters of theology, and the papacy was vacant from 1268 to 1271. This move failed to restore order in the university, and for the next seven years the controversy raged between the faculty of theology and the faculty of arts, as well as among members of the faculties. Such was the situation when Tempier again intervened, this time in a more decisive manner. The work of compiling the syllabus in 1277 was completed within three weeks of the arrival of the papal bull ordering the investigation, and the resulting document suggests that the investigation was carried out in a somewhat helter-skelter fashion by several masters working individually. No ostensible effort was made to introduce a logical order among the propositions. Moreover, their precise meaning remains in some instances obscure due to the lack of any immediate context. It is often difficult to discern the texts from which the propositions were extracted, and modern conjectures about the sources of specific propositions are often contested. Despite the chaotic appearance of the document, indicating great haste in its composition, it is nevertheless likely that the investigation had been initiated by Tempier and a papal legate, Simon de Brion, even prior to the arrival of the letter from John XXI. It is evident, in any case, that Tempier, by censuring these propositions in his own name, exceeded the mandate received from Rome to investigate the errors and their authors.

The condemnation of 1277 appears first of all as an attempt by Tempier to suppress those theses, such as the eternity of the world or the unicity of the intellect, that manifestly contradict Christian doctrine and imply that, when Christian doctrine and philosophy contradict one another, philosophy discovers the truth. In short, the condemnation appears first of all to combat what, since Ernst Renan in the nineteenth century, has commonly been called Latin Averroism. Modern historians, however, who have endeavored to ascertain from whose work each condemned proposition was taken, have inevitably found that the probable sources, masters in the faculty of arts such as Siger of Brabant or Boethius of Dacia, repeatedly affirmed the truth of faith whenever faith and philosophy were found opposed (they did not absurdly affirm two contradictory truths, as Tempier alleges). Thus, on the basis of the condemned propositions, one cannot safely infer the existence of a school of Latin Averroism, and Latin Averroism is now regarded by many as an historiographical fiction. One might conjecture, with Tempier himself, that his opponents dissimulated their true beliefs as a practical necessity. Or one might conclude that Tempier incorrectly attributed these propositions to perceived enemies and reacted to a largely illusory threat. If it be granted that the masters of the arts faculty were sincere in their professions of faith, nevertheless they so far advanced the autonomy of philosophical inquiry and so fully praised the excellence of the philosophical life that their teachings must have appeared threatening to certain masters in the faculty of theology and prelates such as the bishop. The precise nature and extent of the threat that philosophizing masters posed to Christian doctrine are debated up to the present day.

It must not be thought, however, that the condemnation represents simply a reaction of theology against philosophy, as many members of the faculty of theology were Aristotelians as well. The condemnation also appears intended to restrict theologians in certain lines of inquiry and to ensure the preeminence of a relatively more traditional theology against the specific Aristotelianism of Albert, Aquinas, and their followers. Of the 219 propositions incriminated in 1277, marginal notes in several manuscripts show that 11 propositions were understood at the time to be directed against Aquinas's teaching (Props. 42, 43, 46, 53, 74, 79, 146, 147, 162, 163, and 169 in the order given here), and other propositions are generally regarded as reflecting his doctrine (Props. 27, 50, 54, 55, 110, 115, 116). Finally, the two intentions we have attributed to the condemnation—to curtail the freedom exercised by philosophizing masters in the faculty of arts, and to discourage certain Aristotelian innovations in theology—may not have appeared as distinct to Tempier and his colleagues as they do to us now.

Tempier's resounding condemnation was the most severe that the thirteenth century had known. Despite its purely local character, it had broad repercussions throughout the West. In the same year, propositions were also condemned in Oxford by Robert Kilwardby, the archbishop of Canterbury. The propositions condemned in Paris and Oxford in 1277 were combined with those condemned in Paris in 1241 and 1270, and manuscripts of the collected propositions were widely distributed. The condemnations provided a harsh, if momentary response to the threat posed to orthodoxy by philosophy. Disciplinary procedures at this time appear to have put an end to the career of Siger of Brabant, who had taught in Paris from ca. 1265 and to whom several propositions condemned in 1270 were attributed. Siger was summoned to appear before the inquisitor in 1276, several months prior to the condemnations. No record remains of the outcome of the procedure, but later (prior to 1284) he appeared in Italy, where it seems he was stabbed to death by a mad cleric. The conventional conjecture is that he had left France to appeal to Rome, but to what end we do not know.[1] The condemnations also impeded the spread of Thomism and gave a new impetus to the eclectic Aristotelianism favored by men such as Tempier, the Franciscan John Peckham, and the secular masters. Finally, it created an atmosphere of uneasiness that persisted for many years in university circles.

The 219 propositions were translated here for the first time into English from the edition by P. Mandonnet, OP, *Siger de Brabant et l'averroïsme latin au XIIIme siècle*, pt. 2, *Textes inédits*, 2nd ed. (Louvain: Institut Supérieur de Philosophie de l'Université, 1908), 175–91. This translation has been modified primarily in order to bring it into accord with the critical edition of David Piché and Claude LaFleur, *La condamnation parisienne de 1277* (Paris: J. Vrin, 1999), most notably resulting, first, in changes to propositions 7, 8, 79, and 144 and, second, in an additional proposition appended to proposition 179. For ease of study we have retained Mandonnet's ordering of the propositions as well as his section titles. The reader should be aware, however, that this ordering explicitly separates philosophy from theology in a manner not found in the original list, and perhaps contrary to the spirit of the edict of condemnation. The numbers in parentheses at the end of each proposition are those of the original list.

STEPHEN, by divine permission unworthy servant of the church of Paris, sends greetings in the son of the glorious Virgin to all those who will read this letter.

We have received frequent reports, inspired by zeal for the faith, on the part of important and serious persons to the effect that some students of the arts in Paris are exceeding the boundaries of their own faculty and are presuming to treat and discuss, as if they were debatable in the schools, certain obvious and loathsome errors, or rather *vanities and lying follies* [Ps. 39:5 in Vulgate], which are contained in the roll joined to this letter. These students are not hearkening to the admonition of Gregory, "Let him who would speak wisely exercise great care, lest by his speech he disrupt the unity of his listeners," particularly when in support of the aforesaid errors they adduce pagan writings that—shame on their ignorance—they assert to be so convincing that they do not know how to answer them. So as not to appear to be asserting what they thus insinuate, however, they conceal their answers in such a way that, while thinking to avoid Scylla, they fall into Charybdis. For they say that these things are true according to philosophy but not according to the Catholic faith, as if there were two contrary truths and as if the truth of Sacred Scripture were contradicted by the truth in the sayings of the accursed pagans, of whom it is written, *I will destroy the wisdom of the wise* [1 Cor. 1:19; cf. Isa. 29:14], inasmuch as true wisdom destroys false wisdom. Would that such students listen to the advice of the wise man when he says: *If you have understanding, answer your neighbor; but if not, let your hand be upon your mouth, lest you be surprised in an unskillful word and be confounded* [Ecclus. or Sirach 5:14].

Lest, therefore, this unguarded speech lead simple people into error, we, having taken counsel with the doctors of Sacred Scripture and other prudent men, strictly forbid these and like things and totally condemn them. We excommunicate all those who shall have taught the said errors or any one of them, or shall have dared in any way to defend or uphold them, or even to listen to them, unless they choose to reveal themselves to us or to the chancery of Paris within seven days; in addition to which we shall proceed against them by inflicting such other penalties as the law requires according to the nature of the offense.

By this same sentence of ours we also condemn the book *De Amore*, or *De Deo Amoris*,

1. A less dramatic picture can be drawn from the same scanty evidence: there is reason to believe that Siger might have left Paris as early as 1275 for other reasons; furthermore, since subsequent documents show that one of the masters who was summoned to appear with Siger in 1276 was teaching in Paris in the 1280s, and there is no record of a decision against Siger, we may infer that this other master and Siger were acquitted in 1276–1277, in which case, there would have been no cause for him to make an appeal in Rome (J. M. M. H. Thijssen, *Censure and Heresy at the University of Paris, 1200–1400* [Philadelphia: University of Pennsylvania Press, 1998], 44–47).

which begins with the words, *Cogit me multum,* and so on, and ends with the words, *Cave, igitur, Galtere, amoris exercere mandata,* and so on, as well the book of geomancy that begins with the words, *Existimaverunt Indi,* and so on, and ends with the words, *Ratiocinare ergo super eum invenies,* and so on. We likewise condemn the books, scrolls, and leaflets dealing with necromancy, or containing experiments in fortunetelling, invocations of devils or incantations endangering lives, or in which these and similar things evidently contrary to the orthodox faith and good morals are treated. We pronounce the sentence of excommunication against those who shall have taught the said scrolls, books, and leaflets, or listened to them, unless they reveal themselves to us or to the chancery of Paris within seven days in the manner described earlier in this letter; in addition to which we shall proceed to inflict such other penalties as the nature of the offense demands.

Given in the year of the Lord 1276, on the Sunday on which *Laetare Jerusalem* is sung at the court of Paris.

I
ERRORS IN PHILOSOPHY

On the Nature of Philosophy

1. That there is no more excellent state than to study philosophy. (40)
2. That the only wise men in the world are the philosophers. (154)
3. That in order to have some certitude about any conclusion, man must base himself on self-evident principles.—The statement is erroneous because it refers in a general way both to the certitude of apprehension and to that of adherence. (151)
4. That one should not hold anything unless it is self-evident or can be manifested from self-evident principles. (37)
5. That man should not be content with authority to have certitude about any question. (150)
6. That there is no rationally disputable question that the philosopher ought not to dispute and determine, because reasons are derived from things. It belongs to philosophy under one or another of its parts to consider all things.[2] (145)
7. That, aside from the philosophic disciplines, all the sciences are without necessity, and that they are necessary only on account of human custom. (24)

On the Knowability of God

8. That our intellect by its own natural power can attain to a knowledge of the essence of the first cause.—This does not sound well and is erroneous if what is meant is immediate knowledge. (211)
9. That we can know God by His essence in this mortal life. (36)
10. That nothing can be known about God except that He is, or His existence. (215)

On the Nature of God

11. That the proposition, "God is being per se positively," is not intelligible; rather God is being per se privatively. (216)
12. That the intellect by which God understands Himself is by definition different from that by which He understands other things.—This is erroneous because, although the proper reason of His understanding is different in each case, the intellect is not other by definition. (149)

2. Cf. Aristotle *Metaphysics* 4.2 1004a34.

On Divine Science

13. That God does not know things other than Himself. (3)
14. That God cannot know contingent beings immediately except through their particular and proximate causes. (56)
15. That the first cause does not have science of future contingents. The first reason is that future contingents are not beings. The second is that future contingents are singulars, but God knows by means of an intellectual power, which cannot know singulars. Hence, if there were no senses, the intellect would perhaps not distinguish between Socrates and Plato, although it would distinguish between a man and an ass. The third reason is the relation of cause to effect; for the divine foreknowledge is a necessary cause of the things foreknown. The fourth reason is the relation of science to the known; for even though science is not the cause of the known, it is determined to one of two contradictories by that which is known; and this is true of divine science much more than of ours. (42)

On Divine Will and Power

16. That the first cause is the most remote of all beings.—This is erroneous if understood precisely to mean that it is not the most proximate. (190)
17. That what is impossible absolutely speaking cannot be brought about by God or by another agent.—This is erroneous if we mean what is impossible according to nature. (147)
18. That what is self-determined, like God, either always acts or never acts; and that many things are eternal. (52)
19. That an active potency that can exist without acting is mixed with passive potency.—This is erroneous if any operation whatsoever is understood here. (68)
20. That God of necessity makes whatever comes immediately from Him.—This is erroneous whether we are speaking of the necessity of coercion, which destroys liberty, or of the necessity of immutability, which implies the impossibility of doing otherwise. (53)
21. That from a previous act of the will nothing new can proceed unless it is preceded by a change. (39)
22. That God cannot be the cause of a newly-made thing and cannot produce anything new. (48)
23. That God cannot move anything irregularly, that is, in a manner other than that in which He does, because there is no diversity of will in Him. (50)
24. That God is eternal in acting and moving, just as He is eternal in existing; otherwise He would be determined by some other thing that would be prior to Him. (51)
25. That God is infinite with respect to power, not because He makes something out of nothing, but because He maintains infinite motion. (62)
26. That God has infinite power in duration, not in action, since there is no such infinity except in an infinite body, if there were such a thing. (29)

On the Causation of the World

27. That the first cause cannot make more than one world. (34)
28. That from one first agent there cannot proceed a multiplicity of effects. (44)
29. That the first cause would be able to produce an effect equal to itself if it did not limit its power. (26)
30. That the first cause cannot produce something other than itself, because every difference between maker and made is through matter. (55)
31. That in heavenly things there are three principles: the subject of eternal motion, the soul of the heavenly body, and the first mover as desired.—The error is in regard to the first two. (95)
32. That there are two eternal principles, namely, the body of the heaven and its soul. (94)

On the Nature of the Intelligences

33. That the immediate effect of the first being has to be one only and most like unto the first being. (64)
34. That God is the necessary cause of the first intelligence, which cause being posited, the effect is also posited; and both are equal in duration. (58)
35. That God never created an intelligence more than He now creates it. (28)
36. That the absolutely first unmoved being does not move save through the mediation of something moved, and that such an unmoved mover is a part of that which is moved of itself. (67)
37. That the first principle is not the proper cause of eternal beings except metaphorically, in so far as it conserves them, for unless it was, they would not be. (45)
38. That the intelligences, or separated substances, which they say are eternal, do not have an efficient cause properly speaking, but only metaphorically, in so far as they have a cause conserving them in existence; but they were not newly-made, because then they would be mutable. (70)
39. That all the separated substances are coeternal with the first principle. (5)
40. That everything that does not have matter is eternal, because that which was not made through a change in matter did not exist previously; therefore it is eternal. (80)
41. That the separated substances, having no matter through which they would be in potency before being in act and being from a cause that always exists in the same manner, are therefore eternal. (72)
42. That God cannot multiply individuals of the same species without matter. (96)
43. That God could not make several intelligences of the same species because intelligences do not have matter. (81)
44. That no change is possible in the separated substances; nor are they in potency to anything because they are eternal and free from matter. (71)
45. That the intelligence is made by God in eternity because it is totally immutable; the soul of the heaven, however, is not. (83)
46. That the separated substances are the same as their essences because in them that by which they are and that which they are, is the same. (79)
47. That the knowledge (*scientia*) of the intelligence does not differ from its substance, for where there is no distinction between known and knower, there is no distinction of thing known either. (85)
48. That an angel does not understand anything new. (76)
49. That the separated substances are infinite in act; for infinity is not impossible except in material things. (86)
50. That if there were any separated substance that did not move some body in this sensible world, it would not be included in the universe. (77)
51. That the eternal substances separated from matter have all the good possible to them when they are produced and do not desire anything that they do not have. (78)
52. That the separated substances, in so far as they have a single appetite, do not change in their operation. (69)
53. That an intelligence, an angel, or a separated soul is nowhere. (218)
54. That the separated substances are nowhere according to their substance.—This is erroneous if so understood as to mean that substance is not in a place. If, however, it is so understood as to mean that substance is the reason for being in a place, it is true that they are nowhere according to their substance. (219)
55. That the separated substances are somewhere by their operation, and that they cannot move from one extreme to another or to the middle except in so far as they can will to operate either in the middle or in the extremes.—This is erroneous if so understood as to mean that without operation a substance is not in a place and that it does not pass from one place to another. (204)

On the Function of the Intelligences

56. That separated substances by means of their intellect cause things. (73)
57. That an intelligence receives its existence from God through mediating intelligences. (84)
58. That the higher intelligences create rational souls without the motion of the heaven, whereas the lower intelligences create vegetative and sensitive souls through the medium of heavenly motion. (30)

59. That an angel is not in potency to opposite acts immediately but only through the mediating agency of something else, such as a sphere. (75)

60. That the higher intelligences are not the cause of anything new in the lower intelligences, and that the higher intelligences are the cause of eternal knowledge for the lower intelligences. (82)

61. That since an intelligence is full of forms, it impresses these forms on matter by using the heavenly bodies as instruments. (189)

62. That external matter obeys the spiritual substance.—This is erroneous if understood absolutely and according to every mode of change. (210)

63. That the higher intelligences impress things on the lower, just as one intellective soul impresses things on another and even on a sensitive soul; and that through such an impression a spellbinder is able to cast a camel into a pitfall just by looking at it. (112)

On the Heaven and on the Generation of Lower Beings

64. That God is the necessary cause of the motion of the higher bodies and of the union and separation occurring in the stars. (59)

65. That if at one time all the causes were at rest, it is necessary to assert that God is mobile. (57)

66. That God could not move the heaven in a straight line, the reason being that He would then leave a vacuum. (49)

67. That the first principle cannot produce generable things immediately because they are new effects and a new effect requires an immediate cause that is capable of being otherwise. (54)

68. That the first principle cannot be the cause of diverse products here below without the mediation of other causes, inasmuch as nothing that transforms, transforms in diverse ways without being itself transformed. (43)

69. That God cannot produce the effect of a secondary cause without the secondary cause itself. (63)

70. That God is able to produce contraries, that is, through the medium of a heavenly body which occupies diverse places. (61)

71. That the nature that is the principle of motion in the heavenly bodies is a moving intelligence.—This is erroneous if what is meant is the intrinsic nature, which is act or form. (213)

72. That the heavenly bodies have of themselves eternity of substance but not eternity of motion. (93)

73. That the heavenly bodies are moved by an intrinsic principle, which is the soul, and that they are moved by a soul and an appetitive power, like an animal. For just as an animal is moved by desiring, so also is the heaven. (92)

74. That an intelligence by its will alone moves the heaven. (212)

75. That the soul of the heaven is an intelligence, and that the heavenly spheres are not instruments but organs of the intelligences, just as the ear and the eye are organs of the sensitive power. (102)

76. That the intelligence moving the heaven influences the rational soul, just as the body of the heaven influences the human body. (74)

77. That the heaven is never at rest because the generation of lower beings, which is the end of the motion of the heaven, must not cease. Another reason is that the heaven has its existence and its power from its mover and the heaven preserves these through its motion. Hence if it ceased to move, it would cease to be. (186)

78. That there would be nothing new if the heaven were not varied with respect to the matter of generable things. (88)

79. That if the heaven stood still, fire would not burn flax because nature would not exist. (156)

80. That the reasoning of the Philosopher proving that the motion of the heaven is eternal is not sophistic, and that it is surprising that profound men do not perceive this. (91)

81. That a sphere is the immediate efficient cause of all forms. (106)

82. That if in some humor by the power of the stars such a proportion could be achieved as is found in the seed of the parents, a man could be generated from that humor; and that a man could be adequately generated from putrefaction. (188)

On the Eternity of the World

83. That the world, although it was made from nothing, was not newly-made, and, although it passed from nonbeing to being, the nonbeing did not precede being in duration but only in nature. (99)

84. That the world is eternal because everything which has a nature by which it is able to exist for the whole future has a nature by which it was able to exist in the whole past. (98)

85. That the world is eternal as regards all the species contained in it, and that time, motion, matter, agent, and receiver are eternal, because the world comes from the infinite power of God and it is impossible that there be something new in the effect without there being something new in the cause. (87)

86. That eternity and time have no existence in reality but only in the mind. (200)

87. That nothing is eternal from the standpoint of its end that is not eternal from the standpoint of its beginning. (4)

88. That time is infinite as regards both extremes, for although it is impossible for an infinity to be passed through when one of its parts had to be passed through, it is not impossible for an infinity to be passed through when none of its parts had to be passed through. (205)

89. That it is impossible to refute the arguments of the Philosopher concerning the eternity of the world unless we say that the will of the first being embraces incompatibles. (89)

90. That the universe cannot cease to exist because the first agent is able to cause transmutations one after another eternally, now into this form, now into that; and similarly it is of the nature of matter to undergo change. (203)

91. That there has already been an infinite number of revolutions of the heaven, which it is impossible for the created intellect but not for the first cause to comprehend. (101)

92. That with all the heavenly bodies coming back to the same point after a period of thirty-six thousand years, the same effects as now exist will reappear. (6)

On the Necessity and Contingency of Things

93. That some things can take place by chance with respect to the first cause, and that it is false that all things are preordained by the first cause, because then they would come about by necessity. (197)

94. That fate, which is the disposition of the universe, proceeds from divine providence, not immediately, but mediately through the motion of the higher bodies, and that this fate does not impose necessity upon the lower beings, since they have contrariety, but upon the higher. (195)

95. That for all effects to be necessary with respect to the first cause, it does not suffice that the first cause itself be not impedible, but it is also necessary that the intermediary causes be not impedible.—This is erroneous because then God could not produce a necessary effect without posterior causes. (60)

96. That beings depart from the order of the first cause considered in itself, although not in relation to the other causes operating in the universe.—This is erroneous because the order of beings to the first cause is more essential and more inseparable than their order to the lower causes. (47)

97. That it would belong to the dignity of the higher causes to be able to commit errors and produce monsters unintentionally, since nature is able to do this. (196)

98. That, among the efficient causes, the secondary cause has an action that it did not receive from the first cause. (198)

99. That there is more than one prime mover. (66)

100. That, among the efficient causes, if the first cause were to cease to act, the secondary cause would not, as long as the secondary cause operates according to its own nature. (199)

101. That no agent is in potency to one or the other of two things; on the contrary, it is determined. (160)

102. That nothing happens by chance, but everything comes about by necessity, and that all the things that will exist in the future will exist by necessity, and those that will not exist are impossible, and that nothing occurs contingently if all causes are considered.—This is erroneous because the concurrence of causes is included in the definition of chance, as Boethius says in his book *On Consolation*.[3] (21)

3. Boethius *De Consolatione Philosophiae* v. Prose 2.

103. That the necessity of events comes from the diversity of places. (142)
104. That the differences of condition among men, both as regards spiritual gifts and temporal assets, are traced back to the diverse signs of the heaven. (143)
105. That at the time of the generation of a man in body, and hence in soul, which follows upon body, there is in him a disposition produced by the order of the higher and lower causes by which he is inclined to certain actions and events.—This is erroneous unless it is understood of natural events and by way of disposition. (207)
106. That one attributes health, sickness, life, and death to the position of the stars and the glance of fortune by saying that if fortune looks down on him he will live, if it does not, he will die. (206)
107. That God was not able to make prime matter save through the mediation of a heavenly body. (38)

On the Principles of Material Things

108. That, just as nothing can come from matter without an agent, so also nothing can come from an agent without matter, and that God is not an efficient cause except with respect to that which has its existence in the potency of matter. (46)
109. That a form that has to exist and come to be in matter cannot be produced by an agent that does not produce it from matter. (103)
110. That forms are not divided except through matter.—This is erroneous unless one is speaking of forms educed from the potency of matter. (191)
111. That the elements were produced from chaos by a first generation, but they are eternal. (202)
112. That the elements are eternal. They were nevertheless newly produced in the disposition that they now possess. (107)

On Man and the Agent Intellect

113. That a man is a man independently of the rational soul. (11)
114. That by nutrition a man can become other numerically and individually. (148)
115. That God could not make several numerically different souls. (27)
116. That individuals of the same species, like Socrates and Plato, differ solely by the position of their matter, and that since the human form existing in each is numerically the same, it is not surprising that the same being numerically is in different places. (97)
117. That the intellect is numerically one for all, for although it may be separated from this or that body, it is not separated from every body. (32)
118. That the agent intellect is a certain separated substance superior to the possible intellect, and that it is separated from the body according to its substance, power, and operation and is not the form of the human body. (123)
119. That the motions of the heaven are for the sake of the intellectual soul, and the intellectual soul or intellect cannot be educed except through the mediation of a body. (110)
120. That the form of man does not come from an extrinsic source but is educed from the potency of matter, for otherwise the generation would not be univocal. (105)
121. That no form coming from an extrinsic source can form one being with matter; for that which is separable does not form one being with that which is corruptible. (111)
122. That from the sensitive and intellectual parts of man there does not result a unity in essence, unless it be a unity such as that of an intelligence and a sphere, that is, a unity in operation. (13)
123. That the intellect is not the act of the body, except in the way the helmsman [is the act] of the ship, and that it is not an essential perfection of man. (7)
124. That humanity is not the form of a thing but of the mind. (104)
125. That the operation of the non-united intellect is joined to the body in such a way that the operation is that of a thing that does not have a form by which it operates.—The statement is erroneous because it asserts that the intellect is not the form of man. (119)
126. That the intellect, which is man's ultimate perfection, is completely separated. (121)
127. That the human soul is in no way mobile according to place, either essentially or accidentally,

and if it is placed somewhere by means of its substance, it will never move from one place to another. (108)

128. That the soul would never move unless the body moved, just as a heavy or a light thing would never move unless the air moved. (214)

129. That the substance of the soul is eternal, and that the agent intellect and the possible intellect are eternal. (109)

130. That the human intellect is eternal because it comes from a cause that is always the same and because it does not have matter by means of which it is in potency prior to being in act. (31)

131. That the speculative intellect is simply eternal and incorruptible; with respect to this or that man, however, it is corrupted when the phantasms in him are corrupted. (125)

132. That the intellect puts on the body when it so desires and does not put it on when it does not desire it. (8)

133. That the soul is inseparable from the body, and that the soul is corrupted when the harmony of the body is corrupted. (116)

134. That the rational soul, when it departs from an animal, still remains a living animal. (114)

135. That the separated soul is not alterable, according to philosophy, although according to the faith it is altered. (113)

136. That the intellect can pass from body to body, in such a way that it is successively the mover of different bodies. (193)

137. That the generation of man is circular, inasmuch as the form of man returns many times to the same portion of matter. (10)

138. That there was no first man, nor will there be a last; indeed, the generation of man from man always was and always will be. (9)

139. That although the generation of men could cease, by the will of the first agent it will not cease, for the first sphere promotes the generation not only of the elements but also of men. (137)

On the Operation of the Human Intellect

140. That the agent intellect is not united to our possible intellect, and that the possible intellect is not united to us substantially. And if it were united to us as a form, it would be inseparable. (118)

141. That the possible intellect is nothing in act before it understands, because in the case of an intelligible nature, to be something in act is to be actually understanding. (126)

142. That the possible intellect is simply inseparable from the body as regards that act which is the reception of species and as regards judgment, which comes about through the simple acquisition of species or the composition of intelligibles.—This is erroneous if understood of every kind of reception. (122)

143. That a man is said to understand to the same extent that the heaven is said to understand, or to live, or to move of itself, that is, because the agent performing these actions is united to him as mover to moved and not substantially. (14)

144. That from the thinking thing and what is thought there results one substance, inasmuch as the intellect formally becomes the intellected things themselves. (127)

145. That the intellectual soul by knowing itself knows all other things; for the species of all things are co-created with it. But this knowledge does not belong to our intellect in so far as it is ours but in so far as it is the agent intellect. (115)

146. That the fact that we understand less perfectly or more perfectly comes from the passive intellect, which he says is a sensitive power.—This statement is erroneous because it asserts that there is a single intellect in all men or that all souls are equal. (187)

147. That it is improper to maintain that some intellects are more noble than others because this diversity has to come from the intelligences, since it cannot come from the bodies; and thus noble and ignoble souls would necessarily belong to different species, like the intelligences.—This is erroneous, for thus the soul of Christ would not be more noble than that of Judas. (124)

148. That the knowledge of the teacher and the student is numerically one. The reason for which the intellect is thus one is that a form is multiplied only because of the fact that it is educed from the potency of matter. (117)

149. That the intellect of the dead Socrates does not have the knowledge of those things of which it once had knowledge. (41)

On the Human Will

150. That that which by its nature is not determined to being or nonbeing is not determined except by something that is necessary with respect to itself. (128)

151. That the soul wills nothing unless it is moved by another besides itself. Hence the following proposition is false: the soul wills by itself.—This is erroneous if what is meant is that the soul is moved by another, namely, by something desirable or an object in such a way that the desirable thing or object is the whole reason for the movement of the will itself. (194)

152. That all voluntary movements are reduced to the first mover. This is erroneous unless one is speaking of the simply first, uncreated mover and of movement according to its substance, not according to its deformity. (209)

153. That the will and the intellect are not moved in act by themselves but by an eternal cause, namely, the heavenly bodies. (133)

154. That our will is subject to the power of the heavenly bodies. (162)

155. That a sphere is the cause of a doctor's willing to cure. (132)

156. That the effects of the stars upon free choice are hidden. (161)

157. That when two goods are proposed, the stronger moves more strongly.—This is erroneous unless one is speaking from the standpoint of the good that moves. (208)

158. That in all his actions man follows his appetite and always the greater appetite.—This is erroneous if what is meant is the greater in moving power. (164)

159. That the appetite is necessarily moved by a desirable object if all obstacles are removed.—This is erroneous in the case of the intellectual appetite. (134)

160. That it is impossible for the will not to will when it is in the disposition in which it is natural for it to be moved and when that which by nature moves remains so disposed. (131)

161. That in itself the will is undetermined to opposites, like matter, but it is determined by a desirable object as matter is determined by an agent. (135)

162. That the knowledge of contraries alone is the cause for which the rational soul is in potency to opposites, and that a power that is simply one is not in potency to opposites except accidentally and by reason of something else. (173)

163. That the will necessarily pursues what is firmly held by reason, and that it cannot abstain from that which reason dictates. This necessitation, however, is not compulsion but the nature of the will. (163)

164. That man's will is necessitated by his knowledge, like the appetite of a brute. (159)

165. That after a conclusion has been reached about something to be done, the will does not remain free, and that punishments are provided by law only for the correction of ignorance and in order that the correction may be a source of knowledge for others. (158)

166. That if reason is rectified, the will is also rectified.—This is erroneous because contrary to Augustine's gloss on this verse from the Psalms: *My soul hath coveted to long*, and so on [Ps. 118:20], and because according to this, grace would not be necessary for the rectitude of the will but only science, which was the error of Pelagius.[4] (130)

167. That there can be no sin in the higher powers of the soul. And thus sin comes from passion and not from the will. (165)

168. That a man acting from passion acts by compulsion. (136)

169. That as long as passion and particular science are present in act, the will cannot go against them. (129)

On Ethics or Moral Matters

170. That all the good that is possible to man consists in the intellectual virtues. (144)

171. That a man who is ordered as to his intellect and his affections, in the manner in which this

4. Pelagius, a British or perhaps Irish lay monk who came to Rome and then to North Africa at the beginning of the fifth century, opposed Augustine's doctrine of grace and free will on the ground that, by extolling divine grace, it minimized man's responsibility and jeopardized the entire moral order. He was condemned by the councils at Carthage in 416 and 418. Pelagianism, the heresy to which he gave his name, was again censured at the Council of Ephesus in 431.

can be sufficiently accomplished by means of the intellectual and moral virtues of which the Philosopher speaks in the *Ethics,* is sufficiently disposed for eternal happiness. (157)

172. That happiness is had in this life and not in another. (176)

173. That happiness cannot be infused by God immediately. (22)

174. That after death man loses every good. (15)

175. That since Socrates was made incapable of eternity, if he is to be eternal it is necessary that he be changed in nature and species. (12)

176. That God or the intelligence does not infuse science into the human soul during sleep except through the mediation of a heavenly body. (65)

177. That raptures and visions are caused only by nature. (33)

178. That by certain signs one knows men's intentions and changes of intention, and whether these intentions are to be carried out, and that by means of these prefigurations one knows the arrival of strangers, the enslavement of men, the release of captives, and whether those who are coming are acquaintances or thieves. (167)

179. That natural law forbids the killing of irrational animals, although not only these.[5] (20)

II
ERRORS IN THEOLOGY

On the Christian Law

180. That the Christian law impedes learning. (175)

181. That there are fables and falsehoods in the Christian law just as in others. (174)

182. That one does not know anything more by the fact that he knows theology. (153)

183. That the teachings of the theologian are based on fables. (152)

184. That what is possible or impossible absolutely speaking, that is, in every respect, is what is possible or impossible according to philosophy. (146)

On the Dogmas of the Church

185. That God is not triune because trinity is incompatible with the highest simplicity; for where there is a real plurality there is necessarily addition and composition. Take the example of a pile of stones. (1)

186. That God cannot beget his own likeness, for what is begotten from something has some origin on which it depends; and that in God to beget would not be a sign of perfection. (2)

187. That creation should not be called a change to being.—This is erroneous if understood of every kind of change. (217)

188. That it is not true that something comes from nothing or was made in a first creation. (185)

189. That creation is not possible, even though the contrary must be held according to the faith. (184)

190. That he who generates the world in its totality posits a vacuum, because place necessarily precedes that which is generated in it; and so before the generation of the world there would have been a place with nothing in it, which is a vacuum. (201)

191. That the natural philosopher has to deny absolutely the newness of the world because he bases himself on natural causes and natural reasons, whereas the faithful can deny the eternity of the world because he bases himself on supernatural causes. (90)

192. That the theologians who say that the heaven rests at one time or another argue from a false supposition, and that to say that the heaven exists and does not move is to utter contradictories. (100)

193. That it is possible for a universal deluge of fire to come about naturally. (182)

5. In four manuscripts is found an additional condemned article pertaining to ethics: "220. That charity is not a greater good than perfect friendship."

194. That a material form cannot be created. (192)
195. That without a proper agent, such as a father and a man, God could not make a man. (35)
196. That to make an accident exist without a subject has the nature of an impossibility implying contradiction.[6] (140)
197. That God cannot make an accident exist without a subject or make more than one dimension exist simultaneously.[7] (141)
198. That an accident existing without a subject is not an accident except in an equivocal sense, and that it is impossible for quantity or dimension to exist by itself, for this would make it a substance. (139)
199. That since God is not related to beings as a material or formal cause, he does not make an accident exist without a subject, inasmuch as it is of the nature of an accident to exist actually in a subject. (138)

On the Christian Virtues

200. That no other virtues are possible except the acquired or the innate. (177)
201. That one should not be concerned about the faith if something is said to be heretical because it is against the faith. (16)
202. That one should not pray. (180)
203. That one should not confess except for the sake of appearance. (179)
204. That one should not care about burial. (155)
205. That simple fornication, namely, that of an unmarried man with an unmarried woman, is not a sin. (183)
206. That a sin against nature, such as abuse in intercourse, is not against the nature of the individual, although it is against the nature of the species. (166)
207. That the pleasure in sexual acts does not impede the act or the use of the intellect. (172)
208. That continence is not essentially a virtue. (168)
209. That chastity is not a greater good than perfect abstinence. (181)
210. That perfect abstinence from the act of the flesh corrupts virtue and the species. (169)
211. That humility, in the degree to which one does not show what he has but depreciates and lowers himself, is not a virtue.—This is erroneous if what is meant is: neither a virtue nor a virtuous act. (171)
212. That one who is poor as regards the goods of fortune cannot act well in moral matters. (170)

On the Last Ends

213. That death is the end of all terrors.—The statement is erroneous if it excludes the terror of hell, which is the last. (178)
214. That God cannot grant perpetuity to a changeable or corruptible thing. (25)
215. That it does not happen that a corrupted body recurs numerically the same, and it will not rise numerically the same. (17)
216. That a philosopher must not concede the resurrection to come, because it cannot be investigated by reason.—This is erroneous because even a philosopher must *bring his mind into captivity to the obedience* to faith [cf. 2 Cor. 10:5]. (18)
217. That to say that God gives happiness to one and not to another is devoid of reason and fictitious. (23)
218. That nothing can be known about the intellect after its separation. (120)
219. That the separated soul in no way suffers from fire. (19)

6. Propositions 196–199 are directed implicitly against the theological doctrine of the Eucharist, which states that the accidents of bread and wine are left without any subject of inherence once the substance of the bread and wine has been converted into the body and blood of Christ. See Thomas Aquinas *Summa Theologiae* 3.75–77.

7. The allusion is to the teaching according to which the quantity of Christ is present in the Eucharist despite the fact that the quantity or dimensions of the bread remain unchanged. See Thomas Aquinas *Summa Theologiae* 3.76.4.

TWENTY-FIVE

GILES OF ROME

On Ecclesiastical Power

Translated by R. W. Dyson

Of the birth and early education of Giles of Rome (Aegidius Romanus, 1243/7–1316) nothing certain is known. The tradition that he was a member of the illustrious Colonna family is now generally held in suspicion. He entered the Order of the Augustinian Hermits at an early age and was sent to Paris, where he studied theology and likely attended the lectures of Thomas Aquinas during the latter's second stay there (1269–1272). Giles's earlier works include the most influential medieval commentary on Aristotle's *Rhetoric.* Also attributed to him is *The Errors of the Philosophers* (ca. 1270): this treatise culls from the works of Aristotle, Averroes, Maimonides, and others propositions that contradict Christian doctrine (Giles's authorship, however, has been questioned). In 1277, after the general decree of March 7 promulgated by the bishop, Giles was separately examined for fifty-one articles taken from his commentary on the first book of the *Sentences;* the censured articles were often similar to suspected propositions in the works of Thomas. Giles did not recant the fifty-one articles and defended himself before the investigating body. While the process against him seems to have been suspended, his university career abruptly ended. According to a tradition that is not well documented, he then became the tutor of the son of King Philip III of France, the future Philip the Fair. At the request of the king, Giles composed for the prince *On the Government of Princes* (*De Regimine Principum,* ca. 1280), one of the most widely read political works of the Middle Ages. This work makes extensive use of arguments from Aristotle's *Ethics, Politics,* and *Rhetoric;* it very rarely cites the Bible and touches not at all upon the question of ecclesiastical power. Giles develops an account of hereditary kingship adaptable to the practice of monarchy in medieval Europe, in which the king's authority is superior to positive, civil laws, but subordinate to natural law and divine law. Within little more than a century this work was translated into many vernaculars (French, Italian, Hebrew, Castilian, English, and maybe Portuguese), and it is preserved in over 350 manuscripts.

Giles returned to Italy in 1281, holding several offices within his order. After the death in 1285 of Pope Martin IV (Simon de Brion, the former papal legate associated with Tempier's investigations in 1277), the new pope, Honorius IV, ordered a commission in Paris to reexamine Giles's writings: as a result he resumed teaching, became a master of theology, and was permitted to teach several doctrines condemned in 1277. A well-known contemporary, Godfrey of Fontaines, acclaimed Giles as the greatest teacher at the University of Paris;

he produced numerous theological works and engaged in noted debates with Henry of Ghent on subjects in metaphysics. In 1287, Giles's works were made the official doctrine of the Augustinian order. In 1292 he became superior general of his order, and after the election of his associate, Benedetto Caetano, as Pope Boniface VIII, Giles was appointed archbishop of Bourges (1295). From this time on he was often at the papal court. During the second of Boniface's well-publicized quarrels with Philip the Fair (1301–1302) Giles wrote *On Ecclesiastical Power* (*De Ecclesiastica Potestate*), perhaps the most thorough defense of unlimited papal supremacy written by a theologian in the Middle Ages. The treatise provided the theoretical foundation for Boniface's famous bull, *Unam Sanctam* (1302), which marked the zenith in the assertions of the ecclesiastical polity to temporal power. After Boniface's death in 1303, Giles's influence in the curia waned, although he served on commissions to examine the writings of John of Paris and Peter John Olivi. Giles died in Avignon.

The avowed aim of *On Ecclesiatical Power* is to claim for the pope the greatest extension of power and jurisdiction in all areas of human life, and to make these prerogatives known to the entire Christian people. The treatise is divided into three books. Book 1 examines ecclesiastical authority in relation to the material sword and secular power. Book 2 studies the same authority in relation to temporal goods. Book 3 answers objections that may be raised against the position upheld by the author and, building upon the language of prior papal decrees, develops a detailed theory in which the church exercises an occasional, supreme jurisdiction (when "reasonable cause emerges"). Although Giles was a student of Aquinas and a disciple of Augustine (who is often quoted in the treatise), he goes far beyond either of his masters in his vigorous defense of papal absolutism, employing theological arguments to sustain and deepen assertions from the canon law and decretals. Giles's views on this matter are more akin to those of Hugh of St. Victor and Roger Bacon.

The selections given here were translated by R. W. Dyson from his own critical edition; the translation and the critical edition appear together in R. W. Dyson, *Giles of Rome's On Ecclesiastical Power: A Medieval Theory Of World Government* (New York: Columbia University Press, 2004). The page numbers in the Latin text of Dyson's edition are indicated by italicized numbers within our text. Book 1, Chapter 5 explains the superiority of priestly power to royal power, in part, on the basis of the inherently unjust nature of temporal power divorced from priestly power. Book 2, Chapter 6 grounds the superiority of the ecclesiastical power in the ranking of natural powers and in the hierarchy of the arts and sciences. Book 3, Chapter 9 explicates the idea of the fullness of power (*plenitudo potestatis*).

Book 1, Chapter 5: *In which new arguments are adduced showing that priestly power is superior to and greater in dignity than all royal power.*

There can be no doubt among wise men that priestly power precedes royal and earthly power in dignity and nobility. We can show this in four ways: first, from the payment of tithes; second, from blessing and sanctification; third, from the inception of power itself; fourth, from the government of things themselves[1] . . . [*22*] . . .

The third way is derived from the institution of power itself. And, in the same book and in the same part, Hugh touches upon this way also, saying: "Moreover, that the spiritual power is greater in dignity and might than the earthly is manifestly shown among that ancient people of the Old Testament, where, first, priesthood was instituted by God and, subsequently, royal power was ordained through priesthood at the command of God."[2] Royal power must therefore acknowledge priestly dignity as superior, as being that through which it was instituted at the command of God. And if it be said that not all royal power was instituted through priesthood, we shall reply that any royal power not instituted through priesthood was either not rightful, in that it was more robbery than power; or was united with priesthood; or was the successor of that which had been instituted through priesthood. For where there were kingdoms of the gentiles under the law of nature, almost all such kingdoms came into being through invasion and usurpation. Thus Nimrod, of whom we read that he was the first king, whose reign began in Babylon, as can be gathered from Genesis 10, made himself king by invasion and usurpation; and so it

1. The first two arguments are omitted.

2. Hugh of St. Victor *De Sacramentis Fidei Christianae* 2.2.3 (Patrologia Latina, ed. J.-P. Migne [hereafter PL], 176:417).

is said of him in the same place [*24*] that he began to be mighty on earth [Gen. 10:8]: he acquired his kingdom through civil might and not through justice.[3] But according to Augustine in *De civitate Dei,* kingdoms without justice are great bands of robbers.[4] And although such men [as Nimrod] are called kings, they are not kings, but thieves and robbers.

Kingship not instituted through priesthood, therefore, was either not kingship, but robbery, or was united with priesthood. For even before Saul was instituted and appointed as king through Samuel as through a priest of God [1 Sam. 10:1], Melchizedek was king of Salem. But this Melchizedek, while he was a king, was also a priest. And so, in the same place, it is said that he was a priest of the Most High God [Gen. 14:18]. In this case, therefore, kingship did not exist without priesthood, but was united with priesthood, so that priesthood might here be superior to [mere] kingship [by virtue of the combination of spiritual and temporal power]. But modern kingships are the successors of kingships instituted through priesthood. For the kingship [of Saul] was instituted through priesthood before such kingships were in being. And since former things are the patterns and a mirror of later, all later kingships must be referred back to the first, which was instituted through priesthood at the command of God. When we speak of kingship, then, we are speaking of rightful kingship and of that which is separate from priesthood.

But, as is clear from what has been said, we find four kinds of kingship, namely: the kingship of usurpation, which is robbery; kingship united with priesthood; kingship instituted through priesthood; and kingship which is the successor of that so instituted. Thus, if there be a kingship of usurpation, it is not the kind of kingship of which we are speaking, because it is not rightful. Moreover, kingship which is united with priesthood is not that of which we are speaking, because it is not separate from priesthood. Rather, we are speaking of kingship which has been instituted through priesthood or which is the successor of that so instituted. Hence it is clear that the beginning of right rule, insofar as kingship and priesthood are two separate swords, derives its origin from priesthood. Let kings therefore acknowledge themselves to be instituted through priesthood. For if we give diligent attention to whence royal power has come and to whence it has been instituted, it follows that, because it has been instituted through priesthood, royal power should be subject to priestly power, and especially to the power of the Supreme Priest.

The fourth way is derived from the government of things themselves. Therefore, if we wish to see which power stands under which power, we must pay attention to the government of the whole mechanism of the world. And we see in the government of the universe that the whole of corporeal substance is governed through the spiritual. Inferior bodies are indeed ruled through superior, and the more gross through the more subtle and the less potent through the more potent; but the whole of corporeal substance is nonetheless ruled through the spiritual, and the whole of spiritual substance by the Supreme Spirit: [*26*] that is, by God. Hence Augustine, at *De Trinitate* 3:4, says that "certain more gross and inferior bodies are filled in a certain order through the more subtle and the more potent; but all bodies through spirit, and the whole of creation by its Creator." And what we see in the order and government of the universe we must picture to ourselves in the government of the commonwealth and in the government of the whole Christian people. For that same God Who is the universal Director of the whole mechanism of the world is the special governor of His Church and of His faithful people.

And so if the whole universe, of which God has the general care, is so well ordered that inferior bodies are under superior and all bodies are under the spiritual and spiritual substance itself is under the Supreme Spirit; that is, under God; then it is wholly inconsistent to say that the faithful people, and the Church herself, whom God has chosen for Himself; having neither spot nor blemish,[5] is not well ordered; and that she is not wholly and entirely united and joined in the same way, and that the order of the universe, which, as Augustine maintains in the *Enchiridion,* is a most beautiful order and an astonishing beauty:[6] that this astonishing beauty, this most beautiful order, is not

3. Gen. 10:8–10; cf. Peter Comestor *Historia Scholastica,* PL 198:1088.

4. *De Civitate Dei* 4.4 (Corpus Christianorum Series Latina [hereafter CCSL] 47:101).

5. Cf. Eph. 5:27.

6. *Enchiridion* 3.10 (CCSL 46:53).

reflected in the Church. And so just as, in the universe itself, inferior bodies are ruled through superior and the weaker through the more potent, so, among the Christian people, among the faithful themselves, inferior temporal lords are ruled through superiors and the less potent through the more potent. And just as, in the universe itself, the whole of corporeal substance is ruled through spiritual—for the heavens themselves, which are supreme among corporeal substances and which have influence over all bodies, are governed through spiritual substances: through the intelligences which move them;[7] so, among the faithful themselves, all temporal lords and every earthly power must be ruled and governed through the spiritual and ecclesiastical power, and especially through the Supreme Pontiff, who holds the supreme and highest rank in the Church and in spiritual power. But the Supreme Pontiff himself must be judged only by God. For, as we have said above,[8] it is he who judges all things and is judged by no one: that is, by no mere man, but by God alone...[9] [28]...

Nor would it avail if anyone were to say that, though the whole of earthly power must be under the spiritual, this is to be understood with respect to the articles of faith, and not with respect to temporal and earthly power. For those who speak thus do not grasp the force of the argument. For bodies, inasmuch as they are bodies, are placed under spirits. And just as the movements of bodies themselves, and especially the movements of the higher bodies, are governed through ruling spirits and through the intelligences which move the spheres, so temporal powers, inasmuch as they are temporal, and especially the supreme temporal powers, will be subject to judgment by the spiritual power; and especially by the power of the Supreme Pontiff, who is the most sublime and supreme spiritual power in the Church. Inferior temporal lords, if they offend, will be subject to the judgment of superior temporal lords. But superior temporal lords themselves, because they have no superiors among temporal lords, will be subject to the judgment of the spiritual power. But the spiritual power itself, and especially the power of the Supreme Priest, will be subject to judgment by no one except God alone; for it has no man, but God, as its superior.

Book 2, Chapter 6: *That the earthly power is rightly and properly the servant of the spiritual power in itself and in what belongs to it, because it is more particular, and because it prepares material, and because it comes less close to attaining what is best.*

Because the earthly power has lordship over temporal things, we have therefore endeavored in the various chapters of this short work to show more clearly how such power is rightly and properly subject to the spiritual power, so that we may be able to infer from this that the spiritual power will have lordship not only over the earthly power, but also over temporal things, since ecclesiastical authority is shown to have both temporal things and their lords as its subjects.

Now in the heading of this chapter we have noted some three ways in which our proposition can be made clear, which three ways are derived from what we see in other powers. For, in order that it may not avail anyone to resist us in this matter, we wish to show through what we see in other powers that the earthly power must be subject to the spiritual power, so that, from this, we may draw the further conclusion that earthly and temporal things are themselves placed under the jurisdiction and lordship of the Church. Furthermore, it will be possible to show from these observations that, by the disposition of God, these two powers are mutually ordered in such a way that the one does not impede the other, but assists it, and that the one does not take away the right of the other, but that each, [*114*] by observing its proper limit, enjoys and uses its own right: so that, if the earthly power serves the spiritual, the right of the earthly power is not taken away by this, since it is rightly and properly bound to serve the spiritual power. And if, for just and urgent cause, the Church were to concern herself with the affairs of the empire, or with the empire itself, or even, for just and urgent cause, were to transfer the empire, she would inflict injustice on no one by this.[10] For she is competent to do this as of right, and he who makes use of his own right is said to inflict

7. Cf Aquinas *Summa Theologiae* 1.115.3.

8. *On Ecclesiastical Power* 1.2.

9. Two paragraphs are omitted here.

10. According to a well-established tradition, when Leo III crowned Charlemagne on Christmas Day, AD 800, the Roman Empire was transferred (*translatio imperii*) from Byzantium to the West (*On Ecclesiastical Power*, trans. R. W. Dyson [New York: Columbia University Press, 2004], xxiii n. 41).

injustice on no one.[11] For it was said in the previous chapter that the strict duty of the ecclesiastical power requires this: that, though it may possess all things in the sense of exercising lordship, it may have nothing temporally—that is, in the sense of being anxious. Rather, it must entrust anxiety for temporal possessions to the laity, so that it may attend more freely to spiritual matters. Nonetheless, for just and urgent cause, as we have proved by the authority of Bede, this strict duty can sometimes be set aside, so that the Church may justly concern herself even with temporal matters and with those things which belong to the right of the empire.

Let us come, therefore, to our proposition, and make clear the statements contained in the heading of this chapter. To this end, we shall distinguish four kinds of power (*potestas*), and we shall show that, in each kind, some powers are superior and others inferior, and also that, in each such kind, the inferior powers are always the servants of the superior. By way of describing power, then, let us say that power is nothing other than that through which someone is said to be powerful. Therefore, just as whiteness is that through which something is said to be white and blackness is that through which something is said to be black, so power is that through which someone is said to be powerful.

Moreover, we see that it is through natural forces (*virtutes naturales*) that natural causes are powerful. For example, fire is able to heat through heat and through the heating force which it has; and water is able to cool through a cooling force; and the heaven is able to influence these inferior agents through the force which it has. Thus, each natural thing is powerful through its force and through its potency. And just as natural causes are powerful through natural forces, so artists are powerful through the arts: for example, a lute-player is able to play the lute properly through the art of lute-playing, but he who lacks this art cannot play the lute properly. Third, the wise are powerful through the sciences: for example, one man may be powerful in understanding the parts and properties of body in motion through natural philosophy, and another may be powerful, through the other sciences, in examining and understanding those phenomena which are explained by the other sciences. And princes are powerful through the ruling powers, whether these ruling powers be material or spiritual, so that each may enjoy his own right and each may rule by virtue of his own ruling power.

Therefore, four kinds of power have been distinguished. One kind of power consists in natural forces, another in the arts, a third in the sciences, and a fourth in the ruling powers and governments of men. And each of these powers consists [*116*] in a certain order and proportion. Thus, natural power is the proportionate production of natural effects; and artistic power is right reason or order applied to the production of that which can be made by art; and scientific power is right reason applied to the study of that which can be investigated; and the power of ruling is ordered and right reason applied to the government of men. And because we have undertaken the present treatise in order to say something of the ruling powers (*principatus*), which are powers (*potestas*) of a kind, we must also consider the other powers if we wish diligently to examine what order there may be among the ruling powers and governments of men. For to the extent that we examine the other powers, we shall be able to show something of the ruling powers and governments of men.

And so we see, among the natural powers, that some of them are superior and others inferior: that the forces of heaven are superior to those of the elements. For the forces of the elements do not act except by the force of heaven since, as is taught in natural philosophy, fire would not act in such a way as to generate fire, or would not be able to generate fire, except by the force of heaven; and so the heaven and fire generate fire.[12] And what has been said of the elements must be understood to be true also of compounds. For example, according to the order which we see, a horse would not be able to generate a horse except by the force of the sun. And so too with the other animals: sun and horse generate a horse, and sun and lion generate a lion, as it is the task of the natural sciences to show. The force of heaven, therefore, as more general and more universal, is lord of all other forces, whether these forces be those of elements or of compounds.

And just as among natural things we see that some are superior and others inferior, so also among the

11. Cf. Justinian *Digesta* 50.17.55 (*The Digest of Justinian,* ed. T. Mommsen and P. Krueger [Philadelphia: University of Pennsylvania Press, 1985]).

12. Cf. Averroes's commentary on Aristotle's *De Caelo* 2.1 284a1 (*Aristotelis Opera cum Averrois Commentariis,* 5:125) and *Metaphysics* 12.3 1070a (*Aristotelis Opera cum Averrois Commentariis,* 8:304); Aquinas *Summa Theologiae* 1.115.3.

arts some are superior and others inferior. For example, just as there is a certain art of bridle-making, so also is there a certain art of knowing how to make use of an army; and these two arts are not to be linked together as equals. Rather, the one art is under the other: bridle-making is under warfare, for the art of bridle-making is that of making such a bridle as will be of use to the soldier.[13] It is not in this way, however, that the inferior [natural] forces serve the heavenly; for those inferior forces serve the heavenly in that they act more particularly, whereas bridle-making is subservient to warfare in that it prepares its material. But the heaven exerts influence upon all things and assists all things, for it assists both elements and compounds: it assists water to cool and fire to heat; it assists the horse to generate a horse and the lion to generate a lion. For neither the lion nor the horse nor the other compounds could produce anything naturally except by the force of heaven; and neither water nor fire nor the other elements could produce anything except by the force of heaven.

The force of heaven, then, is general, and so has lordship, whereas those inferior forces [*118*] which are either of elements or of compounds are particular, and are therefore servants. But, in the arts, you can assign the reason and cause whereby bridle-making serves warfare rather to the preparation of material than to the particularity of the agent. For there may be various other animals apart from horses for which bridles can be made, which animals may not be the instruments of war or battle. Therefore, although the inferior [natural] forces are particular in relation to the heaven and so can do nothing except by its force, it nonetheless cannot be that bridle-making is particular in relation to warfare in the sense of producing nothing except that which is of use to the soldier. Bridle-making does indeed serve warfare; but by preparing material for it. And, in order to prepare material for it, it orders itself and what belongs to it towards warfare. Therefore, we shall say that a horse is a kind of material with which soldiers occupy themselves; but a horse is not a kind of material prepared and disposed in such a way as to serve the soldier unless it has a bridle, just as a boat would not be disposed in such a way as to serve the sailor unless it had a rudder. Thus, bridle-making serves warfare by preparing material. So also stone-cutting serves building by disposing material, for he who cuts stone serves the builder by preparing material for him.

The reasons and causes have been assigned, then, whereby, among natural things and in the arts, one agent serves another. And, in the sciences, we can assign a third reason and cause whereby one is the servant of another. For, among the sciences discovered by man, each is the servant of metaphysics: not only because metaphysics is more general and more universal than the other sciences, but also because it more completely attains what is best. For among the sciences discovered by man, metaphysics is more able to contemplate God, Who is the most perfect among beings, than any of the other sciences. And so it is that, since theology attains what is best more completely than metaphysics and any other science, she is mistress of the sciences and makes use of all the sciences in her service, so that metaphysics herself is her handmaid and servant. For if metaphysics, or any science discovered by man, contemplates God, this is so only to the extent that He can be contemplated by rational means; but theology contemplates God as He is known with the aid of Divine revelation. And since many more things can be known, and are known, of God through revelation than by effort of reason; it follows that theology attains what is best more completely, and can contemplate many more aspects of God, than any other science, and so is goddess and mistress of the sciences; all of which other sciences are her handmaids. And so she sends to summon them all to the citadel and to the walls of the city as handmaids; for she makes use of them all in her service, so that they may all defend the citadel and the walls of the city: that is, so that they may all defend theology, which we are calling a kind of citadel and a kind of walled city, lest she be attacked by her adversaries. Thus, in the Song of Songs,[14] she is likened to the Tower of David which was adorned with battlements upon which were many bucklers and all the arms of valiant men, so that the arguments [*120*] of the philosophers might not disturb nor suffice to invade her. And all these remarks can be applied to theology and to the Church alike.[15]

13. Cf. Aristotle *Nicomachean Ethics* 1.1 1094al0.

14. Cf. Cant. [Song of Solomon] 4:4.

15. The thought of this paragraph seems somewhat confused, but the point is evidently that just as metaphysics, though the highest of the sciences discovered by man, is nonetheless subject to theology, even the highest of earthly powers is subject to the Church. Cf. Aquinas *Summa Theologiae* 1.1.6. See also below.

Therefore, we have distinguished four kinds of power. For we have said that some powers are natural forces, others are the creations of art, others are the rational operations of the sciences, and others are the ruling powers and governments of men. And, as to the first three kinds, we have assigned three reasons for their subjection and lordship, and three causes. As to the natural forces, we have assigned generality and limitation as the reason and cause by virtue of which they are under the lordship of the forces of heaven. Thus, the forces of heaven have lordship because they are general, whereas the inferior forces serve because they are limited and particular. And, as to the creations of art, we have assigned the preparation of materials as such a reason and cause. Thus, stone-cutting is the servant of building and bridle-making of warfare because they prepare and dispose material for them. And, as to the rational operations of the sciences, we have assigned nearness to what is best as the reason and cause; for that science which attains what is best more completely is lord, and the others are its handmaids.

But in the case of powers of the fourth kind—the ruling and governing powers—we shall say that all three of these causes come together at once. For we shall say that earthly power and rule must obey and serve spiritual power and rule for all three of the reasons so far given: because it is more particular, and because it disposes and prepares material, and also because the one does not come near to or attain what is best as does the other.

Now the ecclesiastical power is more universal than the earthly because the Church herself is said to be Catholic, that is, universal, as Isidore says in the final chapter of *Etymologiae* 7; for he says that 'catholic' is to be translated as 'universal' or 'general' and he adds that 'catholic' is the Greek word for 'universal'.[16] Therefore, if it is an article of faith that we must believe in the Holy Catholic Church, he is not truly faithful who does not believe the Church to be Catholic, that is, universal, and Holy, that is, established and made firm because founded upon a firm Rock; or Holy, that is, pure and spotless, according to what is said in Ephesians 5: *That Christ might present it to Himself as a glorious Church, having no spot or blemish* [Eph. 5:2]. The Church, therefore, is Holy and Catholic, that is, universal; but she would not be truly universal if she did not rule universally over all things.

But the remaining ruling powers are particular, for none of them is a power without which a man cannot obtain salvation. And this is especially so if we speak of secular rulers and earthly powers, for he who withdraws himself from these comes nearer to salvation. For the clergy, who are not under the earthly power, are in a more perfect state [*122*] than are the laity, who are placed under the earthly power. Thus, the earthly power is not universal in such a way that no one can obtain salvation unless he is under it. On the contrary, as we have said, the clergy, who are not under the earthly power, are in a more perfect state than the laity....[17]

The earthly power, therefore, is particular, because it does not have power over all men; but the ecclesiastical power is universal. This was prefigured in the book [*124*] of Numbers, when the Levites, that is, the clergy, were given the surrounding lands under every part of heaven. In this it was prefigured that the Church, who was to succeed to the Levites who served the altar, was to have lordship over the whole world and in every part thereof. For, as of right, every man is under that without which he cannot obtain salvation. Thus, the Church must have lordship over the whole world, and all men must be under her; for those who are not under her will find the gates of heaven closed, and so will not gain entry into the Kingdom of Heaven.

And this universal lordship of the Church was not only prefigured in the Old Law, but has been made manifest among the articles of faith: which must be interpreted not narrowly, but broadly, since upon them are founded all the things which are to be believed and the entire Christian faith. And every true Christian must confess this article: that the Church is Holy and Catholic. But she would not be Catholic—that is, universal—if she did not have lordship equally over all the faithful and over all the possessions of the faithful. For the Church is Catholic because she exercises a universal lordship, and the faithful themselves are Catholics because of their universal subjection to the Church. Let no one say that he is a Catholic, then,

16. *Etymologiae* 7.14.4 (PL 82:294).

17. Two paragraphs are omitted. They argue that the earthly power not only has no power over the Levites (Num. 35:2–8), that is, the priesthood, but also no power over those who had shed blood and then taken refuge in the six towns possessed by the Levites. In the same biblical passage the Levites were granted land in every direction around the towns.

if he is not subject to the Universal Church; and let no one confess the Church to be Catholic unless he confesses that she has a universal lordship. But no one is universally subject to the Church unless he places himself and what is his under the Church: first himself, indeed, and then what is his. For, as is established in Genesis 4, the Lord was mindful of Abel and of his offerings [Gen. 4:4]: of Abel first, therefore, and of his offerings afterwards. Therefore, the faithful must subject first themselves and then what is theirs to the Church; for both belong to the Church: the faithful and the possessions of the faithful. The apostles also desired to have both and to be lords of both: not in order to exalt themselves, but in order to extend the Church and to make her universal and Catholic. And so a gloss on 2 Corinthians 6 says that it was the glory of the apostles "to possess both things and their lords."[18]

Let us turn again to our proposition, therefore, and say that almost every word of this argument supports the conclusion that the earthly power, both in itself and in what belongs to it, must be subject to the ecclesiastical power. Nonetheless, in order to pursue our subject matter as described in the heading of this chapter, we shall [adduce still further arguments to] indicate that, as is clear from what has been said, ecclesiastical lordship is universal whereas earthly lordship is particular.

For ecclesiastical lordship imitates the forces of heaven, whose task it is to exert influence over all things; but earthly lordship imitates those inferior forces whose task it is to bring about particular effects. Thus, fire heats in such a way that it cannot of itself be said to cool; and water cools in such a way that it cannot of itself be said to heat. But the force of heaven accomplishes both. For it assists water to cool since, according to the order that we see, water could not cool if the force of heaven were withdrawn. And, in the same way, it assists fire to heat. For all these [*126*] inferior forces, as servants of heaven, effect whatever they accomplish through the power of heaven. And so earthly lords, as the Church's servants in all their actions and in everything that belongs to them, must acknowledge that the Church is Catholic and universal: that is, universal in lordship. Thus, the earthly power will be under the ecclesiastical as the particular is under the universal, which form of subjection is displayed by the inferior [natural] forces relative to the heavenly.

Second, the earthly power will be under the ecclesiastical as an art which prepares material is under that for which it prepares it. For it pertains to the earthly power to receive the material sword through the Church and under the Church, and to exercise lordship over material things and temporal affairs, and, so far as lay persons and the property over which they have received power are concerned, over human bodies also. Therefore, it will be the duty of the earthly power to do justice in these respects, so that no one may injure another in his own body or in his own property, but every citizen and every faithful man may enjoy his goods. Therefore, it is the duty of the earthly power to prepare material so that the ruler of the Church may not be impeded in spiritual tasks. For the body was made to serve the soul and temporal goods to serve the body. The body is therefore well disposed when it serves the soul well, and temporal goods are well disposed and ordered when they are ordered to the requirements of bodily life and the needs of human bodies. Therefore, the whole duty of the earthly power is to govern and rule these external and material goods in such a way that the faithful are not impeded in the peace of conscience and in peace of soul and in tranquillity of mind. For, in this way, not only have justice and peace kissed[19] in those things which are of God—since unless we live justly with God we shall not have peace with Him—but also justice among these external goods conduces greatly to tranquillity of soul and to peace of mind. For if all men were perfect in their suffering of injustice in the way described in Matthew 5—*If someone shall strike you on your right cheek, turn to him the other also; and if someone shall sue you at law and take away your coat, let him have your cloak also* [Matt. 5:39–40]—then perhaps there would be no need of earthly justice. But since not all men are thus perfect, and since it is good to restrain injustice not only so that victims may not suffer harm, but also so that offenders may not inflict it, there was a need to institute the earthly power to preserve justice as between bodies and temporal things, to preserve tranquillity of soul and peace of mind, and to preserve tranquillity in spiritual matters.

Above all, therefore, the task of earthly princes is to dispose and prepare material for the ruler of the Church. Therefore, they preserve justice in the temporal and material spheres so that peace

18. *Glossa Ordinaria*, PL 114:560.

19. Cf. Ps. 85:10 [Ps. 84:11 in Douay-Rheims].

of mind and tranquillity may be preserved in the spiritual, and so that he who exercises lordship spiritually may exercise lordship more freely. Therefore, just as bridle-making, by placing a bridle on a horse, prepares the horse for the soldier so that it may serve him more freely, so the earthly power, [*128*] by placing a bridle on the laity so that they may not offend against the Church or each other, disposes them so that they may be the more freely subject to the ecclesiastical power. And just as stone-cutting, by cutting stones, disposes them so that the builder may make from those stones a commodious and well-arranged house, so—since the faithful people are the members of which the body of the Church is composed, and are the stones of which the spiritual temple which is the Church is assembled, whose cornerstone and foundation is Christ, according to Ephesians 2: *Christ Jesus Himself being the chief cornerstone, upon Whom the whole building grows into a holy temple in the Lord, upon Whom also you are built together*, and so on [Eph. 2:20–22]—the earthly power, by means of justice in external goods, cuts and disposes these stones for the sake of peace of mind and tranquillity of soul, so that a spiritual temple may be the more freely and easily built from them.

It is clear, therefore, that earthly power and the art of governing a people by earthly power is the art of disposing material for the sake of the disposition of the ecclesiastical power. And so, just as bridle-making is subordinate to warfare, and just as stone-cutting is subject to building, so that all that they do is subject to the command and will of the superior arts and they subordinate all their tools and all their instruments to their command and will: so the art of exercising lordship by means of earthly power, and the earthly power itself, must be so subject to the ecclesiastical power that it subordinates itself and all its instruments and tools to the service and to the command of the spiritual power. And because the instruments and tools of the earthly power are civil might (*potentia*), the weapons of War, the temporal goods which it has, and the laws and constitutions which it establishes, it must therefore subordinate itself and all these things which it has as instruments and tools to the service and will of the ecclesiastical power. Thus, secular power, in itself and with all the instruments just mentioned, is subject to the ecclesiastical power.

Third, the earthly power will be under the ecclesiastical as that which attains what is best is under that which attains it more completely. We see this mode of subjection in the sciences; for metaphysics, which is concerned with God, is the goddess of the sciences discovered by man, and all other such sciences are under metaphysics and serve her, and she herself directs the other sciences. According to this same mode, the ecclesiastical power, which is spiritual and concerned with those things which are of God, is mistress over the earthly power, and it rests with her to direct such power; and the earthly power must be subject to the command of the priest.

Open your eyes, therefore, and see: ask the forces of nature and they will proclaim it to you;[20] consider the ways of the arts and they will tell you; attend to the investigations of the sciences and they will show you. You see, among the forces of nature, that the particular and earthly forces are subject in themselves and in what belongs to them to the universal and heavenly forces. You see also in the arts that those arts which prepare material are subordinate in themselves and in what belongs to them to those for which they prepare material. You see moreover, [*130*] in the investigations of the sciences, that the science which attains what is best more completely is mistress of the other sciences. And since all these things come together in the ecclesiastical power in relation to the earthly—because the earthly power is more particular, disposes material, and attains what is best less completely—it is thus demonstrated and shown clearer than clearly that such power is, in itself and in what belongs to it, subject and subservient to the ecclesiastical power.

Book 3, Chapter 9: *What fullness of power is, and that fullness of power truly resides in the Supreme Pontiff.*

Because we have spoken in many chapters of fullness of power, we therefore wish in the present chapter to show what fullness of power is. Also, we shall show that there is such fullness in the Supreme Pontiff, by reason of which his power is without limit of number, weight, and measure, as will appear in the final chapter.

Many illustrations might be adduced to show what fullness of power is. For our present purpose, however, let it suffice to show only this: that fullness of power resides in some agent when that

20. Cf. Deut. 32:7; 2 Kings 19:16.

agent can do without a secondary cause whatever it can do [*362*] with a secondary cause. For if an agent does not have such power, it follows that it does not have a full power because it does not have a power in which all power is contained. Thus, inasmuch as the Supreme Pontiff has a power in which all power is contained, we say that he has a full power. And, so that we may pass to the government of men by way of those natural phenomena which we see in the government of the world, we shall say that fullness of power does not reside in the heaven [i.e. in the natural order] nor in any secondary agent whatsoever; for the heaven cannot do without a secondary cause what it can do with a secondary cause. For example, although the heaven and a lion bring about the generation of a lion, the heaven could not produce a lion without a lion, nor could it produce a horse without a horse. In God Himself, however, there is fullness of power, for whatever He can do with a secondary cause He can do without a secondary cause. And so the power of all agents is contained in the Primary Agent, that is, in God; for, in bringing forth the world, He brought forth a man without a preexisting man and a horse without a preexisting horse. Now, indeed, He brings forth a horse by means of a horse, but, if He wished and when He wished, He could do this without seed; and an ox by means of an ox, but He could make an ox without an ox, for He could make a calf out of a block of wood, or He could make a calf out of nothing, and the result would come about just as He willed.[21] And, although He can do all things, He nonetheless directs things in such a way that He allows them to pursue their own courses. Sometimes, however, God performs a miracle, or even miracles, so that He may act beyond the ordinary course of nature and not according to the established common laws of nature.

So also, to such extent as there is power within the Church, the Supreme Pontiff has fullness of power, and he can do without a secondary cause whatever he can do with a secondary cause. For example, the election of a bishop depends upon the ordinance of the Supreme Pontiff as to how the election of prelates is to be conducted and as to what manner of men the electors should be in respect of zeal and merit and number, so that there should be such a number of electors, and electors of such a kind, as to ensure that he who is elected is properly chosen. Thus, such election depends upon the establishing and ordaining of the mode of election by the Supreme Pontiff [as by a primary cause], just as the production of natural things depends upon God as a primary cause, Who establishes His laws for natural things, which regulate how they act and how they produce their effects. And the election of a prelate depends also upon the assent of the Canons and upon their choice as upon a secondary cause, just as the production of natural things depends upon natural things themselves, which are under one primary agent: that is, under God.

Truly, therefore, to such extent as there is power within the Church, fullness of power resides in the Supreme Pontiff; for he can do without a secondary cause whatever he can do with a secondary cause. For he could make provision [of a bishop] for any church without election by the chapter, and, by so doing, he would not act according to the established common laws, but according to his fullness of power. [*364*] For, as we have said, the election of a prelate is brought about as by a primary cause—by the Supreme Pontiff establishing how the election is to be conducted—and by a secondary cause, namely, by the choice of the electors according to the form given to them. But the Supreme Pontiff could provide a prelate for any church without this secondary cause: that is, without the choice of the electors. And what has been said of the election of a prelate is true of the other things which are done in the Church: that the Supreme Pontiff, as having fullness of power, in whom all the power of the Church is acknowledged to reside, can act without other agents.

The Supreme Pontiff should note, however, that God, Who has all power not only conditionally (that is, with respect to this or with respect to that) but absolutely, nonetheless almost always acts according to the laws which He has established for things, lest the works of His wisdom should be in vain; and He almost always observes the laws [of nature] in order to accomplish the effects of secondary agents by means of secondary agents. For He warms by means of fire, and He cools by means of water; for it cannot come about according to the laws established for things that what is in fire is not warmed and that what is in water is not cooled. And again, it cannot come about according to these laws that he who walks upon water does not wet his feet. Sometimes, however, albeit rarely, He brings about a state of affairs beyond

21. Cf. *On Ecclesiatical Power* 1.5, p. 33.

these common laws, such that what is in fire is not burned and that someone may walk upon water with dry feet.[22]

So also, the Supreme Pontiff, because it is his task to establish laws regulating how the Church must be governed, should indeed govern the Church according to these laws, and should permit chapters to conduct their own elections and prelates to exercise their own functions and the other persons who are in the Church to perform their tasks according to the form given to them. For reasonable cause, however, he can act beyond these common laws without other agents; for the power of all other agents is contained in him, in that there is in him all the power of all the agents within the Church. And so, for this reason, it may be said that fullness of power resides in him[23]... [*366*]...

In the heaven, therefore, there is not fullness of power with respect to the production of natural phenomena, for neither in the production of perfect things nor even of imperfect can it do without a secondary cause what it can do with a secondary cause.[24] In God, however, there is fullness of power absolutely; for He can do without a secondary cause all that He can do with a secondary cause, nor does He need secondary agents in the production of any effect whatsoever. But the fact that He brings about His effects by means of secondary agents is due not to any need on His part, but to His goodness. For He wishes to share His dignity with His creatures, and He desires that His creatures should not be idle and in vain, and He desires that they should perform their own functions and their own tasks.

But there is fullness of power in the Supreme Pontiff not in every way, but to such extent as there is power within the Church, in that all the power which is in the Church is contained in the Supreme Pontiff. And we say 'all the power which is in the Church' because if there is any power which Christ has retained to Himself and not communicated to the Church, it cannot be that such power is in the Supreme Pontiff. For example, Christ could give the effect of a sacrament without the [actual performance of the] sacrament. For when a child is born, he cannot have the baptism of the Spirit, which baptism one may have by desire, for he does not have the use of reason. If, therefore, he did not have the baptism of blood (as he would not unless he were slain for Christ), and he did not have the baptism of water, and so had baptism neither by desire nor of blood nor of water,[25] Christ could still confer the effect of baptism upon such a newborn child and give him the grace of baptism without [the fact of] baptism; for Christ has not fettered His own power by the sacraments: for He can confer the effect of a sacrament without the sacrament itself. But Christ has not communicated the power to do this to the Church; and so it cannot be that such power is contained in the Supreme Pontiff. Thus, the Supreme Pontiff has fullness of power, and he has all power: not in every way whatever, but he has all the power which has been communicated to the Church and which is in the Church. [*368*]

Therefore, just as, in God, there is fullness of power absolutely, since God can do whatever any agent can do, and whatever He can do by means of any agents He can do without those agents, so the Supreme Pontiff has fullness of power to such extent as there is power in the Church, since whatever any ecclesiastic can do the Supreme Pontiff can do. Hence, he is said to be the ordinary judge everywhere; and whatever the Supreme Pontiff can do by means of any ecclesiastics he can do without them. Nonetheless, as God's most beloved Vicar, he must be His imitator: he must not make use of this fullness of power without distinction and indiscriminately, but only on the examination of certain causes. For where just and reasonable cause has emerged, he can make use of this power freely; for where there is a holy intention, where there is the spirit of the Lord, there is also liberty.[26] And, by the use of this power, their own functions are indeed removed from many members of the Church, so that, if the Supreme Pontiff makes provision [of a bishop] for any church without consulting the Canons, he can indeed do this by reason of his fullness of power, but, when he acts in this way, their own functions are removed from the Canons.

If, therefore, as we have noted above, God, Who has all power absolutely, [nonetheless] governs the

22. Cf. Dan. 3:20; Matt. 14:25–31.

23. Two paragraphs omitted.

24. The omitted paragraphs argue: "In the production of a horse [a perfect thing], the heaven operates as a superior cause and the seed of the horse... as an inferior cause"; in "those [imperfect things] generated from putrefaction... the heaven [again] operates as a superior cause and the putrefaction as an inferior cause"; in neither case can the heaven produce the animal without the inferior cause.

25. Cf. Aquinas *Summa Theologiae* 3.66.11 and 12.

26. Cf. 2 Cor. 3:17.

world according to the laws which He has established for things, and does not use His fullness of power to act beyond the usual course of things without distinction and indiscriminately, but acts beyond these established laws and beyond this usual course only when reasonable cause emerges, so also the Supreme Pontiff, as God's imitator, if he has established a law under which the Canons may elect their own pastor, or under which certain ecclesiastics may carry out certain tasks, should govern the Church according to these established laws, according to this usual course. When reasonable cause emerges, however, he is free to use his power to act beyond these laws and beyond this usual course.

But there is another cause and another reason why it behooves the Supreme Pontiff to act according to the established laws and according to the normal course. For what Aristotle says in the *Politics* is especially true of the Supreme Pontiff. For he maintains that every prince must be a man of many eyes, of many hands, and of many feet.[27] He must indeed be a man of many eyes, because he must gather to himself many industrious and wise men, through whom he may see those things which pertain to the government of his principality. He must be a man of many hands, for he must gather to himself vigorous and powerful men through whom he may do those things which must be done. And he must be a man of many feet, for he must gather to himself many firm and steadfast men, so that his principality may not stumble. This, therefore, is not to remove their functions from others; rather, it is to encourage them to perform their proper activities. It is to encourage the eyes to see: that is, the wise to deliberate. It is to encourage the hands to grasp: that is, the powerful to act. It is to encourage the feet, whose task it is to support all else, [*370*] to walk steadfastly and firmly towards what is good.

Let us return to our proposition, therefore, and say that, although fullness of power does not reside in the material heaven because it cannot bring about those natural effects without inferior causes which it can with such inferior causes, nonetheless, in the Supreme Pontiff, there is fullness of power: not absolutely and as such, nor in every way whatsoever, but to such extent as there is power within the Church. For whatever he can do with other ecclesiastics he can do without them. If we wish to investigate the cause of this, we shall say that it does not rest with the heaven to give laws to natural things; rather, it is its task to act according to the established laws of nature. And so miracles cannot come about simply by the power of heaven, for a miracle is an act beyond the given laws of nature. But it rests with the Supreme Pontiff to lay down laws and to give laws to all ecclesiastics and to the whole Church. And so he is above such laws, and there is in him a fullness of power such that he may act beyond the laws.

Thus, two senses have been assigned to fullness of power. The first is that it can do without a secondary cause all that it can do with a secondary cause; for God can do without natural agents whatever He can do with them. So too, the Supreme Pontiff can do without any persons whatsoever whatever he might do with them. But the other sense is that, just as God gives natural laws to natural things—for example, He gives the law to fire that it may heat and to water that it may cool—and yet there is fullness of power in Him because He can act beyond these laws, so the Supreme Pontiff gives positive moral laws to the nations or to men, yet there is nonetheless fullness of power in him because he can act beyond those laws.

27. Aristotle *Politics* 3.16 1287b30.

TWENTY-SIX

PTOLEMY OF LUCCA

On the Government of Rulers

Translated by James M. Blythe

Ptolemy (Tolomeo Fiadoni) was born in Lucca ca. 1236 and joined the Dominican order in his youth. He likely studied under Thomas Aquinas in Rome, 1265–1268, and in Naples, 1272–1274, becoming Thomas's friend and confessor. In 1288 he was made prior of the Dominican house in Lucca, serving there intermittently over the following fifteen years; he was also prior at Santa Maria Novella in Florence, 1301–1302. From 1309 he lived in Avignon, the location of the papal court of Clement V. There Ptolemy befriended Jacques Duèze, who was elected in 1316 as Clement's successor, John XXII. In 1318 the pope appointed Ptolemy bishop of Torcello, near Venice. Ptolemy became embroiled in a quarrel with the neighboring patriarch of Grado over the appointment of an abbess, ca. 1320. Multiple charges were brought against him, he was excommunicated in 1321, and at some point imprisoned. The pope made inquiries into the matter in 1322 and, although the details remain unclear, the charges were dropped, and Ptolemy was freed. He died in Avignon in 1327.[1]

Ptolemy completed *On the Government of Rulers* (*De Regimine Principum*) no later than 1303. He also wrote a shorter political work treating the authorities of the empire and of the papacy, *De Iurisdictione Imperii et Auctoritate Summi Pontificis* (also known as *Determinatio Compendiosa de Iuribus Imperii*, ed. M. F. Krammer, in *Fontes Iuris Germanici Antique in Usum Scholarum ex Monumentis Germaniae Historicis Separatim Editi* [Hanover and Leipzig: Bibliophilus Hahnianus, 1909]). This work is commonly thought to have been written between 1277 and 1281. There is some overlap between the two works (compare, for example, *Determinatio Compendiosa*, chaps. 18–23 with *De Regimine* 3.1–6), but *On the Government of Rulers* discusses a broader range of political associations and shows a more pronounced influence of Aristotle's *Politics*. In accord with the conventional dating of the two works, *On the Government of Rulers* marks a development in Ptolemy's thought toward a greater appreciation of political rule.[2] Ptolemy's fame has rested largely on his work as a historian:

1. The biographical details have been generously provided by James M. Blythe; see his *Life and Works of Tolomeo Fiadoni (Ptolemy of Lucca)* (Turnhout: Brepols, 2009).

2. According to an alternative view advanced by J. Miethke, the *Determinatio Compendiosa* was not completed until 1300 (*De potestate papae: Die päpstliche Amtskompetenz im Widerstreit der politischen Theorie von Thomas von Aquin bis Wilhelm von Ockham* [Tübingen: Mohr Siebeck, 2000], 86–93). Also see J. M. Blythe and J. La Salle, "Was Ptolemy of Lucca a Civic Humanist? Reflections on a Newly-Discovered Manuscript of Hans Baron," *History of Political Thought* 26 (2005): 237–65.

he wrote chronicles on Tuscany, seen in the light of wider events, and a history of the church (*Historia Ecclesiastica Nova: Nebst Fortsetzungen bis 1329*, ed. O. Clavuot and L. Schmugge [Hanover: Hahnsche Buchhandlung, 2009]).

Ptolemy's *On the Government of Rulers* is a continuation of Aquinas's *On Kingship, to the King of Cyprus* (*De Regno ad Regem Cypri*), which his teacher had begun either ca. 1267 or 1271–1273 but did not complete.[3] Many manuscripts and the vast majority of early printed editions contained both Aquinas's part (through Book 2, Chapter 4) and Ptolemy's continuation (through Book 4), generally without attributing the continuation to Ptolemy. *On the Government of Rulers* appears to have enjoyed a wide readership and exerted varying degrees of influence on the English jurist John Fortescue (ca. 1394–1476); Isaac Abravanel (1437–1508), whose work appears in this volume; and Girolamo Savonarola (ca. 1452–1498), the Dominican preacher and de facto leader of Florence in 1494–1498.[4] Ptolemy's treatment of Roman virtues may have influenced Dante's thinking on the same subject, especially in Book 2 of the *Monarchy*, although it is also possible that they worked from common sources.[5] The overarching subject of Ptolemy's portion of the book is lordship (*dominium*). Book 3 begins by describing the source of all lordship; it subsequently lists the types of lordship and focuses on a particular form, regal lordship, as well as several variations on that form. Book 4 discusses the other fundamental form of lordship, political lordship. This overarching contrast between regal lordship and political lordship appears to follow Thomas's distinction between kingly rule and political rule (*Commentary on the Politics* 1.1.6), which, in turn, is based on Aristotle's observations that perfect kingship is beyond the law, whereas political arrangements operate through the law. Ptolemy's treatment of political rule in the extended treatise contrasts with Aquinas's narrower focus on kingship in the prior, incomplete form of the treatise. Ptolemy's interest in political rule seems to have been prompted by his experience of northern Italian civic republics or "communes." His interest in ancient Roman examples and sources (e.g., Sallust, Cicero, Seneca) is characteristic of the protohumanist literary culture of the communes. Italy in the previous century had suffered from periodic strife between, on the one hand, supporters of the papacy and the quasi-republican governments of the communes (the Guelphs) and, on the other, supporters of the empire and the aristocrats or *signori* who often subverted the quasi-republican governments of the communes (the Ghibellines). Ptolemy's politics are decidedly Guelph, as he explores political rule as well as "regal and sacerdotal" rule—that is, a republicanism appropriate to healthy cities as well as the universal monarchy of Christ. This hybrid political teaching is illuminated not only by philosophical and historical sources, but also by passages from Augustine's *City of God*, ecclesiastical histories, and the Bible.

The selections from *On the Government of Rulers* given here are reprinted from the translation of James M. Blythe: *On the Government of Rulers: De Regimine Principum* (Philadelphia: University of Pennsylvania Press, 1997). The translation is principally based on Thomas Aquinas, *Opuscula Omnia necnon Opera Minora*, vol. 1, *Opuscula Philosophica*, ed. R. P. Joannes Perrier (Paris: P. Lethielleux, 1949), but draws on Thomas Aquinas, *Politica Opuscula Duo*, ed. Joseph Mathis (Turin and Rome: Marietti, 1948, 1971). The paragraph numbering here follows the Blythe translation; the paragraph numbers of the Perrier Latin edition are given in brackets. In order to make accessible several principal threads running through Ptolemy's lengthy work, space is conserved here by omitting paragraphs from some chapters and by omitting or abbreviating (and thus modifying) several informative footnotes in Blythe's edition; the reader is encouraged to consult the original

3. *De Regno* appears in some manuscripts under the same title as the complete work, *De Regimine Principum*. *De Regno* ends with Book 2, Chapter 8, as numbered in the Leonine edition, or Book 2, Chapter 4 in those editions that contain Ptolemy's continuation. The conventional date for *De Regno* is 1267; the later date is argued by C. Flüeler (*Rezeption und Interpretation der aristotelischen Politica im späten Mittelalter* [Amsterdam and Philadelphia: B. R. Grüner, 1992], 27–28).

4. Felix Gilbert, "Sir John Fortescue's 'Dominium Regale et Politicum,'" *Mediaevalia et Humanistica* 2 (1943): 88–97; also Thomas M. Osborne Jr., "*Dominum Regalem et Politicum:* Sir John Fortescue's Response to the Problem of Tyranny as Presented by Thomas Aquinas and Ptolemy of Lucca," *Mediaeval Studies* 62 (2000): 161–88; David Wootton, "The True Origins of Republicanism: The Disciples of Baron and the Counter-example of Venturi," in *Il repubblicanesimo moderno: L'idea di repubblica nella riflessione storica di Franco Venturi*, ed. Manuela Albertone (Naples: Bibliopolis, 2006), 271–304.

5. Compare *On the Government of Rulers* 3.4–6 and *Determinatio Compendiosa*, chaps. 21–23 with *Convivio* 4.5 and *Monarchia* 2.5; see Theodore Silverstein, "On the Genesis of *De Monarchia*, II, v," *Speculum* 13 (1938): 326–49; Charles Davis, *Dante's Italy and Other Essays* (Philadelphia: University of Pennsylvania Press, 1984), 263–69, 273–75.

edition. Chapters 8 and 9 from Book 2 introduce in passing the opposition between political lordship and despotic lordship. From Book 3, Chapters 1 and 2 demonstrate the source of all lordship in God; Chapter 9 discusses why lordship belongs to human beings by nature; Chapter 10 lists the four types of lordship; Chapter 11 distinguishes regal rule from despotic rule, but then explains the circumstances under which the latter is "reduced" to the former; Chapter 13, picking up on a theme introduced in Chapter 10, attributes to Christ and his vicars the most complete form of regal lordship. In Book 4, Chapters 1 and 23 expand Ptolemy's account of political lordship.

BOOK TWO

Chapter Eight

Ministers are necessary for the government of a kingdom or any other lordship. An incidental distinction between two lordships—political and despotic—and many reasons to show that political lordship must necessarily be mild.

1. [69] The king must be strengthened with ministers as well as with wealth. In speaking about this in Ecclesiastes, the great king Solomon said: *I possessed servants and maids and an exceedingly great household* [Eccles. 2:7]. But that which is possessed seems to be under the lordship of the one who possesses it, and so I must incidentally make the following distinction about lordship. Although in Book 5 of the *Politics* Aristotle supposes that there are many forms of rule, which I have already described and will discuss again, elsewhere in the same work he supposes that there are only two, political and despotic,[6] each of which has its own distinctive ministers. Political rule exists when a region, province, city, or town is governed by one or many according to its own statutes, as happens in regions of Italy and especially in Rome, which for the most part has been governed by senators and consuls ever since the city was founded. Political lordship is more suitable for producing a certain civility in governing, because in it there is an uninterrupted alternation of government over citizens and foreigners alike, as 1 Maccabees [8:16] says about the Romans: *they annually commit their magistracy to one person, who exercises lordship over all their land.*

2. [70] There are two reasons why the subjects of political lordship cannot be rigidly corrected, as they could be under a regal lordship. One reason has to do with the part that governs. Its government is temporary, and when it considers that its lordship will end after such a brief time it is less anxious to be harsh with those subject to it. This is why the judges of the people of Israel, who judged politically, were more moderate in their judgments than the succeeding kings. Samuel, who judged these people for a time, said to them, when he wanted to show that his government had been political and not regal (although the people had now chosen the latter): *Speak of me in the presence of the Lord and his Christ and say whether I have taken anyone's cow or ass, whether I have slandered anyone, whether I have oppressed anyone, whether I have accepted a gift from anyone's hands* [1 Sam. 12:3]. Those who have royal lordship do all of this, as I will make clear below and as this prophet shows in 1 Kings [1 Samuel].[7]

3. Moreover, the mode of governing in those places where lordship is political is mercenary, since lords are employed for pay. When wages are fixed ahead of time for an end, lords are not as intent on governing their subjects, and, in consequence, the rigor of correction is tempered. The Lord refers to these things in John: *Mercenaries, and those who are not shepherds, who do not have the obligation of caring for the sheep,* because they are put in charge of them only for a time, *see a wolf and flee. And mercenaries flee because they*

6. On the distinction of despotism from political rule, see *Politics* 1.3 1253b18–21, 1.7 1255b17–40. Book 5 discusses a variety of governments with regard to the different kinds of revolutions that may arise in them and how to avoid them, but Books 3.6 through 4.10 would seem to be a better reference. In 1.2, the author of the first part repeated Aristotle's sixfold classification of polities from *Politics* 3.7 1279a.

7. In the Ptolemy selections, Bible citations are translated literally; the now conventional titles of books are given in brackets; the location of chapter and verse corresponds to the Vulgate or Douay-Rheims translations.

are mercenaries [John 10:12–13], as if the wages were the end of rule in themselves and the subjects a secondary matter. For this reason ancient Roman leaders, such as Marcus Curius, Fabricius, and many others, as Valerius Maximus writes, took care of the Republic with their own riches, which made them more bold and more solicitous for the care of the polity, as if their whole intention and inner disposition were directed to that.[8] This verifies Cato's opinion, which Sallust relates in *The War with Catiline*: "The Republic, which had once been small, was made great because they displayed industry at home, just command abroad, a free spirit in counseling, and were addicted neither to lust nor transgressions."[9]

4. [71] The second reason why political lordship must be moderate and be exercised with moderation comes from its subjects, since, by nature, their disposition is suited to such a government. Ptolemy proves in his *Quadripartus* that the various constellations divide human beings into distinct regions with respect to the government of mores, and that the lordship of the stars above always circumscribes human command of will.[10] The Roman regions are situated under Mars, and so they are not as easily subjected as others. For the same reason, the Roman nation is not accustomed to be satisfied with its boundaries, and it can only be subjected when it cannot resist. Because it is unable to endure a foreign will, it is grudging of any superior. As is written in 1 Maccabees [8:14], of those who presided among the Romans: *no one wore a diadem or assumed the purple,* and the effect of such humility is that *there is neither ill will nor jealousy among them.* Therefore, they exercised governance with a certain forgiving spirit, as the nature of that region's subjects requires. As Cicero relates in his *Philippics,* they needed no protection from those with arms, but only the love and benevolence of the citizens, for it is this, not arms, which fortifies the ruling element.[11] Sallust reports Cato's opinion of the ancient Roman Fathers, which is to the same effect.[12]

5. Likewise, the subjects of a political government develop confidence from being released from the lordship of kings and from exercising lordship themselves at suitable times, and this makes them bold in pursuing liberty, so as not to be forced to submit and bow down to kings. For this reason political government must necessarily be mild.

6. [72] Moreover, this is a sure mode of governing because it is according to the form of the laws of the commune or the municipality, to which the rector is bound. But for this reason the ruler's prudence is not free, and, therefore, it is more remote from the divine and imitates it less. Although laws originate in natural law, as Cicero proves in his treatise *On Laws,*[13] and natural law derives from divine law, as the prophet David declares: *The light of your countenance is signed on us, Lord* [Ps. 4:7]; nevertheless they fail in particular acts, for which legislators cannot provide, since they are ignorant of future events. Thus, political government results in a certain weakness, since political rectors judge the people by the laws alone. This weakness is eliminated in regal lordship since the rulers, not being obligated by the laws, may judge by what is in their hearts,[14] and they therefore more closely follow divine providence *which has care of all things,* as is said in the Book of Wisdom [12:13].

7. All this makes clear what sort of rule political rule is and its mode of governing. Now I must consider despotic rule.

Chapter Nine

What despotic rule is and how it is reduced to regal rule. An incidental comparison of political and despotic rule in different regions and times.

1. [73] Here let me note that what is called despotic rule is the relationship of a lord to a servant. This title comes from the Greek, and to this day lords of that province are called despots. We can reduce that rule to regal rule, as Sacred Scripture makes clear.

2. Someone may object that Aristotle contrasts regal and despotic rule.[15] I will explain this in

8. Valerius Maximus *Memorable Deeds and Sayings* 4.3.5 (for Manius Curius [not Marcus]), 4.3.6 (for Gaius Fabricius Luscinus), 4.8 (on liberality).

9. Sallust *The War with Cataline* 52.21.

10. Claudius Ptolemaeus *Quadripartus* (or *Tetrabiblos*) 2.3–4.

11. Cicero *Philippics* 2.41.

12. Sallust *The War with Cataline* 52.21.

13. Cf. Cicero *On Laws* (*De Legibus*) 1.15.

14. *The Body of Civil Law: Codex* 6.23.19.1 (law is in the ruler's heart); *Digest* 1.3.31, 32.1.23; *Codex* 6.23.3; *Institutes* 2.17.8 (the ruler is free of the laws).

15. Aristotle *Politics* 1.5 1254b2–5.

the next book, when I have assembled the material necessary to understand it, but for now it will suffice to prove what I have said using divine Scripture. Samuel, a prophet of the Israelite people, handed down regal laws, and these were the laws that introduced servitude. The people had petitioned Samuel for a king, since he was in his declining years and his sons were not exercising just lordship in a political mode, as the other judges of this people had done. When Samuel consulted the Lord, he answered: *Hear the voice of the people in those things which they say.... But call them to witness and preach the law of a king to them:... "He will take away your sons and put them in his chariots and he will make for himself chariots and horsemen and those to run before his teams of horse... and appoint plowmen for his fields and reapers for his crops and forgers for his arms; he will also make your daughters into maids, perfumers, and bakers of bread"* [1 Sam. 8:7–13]. 1 Kings [1 Samuel] also relates other conditions that pertain to servitude, with the intention of showing that political government, which Samuel's government and that of the other judges had been, was more fruitful to the people.

3. Nevertheless, I showed the contrary above.[16]

4. [74] To clear up this contradiction I need to let you know that political government is placed ahead of royal government for two reasons. First, if we refer lordship to the integral state of human nature, called the State of Innocence, in which there was political, not regal lordship, there was no lordship then that involved servitude, but rather preeminence and subjection existed according to the merits of each for disposing and governing the multitude, so that whether in influencing or receiving influence each was disposed proportionately according to its own nature.[17] Therefore, political government was better for wise and virtuous persons, such as the ancient Romans, since it imitated this state of nature.

5. But because *the perverse are corrected with difficulty and the number of fools is infinite,* as is said in Ecclesiastes [1:15], in corrupt nature regal government is more fruitful, because it is necessary for human nature to be disposed in such a way to, as it were, restrain its flux within limits. This gives rise to the exalted royal dignity, of which it is written in Proverbs [20:8]: *The king who sits on the throne of judgment scatters all evil with his gaze.* Therefore, the rod of discipline, which everyone fears, and rigor of justice are necessary in the governance of the world, because through them the people and the uneducated multitude are better governed. This is why Paul said in Romans [13:4], speaking of the rectors of the world: *they do not bear the sword without cause... they are avengers in wrath against those who act badly.* And Aristotle says that the penalties imposed by laws were instituted to serve as medicine.[18] In this respect regal lordship excels.[19]

BOOK THREE

Chapter One

In this first chapter I consider and prove that all dominion is from God by considering the nature of being.

1. [99] The *heart of a king is in the hand of God, and it will go wherever he has willed,* as is written in Proverbs [21:1]. Cyrus, king of the Persians, that great monarch of the east, announced this in a public edict after his victory over Babylon, which he razed to its foundation, and after the slaying of its king, Belshazzar, as the histories tell us: *Cyrus the Persian says these things: The Lord God of heaven has given all the kingdoms of the world to me.*[20] It is apparent that all lordship comes from God, as from that First One who exercises lordship. We can show this in the three ways touched

16. Presumably a reference to Book 1 (attributed to Aquinas), which praises kingship.

17. Cf. Thomas Aquinas *Summa Theologiae* 1.96.4 and *Scriptum super Sententiis* 2 d. 44 q. 1 a. 3.

18. Aristotle *Nicomachean Ethics* 10.9 1180b23–28.

19. One paragraph is omitted. The paragraph, similar to 2.8.4 [71] above, argues that the situation of a region with respect to the stars affects whether political or regal lordship is more appropriate.

20. Ezra 1:2; 2 Chron. 36:23. For the name Belshazzar, see Dan. 5:1–30. In actuality the last king of Babylon was Nabodinus (ca. 556–539 BC). Belshazzar was his son and heir and apparently commander of part of the Babylonian armies.

on by Aristotle, that is, with regard to being, to motion, and to ends.

2. With regard to being, since all being must be reduced to the First Being, which is the origin of all being, as all heat is reduced to the heat of fire, as Aristotle makes clear.[21] For this reason, all being derives from the First Being, as does lordship, since it is founded on being. To the extent that it is founded on a more noble being, it comes before the others to exercise lordship over persons who are equal by nature, so that there is no cause for pride, but rather a cause for humanely exercising governance over the people, as Seneca says in his letter to Lucilius.[22] On this account it is said in Ecclesiasticus: *Did they make you rector? Don't exalt yourself, but be among them as if you were one of them* [Sirach 32:1]. Thus, all being derives from that being which is the First Cause, and all lordship that a creature exercises derives from God as from that one who first exercises lordship and as from the First Being.

3. [100] Further, every multitude proceeds from one and is measured by one, as Aristotle makes clear.[23] Therefore, the multitude of those who exercise lordship takes its origin in the same way, from the one who exercises governance, which is God. We see the same thing in regal courts, in which there are many who exercise governance in various offices, yet all derive from one, namely the king. On that account Aristotle says that God or the Prime Cause stands in the same relationship to the whole universe as a leader, from whom the whole multitude of a camp derives, stands in relationship to the whole army.[24] In Exodus, Moses himself calls God the leader of the people: *In your mercy,* he says, *You have been a leader to your people that you have redeemed* [Exod. 15:13]. All lordship, therefore, takes its origin from God.

Chapter Two

I prove the same thing by considering the movement of any created nature.

1. [101] We can prove that lordship comes from God not only by reason of being, but also by reason of movement. First, we must take up Aristotle's argument that since everything that moves is moved by something, and it is impossible to regress infinitely through a series of moving things and things moved, it is necessary to come to some immovable Prime Mover, which is God, or the First Cause.[25] But kings, rulers, and all who have precedence are among those persons who possess reason for movement to a greater degree than others, whether they exercise governance, judge, defend, or engage in other acts pertaining to the responsibility of government. As Seneca says of Caesar in his little book *On the Shortness of Life, to Paulinus,* when he exhorts Paulinus to have contempt for the world: "When you want to forget everything else, think of Caesar.... All things are permitted to the one who is Caesar, but for this reason many things are not permissible for him. Caesar's vigilance defends the homes of all, his labor defends the repose of all, and his activity defends the leisure of all. For this, Caesar has dedicated himself to the world, has robbed himself from himself, and acts by the custom of the stars, which, unresting, always follow their courses."[26]

2. Therefore, if kings and other lords have so much reason for movement, they cannot perfect this movement other than through the influence and virtue of the Prime Mover, which is God, as I proved above. On this account, when the author of the Book of Wisdom (in which the effects of divine virtue acting through divine wisdom are enumerated) wants to show how all things participate in the influence of divine movement, he adds immediately: *Wisdom is more active than all other active things, for it reaches everywhere on account of its purity* [Wisdom 7:24], identifying as "purity" the absolute, surpassing, and unmixed divine virtue directed toward moving all things toward a likeness of corporal light, which in this regard imitates the divine nature.

3. [102] There is another argument with regard to movement. Every primary cause has more influence over what it causes than a secondary cause

21. Aristotle *Metaphysics* 2.2 994a1–994b30. Aristotle mentions the First Cause here but does not specifically mention being as such or heat.

22. Seneca *Letters to Lucilius* esp. 47 and 90. The fact that Ptolemy does not cite Letter 90 elsewhere, when it so clearly bears on his concerns and ideas, suggests that that this letter was not available to him.

23. Aristotle *Metaphysics* 10.1 1052b32–1053a2.

24. Ibid. 12.9 1075a13–15.

25. Aristotle *Physics* 8.6 258b10–259a20; cf. Thomas Aquinas *Summa Theologiae* 1.2.3.

26. Seneca *On the Shortness of Life, to Paulinus* 7.1–2.

does. Since the Primary Cause is God, and since all things are moved by virtue of the Prime Cause, all things receive the influence of its movement, and, therefore, the movement of lords derives from the virtue of God and from his moving.

4. Further, if there is an order among corporal movements, so much more will there be an order among spiritual ones. If we consider bodies, we see that inferior ones are moved by superior ones and that all movements are ultimately reduced to the movement of the supreme body, which is the ninth sphere, according to Ptolemy in *Almagest,* but the eighth according to Aristotle.[27] If, therefore, all corporal movements are regulated by the first movement and receive their capacity to influence movement from it, it is true of spiritual substances to a much greater degree since they are more similar to the first movement. Because of this, they are more fit to receive the influence of the first and supreme mover or motion, which is God. The Blessed Dionysius himself tells us about this movement in his books *On the Divine Names* and *On the Celestial Hierarchy,* where he distinguishes the same kinds of motion among spiritual substances as among corporal bodies: circular, right, and oblique.[28] These spiritual movements consist of certain illuminations that they receive from superior ones for the purpose of acting, as the same doctor explains, but in order to receive such illuminations it is necessary to have a disposition of mind suited to the influence of that movement.

5. [103] Kings, rulers, and others exercising lordship in the world are among those who ought to be more prepared for this, both because they have been trained to perform the universal actions of government (for which reason their minds are more elevated to the divine) and also because it is incumbent on them to dispose themselves to provide the care imposed on them in exercising governance over their flocks and in doing other things necessary for the acts of government (these things are above rulers and beyond their particular natures). Through such movement they should be sufficiently led to the divine influence.

6. King David disposed himself in this way, and through the movement of prophetic illumination he earned the spirit of prophetic understanding in his psalms beyond that of all other kings, even above that of the prophets, as the doctors of Sacred Scripture tell us. But, for acting in a contrary manner, the heathen rulers, whom the prophet David mentions, such as Nebuchadnezzar and his son Belshazzar, deserved to be overshadowed.[29] The influence of divine illumination affected their fantasy with imaginary visions, as the book of Daniel shows clearly,[30] to let them know what they should do in their regal government, but because their minds were embroiled in the darkness of sin and not properly disposed, their minds could not apprehend the meaning of these visions. They lacked the light of the prophet Daniel, to whom was given the spirit of understanding those things to be interpreted, in order to verify what Solomon said in the book of Proverbs [8:14–16]: *Counsel and impartiality are mine, prudence is mine, and fortitude is mine. Through me kings reign and those who institute laws decree what is just. Through me rulers command and the mighty decree justice.*[31]

7. These things make it clear how we can show that all lordship is from God by considering movement.

Chapter Nine

Human beings naturally exercise lordship over the animals of the forest and other irrational things. Many reasons prove this.

1. [125] Now I must attend to the diverse species of exercising lordship, classified according to the various modes and ranks of lordship and rule among human beings. First, there is a certain general species that pertains to all, which belongs to humans by nature, as Augustine and Aristotle tell us.[32] Scripture confirms this, when in creating the nature appointed for humans, God said: *Exercise lordship*

27. Eight moving spheres are required to account for the motions of the sun, the moon, the five visible planets, and the daily motion of the fixed stars; Ptolemy notes an additional motion of the fixed stars, i.e., the precession of the equinoxes, which was not known to Aristotle. Cf. Ptolemy *Almagest* 1.8, 7.2; Aristotle *On the Heavens* 2.12 292b1–25.

28. Pseudo-Dionysius the Areopagite *On the Divine Names* 4.8–9. "Divine minds are moved in a circular direction by being united to the illuminations of the Beautiful and Good, without beginning or end; in a direct line whenever they advance to help a subordinate by accomplishing everything directly; in a spiral direction since, even in providing for the more indigent, they remain fixedly, in identity, around the Good and the Beautiful because of their identity."

29. See 3.1.1 and Dan. 5 for Belshazzar. Confusingly, in Dan. 4, Daniel himself is called Belteshazzar, and in the Vulgate both are called Balthasar. The confused account in Daniel calls Belshazzar Nebuchadnezzar's son, although at most he was his grandson.

30. Dan. 2.1 ff., 4.1 ff., 5.5 ff.

31. The personification of Wisdom, which is God, is speaking.

32. Augustine *The City of God* 19.5; Aristotle *Politics* 1.2 1253a2–18.

over the fish of the sea and the flying things of the heavens and all animals which move over the earth [Gen. 1:28]. These words show that he gave this power to human nature as he instituted it. He said, *Let the earth put forth the green herb* [Gen. 1:11], which implies that he gave the power of germinating to trees. Similarly, he then said: *Exercise lordship over the fish of the sea,* etc. Thus, from all the things that I have said, it is clear that the lordship of human beings over other, inferior creatures is natural. By the same reasoning Aristotle proves that hunting and fowling come from nature.[33] Augustine proves the same thing by citing the lordship that the ancient Fathers were accustomed to have as herders of cattle, which I defined above as natural wealth...[34]

3. [126] I can give three reasons why that lordship was suitably conferred when humans were first instituted. First, it follows from a consideration of the process of nature itself. Just as in the generation of things, in which we understand there to be a certain order of advancement from the imperfect to the perfect, since matter exists on account of form and the more imperfect form exists on account of the more perfect, so also in the use of natural things such an order is present, since more imperfect things exist for the use of those that are more perfect. Plants use the land for their own nutrition, but animals use plants, and humans use both plants and animals. Therefore, I conclude that humans naturally exercise lordship over animals. It is with this reason, as I mentioned above, that Aristotle proves that the hunting of animals of the forest is naturally just, because by it humans lay a legal claim for themselves to that which naturally is theirs.[35]

4. Second, it follows from a consideration of the order of divine providence which always governs inferior things through superior ones. Humans are above other animals, since they are made in the image of God, and so human governance suitably subjects other animals.

5. Third, it follows from a consideration of the peculiar nature of humans and other animals. In other animals we may discover a certain participation in prudence toward particular acts according to a natural faculty of judgment, but in humans we find a useful prudence which comes from the rational ability of doing things. But all that exists only through participation is subjected by that which exists essentially and universally. Thus, it is clear that other animals are naturally subject to humans.

6. [127] The truth of whether the lordship of human being over human being is natural or whether it is merely permitted or foreseen by God can be deduced from what I have already said. If we speak of lordship involving the mode of servile subjection, this was introduced only on account of sin, as I said above,[36] but if we speak of lordship as it pertains to the office of counseling and directing, this mode can be called natural, because it existed even in the State of Innocence. This is also Augustine's opinion.[37] Therefore, the second kind of lordship pertains to human beings, as naturally social or political animals, as I said above.[38]

7. Moreover, it is necessary that a society be mutually ordained, and in all cases involving things that are mutually ordained, one thing must always be the principal and first directing thing, as Aristotle tells us.[39] This follows from the very raison d'être (*ratio*) of order or nature. As Augustine writes: "Order is the disposition of equal and unequal things giving to each its due."[40] It is therefore manifest that the word "order" itself implies inequality, and this is so by the raison d'être of lordship. By this argument the lordship of human over human is natural, lordship exists even among the Angels, it existed in the First State, and it exists even now. We must now consider sequentially the various kinds of lordship according to their own dignities and ranks.

33. Aristotle *Politics* 1.8 1256a30–b23.

34. Augustine *The City of God* 19.15; *On the Government of Rulers* 2.6.1, 3.

35. *On the Government of Rulers* 3.9.1; Aristotle *Politics* 1.8 1256a30–b23.

36. *On the Government of Rulers* 2.9.4–5; also 3.7.1: "In Sacred Scripture we find another reason for which God permitted lordship, that is, on account of the merit of the peoples, and this is not contrary to the opinions of the philosophers and the wise ones of this world. The blessed Augustine gives this reason, when he proves that servitude was introduced on account of sin [*The City of God* 19.15]. This is obvious since... those who first exercised lordship in the world were iniquitous persons, such as Cain, Nimrod, Belus, Ninus, and his wife Semiramis...."

37. Augustine *The City of God* 19.14–15.

38. *On the Government of Rulers* (or *On Kingship, to the King of Cyprus*) 1.1.3, 3.5.3.

39. Aristotle *Politics* 1.5 1254a20–25.

40. Augustine *The City of God* 19.13.

Chapter Ten

Distinctions of human lordship according to rank and dignity. How the pope's lordship is preferred to all other lordship.

1. [128] We can subdivide lordship into four types by the same criterion. One type is sacerdotal and regal at the same time, another is regal alone, under which we include imperial, a third is political, and the fourth has to do with household management.

2. I mention sacerdotal and regal first for a number of reasons, but especially since it exists by the divine institution of Christ. Since all power was conferred on him by virtue of his humanity, he communicated all this power to his vicar when he said, as we read in Matthew: *I say to you: "you are Peter, and on this rock I will build my Church, and the gates of Hell will not prevail against it. And I will give you the keys to the kingdom of heaven, and whatever you bind on earth will be bound in heaven, and whatever you loose on earth will be loosed in heaven"* [Matt. 16:18–19]. All four clauses of this statement signify the lordship of Peter and his successors over all the faithful, and because of this the Supreme Pontiff, the Roman Bishop, can deservedly be called king and priest. If our Lord Jesus Christ is called king and priest, as Augustine proves,[41] it does not seem unsuitable to apply the same titles to his successor. This is clear enough from what I have said, but in order to adduce more reasons we must go back to the four clauses that I just mentioned, of which the first refers to the magnitude of the title given, the second to the fortitude of lordship, the third to the amplitude of lordship, and the fourth to the fullness of lordship....

10. [132] I must note that this divine institution cannot be abandoned, since Christ elevated his vicars solely as dispensers and ministers, as Paul said in 1 Corinthians: *Let one so judge us, as ministers of Christ and dispensers of the mysteries of God* [1 Cor. 4:1]. For Christ alone founded the Church whose ministry he committed to Peter: *For no one can lay another foundation except the one that was laid, which is Christ Jesus* [1 Cor. 3:11]. For this reason the Sacred Doctors attribute a certain power to Christ, which they call "excellent," which neither Peter nor his successors had. Thus the power of Peter and his successors is not equal to that of Christ; on the contrary, Christ's power totally transcends Peter's. For example, Christ could save someone without baptism, for which reason Jerome says in commenting on Matthew: "He healed no one in body whom he did not heal in mind, yet he did this without baptism, which Peter could not do."[42] For Peter baptized Cornelius the Centurion and his whole household, as we read in Acts, even after the Advent of the Holy Spirit.[43] Christ could change the form and matter of the sacraments, which neither Peter nor his successors could do.

11. This suffices for the present, and I will leave for the wise the other and more subtle things that could be said. Nevertheless, the conclusion of this chapter, that the Vicar of Christ ought to be preferred to all other lords, should stand for the reasons I have given.

Chapter Eleven

What regal lordship consists of, how it differs from political lordship, and how it is distinguished in different ways in different regions.

1. [133] Now we must go on to regal lordship, and we must distinguish it with respect to various regions and with respect to the ways it is described in various sources. First, in Sacred Scripture, Moses tells us the laws of regal lordship in one way in Deuteronomy, and the Prophet Samuel in another way in 1 Kings [1 Samuel], but both do this in the persona of God. In Deuteronomy, God ordains the king for the utility of his subjects, which, as Aristotle tells us,[44] is characteristic of

41. Ibid. 17.6, 17.17.

42. The quotation has not been located in Jerome's *Commentary on Matthew.*

43. Acts 10:44–48.

44. Aristotle *Nicomachean Ethics* 8.10 1160b1–3; cf. *Politics* 3.7 1279a32.

kings. *When a king has been constituted,* Moses says, *he will not multiply horses for himself, nor, being puffed up by the size of his cavalry, lead the people back into Egypt. He will not have many wives who will attract his spirit, nor an immense amount of silver or gold* [Deut. 17:16–17]. This book also tells us how he wanted the king to understand this: *he will copy this law of Deuteronomy for himself... and he will keep it with him and read it all the days of his life, so that he might learn to fear the Lord his God and guard his words and ceremonies* [Deut. 17:18–19] so that he can direct the people according to divine law. So also King Solomon at the beginning of his government asked God for wisdom to direct his lordship for the utility of his subjects, as is written in 3 Kings [1 Kings 3:9]. Moses added in Deuteronomy: *Let his heart not be lifted over-flowingly over his brothers, nor incline to the right or the left, so that he and his son may reign for a long time over Israel* [Deut. 17:20]. But in 1 Kings [1 Samuel] the laws of a kingdom are handed down more for the utility of the king, as I made clear above,[45] where I quoted those words as clearly pertaining to a servile condition. Nevertheless, Samuel says that the laws that he hands down are regal, even though they are completely despotic.

2. [134] In the *Ethics* Aristotle is more in accord with the first set of laws. He posits three things about a legitimate king: first, he principally intends the good of his subjects; second, he is found to be sufficient in himself and to excel superabundantly in all good qualities, not burdening his subjects; and third, he undertakes the care of his subjects so that they may function well, just as shepherds act toward their sheep.[46]

3. From this it is clear that in this mode despotic is much different from regal, as Aristotle seems to say.[47] Likewise, it is clear that the kingdom does not exist on account of the king but rather the king on account of the kingdom, because it is for this that God provided for kings to govern and exercise governance over their kingdoms and preserve everyone according to their own right, and this is the end of government. If they do otherwise and turn things to their own advantage, they are not kings but tyrants...[48]

4. [135] Moreover, human beings constitute a kingdom just as walls a home and members the human body, as Aristotle says.[49] Therefore, it is necessary for the king to keep them safe if the government is to be prosperous. Hence, the common good of any kind of rule includes the participation of divinity; as Aristotle says, the common good is a divine good.[50] Just as God, who is *King of Kings and Lord of those exercising lordship* [1 Tim. 6:15; Rev. 19:16] by whose virtue rulers command, as I proved above,[51] governs us and exercises governance over us not for himself but for our salvation, so too should kings and others exercising lordship in the world. But since no one ever provides their own pay for being in the military, and because by natural right all should receive a wage for their labor, as Paul proves in 1 Corinthians [9:7], we hold that it is permissible for rulers to collect tributes and annual poll taxes from their subjects. After Paul proved to the Romans that God provided for all lordship, he finally persuaded them to return payment according to their labor: *Therefore, you are responsible for tributes, for they are ministers of God serving him in this* [Rom. 13:6]. Augustine proves this same thing, commenting on these same words of Paul in *On the Words of the Lord.*[52] Therefore, we must conclude that legitimate kings ought to govern and exercise governance according to the form described in Deuteronomy....

9. [138] In John's opinion, those who seek more for themselves than the pay publicly decreed are to be condemned as calumniators and violent extortionists. From this, despotic rule is reduced to regal rule in two ways, but especially by reason of transgression, on account of which servitude was introduced, as Augustine says.[53] Although there had been lordship even in the First State, it existed only in the offices of counseling and directing, and not out of lust for exercising lordship or with the intention of subjecting anyone servilely, as I said above.[54] But the laws of regal lordship that the Prophet Samuel passed on to the Israelite people were given with the following consideration: that

45. *On the Government of Rulers* 2.9.2.

46. Aristotle *Nicomachean Ethics* 8.10 1160b1–7, 8.11 1161a11–15.

47. Aristotle *Politics* 1.1 1252a8–18; cf. 1.5 1254b3–7.

48. A quotation (Ezek. 34:2–4) and subsequent comment are omitted.

49. Aristotle *Politics* 3.1 1274b39.

50. Aristotle *Ethics* 1.1 1094b10.

51. *On the Government of Rulers* 3.1–3.

52. Cf. Augustine *Sermon* 90.10 and *Exposition of Certain Propositions from the Epistle to the Romans* 72–75. *On the Words of the Lord* was a name given to some of his epistles on the New Testament (now *Sermons* 51–147A), but a quotation of Rom. 13:6 has not been found there.

53. Augustine *The City of God* 19.15.

54. *On the Government of Rulers* 3.9.6.

this people, on account of its ingratitude and because it was stiff-necked, deserved to have such laws. For sometimes when a people does not know the benefit of a good government it is expedient to exercise tyranny over it, because even tyrannies are the instruments of divine justice.[55] For this reason, certain islands and provinces, according to what the histories relate, always had tyrants on account of the evil of the people, because they could not be governed otherwise than with an iron rod. In such ill-tempered regions, despotic rule is necessary for kings, not according to the nature of regal lordship, but according to the merits and pertinacity of the subjects, and this is the reason Augustine gives.[56] When Aristotle distinguishes the types of kingdoms, he also shows that among certain barbarous nations regal lordship is altogether despotic, because otherwise they could not be governed, and that this kind of lordship flourishes especially in Greece and among the Persians, at least with regard to popular government.[57]

10. This is all I have to say at this point about regal lordship, and how despotic rule is reduced to it, and for what reason it is opposed to political rule, but I will show this still more clearly in a later chapter on political lordship.

Chapter Thirteen

How Christ's monarchy excels in three ways, and how Octavian Caesar stood in the place of Christ.

1. [142] This fifth monarchy, which according to the Truth succeeded that of the Romans, surpasses all the others in three ways. First, from the number of its years, because it lasted longer, lasts up to the present time, and will last until the renovation of the world, as is clear from the vision of Daniel that I mentioned above and about which I will now say more.[58]

2. Second, its excellence is apparent from the universality of its lordship, because: *their sound went out to all the earth and their words to the ends of the globe* [Ps. 18:5]. There is no corner of the world and no region in which the name of Christ is not adored. As Paul maintains: He *subjected all things beneath his feet* [1 Cor. 15:26]. The prophet Malachi also points to that lordship when he says: *The Lord of Armies says: "From the rising to the setting of the sun, my name is great among the nations, and in every place a clean oblation is sacrificed and offered to my name, because my name is great among the nations"* [Malachi 1:11].

3. These words make it sufficiently clear that Christ's lordship is ordained to the salvation of the spirit and to spiritual goods, as we will soon see, although it is not excluded from temporal matters in so far as they are ordained to spiritual things. Thus it is that although Christ was adored by the Magi[59] and glorified by the Angels as a sign of his universal lordship, he nevertheless lay in a humble place wrapped in ordinary swaddling clothes. Persons are drawn to virtue better in this way than by force of arms. He intended this, although more often he used his might as the true Lord.

4. Therefore, he lived in humility and sustained the lordship of Augustus so that the whole globe might be counted at the time of the birth of the Lord, as the Evangelist Luke testifies [Luke 2:1]. A poll tax or tribute was levied based on this count, as the histories tell us, in recognition of the servitude that was owed.[60] There is a mystery in this, since he who was born was true Lord and Monarch of the world, and Augustus stood in his place, although he did this not through his understanding but through the motion of God, in the same way as Caiaphas prophesied.[61] Feeling this instinctively, Caesar Augustus issued a mandate, as the histories relate, that none of the Roman people should call him "Lord." Augustus, who subjugated the whole earthly globe, held the position of monarchy for fourteen years after the nativity of Christ, the True Lord, and he ruled for a total of fifty-six years and six months as described in accounts of the acts of the Roman rulers. Tiberius, who succeeded Augustus, as the histories relate, wanted to translate Christ, as True Lord, to a place among the gods, but he was impeded in this by a proud and haughty senate impatient of any lordship.[62]

55. *Ibid.* 3.7.2. There Ptolemy cites, among others, Isa. 10:5–6.
56. Augustine *The City of God* 19.15.
57. Aristotle *Politics* 3.14 1285a16–b4.
58. *On the Government of Rulers* 3.10.9; and below, 3.13.6.
59. Matt. 2:11.
60. Peter Comestor *Scholastic History,* On the Gospels, 4.
61. Cf. John 11:49–52.
62. Cf. Orosius *Seven Books of History against the Pagans* 7.4; Gregory of Tours *History of the Franks* 1.24.

5. [143] Third, the greater excellence of Christ's monarchy over the other four that preceded it is apparent from the dignity of the one who exercises lordship, since that one is both God and human. By this consideration the human nature in Christ participates in infinite virtue, which means that it is a greater and higher fortitude and virtue than human fortitude and virtue. The prophet Isaiah describes this in speaking of the temporal virtue of Christ, for which virtue we call him "Monarch": *A little one was born to us, and a son was given to us, and rule was put on his shoulders; and his name will be called Admirable, Counselor, Strong God, Father of the Future Age, Ruler of Peace. His empire will be multiplied, and there will be no end of peace* [Isaiah 9:6–7]. In these words Isaiah touches on all the things that are required for a true ruler; though, to be sure, he transcends the limits of all other lords, as I will declare in the following chapter, and as is clear to anyone who looks.

6. Therefore, this rule or monarchy brings to naught and destroys all other lordship, because all kingdoms are subjected to the same one, as the same prophet foretold: *"I am alive," says the Lord, "because every knee will be bowed to me"* [Isaiah 45:23–24].[63] And the Apostle Paul writes in Philippians [2:10]: *In the name of Jesus every knee should be bent, all those that are celestial, earthly, or infernal.* After he has explained the vision in Nebuchadnezzar's dream, Daniel concludes about this monarchy: *In those days,* that is, after the four monarchies of the Assyrians, the Persians and the Medes, the Greeks, and the Romans, *God will raise up the kingdom of heaven, which will not dissipate in eternity, and his kingdom will not be handed over to another, and it will crush all these kingdoms and itself stand through eternity* [Dan. 2:44].[64] Indeed, the reason it will last through eternity is at hand, because that one is joined to eternal rule, since he is both Lord God and human.

7. We have now come full circle, because I proved above that all lordship takes its origin from God. Rule is bounded by this true rule, to mention human motions, as by something immovable beyond which there is no motion. We must conclude from these things that this Lordship can not fail.

BOOK FOUR

Chapter One

The difference between the rule of a kingdom and political rule, and two kinds of political rule.

1. [174] *You will constitute them as rulers over all the earth; they will be mindful of your name, Lord.*[65] Although God instituted all lordship or rule, as I said above, Aristotle and Sacred Scripture tell us about different modes of lordship. Since I have already treated the monarchy of one—namely the lordship of the Highest Pontiff, regal lordship, and imperial lordship—and their nature and the things that go along with them,[66] I think that it is now time to treat the lordship of many, which we call by the common name "political." I described this earlier in two ways: with respect to the mode of elevating those who rule and with respect to the mode of life under political rule.[67] The mode of elevation to this rank is elective, and someone from any stock at all is eligible, not just one selected by birth, as is the case with kings. This is what the words of constitution mean: *You will constitute them as rulers,* and it adds, *over all the earth,* showing the general regulation in political rule, which extends to any human stock. Not just any person should be chosen, but one who is virtuous. This refers to the mode of living, for which reason the Psalm adds: *they will be mindful of your name, Lord,* in consideration of the divine and of

63. The Vulgate actually says: "The word of justice will go out of my mouth and it will not return, because every knee will be bowed to me and every tongue will swear!"

64. In Dan. 2:31–45 a vision of a statue made of four materials is interpreted as referring to four monarchies; Ptolemy, consonant with a long-standing but varying medieval tradition, identifies the four historical monarchies and takes the fifth monarchy to be the kingdom of Christ. Cf. *On the Government of Rulers* 3.10.9, esp. note 162; Jerome *Commentary on Daniel* 2:31–40; Peter Comestor *Scholastic History,* On the Book of Daniel; and Orosius *Seven Books of History against the Pagans* 7.2.

65. A paraphrase of Ps. 44.17–18: "You will place them as princes in the whole earth; I [some versions have 'they'] will think of your name in all generations to come."

66. Imperial lordship stands in the middle between regal lordship and political lordship: political, because the emperors were elected; regal, because they were not bound by laws (*On the Government of Rulers* 3.12, 3.20).

67. *On the Government of Rulers* 3.20 (election); 2.8–10 (way of life).

his precepts, which serve as right reason to those who govern for what must be done. Proverbs says that *the mandate of the Lord is a lamp, and his law a light* [6:23][68] and Valerius Maximus writes that Caesar fostered virtues and punished vices by celestial providence.[69]

2. [175] Therefore, in the present book I will treat this rule, which Aristotle and I distinguished as follows:[70] if a few virtuous ones guide a government it is called "aristocracy" (as was the case in the city of Rome under the two consuls and the dictator just after the expulsion of the kings), but if many guide it (which the histories relate happened in the course of time in the same city under the consuls, dictators, and tribunes, and afterward under the senators) they call such a government a "polity" from the word "*polis.*" This word means "plurality" or "city," because this government is characteristic of cities, as we see especially in parts of Italy. Such a government also once thrived in Athens after the death of Codrus, as Augustine reports,[71] for at that time the Athenians abandoned regal lordship and elevated magistrates of the republic, just as in Rome. In either of these two modes, political rule is distinguished from kingdom or monarchy, and the opposite of each of these is also distinguished from the opposite of kingdom or monarchy, because the opposites of two opposite propositions are still opposite.[72] As Aristotle mentions, both these are kinds of political rule, as distinguished from regal or despotic rule, because both include plurality.[73]

3. [176] I must now consider all the ways in which political rule differs from regal, imperial, or monarchical rule, which to some extent can be seen from what I have said above in Books 1 and 3.[74] One difference is that political rectors are bound by laws and cannot proceed beyond them in seeking justice, but this is not the case with kings and other monarchical rulers, because laws are hidden in their hearts and applied in each individual case, and what pleases the ruler is held to be law.[75] This is what the laws of nations tell us, but we do not find the same thing said about political rectors, because they do not dare to do anything new beyond the written laws.

4. In 1 Maccabees [8:15] it is written that the Romans *held court to consult daily with the 320, always taking counsel about matters concerning the multitude so that they might do those things that were worthy.* Considering this, I hold that in the Roman government, lordship was political from the expulsion of the kings up to the usurpation of empire. This happened when Julius Caesar, after he had prostrated his enemies, after Pompey and his sons had been killed, and after he had subjugated the globe, took up sole lordship for himself in the form of monarchy and converted a polity into a despotic or tyrannical rule. As the histories tell us, after these events Caesar seemed inclined to be contemptuous of the senators; thus provoked, the great ones of the city, instigated by Brutus and Cassius and most of the senate, ran him through with twenty-four daggers in the Capitol.[76]

5. I should add that although the book of Maccabees says that one person exercised lordship in a given year [Macc. 8:16], as happens in the cities of Italy even now, government depended on the many, and therefore it was not called regal but political. This is also true of the judges of the Israelite people since they did not govern regally but politically, as I said above.[77] Cities live politically in all regions, whether in Germany, Scythia, or Gaul, although they may be circumscribed by the might of the king or emperor, to whom they are bound by established laws.

6. [177] Still another difference is that rectors more often are examined to see if they have judged well or governed according to the laws handed down to them, and if not they are subjected to penalties. It is written in 1 Kings that Samuel himself, because he had judged the Israelite people in a political mode, exposed himself to such a sentence after Saul had been elevated as king: *Behold,* he said, *I am here; speak of me before the Lord and his Christ,* namely Saul, *whether I have taken anyone's ox, whether I have slandered anyone, whether I have oppressed anyone,*

68. The words "of the Lord" and "his" do not appear in the Vulgate.

69. Valerius Maximus *Memorable Deeds and Sayings,* preface.

70. *On the Government of Rulers* (or *On Kingship, to the King of Cyprus*) 1.2; Aristotle *Politics* 3.7 1279a22–b10.

71. Augustine *The City of God* 18.20.

72. That is, the forms of rule opposite to aristocracy and polity, namely, oligarchy and democracy, are also distinct from the opposite of monarchy, namely, tyranny.

73. From his references to Books 1 and 3 of Aristotle's *Politics* (found in the Latin), Ptolemy must have 1.1 1252a9–17 and 3.7 1279a22–b10 in mind, but Aristotle does not say exactly what is attributed to him.

74. *On the Government of Rulers* 3.10–3.22, esp. 3.20. In Book 1 no distinction is made between political and nonpolitical rule.

75. Cf. *The Body of Civil Law: Institutes* 1.2.6; *Digest* 1.4.1.

76. Eutropius *A Brief History of Rome* 6.25.

77. *On the Government of Rulers* 2.8.2, 2.9.2.

whether I have accepted a gift from anyone's hands [1 Samuel 12:2–3]. The histories also tell us this about the Roman consuls, which is why Scipio Africanus left Rome when his impious rivals accused him of being corrupted by money, and eventually such false accusations led to civil wars. Such examinations have no place among kings or emperors, except that regions now and then rebel against them if they overstep the rights of the kingdom, as happens frequently, in parts of Spain and Hungary.[78] In the east also they fairly often plot the death of their lord, as Egyptians do against the sultan, and the Persians and Assyrians against the Tartar rulers.[79]

Chapter Twenty-Three

What the perfect polity consists of, from which it receives political happiness, namely when the parts of the polity are well disposed and mutually interrelated.

1. [242] Since, when I consider a polity, I refer to a city, the mode of proceeding to discuss a polity depends on the quality of the city. A city, as Augustine says, "is a multitude of human beings bound together by some chain of society, which is rendered blessed through true virtue."[80] This definition does not clash with Aristotle's opinion, which places political felicity in the perfect government of the polity.[81] For the virtue by which a political rector exercises governance over a city is the architect of all other virtues of the citizens, because the other civil virtues are ordained to that virtue, just as the equestrian virtue and that of archers are ordained to the military virtue. Therefore, political felicity consists in its operation, since it is the supreme virtue, as Aristotle seems to imply in the passage just cited. The true and perfect polity is like the well-disposed body, in which the organic strengths have perfect vigor. If the supreme virtue, which is reason, directs other inferior potencies and they are moved by its command, then a certain pleasantness and perfect pleasure of strengths arises in both, and this we call harmony. Augustine says that a well-disposed republic or city can be compared to a voice in a melody, in which, with diverse, mutually proportionate sounds, a song becomes pleasant and delectable to the ears.[82]

2. This was characteristic of the State of Innocence, which was regulated by the virtue of original justice beyond the act of divine cognition. This causes contemplative felicity, and it is in this way that perfect men want nothing except that which the regulation of reason mandates and what pleases God, according to a certain participatory virtue found in them. For this reason the philosopher Plutarch was motivated to compare the republic or polity to a natural and organic body, in which motions depend on the movement of one or two parts, such as the heart and brain, and yet every part of the body has a proper function corresponding to the first motions and assisting in the ministry of the others.[83] Hence, this body shows itself to be animated through the benefit of the divine gift, and this happens with the greatest equity through the rudder of reason with the approval of God. Paul confirms this in 1 Corinthians, when he shows that the whole Church is one body distinguished in parts but united by the chain of charity.[84] Therefore, in a true civility or polity it is required that the members be conformed to the head and not mutually discordant and that all things be disposed in civility, as I just said...

4. [244] Besides, order is "the disposition of equal and unequal things giving to each its due," as Augustine says.[85] According to this definition there are various ranks in a polity, with respect to the execution of offices as well as to the subjection or obedience of the subjects, so that there is a perfect social congregation when all are properly

78. Ptolemy is probably thinking especially of the imposition of the Golden Bull, a charter of rights, on King Andrew II by the Hungarian nobles in 1222.

79. The word "Tartar" was used imprecisely in the Middle Ages for a variety of Turkic and Mongolian peoples, and not just for the Tatars proper of Russia. At the time, Mongols were in control of both Persia and Mesopotamia (Ptolemy's "Assyrians").

80. Augustine *The City of God* 15.8. The second clause is not in 15.8.

81. Cf. Aristotle *Nicomachean Ethics* 1.9 1099b30 ff; cf. Thomas Aquinas *Commentary on the Ethics* 1.14.

82. Augustine *The City of God* 2.21, quoting Scipio Africanus in Cicero's *On the Republic* 2.42.69.

83. (Pseudo-)Plutarch, "The Instruction of Trajan," as reported in John of Salisbury *Policraticus* 5.2, 5.9, 6.20, and passim. John may have manufactured this source himself.

84. Cf. 1 Cor. 12:12–14.

85. Augustine *The City of God* 19.13.

disposed and operate properly in their own states. Just as a building is stable when its parts are well laid down, so also a polity has firmness and perpetuity when all, whether rectors, officials, or subjects, work properly in their own ranks, as the action of their condition requires. Because there is nothing repugnant there, there will be the greatest pleasantness and perpetual firmness of state, which is characteristic of political felicity, as Aristotle tells us.

[5] In Exodus, Moses' relative Jethro describes for us just such rectors of the city or polity as those, for the purpose of preserving the people in peace: *Provide from the plebeians mighty men who fear the Lord, in whom there is truth, and who hate avarice, and constitute from them tribunes and centurions and ones set over fifty and over ten who may judge the people at all times.* Afterward he adds, *If you do this, you will fulfill the command of the Lord; you will be able to sustain his precepts, and all the people will return in peace to their own place,*[86] as if all things would exist in the certain mental pleasantness and temporal peace from which human felicity arises, if such ones as are ordained here were governors of the republic. The Roman rectors were such as these, Sallust says, for which reason the Republic went from small to great, because they manifested: "industry at home, just command abroad, a free spirit in counseling, and were addicted neither to lust nor transgressions."[87] In these phrases Sallust shows us the acts of a virtuous government, from which comes the perfect and happy polity.

86. Exod. 18:21–23. The quote is not exact.

87. Sallust *The War with Cataline* 52.21. See above 2.8.3, 3.4.3, 3.20.5.

TWENTY-SEVEN

DANTE ALIGHIERI

Monarchy

Translated by Philip H. Wicksteed

Dante Alighieri (1265–1321) was descended from an ancient Florentine family that for several generations had belonged to the burgher rather than the knightly class. Apart from his love for Beatrice at a tender age, nothing definite is known about his early years. In his grief after the death of Beatrice in 1290, Dante found relief in his study of philosophy, first encountered in Boethius's *Consolation of Philosophy* and Cicero's *On Friendship,* as he related later in *The Banquet* (*Il Convivio,* written 1304–1307). For two and a half years he frequented "the schools of the religious" and "the disputations of the philosophers," probably at the schools of the Dominican Santa Maria Novella and the Franciscan Santa Croce (*Banquet* 2.12.7). From 1295 onward, he took an active part in Florentine politics as a member of the guild of physicians and apothecaries and showed himself a firm opponent of papal interference in temporal matters. Along with two other envoys, he went to Rome in 1301, in a vain attempt to dissuade Boniface VIII from calling in a French army under Charles of Valois to liquidate the antichurch party in Florence. In 1302 he was charged with corrupt practices ("barratry") in and out of office, as well as with offenses against the Guelph party, and condemned to pay a fine of 5,000 florins. The real reason for his conviction appears to have been his outspoken criticism of the policies of the pope and his Florentine supporters. When he refused to submit, his property was confiscated, and he himself was forced into exile. He spent the following years traveling through Italy, seeking refuge and performing occasional diplomatic services. According to several fourteenth-century sources (Boccaccio, Villani), he spent some time in Paris, perhaps between 1309 and 1310, although the evidence is scanty.[1] Emperor Henry VII's campaign in Italy in 1310 revived Dante's hopes for an improvement of the political situation in his country. These hopes were dashed when the emperor, whom Dante had induced to besiege Florence ("destroy the poisonous hydra"), died in 1313. In 1315, the sentence pronounced against Dante by his native city was renewed. Because the *Monarchy* shows similarities to three political letters that Dante wrote during Henry's campaign, the

1. Giorgio Petrocchi, *Vita di Dante* (Rome and Bari: Economia Laterza, 1993), 103.

treatise is often thought to have been written as early as 1311. Yet because the fifth canto of *Paradiso* is referenced in *Monarchy* 1.12 (in a passage that was restored to the treatise in the last two critical editions), the treatise seems to have been written no earlier than 1314 and perhaps as late as 1319. After a sojourn in Verona under the imperial vicar Can Grande della Scala, Dante settled at Ravenna, ca. 1318, and devoted the last years of his life to the completion of his greatest work, the *Divine Comedy.*

The *Monarchy,* like Marsilius's *Defender of the Peace,* attained notoriety among the many pamphlets and documents drafted in the public-relations battles in the late 1320s that accompanied the political struggle between Emperor Ludwig of Bavaria and Pope John XXII. In 1329 the treatise was publicly burned in the marketplace of Bologna by the papal legate, Cardinal Bertrand du Poujet, who had been appointed several years before to advance Guelph policies in northern Italy and to suppress heresy. Around the same time Guido Vernani of Rimini, formerly a lecturer in theology at the Dominican *studium* in Bologna, wrote *De Reprobatione Monarchiae,* a point-by-point rebuttal of Dante's treatise.[2] Vernani, a tolerably competent but undistinguished scholar, noted Dante's open reference in chapter 1.3 to Averroes's teaching regarding the "possible intellect" and drew the conclusion that Dante adhered to Averroes's doctrine of a single, separate possible intellect for all humankind. Vernani's conclusion may appear rash, as Averroes's teaching on the intellect and the soul is explicitly criticized by Dante in the *Purgatorio* (25.61–78), but Vernani's treatise nevertheless shows that the treatise may have been burned for its doctrinal errors as much as for its controversial political stance. The treatise continued to exert a circuitous influence for at least two centuries. In the Renaissance it was translated into Italian several times, including once by Marsilio Ficino. The first printed edition appeared in 1559 during the Reformation; soon after (1564) it was placed on the Index of Prohibited Books, to be removed again in the nineteenth century. The final rehabilitation came when Benedict XV extolled Dante's works in his encyclical letter *In Praeclara* (1921).

The *Monarchy* is divided into three books. Book 1 sets forth the necessity of a universal temporal monarchy for the well-being of the world. Book 2 establishes the right of the Roman people to this dignity. Book 3 argues that the monarch receives his authority not through the mediation of the supreme pontiff, but immediately from God. Upon this threefold division a second structure is also imposed: the first and last parts of the treatise, Chapters 1.1–15 and 3.12–16, argue from reason; Chapters 1.16–2.9 and 3.10–11 argue from "human deeds," and Chapters 2.10–3.9 argue from the "principles of Christian faith." Book 1 is reproduced here in its entirety, along with Chapters 12 and 16 from Book 3, which are also argued from reason. The work as a whole, at once a treatise and a tract for the times, purports to disclose "truths unattempted by others." Accordingly, Dante's appropriation of Aristotle's "total kingship" departs radically from the teaching of his master, as he advocates the establishment of a world government as a means of eliminating strife among cities and nations. In what ways and to what degree Dante's ultimate intention regarding total kingship differs from Aristotle's own has to be assessed in the light of Dante's immediate intention of limiting the role of the papacy in political and temporal affairs.

The following translation is based on that of Philip H. Wicksteed: *The Latin Works of Dante* (London, 1904), 127–72, 262–65, and 275–79; the translation has been extensively revised by both the previous and the current editors, rendering it more literal and bringing it into accord with the Latin edition of Prue Shaw, *Monarchia,* Cambridge Medieval Classics 4 (Cambridge: Cambridge University Press, 1995). This edition was based upon the critical edition of Pier Giorgio Ricci, *Monarchia* (Arnoldo Mondadori Editore, 1965), although it included emendations that were documented in the subsequent critical edition of Prue Shaw, *Monarchia* (Birmingham, UK: Scholarly Digital Editions, 2006). Also frequently consulted for the present version was the annotated edition of Bruno Nardi, *Dante Alighieri—Opere minori,* vol. 2 (Milan: Ricciardi, 1979). The numbers in brackets within the text indicate the subsections of these editions; the chapter numbering follows the Shaw edition.

2. For an English translation, see *The Monarchia Controversy,* trans. Anthony K. Cassell (Washington, DC: The Catholic University of America Press, 2004). Some of the biographical details reported here are derived from Cassell's commentary. Additional information on the contest between Ludwig and John XXII may be found in the biographical introduction to Marsilius of Padua in this volume.

BOOK ONE

1

It seems to be of the utmost importance to all men on whom the Higher Nature[3] has stamped the love of truth to work in advance for their descendants, so that posterity may have from them something by which to be enriched, just as they themselves have been enriched by the work of the ancients. [2] For let there be no doubt in the mind of the man who is imbued with public teachings and yet does not care to contribute anything to the commonweal that he is falling far short of his duty. He is not indeed *a tree by the streams of waters, bearing its fruit in its season* [Ps. 1:3], but rather a destructive whirlpool, always sucking in and never pouring back what it has swallowed. [3] Reflecting then, as I often do, upon these things, lest I should one day be convicted of the charge of the buried talent,[4] I long not only to burgeon but also to bear fruit in the public interest and to set forth truths unattempted by others. [4] For what fruit would one bear by demonstrating anew one of Euclid's theorems, or by setting about the task of re-expounding the doctrine of happiness already expounded by Aristotle, or by undertaking once again the apology of old age, which Cicero had defended? None whatsoever. That boring superfluousness would rather provoke disgust.

[5] And since among other hidden and useful truths the knowledge of the temporal monarchy is the most useful and the most concealed, and since it has not been attempted by anyone (because it stands in no direct relation to gain), I propose to extract it from its recesses, so that I may both keep a useful vigil for the world and become the first to win for my glory the palm of so great a prize.[5] [6] The task is indeed arduous and beyond my strength, but in undertaking it I trust not so much in my own power as in the light of that Giver *who gives to all liberally and does not upbraid* [James 1:5].

2

We must first consider what is meant by 'temporal monarchy' in outline, so to speak, and according to its intention. [2] The temporal monarchy, which is called 'the Empire', is thus a single principality extending over all persons in time or in and over the things that are measured in time. [3] Now there are three main questions to be raised concerning this temporal monarchy. First, we may inquire and examine whether it is necessary for the well-being of the world; secondly, whether the Roman people rightfully claimed for itself the office of monarch; and thirdly, whether the authority of the monarch depends upon God immediately or upon some minister or vicar of God.

[4] But inasmuch as every truth that is not a principle derives its evidence from the truth of some principle, it is necessary in any inquiry that we have knowledge of the principle to which we may return by analysis in order to arrive at certitude concerning all the propositions that are afterwards laid down. And since the present treatise is an inquiry of some sort, it seems that before all else we must examine closely the principle in virtue of which what follows may be established. [5] We should know, then, that there are some things that are not in any way subject to our power and that we can only think over but cannot act upon, such as mathematics, physics, and things divine. But there are other things that are subject to our power and that we can not only think over but also act upon; and in this case, the action is not undertaken for the sake of speculation, but speculation for the sake of action, for in such things the end is action. [6] Hence, since the present matter is political, and indeed the source and principle of correct polities, and since everything political is subject to our power, it is obvious that the present matter is not ordered primarily to speculation but to action. [7] Moreover, since in matters of action the ultimate end is the principle and cause of all things (for it first moves the agent), it follows that every reasoning about the means to an end

3. Cf. Dante *Purgatory* 16.79, where God is referred to as "miglior natura," or superior nature; cf. also *The Banquet* 1.1, where Dante cites Aristotle *Metaphysics* 1.1 980a20.

4. Cf. Matt. 25:25.

5. Cf. 1 Cor. 9:24.

must be derived from the end itself. Thus there will be one way of cutting wood to build a house and another to build a ship. [8] Hence that which is the universal end of the society of the human race, if there is such an end, will be in this case the principle by means of which all things that we have to prove below will be made sufficiently clear.[6] Now it would be foolish to suppose that there is an end for this or that society and no one end for all of them.

3

Now, then, we must consider what is the end of human society as a whole; once we have seen that, more than half of our work will be done, as the Philosopher says in the *Nicomachean Ethics.*[7] [2] And in order to clarify the point in question, we must observe that, just as nature produces the thumb for a certain end, and the whole hand for a different end, and the arm for another different from both, and the whole human for an end that again differs from all the others; so it orders the individual human to one end, the domestic community to another, the village to a third, the city to another, the kingdom yet to another, and lastly there is the best end for which God eternal, by His art, which is nature, brings into being the human race in its universality. And this last end is what we are seeking here as the guiding principle of our investigation. [3] Accordingly, we have to know first of all that "God and nature make nothing in vain,"[8] but whatever comes into being is ordered to some operation. For the ultimate end in the intention of the creator as creator is not some created essence, but rather the proper operation of the essence. Hence it is not the proper operation that comes into being for the sake of the essence, but the latter for the sake of the former. [4] There is, then, a certain operation proper to humanity as a whole to which the totality of men itself in all its multiplicity is ordered, and neither one human, nor one family, nor one village, nor one city, nor any particular kingdom can achieve this operation. Now what this operation is, will become clear if the ultimate potentiality of all of humanity can be manifested. [5] I say, therefore, that no power that is shared by several specifically distinct beings is the ultimate potentiality of any one of them. For since that which is thus ultimate is constitutive of the species, it would follow that one essence would be specified for several species, which is impossible. [6] The ultimate power in a human being, then, is not being itself, taken absolutely—for even taken as such, it is shared by the elements; nor is it compound being, for this is also found in minerals; nor is it animated being, for this is also in plants; nor is it apprehension, for apprehension is also shared by the lower animals; rather it is apprehension by means of the possible intellect, which belongs to no other save man, either above or below him. [7] For although there are other essences that share in the intellect, their intellect is not a possible intellect like man's, since these essences are intellectual species and nothing else, and their being is nothing other than the act of understanding what it is that they are; this act is without interruption, otherwise they would not be everlasting. It is clear then that the ultimate potentiality of humanity as such is an intellectual potentiality or power. [8] And since that potentiality cannot all be reduced to actuality at the same time by one human or by any of the particular groups distinguished above, there must be a multiplicity in the human race by which precisely the whole of this potentiality may be actualized, just as there must be a multiplicity of generable things in order that the whole potentiality of prime matter may always be in act; otherwise we would have to concede the existence of a separate potentiality, which is impossible. [9] Averroes agrees with this view in his commentary on the treatise *On the Soul.*[9] Moreover, the intellectual power of which I am speaking is ordered not only to universal forms of species, but also by a kind of extension to particulars. Hence it is commonly said that the speculative intellect

6. "Society" translates *civilitas.* The Greek word *politeia* was occasionally rendered by *civilitas* (especially in reference to *Ethics* 2.1 1103b3–7; compare Dante's *Epistolae* 1.5–8), but *politeia* understood as "constitution" or "regime" was more often simply transliterated as *politia* (L. Minio-Paluello, "Tre Note alla 'Monarchia,'" in *Medioevo e Rinascimento* [Florence: G. C. Sansoni, 1955], 285–96). Minio-Paluello argues that here *civilitas* is equivalent to *civitas.* Cf. *The Banquet* 4.4.

7. Cf. Aristotle *Nicomachean Ethics* 1.7 1098b6.

8. Cf. Aristotle *De Caelo* 1.4 271a33.

9. Cf. Averroes *Commentarium Magnum in Aristotelis De Anima Libros* 3 t.c. 5.

becomes practical by extension[10] and so has as its end doing and making. [10] I say this because there are things to be done, which are regulated by political prudence, and things to be made, which are regulated by art, all of which serve speculation as the greatest good for which the Supreme Goodness has brought the human race into being. This already enables us to understand the statement of the *Politics* that "the intellectually vigorous by nature rule over the others."[11]

4

It has been sufficiently shown, therefore, that the proper work of the human race taken as a whole is to actualize at all times the entire potentiality of the possible intellect, primarily for speculation, and secondarily—by extension and for the sake of the other—for action. [2] Since it is with the whole as it is with the part, and since the individual man is "perfected in prudence and wisdom by means of sitting and being still,"[12] it is evident that the human race is most freely and favorably disposed toward its own proper work—which is almost divine (according to the words: *Thou hast made him a little lower than the angels* [Ps. 8:6 in Vulgate; Heb. 2:7])—in the stillness or tranquillity of peace. Hence it is clear that of all the things that are ordered to our happiness, universal peace is the best. [3] That is why there rang out to the shepherds from on high, not riches, not pleasures, not honors, not length of life, not health, not strength, not beauty, but peace. For the heavenly host proclaimed: *Glory to God in the highest, and on earth peace to men of good will* [Luke 2:14]. [4] That is why also He who is the salvation of men used the salutation, *Peace be with you* [Luke 24:36; John 20:21, 26]. For it was fitting that the Supreme Savior should utter the supreme salutation. His disciples and Paul likewise sought to preserve this custom in their own salutations, as everyone can see.[13] [5] From what we have said, then, the means are clear by which the human race better and indeed best achieves its proper work. And as a result, we have perceived the most proximate way of attaining that to which all our deeds are ordered as to their ultimate end, namely, universal peace, which may serve as the principle upon which the following arguments are based. [6] This principle was needed, we said, as a standard set before us into which whatever has to be proved must be resolved as into the most obvious truth.

5

To sum up, then, what we have been saying since the beginning, there are three main questions to be raised and inquired into concerning the temporal monarchy, more commonly called the Empire; and these questions, as we stated earlier, we propose to investigate in the light of the principle laid down and according to the order that has already been indicated. [2] The first question therefore is whether the temporal monarchy is necessary for the well-being of the world. Against its being necessary there is no force of reason or of authority, whereas there are indeed very strong and lucid arguments to show that it is. The first of these arguments may be drawn from the authority of the Philosopher in his *Politics*.[14] [3] For there his venerable authority asserts that when several things are ordered to one thing, one of them must regulate or rule and the others be regulated or ruled. To this not only the illustrious name of the author but inductive reasoning forces us to assent. [4] For if we consider one man, we shall see that this comes to pass in him; indeed, since all his powers are ordered to happiness, the intellectual power itself regulates and rules all the others; otherwise he cannot attain happiness. [5] If we consider one household, the end of which is to prepare its members to live well, there must be one to regulate and rule, who is called the *paterfamilias*, or someone who takes

10. This phrase was inserted into an early translation of Aristotle's *De Anima* 3.7 431b9–11 and became widely known, even though it was subsequently removed in the translation of William of Moerbeke (Minio-Paluello, "Tre Note all 'Monarchia,'" 277–85).

11. Cf. Aristotle *Politics* 1.2 1252a31; cf. also 1.5 1254a17 ff.; and Letter to Can Grande, *Epistola* 13.2.7.

12. Aristotle *Physics* 7.3 247b11–12.

13. Cf. Gal. 1:3; Eph. 1:2; 1 Pet. 1:2; 2 John 1:3.

14. Cf. Aristotle *Politics* 1.5. 1254a28; the preface to Thomas Aquinas *Commentary on the Metaphysics.*

his place; according to the words of the Philosopher, "every household is ruled by the oldest."[15] And it pertains to him, as Homer says, to rule over all and to impose laws on others.[16] [6] Hence the proverbial curse: "May you have an equal in your home." If we consider one village, the end of which is convenient assistance as regards both persons and things, one person has to regulate the others, whether he be appointed by someone else or rise to pre-eminence out of themselves with the consent of others; otherwise not only do they fail to achieve that mutual sufficiency, but sometimes, when several strive for pre-eminence, the whole village is brought to ruin. [7] And if we consider one city, the end of which is to live well and self-sufficiently, there must be a single rule (*regimen*); and this applies not only to a correct regime (*politia*), but even to a corrupt one. For if it be otherwise, not only is the end of the civil life thwarted, but even the city ceases to be what it was. [8] Finally, if we consider one particular kingdom, the end of which is the same as that of the city, but with greater assurance of its tranquillity, there must be one king to rule and govern; otherwise, not only do the people living in the kingdom fail to reach the end, but the kingdom itself lapses into ruin, according to the words of the infallible truth: *Every kingdom divided against itself shall be laid waste* [Matt. 12:25; Luke 11:17]. [9] If such is the case, then, in these and in all things that are ordered to some one thing, the proposition laid down above is true. Now it is evident that the entire human race is ordered to one thing, as we have already shown. Therefore there must be one regulating or ruling, and this one ought to be called the monarch or emperor. [10] Thus it is clear that for the well-being of the world there must be a monarchy or empire.

6

Furthermore, the relation of the partial order to the total order is the same as that of the part to the whole. The part is related to the whole as to its end and greatest good. Therefore the order in the part is also related to the order in the whole as to its end and greatest good. From this we gather that the goodness of the partial order does not exceed the goodness of the total order, but rather the contrary. [2] Since then we may discover a twofold order in things, namely, the order of the parts among themselves and the order of the parts to some one thing that is not a part (for instance the order of the parts of an army among themselves and their order to the general), the order of the parts to that one thing is the superior order, as being the end of the other; for the other exists for its sake and not conversely. [3] Hence, if the form of this order is found in the parts of the human collectivity, much more must it be found in the collectivity or totality itself, in virtue of the previously advanced syllogism, since it is the superior order or form of the order. But it is found in all the parts of the human collectivity, as is sufficiently clear from what has been said in the preceding chapter. Therefore it ought to be found in the totality itself. [4] And thus all the parts mentioned earlier, which are inferior to the kingdoms, and the kingdoms themselves should be ordered to a single prince or to a single principality, that is to say, to the monarch or the monarchy.

7

Moreover, the human totality is a whole of some sort in relation to certain parts, and it is a part of some sort in relation to a certain whole. It is indeed a whole in relation to particular kingdoms and nations, as shown above, and it is a part in relation to the universe as a whole. This is self-evident. [2] The human totality therefore is said to be properly related to its whole in the same way that its own lower parts are properly related to the human totality itself. Its parts are related to it by means of a single principle, as may easily be gathered from what has been said earlier. The totality itself therefore is properly related, absolutely speaking, to the universe or to its prince, who is

15. Aristotle *Politics* 1.2 1252b21.

16. Cf. Homer *Odyssey* 9.114, cited in Aristotle *Politics* 1.2 1252b23.

God and the Monarch, by means of one principle only, namely, a single prince. [3] Hence it follows that the monarchy is necessary to the world for its well-being.

8

Furthermore, all things have a good and perfect disposition when they exist as the first agent, who is God, intended them to be. And this is self-evident to all save those who deny that the divine goodness attains the height of perfection. [2] It is God's intention that every caused being should reflect the divine likeness in the degree to which its proper nature is capable of receiving it. For that reason it was said: *Let us make man after our image and likeness* [Gen. 1:26]. And although *after our image* cannot be said of the things lower than man, yet *after our likeness* can be said of anything whatever, since the universe in its entirety is nothing other than a certain trace of the divine goodness. The human race therefore has a good and perfect disposition when, in so far as it is capable, it resembles God. [3] But the human race most resembles God when it is most one; for it is in Him alone that the true form (*ratio*) of the one exists. That is why it is written: *Hear, Israel, the Lord your God is one* [Deut. 6:4]. [4] But the human race is most one when it is all united in one, and this cannot be except when it is totally subject to one prince, as is self-evident. [5] It is when subject to one prince, therefore, that human race most resembles God and, as a result, best conforms to the divine intention; and this is to be in a good and perfect condition, as was proved at the beginning of the chapter.

9

Likewise every son has a good and perfect disposition when he follows the trail of a perfect father, in so far as his own nature allows. The human race is the son of heaven, which is most perfect in all its work; for "man is begotten by man and the sun," according to Book 2 of the *Physics*.[17] The human race has a perfect disposition, therefore, when it follows the trail of heaven, in so far as its own nature allows. [2] And since the whole heaven in all its parts, motions, and movers, is regulated by a single motion—namely, that of the first moved—and by a single mover—who is God, as human reason discovers very clearly through philosophy—the human race is perfect, if our reasoning is correct, when it is regulated in its movers and its motions by a single prince as by a single mover, and by a single law as by a single motion. [3] Hence it appears necessary for the well-being of the world that there should be a monarchy or single principality, which is called the Empire. This is the argument that Boethius was sighing forth when he said: "How happy you would be, oh race of men, if the love by which heaven is ruled, also ruled your minds."[18]

10

Furthermore, wherever disputes may arise, there must be judgment; otherwise there would be something imperfect without its proper perfecting element, which is impossible since God and nature do not fail in things necessary.[19] [2] Between any two princes, one of whom is in no way subject to the other, a dispute may arise either through their own fault or that of their subjects, as is self-evident. Between such princes, therefore, there must be judgment. [3] And since one cannot take cognizance of the affairs of the other, one not being subject to the other (for an equal has no imperium over his equal), there has to be a third of wider jurisdiction who, within

17. Aristotle *Physics* 2.2 194b13; cf. also *Metaphysics* 12.5 1071a13–17.

18. Boethius *De Consolatione Philosophiae* 2, Poem 8; cf. *Paradiso* 33.143–45.

19. Cf. Aristotle *De Anima* 3.9 432b21.

the compass of his right, may exercise his rule over both. [4] And this person will either be the monarch or not. If he is, the proposition is established. If not, he will again have a coequal outside the compass of his jurisdiction; then a third will again be necessary. [5] And so either we shall go on to infinity, which cannot be, or we must come to a first and highest judge, by whose judgment all disputes may be settled, either mediately or immediately; and this person will be the monarch or emperor. Monarchy is therefore necessary to the world. [6] The Philosopher perceived this argument when he said: "Beings do not want to be badly disposed; but a multiplicity of principalities is an evil; therefore let there be a single prince."[20]

11

In addition, the world is best disposed when in it justice is strongest. Hence Virgil, wishing to praise that age which seemed to be emerging in his own day, sang in his *Bucolics:* "Already, too, the Virgin is returning, the Saturnian kingdoms come again."[21] For by "Virgin" was meant justice, which was also called Astraea.[22] By "Saturnian kingdoms" was meant the best age, which was also called the golden age. [2] Justice is strongest only under a monarch. For the best disposition of the world, therefore, a monarchy or empire is required. [3] In order to establish the subsumed premise, we have to know that justice of itself and considered in its proper nature is a certain rectitude or rule excluding deviations on either side; and thus it is not susceptible of more or less, any more than is whiteness considered in the abstract. [4] For there are certain forms of this kind, which, although subject to composition, consist in a simple and invariable essence, as the Master of the Six Principles rightly says.[23] Such qualities are nevertheless susceptible of more or less with respect to the subjects to which they are united, according to the greater or lesser admixture of their contraries in these subjects. [5] Hence where there is least of the contrary of justice admixed, both as regards the habitus and as regards operation, there justice is strongest.[24] And then it may truly be said of it, as the Philosopher remarks: "Neither Hesperus nor Lucifer is so wonderful."[25] For then it is like Phoebe gazing across the horizon at her brother in the purple glow of the morning calm.[26] [6] As regards habitus then, justice sometimes finds opposition in the will, for where the will is not free from all greed, even though justice is present, nevertheless it is not altogether there in the radiance of its purity; for it has a subject that, however slightly, resists it to some extent. That is why those who attempt to inspire the judge with passion are rightly rebuffed.[27] [7] As regards operation, on the other hand, justice finds opposition in relation to power. For since justice is a virtue that is related to others, how can anyone act in accordance with it if he does not have the power of rendering to each his due? Hence it is obvious that the more powerful the just man is, the broader his justice will be when he acts.

[8] On the basis of this statement, then, we argue as follows: justice is strongest in the world when it exists in the most willing and most powerful subject; the monarch alone is such a subject; therefore justice is strongest in the world only when it exists in the monarch. [9] This prosyllogism is in the second figure,[28] with intrinsic negation, and is similar to this one: all B is A; only C is A; therefore, only C is B. That is: All B is A;

20. Aristotle *Metaphysics* 12.10 1076a4. In the last part of the sentence Aristotle is quoting Homer's *Iliad* 2.204.

21. Virgil *Eclogues* 4.6.

22. According to one account, Astraea, the star maiden, was the daughter of Zeus and Themis and as such was identified with *Dikē,* Justice. She lived among men in the golden age and, at the end of that age, was the last of the gods to withdraw into the sky, where she shines as the constellation of the Virgin (cf. Ovid *Metamorphoses* 1.149–50). Saturn was an ancient Italian god of seedtime and harvest, later identified with the Greek Kronos. Thrust out by Zeus, he came across the sea to Italy and brought to that country, over which he ruled as king, the blessings of agriculture. His reign was regarded as the golden age of Italy.

23. Cf. Gilbert de la Porrée (ca. 1076–1154) *Liber de Sex Principiis* 1.1.

24. The *habitus* (in Greek, *hexis*) is the disposition to perform a virtuous or vicious action; cf. Aristotle *Nicomachean Ethics* 2.5 1105b21.

25. Aristotle *Nicomachean Ethics* 5.1 1129b28. Hesperus is the evening star, and Lucifer the morning star.

26. Phoebe, the moon goddess, was the sister of Phoebus or Apollo, the sun god.

27. Cf. Aristotle *Rhetoric* 1.1 1354a24.

28. Cf. Aristotle *Prior Analytics* 1.5.

nothing except C is A; therefore nothing except C is B. [10] The first proposition is clear from the preceding explanation. The other is manifested as follows, first as regards the will, then as regards power. [11] In order to establish the first point, we should note that what is most contrary to justice is greed, as Aristotle points out in the fifth book of the *Nicomachean Ethics*.[29] If greed is removed altogether, nothing is left to oppose justice. Hence it is the opinion of the Philosopher that those things that can be determined by law should in no way be left to the judge, and this for fear of greed, which readily twists the minds of men.[30] Thus where there is nothing that can be desired, there it is impossible for greed to be; for when their objects are destroyed, the passions cannot exist. [12] But the monarch has nothing that he can desire, for his jurisdiction is bounded by the ocean alone, which is not the case with other princes, whose principalities are bounded by others, as for instance the King of Castile's by that of the King of Aragon. From this it follows that the monarch can be the purest subject of justice among mortals. [13] In addition, just as greed, however slight, clouds the habitus of justice, so charity or right love sharpens and brightens it. Thus the person in whom right love is most capable of inhering is also the person in whom justice can occupy the strongest place. Such is the monarch. When he exists, therefore, justice is or can be strongest. [14] Now that right love produces the effect just mentioned may be shown from the following. Greed, scorning the good in itself of men, seeks other things; but charity, scorning all other things, seeks God and man and, consequently, the good of man. And since, among the various goods of man, the most important is to live in peace (as we were saying earlier), and since this is brought about above all and most potently by justice, charity will chiefly lend vigor to justice, and the stronger it is, the more. [15] And that of all men the monarch is the one in whom right love should most inhere, is manifested as follows. The closer anything lovable is to the lover, the more it is loved. But men are closer to the monarch than to other princes. Therefore they are or ought to be most loved by him. The first proposition is evident if we consider the nature of passives and actives. The second becomes apparent from the fact that men come into contact with other princes only in part, whereas they come into contact with the monarch according to their totality. [16] And again, they come into contact with other princes through the monarch, and not conversely. And thus the care of all men is found primarily and immediately in the monarch, and in other princes only through the monarch, inasmuch as their care is derived from that supreme care. [17] In addition, the more universal a cause is, the more fully it has the form of a cause, for the lower cause is a cause only through the higher, as is clear from *De Causis*;[31] and the more a cause is a cause, the more it loves its effect, since such love is a property of the cause as such. [18] Hence since among mortals the monarch is the most universal cause by which men may live well, for other princes are so through him, as we have already said, it follows that the good of men is most loved by him. [19] Now who, with the exception of the man who is ignorant of the meaning of the word, has any doubt that the monarch has the greatest power to effect justice? For if he is a monarch, he could not possibly have enemies. [20] The subsumed premise having been sufficiently explained, the conclusion is certain, namely, that for the best disposition of the world it is necessary that the monarchy exist.

12

Furthermore, the human race is best disposed when it is most free. This will become evident if the principle of freedom is made clear. [2] Hence we will have to know that the first principle of our freedom is freedom of choice, which many have on their lips but few in their minds. For they get as far as saying that free choice is free judgment on the part of the will. And what they say is true, but

29. Cf. Aristotle *Nicomachean Ethics* 5.2 1130a19.

30. Cf. Aristotle *Rhetoric* 1.1 1354a31.

31. *Liber de Causis* 1.16. This work was put together in Arabic by an unknown philosopher ca. 850 and consists for the most part of excerpts from Proclus's *Elements of Theology*. The work exerted a considerable influence in the Christian world through Gerard of Cremona, who translated it into Latin at Toledo between 1167 and 1187 and attributed it to Aristotle. William of Moerbeke's translation of Proclus's *Elements of Theology* into Latin in 1268 revealed to Thomas Aquinas and medieval philosophers generally the true character of the *Liber de Causis*.

they are far from understanding what is meant by these words, as is constantly the case with our logicians in regard to certain propositions introduced by way of example in logic—for instance, the three angles of a triangle are equal to two right angles. [3] I say therefore that between apprehension and appetite lies judgment. For first a thing is apprehended; once apprehended, it is judged good or bad; and finally the one who judges either pursues it or shuns it. [4] If, then, the judgment moves the appetite altogether and is in no way anticipated by it, it is free. But if the judgment is moved by an appetite that anticipates it in any way whatever, it cannot be free, for it does not move of itself, but is drawn captive by another. [5] And hence it is that brutes cannot have free judgment, because their judgments are always anticipated by their appetite. And hence it too can be shown that the intellectual substances, whose wills are immutable, as well as the separated souls who depart from here well, do not lose their freedom of choice because of the immutability of their wills, but retain it in its most perfect and efficacious form.

[6] Having seen all this, we may further show that this freedom or this principle of all our freedom is the greatest gift conferred by God on human nature—as I already said in the Paradise of my *Comedy*[32]—for through it we are rendered happy here as men, through it we are rendered happy elsewhere as gods. [7] And if this is so, who would not agree that the human race is best disposed when it enjoys the fullest use of this principle? [8] But it is under a monarch that it is most free. In order to grasp this, we have to know that to be free is to exist "for one's own sake and not for the sake of some other," as the Philosopher would have it in his treatise *De Simpliciter Ente.*[33] For that which exists for the sake of something else is determined by that for the sake of which it exists, as a road is determined by its goal. [9] Only when a monarch has imperium does the human race exist for its own sake and not for the sake of something else; for it is only then that perverted regimes—namely, democracies, oligarchies, and tyrannies (all of which force the human race into slavery, as is obvious to anyone who runs through all of them)—are rectified, and that kings, aristocrats (who are called *optimates*), and zealots of the people's freedom rule politically. For since the monarch has the greatest love of men, as already indicated, he wants all men to become good, which cannot happen within perverted regimes. [10] That is why the Philosopher says in his *Politics* that "under a perverted regime a good man is a bad citizen, but under a correct one the good man and the good citizen are identical."[34] And correct regimes such as these aim at freedom, namely, that men may exist for their own sakes. [11] For the citizens are not there for the sake of the consuls, nor the nation for the sake of the king, but conversely the consuls for the sake of the citizens and the king for the sake of the nation. For just as the regime is not established for the sake of the laws, but rather the laws for the sake of the regime, so too those who live according to law are not ordered to the legislator, but rather he to them, as the Philosopher again says in what has been left by him on the present matter.[35] [12] Hence it is also clear that, although the consul or the king is the master of the others as regards the way, yet as regards the end he is their servant, and the monarch most of all, for he must be regarded without doubt as the servant of all men. Hence, too, we can already see that in establishing laws, the monarch is determined by the end set before him. [13] The human race, therefore, is best disposed when it exists under a monarch; from this it follows that for the well-being of the world the existence of the monarchy is necessary.

13

Further, he who is himself capable of being best disposed for ruling is also capable of disposing others best. For in every action the chief intent of the agent, whether acting by necessity of nature or by choice, is to unfold its own likeness. [2] Hence every agent, in so far as it acts, experiences pleasure. For since everything that exists desires its own being, and since by acting the agent's being is in a certain way expanded, pleasure of necessity follows; for pleasure always attaches to the

32. *Paradise* 5.19–24.

33. Aristotle *Metaphysics* 1.2 982b25; on the title, *De Simpliciter Ente* (*On Being Simply*), cf. Aristotle *Metaphysics* 4.1 1003b23.

34. Cf. Aristotle *Politics* 3.4 1276b30; *Nicomachean Ethics* 5.2 1130b28; Thomas Aquinas *Commentary on the Nicomachean Ethics* 5.3.14.

35. Cf. Aristotle *Politics* 4.1 1289a13–15.

thing desired. [3] Nothing acts, therefore, unless it is already itself what the thing acted upon is to become. That is why the Philosopher says in his work *De Simpliciter Ente:* "Everything that is led from potency to act is led thereto by something that is already in act what the other is to become,"[36] for if anything attempted to act otherwise, the attempt would be vain. [4] And thus may be refuted the error of those who think that by speaking well and acting badly they can inform others with life and morals, and who fail to perceive that the hands of Jacob were more persuasive than his words, although the former urged what was false and the latter what was true. Hence the Philosopher says in the *Nicomachean Ethics:* "For in the things that concern passions and actions, words are less convincing than deeds."[37] [5] Hence also it was said from heaven to the sinner David: *Why do you talk of my righteousness?* [Ps. 49:16], as if to say, "In vain do you speak, so long as you yourself are other than that which you speak." From this we gather that he who would dispose others best must himself be best disposed. [6] But the monarch alone is the one who is capable of being best disposed to rule. This is shown as follows. A thing is easily and perfectly disposed for a habitus and an operation in the degree to which there is in it nothing contrary to such a disposition. That is why those who have never been taught anything arrive at the habitus of philosophical truth more easily and perfectly than those who have been taught for a long time and are imbued with false opinions. For this reason Galen says rightly: "Such persons need twice as much time to acquire science."[38] [7] Since, then, the monarch cannot have any occasion for greed, or at any rate the least occasion among mortals, as has been shown above, which is not the case with the other princes, and since greed itself alone corrupts judgment and impedes justice, it follows that the monarch can be either entirely or most of all well disposed to rule, because of all the rest he is capable of the highest degree of judgment and justice. These two qualities belong most fittingly to the legislator and to the executor of the law, as that most holy king testified when he requested of God the things that are fitting for a king and the son of a king. *God,* he said, *give Your judgment to the king and Your justice to the king's son* [Ps. 71:1]. [8] The subsumed premise rightly states, therefore, that the monarch alone is the one who is best disposed for ruling. Thus the monarch alone is capable of disposing others best. From this it follows that for the best disposition of the world monarchy is necessary.

14

Also, it is better that what is capable of being done by one should be done by one rather than by more than one. This is shown as follows. Let A be the one by which a thing can be done, and let A and B be more than one by which in like manner the same thing can be done. If then that same thing that is done by A and B can be done by A alone, B is called in in vain, because nothing follows from its being called in, inasmuch as that same thing was being done by A alone. [2] And since every such calling in is useless or superfluous, and everything superfluous is displeasing to God and nature, and everything displeasing to God and nature is bad, as is self-evident, it follows not only that it is better for it to be done by one if it can be than to be done by more than one, but further that it is good for it to be done by one and bad absolutely for it to be done by more than one. [3] Moreover, a thing is said to be better for being closer to the best, and the end has the form of what is best; but to be done by one is closer to the end, therefore it is better. And that it is closer is clear from the following. Let the end be C, the being done by one, A, and being done by more than one, A and B. It is evident that the way from A through B to C is longer than from A alone to C. [4] But the human race can be ruled by one supreme prince, who is the monarch. In this respect it should of course be noted that when we say the human race can be ruled by a single supreme prince, we do not mean that the minutest decisions of each municipality could emanate directly from this single ruler, since municipal laws also are sometimes deficient and need direction, as is clear from the Philosopher, who commends *epieikeia* [equity] in the fifth book of the *Nicomachean Ethics.*[39] [5] For nations, kingdoms, and cities have their own

36. Aristotle *Metaphysics* 9.8 1049b24.
37. Aristotle *Nicomachean Ethics* 10.1 1172a34.
38. Galen *De Cognoscendis Morbis* 10.
39. Cf. Aristotle *Nicomachean Ethics* 5.10 1137b26.

characteristics, which have to be regulated by different laws. For a law is a rule (*regula*) to direct life. [6] Indeed, the Scythians,[40] who live outside the seventh circle and experience great inequalities of days and nights and are oppressed by an almost intolerable chill of frost, have to be regulated in a different way from the Garamantes, who live under the equinoctial circle and always have the light of day equal in length to the darkness of night and, because of the excessive heat of the air, cannot wear clothes. [7] Rather one must understand that the human race, in the things that are common and apply to all, should be ruled by him and guided to peace by a common rule. And particular princes ought to receive this rule or law from him, just as, to arrive at a practical conclusion, the practical intellect receives the major proposition from the speculative intellect, subsumes a particular proposition that is properly its own, and draws its conclusion concerning a particular action. [8] And not only is this possible for one, but it must of necessity proceed from one, so that all confusion concerning the universal principles may be removed. [9] Moses writes in the Law that this is also what he himself did;[41] for, having chosen chiefs from the tribes of the sons of Israel, he left the minor decisions to them and reserved the higher and more common ones for himself alone, and the chiefs made use of these more common decisions throughout their tribes according to their applicability to each of them. [10] It is better, therefore, that the human race be ruled by one than by several, and thus by the monarch, who is a single prince; and if better, then more acceptable to God, since God always wills what is better. And since when there are only two alternatives better and best are the same, it follows that between "one" and "several," "one" is not only more acceptable to God, but most acceptable. [11] Hence it follows that the human race is most perfect when it is ruled by one. And thus for the well-being of the world it is necessary that there should be a monarchy.

15

Likewise, I affirm that being and oneness and goodness are related in order of priority according to the fifth sense of "prior."[42] For being by nature is prior to oneness, and oneness is prior to goodness; for that which "is" most, is most one; and what is most one, is most good. And the further that anything is removed from maximal being, the further also is it removed from being one and consequently from being good. [2] That is why in every genus of things that which is most one is best, as the Philosopher would have it in his work *De Simpliciter Ente.*[43] Hence it is that "being one" appears to be the root of that which is "being good," and "being many" the root of that which is "being bad." That is why Pythagoras, in his correlations, placed one on the side of the good and many on the side of evil, as is clear from the first book of the *De Simpliciter Ente.*[44] [3] From this we can see that to sin is nothing other than to reject the one and to go on to seek the many. And this the Psalmist perceived when he said: *They are multiplied in the fruit of corn and wine and oil* [Ps. 4:8]. [4] It is clear, then, that everything that is good is good in virtue of its being one. And since concord as such is a good, it is evident that it consists in some unity, as in its proper root. [5] This root we shall discover if we consider the nature or definition of concord. Concord is indeed the uniform motion of several wills. From this definition it becomes apparent that the unity of wills, which we are given to understand by uniform motion, is the root of concord or is in fact concord itself. [6] For just as we would call a number of clods concordant because they are descend together toward the center, and a number of flames concordant because they all ascend together toward the circumference, if they did this of their own will, so we call a number of men concordant when, as regards the act of the will, they move together toward a single thing that is formally present in their wills—just as a single quality, namely, heaviness, is formally present in the clods and another, namely, lightness, in the flames. [7] For the power to will is a certain potentiality, but its form is the concept

40. In antiquity, "Scythian" was a general designation for the nomadic tribes of the north of Europe, beyond the Black Sea. The Garamantes were a tribe of the interior of Africa, beyond the Gaetulians, in that part of Libya today called the Fezzan.

41. Cf. Exod. 18:17–26.

42. Cf. Aristotle *Categories* chap. 12 14a26–b22.

43. Cf. *Metaphysics* 5.16 1021b30, 10.2 1054a9–13; consider as well Thomas Aquinas *Summa Theologiae* 1.5.2, 1.11.4.

44. Aristotle *Metaphysics* 1.5 986a23–27.

of the good that is apprehended; and this form, like other forms, although one in itself, is multiplied according to the multiplicity of the matter in which it is received, as are the soul and number and the other forms subject to composition.

[8] With these preliminary remarks in mind, in order to manifest what will be the major premise of our thesis, we argue as follows. All concord depends on unity in the wills. The human race when best disposed is a certain concord. For just as one man when best disposed both as to soul and body is a certain concord, and likewise a family, a city, and a kingdom, so also is the whole human race. The human race, therefore, when best disposed depends upon the unity of wills. [9] But this cannot be unless there is one will dominating and ordering (*domina et regulatrix*) all the others to one thing, inasmuch as the wills of mortals, because of the seductive pleasures of youth, are in need of direction, as the Philosopher teaches in the last book of the *Nicomachean Ethics.*[45] Nor can that one will exist unless there be one prince of all, whose will may dominate and regulate all the others. [10] Now if all the above conclusions are true—and they are—it is necessary for the best disposition of the human race that there should be a monarch in the world and consequently for the well-being of the world that there should be a monarchy.

16

All the reasons set forth above are confirmed by a memorable experience, namely, the state of mortals that the Son of God, who was to assume man for man's salvation, either awaited or, when he so willed, arranged. For if we go through all the states and periods of man from the fall of our first parents, which was the point at which we deviated and began to wander, we shall find that the world was never quiet on every side except under the monarch *divus* Augustus, when there existed a perfect monarchy. [2] That the human race was then happy in the tranquillity of universal peace, to this fact all historians, the famous poets, and even the scribe of the gentleness of Christ[46] deigned to bear witness. Finally, Paul too referred to that most happy state as the *fulness of time* [Gal. 4:4]. Truly the time and all temporal things were full, for no ministry to our happiness was vacant of its minister. [3] But what the state of the world has been since that seamless garment first suffered rending by the nail of greed[47] we may read; would that we might not also see!

[4] O race of men, how many losses must you suffer, in how many storms and shipwrecks must you be tossed, so long as, transformed into a beast of many heads, you strive after diverse things? [5] You are sick in either intellect, sick likewise in affection. You do not minister to the higher intellect by means of indestructible arguments, nor to the lower by the evidence of experience, nor even to your affection by the sweetness of divine persuasion, even though through the trumpet of the Holy Spirit the words are sounded to you: *Behold, how good and how pleasant it is for brothers to dwell together in unity* [Ps. 132:1].

BOOK THREE

12

Their argument from reason is this.[48] They take their first principle from the tenth book of the *First Philosophy,* and say that all things which are of one kind are reduced to the unit which is the measure of all that come under that class.[49] But all men are of one kind; therefore they must be reduced to one as the measure of them all. [2] And since the supreme pontiff and the emperor

45. Cf. Aristotle *Nicomachean Ethics* 10.9 1179b31.

46. I.e., the apostle Luke; cf. Luke 2:14.

47. Cf. John 19:23. The seamless garment is the Roman Empire, which had been allegedly divided according to the donation of Constantine; cf. *Monarchy* 3.10.

48. In the previous eight chapters Dante refuted arguments based on scripture (3.4–9) and arguments based on history (3.10 and 11) that maintained that the authority of the emperor depends on that of the pope. The present chapter refutes an argument for the same thesis based on reason.

49. Cf. Aristotle *Metaphysics* 5.7 1016a19–1017a2, 10.2 1053a18–20, 1053b20–28.

are men, if that conclusion is true they must be reduced to one man; and since the pope must not be reduced to any other, it remains that the emperor, together with all others, must be reduced to him, as the measure and rule (*regula*). Whence again their contention follows. [3] To refute this argument, I say that when they declare that "all things which are of one kind ought to be reduced to some unit of that kind which is the standard therein," they speak truly. And in like manner they speak truly when they say that all men are of one kind. And they likewise draw a true conclusion when they infer from this that all men must be reduced to a standard unit in their kind. But when from this conclusion they draw the further inference about the pope and emperor, they fall into a fallacy *secundum accidens.* [4] To demonstrate which, be it known that it is one thing to be a man and another thing to be pope. And in like manner it is one thing to be a man and another to be emperor; just as it is one thing to be a man and another to be a father and a lord (*dominus*). [5] For a man is what he is through the substantial form from which he acquires his species and genus, and by which he is brought under the category of substance. But a father is what he is through an accidental form, which is the relation from which he acquires a certain species and genus and [by which] he is brought under the class "with respect to" or "relation." Otherwise, since no accidental form exists in itself, apart from the foundation of the substance that underlies it, everything would fall within the category of substance; and this is false. [6] Since, then, the pope and emperor are what they are through certain relations (to wit papacy and imperium, the one relation coming under the scope of fatherhood and the other under the scope of lordship), it is clear that the pope and emperor, as such, must come under the category of relation, and are consequently to be reduced to something which exists under that class. [7] Wherefore I maintain that there is one standard to which they must be reduced as men, and another to which they must be reduced as pope and emperor. For as men they have to be referred to the best man who is the standard of all the others and the idea, so to speak, that is, to him—whoever he may be—who is most supremely one in his own kind, as may be gathered from the last book of the *Nicomachean Ethics.*[50] [8] In so far as they are relational (which they obviously are) either they must be reduced the one to the other (if one is subordinated to the other, or if through the nature of their relation they share in a species), or there is some third thing to which they must be reduced as to a common unity. [9] But it cannot be said that one is subordinated to the other; for in that case one could be predicated of the other, which is false; for we do not say "the emperor is a pope," nor the converse. Nor can it be said that they are of the same species, since the meaning of "pope," as such, is one, and of "emperor" another. Therefore they must be reduced to something in which they will find their union.

[10] As to which, be it known that as relation is to relation so is related thing to related thing. If therefore papacy and imperium, being relations of superposition, are to be reduced to the relationship of superposition from which they descend with their specific differences, then the pope and emperor (each being relational) will have to be referred to some unity in which that very relationship of superposition is found without further specific differences. [11] And this will be either God himself in whom every relationship is universally united, or some substance inferior to God in which the relationship of superposition, descending from relationship simply, is particularized by its specific differences. [12] And thus it is clear that the pope and emperor, as men, must be reduced to one, but as pope and emperor to another; and thus we have elucidated the appeal to reason.

16

Although in the preceding chapter it has been shown by reduction to an absurdity that the authority of the Empire is not derived from the authority of the supreme pontiff, yet it has not been fully proved, save by consequential inference, that it depends immediately on God. For it follows that if it does not depend on the vicar of God, it depends on God. [2] And so, for the perfect establishment

50. Cf. Aristotle *Nicomachean Ethics* 10.7 1177a13 ff., 10.8 1178a9 ff.

of our thesis, there must be a *positive* proof that the emperor or monarch of the world stands in immediate relation to the prince of the universe, who is God. [3] Now in order to understand this we have to know that man alone among all beings occupies a middle position between corruptible and incorruptible things. That is why he is rightly likened by philosophers to the horizon, which joins two hemispheres.[51] [4] For man, if considered according to each essential part, that is, soul and body, is corruptible with respect to the one, namely the body, but with respect to the other, namely the soul, he is incorruptible. For that reason the Philosopher in the second book of *On the Soul* rightly says of the soul, in that it is incorruptible: "And it alone, as perpetual, is capable of being separated from the corruptible."[52] [5] If man, then, is a kind of mean between corruptible and incorruptible beings, since every mean savors of the nature of extremes, it is necessary that man should savor of either nature. [6] And since every nature is ordered to some ultimate end, it follows that there exists a twofold end of man, so that just as he alone among all beings is ordered to two ultimate ends, one of which is his end as a corruptible being and the other his end as an incorruptible being.

[7] That ineffable providence, then, has set before man two ends toward which he must tend, namely, the happiness of this life, which consists in the exercise of his proper power and is figured by the earthly paradise, and the happiness of the eternal life, to which his proper power cannot ascend without the assistance of the divine light; and this happiness is what we are given to understand by the heavenly paradise. [8] Now we have to arrive at the twofold happiness, just as we arrive at diverse conclusions, by diverse means. We arrive at the first through the teachings of philosophy, provided we follow them by acting in accordance with the moral and intellectual virtues. We arrive at the second through spiritual teachings, which transcend human reason, provided we follow them by acting in accordance with the theological virtues, namely, faith, hope, and charity. [9] Thus, although these ends and these means have been made plain to us—in one case by human reason, which the philosophers have wholly brought to our knowledge, and in the other case by the Holy Spirit, who, through the prophets and the sacred writers, through Jesus Christ, the Son of God coeternal with the Spirit, and through His disciples, has revealed the truth that is beyond our nature but necessary to us—nevertheless human greed would cast them aside if men, like horses going astray in their brutishness, were not held in the way *by bit and rein* [Ps. 31:9]. [10] That is why man needed twofold direction corresponding to his twofold end, namely, the supreme pontiff to lead the human race to eternal life in accordance with what has been revealed, and the emperor to direct the human race to temporal happiness in accordance with the teachings of philosophy. [11] And since none or few, and these with extreme difficulty, could reach this port, were not the waves of seductive greed assuaged and the human race free to rest in the tranquillity of peace, this is the standard for which he who has charge of the world and is called the Roman Prince should chiefly strive—namely, that on this threshing floor of mortality, life should be lived in freedom and in peace. [12] And since the disposition of this world follows the disposition that inheres in the rotation of the heavens, in order to accomplish this end, namely, that the teachings conducive to freedom and peace should be applied with due reference to time and place, it is necessary for the supervisor to be arranged by Him who personally looks upon the whole disposition of the heavens. And this is He alone who so preordained that disposition that by it He Himself in His providence might weave all things together in their proper order. [13] If this is so, God alone chooses, He alone confirms, since He has no superior. From this we may further gather that neither they who are now called "electors" nor others of any kind who have been in the past should be so called; but rather they should be reckoned as the "heralds of divine providence." [14] Hence it happens that those to whom has been granted the honor of proclaiming this office are subject from time to time to dissent, because either all or some of them are clouded by the mists of greed and fail to discern the features of the divine dispensation. [15] Thus it is plain that the authority of the temporal monarch descends upon him without any intermediary from the source of all authority, which source, although undivided in the citadel of its simplicity, flows into multiple channels out of the abundance of its goodness.

[16] And now it seems to me that I have sufficiently attained the goal that I set for myself.

51. *Liber de Causis* 2.22.

52. Aristotle *De Anima* 2.2 413b26.

For I have searched out the truth concerning the three questions that were raised: whether the office of monarch is necessary for the well-being of the world, whether the Roman people rightfully claimed the Empire for itself, and finally whether the authority of the monarch derives immediately from God or from someone else. [17] The truth of this last question is not to be taken so strictly as to mean that the Roman Prince is not subject in some things to the Roman Pontiff, inasmuch as mortal happiness is in some way ordered to immortal happiness. [18] Let Caesar, therefore, observe that reverence toward Peter which a first-born son should observe toward a father, so that, illuminated by the light of paternal grace, he may with greater power enlighten the world over which he has been set by Him alone who steers all things spiritual and temporal.

TWENTY-EIGHT

MARSILIUS OF PADUA

The Defender of the Peace

Translated by Alan Gewirth

Marsilius (or Marsilio dei Mainardini, ca. 1275/80–1342) was born into a family of notaries in the administrative class of the commune of Padua. In his native city he befriended Albertino Mussato, a protohumanist poet and historian noted for his vigorous defense of Paduan liberty. As a young student, Marsilius appears to have hesitated between law and medicine and finally decided in favor of the latter. He first appears in the historical record as rector of the University of Paris from December 1312 to March 1313. In the course of his education he became acquainted with reputed Averroists, such as Peter of Abano, who hailed from Padua, and Jean of Jandun, whom he met in Paris. Pope John XXII promised Marsilius a canonry in 1316 and in 1318 reserved for him the first vacant benefice at Padua, which would have supported him in his studies; neither came into his possession, however, and he appears not to have taken orders. In 1319, Marsilius represented Matteo Visconti of Milan and Can Grande of Verona when they offered the captaincy of the Ghibelline League to Count Charles of La Marche (later Charles IV of France); this diplomatic effort, opposed by the pope, did not succeed.

In the following years, Marsilius returned to Paris where he devoted himself to teaching and the practice of medicine. The *Defensor Pacis* (*Defender of the Peace*), his major work, was completed in June 1324 and dedicated to the emperor, Ludwig of Bavaria. At that time Ludwig was quarreling with the pope, who, not acknowledging the emperor's election and thus regarding the imperial throne as vacant, had appointed himself imperial vicar. Two years later, when Marsilius's authorship of the *Defensor Pacis* became known, he fled with Jean of Jandun to the court of Ludwig at Nuremberg. In 1327, John XXII, presiding in Avignon, condemned five propositions from the *Defensor* and excommunicated its author.[1] In 1327 and 1328, Marsilius accompanied Ludwig to Rome on his ill-fated expedition to strengthen the Ghibelline position in Italy and establish the legitimacy of his imperial office. The spectacular

1. The propositions condemned by the pope had brought into question the primacy of the pope over other priests and had maintained the coercive power of the emperor over the church, especially the power to appoint, remove, or punish a pope (Carlo Pincin, *Marsilio* [Turin: Edizioni Giappichelli, 1967], 156–57). These condemned statements were drawn from the Second Discourse of the *Defender of the Peace* rather than the First Discourse (the source of most passages included here), although the philosophical basis of the condemned propositions (as opposed to their scriptural warrants) may be found in the First Discourse.

events of those years may be viewed as an attempt to put Marsilius's antipapal doctrines into practice. While it was customary for the emperor to be crowned in Rome by the pope, Ludwig was crowned by Sciarra Colonna in the name of the Roman people, and the emperor in turn, acting "by our authority together with the entire clergy and Roman people," deposed John XXII and named a new pope. Marsilius was appointed spiritual vicar of the city. By August 1328, however, Ludwig, lacking resources and the active support of his Ghibelline allies, was compelled to withdraw first from Rome and, in the following year, from Italy. Marsilius returned with him to Bavaria, where he spent the rest of his life. In 1336–1337, Ludwig, negotiating with John's successor, Benedict XII, distanced himself from Marsilius and other scholars in his court, including William of Ockham. In 1340–1341, however, Marsilius was again active on behalf of the emperor, writing the *Defensor Minor,* a shorter work that recapitulated arguments from the *Defensor Pacis* and addressed the legal issues regarding the imminent marriage of Ludwig's son to a countess of Tyrol.

The *Defensor Pacis* is divided into three discourses (*Dictiones*) of unequal length. The First Discourse sets forth Marsilius's views on the nature and causes of civil society by means of arguments drawn from reason (cf. 1.1.8). One effect of this account of civil society is quietly to undermine any rational grounds for the doctrine of the papal plenitude (or fullness) of power, for example, by distinguishing "law" in the proper sense, a coercive command, from divine law, which provides lessons and admonitions. Much of the First Discourse is reproduced here, with the exception of Chapters 14–19. The omitted chapters deal with the general question of the efficient cause of rulership and, specifically, with the qualities of the ruler, his election, the unity of government in the state, and the correction of rulers. The Second Discourse, which constitutes the major portion of the work, is a long indictment of the doctrine of papal plenitude of temporal and coercive power, regarded by Marsilius as the singular cause of strife and discord in cities and states. In this part, Marsilius's argument is based primarily on scripture and various other Christian authorities. From the Second Discourse one chapter is reproduced here, which treats the diverse meanings of "right," including "natural right." The Third Discourse sums up briefly the results of the preceding discourses and draws a number of conclusions from them.

Marsilius's stated aim is not to set forth a complete political philosophy, but to deal with one specific evil that Aristotle, as a pagan living in pre-Christian times, could not have foreseen: the encroachments of the papacy in the spiritual and temporal spheres and the dire consequences of these abuses for the peace of society. Yet this single extension of Aristotle's thought brings Marsilius to his one flagrant deviation from Aristotle: in sharply segregating coercive human law from evangelical law or canon law, Marsilius defines the sole source of human law, the "legislator," as "the people or the whole body of citizens, or the weightier part thereof," taking "into consideration the quantity and the quality of the persons" (1.12.3). To some readers this appears to be a bold expression of popular sovereignty, an anticipation of modern democratic thought, arising from Marsilius's roots in the civic republic of Padua. Others, taking note of Marsilius's service to the Ghibelline *signori* and the emperor, point out that the legislator may, in practice, be a single person such as the emperor (especially in the Second Discourse and the *Defensor Minor*). This ineradicable ambiguity in the doctrine of the "legislator" is ultimately involved in the question of the Averroism of the *Defensor Pacis.* The suspicion of Averroism is prompted by the unwavering secularism of the First Discourse and the unrelenting application of its findings to the church in the Second. The conventional subjects of "Latin Averroism," however—the unicity of the intellect, the eternity of the world—are not present. More importantly, there is little direct evidence here of Boethius's enthusiasm for philosophizing as the highest way of life, or Alfarabi's assertion that the philosopher and the ruler (in the complete sense) are the same. Alfarabi's teaching even appears to be precluded by Marsilius's distinctive understanding of the "legislator," since for him the term properly refers to the weightier part of the whole body of citizens rather than to the philosopher. Since Marsilius employs this antimonarchic or antiaristocratic principle in order to oppose the ecclesiastical encroachment of political power, the question remains: Does he intend this same antiaristocratic principle to apply equally to the elevation of philosophy over the common life of man, as it is asserted by Alfarabi or Boethius? However this particular issue is understood, Marsilius's doctrines earned him an infamous name in the fourteenth century, and yet despite this infamy, they exerted a profound influence on the conciliar movement of the fifteenth century and ultimately on the political theology of the Reformation.[2]

The following translation is that of Alan Gewirth, *Marsilius of Padua*, vol. 2, *The Defender of Peace* (New York: Columbia University Press, 1956), 3–55 and 187–92, with minor revisions by the editor. Gewirth's translation was made from the critical edition by C. W. Previté-Orton, *The Defensor Pacis of Marsilius of Padua* (Cambridge: Cambridge University Press, 1928). In a few cases, which are indicated in the footnotes, emendations of Previté-Orton's text have been adopted from the edition of the *Defensor Pacis* by R. Scholz (Hanover, 1932), and from Dino Bigongiari, "Notes on the Text of the Defensor Pacis," *Speculum* 7 (1932): 36–49. The divisions into discourses, chapters, and sections are those of Marsilius. The italic page numbers in brackets refer to Previté-Orton's edition.

DISCOURSE 1

Chapter 1. On the General Aim of the Discussion, the Cause of That Aim, and the Division of the Book

> *"Tranquillity, wherein peoples prosper and the welfare of nations is preserved, must certainly be desirable to every state. For it is the noble mother of the good arts. Permitting the steady increase of the race of mortals, it extends their means and enhances their manners. And he who is perceived not to have sought for it is recognized to be ignorant of such important concerns."*[3]

1. The benefits and fruits of the tranquillity or peace of civil regimes were set forth by Cassiodorus in this passage of his first epistle. Exhibiting through these very great goods the greatest good of man, sufficiency of life, which no one can attain without peace and tranquillity, Cassiodorus aimed thereby to arouse in men the desire to have peace with one another and hence tranquillity. In this aim he was in accord with what the blessed Job said in his twenty-second chapter: *Be at peace, and thereby thou shalt have the best fruits* [Job 22:21]. Indeed, it was for this reason that Christ, son of God, decreed that peace would be the sign and messenger of his new birth, [*2*] when, in the same message, he wanted the heavenly choir to sing: *Glory to God in the highest: and on earth peace to men of good will* [Luke 2:14]. For this same reason, too, he often wished peace to his disciples. Whence John: *Jesus came and stood amid his disciples and said, "Peace be to you"* [John 20:19]. Counseling them concerning the maintenance of peace with one another, he said, in Mark: *Have peace among you* [Mark 9:50]. And he taught them not only to have peace among themselves, but also to wish it to others; whence in Matthew: *When you come into the house, salute it, saying: "Peace be to this house"* [Matt. 10:12; Luke 10:5]. Peace, again, was the heritage which he bequeathed to his disciples at the time of his passion and death, when he said, in the fourteenth chapter of John: *Peace I leave with you; my peace I give unto you* [John 14:27]. And like Christ, his true heirs and imitators, the apostles, wished peace to the men to whom they sent epistles containing evangelical lessons and admonitions, for they knew that the fruits of peace would be the greatest goods, as was shown from Job and more fully exhibited through Cassiodorus.

2. Since, however, "contraries are [essentially] productive of contraries,"[4] from discord, the opposite of tranquillity, the worst fruits and troubles will befall any civil regime or state. This can readily be seen, and is obvious to almost all men, from the example of the Italian state. For while the inhabitants of Italy lived peacefully together, they experienced those sweet fruits of peace which have been mentioned above, and from and in those fruits they made such great progress that they brought the whole habitable world under their sway. But when discord and strife arose among them, their state was sorely beset by all kinds of hardships and troubles and underwent the dominion of hateful foreign nations. And in the same way Italy is once again battered on all sides because of strife and is almost destroyed, so that it can easily be invaded by anyone who wants to seize it and who has any power at all. Nor is such an outcome astonishing, for, as Sallust attests, writing about Jugurtha: "By

2. P. Sigmund, "The Influence of Marsilius on Fifteenth-Century Conciliarism," *Journal of the History of Ideas* 23 (1962): 393–402.

3. Cassiodorus *Variae* 1.1.

4. Aristotle *Politics* 5.8 1307b29.

concord small things increase, by discord great things [3] perish."[5] Misled through discord into the bypath of error, the Italian natives are deprived of the sufficient life, continuously undergoing the gravest hardships instead of the quiet they seek, and the harsh yoke of tyrants instead of liberty; and finally, they have become so much unhappier than citizens of other states that their ancestral name, which used to give glory and protection to all who appealed to it, is now, to their ignominy, cast into their teeth by the other nations.

3. Into this dire predicament, then, the miserable men are dragged because of their discord and strife, which, like the illness of an animal, is recognized to be the diseased disposition of the civil regime. Although strife has numerous original causes, many of which are not unrelated, almost all those which can emerge in the usual ways were described by the foremost of the philosophers in his *Civil Science.*[6] Besides these, however, there is one singular and very obscure cause by which the Roman empire has long been troubled and is still troubled.[7] This cause is very contagious and prone to creep up on all other cities and states; in its greediness it has already tried to invade most of them. Neither Aristotle nor any other philosopher of his time or before could have discerned the origin and species of this cause. For it was and is a certain perverted opinion (to be exposed by us below) which came to be adopted as an aftermath of the miraculous effect produced by the supreme cause long after Aristotle's time; an effect beyond the power of the lower nature and the usual action of causes in things. This sophistic opinion, wearing the guise of the honorable and beneficial, is utterly pernicious to the human race and, if unchecked, will eventually bring unbearable harm to every city and country.

4. The fruits of peace or tranquillity, then, are the greatest goods, as we have said, while those of its opposite, strife, are unbearable evils. Hence we ought to wish for peace, to seek it if we do not already have it, to conserve it once it is attained, and to repel with all our strength the strife which is opposed to it. To this end individual brethren, and in even greater degree groups and communities, are obliged to help one another, both from the feeling of heavenly love and from the bond or

5. Sallust *Jugurtha* 10.6.

6. Cf. Aristotle *Politics* bk. 5 passim.

7. The cause of strife to which Marsilius alludes here is described at greater length in 1.19.12–13: "This wrong opinion of certain Roman bishops [that is, that they have total coercive temporal jurisdiction over the Roman ruler and over every human creature] and also perhaps their perverted desire for rulership, which they assert is owed to them because of the plenitude of power given to them, as they say, by Christ—this is that singular cause which we have said produces the intranquillity or discord of the city or state. For it is prone to creep up on all states, as was said in our introductory remarks, and by its hateful action it has for a long time distressed the Italian state, and has kept and still keeps it from tranquillity or peace, by preventing with all its force the appointment or institution of the ruler, the Roman emperor, and his functioning in the said empire. From lack of this function, which is the just regulation of civil acts, there readily emerge injuries and contentions, and these, if not measured by a standard of justice or law because of the absence of the measurer, cause fights, whence there have resulted the separation of citizens and finally the destruction of the Italian polities or cities, as we have said. With this opinion, therefore, and perhaps also with what we have called a desire for ruling, the Roman bishop strives to make the Roman ruler subject to him in coercive or temporal jurisdiction, whereas that ruler neither rightly ought to be, as we shall clearly show below, nor wishes to be subject to him in such judgment. From this there has arisen so much strife and discord that it cannot be extinguished without great peril to souls and bodies and expenditure of wealth.

"For the office of coercive rulership over any individual, of whatever condition he may be, or over any community or group, does not belong to the Roman or any other bishop, priest, or spiritual minister, as such, has been demonstrated in Chapters 15 and 17 of this discourse. And this was what Aristotle held with respect to the priesthood in any law or religion, when he said in the fourth book of the *Politics* [1299a16 ff.]: 'Hence not all those who are elected or chosen by lot are to be regarded as rulers. Consider the priests in the first place. These must be regarded as different from the political rulers,' and so on. 'And of the superintendent functions,' that is, offices, 'some are political,' and so on. And a little below he adds: 'And other offices are economic.'

"13 Since this pernicious pestilence, which is completely opposed to all the peace and happiness of man, could well infect with a disease of the same corrupt root the other states of faithful Christians throughout the world, I consider it supremely necessary to repel it, as I said in my introductory remarks. This is to be done first by tearing away the mask of the aforementioned false opinion, as the root of the past and future evils; and then by checking, through external action if necessary, its ignorant or unjust patrons or expositors and stubborn defenders. To these tasks all men are obligated who have the knowledge and ability to thwart this evil; and those who neglect or omit them on whatever grounds are unjust, as Tully attested in the treatise *On Duties,* Book 1, Chapter 5, when he said: 'There are two kinds of injustice: one, of those men who inflict it; the other, of those who do not drive away the injury from those upon whom it is inflicted, if they can.' See, then, according to this notable statement of Tully, that not only those who inflict injury on others are unjust, but also those who, while having the knowledge and ability to prevent men from inflicting injury on others, do not do so. For every man is obligated to do this for another by a certain quasi-natural law, the duty of friendship and human society. And lest I myself, by knowingly transgressing this law, be called unjust at least to myself, I propose to drive away this pestilence from my brethren, the Christian believers, first by teaching, and then by external action so far as I may be able. For, as I seem indubitably to see, there has been given to me from above the power to discern and unmask the sophism which has sustained in the past, and by which they will strive to sustain, the wrong opinion, and perhaps also the perverted desire, of certain former Roman bishops and of the present one with his accomplices. It is this opinion and desire which is the parent of the scandals mentioned above."

law [4] of human society. This admonition Plato also gives us, as Tully attests in the first book of his treatise *On Duties,* when he said: "We were not born for ourselves alone; to part of us our native land lays claim, and to part, our friends." To this sentence Tully adds: "And so, as the Stoics were wont to say, the things that grow in the earth are all created for the use of men; but men are born for the sake of men. In this we ought to follow the lead of nature, and to bring forth common utilities for all."[8] But it would be no small common utility, indeed it is rather a necessity, to unmask the sophism of this singular cause of wars which threatens no small harm to all states and communities. Hence, whoever is willing and able to discern the common utility is obliged to give this matter his vigilant care and diligent efforts. For while this sophism remains concealed, this pestilence can in no way be avoided, nor its pernicious effect be completely uprooted from states or cities.

5. This task should not be neglected by anyone because of fear or laziness or any other evil disposition. For, as it is written in the second epistle to Timothy: *God has not given us the spirit of fear, but of power and of love* [2 Tim. 1:7]: the power and love, I say, of spreading the truth; whence the Apostle continues: *Be not thou therefore ashamed of the testimony of our Lord.* This was the testimony of the truth, for the bearing of which Christ said he had come into the world when he stated, in the eighteenth chapter of John: *For this was I born and for this came I into the world, that I should give testimony to the truth* [John 18:37]: that truth, namely, which leads the human race to eternal salvation. Following the example of Christ, therefore we must strive to teach the truth whereby the aforesaid pestilence of civil regimes may be warded off from the human race, especially the worshipers of Christ—the truth which leads to the salvation of civil life, and which also is of no little help for eternal salvation. Such striving is all the more obligatory for that person in whom the giver of graces has inspired a greater understanding of these things; and he who has the knowledge and the ability for this, but yet, like an ingrate, neglects it, commits a grave sin, as James attested in the fourth chapter of his canonic epistle, when he said: *To him who knoweth to do good and doeth it not, to him it is sin* [Jas. 4:17]. For this evil, the common enemy of the human race, will not be completely cut down, nor will the pernicious fruits which it has thus far produced [5] be arrested, unless the iniquity of its cause or root is first revealed and denounced. For by no other path can the coercive power of rulers safely enter upon the final rout of the shameful patrons and stubborn defenders of this evil.

6. And so I, a son of Antenor,[9] heeding and obeying the aforesaid admonitions of Christ, of the saints, and of the philosophers, moved also by the spirit of an understanding of these things (if any grace has been given me), and of confidence sent to me from above (for as James attests in the first chapter of his epistle: *Every best gift and every perfect gift is from above, coming down from the Father of lights* [Jas. 1:17]); acting from reverence for the giver, from love of spreading the truth, from fervent affection for country and brethren, from pity for the oppressed, from a desire to save them, to recall the oppressors from the bypath of error, and to arouse the resistance of those who suffer such things when they can and should combat them; and beholding in you especially, most exalted Ludwig, emperor[10] of the Romans, God's servant, who shall give to this task that external fulfilment of it which you desire, and who by some special ancient birthright, as well as by your singularly heroic native disposition and outstanding virtue, have a firmly ingrained love of wiping out heresies, upholding and preserving the catholic truth and every other worthy discipline, uprooting vice, encouraging virtuous pursuits, extinguishing strife, and spreading and nourishing peace or tranquillity everywhere—I have written down the sentences which follow, after a period of diligent and intense study, thinking that these may be of some help to your vigilant majesty, who bestows careful attention upon the above-mentioned evils and others which may occur, as well as upon all matters affecting the public welfare.

7. It is my purpose, therefore, with God's help, [6] to expose only this singular cause of strife. For to reiterate the number and nature of those causes which were set forth by Aristotle would be superfluous; but this cause which Aristotle could not have known, and which no one after him who

8. Cicero *De Officiis* 1.7.22. Cf. Plato *Epistles* 9 358A; *Laws* 11 923A.

9. Antenor was the legendary founder of Padua. Cf. Virgil *Aeneid* 1.242–49.

10. This is the only place in the *Defender* where Marsilius refers to Ludwig as emperor.

could know it has undertaken to investigate, we wish to unmask so that it may henceforth be readily excluded from all states or cities, and virtuous rulers and subjects live more securely in tranquillity. This is the desirable outcome which I propose at the beginning of this work; an outcome necessary for those who would enjoy civil happiness, which seems the best of the objects of desire possible to man in this world, and the ultimate aim of human acts.

8. I shall divide my proposed work into three discourses. In the first I shall demonstrate my views by sure methods discovered by the human intellect, based upon propositions self-evident to every mind not corrupted by nature, custom, or perverted disposition. In the second discourse, the things which I shall believe myself to have demonstrated I shall confirm by established testimonies of the eternal truth, and by the authorities of its saintly interpreters and of other approved teachers of the Christian faith, so that this book may stand by itself, needing no external proof. From the same source too I shall refute the falsities opposed to my conclusions, and expose the intricately obstructive sophisms of my opponents. In the third discourse, I shall infer certain conclusions or useful lessons which the citizens, both rulers and subjects, ought to observe, conclusions having an evident certainty from our previous findings. Each of these discourses I shall divide into chapters, and each chapter into more or less paragraphs depending upon the length of the chapter. One advantage of this division will be ease for the readers in finding what they look for when they are referred from later to earlier discourses and chapters. From this will follow a second advantage: a shortening of the volume. For when we assume in later pages some truth, either for itself or for the demonstration of other things, whose proof or certainty has been sufficiently set forth in preceding sections, instead of trifling with the proof all over again, we shall send the reader back to the discourse, chapter, and paragraph in which the proof was originally given, so that thus he may easily be able to find the certainty of the proposition in question. [*7*]

Chapter 2. On the First Questions in This Book, and the Distinction of the Various Meanings of the Term "State"

1. Entering upon our proposed task, we wish first to show what are the tranquillity and intranquillity of the state or city (*regni vel civitatis*); and first the tranquillity, for if this be not clear, one is necessarily ignorant also of what is intranquillity. Since, however, both of these seem to be dispositions of the city or state (let this be assumed from Cassiodorus), we shall consequently make clear what must be revealed at the very outset; namely, what is the state or city, and why. Through this, the definitions of tranquillity and of its opposite will be more readily apparent.

2. Following the aforesaid order for the definition of the tranquillity of the city or state, we must notice, in order to prevent ambiguity from entering our project, that the term "state" (*regnum*) has many meanings. In one sense it means a number of cities (*civitatum*) or provinces contained under one regime; in which sense a state does not differ from a city with respect to species of polity but rather with respect to quantity. In another sense the term "state" signifies a certain species of temperate polity or regime, which Aristotle calls "temperate monarchy" (*monarchiam temperatam*);[11] in this sense a state may consist in a single city as well as in many cities, as was the case around the time of the rise of civil communities, for then there was usually one king in a single city. The third and most familiar sense of this term is a combination of the first and the second. In its fourth sense it means something common to every species of temperate regime, whether in a single city or in many; it was in this sense that Cassiodorus used it in the passage we quoted at the beginning of this book, and this, too, is the sense in which we shall use the term in our discussions of the matters under inquiry.[12]

11. Cf. Aristotle *Politics* 3.7 1279a34; 5.8 1307b30.

12. The decision to use the term *regnum* to mean "something common to every species of temperate regime" is unique among the medieval Aristotelians in two respects, for the others use the term in Marsilius's third sense alone, that is, as signifying a *royal monarchy* composed of a *number of cities*.

3. Now we must define tranquillity and its opposite. [8] Let us assume with Aristotle in his *Politics,* Book 1, Chapter 2, and Book 5, Chapter 3, that the city is like an animate nature or animal.[13] For just as an animal well disposed in accordance with nature is composed of certain proportioned parts ordered to one another and communicating their functions mutually and for the whole, so too the city is constituted of certain such parts when it is well disposed and established in accordance with reason. The relation, therefore, of the city or state and its parts to tranquillity will be seen to be similar to the relation of the animal and its parts to health. The trustworthiness of this inference we can accept from what all men comprehend about each of these relations. For they think that health is the best disposition of an animal in accordance with nature, and likewise that tranquillity is the best disposition of a city established in accordance with reason. Health, moreover, as the more experienced physicists describe it, is the good disposition of the animal whereby each of its parts can perfectly perform the operations belonging to its nature; according to which analogy tranquillity will be the good disposition of the city or state whereby each of its parts will be able perfectly to perform the operations belonging to it in accordance with reason and its establishment. And since a good definition consignifies contraries, intranquillity will be the diseased disposition of the city or state, like the illness of an animal, whereby all or some of its parts are impeded from performing the operations belonging to them, either entirely or to the extent required for complete functioning.

In this general way, then, we have defined tranquillity and its opposite, intranquillity. [9]

Chapter 3. On the Origin of the Civil Community

1. Having defined tranquillity as the good disposition of the city for the functioning of its parts, we must now examine what the city is in itself, and why;[14] what and how many are its primary parts;[15] what is the function appropriate to each part,[16] their causes,[17] and their order in relation to one another.[18] For these are the main points required for the perfect determination of tranquillity and its opposite.

2. However, before discussing the city and its species or modes, since the city is the perfect community we must first trace the origin of civil communities and of their regimes and modes of living. From the imperfect kinds, men have advanced to perfect communities, regimes, and modes of living in them. For from the less to the more perfect is always the path of nature and of its imitator, art.[19] And men do not think that they have scientific knowledge of each thing unless they "know its first causes and first principles down to the elements."[20]

3. Following this method, then, we must note that civil communities had small beginnings in diverse regions and times, and growing gradually came at length to completion, just as we said happens in every process of nature or of art. For the first and smallest combination of human beings, wherefrom the other combinations emerged, was that of male and female, as the foremost of the philosophers says in the *Politics,* Book 1, Chapter 1,[21] and as appears more fully from his *Economics.*[22] From this combination there were generated other humans, who first occupied one household; from these, more combinations of the same kind were formed, and so great was the procreation of children that a single household did not suffice for them, [10] but many households had to be made. A number of these households was called a village or hamlet, and this was the first community, as is also written in the above-cited treatise.[23]

4. So long as men were in a single household, all their actions, especially those we shall henceforth call "civil," were regulated by the elder among them as being more discerning, but apart from laws or customs, because these could not yet have been discovered. Not only were the men of a single household ruled in this way, but the first community too, called the village, was ruled in almost the same manner, although in some things it was ruled differently. For although the head of a single

13. Cf. Aristotle *Politics* 1.5 1254a31 ff.; 5.3 1302b34 ff.; 4.4 1290b24 ff.

14. Cf. below, 1.4.1–2.

15. 1.4.3–4; 1.5.1.

16. 1.5.5–13; 1.6.

17. 1.7.

18. 1.8.1; 1.15.14.

19. Cf. Aristotle *Physics* 2.8 199a9 ff.

20. Aristotle *Physics* 1.1 184a13.

21. Aristotle *Politics* 1.2 1252a26 ff.

22. Pseudo-Aristotle *Economics* 1.3 1343b8 ff.

23. Aristotle *Politics* 1.2 1252b9 ff.

household might have been allowed to pardon or to punish domestic injuries entirely according to his own will and pleasure, this would not have been allowed the head of the first community called the village. For in this community the elder had to regulate matters of justice and benefit by some reasonable ordinance or quasi-natural law, because thus it seemed appropriate to all by a certain equity, not as a result of prolonged inquiry, but solely by the common dictate of reason and a certain duty of human society.

The cause of this difference of regime in a single household and in a village is and was as follows. If someone in the single and first household or domestic family had killed or otherwise offended his brother, then the head of the household, if he so desired, was allowed not to give the wrongdoer the extreme penalty without any dangerous consequences resulting therefrom, because the injury seemed to have been done to the father alone, who forgave it; and because of the paucity of men; and again because it was less unfortunate and sorrowful for the father to lose one son than two. Our first ancestor, Adam, seems to have acted in this way when his first-born son, Cain, killed his brother Abel. For there is properly no civil justice of a father in relation to his son, as Aristotle wrote in Book 4 of the *Ethics,* the treatise on justice.[24] On the other hand, in the first community, the village or hamlet, such procedure was not and would not be allowed, because the case here was different from that of the family; indeed, unless injuries were avenged or equalized by the elder, there would have arisen fighting and the separation of the villagers.

Villages having multiplied and the community grown larger [*11*] because of increasing procreation, they were still ruled by one man, either because of a lack of many prudent men or through some other cause, as is written in the *Politics,* Book 3, Chapter 9.[25] The ruler, however, was the elder or the man who was regarded as better, although the regulations of these communities were less imperfect than those by which the single village or hamlet was ordered. Those first communities, however, did not have so great a differentiation and ordering of parts, or so large a quantity of necessary arts and rules of living, as were gradually to be found afterwards in perfect communities. For sometimes the same man was both ruler and farmer or shepherd, like Abraham and several others after him; but in perfect communities this was not expedient nor would it be allowed.

5. These communities having gradually increased, men's experience became greater, more perfect arts and rules and ways of living were discovered, and also the parts of communities were more fully differentiated. Finally, the things which are necessary for living and for living well were brought to full development by men's reason and experience, and there was established the perfect community, called the city, with the differentiation of its parts, to the discussion of which we shall now proceed.

Let this much suffice, then, concerning the rise of the civil community.

Chapter 4. On the Final Cause of the City and of Its Civil[26] Requirements, and the Differentiation in General of Its Parts

1. The city, according to Aristotle in the *Politics,* Book 1, Chapter 1, is "the perfect community having the full limit of self-sufficiency, which came into existence for the sake of living, but exists for the sake of living well."[27] This phrase of Aristotle—"came into existence for the sake of living, but exists for the sake of living well"—signifies [*12*] the perfect final cause of the city, since those who live a civil life not only live, which beasts or slaves do too, but live well, having leisure for those liberal functions in which are exercised the virtues of both the practical and the theoretic soul.

2. Having thus determined the end of the city to be living and living well, we must treat first of living and its modes. For this, as we have said, is the purpose for the sake of which the city was established, and which necessitates all the things which exist in the city and are done by the association of men in it. Let us therefore lay this down as the principle of all the things which are to be

24. Aristotle *Nicomachean Ethics* 5.6 1134b9 ff.; cf. 5.11 1138b6. Marsilius regularly refers to Book 5 of the *Ethics* as Book 4.

25. Aristotle *Politics* 3.14 1285a2 ff.; cf. 3.15 1286b8 ff.

26. Reading, with Scholz, *civilium* for *scibilium.*

27. Aristotle *Politics* 1.2 1252b27.

demonstrated here, a principle naturally obtained, held, and freely granted by all: that all men not deformed or otherwise impeded naturally desire a sufficient life, and avoid and flee what is harmful thereto.[28] This has been acknowledged not only with regard to man but also with regard to every genus of animals, according to Tully in his treatise *On Duties,* Book 1, Chapter 3, where he says: "It is an original endowment which nature has bestowed upon every genus of living things, that it preserves itself, its body, and its life, that it avoids those things which seem harmful, and that it seeks and obtains all those things which are necessary for living."[29] This principle can also be clearly grasped by everyone through sense induction.

3. But the living and living well which are appropriate to men fall into two kinds, of which one is temporal or earthly, while the other is usually called eternal or heavenly. However, this latter kind of living, the eternal, the whole body of philosophers were unable to prove by demonstration, nor was it self-evident, and therefore they did not concern themselves with the means thereto. But as to the first kind of living and living well or good life, that is, the earthly, and its necessary means, this the glorious philosophers comprehended almost completely through demonstration. Hence for its attainment they concluded the necessity of the civil community, without which this sufficient life cannot be obtained. [*13*] Thus the foremost of the philosophers, Aristotle, said in his *Politics,* Book 1, Chapter 1: "All men are driven toward such an association by a natural impulse."[30] Although sense experience teaches this, we wish to bring out more distinctly that cause of it which we have indicated, as follows: Man is born composed of contrary elements, because of whose contrary actions and passions some of his substance is continually being destroyed; moreover, he is born "bare and unprotected" from excess of the surrounding air and other elements, capable of suffering and of destruction, as has been said in the science of nature.[31] As a consequence, he needed arts of diverse genera and species to avoid the aforementioned harms. But since these arts can be exercised only by a large number of men, and can be had only through their association with one another, men had to assemble together in order to attain what was beneficial through these arts and to avoid what was harmful.

4. But since among men thus assembled there arise disputes and quarrels which, if not regulated by a norm of justice, would cause men to fight and separate and thus finally would bring about the destruction of the city, there had to be established in this association a standard of justice and a guardian or maker thereof. And since this guardian has to restrain excessive wrongdoers as well as other individuals both within and outside the city who disturb or attempt to oppress the community, the city had to have within it something by which to resist these. Again, since the community needs various conveniences, repairs, and protection of certain common things, and different things in time of peace and in time of war, it was necessary that there be in the community men to take care of such matters, in order that the common necessity might be relieved when it was expedient or needful. But beside the things which we have so far mentioned, which relieve only the necessities of the present life, there is something else which men associated in a civil community need for the status of the future world promised to the human race through God's supernatural revelation, and which is useful also for the status of the present life. [*14*] This is the worship and honoring of God, and the giving of thanks both for benefits received in this world and for those to be received in the future one. For the teaching of these things and for the directing of men in them, the city had to designate certain teachers. The nature and qualities of all these and the other matters mentioned above will be treated in detail in the subsequent discussions.

5. Men, then, were assembled for the sake of the sufficient life, being able to seek out for themselves the necessaries enumerated above, and exchanging them with one another. This assemblage, thus perfect and having the limit of self-sufficiency, was called the city, whose final cause as well as that of its many parts has already been indicated by us in some measure, and will be more fully distinguished below. For since diverse things are necessary to men who desire a sufficient life, things which cannot be supplied by men of one order or office, there had to be diverse orders or offices of men in this association, exercising or supplying such diverse things which men need for sufficiency of life. But these diverse orders or offices of men are none other than the many and distinct parts of the city.

28. Reading, with Scholz, *huic* for *hinc.*

29. Cicero *De Officiis* 1.4.11.

30. Aristotle *Politics* 1.2 1253a29.

31. Aristotle *On the Parts of Animals* 4.10 687a25.

Let it suffice, then, to have covered thus in outline what the city is, why there came about such an association, and the number and division of its parts.

Chapter 5. On the Differentiation of the Parts of the City, and the Necessity of Their Separate Existence for an End Discoverable by Man

1. We have now treated in general of the parts of the city, in whose perfect action and intercommunication, without external impediment, we have said that the tranquillity of the city consists. But we must now continue our discussion of them, since the fuller determination of these parts, with respect both to their functions or ends and to their other appropriate causes, will make more manifest the causes of tranquillity and of its [*15*] opposite. Let us say, then, that the parts or offices of the city are of six kinds, as Aristotle said in the *Politics,* Book 7, Chapter 7: the agricultural, the artisan, the military, the financial, the priestly, and the judicial or deliberative.[32] Three of these, the priestly, the warrior, and the judicial, are in the strict sense parts of the city, and in civil communities they are usually called the honorable class (*honorabilitatem*). The others are called parts only in the broad sense of the term, because they are offices necessary to the city according to the doctrine of Aristotle in the *Politics,* Book 7, Chapter 7.[33] And the multitude belonging to these offices are usually called the vulgar. These, then, are the more familiar parts of the city or state, to which all the others can appropriately be reduced.

2. Although the necessity of these parts has been indicated to a certain extent in the preceding chapter, we wish to indicate it again more distinctly, assuming this proposition as having been previously demonstrated from what is self-evident, namely, that the city is a community established for the sake of the living and living well of the men in it. Of this "living" we have previously distinguished two kinds: one, the life or living of this world, that is, earthly; the other, the life or living of the other or future world. From these kinds of living, desired by man as ends, we shall indicate the necessity for the differentiation of the parts of the civil community. The first kind of human living, the earthly, is sometimes taken to mean the being of living things, as in Book 2 of the treatise *On the Soul:* "For living things, living is their being";[34] in which sense life is nothing other than soul. At other times, "living" is taken to mean the act, the action or passion, of the soul or of life.[35] Again, each of these meanings is used in two ways, with reference either to the numerically same being or to the being that is common to many individuals and that is called specific. And although each of these kinds of living, both as proper to man and as common to him and to the other animate things, depends upon natural causes, yet we are not at present considering it in so far as it comes from these causes; the natural science of plants and animals deals with this. Rather, our present concern is with these causes in so far as [*16*] they receive fulfilment "through art and reason," whereby "the human race lives."[36]

3. Hence, we must note that if man is to live and to live well, it is necessary that his actions be done and be done well; and not only his actions but also his passions. By "well" I mean in proper proportion. And since we do not receive entirely perfect from nature the means whereby these proportions are fulfilled, it was necessary for man to go beyond natural causes to form through reason some means whereby to effect and preserve his actions and passions in body and soul. And these means are the various kinds of functions and products deriving from the virtues and arts both practical and theoretic.

4. Of human actions and passions, some come from natural causes apart from knowledge. Such are those which are effected by the contrariety of the elements composing our bodies, through their intermixture. In this class can properly be placed the actions of the nutritive part. Under this head also come actions effected by the elements surrounding our body through the alteration of their qualities; of this kind also are the alterations effected by things entering human bodies, such as food, drink, medicines, poisons, and other similar

32. Aristotle *Politics* 7.8 1328b2 ff.

33. Ibid. 7.7 1328a2 ff.

34. Aristotle *De Anima* 2.4 415b14.

35. Cf. Aristotle *De Anima* 2.1 412a10 ff.

36. Aristotle *Metaphysics* 1.1 980b27. Cf. *Politics* 7.13 1332b3–6.

things. But there are other actions or passions which are performed by us or occur in us through our cognitive and appetitive powers. Of these some are called "immanent" because they do not cross over (*non transeunt*) into a subject other than the doer, nor are they exercised through any external organs or locomotive members; of this kind are the thoughts and desires or affections of men. But there are other actions and passions which are called "transitive" because they are opposed in either or in both respects to the kind which we have just described.

5. In order to proportion all these actions and passions, and to fulfil them in that to which nature could not lead, there were discovered the various kinds of arts and other virtues, as we said above, and men of various offices were established to exercise these for the purpose of supplying human needs. [*17*] These orders are none other than the parts of the city enumerated above. For in order to proportion and preserve the acts of the nutritive part of the soul, whose cessation would mean the complete destruction of the animal both individually and as a species, agriculture and animal husbandry were established. To these may properly be reduced all kinds of hunting of land, sea, and air animals, and all other arts whereby food is acquired by some exchange or is prepared for eating, so that what is lost from the substance of our body may thereby be restored, and the body be continued in its immortal being so far as nature has permitted this to man.

6. In order to moderate the actions and passions of our body caused by the impressions of the elements which externally surround us, there was discovered the general class of mechanics, which Aristotle in the *Politics,* Book 7, Chapter 6, calls the "arts."[37] To this class belong spinning, leathermaking, shoemaking, all species of housebuilding, and in general all the other mechanical arts which subserve the other offices of the city directly or indirectly, and which moderate not only men's touch or taste but also the other senses. These latter arts are more for pleasure and for living well than for the necessity of life, such as the painter's art and others similar to it, concerning which Aristotle says in the *Politics,* Book 4, Chapter 3: "Of these arts some must exist from necessity, and others are for pleasure and living well."[38] Under this class is also placed the practice of medicine, which is in some way architectonic to many of the abovementioned arts.

7. In order to moderate the excesses of the acts deriving from the locomotive powers through knowledge and desire, which we have called transitive acts and which can be done for the benefit or for the harm or injury of someone other than the doer for the status of the present world, there was necessarily established in the city a part or office by which the excesses of such acts are corrected and reduced to equality or due proportion. For without such correction the excesses of these acts would cause fighting and hence the separation of the citizens, and finally the destruction of the city and loss of the sufficient life. This part of the city, together with its subsidiaries, is called by Aristotle the "judicial" or "ruling" and "deliberative" part, and its function is to regulate matters of justice and the common benefit. [*18*]

8. In addition, since the sufficient life cannot be led by citizens who are oppressed or cast into slavery by external oppressors, and also since the sentences of the judges against injurious and rebellious men within the city must be executed by coercive force, it was necessary to set up in the city a military or warrior part, which many of the mechanics also subserve. For the city was established for the sake of living and living well, as was said in the preceding chapter; but this is impossible for citizens cast into slavery. For this, as the excellent Aristotle said, is contrary to the nature of the city. Hence, indicating the necessity for this part, he said in the *Politics,* Book 4, Chapter 3: "There is a fifth class, that of the warriors, which is not less necessary than the others, if the citizens are not to be slaves of invaders. For nothing is more truly impossible than for that which is by nature slavish to be worthy of the name 'city'; for a city is self-sufficient, but a slave is not self-sufficient."[39] The necessity for this class because of internal rebels is treated by Aristotle in the *Politics,* Book 7, Chapter 6.[40] We have omitted the quotation of this passage here for the sake of brevity, and because we shall quote it in Chapter 14 of this discourse, paragraph 8.

9. Again, since in some years on earth the harvests are large, and in others small; and the city is sometimes at peace with its neighbors, and sometimes not; and it is in need of various common services such as the construction and repair

37. Aristotle *Politics* 7.8 1328b6.

38. Ibid. 4.4 1291a2–4.

39. Ibid. 4.4 1291a6.

40. Ibid. 7.8 1328b7.

of roads, bridges, and other edifices, and similar things whose enumeration here would be neither appropriate nor brief—to provide all these things at the proper time it was necessary to establish in the city a treasure-keeping part, which Aristotle called the "money class." This part gathers and saves monies, coins, wines, oils, and other necessaries; it procures from all places things needed for the common benefit, and it seeks to relieve future necessities; it is also subserved by some of the other parts of the city. Aristotle called this the "money" part, since the saver of monies seems to be the treasurer of all things; for all things are exchanged for money. [*19*]

10. It remains for us to discuss the necessity of the priestly part. All men have not thought so harmoniously about this as they have about the necessity of the other parts of the city. The cause of this difference was that the true and primary necessity of this part could not be comprehended through demonstration, nor was it self-evident. All nations, however, agreed that it was appropriate to establish the priesthood for the worship and honoring of God, and for the benefit resulting therefrom for the status of the present or the future world. For most laws or religions[41] promise that in the future world God will distribute rewards to those who do good and punishment to doers of evil.

11. However, besides these causes of the laying down of religious laws, causes which are believed without demonstration, the philosophers, including Hesiod, Pythagoras, and several others of the ancients, noted appropriately a quite different cause or purpose for the setting forth of divine laws or religions—a purpose which was in some sense necessary for the status of this world. This was to ensure the goodness of human acts both individual and civil, on which depend almost completely the quiet or tranquillity of communities and finally the sufficient life in the present world. For although some of the philosophers who founded such laws or religions did not accept or believe in human resurrection and that life which is called eternal, they nevertheless feigned and persuaded others that it exists and that in it pleasures and pains are in accordance with the qualities of human deeds in this mortal life, in order that they might thereby induce in men reverence and fear of God, and a desire to flee the vices and to cultivate the virtues. For there are certain acts which the legislator cannot regulate by human law, that is, those acts which cannot be proved to be present or absent to someone, but which nevertheless cannot be concealed from God, whom these philosophers feigned to be the maker of such laws and the commander of their observance, under the threat or promise of eternal reward for doers of good and punishment for doers of evil. Hence, they said of the variously virtuous men in this world that they were placed in the heavenly firmament; and from this were perhaps derived the names of certain [*20*] stars and constellations. These philosophers said that the souls of men who acted wrongly entered the bodies of various brutes; for example, the souls of men who had been intemperate eaters entered the bodies of pigs, those who were intemperate as regards [the pleasures of] the sense of touch and sexual matters entered the bodies of goats, and so on, according to the proportions of human vices to their condemnable properties. So too the philosophers assigned various kinds of torments to wrongdoers, like perpetual thirst and hunger for intemperate Tantalus: water and fruit were to be near him, but he was unable to drink or eat these, for they were always fleeing faster than he could pursue them. The philosophers also said that the infernal regions, the place of these torments, were deep and dark; and they painted all sorts of terrible and gloomy pictures of them. From fear of these, men eschewed wrongdoing, were instigated to perform virtuous works of piety and mercy, and were well disposed both in themselves and toward others. As a consequence, many disputes and injuries ceased in communities. Hence too the peace or tranquillity of cities and the sufficient life of men for the status of the present world were preserved with less difficulty; which was the end intended by these wise men in laying down[42] such laws or religions.

12. Thus there existed a handing-down of such precepts by the gentile priests; and for the teaching of them they established in their communities temples in which their gods were worshiped. They also appointed teachers of these laws or traditions, whom they called priests (*sacerdotes*), because they handled the sacred objects of the temples, like the books, vases, and other such things subserving divine worship.

13. These affairs they arranged fittingly in accordance with their beliefs and rites. For as priests

41. Literally, "sects" (*sectae*). Marsilius uses this term regularly to refer to any system of religious law. See below, 1.5.13; 1.10.5, 7.

42. Reading, with Bigongiari (p. 37), *ex positione* for *expositione*.

they appointed not anyone at all, but only virtuous and esteemed citizens who had held military, judicial, or deliberative office, and who had retired from secular affairs, being excused from civil burdens and offices because of age. For by such men, removed from passions, and in whose [*21*] words greater credence was placed because of their age and moral dignity, it was fitting that the gods should be honored and their sacred objects handled, not by artisans or hirelings who had exercised lowly and defiling offices. Hence it is said in the *Politics,* Book 7, Chapter 7: "Neither a farmer nor an artisan should be made a priest."[43]

14.[44] Now correct views concerning God were not held by the gentile laws or religions and by all the other religions which are or were outside the catholic Christian faith or outside the Mosaic law which preceded it or the beliefs of the holy fathers which in turn preceded this—and, in general, by all those doctrines which are outside the tradition of what is contained in the sacred canon called the Bible. For they followed the human mind or false prophets or teachers of errors. Hence too they did not have a correct view about the future life and its happiness or misery, nor about the true priesthood established for its sake. We have, nevertheless, spoken of their rites in order to make more manifest their difference from the true priesthood, that of the Christians, and the necessity for the priestly part in communities.

Chapter 6. On the Final Cause of a Certain Part of the City, the Priesthood, Shown from the Immediate Teaching or Revelation of God, but Incapable of Being Proved by Human Reason

1. It remains now to discuss the final cause for which the true priesthood was established in communities of the faithful. This was in order to moderate human acts both immanent and transitive controlled by knowledge and desire, according as the human race is ordered by such acts toward the best life of the future world. Hence it must be noted that although the first man, Adam, was created principally for the glory of God, just as were the other creatures, nevertheless, unlike the other species of corruptible things, he was created uniquely in God's image and likeness, so that he might be capable of participating [*22*] in eternal happiness after the life of the present world. Also he was created in a state of innocence or original justice and also of grace, as is plausibly said by some of the saints and certain leading teachers of the sacred Scriptures. Now if Adam had remained in this state, the establishment or differentiation of civil offices would not have been necessary for him or for his posterity, because nature would have produced for him the advantages and pleasures of the sufficiency of this life in the earthly or pleasurable paradise, without any suffering or fatigue on his part.

2. But because Adam corrupted his innocence or original justice and grace by eating of the forbidden fruit, transgressing thereby a divine commandment, he sank suddenly into guilt and misery, and was punished by being deprived of eternal happiness, the end to which he had been ordered with all his posterity by the beneficence of glorious God. His desert for transgressing this commandment was also to propagate all his posterity in lust. Every man after him was likewise conceived and born in lust, contracting therefrom the sin which in the law of the Christians is called "original." The only exception was Jesus Christ who, without any kind of sin or lust, was conceived by the Holy Spirit and born of the Virgin Mary; which came about when one of the three divine persons, the Son, true God in the unity of his person, assumed a human nature. As a result of this transgression of its first parents, the whole posterity of mankind was weakened in soul and is born weak, whereas it had previously been created in a state of perfect health, innocence, and grace. It was also because of this guilt that the human race was deprived of its best end to which it had been ordered.

3. But it is proper to God to have compassion for the human race, which He made in His own image, and which He had foreordained to a happy and eternal life. Hence God, who "never does anything in vain and never is lacking in necessaries,"[45] willed to remedy the human plight by giving certain

43. Aristotle *Politics* 7.9 1329a28.

44. This paragraph division is from Scholz.

45. Aristotle *De Anima* 3.9 432b22. Cf. *De Caelo* 1.4 271a34; *Politics* 1.1 1253a9.

commands which men were to obey and observe, and which would counteract the transgression and heal the disease of the guilt resulting from it. Like an expert physician, He proceeded in a very orderly manner from the easier to the more difficult steps. For He first commanded men [*23*] to observe the rite of holocausts, sacrificing the first fruit of the earth and the first-born of the animals, as if He wanted to test human penitence and obedience. This rite the ancient fathers observed with reverence for God, with faith, obedience, and thankfulness, down to the time of Abraham. To him God gave an additional command, more difficult than the first: the circumcision of the whole male sex in the flesh of the foreskin. By this command God seemed again to be testing even more severely human penitence and obedience. These commands were observed by some men down to the time of Moses, through whom God handed down to the people of Israel a law wherein He set forth, in addition to the previous commands, further ones for the status of both the present and the future world; and He appointed priests and levites as ministers of this law. The utility of observing all the prior commands and the Mosaic law was that men would be purged of sin or guilt, both original and actual or freely committed, and would escape and be preserved from eternal and temporal sensory punishment of the other world, although by observing these commands they would not merit eternal happiness.

4. It was such happiness, however, to which merciful God had ordered the human race and which He wished to restore to it after leading it back from the fall, following the appropriate order. Hence, most recently of all, through His son Jesus Christ, true God and true man in unity of person, He handed down the evangelical law, containing commands and counsels of what must be believed, done, and avoided. By observance of these, not only are men preserved from sensory punishment, as they had been by observance of the prior commands, but also through God's gracious ordainment they merit, by a certain congruity, eternal happiness. And for this reason the evangelical law is called the law of grace, both because through the passion and death of Christ the human race was redeemed from its guilt and from the penalty of losing eternal beatitude which it had incurred as a result of the fall or sin of its first parents; and also because, by observing this law and receiving the sacraments established with it and in it, we are given divine grace, after it is given it is strengthened in us, and when we lose it, it is restored to us. Through this grace, by the ordainment of God and with the merit of [*24*] the passion of Christ, our works come by a certain congruity (as we have said) to merit eternal happiness.

5. Through Christ's passion the grace whereby men are able to merit a blessed life was received not only by those who came after but also by those who had observed the first commands and the Mosaic law. Before Christ's advent, passion, death, and resurrection, they had been deprived of this beatitude in the other world, in the place called limbo. But through Christ, they received the promise given to them by God, although in the prior commands of the prophets and of the Mosaic law such a promise had been handed down to them in a veiled and enigmatic manner, for *all these things happened to them in figure* [1 Cor. 10:11], as the Apostle said to the Hebrews.[46]

6. This divine procedure was very appropriate, for it went from the less to the more perfect and finally to the most perfect of the things appropriate to human salvation. Nor should it be thought that God could not have bestowed immediately at the outset, had He so wished, a perfect remedy for the fall of man. But He acted as He did because He so willed it and it was fitting, as required by men's sin, lest a too easy pardon be the occasion for further sinning.

7. As teachers of this law, and as ministers of its sacraments, certain men in the communities were chosen, called priests and deacons or levites. It is their office to teach the commands and counsels of the Christian evangelical law, as to what must be believed, done, and spurned, to the end that a blessed state be attained in the future world, and the opposite avoided.

8. The end of the priesthood, therefore, is to teach and educate men in those things which, according to the evangelical law, it is necessary to believe, do, and omit in order to attain eternal salvation and avoid [eternal] misery.

9. To this office appropriately pertain all the disciplines, theoretic and practical, discovered by the human mind, which moderate human acts both immanent and transitive arising from desire and knowledge, and which make man well disposed [*25*] in soul for the state of both the present

46. Marsilius refers here only to the general argument of the Epistle to the Hebrews.

and the future world. We have almost all these disciplines through the teaching of the admirable Philosopher and of other glorious men; however, we have omitted to enumerate them here, both for the sake of brevity and because it is not necessary to our present consideration.

10.[47] With respect to this chapter and the one following, we must understand that the causes of the offices of the city, in respect of each kind of cause, differ according as they are offices of the city and according as they are habits of the human body or mind. For according as they are habits of the human body or soul, their final causes are the functions which are immediately and essentially forthcoming from them. For example, the final cause of the shipbuilding part of the city is a ship; of the military part, the use of arms and fighting; of the priesthood, the preaching of the divine law and the administration of the sacraments in accordance with it; and so on with all the rest. But according as they are offices determined and established in the city, their final causes are the benefits and sufficiencies which perfect human actions and passions, and which are forthcoming from the functions of the aforesaid habits, or which cannot be had without them. For example, from fighting, which is the act or end of the military habit, freedom is forthcoming and is preserved for men in the city, and this freedom is the end of the acts and functions of the military. So too from the function or end of the housebuilding part, which is a house, there is forthcoming to men or to the city protection from the harmful impressions of the air, the hot, the cold, the wet, or the dry, which protection is the final cause for whose sake the housebuilding office was established in the city. In the same way, from observance of the divine law, which is the end of the priesthood, eternal happiness is forthcoming to men. Similar considerations apply to all the other parts or offices of the city. And the other kinds of causes of these offices—the material, formal, and efficient causes—are distinguished in the same or a similar manner, as will appear in the following chapter.

We have now finished our discussion of the number of the parts of the city, their necessity, and their differentiation through the sufficiencies which are their ends. [*26*].

Chapter 7. On the Other Kinds of Causes of the Separate Existence of the Parts of the City, and the Division of Each Kind in Two Ways Relevant to Our Purpose

1. We must now discuss the other causes of the offices or parts of the city. First we shall speak about their material and formal causes; then we shall inquire into their efficient cause. And since in things completed by the human mind the matter actually exists prior to the form,[48] let us first discuss the material cause. The proper matter of the different offices, according as the offices mean habits of the soul, is men inclined from their generation or birth to different arts or disciplines. For "nature is not lacking in necessaries,"[49] and is more solicitous for what is more noble;[50] among corruptible things, the most noble is the human species, which, perfected by different arts or disciplines, is the matter wherefrom must be established the city and its distinct parts necessary for the attainment of sufficiency of life, as was shown in Chapters 4 and 5 of this discourse. Hence nature herself initiated this differentiation in the generation of men, producing some who in their natural dispositions were apt for and inclined toward farming, others toward military pursuits, and still others toward the other genera of arts and disciplines, but different men toward different ones. Nor did she incline only one individual toward one species of art or discipline, but rather many individuals toward the same species, to the extent necessary for sufficiency of life. Hence, she generated some men apt for prudence, since the judicial and deliberative part of the city must be composed of prudent men; some men apt for strength and courage, since the military part is appropriately composed of such men. So too she adapted the other men to the other genera of practical and theoretic habits which are necessary or appropriate for living and living well, so that out of the diversity of the natural inclinations toward habits [*27*] of diverse genera and species in

47. This paragraph division is from Scholz.

48. Aristotle *Metaphysics* 7.7 1032b31.

49. Aristotle *De Anima* 3.9 432b22. See above, 1.6.3.

50. Aristotle *On the Parts of Animals* 4.10 686a25 ff.

all men, she perfected what was necessary for the diversity of the parts of the city.

The material causes of the offices of the city, according as the offices mean parts of the city, are almost apparent already. For these are men habituated by the arts and disciplines of diverse genera and species, from whom the diverse orders or parts are established in the city for the sake of the sufficiencies or ends forthcoming from their arts and disciplines. Considered in this way, as having been established in the city for this purpose, the parts of the city are properly called offices, in the sense of services, for they are ordered toward human service.

2. The formal causes of the offices of the city, according as they are habits of the human mind, are none other than these very habits. For these habits are themselves the forms of those who have them; they fulfil or perfect the human inclinations which exist by nature. Hence it is said in the *Politics,* Book 7, last chapter: "Every art and discipline aims to supply what nature lacks."[51] On the other hand, according as the offices of the city are established parts of the city, their formal causes are the commands which the efficient cause has given to or impressed upon the men who are appointed to exercise determinate functions in the city.

3. The efficient or productive causes of the offices, according as they mean habits of the soul, are the minds and wills of men through their thoughts and desires, individually or collectively. Also, in the case of certain offices, an added principle is the movement and exercise of the bodily organs. But the efficient cause of the offices, according as they are parts of the city, is frequently and in most cases the human legislator, although formerly, rarely and in very few cases, the immediate efficient cause was God, without human determination, as will be said in Chapter 9 of this discourse and as will appear more fully from Chapter 12 of this discourse and Chapter 15 of Discourse 2.[52] With regard to the priesthood, however, there is a different manner of establishment, which will be sufficiently discussed in Chapters 15 and 17 of Discourse 2.

In this way, then, we have discussed the parts of the city and the necessity of their establishment from the three other kinds of cause. [*28*]

Chapter 8. On the Genera of Polities or Regimes, the Temperate and the Diseased, and the Division of Their Species

1. We must now show with greater certainty what was already shown to some extent above, that the establishment and differentiation of the parts of the city are brought about by an efficient cause which we have previously called the legislator. The same legislator establishes these parts, and differentiates and separates them as nature does with an animal, by first forming or establishing in the city one part which in Chapter 5 of this discourse we called the ruling or judicial part,[53] and through this the other parts, as will be indicated more fully in Chapter 15 of this discourse. Hence we must first say something concerning the nature of this ruling part. For since it is the first part of the city, as will appear below, the appropriate procedure will be to go from the indication of its efficient cause to the indication of the efficient cause which establishes and differentiates the other parts of the city.

2. There are two genera of ruling parts or governments, one well tempered, the other diseased. With Aristotle in the *Politics,* Book 3, Chapter 5,[54] I call that genus "well tempered" in which the ruler governs for the common benefit, in accordance with the will of the subjects; while the "diseased" genus is that which is deficient in this respect. Each of these genera, again, is divided into three species: the temperate into kingly monarchy (*regalem monarchiam*), aristocracy, and polity; the diseased into the three opposite species of tyrannical monarchy, oligarchy, and democracy. And each of these again has sub-species, the detailed discussion of which is not part of our present task. For Aristotle gave a sufficient account of them in Books 3 and 4 of his *Politics.*

3. To obtain a fuller knowledge of these species of government, which is necessary for the clear understanding of what follows, let us define each species in accordance with the view of Aristotle. A *kingly monarchy,* then, is a temperate [*29*] government wherein the ruler is a single man who rules

51. Aristotle *Politics* 7.17 1337a1.

52. Reading, with Scholz, "2e" after "15°." The passages referred to are 1.9.2; 1.12.1; 2.15.2 ff.

53. 1.5.7.

54. Aristotle *Politics* 3.7–8 1279a17 ff.

for the common benefit, and in accordance with the will or consent of the subjects. *Tyranny,* its opposite, is a diseased government wherein the ruler is a single man who rules for his own private benefit apart from the will of his subjects. *Aristocracy* is a temperate government in which the honorable class (*honorabilitas*) alone rules in accordance with the will or consent of the subjects and for the common benefit. *Oligarchy,* its opposite, is a diseased government in which some of the wealthier or more powerful rule for their own benefit apart from the will of the subjects. A *polity,* although in one sense it is something common to every genus or species of regime or government, means in another sense a certain species of temperate government, in which any citizen participates in some way in the government or in the deliberative function in turn according to his rank and ability or condition, for the common benefit and with the will or consent of the citizens. *Democracy,* its opposite, is a government in which the vulgar or the multitude of the needy establish the government and rule alone, apart from the will or consent of the other citizens and not entirely for the common benefit according to proper proportion.

4. As to which of the temperate governments is best or which of the diseased governments is worst, and the relative goodness or badness of the other species, the discussion of these points is not part of our present concern. Let it suffice to have said this much about the division of governments into their species and the definition of each.

Chapter 9. On the Methods of Establishing a Kingly Monarchy, and Which Method Is the More Perfect;[55] Also on the Methods, of Establishing the Other Kinds of Regime or Polity, Both Temperate and Diseased

1. Having determined these points, we must now discuss the methods of effecting or establishing the ruling part (*partem principantem*) [of the city]. For from the better or worse nature of these methods, viewed as actions[56] emerging from that nature to the civil regime, we must infer the efficient cause by which [*30*] these methods and the ruling part established by them will emerge more advantageously to the polity.

2. In this book we are considering the causes and actions by which the ruling part must in most cases be established. First, however, we wish to indicate the method and cause by which this part has been established in the past, although rarely, in order to distinguish this method or action, and its immediate cause, from those by which the government must regularly and in most cases be established, and which we can prove by human demonstration. For of the former method no certain comprehension can be had through demonstration. This method or action, with its immediate cause, by which the ruling part and other parts of the city, especially the priesthood, were formed in the past, was the divine will commanding this either through the determinate oracle of some individual creature or else perhaps immediately through itself alone. It was by this method that the divine will established the government of the people of Israel in the person of Moses and of certain other judges after him, and also the priesthood in the person of Aaron and his successors. With respect to this cause and its free action, as to why it did or did not operate in one way or another, we can say nothing through demonstration, but we hold it by simple belief apart from reason. There is, however, another method of establishing governments which proceeds immediately from the human mind, although perhaps from God as remote cause, who grants all earthly rulership, as is said in the nineteenth chapter of John [cf. John 19:11], and as the Apostle clearly states in the thirteenth chapter of the epistle to the Romans [cf. Rom. 13:1] and St. Augustine in the *City of God,* Book 5, Chapter 21. However, God does not always act immediately; indeed in most cases, nearly everywhere, He establishes governments by means of human minds, to which He has granted the discretionary will for such establishment. And as for this latter cause, what it is, and by what kind of action it must establish such things, this can be indicated with human certainty from what is better or worse for the polity. [*31*]

3. Omitting, then, that method of which we cannot attain certain knowledge through demonstration,

55. Reading, with Bigongiari (p. 39) and MSS, *perfectioris* for *perfectionis.*

56. Reading, with Bigongiari (p. 40) and MSS, *actionum* for *actionibus;* hence also *provenientium* for *provenientibus.*

we wish first to present those methods of establishing governments (*principatus*) which are effected immediately by the human will;[57] next we shall show which of these is the more certain and the simpler.[58] Then, from the better nature of that method we shall infer the efficient cause from which alone it must and can emerge.[59] From these points, consequently, will appear the cause which must move to the best establishment and determination of the other parts of the city.[60] Finally we shall discuss the unity of the government,[61] through which it will also be apparent what is the unity of the city or state.[62]

4. In pursuit of this program, then, we shall first enumerate the methods of establishing kingly monarchy, by speaking of their origins. For this species of government seems rather kindred to us, and directly connected with the rule of the family, as is clear from what we said in Chapter 3. After the determination of this point, the methods of establishing the other divisions of government will be made clear.

There are five methods of establishing kingly monarchies, according to Aristotle's *Politics,* Book 3, Chapter 8.[63] One is when the monarch is appointed for one determinate function with respect to the ruling of the community, such as the leadership of the army, either with hereditary succession or for his own lifetime only. It was by this method that Agamemnon was made leader of the army by the Greeks. In modern communities this office is called the captaincy or constabulary.[64] This leader of the army had no judicial power in time of peace, but when the army was fighting a war he had the supreme authority to kill or otherwise punish transgressors.

Another method is that whereby certain monarchs rule in Asia; they receive their dominating authority through hereditary succession, and while they rule according to law, this law is like that of despots, being for the monarch's benefit rather than completely for the community's. The inhabitants of that region endure such rule "without protest,"[65] because of their barbaric [*32*] and slavish nature and the influence of custom. This rule is kingly in that it is native to the country and is over voluntary subjects, because, for example, the monarch's ancestors had been the first inhabitants of the region. But it is also in a sense tyrannical, in that its laws are not completely for the common benefit but for that of the monarch.

A third method of kingly government is when the ruler receives his authority through election rather than hereditary succession, but governs according to a law which is not completely for the common benefit but rather for that of the monarch, like the law of tyrants. Aristotle, therefore, called this species of government an "elective tyranny,"[66] a tyranny because the law was despotic, and elective because it was not over involuntary subjects.

A fourth method is that whereby a ruler is elected with subsequent hereditary succession, and governs according to laws which are completely for the common benefit; this method was used "in heroic days,"[67] as Aristotle says in the chapter previously mentioned. Those days were called "heroic" either because the stars then produced men who were believed to be "heroes," that is, divine, on account of their exceeding virtue; or because such men and not others were named rulers on account of their exceeding virtues and beneficial deeds, in that they brought together a scattered multitude and assembled it into a civil community, or they freed the region of oppressors by fighting and strength of arms, or perhaps they bought the region or acquired it by some other appropriate method and divided it among the subjects. At any rate these men were made rulers with subsequent hereditary succession, because of their bestowal of great benefits or their excess of virtue over the rest of the multitude, as Aristotle also said in the *Politics,* Book 5, Chapter 5.[68] Under this species of monarchy, Aristotle perhaps included that in which someone is elected only for his own lifetime or a part of his lifetime; or else he designated it through the combination of this fourth species and the one called elective tyranny, because it shares features of both.

57. 1.9.4–6.
58. 1.9.7.
59. 1.15.1–3. Cf. 1.10.1; 1.14.1.
60. 1.15.4–10.
61. 1.17.1–9.
62. 1.17.11.
63. Aristotle *Politics* 3.14 1284b35 ff.
64. Marsilius's terms are *capitaneatus* and *constabiliaria.* The former designated a position of army leadership; see Du Cange, *Glossarium,* s.v. *capitaneatus, capitaneus.* Du Cange has no entry for *constabiliaria,* but for the seemingly related terms *constabularia* and *contestabiliaria* (the latter found in some MSS of the *Defensor* instead of *constabiliaria*), Du Cange refers to *comes stabuli,* meaning the custodian of the royal stable, and gives a large number of citations, s.v.
65. Aristotle *Politics* 3.14 1285a23.
66. Ibid. 3.14 1285a32.
67. Ibid. 3.14 1285b4.
68. Ibid. 5.10 1310b10 ff.

There is and was a fifth method of kingly monarchy, whereby the ruler is made [33] lord (*dominus*) over everything in the community, disposing of things and persons according to his own will, just as the head of a family disposes at will of everything in his own household.[69]

5. To make clearer these concepts of Aristotle, and to summarize all the methods of establishing the other kinds of government, we shall say that every government is over either voluntary or involuntary subjects. The first is the genus of well-tempered governments, the second of diseased governments. Each of these genera is divided into three species or modes, as was said in Chapter 8. And since one of the species of well-tempered government, and perhaps the more perfect, is kingly monarchy, let us resume our previous statements about its various modes, by saying that the king or monarch either is named by the election of the inhabitants or citizens, or duly obtains the rulership without their election. If without the election of the citizens, this is either because he or his ancestors first inhabited the region, or because he bought the land and jurisdiction, or acquired it by a just war or by some other lawful method, such as by gift made to him for some great service. Each of these kinds of monarchy participates so much the more in true kingship, the more it is over voluntary subjects and according to law made for the common benefit of the subjects; and it savors so much the more of tyranny the more it departs from these features, that is, the consent of the subjects and law established for their common benefit. Hence it is written in the *Politics*, Book 4, Chapter 8: "These," that is, monarchies, "were kingly because they were according to law, and ruled voluntary subjects; but they were tyrannical because they ruled despotically and in accordance with their," that is, the monarchs', "own judgment."[70] These two features, then, distinguish temperate from diseased government, as is apparent from the clear statement of Aristotle, but absolutely or in greater degree it is the consent of the subjects which is the distinguishing criterion.[71] Now if the ruling monarch is elected by the inhabitants, it is [34] either with all his posterity succeeding him or not. If the latter, this may be in several ways, as he is named either for his own lifetime alone, or for his own lifetime and that of one or more of his successors, or not for the whole lifetime either of himself or of any of his successors but only for some determinate period, such as one or two years, more or less. Again, he is named to exercise either every judicial office, or only one office such as leading the army.

6. The elected and the non-elected kingly monarchs agree in that each rules voluntary subjects. They differ, however, in that the non-elected kings for the most part rule less voluntary subjects, and by laws which are less politic for the common benefit, as we said before in the case of the barbarians. The elected kings, on the other hand, rule more voluntary subjects, and by laws which are more politic, in that they are made for the common benefit, as we have said.

7. From these considerations it is clear, and will be even more apparent in the sequel, that the elected kind of government is superior to the non-elected. This is also the view of Aristotle in that passage of the *Politics*, Book 3, Chapter 8, which we cited above with reference to those who were made rulers in the heroic days.[72] Again, this method of establishing governments is more permanent in perfect communities. For at some time or other it becomes necessary to have recourse to this from among all the other methods of establishing governments, but not conversely. For example, if hereditary succession fails, or if for some reason the multitude cannot bear the excessive malice of that family's rule, they must then turn to the method of election, which can never fail so long as the generation of men does not fail. Moreover, by the method of election alone is the best ruler obtained. For it is expedient that the ruler be the best man in the polity, since he must regulate the civil acts of all the rest. [35]

8. The method of establishing the other species of temperate government is usually election; in some cases the ruler is chosen by lot,[73] without subsequent hereditary succession. Diseased governments, on the other hand, are usually established by fraud or force or both.[74]

9. Which of the temperate governments is better, monarchy or one of the other two species, aristocracy or polity; and again, which of the monarchies is better, the elected or the non-elected; and moreover, which of the elected monarchies, that established with hereditary succession ensuing

69. See Aristotle *Politics* 3.16–17 1287a1 ff.

70. Aristotle *Politics* 4.10 1295a15.

71. See above, 1.8.2.

72. Aristotle *Politics* 3.14 1285b2; above, para. 4.

73. Aristotle *Politics* 2.6 1266a9; 6.2 1317b21, 1318a2.

74. Ibid. 5.4 1304b8.

or that in which one man alone is named without such succession; which in turn is divided into the further alternatives of whether it is better to name the ruler for a whole lifetime, either of himself alone or of some of his successors also, or only for some determinate period, such as one or two years, more or less—in all these questions there is room for inquiry and reasonable doubt.[75] It must be held without doubt, however, in accordance with the truth and the manifest view of Aristotle, that election is the more certain standard of government, as will be more fully shown in Chapters 12, 16, and 17, of this discourse.

10. We must not overlook, however, that different multitudes in different times and places are inclined toward different kinds of polity and government, as Aristotle says in the *Politics,* Book 3, Chapter 9.[76] Legislators and institutors of governments must hearken to this fact. For just as not every man is inclined toward the best discipline or study, whereupon it is appropriate that he be directed toward the acquisition not of that discipline but of some other good one for which he is more fitted, so too a multitude in some time or place may perhaps not be inclined to accept the best kind of government, and therefore recourse must first be had to that kind of temperate government which is more appropriate to it. For example, before the monarchy of Julius Caesar, the Roman people were for a long time unwilling to accept any definite monarch, either with hereditary succession or even one who was named only for his own lifetime. The reason for this was [*36*] perhaps that there was a large number of heroic men worthy of rulership among them, both families and individuals.

11. From these conclusions, then, it emerges clearly that those who ask which monarch is better for a city or state, the one who rules through election or the one who rules through hereditary succession, do not put the question in the proper way. What they must correctly ask first is, which monarch is better, the elected or the non-elected. And if the elected, again which, the one who is named with hereditary succession ensuing or the one who is named without hereditary succession. For although a non-elected monarch almost always transmits the rulership to his heir, not every elected monarch does so, but only the one who is named to rule with hereditary succession ensuing.

Let these, then, be our conclusions about the methods of establishing governments, and that the absolutely better method is election.

Chapter 10. On the Distinction of the Meaning of the Term "Law," and on the Meaning Which Is Most Proper and Intended by Us

1. Since we have said that election is the more perfect and better method of establishing governments, we shall do well to inquire as to its efficient cause, wherefrom it has to emerge in its full value; for from this will appear the cause not only of the elected government but also of the other parts of the polity. Now a government has to regulate [*37*] civil human acts (as we demonstrated in Chapter 5 of this discourse),[77] and according to a standard (*regulam*) which is and ought to be the form of the ruler, as such. We must, consequently, inquire into this standard, as to whether it exists, what it is, and why. For the efficient cause of this standard is perhaps the same as that of the ruler.

2. The existence of this standard, which is called a "statute" or "custom" and by the common term "law," we assume as almost self-evident by induction in all perfect communities. We shall show first, then, what law is;[78] next we shall indicate its final cause or necessity;[79] and finally we shall demonstrate by what person or persons and by what kind of action the law should be established;[80] which will be to inquire into its legislator or efficient cause, to whom we think it also pertains to elect the government, as we shall show subsequently by demonstration.[81] From these points there will also appear the matter or subject of the aforesaid standard which we have called law. For this matter is the ruling part, whose function it is to regulate the political or civil acts of men according to the law.

3. Following this procedure, then, we must first distinguish the meanings or intentions of this term "law," in order that its many senses, may not lead to confusion. For in one sense it means

75. See above, 1.8.4.
76. Aristotle *Politics* 3.14 1284b39, 1285a19.
77. See above, 1.5.7.
78. 1.10.
79. 1.11.
80. 1.12–13.
81. 1.14; 1.15.3.

a natural sensitive inclination toward some action or passion. This is the way the Apostle used it when he said in the seventh chapter of the epistle to the Romans: *I see another law in my members, fighting against the law of my mind* [Rom. 7:23]. In another sense this term "law" means any operative habit and in general every form, existing in the mind, of a producible thing, from which as from an exemplar or measure there emerge the forms of things made by art. This is the way in which the term was used in the forty-third chapter of Ezekiel: *This is the law of the house... And these are the measurements of the altar* [Ezek. 43:12–13]. In a third sense "law" means the standard containing admonitions for voluntary human acts according as these are ordered toward glory or punishment in the future world. In this sense the "Mosaic Law" was in part called a law, just as the "Evangelical Law" in its [*38*] entirety is called a law. Hence the Apostle said of these in his epistle to the Hebrews: *Since the priesthood has been changed, it is necessary that there be a change of the law also* [Heb. 7:12]. In this sense "law" was also used for the evangelic discipline in the first chapter of James: *He who has looked into the perfect law of liberty, and has continued therein... this man shall be blessed in his deeds* [Jas. 1:25]. In this sense of the term law all religions, such as that of Muhammad or of the Persians, are called laws in whole or in part, although among these only the Mosaic and the evangelic, that is, the Christian, contain the truth. So too Aristotle called religions "laws" when he said, in the second book of his *Philosophy:* "The laws show how great is the power of custom";[82] and also in the twelfth book of the same work: "The other doctrines were added as myths to persuade men to obey the laws, and for the sake of expediency."[83] In its fourth and most familiar sense, this term "law" means the science or doctrine or universal judgment of matters of civil justice and benefit, and of their opposites.

4. Taken in this last sense, law may be considered in two ways. In one way it may be considered in itself, as it only shows what is just or unjust, beneficial or harmful; and as such it is called the science or doctrine of right (*juris*). In another way it may be considered according as with regard to its observance there is given a command coercive through punishment or reward to be distributed in the present world, or according as it is handed down by way of such a command; and considered in this way it most properly is called, and is, a law. It was in this sense that Aristotle also defined it in the last book of the *Ethics,* Chapter 8, when he said: "Law has coercive force, for it is discourse emerging from prudence and understanding."[84] Law, then, is a "discourse" or statement "emerging from prudence and" political "understanding," that is, it is an ordinance made by political prudence, concerning matters of justice and benefit and their opposites, [*39*] and having "coercive force," that is, concerning whose observance there is given a command which one is compelled to observe, or which is made by way of such a command.

5. Hence not all true cognitions of matters of civil justice and benefit are laws unless a coercive command has been given concerning their observance, or they have been made by way of a command, although such true cognition is necessarily required for a perfect law. Indeed, sometimes false cognitions of the just and the beneficial become laws, when there is given a command to observe them, or they are made by way of a command. An example of this is found in the regions of certain barbarians, who cause it to be observed as just that a murderer be absolved of civil guilt and punishment on payment of a fine. This, however, is absolutely unjust, and consequently the laws of such barbarians are not absolutely perfect. For although they have the proper form, that is, a coercive command of observance, they lack a proper condition, that is, the proper and true ordering of justice.

6. Under this sense of law are included all standards of civil justice and benefit established by human authority, such as customs, statutes, plebiscites, decretals, and all similar rules which are based upon human authority as we have said.

7. We must not overlook, however, that both the evangelical law and the Mosaic, and perhaps the other religions as well, may be considered and compared in different ways in whole or in part, in relation to human acts for the status of the present or the future world. For they sometimes come, or have hitherto come, or will come, under the third sense of law, and sometimes under the last, as will be shown more fully in Chapters 8 and 9 of Discourse 2. Moreover, some of these laws are true, while others are false fancies and empty promises.

It is now clear, then, that there exists a standard or law of civil human acts, and what this is. [*40*]

82. Aristotle *Metaphysics* 2.3 995a4.

83. Ibid. 12.8 1074b3.

84. Aristotle *Nicomachean Ethics* 10.9 1180a21.

Chapter 11. On the Necessity for Making Laws (Taken in Their Most Proper Sense); and That No Ruler, However Virtuous or Just, Should Rule without Laws

8. Having thus distinguished these various meanings of "law," we wish to show the end or necessity of law in its last and most proper sense. The principal end is civil justice and the common benefit; the secondary end is the security of rulers, especially those with hereditary succession, and the long duration of governments. The primary necessity of the law, then, is as follows: It is necessary to establish in the polity that without which civil judgments cannot be made with complete rightness, and through which these judgments are properly made and preserved from defect so far as it is humanly possible. Such a thing is the law, when the ruler is directed to make civil judgments in accordance with it. Therefore, the establishment of law is necessary in the polity. The major premise of this demonstration is almost self-evident, and is very close to being indemonstrable. Its certainty can and should be grasped from Chapter 5, paragraph 7 of this discourse. The minor premise will now be proved in this way: To make a good judgment, there are required a right disposition (*affectio*) of the judges and a true knowledge of the matters to be judged; the opposites of which corrupt civil judgments. For if the judge has a perverted disposition, such as hate, love, or avarice, this perverts his desire. But such dispositions are kept away from the judgment, and it is preserved from them, when the judge or ruler is directed to make judgments according to the laws, because the law lacks all perverted disposition; for it is not made useful for friend or harmful for foe, but universally for all those who perform civil acts well or badly. For all other things are accidental to the law and are outside it; but they are not similarly outside the judge. Persons involved in a judgment can be friendly or inimical to the judge, helpful or harmful to him, by making him a gift or a promise; and in other ways too they can arouse in the judge a disposition which perverts his judgment. Consequently, no judgment, so far as possible, should be entrusted [*41*] to the discretion of the judge, but rather it should be determined by law and pronounced in accordance with it.

2. This was also the view of the divine Aristotle in the *Politics,* Book 3, Chapter 9, where he purposely asks whether it is better for a polity to be ruled by the best man without law or by the best laws; and he replies as follows: "That is better," that is, superior for judging, "which entirely lacks the passionate factor," that is, the disposition which may pervert the judgment, "than that to which passion is natural. But law does not have this," that is, passion or disposition, "while every human soul must necessarily have it";[85] and he said "every," not excepting anyone, however virtuous. He repeats this view in the *Rhetoric,* Book 1, Chapter 1: "Most of all" is this required, that is, that nothing be left to the discretion of the judge, to be judged apart from the law, "because the judgment of the legislator," that is, the law, "is not partial," that is, it is not made on account of some one particular man, "but is concerned with future and universal matters. Now the judge and the magistrate judge about present and determinate matters, with which love and hate and private benefit are often involved, so that they cannot sufficiently see the truth, but instead have regard in their judgments to their own private pleasure and displeasure."[86] He also makes this point in Book 1, Chapter 2 of the same treatise: "We do not render the same judgments when we are pleased as when we are pained, when we love as when we hate."[87]

3. A judgment is also corrupted through the ignorance of the judges, even if they be of good disposition or intention. This sin or defect is removed and remedied by the law, for in the law is determined well-nigh perfectly what is just or unjust, beneficial or harmful, with regard to each civil human act. Such determination cannot be made so adequately by any one man, however intelligent he may be. For no single man, and [*42*] perhaps not even all the men of one era, could investigate or remember all the civil acts determined in the law; indeed, what was said about them by the first investigators and also by all the men of the same era who observed such acts was meager and imperfect, and attained its completion only subsequently through the additions made by later investigators. This can be sufficiently seen from experience, in the additions, subtractions, and complete changes sometimes made in the laws

85. Aristotle *Politics* 3.15 1286a17.

86. Aristotle *Rhetoric* 1.1 1354b4 ff.

87. Ibid. 1.2 1356a14.

in different eras, or at different times within the same era.

Aristotle also attests to this in the *Politics*, Book 2, Chapter 2, when he says: "We must not ignore that attention must be paid to the long time and many years of the past, in which it would not have remained unknown if these things were good,"[88] that is, the measures which are to be established as laws. He says the same thing in the *Rhetoric*, Book 1, Chapter 1: "Laws are made after long study."[89] This is also confirmed by reason, since the making of laws requires prudence, as we saw above from the definition of law, and prudence requires long experience, which, in turn, requires much time. Hence it is said in the sixth book of the *Ethics*: "A sign of what has been said is that while youths may become geometers, and be learned and wise in such sciences, they do not seem to become prudent. The cause is that prudence is of singular things which become known through experience; but a youth is not experienced, for experience requires a long time."[90] Consequently, what one man alone can discover or know by himself, both in the science of civil justice and benefit and in the other sciences, is little or nothing. Moreover, what is observed by the men of one era is quite imperfect by comparison with what is observed in many eras, so that Aristotle, discussing the discovery of truth in every art and discipline, wrote as follows in the *Philosophy*, Book 2, Chapter 1: "One man," that is, one discoverer of any art or discipline, "contributes to it," [*43*] that is, discovers about it by himself alone, "little or nothing, but by the contributions of all a great deal is accomplished."[91] This passage is clearer in the translation from the Arabic, in which it reads as follows: "Each of them," that is, each of the discoverers of any art or discipline, "comprehends little or nothing about the truth. But when a collection is made from among all who have achieved some comprehension, what is collected will be of considerable quantity."[92] This may especially be seen in the case of astrology.

It is in this way, then, by men's mutual help and the addition of later to earlier discoveries, that all arts and disciplines have been perfected. Aristotle indicated this in a general way (*figuraliter*) with regard to the discovery of music in the same place cited above, when he said: "If there had been no Timotheus, we should be lacking much melody; but if there had been no Phrynes, there would have been no Timotheus";[93] that is, Timotheus would not have been so accomplished in melody if he had not had the melodies previously discovered by Phrynes. Averroes expounds these words as follows in the second book of his *Commentary*: "And what he," that is, Aristotle, "says in this chapter is clear. For no one can discover by himself the larger part of the practical or considerative," that is, theoretic, "arts, because these are completed only through the assistance which an earlier investigator gives to the one following him."[94] And Aristotle says the same thing in the second book of the *Refutations*,[95] last chapter, concerning the discovery of rhetoric and of all other disciplines, whatever the case may have been with regard to the discovery of logic, whose complete development he ascribed to himself alone without the discovery or assistance of any predecessor; in which he seems to have been unique among men. He also makes the same point in the *Ethics*, Book 8, Chapter 1: "Two persons are better able to act and to understand"[96] [than one alone]. But if two, then more than two, both simultaneously and successively, can do more than one man alone. And this is what Aristotle says with regard to our present subject in the *Politics*, Book 3, Chapter 9: "It will appear most unreasonable if one man should perceive better, judging with only two [*44*] eyes and two ears and acting with only two hands and feet, than many persons with many such organs."[97]

Since, then, the law is an eye composed of many eyes, that is, the considered comprehension of many comprehenders for avoiding error in civil judgments and for judging rightly, it is safer that these judgments be made according to law than

88. Aristotle *Politics* 2.5 1264a1.

89. Aristotle *Rhetoric* 1.1 1354b3.

90. Aristotle *Nicomachean Ethics* 6.9 1142a12.

91. Aristotle *Metaphysics* 2.1 993b2.

92. For the translation from the Arabic, see *Aristotelis Opera*, ed. Manardus (Venice, 1560), vol. 4, fol. 47v; A. Brett (ed. and trans., *The Defender of the Peace* [Cambridge: Cambridge University Press, 2005]) cites *Aristotelis Opera cum Averrois Commentariis*, ed. Marco Antonio Zimara (Venice, 1562–1574; Frankfurt am Main: Minerva, 1962), vol. 8, *Metaphysicorum Libri XIV*, bk. 2, chap. 1, fol. 28v.

93. Aristotle *Metaphysics* 2.1 993b15; inserting, with Bigongiari (p. 42), *non* before Phrynes.

94. Averroes *Commentarius in Aristotelis Metaphysicam* 2.1, in *Aristotelis Opera*, ed. Manardus (Venice, 1560), vol. 4, fol. 49r; or *Aristotelis Opera cum Averrois Commentariis*, ed. Zimara, vol. 8, *Metaphysicorum Libri XIV*, book 2, chap. 1, fol. 29r.

95. Aristotle *On Sophistical Refutations* 34 183b34 ff.

96. Aristotle *Nicomachean Ethics* 8.1 1155a16.

97. Aristotle *Politics* 3.16 1287b26.

according to the discretion of the judge. For this reason it is necessary to establish the law, if polities are to be ordered for the best with regard to their civil justice and benefit; for through the law, civil judgments are preserved from the ignorance and perverted disposition of the judges. This was the minor premise of the demonstration by which we have tried from the beginning of this chapter to prove the necessity of the laws. As to the method by which a dispute or civil lawsuit is to be decided or judged when it is not determined by law, this will be discussed in Chapter 14 of this discourse.[98] Laws, therefore, are necessary in order to exclude malice and error from the civil judgments or sentences of the judges.

4. For these reasons, Aristotle counseled that no judge or ruler should be granted the discretionary power to give judgments or commands without law, concerning those civil affairs which could be determined by law. Hence he said in the *Ethics,* Book 4, Chapter 5, the treatise on justice: "We must not allow man to rule, but" in accordance with "reason,"[99] that is, law; and Aristotle indicated the cause which we pointed out above, the perverted disposition which can be had by man. In the *Politics,* Book 3, Chapter 6, he said: "The first question shows plainly above all that laws rightly made should govern,"[100] that is, that rulers should govern in accordance with laws. Again in the same treatise, Book 3, Chapter 9, he said: "He who orders the mind to rule seems thereby to order God and the laws to rule; but he who orders man to rule," that is, without law, according to his own discretion, "instigates a beast";[101] and shortly thereafter he indicated the ground for this: "Hence the law is reason without appetite,"[102] [*45*] as if to say that the law is reason or knowledge without appetite, that is, without any affective disposition. He repeated this view also in the *Rhetoric,* Book 1, Chapter 1: "It is best, therefore, for rightly-made laws to determine as many matters as possible and to entrust as little as possible to the judges";[103] giving the reasons adduced above, the exclusion from civil judgments of the judges' malice and ignorance, which cannot arise in the law as they do in the judge, as we have shown above. And even more clearly Aristotle says in the *Politics,* Book 4, Chapter 4: "Where the laws do not govern," that is, where rulers do not govern in accordance with the laws, "there is no polity," that is, none which is temperate. "For the law should govern all things."[104]

5. It still remains to show that all rulers should govern according to law and not without it, and especially those monarchs who rule with hereditary succession, in order that their governments may be more secure and longer lasting. This was the second reason for the necessity of laws which we indicated at the beginning of this chapter. This may be seen first of all from the fact that, when rulers govern according to law, their judgments are preserved from the defect which is caused by ignorance and perverted disposition. Hence the rulers are regulated both in themselves and in relation to their citizen subjects, and they suffer less from sedition and from the consequent destruction of their governments which they would incur if they acted badly according to their own discretion, as Aristotle clearly says in the *Politics,* Book 5, Chapter 5: "For a kingdom is destroyed least of all by external forces: its destruction most usually comes from within itself. It is destroyed in two ways: one is when those who share the ruling power quarrel among themselves, the other is when they try to govern tyrannically, by controlling more things, and contrary to the law. Kingdoms no longer occur these days, but if monarchies occur, they are rather tyrannies."[105]

6. Someone will raise an objection about the best man, who lacks ignorance [*46*] and perverted disposition.[106] As for us, however, we reply that such a man happens very rarely, and that even when he does he is not as free [from ignorance and passion] as the law itself, as we proved above from Aristotle, from reason, and from sense experience. For every soul sometimes has a vicious disposition. We can readily accept this from the thirteenth chapter of Daniel; for it is there written that two elders came full of wicked device against Susanna, to put her to death [Dan. 13:28]. Now these were old men and priests and judges of the people that year: nevertheless they bore false witness against her because she would not acquiesce to their vicious lust. If, then, old priests, about whom it would least be expected, were corrupted by carnal lust, what should be thought of other men, and how much more will they be corrupted by avarice and other vicious

98. See below, 1.14.3–6.
99. Aristotle *Nicomachean Ethics* 5.6 1134a35.
100. Aristotle *Politics* 3.11 1282b1.
101. Ibid. 3.16 1287b28.
102. Ibid. 3.16 1287a32.
103. Aristotle *Rhetoric* 1.1 1354b32.
104. Aristotle *Politics* 4.4 1292a32.
105. Ibid. 5.10 1312b38.
106. Cf. Aristotle *Politics* 3.13 1284b3 ff.; 3.17 1288a15 ff. Cf. also Dante *Monarchia* 1.11 and 13.

dispositions? Certainly, no one, however virtuous, can be so lacking in perverted passion and ignorance as is the law. Therefore, it is safer that civil judgments be regulated by the law than that they be entrusted to the discretion of a judge, however virtuous (*studiosi*) he may be.

7. Let us assume, however, although it is most rare or impossible, that there is some ruler so heroic that in him neither passion nor ignorance finds a place. What shall we say of his sons, who are unlike him and who, ruling in accordance with their own discretion, will commit excesses which result in their being deprived of the rulership? Someone may say that the father, who is the best of men, will not hand over the government to such sons. This reply, however, is not to be granted, for two reasons: first, because it is not in the father's power to deprive his sons of the succession, since the rulership is a hereditary possession of his family, and second, because even if it were in the father's power to transfer the rulership to whomever he wanted, he would not deprive his sons of it no matter how vicious they were. Hence, Aristotle answers this objection as follows in the *Politics,* Book 3, Chapter 9: "It is difficult to believe this," that is, that the father will deprive his sons of the rulership, "as it would require a greater virtue than human nature is capable of."[107] For this reason it is more expedient for rulers [*47*] that they be regulated and limited by law, than that they make civil judgments according to their own discretion. For when they act according to law, they will do nothing vicious or reprehensible, so that their rule will be made more secure and longer lasting.

8. This was the counsel which the distinguished Aristotle gave to all rulers, but to which they pay little heed. As he said in the *Politics,* Book 5, Chapter 6: "The fewer things the rulers control," that is, without law, "the longer must every government endure, for they," that is, the rulers, "become less despotic, they are more moderate in their ways and are less hated by their subjects."[108] And then Aristotle adduces the testimony of a certain very prudent king called Theopompus, who gave up some of the power which had been granted to him. We have thought it appropriate to quote Aristotle's words here because of this ruler's uniqueness and his outstanding virtue, almost unheard of in anyone else throughout the ages. This is what Aristotle said: "Theopompus exercised moderation," that is, he lessened his power, which may perhaps have seemed excessive, "among other ways by establishing the office of the ephors: for by diminishing his power he increased his kingdom in time," that is, he made it more durable; "hence in a way he made it not smaller but greater. When his wife asked him whether he was not ashamed to give his children a smaller kingdom than he had received from his father, he replied, 'Not at all, for the power I give to them will be more lasting.'"[109] O heroic voice, proceeding from Theopompus' unheard-of prudence, a voice which should be heeded by all those who wish to wield plenitude of power over their subjects apart from laws! Many rulers, not heeding this voice, have been destroyed. And we ourselves have seen that from lack of attention to this voice not the least of kingdoms in modern times almost underwent a revolution, when its ruler wished to impose upon his subjects an unusual and illegal tax.[110] [*48*]

It is clear, then, from what we have said, that laws are necessary in polities if they are to be ordered with entire rightness and their governments are to be longer lasting.

Chapter 12. On the Demonstrable Efficient Cause of Human Laws, and Also on That Cause Which Cannot Be Proved by Demonstration: Which Is to Inquire into the Legislator. Whence It Appears Also That Whatever Is Established by Election Derives Its Authority from Election Alone apart from Any Other Confirmation

1. We must next discuss the efficient cause of the laws which is capable of demonstration. For I do not intend to deal here with that institution of laws which can be effected by the immediate act or oracle of God apart from the human will, or which has been so effected in the past. Such, we said, was the establishment of the Mosaic law.[111] But I shall not deal with it here even in so far as

107. Aristotle *Politics* 3.15 1286b26.

108. Ibid. 5.11 1313a20.

109. Ibid. 5.11 1313a26.

110. This is a reference to the leagues formed in France to protest against Philip the Fair's new taxation in 1314.

111. Cf. above, 1.9.2; also 1.6.3.

it contains commands with regard to civil acts for the status of the present world. I shall discuss the establishment of only those laws and governments which emerge immediately from the decision of the human mind.

2. Let us say, to begin with, that it can pertain to any citizen to discover the law taken materially and in its third sense, as the science of civil justice and benefit.[112] Such inquiry, however, can be carried on more appropriately and be completed better by those men who are able to have leisure, who are older and experienced in practical affairs, and who are called "prudent men," [*49*] than by the mechanics who must bend all their efforts to acquiring the necessities of life. But it must be remembered that the true knowledge or discovery of the just and the beneficial, and of their opposites, is not law taken in its last and most proper sense, whereby it is the measure of civil human acts, unless there is given a coercive command as to its observance, or it is made by way of such a command, by someone through whose authority its transgressors must and can be punished.[113] Hence, we must now say to whom belongs the authority to make such a command and to punish its transgressors. This, indeed, is to inquire into the legislator or the maker of the law.

3. Let us say, then, in accordance with the truth and the counsel of Aristotle in the *Politics,* Book 3, Chapter 6,[114] that the legislator, or the primary and proper efficient cause of the law, is the people or the whole body of citizens, or the weightier part thereof, through its choice or will expressed by words in the general assembly of the citizens, commanding or determining that something be done or omitted with regard to civil human acts, under a temporal pain or punishment. By the "weightier part" I mean to take into consideration the quantity and the quality of the persons in that community over which the law is made. The aforesaid whole body of citizens or the weightier part thereof is the legislator regardless of whether it makes the law directly by itself or entrusts the making of it to some person or persons, who are not and cannot be the legislator in the absolute sense, but only in a relative sense and for a particular time and in accordance with the authority of the primary legislator. And I say further that [*50*] the laws and anything else established through election must receive their necessary approval by that same primary authority and no other, whatever be the case with regard to certain ceremonies or solemnities, which are required not for the being of the matters elected but for their well-being, since the election would be no less valid even if these ceremonies were not performed. Moreover, by the same authority must the laws and other things established through election undergo addition, subtraction, complete change, interpretation, or suspension, in so far as the exigencies of time or place or other circumstances make any such action opportune for the common benefit. And by the same authority, also, must the laws be promulgated or proclaimed after their enactment, so that no citizen or alien who is delinquent in observing them may be excused because of ignorance.

4. A citizen I define in accordance with Aristotle in the *Politics,* Book 3, Chapters 1, 3, and 7, as one who participates in the civil community in the government or the deliberative or judicial function according to his rank.[115] By this definition, children, slaves, aliens, and women are distinguished from citizens, although in different ways. For the sons of citizens are citizens in proximate potentiality, lacking only in years. The weightier part of the citizens should be viewed in accordance with the honorable custom of polities, or else it should be determined in accordance with the doctrine of Aristotle in the *Politics,* Book 6, Chapter 2.[116]

5. Having thus defined the citizen and the weightier part of the citizens, let us return to our proposed objective, namely, to demonstrate that the human authority to make laws belongs only to the whole body of the citizens or to the weightier part thereof. First we shall try to prove that this is so. The absolutely primary human authority to make or establish human laws belongs only to those men from whom alone the best laws can emerge. But these are the whole body of the citizens, or the weightier part thereof, which represents that whole body; since it is difficult or impossible for all persons [*51*] to agree upon one decision, because some men have a deformed nature, disagreeing with the common decision through singular malice or ignorance. The common benefit should not, however, be impeded or neglected because of the unreasonable protest or opposition of these men. The authority to make or establish laws, therefore,

112. Cf. above, 1.10.3.

113. Cf. above, 1.10.4–5.

114. Aristotle *Politics* 3.11 1281a39 ff.

115. Ibid. 3.1 1275a22, 1275b19; 3.3 1277b33; 3.13 1283b42.

116. Ibid. 6.3–4 1318a3 ff.

belongs only to the whole body of the citizens or to the weightier part thereof.

The first proposition of this demonstration is very close to self-evident, although its force and its ultimate certainty can be grasped from Chapter 5 of this discourse. The second proposition, that the best law is made only through the hearing and command of the entire multitude, I prove by assuming with Aristotle in the *Politics,* Book 3, Chapter 7, that the best law is that which is made for the common benefit of the citizens. As Aristotle said: "That is presumably right," that is, in the laws, "which is for the common benefit of the city and the citizens."[117] But that this is best achieved only by the whole body of the citizens or by the weightier part thereof, which is assumed to be the same thing, I show as follows: That at which the entire body of the citizens aims intellectually and affectively is more certainly judged as to its truth and more diligently noted as to its common utility. For a defect in some proposed law can be better noted by the greater number than by any part thereof, since every whole, or at least every corporeal whole, is greater in mass and in virtue than any part of it taken separately. Moreover, the common utility of a law is better noted by the entire multitude, because no one knowingly harms himself.[118] Anyone can look to see whether a proposed law leans toward the benefit of one or a few persons more than of the others or of the community, and can protest against it. Such, however, would not be the case were the law made by one or a few persons, considering their own private benefit rather than that of the community. This position is also supported by the arguments which we advanced in Chapter 11 of this discourse with regard to the necessity of having laws.

6. Another argument to the principal conclusion is as follows. The authority to make the law belongs only to those men whose making of it will cause the law to be better observed or [52] observed at all. Only the whole body of the citizens are such men. To them, therefore, belongs the authority to make the law. The first proposition of this demonstration is very close to self-evident, for a law would be useless unless it were observed. Hence Aristotle said in the *Politics,* Book 4, Chapter 6: "Laws are not well ordered when they are well made but not obeyed."[119] He also said in Book 6, Chapter 5: "Nothing is accomplished by forming opinions about justice and not carrying them out."[120] The second proposition I prove as follows. That law is better observed by every citizen which each one seems to have imposed upon himself. But such is the law which is made through the hearing and command of the entire multitude of the citizens. The first proposition of this prosyllogism is almost self-evident; for since "the city is a community of free men," as is written in the *Politics,* Book 3, Chapter 4,[121] every citizen must be free, and not undergo another's despotism, that is, slavish dominion. But this would not be the case if one or a few of the citizens by their own authority made the law over the whole body of citizens. For those who thus made the law would be despots over the others, and hence such a law, however good it was, would be endured only with reluctance, or not at all, by the rest of the citizens, the more ample part. Having suffered contempt, they would protest against it, and not having been called upon to make it, they would not observe it. On the other hand, a law made by the hearing or consent of the whole multitude, even though it were less useful, would be readily observed and endured by everyone of the citizens, because then each would seem to have set the law upon himself, and hence would have no protest against it, but would rather tolerate it with equanimity. The second proposition of the first syllogism I also prove in another way, as follows. The power to cause the laws to be observed belongs only to those men to whom belongs coercive force over the transgressors of the laws. But these men are the whole body of citizens or the weightier part thereof. Therefore, to them alone belongs the authority to make the laws.

7. The principal conclusion is also proved as follows. That practical matter whose proper establishment is of greatest importance for the common sufficiency of the citizens in this life, and whose poor establishment [53] threatens harm for the community, must be established only by the whole body of the citizens. But such a matter is the law. Therefore, the establishment of the law pertains only to the whole body of the citizens. The major premise of this demonstration is almost self-evident, and is grounded in the immediate truths which were set forth in Chapters 4 and 5 of this discourse. For men came together to

117. Ibid. 3.13 1283b40.

118. Cf. 1.12.8.

119. Aristotle *Politics* 4.8 1294a3.

120. Ibid. 6.8 1322a5.

121. Ibid. 3.6 1279a21.

the civil community in order to attain what was beneficial for sufficiency of life, and to avoid the opposite. Those matters, therefore, which can affect the benefit and harm of all ought to be known and heard by all, in order that they may be able to attain the beneficial and to avoid the opposite. Such matters are the laws, as was assumed in the minor premise. For in the laws being rightly made consists a large part of the whole common sufficiency of men, while under bad laws there arise unbearable slavery, oppression, and misery of the citizens, the final result of which is that the polity is destroyed.

8. Again, and this is an abbreviation and summary of the previous demonstrations: The authority to make laws belongs only to the whole body of the citizens, as we have said, or else it belongs to one or a few men.[122] But it cannot belong to one man alone for the reasons given in Chapter 11 and in the first demonstration adduced in the present chapter; for through ignorance or malice or both, this one man could make a bad law, looking more to his own private benefit than to that of the community, so that the law would be tyrannical. For the same reason, the authority to make laws cannot belong to a few; for they too could sin, as above, in making the law for the benefit of a certain few and not for the common benefit, as can be seen in oligarchies. The authority to make the laws belongs, therefore, to the whole body of citizens or to the weightier part thereof, for precisely the opposite reason. For since all the citizens must be measured by the law according to due proportion, and no one knowingly harms or wishes injustice to himself, it follows that all or most wish a law conducing to the common benefit of the citizens.

9. From these same demonstrations it can also be proved, merely by changing the minor term, that the approval, interpretation, and suspension of the laws, and the other matters set forth in paragraph 3 of this same chapter, [*54*] pertain to the authority of the legislator alone. And the same must be thought of everything else which is established by election. For the authority to approve or disapprove rests with those who have the primary authority to elect, or with those to whom they have granted this authority of election. For otherwise, if the part could dissolve by its own authority what had been established by the whole, the part would be greater than the whole, or at least equal to it.

The method of coming together to make the laws will be described in the following chapter.

Chapter 13. On Some Objections to the Statements[123] Made in the Preceding Chapter, and Their Refutation, together with a Fuller Exposition of the Proposition

1. Objections will be made to our above statements, to the effect that the authority to make or establish laws does not belong to the whole body of the citizens. The first objection is that those who for the most part are vicious and undiscerning should not make the law. For these two sins, malice and ignorance, must be excluded from the legislator, and it was to avoid them in civil judgments that we upheld the necessity of law in Chapter 11 of this discourse. But the people or the whole body of citizens have these sins; for men for the most part seem to be vicious and stupid: *The number of the stupid is infinite* [Eccles. 1:15], as it is said in the first chapter of Ecclesiastes. Another objection is that it is very difficult or impossible to harmonize the views of many vicious and unintelligent persons; but such is not the case with the few and virtuous. It is more useful, therefore, that the law be made by the few than by the whole body of the citizens or the exceeding majority of them. Again, in every civil community the wise and learned are few in comparison with the multitude of the unlearned. Since, therefore, the law is more usefully made by the wise and learned than by the unlearned and uncultivated, it seems that the authority to make laws belongs to the few, not to the many or to all. Furthermore, that which can be done by fewer persons is needlessly done by more. Since, therefore, the law can be made by the wise, who are few, as has been said, the entire multitude or the greater part of it would needlessly be occupied therein. [*55*] The authority to make the laws does not belong, therefore, to the whole body of the citizens or to the weightier part thereof.

122. Reading, with Scholz, full stop after *pauciores.*

123. Reading, with Scholz, *ad dicta* for *addicta.*

2. From what we assumed above as the principle of all the things to be demonstrated in this book, namely, that all men desire sufficiency of life and avoid the opposite,[124] we demonstrated in Chapter 4 the civil association of men, inasmuch as through such association they can attain this sufficiency, and without it they cannot. Hence too Aristotle says in the *Politics,* Book 1, Chapter 1: "There is in all men a natural impulse toward such a community,"[125] that is, the civil community. From this truth there necessarily follows another, which is presented in the *Politics,* Book 4, Chapter 10, namely, that "that part of the city which wishes the polity to endure must be weightier than the part which does not wish it."[126] For the same specific nature according to the greater part of itself never desires a thing and immediately at the same time that thing's destruction, since such a desire would be futile. Indeed, those who do not wish the polity to endure are classed among the slaves, not among the citizens, as are certain aliens. Hence Aristotle says in the *Politics,* Book 7, Chapter 13: "Everyone in the country unites with the subjects in the desire to have a revolution," and then he adds: "It is impossible that there be so many persons in the government," that is, rebellious, or not caring to live a civil life, "that they are stronger than all the others,"[127] that is, than those who wish to carry on a political life (*politizare*). Why this is impossible is obvious; for it would mean that nature errs or is deficient for the most part. If, therefore, the weightier multitude of men wish the polity to endure, as seems to have been well said, they also wish that without which the polity cannot endure. But this is the standard of the just and the beneficial, handed down with a command, and called the law; for "it is impossible for the best-ruled city," that is, the city governed according to virtue, "not to be well ordered by laws," as is said in the *Politics,* Book 4, Chapter 7,[128] and as we demonstrated in Chapter 11 of this discourse. Therefore, the weightier multitude of the city wishes to have law, or else there would occur deformity in nature and art in most cases; the impossibility of which is assumed from natural science.[129] [*56*]

With these manifest truths I again assume that common conception of the mind, that "every whole is greater than its part," which is true with respect both to magnitude or mass and to practical virtue and action. From this it clearly follows of necessity that the whole body of the citizens, or the weightier multitude thereof, which must be taken for the same thing, can better discern what must be elected and what rejected than any part of it taken separately.

3. Now that we have laid down these obvious truths, it is easy to refute the objections whereby one might try to prove that the making of the law does not pertain to the whole body of the citizens or the weightier multitude thereof but rather to a certain few. As for the first objection, that the authority to make laws does not belong to those who in most cases are vicious and undiscerning, this is granted. But when it is added that the whole body of citizens is such, this must be denied. For most of the citizens are neither vicious nor undiscerning most of the time; all or most of them are of sound mind and reason and have a right desire for the polity and for the things necessary for it to endure, like laws and other statutes or customs, as was shown above. For although not every citizen nor the greater number of the citizens be discoverers of the laws, yet every citizen can judge of what has been discovered and proposed to him by someone else, and can discern what must be added, subtracted, or changed. Hence in the major premise's reference to the "undiscerning," if what is meant is that because most of the citizens cannot discover the law by themselves, therefore they ought not to establish the law, this must be denied as manifestly false, as is borne out by sense induction and by Aristotle in the *Politics,* Book 3, Chapter 6. By induction we can see that many men judge rightly about the quality of a picture, a house, a ship, and other works of art, even though they would have been unable to discover or produce them. Aristotle also attests to this in the place just cited, answering the proposed objection with these words: "About some things the man who made them is not the only or the best judge."[130] He proves this in many species of arts, and indicates that the same is true for all the others. [*57*]

4. Nor is this position invalidated by those who say that the wise, who are few, can discern what

124. Cf. above, 1.4.2.

125. Aristotle *Politics* 1.2 1253a29.

126. Ibid. 4.12 1296b14.

127. Ibid. 7.14 1332b29 ff.

128. Ibid. 4.8 1293b42.

129. Aristotle *Physics* 2.8 199a9 ff.; *Nicomachean Ethics* 1.9 1099b20–24.

130. Aristotle *Politics* 3.11 1282a17.

should be enacted with regard to practical matters better than can the rest of the multitude. For even if this be true, it still does not follow that the wise can discern what should be enacted better than can the whole multitude, in which the wise are included together with the less learned. For every whole is greater than its part both in action and in discernment. This was undoubtedly the view of Aristotle in the *Politics,* Book 3, Chapter 6, when he said: "The multitude is justly dominant in the more important matters," that is, the multitude or the whole body of citizens or the weightier part thereof, which he here signifies by the term "multitude," should justly be dominant with respect to the more important matters in the polity; and he gives this reason: "The people is composed of many persons including the council and the judiciary and the honorable class, and all of these together are more ample than any single person or group, including the few rulers who hold high governmental offices."[131] He means that the people, or the multitude composed of all the groups of the polity or city taken together, is more ample than any part of it taken separately, and consequently its judgment is more secure than that of any such part, whether that part be the common mass, which he here signified by the term "council" (*consilium*), such as the farmers, artisans, and others of that sort; or whether it be the "judiciary," that is, those officials who assist the ruler in judicial functions, as advocates or lawyers and notaries; or whether it be the "honorable class," that is, the group of the best men, who are few, and who alone are appropriately elected to the highest governmental offices; or whether it be any other part of the city taken separately. Moreover, even if we assume what is indeed true, that some of the less learned do not judge about a proposed law or some other practical matter as well as do the same number of the learned, still the number of the less learned could be increased to such an extent that they would judge about these matters as well as, or even better than, the few who are more learned. Aristotle stated this clearly in the place cited above when he undertook to confirm this view: "If the multitude be not too vile, each member of it will indeed be a worse judge than those who have knowledge; but taken all together they will be better judges, or at least not worse."[132]

As for the passage quoted from the first chapter of Ecclesiastes that the number of the stupid is infinite, [58] it must be replied that by "stupid" was meant those who are less learned or who do not have leisure for liberal functions, but who nevertheless share in the understanding and judgment of practical matters, although not equally with those who have leisure. Or perhaps the wise author, as Jerome says in his commentary thereon, meant by "stupid" the unbelievers who, however much they may know the worldly sciences, are stupid in an absolute sense, in keeping with the statement of the Apostle in the first epistle to the Corinthians: *The wisdom of this world is stupidity with God* [1 Cor. 3:19].

5. The second objection carries little weight, for even though it be easier to harmonize the views of fewer persons than of many, it does not follow that the views of the few, or of the part, are superior to those of the whole multitude, of which the few are a part. For the few would not discern or desire the common benefit as well as would the entire multitude of the citizens. Indeed, it would be insecure, as we have already shown, to entrust the making of the law to the discretion of the few. For they would perhaps consult therein their own private benefit, as individuals or as a group, rather than the common benefit, as is quite apparent in those who have made the decretals of the clergy, and as we shall make sufficiently clear in Chapter 28 of Discourse 2. By this means the way would be opened to oligarchy, just as when the power to make the laws is given to one man alone the opportunity is afforded for tyranny, as we showed above in Chapter 11, paragraph 4, where we quoted from the fourth book of Aristotle's *Ethics,* the treatise on justice.

6. The third objection can be easily refuted from what we have already said: for although the laws can be better made by the wise than by the less learned, it is not therefore to be concluded that they are better made by the wise alone than by the entire multitude of citizens, in which the wise are included. For the assembled multitude of all of these can discern and desire the common justice [59] and benefit to a greater extent than can any part of that multitude taken separately, however prudent that part may be.

7. Hence those do not speak the truth who hold that the less learned multitude impedes the choice

131. Ibid. 3.11 1282a38 ff.

132. Ibid. 3.11 1282a15.

and approval of the true or common good; rather, the multitude is of help in this function when it is joined to those who are more learned and more experienced. For although the multitude cannot by itself discover true and useful measures, it can nevertheless discern and judge the measures discovered and proposed to it by others, as to whether they should be added to, or subtracted from, or completely changed, or rejected. For many things which a man would have been unable to initiate or discover by himself, he can comprehend and bring to completion after they have been explained to him by someone else. For the beginnings of things are the most difficult to discover; as Aristotle says in the second book of the *Refutations,* last chapter: "Most difficult is it to see the beginning,"[133] that is, of the truth proper to each discipline. But when this has been discovered, it is easy to add the remainder or to extend it. Hence, while only the best and most acute minds can discover the principles of the sciences, the arts, and other disciplines, nevertheless when these principles have been discovered, additions can be made to them by men of humbler mind. Nor should the latter be called undiscerning because they cannot discover such principles by themselves; on the contrary, they should be numbered among good men, as Aristotle said in the *Ethics,* Book 1, Chapter 2: "That man is best who has achieved an understanding of all things by himself. But he too is good who hearkens to the wise words of another,"[134] that is, by listening to him attentively and not contradicting him without reason.

8. It is hence appropriate and highly useful that the whole body of citizens entrust to those who are prudent and experienced the investigation, discovery, and examination of the standards, the future laws or statutes, concerning civil justice and benefit, common difficulties or burdens, and other similar matters. Either some of these prudent and experienced men may be elected by each of the primary parts of the city enumerated in Chapter 5, paragraph 1, according to the proportion of each part; [*60*] or else all these men may be elected by all the citizens assembled together. And this will be an appropriate and useful method whereby to come together to discover the laws without detriment to the rest of the multitude, that is, the less learned, who would be of little help in the investigation of such standards, and would be disturbed in their performance of the other functions necessary both to themselves and to others, which would be burdensome both to each individual and to the community.

After such standards, the future laws, have been discovered and diligently examined, they must be laid before the assembled whole body of citizens for their approval or disapproval, so that if any citizen thinks that something should be added, subtracted, changed, or completely rejected, he can say so, since by this means the law will be more usefully ordained. For, as we have said, the less learned citizens can sometimes perceive something which must be corrected in a proposed law even though they could not have discovered the law itself. Also, the laws thus made by the hearing and consent of the entire multitude will be better observed, nor will anyone have any protest to make against them.

These standards, the future laws, will thus have been made public, and in the general assembly of the citizens those citizens will have been heard who have wanted to make some reasonable statements with regard to them. Then there must again be elected men of the qualities, and by the method, indicated above, or else the aforesaid men must be confirmed; and they, representing the position and authority of the whole body of the citizens, will approve or disapprove in whole or in part the aforementioned standards which had been investigated and proposed, or else, if it so wishes, the whole body of the citizens or the weightier part thereof will do this same thing by itself. After this approval, the aforesaid standards are laws and deserve to be so called, not before; and after their publication or proclamation, they alone among human commands make transgressors liable to civil guilt and punishment. [*61*]

We think we have adequately shown, then, that the authority to make or establish the laws, and to give a command with regard to their observance, belongs only to the whole body of the citizens or to the weightier part thereof as efficient cause, or else to the person or persons to whom the aforesaid whole body has granted this authority.

133. Aristotle *On Sophistical Refutations* 34 183b24.

134. Aristotle *Nicomachean Ethics* 1.2 1095b10, quoting Hesiod *Works and Days* 293.

DISCOURSE 2

Chapter 12. On the Differentiation of the Meanings of Certain Terms Necessary for the Determination of Questions concerning the Status of Supreme Poverty

3. We shall begin by distinguishing the meanings of "right" (*jus*), since we shall need these in the distinctions and definitions of the other terms, and not conversely. (i) "Right," then, in one of its senses means law taken [*214*] in the third and last sense of "law" (*lex*), which we discussed in Chapter 10 of Discourse 1.[135] This is twofold, one human, the other divine, and the latter at a particular time and in a particular way comes under the last meaning of law, as has been said above.[136] The nature and quality of these laws, how they agree and how they differ, have been sufficiently discussed in Chapters 8 and 9 of this discourse. But reconsidering them again in relation to our present purpose, let us say that these laws agree in this respect first of all, that each is a command or prohibition or permission of acts whose nature it is to emerge through the control of the human mind. But the laws differ in that the human is coercive in this world over those who transgress it, while the second, the divine, is not coercive in this world, but in the future world only. The word "command" also is used in two senses. In one sense it is used actively, referring to the act of the commander; it is in this sense that we say that the expressed will of a man who holds power, such as a king or other ruler, is a command. In another sense, "command" refers to what is willed by the act of the commander; in this sense we say that the servant has done the command of the master—not that the servant has done the master's act, which is to command or order, but that the servant has done what was willed by the master's act or command. And therefore, whenever this word "command" refers to the commander, it means the same as the act of commanding; whenever it refers to the subject, it means the same as what is willed by the act of commanding, and is then used passively.

This word "command," then, taken actively and in the general sense, means the legislator's ordinance or statute, both affirmative and negative, obliging the transgressor to punishment. But in modern usage it is properly taken for an affirmative statute. For usage has brought it about that an affirmative statute does not have a specific name of its own, but has kept the general name of "command"; but a negative statute does have a specific name of its own, for it is called a "prohibition."

I call an "affirmative statute" one which orders something to be done; a "negative statute," one which orders something not to be done. If such an ordinance, which obliges the transgressor to punishment, be affirmative, it is called a "command"; if it be negative, and also thus obliges, it is called a "prohibition." [*215*] Now "prohibition" is used in two senses, actively and passively, as is "command." These two ordinances, which oblige transgressors to punishment, are usually expressed in laws, either in their own proper species or in a similar or analogous one.[137] But in another and stricter sense, "command" and "prohibition" are used in divine law to refer only to that affirmative or negative statute which obliges the transgressor to eternal punishment. It is in this sense that these words are used by theologians when they say that commands are "necessary for salvation," that is, that observance of them is necessary, if one is to be saved. Whence in Luke, Chapter 18: *If thou wilt enter into life, keep the commandments,*[138] that is, the commands.

4. But there are certain other ordinances, both affirmative and negative, which are expressed or only implied in the laws, and which, whether referring to the same act or to a different one, do not oblige the man who does or omits the act to punishment. Very many acts are the objects of such ordinances, such as the performance or omission of an act of liberality. And it is such acts which are properly said to be "permitted by law," although this word "permission" is sometimes taken in a general sense to refer to statutes which oblige to punishment. For everything which the law commands to be done, it permits to be done, although not conversely; so too, what the law prohibits to be done, it permits not to be done. And again, of these permitted acts, taking "permitted" in its proper

135. Cf. above, 1.10.3–4.

136. Cf. 1.10.7.

137. That is, an act may be commanded (or prohibited) in a law that deals either specifically with that act or with acts similar thereto.

138. While the reference is to Luke 18:18, the passage cited is really Matt. 19:17.

sense as that which does not oblige to punishment, some are meritorious according to divine law and are called "counsels," while others which are not thus meritorious are given the unqualified name of "permissions." And these terms, thus taken in their proper sense, are again used in two ways, actively and passively, as are prohibitions and commands. But these for the most part are not given specific expression in the laws, particularly in human laws, because their number is so large and a general ordinance concerning them is sufficient. For everything which is not commanded or prohibited by the law is understood to be permitted by the ordinance of the legislator. A "command" in accordance with the law, then, in its proper sense is an affirmative statute obliging its transgressor to punishment; a "prohibition" in its proper sense [*216*] is a negative statute obliging its transgressor to punishment; a "permission" in its proper sense is an ordinance of the legislator obliging no one to punishment. We shall henceforth use these terms in these proper senses.

5. From the above, it can readily be seen what is meant by the term "lawful"; for everything which is done in accordance with the command or permission of the law, or which is omitted in accordance with the prohibition or permission of the law, is lawfully done or omitted, and can be called "lawful," while its opposite or contrary is "unlawful."

6. From the above, we can also see what is usually meant by the term "equitable" (*fas*). For in one sense the equitable is the same as the lawful, so that the two are used convertibly. In another sense, the equitable is that which the legislator is reasonably presumed to have permitted in some case, although such an act is generally or regularly prohibited; as, for example, it is equitable to pass through another's field sometimes, or to take what belongs to another without the owner's express consent, although it is not "right" taken regularly in any of the senses given above. For the taking of another's property is regularly prohibited; yet it is equitable in the case where the owner is reasonably presumed to give his consent, even though he does not expressly give it; for which reason there is sometimes need of equity (*epieikeia*) in such cases.[139] Thus, then, in one sense right is the same as law, divine or human, or what is commanded or prohibited or permitted according to these laws.

7. There is also another division of right, and properly of human right, into natural and civil. Natural right (*jus naturale*), according to Aristotle in the fourth book of the *Ethics,* the treatise on justice, is that statute of the legislator with respect to which almost all men agree that it is honorable and should be observed.[140] Examples are that God must be worshiped, parents must be honored, children must be reared by their parents up to a certain age, no one should be injured, injuries must be lawfully repulsed, and the like. Although these depend upon human enactment, they are analogously (*transumptive*) called "natural" rights [*217*] because in all regions they are in the same way believed to be lawful and their opposites unlawful, just as the acts of natural things which are devoid of will are everywhere uniform, like fire, which "burns here just as it does in Persia."[141]

8. However, there are some men who define natural right as the dictate of right reason in practical matters, which they place under divine right; and consequently everything done in accordance with divine law and in accordance with the counsel of right reason is lawful in an absolute sense; but not everything done in accordance with human laws, since in some things the latter fall away from right reason. But the word "natural" is used equivocally here and above. For there are many things which are in accordance with the dictate of right reason, but which are not agreed upon as honorable by all nations, namely, those things which are not self-evident to all, and consequently not acknowledged by all. So too there are some commands, prohibitions, or permissions in accordance with divine law which do not agree in this respect with human law; but since many cases of this are well known, I have omitted to cite examples for the sake of brevity.

9. And hence too, some things are lawful according to human law which are not lawful according to divine law, and conversely. However, what is lawful and what unlawful in an absolute sense must be viewed according to divine law rather than human law, when these disagree in their commands, prohibitions, or permissions.

10. (ii) "Right" is used in a second sense to refer to every controlled human act, power, or acquired habit, internal or external, both immanent and transitive or crossing over into some external thing or something pertaining thereto, like its use

139. Cf. above, 1.14.7. Also Aristotle *Nicomachean Ethics* 5.10 1137a32 ff.

140. See Aristotle *Nicomachean Ethics* 5.7 1134b19.

141. Aristotle *Nicomachean Ethics* 5.7 1134b25.

or usufruct, acquisition, holding, saving, or exchanging, and so on, whenever these are in conformity with right taken in its first sense. What the use or usufruct of a thing is, together with the other lawful or rightful ways of handling things, we shall assume for the present from the science of civil acts. [*218*]

It is in this sense that we usually say: "This is someone's right," when he wishes or handles something in a manner which is in conformity with right taken in the first sense. Hence, such wish or handling is called right because it conforms to the command, prohibition, or permission of right; just as a column is called right (*dextra*) or left because it is situated nearer to the right or the left side of an animal. Right, then, taken in this second sense, is none other than what is willed by the active command, prohibition, or permission of the legislator, and this is what we called above the passive meaning of these three words.[142] And this too is what we previously called lawful.[143]

11. (iii) In another sense this term "right" means the sentence or judgments made by judges in accordance with the law or with right taken in its first sense. It is in this sense that men usually say: "The judge or ruler has done or rendered right to someone," when he has convicted or acquitted someone by a legal sentence.

12. (iv) "Right" is also used to refer to an act or habit of particular justice; in this sense we say that he wishes right or justice who wishes what is equal or proportional in exchanges or distributions.

142. Cf. above, para. 3.

143. Cf. above, para. 5.

TWENTY-NINE

WILLIAM OF OCKHAM

The Dialogue

Translated by John Kilcullen

Of the early life and education of William of Ockham (ca. 1288–1347) nothing certain is known. Having been brought to the Franciscan order in his youth, he likely began his education in logic and philosophy at the Franciscan convent in London. In 1317 Ockham began lecturing in Oxford on the *Sentences* of Peter Lombard; in 1321 he probably returned to the London convent as a lecturer, remaining there until 1324. During this period he composed numerous works, including the *Summa Logicae;* commentaries on Aristotle's *Categories, On Interpretation, Sophistical Refutations,* and *Physics;* and the *Treatise on Predestination and God's Foreknowledge with Respect to Future Contingents.* Although he apparently fulfilled the requirements for the degree of master of theology, he neither received the degree nor occupied a chair of theology at a university. His reputation as a dialectician, his vigorous criticism of his contemporaries (especially Duns Scotus), and the real or apparent novelty of his opinions seem to have aroused considerable antagonism. In 1323 he was asked to explain to a provincial chapter of his order statements he had made that were characteristic of what was later called his "nominalism." In the same year he was accused at the papal court in Avignon of heretical teachings, by someone from England, possibly John Lutterell, a former chancellor of the University of Oxford and himself a controversial figure. Ockham arrived in Avignon in 1324, where a commission was appointed to examine his *Commentary on the Sentences.* None of the doctrines censured by the commission, however, were ever formally condemned. In the same period, the pope had been quarreling with the superior general of the Franciscan order, Michael of Cesena, over the Franciscan practice of apostolic poverty (could it be maintained that the order *as a whole* renounced all possessions?), and in 1327 Cesena was present in Avignon. The year 1328 appears to have been the crucial turning point in Ockham's life. Having been asked by a superior, presumably Cesena, to investigate the question regarding poverty, Ockham (according to a later autobiographical comment) determined that John XXII was a heretic and therefore no longer pope. Cesena, Ockham, and two other Franciscan friars left Avignon under cover of night and journeyed to Pisa, where they joined the emperor, Ludwig of Bavaria, after he had been compelled to withdraw from Rome. Together they withdrew to Munich, where Ockham became one of the intellectual leaders in the struggle of the emperor against the "Church of Avignon," as he called it. Ockham was excommunicated on the grounds that he had left Avignon without permission. Remaining in

Munich until his death, he produced an enormous corpus of writings, which, prompted by the political and ecclesiastical crises, explored property rights, ecclesiology, and the papal and imperial powers. After Ludwig's death in 1347, the friars in Munich who had supported Michael sought reconciliation with the pope and with their order. As their formal submission included a "William of England," it had previously been thought that Ockham too had sought reconciliation. It has since been shown, however, that the "William" of the letter is not Ockham, and that Ockham died in 1347.[1]

The *Dialogue* (*Dialogus de Potestate Papae et Imperatoris*) was conceived as a comprehensive work in which Ockham proposed to include all his major ideas on political matters and, more particularly, on the errors of the papacy and its rights with respect to those of the empire. In the *Dialogue* a student asks questions, and a master recites answers. The work is divided into three parts. Part 1 (1333–1334), the only one to have come down to us in its totality, treats the nature of heresy; the relationship of theology and canon law; papal, conciliar, and ecclesiastical infallibility; the procedure to be followed when a pope falls into heresy; and the punishment of heretics and their accomplices. Part 2 seems to have been planned, but never written (in some manuscripts two pamphlets are inserted in its place). Part 3 (ca. 1338–1346) was intended to have nine tracts, of which we have two, on the power of the pope and the clergy, and on the rights of the Roman Empire. The first tract investigates what sort of "fullness of power" belongs to the papacy (Book 1), whether it is beneficial for the pope to rule the community of the faithful in a kingly fashion (Book 2), whether the pope holds this authority by an ordinance of Christ (Book 4), and what writings must be believed in to answer the prior question (Book 3). Seven chapters of Book 2 are given here in order to exhibit Ockham's employment of Aristotle's accounts of kingship and aristocracy, and the relationship of papal rule to natural justice and positive law.

As the dialectical structure of Book 2 of the first tract is complex, we will briefly sketch the context of the seven chapters reproduced here (6, 9, 13, 17, 20, 24, and 27). Chapters 1 and 2 argue *for* and *against,* respectively, the statement that it is beneficial for the community of the faithful to be ruled by one leader, the supreme pontiff, rather than by several. The arguments *against* are answered in Chapters 18 and 19; the arguments *for* are answered at the end of Book 2, in Chapter 30. According to the first chapter, "it is beneficial for the community of the faithful to be governed in matters relating to the Christian religion under the form of government that most resembles the best secular constitution," which is kingship, "as Aristotle testifies." Between these scattered elements of the overarching dialectical inquiry we find three major digressions pertaining to Aristotle's thought: first, a review of Aristotle's political terms (Chapters 3–8; Chapter 6 on kingship is reproduced here); second, an exploration of whether Aristotle's account of kingship should be applied to the papacy (Chapters 9–17, of which 9, 13, and 17 are reproduced here); third, a discussion of whether it would be just for the church to change regimes from kingship to aristocracy (Chapters 20–27, of which 20, 24, and 27 are reproduced here). It is worth noting that, since the last chapter (30) responds to arguments in the first chapter, the initial statement in favor of kingship within the church (quoted above) is denied at the close of Book 2: "Although kingship is the best constitution in one city, according to Aristotle (who speaks only of constitutions that are observed in cities...), kingship is nevertheless not the best constitution for the whole world or for every part of the world, because the whole world and various kingdoms are better ruled by several, none of whom is superior to another, than by one man alone, for the reasons touched on above."

The second tract of Part 3 shifts focus from the church to the empire. This tract discusses the source of imperial authority and the possibility of its being transferred or terminated, especially by the pope (Book 1); the powers of the emperor over secular persons and things, as distinguished from the pope's power (Book 2); and the powers of the emperor over spiritual persons, especially as regards the election of the pope (Book 3). Book 3, Chapter 6, reproduced here, explicates the several modes of natural law.

In the remaining tracts of Part 3, which were either lost or never written, Ockham had planned to give a historical account of the deeds of John XXII, Ludwig of Bavaria, Benedict XII, Michael of

1. Gedeon Gál, "William of Ockham Died 'Impenitent' in April 1347," *Franciscan Studies* 42 (1982): 90–95.

Cesena, and other figures involved in the controversy in which he himself had taken a prominent part. The vast dimensions of the *Dialogue*, coupled with the fact that the author often sets forth contradictory opinions without openly siding with any one of them, renders an analysis of Ockham's thought particularly difficult. In the prologue to Part 1 the student asks the master not to reveal his own opinions or even his name, first, so that the student may form his own opinions and, second, so that both friends and enemies of the master do not have their reason obstructed by their passions. The student avows himself an eager supporter of the papacy but evinces doubts about the master's position. While Ockham, like Marsilius, was strongly opposed to the indefinite extension of papal powers by earlier or contemporary theologians and canonists, Ockham's criticisms are grounded in a different understanding of the nature and character of political and ecclesiastical associations, and he appears not to have shared the radicalism of Marsilius as regards the powers of the papacy. His *Dialogue* nevertheless supplied the adversaries of the papacy with a wide variety of arguments in favor of their positions. His theological doctrines also prepared the way for Luther and other Reformers. Subsequent thinkers strongly influenced by Ockham or associated with his thought include John Buridan, Peter d'Ailly, and John Gerson.

The selected chapters from the *Dialogue* have been taken from the translation of John Kilcullen, in *A Letter to the Friars Minor and Other Writings*, ed. Arthur Stephen McGrade and John Kilcullen (Cambridge: Cambridge University Press, 1995). The translation was made from the Goldast edition (Melchior Goldast, *Monarchia Sancti Romani Imperii* [Frankfurt, 1614; photographic reprint, Graz, 1960]), although very many variants were adopted by the translator on the basis of a study of the manuscripts.[2] A critical edition of the entire *Dialogue* is being jointly developed by John Kilcullen, George Knysh, Volker Leppin, John Scott, and Jan Ballweg under the auspices of the British Academy.[3] The translation given here has been very slightly modified to conform to the edition being developed online; footnotes have also been added or modified in order to remedy the defects inherent in a partial presentation of Ockham's argument.

PART THREE, TRACT ONE

Book Two, Chapter Six

MASTER: There are two primary kinds of constitutions, just as there are two primary kinds of governments or prelacies and of rulers or prelates or rectors. Every government is either ordered chiefly to the common good or benefit (i.e. the good of the ruler or rulers and also of the subjects) or not ordered to the common good. If it is ordered to the common good the regime is tempered and right; if it is not ordered to the common good the regime is defective and perverted, because it is a corruption and perversion of a regime that is tempered and right and just. Every constitution, therefore, is either tempered and right, or defective and perverted.

There are three principal and unmixed kinds of tempered and right constitutions. The first is when the ruler is one person; this is called royal monarchy, in which one alone rules for the sake of the common good, and not principally on account of his own will and benefit. According to Aristotle, *Ethics*, Book 8, such a constitution is the best, when it takes its best form. It has several forms, according to Aristotle, *Politics*, Book 3, chapter 16.[4] Its most powerful form seems to be when someone reigns and rules in the kingdom not according to law but according to his will. Some understand this as follows. Someone is said to rule and reign according to his will and not according to law if he reigns for the common good of all and is not bound by any purely positive human laws or customs but is above all such laws, though he is bound by the natural laws. And therefore such a king does not have to swear or even promise that

2. Significant corrections to the Goldast edition, with regard to Part 3, Tract 2, Book 3, Chapter 6 (the text used for the translation appearing in the first edition of the *Sourcebook*), were proposed by H. S. Offler, "The Three Modes of Natural Law in Ockham: A Revision of the Text," *Franciscan Studies* 37 (1977): 207–18.

3. http://www.britac.ac.uk/pubs/dialogus.

4. Aristotle *Nicomachean Ethics* 8.10 1160a35–36; *Politics* 3.16 1285a1.

he will observe any laws or customs whatever introduced by human beings, though it is beneficial for him to swear that he will observe the natural laws for the common benefit and that in all things relating to the government he has undertaken he will aim at the common good, not at private good. Such a king can be said to have fullness of power, namely in respect of things relating to the common good and not private good. Such government differs from tyrannical rule because it exists for the common good, whereas tyrannical rule does not exist for the common good. It differs also from despotic rule because despotic rule is chiefly for the ruler's own good, in the same way as lordship over beasts and other temporal things is for the good of the possessor, whereas royal government is for the common good; and therefore it is not properly called despotic rule. Yet such a king is, in a way, the lord over all, but in another way than in a despotic regime. For in a despotic regime the ruler also has so great a lordship that he can use his slaves and any other property whatever that belongs to his rulership of this kind not only for the sake of the common good but also for his own good, as long as he attempts nothing contrary to the divine or natural law; but the ruler in the royal government mentioned above can use subjects and their property however he pleases for the common good but cannot use them however he pleases for his own good, and they are therefore not his slaves but enjoy natural liberty. It belongs to natural liberty that no one can use free persons for the user's advantage, but it is not contrary to natural liberty that someone should use free persons reasonably for the sake of the common good, since everyone is obliged to prefer common to private good.

STUDENT: According to these [ideas] a despotic rulership would be greater and more perfect than such a royal rulership, since it would include greater power. For one who rules despotically can use slaves and their goods for both common and private advantage and a king only for the common advantage; therefore it is greater and more perfect.

MASTER: It is answered that despotic rule is in a way greater, because in a way it extends to more things; but by this very fact it is more imperfect, either because the good of many is better than the good of one or because detriment to the good of many implies no perfection, but rather imperfection. In despotic rule there is detriment to the many from the very fact that the despot can use his subjects and their goods for his own advantage, and therefore such greater power includes the imperfection of a better good, namely of the good of the many. Accordingly despotic rule—not only of a father in a household, but of a king in a kingdom, and consequently of an emperor in the whole world—would be simply more imperfect than such royal rule.

Besides that royal rule there are other royal rulerships that fall short of it in various ways but agree in being kinds of monarchy. For a certain rulership of one monarch falls short of that one in respect of *aiming at the common good,* namely because it was not established wholly on account of the common good but also for the ruler's own good. Such royal government has something of tyrannical or despotical rule and is in some way a mixture of despotic, tyrannical, and royal rule. For inasmuch as in certain respects it aims at the ruler's own good and not the common good it has something of tyranny or despotic rule, but inasmuch as in many things it aims at the common good it has something of tempered and right government—and therefore, since one man rules by himself, it has something of royal government; and therefore it is in a way a mixture of those kinds of rule. And thus some royal rule is called tyrannical by Aristotle. And rule by one man sometimes falls short of the oft-mentioned royal government in respect of *power,* namely because it does not have the fullness of power that the above-mentioned royal government has. Such royal government is said to be "according to law," because, although one man rules, he does not rule according to his will but is bound by certain laws and customs introduced by human beings, which he is obliged to observe, and he is obliged to swear or promise that he will observe them; and the more he is obliged to observe many such laws and customs the more he recedes from the above-mentioned royal government—perhaps these days such royal government does not exist in the whole world.

According to Aristotle no one is worthy of such a kingship unless he excels in wisdom and virtue and all good things both of body and soul, and also in external goods, namely in friends and wealth. Otherwise it is to be feared that he may turn to tyranny. And thus he should have his own property, either from himself or by an allocation made by those he is over, so that he will never appropriate to himself the property of free persons or even accept it in any way, unless evident benefit or manifest necessity demands it.

Chapter Nine

STUDENT: You have explained, I think, according to the opinion of the some, the meanings of the foreign terms that occur more often in the texts of Aristotle quoted and to be quoted, so do not explain any further, but go back to the main inquiry. Bestir yourself and describe how the arguments advanced above in the first and second chapters of this second book in favor of the various conflicting opinions can be answered in accordance with those opinions. But before you relate answers to them, I ask you to bring forward some arguments to prove that it is more beneficial to the whole community of the faithful to be ruled by one than by many.

MASTER: This seems provable as follows...[5] It is more beneficial for the community of the faithful to be ruled by the government that is more like natural government and rule; for just as art, if it is right, imitates nature, so rule, if it is right, imitates and is like natural rule (*principatus*); and consequently the rule that is more like natural rule is more right and more perfect, and consequently more beneficial. But the government or rule of one person, namely when one alone governs many and presides over them, is more like natural rule than the government or rule of many. For such a government is like royal rule, which is rule of one, and royal rule is more like natural rule than aristocratic rule or "constitutional" (*politicus*) rule in the narrow sense, and it is more like the household, in which one head of household rules; and thus the rule of the head of the household seems in a way to be royal, as Aristotle testifies. In *Politics,* Book 1, chapter 10, he says that the head of the household rules the offspring royally, and in the same chapter he says, "Rule over the children is royal, for because he begot them he ruled by virtue of both love and age, which is indeed a royal kind of rule."[6] From these words we gather that royal government is like the household community, in which one rules and not many (either in the first way or in the second). And the household community is natural, according to Aristotle. In *Politics,* Book 1, in the prologue, he says, "The household, therefore, is the community established according to nature for everyday life."[7] These words establish that the household community is in accordance with nature and natural. Royal government, therefore, is more like natural government than aristocracy and "constitution" in the narrow sense, and consequently the government that is more like royal, namely that in which one rules and not many, is more like natural government, and consequently more perfect and better and more beneficial. From this it follows that it is more beneficial for the community of the faithful to be ruled by one than by many, even in the second way.

STUDENT: It seems that the argument is not conclusive, because royal government does not more resemble the household community than does constitutional government in which many rule. According to Aristotle, *Politics,* Book 1, chapters 2 and 10, the household community, which is the "economic" community, has three parts, of which one is despotic, another marital, and the third paternal;[8] and therefore there are in the household three rulerships of different kinds, namely despotic, by which the head of the household rules the slaves, constitutional, by which the head of the household rules the wife, and royal, by which the head of the household rules the children or offspring. Aristotle says: "There were three parts of the economic, one indeed despotic, which we have spoken of above, and one paternal, and the third marital. For he also rules over the wife and offspring as free persons; but he does not rule both in the same way, but the wife 'constitutionally' and the offspring royally." From these words we gather the things that have been said, and it follows that royal government is not more similar than "constitutional" government is to the household community, because just as royal government is like one part, so is "constitutional" government like the other part. Therefore, it seems, royal government is not more like natural government than is "constitutional" government, since the rule by which the head of the household rules his wife in the household, which "constitutional" government resembles, is natural, just as the rule is by which he rules the offspring, which royal government resembles. As

5. One speech each of the master and student has been omitted here; these speeches define two ways in which several persons may rule: separately over separate entities (referred to as the "first way" and pursued in chapter 28), or jointly over a single entity (the "second" way, discussed here).

6. *Politics* 1.12 1259b1, 1259b10–12.

7. Ibid. 1.1 1252b12–14.

8. Ibid. 1.2 1253b7; 1.10 1259a37. The following quotations are taken from *Politics* 1.10 1259a37–b4.

Aristotle testifies in the same chapter, "*By nature* the male is more ruler-like than the female, unless there is something out of the ordinary course of nature, and the elder and fully developed is"—is, namely, more ruler-like—"than the younger and less developed." This implies that the male naturally rules the wife and the father the offspring. Aristotle plainly says this of the male in respect of the wife in *Politics,* Book 1, chapter 3: "And again, the male and the female, the one is *by nature* better and the other worse, the one ruling and the other ruled."[9] These [passages] imply that from the fact that royal government is like natural government it cannot be proved that it is better and more perfect than aristocratic government and "constitutional" government in the narrow sense.

MASTER: Some try to avoid that answer, saying that although both royal and "constitutional" government, and also aristocratic and indeed every right rule, is similar in some way to natural government, royal government is, nevertheless, more like the more perfect and better natural government than is "constitutional" government in the narrow sense. For the rule of the head of a household over the offspring is more rule-like, and more perfect and better, than the rule by which he rules his wife: First, because rule over children is better than rule over a wife, for among the children there are males, who are better than females, as has been proved above from Aristotle, and the rule of better subjects is always better, according to Aristotle, *Politics,* Book 1, chapter 3.[10] Also, because the rule by which the head of household rules his wife is for the sake of the rule by which he rules his offspring, for a wife should be married mainly for having children. Also, because the father naturally loves his children more than his wife, because they are joined to him by natural conjunction and more perfectly than is his wife. And thus in the community of the household the most rule-like and most suitable and most natural rule is that by which the head of the household rules the offspring, and royal government resembles this; royal government is therefore more perfect than the other rulerships in the community of the household.

Further, royal government is more like the natural rule by which the head of the household rules his offspring than "constitutional" rule is like the rule by which the head of the household rules his wife. Royal rule is like paternal rule both as to the unity of the ruler and as to fullness of power, because in each regime there is one ruler with fullness of power over his subjects. But although "constitutional" government is like the rule by which the head of the household rules his wife in that neither ruler has fullness of power, they differ in that the ruler in "constitutional" government is not one but many, where in the natural rule by which the head of a household rules his wife the ruler is one, whether he has several wives or one. And so royal government is more like natural government than is the rule of the head of a household over his wife. From this it follows that it is more beneficial for the community of the faithful to be ruled by one than by many.

Chapter Thirteen

STUDENT: If any other arguments occur to you to prove that no one should be over all the faithful unless he surpasses all in wisdom and virtue, bring them forward.

MASTER: This is again proved as follows. No less wisdom or virtue is needed in one who rules the whole congregation of the faithful in spiritual matters than in a king who presides over his subjects in temporal matters, as Aristotle seems to maintain in *Politics,* Book 7, chapter 13. According to him (in the same place) it is not just for some to rule always (as kings do, and also highest pontiffs) and others always to be subject unless they differ from their subjects as much as gods and heroes differ from men. (Gods and heroes, according to him, simply excel all men.) He says this: "If, therefore, some men differed from others as much as we think gods and heroes differ from men, having simply great superiority, first of body and then of soul, so that the superiority of the rulers in respect of their subjects were undoubted and manifest, it is clear that it would be better for those to rule always for life," etc.[11] For what is more excellent and

9. *Politics* 1.5 1254b12.
10. Ibid. 1.5 1254a25–6.
11. Ibid. 7.14 1332b16–22.

more perfect, while it remains such, is fit to rule whatever lacks such great excellence. When, however, men are not found who differ from others as gods and heroes differ from men, then it is not just that some of the them should rule the others for the whole of their lives, but it is just that all should in some way share in the rulership, namely so that all of those who are equals in wisdom and virtue should rule by turns, first some and then others, as Aristotle in the same place seems to maintain. He says, "But since this is not easily found, and there are no kings (as Scylax says there are in India) who differ so much from their subjects, it is manifest that for many reasons all must share, and must rule and be subject in turn"—namely, so that no one should rule through the whole period of his life, but instead they should sometimes rule and sometimes be subject.[12] He gives a reason for this, saying, "For fairness is: the same for similars." From these words the following argument is drawn. It is unjust that someone should always rule his equals and similars; therefore, when some are similar, it is unjust that some of them should always rule and others always be subject. Therefore it follows that, if among the faithful there are many who are like one another in wisdom and virtue, it is unjust that one of them should rule always, for the whole time of his life, and the others always be subject. Therefore, since the pope should be over all the faithful for the whole time of his life, it is unjust that someone should be made pope if others are found like him in wisdom and virtue. It is therefore unjust that someone should be made pope unless he surpasses all the faithful in wisdom and virtue.

Further, papal government is more perfect than royal government, as Gregory Nazienzen testifies. As we read in dist. 10, c. *Suscipitis,* he says, writing to the emperors of Constantinople, "He also gave power to us; he gave a rulership much more perfect than your rulerships."[13] But no one is worthy of royal rulership unless he surpasses others in wisdom and virtue, in fact in all good things, as Aristotle seems to assert in *Ethics,* Book 8, quoted above in chapter 2 of this second book.[14] This is also proved from the fact that "kingship is established in accordance with aristocracy," according to Aristotle, *Politics,* Book 5, chapter 8.[15] But in aristocracy those rule who are better than the rest, according to Aristotle, *Politics,* Book 4, chapter 5.[16] Therefore in a kingdom, also, no one should rule royally unless he surpasses the rest. And thus when God first appointed a king over his people, he chose the best man of the whole people, as Samuel testifies. In 1 Kings 10 he said of him, i.e., Saul, as he was at the time, "Surely you see him whom the Lord has chosen, that there is none like him among all the people" [1 Samuel 10:24]. Therefore, *a fortiori,* no one is worthy of papal rulership unless he excels all in wisdom and virtue. Therefore when there is not found anyone whose excellence is without doubt and manifestly so great (since the excellence of rulers should be undoubted and manifest, according to Aristotle, as was said above in the first chapter[17]), then no one should be chosen as highest pontiff, but instead several should be appointed who are more excellent than others, who should rule all others aristocratically or "constitutionally."

Chapter Seventeen

STUDENT: Say now how the arguments brought forward above in chapter 13 are answered.

MASTER: They are all based, it seems, on the premise that no one is worthy of royal rulership unless he surpasses all others in wisdom and virtue, as Aristotle seems to think in the *Politics* and also in the *Ethics,* so that no one should be king unless he is the best, and better in wisdom and virtue than all his subjects. To which it is said that this is not,

12. Ibid. 7.14 1332b23–27; the following quotation is from the same passage.

13. Gratian *Decretum* dist. 10, c. 6, col. 20 (the column number refers to *Corpus iuris canonici,* vol. 1, ed. A. Friedberg [Leipzig, 1879; Graz, 1955]); for an English translation, see Gratian, *The Treatise on Laws: Decretum* DD. 1–20, trans. A. Thompson and J. Gordley (Washington, DC: The Catholic University of America Press, 1993), 35. In the 1140s Gratian set in order diverse church canons; this arrangement (formally entitled *Concordia Discordantium Canonum*) formed the basis of canon law. Note that the Friedberg edition does not include the glosses on either work; readers wishing to locate passages of the glosses should consult the appendix to *A Letter to the Friars Minor,* ed. A. S. McGrade and J. Kilcullen.

14. Cf. 3.1 *Dialogue* 1.2, where Ockham cites *Nicomachean Ethics* 8.10 1160b3.

15. *Politics* 5.10 1310b33.

16. Ibid. 4.7 1293b3–5.

17. Not in the first chapter, but in the beginning of this chapter.

according to Aristotle, true universally, without any exception. To make this clear, it is said, it must be known that royal rulership can be obtained in many ways, of which it is enough for the present to enumerate two. One of these is when someone is voluntarily made king by subjects. The other is when someone voluntarily transfers himself from a despotic rule that he has justly obtained to a royal rule. If someone should (as a rule) be appointed to royal government in the first way, then the best man in wisdom and virtue should be appointed, if such a one is found and no just impediment impedes his advancement. If a family is found that in this way excels all others, then (as a rule) it is just that this family should reign. This is what Aristotle means in *Politics,* Book 3, chapter 16, when he says, "When, therefore, it happens that either a whole family or one individual differs in virtue so much that his virtue exceeds that of all others, then it is just that this family should be royal and rule over all, and this one man be king, as was said above."[18] If, however, [such a family or man] is not found, yet many good men are found, then one of them should be appointed, and the others similar and equal to him in wisdom and virtue are obliged to bear his government patiently and willingly for the common good. How he should be appointed you can inquire afterwards, if you like.

If, however, someone comes to royal rulership in the second way (for example, because he first held lordship of the whole region and of all those living there, whether by occupation, by gift, by purchase, by just war, or in any other just way, and afterwards, renouncing despotic rule, is content with royal rulership only—that is, so that he chiefly wishes to rule his subjects for their good and advantage and not, as a despot rules, for his own good), he can justly take possession of a royal rulership even if he is not the best of men, because from the fact that he is giving up part of his right and keeping a part he should not be regarded as unjust, even if he is not the best man.

And Aristotle's suggestion in *Politics,* Book 7, chapter 13, that it is not just for some always to rule unless they differ as much from their subjects as gods and heroes differ from men, is answered in many ways. In one way, that this is true if account is taken only of the merit and worth of the ruler, but not if account is taken of advantage to the common good.

In another way it is said that this is true of natural justice in particular, i.e. that it is not natural justice that they should rule over all others unless they differ in such a way from all the others whom they rule; in this way it is just that the husband should rule over his wife or wives, a father over his children, and the lord over slaves that are naturally slaves, according to Aristotle, *Politics,* Book 1. But it is not true of positive justice. For since it is often just (and natural) that someone should be lord over many who are similar and equal to himself in a perfect community (because those who are similar and equal in virtue are so many that they cannot usefully all rule together, and yet such a community cannot stand without a ruler, according to Aristotle), and yet it is not natural justice that these should rule rather than those, it must therefore be determined by positive justice that these should rule, either simply for the whole of their life or for a time; and thus, though, as Aristotle thinks, it is not natural justice that this man should rule for his whole life those who are his similars and equals, nevertheless it can become, for a reason, positive justice. Aristotle did not intend to deny this.

STUDENT: How can it be natural justice that someone should rule those who are similar to himself, and yet not natural justice that *this* man should rule those who are similar to himself, and not natural justice that *this* [other] man should rule those who are similar to himself, and so on of each man?

MASTER: It is answered that your question arises from an ignorance of elementary matters (namely, of logic) which no one working in any science whatever should fail to know, for otherwise he will argue sophistically when he thinks he is arguing demonstratively. It is said, therefore, that just as, often, both the universal and the particular [proposition] are necessary though each of their singulars is contingent,[19] so it is possible that the

18. *Politics* 3.17 1288a15–20.

19. In Aristotle's terminology (which Ockham says may be improper: *Summa Logicae,* ed. P. Boehner, G. Gál, and S. Brown [St. Bonaventure, NY: St. Bonaventure University, 1974], II, 9.47–66, pp. 274–75; or *Ockham's Theory of Propositions: Part II of the Summa Logicae,* trans. A. J. Freddoso and H. Schuurman [Notre Dame, IN: University of Notre Dame Press, 1980], 110), "Every red thing is colored" is a universal in respect of singular propositions "This red thing is colored," "That red thing is colored," etc. "That every red thing is colored is necessary" may be true, but "This red thing is colored" is contingent (because, according to Aristotle, it will cease to be true when this thing perishes). See *Summa Logicae,* ed. Boehner, Gál, and Brown, II, 9.30–38, p. 274 (or *Ockham's Theory of Propositions,* 109); III–3, 34.30–42, pp. 717–18.

particular is in accordance with natural justice and yet no singular will be in accordance with natural justice.[20] It is therefore possible that it is natural justice that *someone* should rule those who are similar to himself, and yet not natural justice that *this* man should rule those who are similar to himself, and not natural justice that *this* [other] man should rule those who are similar to himself, and so on of each man. And just as it is possible that a categorical proposition about a disjunct term, having as its subject discrete terms contained under some common term,[21] is necessary, and that the corresponding disjunctive with the mode of necessity is nevertheless false, and that therefore none of those singulars is necessary,[22] so it can happen that this is true: "It is natural justice for this man or that man," and so on of each man, "to rule over those who are similar to himself," which is a categorical statement about a disjunct subject, and yet this disjunctive is false, and consequently each singular is false. Therefore, according to them, so that we may reason without any deception in such matters, we must learn most diligently the difference between a disjunctive proposition and one about a disjunct term,[23] and between a proposition about the same terms taken in the sense of composition and in the sense of division (according to some), or between the different senses of such propositions according to amphiboly (according to others).[24] For often, because of ignorance of the difference between such propositions and senses, the meaning of authors is in many matters not known, when they are thought to have had one sense and sometimes have had another, indeed, sometimes the opposite. In such matters various kinds of sophisms are committed (though by many in ignorance) when one sense or equivalent proposition is sophistically inferred from the other, or the converse; or from a proposition taken in one sense, or from one sense, are inferred things that follow not from it but from the other sense—or, conversely, one sense is sophistically inferred from things from which the other sense can by a true argument be inferred. In many other ways also sophisms are committed in such matters because of ignorance of this distinction in sense of propositions that are the same verbally.

STUDENT: You have related two ways of answering Aristotle. Now relate another, if it occurs to you.

MASTER: In another way it is said that for some men (or man) to rule always is not just, unless they differ (or he differs) from the subjects as gods and heroes differ from men, if it is feared with probability that the equals will bring about dangerous dissensions and seditions if they are not honored equally.

STUDENT: In accordance with those [answers], run through the texts brought forward above in chapter 13.

MASTER: This opinion concedes the first text of Aristotle just as it sounds. To the second it is said that when there are many equals in some perfect community, Aristotle maintains that it is beneficial that all should share in rulership "in part"—i.e., sometimes to rule, sometimes to be subject—when it is feared with probability that otherwise, unless each who is equally worthy sometimes rules, dangerous seditions will arise. If, however, there is no fear of such sedition, it is beneficial, if some suitable man is found, that one man should rule all as king, even during his whole life, unless it is presumed that he would wish to convert royal rule into tyranny or there is fear of some other evil that could happen because of some wickedness.

20. According to Ockham there are other modes besides the four famous ones (necessary, contingent, possible, impossible); see *Summa Logicae* II, 1.36–68, pp. 242–43 (or *Ockham's Theory of Propositions,* 80). "In a broad sense, every proposition is called modal in which occurs some term that can belong to a whole proposition": Ockham, *Expositio in Librum Perihermeneias Aristotelis,* ed. Angelo Gambatese and Stephen Brown, vol. 2, *Opera Philosophica* (St. Bonaventure, NY: St. Bonaventure University, 1978) II, 5.87–88, p. 462. "In accordance with natural justice" fits this definition of a mode.

21. E.g., "This man or that man or..."—"this" makes the term discrete (i.e., a term referring to an individual); "man" is a common term.

22. "'This man or that man or...is P' is necessary" may be true, and yet "This man is necessarily P, or that man is necessarily P..." may be false.

23. See Ockham *Summa Logicae* III-4, 5.136–143, pp. 768–69; cf. II, 37.11–18, p. 355 (*Ockham's Theory of Propositions,* 194).

24. Amphiboly and "composition and division" are fallacies arising not from ambiguities of terms but from ambiguities of construction: "composition and division" from uncertainty of punctuation or grouping of words (*Summa Logicae* III-4, 8.3–6, p. 786), amphiboly from ambiguities of syntax. Ockham thinks that some ambiguities commonly classed under "composition and division" cannot easily be exhibited by difference of punctuation and would be better classed under amphiboly (*Summa Logicae* III-4, 5.76–93, 174–199, pp. 766–67, 770; 8.36–43, pp. 787–88).

And to the other argument from Aristotle, that fairness is "the same for similars," the answer was given earlier.[25]

To the other, when it is taken from Aristotle that no one is worthy to rule unless he surpasses all others in good, the answer given is that this is true if only the merit and the personal worth of him who should be king are taken into account, not having regard for the common good.

To the other, when it is taken [as premise] that kingship is established in accordance with aristocracy, in which only those rule who are better than the rest, it is answered that if in some community willing to be ruled aristocratically some few are found who are better than the rest, then it is just that, unless there is some other obstacle, these should rule the rest. If, however, there are not found some few who are better than the rest, but there are many equal in wisdom and virtue, and so many that it would not be beneficial for all of them to rule, then it cannot happen that aristocratic rulers are better than the rest; yet aristocratic government is beneficial for the whole community, if they are not willing to tolerate royal government; and then to appoint some few of the equals to rule all will be more useful than to establish a "constitutional," oligarchic, or democratic regime.

To the statement that God chose as first king of Israel the best man from the whole people, namely Saul, it is answered that Saul was not better in virtue and wisdom than all the others, for Samuel was much better than him, and perhaps many others excelled him in virtue and wisdom. However, it was said that there was no one like him in the whole people on account of his tall stature, because (as we read in that place), "he was taller among all the people by head and shoulders" [1 Samuel 10:23]. Many infer from this that it is not universally and without exception necessary always to choose the better man as king, because Samuel was not chosen as king and yet he was much better than Saul.

STUDENT: Applying the above to the pope, say briefly how what was written before is answered insofar as it seems to prove that no one should be over all the faithful as pope unless he surpasses all in wisdom and virtue.

MASTER: It is said that if some Catholic were found of whom such excellence were known, then, unless some circumstance particularly impeded it, he should be set over the whole community of the faithful; so that if someone else, less perfect, were elected, or even were presiding already, by love of the common good that person would be bound of necessity for salvation to resign in his favor, unless some special reason stood in the way of such resignation. If, however, no one were found who excelled in that way, someone should be appointed from among the equals. For although it is not natural or divine justice that this man should be appointed, it is natural justice that someone should be appointed; and because not all the equals should rule, it is therefore beneficial that someone from among the equals should be promoted by lot, if it cannot reasonably be done otherwise than by lot; just as the apostles, because they judged Matthias and Joseph called Barsabbas to be equal in all respects, gave them lots, and appointed him upon whom the lot fell to the office of the apostle.[26] If, however, some are perceived to be in some ways unequal, though not in wisdom and virtue, then it is possible to take notice of the inequalities, in accordance with the quality of the time: at one time notice can justly be taken of one thing and at another time of the opposite, for at one time notice could be justly taken of the power of friends and at another time of lack of friends. And thus some think it should likewise be said of other things besides wisdom and virtue.

Chapter Twenty

STUDENT: On the occasion of what you have just related I have decided that it should be asked whether, according to that opinion, it is beneficial for the community of the faithful to have the power to change an aristocratic regime (*principatus*) into a regime similar to a royal regime and vice versa, so that it has the power to appoint one highest pontiff who is over all others and power

25. Cf. Chapter 15: "When it is not possible or not useful or less useful, especially to the common good, for equal office and rank to be conferred on equals, then, without any injustice, indeed justly, by election or lot or in any other permissible way, someone can be promoted in rank and offices over his similars and equals. If others were disturbed by this and were provoked into making sedition, they would become dissimilar and unequal in virtue to the other to whom they had before been equal and similar, as being ambitious and envious, preferring their own honor to the common good" (trans. Kilcullen).

26. Acts 1:24.

also to appoint or elect many highest pontiffs at the same time who, with equal power, would together rule aristocratically and be over all the other faithful, so that it can change one regime into another indifferently as seems beneficial, as nations have reasonably changed aristocratic rule into royal rule and vice versa.[27]

MASTER: About this there are various opinions. Keeping to the opinion that asserts that sometimes aristocratic government is better for some than royal government and sometimes royal government is better for the same people, one opinion is that it is beneficial for the community of the faithful to have such power to change aristocratic government into the rule of one highest pontiff and vice versa, according as necessity and the quality of the time demands and requires one regime or the other.

STUDENT: Bring forward some arguments for that opinion.

MASTER: In favor of this opinion [1] the following argument can be given. Just as it is beneficial that human enactments should change with the change of the times (*Extra, De consanguinitate et affinitate, Non debet reprehensibile*), so it is beneficial that human regimes should change with the change of the times.[28] But Christ's Church chiefly has power over human rulerships in respect of all things that are beneficial to it; therefore it has power to change such rulerships.

STUDENT: It could be said that the rulership by which the highest priest rules all the faithful is not human but divine, because it was established by God alone; therefore it is not decent, and consequently not beneficial, that the Church should have power over the papal rulership.

MASTER: This answer is attacked. Although papal rule is divine in that Christ decided that it should exist in the Church, in many respects it seems to be human. For it is for men to decide who should be appointed to it, and who should elect, and who should correct the one appointed if he needs correction, and the like. Therefore, similarly, it will be human in this respect, that it should be decided by men whether one only, or, when beneficial, many, should be appointed to such rulership.

[2] Further, in respect of everything necessary for the things that are special to Christians, provision has been made for the community of the faithful in the best way, and not less well than for any other community or nation; so that in all such matters it has power in respect of all things that are beneficial and as they are beneficial. But if the Church had power to change a regime that began to be less beneficial into another, more beneficial, regime, it would be better provided for than if it did not have such power; therefore, since in such matters it has been provided for in the best way, it has power to change rule by one into rule by many, if it notices that it is more beneficial to be ruled by many in an aristocratic regime than by one alone.

[3] Again, it is not less beneficial for the community of the faithful to have power to abolish regimes that begin to be burdensome or less useful than to have power to abolish burdensome customs, since nothing can do more harm to the Church than a burdensome and useless regime, according to the opinion of Augustine. As we read in dist. 81, *Nemo*, he says: "No one indeed does more harm in the Church than he who, though acting perversely, has the name or order of holiness and priesthood."[29] From this we gather that nothing does more harm to the Church than a perverse ruler and a perverse regime. Therefore, if the Church notices that the Church is ruled perversely or less usefully because of the fact that one by himself rules over all, it is beneficial for it to have power to change such a regime into another that will be more useful for the time.

[4] Besides, it is not beneficial for the Church to be tied to a regime that can be changed into the worst regime; but the regime in which one rules by himself can be changed into the worst regime, as royal government, even though it is the best, can, so far as it depends on the nature of the rulership, be changed into tyranny, which is the worst regime, as Aristotle in the *Ethics* and the *Politics*

27. In the arguments against kingship in Chapter 2, the master cites Aristotle to the effect that aristocracy, rule by several good men, is superior to kingship, the rule of one good man (*Politics* 3.15 1286b5). In the response to this argument in Chapter 19, the master says that aristocracy is sometimes better than kingship, but that kingship is better at other times, and that the ancients changed from one to the other.

28. *Decretales* IV.14.8, col. 703 (again, the column number refers to *Corpus iuris canonici,* vol. 1, ed. Friedberg). The *Decretals* were assembled as a supplement to the *Decretum* by Pope Gregory IX in 1234.

29. *Decretum* dist. 81, c. 2, col. 281.

asserts and plainly proves. Therefore it is not beneficial for the Church for it to be so restricted to the regime in which one rules by himself that it cannot change it into another regime, namely aristocracy, more useful for the time.

[5] Moreover, as the civil law also testifies, "In new matters for decision, to depart from a law that has seemed fair for a long time, the advantage ought to be evident."[30] We gather from this that innovation should be made for the sake of evident advantage, even so as to depart from a law that has seemed fair for a long time. But a law should not be departed from more than a form of government, because in every community nothing can be more necessary to observe than law; for what is incongruous with the law should in no way be observed. Therefore, for the sake of evident advantage, innovation should be made, so as to depart from a form of government that has seemed reasonable and fair for a long time. Therefore, if it appears evident to the Church that for some particular time a greater advantage will come to the Church from an aristocratic regime in which many rule the community of the faithful together than from the rule of one, such innovation should be made, so as to depart from the rule of one which has seemed fair and useful for a long time.

[6] Also, what has been introduced for the support and advantage of certain persons should not be turned to their damage and loss. But the regime to which all the faithful should be subject was introduced for the support and advantage of all the faithful; therefore, if a certain kind of regime begins to be damaging to the faithful, or less useful, it is beneficial that that kind of regime should be changed into another more useful for the time. Therefore the Church has power to establish aristocratic government over all the faithful, if they consider that government by one man is beginning to harm the faithful.

[7] Further, according to Pope Leo, as we read in dist. 45, c. *Licet enim,* "A provision made for concord" should not "tend to harm."[31] This implies that whatever was provided for the sake of concord should be abolished if it tends towards harm. But rule by one highest pontiff was provided for the concord of all the faithful, namely that one should be over others "lest schism occur," according to the gloss in the same place; therefore if rule by one highest pontiff tends towards harm, i.e., toward love of dominating or ruling tyrannically, or even to a dangerous schism among Christians—that is, if a greater and temporarily more powerful, or equal, part of Christians will in no way tolerate the rule of one highest pontiff and yet will tolerate the aristocratic rule of many ruling at the same time, each of whom is highest pontiff, as sometimes there have been several emperors at the same time, and sometimes there are several judges with equal power in the same case—the rule of the one, similar to royal government, should be abolished at least for the time, and an aristocratic regime should be established, at least until those evils or dangers and others like them cease.

[8] Again, when the reason ceases the effect should cease, *Extra, De appellationibus, Cum cessante.*[32] But the common advantage is the reason why one highest pontiff should be over all the faithful. Therefore, if there comes from the rule of one, not common advantage, but common loss, such rule should cease for then. Therefore the community of the faithful then has power to establish another regime.

[9] Further, in all churches what the greater part judges should be observed ought to be observed: *Extra, De his quae fiunt a maiori parti capituli,* c. 1; dist. 65, c. 1, 2, and 3; *Extra, De electione, Licet.*[33] Therefore, if the greater part of the faithful think that an aristocratic regime should be established over the whole community of the faithful, such a regime ought to be established. From this it follows that the Church or community of the faithful has power to establish such a regime.

STUDENT: As the gloss notes upon the quoted chapter, *Extra, De his quae fiunt a maiori parti capituli,* "We do not always conform to the greater part, or the plurality: as here, and in dist. 31, *Nicena,* and above, *De electione, Ecclesia vestra*... It is the rule that we conform to the greater part, but the greater part is that which relies on the greater piety and reason: dist. 9, *Sana quippe;* dist. 40, *Multi* at the end; 4, q. 3, para. *Iurisiurandi.*"[34] The gloss on dist. 40, upon the last

30. *The Digest of Justinian* 1.4.2 (ed. A. Watson [Philadelphia: University of Pennsylvania Press, 1998]).

31. *Decretum* dist. 45, c. 6 (*Licet nonnunquam*), col. 162; the following quotation comes from the gloss, v. *concordiam,* on the same passage: "Namely, that one should rule over others, lest schism occur."

32. *Decretales* II.28.60, col. 437.

33. *Decretales* III.11.1, col. 506; *Decretum* dist. 65, c. 1, 2, and 3, cols. 249–50; *Decretales* I.6.6, col. 51.

34. Gloss s.v. *rationabiliter,* in reference to *Decretales* III.11.1, col. 506.

chapter, also seems to take this view. It says: "Not the more distinguished rank, but the action of a better life, is approved, 23, q. 4, *Sicut,* and 16, q. 1, *Sunt nonnulli.* There is here an argument that the party that relies on the juster reason is called the greater, even if it is the smaller: dist. 31, *Nicena,* 19, *In canonicis;* 4, q. 3, para. 2; and *Extra, De testibus, In nostra.*"[35] By these it is plainly established that we must not always conform to the greater part. Therefore even if the greater part of Christians were to judge that the rule of one should be changed into an aristocratic rule, this should nevertheless not be done.

MASTER: That answer is attacked. Although we should not always conform to the greater part but sometimes to the lesser, nevertheless we should always conform to the greater part unless it is plainly proved by the lesser that we should not conform to the greater part. This is gathered from the gloss on the above quoted chapter of *De his quae fiunt a maiori parte capituli,* which says, after the words quoted above: "The presumption is in favor of the plurality, dist. 61, *Nullus,* at the end, unless the contrary is proved, as is clear here and in dist. 23, *Illud,* and above, *De electione, Dudum.*" In the same place, on the word *Ostensum,* it says: "It is not enough to object, unless it is proved." Since, therefore, it cannot be proved that we must not conform to the greater part of Christians if, for the common utility, they wish to change the rule of one highest pontiff into aristocratic rule, it follows that in this matter we must conform to the greater part of the faithful.

STUDENT: It seems that it could reasonably be shown that in this matter we must not conform to the greater part of Christians if it decides to establish aristocratic government over all the faithful. For in contradicting the greater part the lesser part would rely on a juster argument; for the lesser part would then rely on an ordinance of Christ, which prevails over every human ordinance.

MASTER: To some it seems that, even if Christ had ordained that one highest pontiff should rule over all the faithful, the Church could, for the common utility, establish another regime. This is proved as follows. Necessity and utility are of equal force, as Alexander III seems to suggest, *Extra, De qualitate et aetate praeficiendorum, Quaeris.*[36] But for the sake of necessity it is permissible to act against a divine commandment, even one that is explicit, in things not evil in themselves but evil only because they are prohibited. Therefore, also, for the sake of the common utility it is permissible to act against a commandment of God and an ordinance of Christ. Therefore, even if Christ had ordained that one highest pontiff should be set over all the faithful, it would be permissible for the faithful, for the sake of common utility, to establish some other regime, at least for the time. The major premise seems to have been proved manifestly, and it is also proved from the premise that necessity and piety have equal force, as Gregory IX suggests *Extra, De feriis,* last chapter;[37] but piety includes usefulness; therefore, necessity and utility have equal force, and consequently whatever necessity makes permissible utility also makes permissible. The minor premise is shown in many ways. Bede seems clearly to assert this in his *Commentary on Mark,* quoted in *Extra, De regulis iuris,* c. *Quod non est.*[38] He says, "What is not permissible in the law, necessity makes permissible; for it is also a commandment to observe the Sabbath, but the Machabees fought on the Sabbath without fault." It seems to be clearly established by these words that the Machabees acted licitly, out of necessity, against an explicit divine command. Christ himself also seems to teach this explicitly in Matthew 12[:4] and Luke 6[:4] when he says that David and those who were with him licitly ate the loaves of offering against a divine commandment, for God explicitly commanded that no one except a priest should eat that bread. From these and a great many other [texts] we gather that the rule, "Necessity has no law," which is asserted in *Extra, De consuetudine, Quanto,* and the rule, "Necessity does not submit to law," *Extra, De observatione ieiuniorum,* c. 2, and the rule, "In the laws necessity is excepted," *Extra, De iureiurando, Querelam,* and the like, should be understood not only of positive human laws, but also of positive divine laws, unless in those divine laws the opposite is laid down expressly, so that "necessity does not submit to" *positive divine* "law."[39] (It is

35. Gloss s.v. *in honore,* in reference to *Decretum* dist. 40, c. 12, col. 147.

36. *Decretales* I.14.6, col. 127: "...and the utility of the Church or usefulness persuades."

37. *Decretales* II.9.5, col. 272: "...unless necessity urges, or piety persuades."

38. *Decretales* V.41.4, col. 927.

39. *Decretales* I.4.4, col. 37; III.46.2, col. 650; II.24.10, col. 362.

otherwise with natural law, because to that law necessity does submit, and neither can any necessity excuse.)

[10] Further, it is shown that such an ordinance of Christ would pose no obstacle. Christians in the New Law do not have less power to change the regime of priests than those had who were living under the Old Law. But notwithstanding the commandment of God concerning the appointment of one highest pontiff in Exodus 29[:29–30], also found in the *Decreta,* dist. 21, para. 1, David afterwards appointed several highest pontiffs, as we gather from 1 Paralipomenon 24 [1 Chron. 24:5]; and thus the evangelist Luke, in chapter 2 [3:2], seems to testify that in Christ's time there were several chief priests at the same time. Therefore Christians also have power to appoint several highest pontiffs, even though Christ ordained that some one person should be appointed as highest pontiff.

Chapter Twenty-Four

MASTER: That objection mentions two things, a power to dispense against a commandment of God or of Christ, and a power to interpret a commandment of God or of Christ.[40] As to the [1] first, it is said that no Christians whatever have power to dispense against a commandment of God or of Christ, unless interpretation or declaration of the law is called dispensation. This is how the gloss upon 25, q. 1, c. *Sunt quidam* seems to speak. It says that "the pope dispenses from the gospel by interpreting it."[41] The assertion of some jurists seems to harmonize with this. They say, "Declaration or commutation is called dispensation; thus he," i.e., the pope, "can dispense from a vow, and from things which are done by divine and natural law, provided there is necessity or utility and compensability."[42]

[2] Concerning the power to interpret a commandment of God or of Christ and, consequently, to dispense in the above way, the studious can perceive what should be said (according to a certain opinion) from our extensive disputation concerning the power to interpret the statements and enactments of others in the first part of our dialogue, Book 6.[43] I will relate a few things from it, adding some. It is said, therefore, that interpretation of some statement or commandment or statute, divine or natural or human, is necessary only because of the ignorance of some one for whom an interpretation is necessary, because "where the words are not doubtful there is no room for interpretation," as the gloss notes, *Extra, De consuetudine,* upon the chapter *Cum dilectus.*[44] Interpretation therefore pertains to anyone who knows the true meaning of what has to be interpreted, that is, when someone else is in doubt about its true meaning. But many experts know the true meaning of the commandments of God and Christ. They can interpret those commandments to those who do not know, because such interpretation is nothing but an exposition, clarification, or making manifest of the true meaning of God's commandments. And thus Christians have power sometimes to interpret a divine commandment, namely when they know its true meaning. If, however, the true meaning of some commandment of God were not known, because God's intention in making the commandment was not known and could not be known through reasoning or through other Scriptures but only by a revelation of God—as, according to some, the true literal meaning of many of the prophecies included in the Book of the Apocalypse and in other prophetic writings cannot be known except through a new revelation—then the interpretation of such a commandment must be awaited from God alone. But the meaning of God's commandments or ordinances about preserving patience, not making oaths, not carrying a wallet or a bag,[45] and about appointing a highest pontiff, and of

40. In Chapter 23 the student sees some "plausibility" in the premise that it is "permissible to contravene the words of a commandment of God," but raises objections against it in order to understand it better. He objects that contravening a commandment requires dispensing against it and interpreting it, neither of which are permitted. The commandment ultimately in question is the "ordinance" that established Peter as the highest pontiff (Chapter 21; cf. Matt. 16:18–19).

41. Gloss, v. *Apostoli,* in reference to *Decretum* causa 25, q. 1, c. 6, col. 1008.

42. The source has not been found.

43. See 1 *Dialogue* 6.100.

44. Gloss, v. *iuri communi,* in reference to *Decretales* I.4.8.

45. The list refers to examples discussed in Chapter 22; cf. Matt. 5:34, 39; 10:9–10. See also Luke 22:35.

many other commandments, is known by many Christians, and can be known through reasoning and the Scriptures; Christian experts can therefore interpret such commandments or ordinances, and they ought to be observed according to the true interpretation. And "we must not always stick to the words," even of Christ, "but to the intention," according to the gloss, 23, q. 1, on the chapter *Paratus,* which in that place speaks specifically of the words of Christ.[46]

STUDENT: According to these ideas it would be no more permissible for the pope to interpret the words of God and Christ than for anyone else wise and learned in sacred literature, and we would not have to believe the pope in such matters more than any other wise man.

MASTER: It is answered that it is not permissible for the pope to interpret the words of God or Christ otherwise than it is for another, nor do we have to believe him in such matters more than any other wise man—indeed, in such matters those more expert than the pope should be preferred to the pope himself, as we read in dist. 20, para. 1, where we read that in explaining the sacred Scriptures those who treat of the divine Scriptures are preferred to the highest pontiffs.[47] However, if the pope's exposition or interpretation is Catholic, containing no error, it is in some way more authoritative than the interpretation of another learned man, because from then on it will not be permissible for anyone knowingly to opine and hold the opposite in public. This is not true of the same interpretation if it were only that of another learned man, because if it were not about something that one was obliged to believe explicitly, it would be permissible, despite this interpretation, for another, expressing an opinion in public, to hold the opposite, though not pertinaciously. If, however, the pope's interpretation were erroneous and not in harmony with the truth, it would be permissible for anyone knowing that it is not in harmony with the truth to reject it openly and publicly, and anyone knowing this would be obliged, of necessity for salvation, to attack it, according to place and time.

STUDENT: According to these ideas the pope could in no way dispense against the Lord or the Apostle, or against sacred Scripture. The gloss to 25, q. 1, on the chapter *Sunt quidam,*[48] seems to hold the opposite of this. It says, "It can be maintained that the pope dispenses against the Apostle, but not in matters that pertain to articles of faith."

MASTER: It is said that the gloss here takes "dispense" for interpreting or clarifying the Apostle's meaning; this the pope can do.

STUDENT: In this way the pope can dispense in matters that pertain to the articles of faith, which, however, the gloss denies. For he can clarify the true meaning of things that pertain to the articles of faith, as also of other things.

MASTER: It is answered that he cannot interpret the articles of faith included in the Creed, of which the gloss speaks, otherwise than as they have been interpreted, because in respect of their literal sense they have been sufficiently interpreted and clarified. But the pope can, if he is an expert, interpret in a new interpretation [the sense] of many other things found in the sacred Scriptures, because they are not found in particular to have been interpreted by earlier interpreters in such a way that they do not need, for many simple people, and indeed for experts, a new and explicit interpretation, which many, even learned men, do not know how to gather from all the writings of the highest pontiffs and of those who treat of the divine Scriptures; and none of the highest pontiffs or doctors is, or was, so expert that he has not been and could not be able, continually and always, even if he lived a thousand years or more, to advance in the understanding of divine Scripture, by newly finding Catholic literal senses (which are the foundation of all other senses) by studying the sacred Scriptures; this is because of the difficulty of understanding sacred Scripture in various places.

STUDENT: You have said enough about this objection. Now relate how the first objection I brought forward in the last chapter is answered.[49]

46. Gloss, v. *Si verba,* in reference to *Decretum* causa 23, q. 1, c. 2, col. 891.

47. *Decretum* dist. 20, para. 1, col. 65; *The Treatise on Laws,* p. 84.

48. Gloss, v. *Apostoli,* in reference to *Decretum* causa 25, qu. 1, c. 6, col. 1008.

49. In Chapter 23 the student argues: "Of similars the same judgment must be held," so that "every commandment of God and of Christ obliges in such a way that in no case not expressed by God or by Christ would it be permissible to contravene the divine commandment on account of necessity and utility."

MASTER: To that argument it is said that we should hold a similar judgment about similars when it is not prohibited, either explicitly or implicitly, to hold a similar judgment. However, where it is explicitly or implicitly prohibited to hold a similar judgment about similars, there we should not hold a similar judgment about similars. Because Abraham received the command about sacrificing his son, he was obliged to prepare himself to kill his innocent son; and yet he was obliged to take care not to kill other innocents, because it was commanded to him simply to sacrifice his son, and not others, and he could therefore not have drawn any other meaning from the words of the commandment except that which they first expressed. And they were so explicit, being free from all ambiguity, that there was no room for interpretation, and he could not have drawn any other meaning. And by reasoning, also, he could have drawn no other meaning from these words of God, since he was not ignorant that God was the lord of life and death. Therefore, even if there were a similarity between God's commandment not to dissolve a marriage or not to send away a wife and any other commandment of God, nevertheless, a similar judgment does not and would not have to be held in all respects concerning that commandment and any other commandment of God whatever, because in excepting one special case in which it is permissible to send away a wife Christ prohibited other cases, because "what is conceded of one is denied of the others" (dist. 25, c. *Qualis;*[50] 15, q. 3, *De crimine;* dist. 45, c. *Disciplina;* 1, q. 1, *Per Esaiam*); this rule holds where the argument from the opposite sense holds, which is very strong in the law, as the laws say.[51] But in many other commandments of God and Christ special cases are not excepted explicitly. Therefore in them one case should not be understood to be excepted more than another. We must therefore gather from other places of divine Scripture whether some case should be excepted though it is not expressed, whether there is the same reason for excepting such a case in one commandment and in another, and whether the commandments are similar in kind (for example, whether they are natural commandments or positive commandments or one natural and the other positive). If they are simply commandments of natural law, no case should be excepted for any necessity or utility whatever, unless God specially excepted some case (as, notwithstanding the commandment of purely natural law about not knowingly killing the innocent, God made a special exception in commanding Abraham to sacrifice his son). If, however, they are purely positive commandments, a case of necessity and utility should be excepted in the same way in one as in another, unless it can be especially gathered from the Scripture that in some such commandment a case of necessity and utility should not be excepted. And in that way similar judgment can be held concerning similar commandments.

Chapter Twenty-Seven

STUDENT: You have reported how, according to one opinion, the arguments showing that the faithful cannot appoint several apostolics at the same time are answered. Now relate how answer is made according to the contrary opinion to the contrary arguments brought forward above in chapter 20 of this second book, by which it is shown that it is permissible for the faithful to appoint several rulers over the community of the faithful; either that they can establish another regime than the apostolic, or merely that they can promote several at the same time to the apostolic status.

MASTER: According to those who hold that there can in no way be several apostolics at the same time, [1] the answer made to the first argument is that human enactments that do not conflict with

50. Gloss, v. *Casus* (which mentions the argument from the opposite sense), in reference to *Decretum* dist. 25, c. 4, col. 94; and v. *Negatur,* which seems to be the source of the other references.

51. Gloss, v. *Fortissimum,* in reference to *Digest* 1.21.1.

divine commandments can be changed, and so also it is permissible to interchange regimes that are not at all opposed to a divine ordinance, but not regimes one of which would be in conflict with a divine ordinance. For there to be several apostolics at the same time would conflict with the ordinance of Christ, who appointed one, and therefore it is not permissible to appoint several apostolics at the same time.

[2] To the second it is said that in respect of all necessary things the best provision has been made for the community of the faithful, in that by loving and obeying God "all things work together for the good" of the faithful, according to the Apostle [Rom. 8:28]; and therefore, although sometimes it would be better and more beneficial for several apostolics (rather than one) to preside if it were not against the ordinance of Christ, it is, nevertheless, better and more beneficial for Christians to be subject to and to obey one apostolic rather than several, because of Christ's ordinance.

[3] To the other it is answered that customs that are in harmony with Christ's ordinance, however much they began to be burdensome, could not be abolished by Christians. Just as divine laws given to the Jewish people, though they were burdensome (according to the words of Peter that we read in Acts 15[:10]), could not be abolished by that people, so even if government by one apostolic alone began to be burdensome, it could not be abolished but would have to be borne with, just as bad prelates must be borne with.

[4] To the next it is answered that it is beneficial for the Church, because of the good of obedience, to be bound, if it is God's will, to a regime that can be changed into the worst, just as because of the good of obedience it is beneficial for a church, because of God's commandment, to obey even the worst prelate; and therefore, although the rule of one highest pontiff could be changed by his wickedness into the worst, because he can become a tyrant, nevertheless, because of the good of obedience, it is beneficial for the Church to endure it.

[5] To the next argument it is answered that for the sake of evident utility innovation should be made so as to depart from that human law which has seemed fair for a long time, but for no utility should any departure be made from a divine law that has seemed fair for a long time. So, also, a departure should be made for the sake of evident utility from a regime humanly established, but not from the regime established by Christ, just as it was not permissible for the Jews for any utility to depart from the levitical priesthood. But the apostolic regime was divinely instituted in such a way that one alone should rule. This regime must therefore not be transformed for the sake of any utility into an aristocratic or other regime, and in no way will it be permissible for the faithful to appoint several apostolics.

[6] To the next it is answered that government by a highest pontiff can be damaging to Christians only because of the wickedness of the ruling highest pontiff or because of the wickedness of subjects; that regime must therefore not be changed into another, but those because of whom it tends to harm, or because of whom damage happens to Christians, should be corrected.

[7] Through the same [argument] it is answered to the other, that sometimes when something provided for concord tends to harm because of the wickedness of some, it must not be abolished, but those because of whom it tends to harm must be corrected.

[8] To the next it is said that the effect does not always cease when the cause ceases, as is clear in many cases.

[9] To the next it is answered (as it was answered) that it is not true that we must always conform to the greater part or to the plurality; and therefore, even if the greater part of Christians wished to appoint several apostolics at the same time, we would not be obliged to conform to them, because the lesser part would rely on the greater reason: namely, the ordinance of Christ, who appointed one apostolic alone. To the arguments on the other side it is said that it is *not* permissible to act against an explicit divine commandment for the sake of necessity, except when it can be gathered from the Scriptures that in the divine laws necessity is excepted. But it cannot be established from the Scriptures that any necessity was excepted in Christ's ordinance about appointing one apostolic, and therefore neither because of necessity nor because of utility should several apostolics be appointed.

[10] To the last it is answered that David made that division of the priests by divine inspiration; and therefore, if God ordered it, several apostolics could be appointed, but without a divine commandment this could never lawfully be done.

PART THREE, TRACT TWO

Book Three, Chapter Six

STUDENT: Say how answer is made to my premise that the Romans have the right to elect the highest pontiff neither by divine law nor by human law.

MASTER: To this it is answered that the Romans have the right to elect the highest pontiff by divine law, extending "divine law" to include all natural law.

STUDENT: To me that answer seems obscure. I therefore want it explained, in accordance with that opinion. And first explain, in accordance with it, why it is said, "extending divine law to include *all* natural law," and second why all natural law can be called divine law.

MASTER: The first is said because of the three modes of natural law. For, in one way, that is called natural law which is in conformity with natural reason that in no case fails, such as "Do not commit adultery," "Do not lie," and the like.

In another way, that is called natural law which is to be observed by those who use natural equity alone without any custom and human legislation. This is called "natural" because its contrary is contrary to the state of nature as originally established, and if all men lived according to natural reason or divine law it[52] should not be observed or done. In this second way, and not in the first, all things are common by natural law, because in the state of nature as originally established all things would have been common, and if after the fall all men lived according to reason all things should have been common and nothing owned, for ownership was introduced because of wickedness, 12, q. 1, c. *Dilectissimus.*[53] Isidore speaks in that way in Book 6 of the *Etymologies,* included in the *Decreta,* dist. 1, *Ius naturale,* when he says that according to natural law there is "common possession of all things and the one liberty of all."[54] For common possession of all things and one liberty of all do not exist by natural law in the first way, for then no one could licitly appropriate anything to himself and no one could be made a slave by any law of nations or civil law, because natural law in the first way is immutable, invariable, indispensable, dist. 5, para. *Nunc autem,* dist. 6, para. *His itaque respondetur.*[55] But it is certain that some are made slaves licitly by the law of nations, as blessed Gregory testifies. In 12, q. 2, c. *Cum redemptor,* he says, "It is soundly done if, by the beneficence of the manumitter, men whom from the beginning nature brought forth free, and the law of nations placed under the yoke of slavery, are made free in the nature in which they were born."[56] From these words we gather that by natural law all men are free, and yet by the law of nations some are made slaves. From this it is inferred that natural law, taking the word in one way, is not immutable; rather, it is permissible to enact the contrary, so that the contrary is done by law.

In a third way that is called the natural law which is gathered by evident reasoning from the law of nations or another [law] or from some act, divine or human, unless the contrary is enacted with the consent of those concerned. This can be called natural law "on a supposition": as, according to Isidore (as quoted above), "natural law is the return of a thing deposited or of money lent, the repelling of violence by force." For these are not natural laws in the first way, or in the second way either, because they would not have existed in the state of nature as originally established and would not exist among those who, living according to reason, were content with natural equity alone without any custom and human legislation, because among them nothing would be deposited or lent and no one would inflict force on another. They are therefore natural laws on supposition, because, supposing that things and money have been appropriated by the law of nations or by some human law, then it is gathered by evident reasoning that a thing deposited and money lent should be returned, unless for a reason the contrary is decided by him or those concerned. Similarly, supposing that some one in fact unjustly inflicts violence on another (which is not in accordance with natural law but against natural law), then it

52. The contrary to the state of nature.

53. *Decretum* causa 12, q. 1, c. 2, col. 676.

54. *Decretum* dist. 1, c. 7, col. 2; *The Treatise on Laws,* p. 6.

55. *Decretum* dist. 5, para. *Nunc autem* [*Nunc ad*], col. 7; dist. 6, *His itaque respondetur,* col. 11; *The Treatise on Laws,* pp. 16, 21.

56. *Decretum* causa 12, q. 2, c. 68, col. 709.

is gathered by evident reasoning that it is permissible to repel such violence by force.

Because of these three modes of natural law, they say that the Romans have by divine law the right to elect the highest pontiff, extending "divine law" to *every* natural law. For if it were extended only to natural law spoken of in the first way (as natural law is taken in dist. 5, para. 1, and dist. 6, para. *His itaque respondetur,* and dist. 8, para. *Dignitate vero,* and dist. 9, para. 1, and in many other places), the Romans would not have the right to elect the highest pontiff from divine law alone.[57]

STUDENT: Because I have not elsewhere heard that distinction of natural law, I wish to make objections against it, to understand better from the solution of objections in accordance with that opinion whether it contains anything of the truth. That distinction seems, therefore, to conflict very obviously with Isidore's words in the chapter *Ius naturale* quoted earlier. First, because Isidore says, "Natural law is common to all nations, because it is everywhere held by an instinct of nature and not by any enactment." These words cannot suit the second member of the above distinction, because things whose contrary can be permissible according to the law of nations are not common to all nations and are not held everywhere by an instinct of nature, because they are not held where the contrary is observed according to the law of nations. Also, because Isidore says in the same place, "But this, or anything similar to this, is never regarded as unjust, but as natural and fair." This cannot be true of either the second or the third members. For what is called natural law in the second way can be unjust, because the contrary can be in accordance with the law of nations; for what is contrary to the law of nations must be regarded as unjust. And what is called natural law in the third way can be unjust, because the contrary is in accordance with the law of nature in the second way. For it is in accordance with natural law in the second sense that restitution of money borrowed or of a thing lent should not be made, since it is in accordance with natural law in that sense that no money should be lent and no thing deposited, because according to the natural law, taking the term in that way, all things are common, and thus according to that law no money can be lent and nothing deposited. These are the arguments that move me against the foregoing distinction; but say how they are answered.

MASTER: They are answered in two ways. In one way that some words in the chapter *Ius naturale* should be understood only of natural law spoken of in the first way and others of others, and therefore the words you take in your objection should be understood only of natural law spoken of in the first way, and thus do not seem to establish anything against the foregoing.

In the other way it is said that the words you quote in your objection are said of every natural law, but they should be understood soundly. When, therefore, Isidore says, "Natural law is common to all nations," etc., he means that natural law spoken of in the first way is common to all nations in such a way that all nations are indispensably obliged to it, and therefore "it is had by instinct of nature," that is, of natural reason, which is never mistaken. And natural law spoken of in the second way is common to all nations in such a way that all nations are obliged to it, *unless* for reasonable cause they decide on the contrary, and therefore it exists "by instinct of nature," that is, of natural reason, *until* the contrary is enacted by human ordinance; for reason dictates that all things are common until they are appropriated with the consent of men. But natural law in the third way is common to all nations *on supposition*—namely, if all nations enact or do something from which a [natural] law in that sense is gathered by evident reasoning; and therefore "it is had by an instinct of nature," i.e., of natural reason, *supposing* that from which it is thus inferred.

Similarly it is said of the words you quote second, "But this, or anything similar to this," etc., that they can be understood of the second member, because such a natural law is "never unjust, but is regarded as natural and fair," *unless* the contrary is, for some reasonable cause, established by some human law. Also, natural law spoken of in the third way is in some way "never unjust, but is" always "regarded as natural and fair," because, *supposing* that from which it is inferred by evident reasoning, it is "never unjust but is" always "regarded as natural and fair," *unless* the opposite is decided on by him or those concerned.

STUDENT: It seems that those things are said unsuitably, because according to them the same word

57. *Decretum* dist. 5, para. *Nunc autem,* col. 7; dist. 6, para. *His itaque respondetur,* col. 11; dist. 8, para. *Dignitate vero,* col. 13; dist. 9, para. *Cum ergo,* col. 18; *The Treatise on Laws,* pp. 16, 21, 25, 32, respectively.

occurring once in the foregoing words of Isidore is taken equivocally.

MASTER: This is not regarded as unsuitable, because the gloss on dist. 63, c. *Nosse* notes this. It says, "Note, a word occurring here once is used equivocally, as in dist. 28, *Presbyterium.*"[58]

STUDENT: You have explained in accordance with the opinion stated above why it said that the Romans have the right to elect the highest pontiff by divine law, extending divine law to every natural law. Now say, in accordance with the same opinion, why it says that every natural law can be called a divine law.

MASTER: They say this, first, because every law that is from God, who is the creator of nature, can be called a divine law; but every natural law is from God who is the creator of nature; therefore etc. Also, because every law that is contained explicitly or implicitly in the divine Scriptures can be called a divine law, because "divine law is contained in the divine Scriptures," dist. 8, c. *Quo iure;*[59] but every natural law is contained explicitly or implicitly in the divine Scriptures, because in the divine Scriptures there are certain general propositions from which, either alone or with other [premises], can be inferred every natural law, spoken of in the first way, in the second way, and in the third way, though it may not be found in them explicitly.

STUDENT: You have explained in accordance with the above-stated opinion the two things that seemed obscure to me. Now say, in accordance with the same opinion, how the Romans have from divine law the right to elect the highest pontiff.

MASTER: To this it is said that the Romans have the right to elect the highest pontiff from natural law spoken of in the third way. For *supposing* that someone is to be set over certain persons as prelate, ruler, or rector, it is inferred by evident reason that, unless the contrary is decided on by the person or persons concerned, those whom he is to be set over have the right to elect the one to be set over them, so that no one should be given to them against their will. It seems that this can be proved by numberless arguments and examples, but I will bring forward a few.

An example to this [effect] is that no one should be set over the whole body of mortals except by their election and consent.[60]

Further, what affects all should be dealt with by all; for someone to be set over all affects all, therefore it should be dealt with by all.

Again, to those whom it concerns to make themselves laws it belongs to elect a head, if they wish; but any people and city can make themselves their own law, which is called "civil" law, dist. 1, *Ius civile;* therefore also a people and city can elect themselves a head. And thus it always belongs to those whom someone is to be set over to elect the one to be set over them, unless the contrary is decided on by the person or persons concerned. (This is said because they can, at least in many cases, resign their right and transfer their right to another or to others. In this way, although from natural law spoken of in the third way or in the second way the people had the right to make laws, yet they transferred that power to the emperor, and so it was in his power to transfer the right to elect the emperor to another or to others.) Similarly, if those whom someone is to be set over are in such matters subject to some superior, that superior can decide that they do not have the right to elect, although they had the right to elect by the law of nature spoken of in that way[61]—namely, unless the contrary had been decided on either by themselves or by the superior.

And thus it seems to them that the proposition taken before must be regarded as evident. But the highest pontiff is in a way especially to be set over the Romans, because they do not have another bishop. Therefore, by natural law spoken of in that way—that is, by natural law on supposition, namely, on the supposition that they should have a bishop—they have the right to elect him, unless the contrary is enacted or decided on by the Romans themselves or by some other, superior to the Romans, who has power in this matter. For the Romans themselves can resign their right and also transfer the right to elect the highest pontiff to another; they could also transfer to another the right of appointing the electors of the highest pontiff. Also, someone superior to the Romans who had power in such matters could grant

58. Gloss *in v. clero,* in reference to *Decretum* dist. 63, c. 12, col. 238.

59. *Decretum,* dist. 8, c. 1, col. 12; *The Treatise on Laws,* p. 24.

60. "The whole body of all mortals" is the Roman Empire; it was universally accepted that the Roman emperor should be elected.

61. That is, in the third way.

the right to elect to some persons other than the Romans; but that superior was Christ and not the pope, and therefore Christ and not the pope could deprive the Romans of the right to elect the highest pontiff. But Christ did not deprive the Romans of the right to elect their bishop; for when Christ set blessed Peter over all Christians, giving him power to select a see where he wished in such a way that in that place he would be in a way their own bishop, he did not deprive them of that right, which belongs to all whom some power, secular or ecclesiastical, is to be set over (unless the contrary is determined by those whom that power, secular or ecclesiastical, is to be set over, or by their superior); therefore, since blessed Peter selected the see of Rome, it follows that the Romans have the right to elect the successor of blessed Peter, who in spiritual matters is to be set over them especially. And thus the Romans have by divine law, extending divine law to every natural law, the right to elect the highest pontiff.

STUDENT: It seems that according to that opinion it would be better to say that the Romans have the right to elect their bishop by the law *of nations*, because it is by the law of nations that all of those whom someone is to be set over have the right to elect the person to be set over them unless they resign their right or their superior decides on the contrary.

MASTER: Although many things that belong to the law of nations are natural laws, taking "natural law" in the third way, nevertheless it is more properly said, according to that opinion, that the Romans have the right to elect their bishop by divine law or by natural law spoken of in the third way, rather than by the law of nations; because it does not belong to the law of nations to have a Catholic bishop, but this pertains to the divine law. Also, although it belongs to the law of nations that someone to be set over others should be elected by those whom he is to be set over, it belongs equally to the divine law, because it can be inferred from [premises] found in the sacred Scriptures together with other [premises]. Thus the two suppositions from which it follows that the Romans have the right to elect their bishop belong to the divine law, though in different ways, but only one belongs to the law of nations. And for this reason it is more properly said that the Romans have the right to elect their bishop by divine law or by natural law spoken of in the third way, rather than by the law of nations.

However, since the holders of this theory do not care to contend about words, they say that it is enough for them that the Romans have the right to elect their bishop from this, that they should have a bishop, and that those whom someone is to be set over should elect him unless they resign their right or the contrary is decided on by their superior. But whether it should be said that, properly speaking, the Romans have the right to elect by divine law, or by natural law spoken of in the third way, or by the law of nations, or by the divine law and the law of nations together, does not make much difference. It seems to some, however, that it is properly said that they have the right to elect by divine law and the law of nations together. And therefore when you ask whether they have the right to elect by divine or human law, they say: from neither divine nor human law alone, but from both together, extending human law to [include] the law of nations and not only civil and canon law.[62]

62. According to some of the civil law texts the law of nations is natural law, which implies that it is not human law.

BIBLIOGRAPHY AND FURTHER READING

Primary Sources in English

Alighieri, Dante. *The Banquet* [*Il Convivio*]. Translated by Christopher Ryan. Stanford French and Italian studies, v. 61, Saratoga, CA: ANMA Libri, 1989. (Consult especially chapters 1.1 and 4.4–6.)

——. *Il Convivio.* Edited by Cesare Vasoli and Domenico De Robertis. Vol. 1, pt. 2 of *Dante Alighieri—Opere Minori.* Milan: Riccardo Ricciardi Editore, 1979. (Italian text with excellent notes.)

——. *The Letters of Dante.* Edited by Paget Toynbee. 2nd ed. Oxford: Clarendon Press, 1966. (Letters 5–8 bear on Dante's political thought.)

——. *Monarchia.* Translated and edited by Prue Shaw. Cambridge: Cambridge University Press, 1995.

——. *The Monarchia Controversy: An Historical Study with Accompanying Translations of Dante Alighieri's "Monarchia," Guido Vernani's "Refutation of the Monarchia Composed by Dante," and Pope John XXII's Bull "Si Fratrum."* Translated by Anthony K. Cassell. Washington, DC: The Catholic University of America Press, 2004.

Aquinas, Thomas. *Aquinas against the Averroists: On There Being Only One Intellect.* Translated by Ralph McInerny. West Lafayette, IN: Purdue University Press, 1993.

——. *Aquinas: Political Writings.* Translated by R. W. Dyson. Cambridge: Cambridge University Press, 2002. (Includes *De Regno* and selections from the *Summa Theologiae.*)

——. *Commentary on Aristotle's Politics.* Translated by Richard J. Regan. Indianapolis: Hackett, 2007.

Aquinas, Thomas, Siger of Brabant, and Bonaventure. *On the Eternity of the World (De Aeternitate Mundi).* Translated by Cyril Vollert, Lottie H. Kendzierski, and Paul M. Byrne. 2nd ed. Milwaukee: Marquette University Press, 1984.

Augustine. *The City of God against the Pagans.* Translated by R. W. Dyson. Cambridge: Cambridge University Press. 1998.

——. *Political Writings.* Translated by E. M. Atkins and Robert Dodaro. Cambridge: Cambridge University Press, 2001. (Includes letters and sermons on political subjects.)

——. *Political Writings.* Edited by Ernest L. Fortin and Douglas Kries and translated by Douglas Kries and Michael W. Tkacz, with Roland Gunn. Indianapolis: Hackett, 1994. (Includes abridged translation of *City of God* and other writings.)

Bacon, Roger. *The Opus Maius of Roger Bacon.* Translated by Robert Belle Burke. 2 vols. Philadelphia: University of Pennsylvania Press, 1928; New York: Russell and Russell, 1962.

Giles of Rome. *Errores Philosophorum; Critical Text with Notes and Introduction.* Edited by Josef Koch and translated by John O. Riedl. Milwaukee: Marquette University Press, 1944.

——. "Giles of Rome on the Errors of the Philosophers." Translated by Herman Shapiro. In *Medieval Philosophy: Selected Readings from Augustine to Buridan,* 384–413. New York: Modern Library, 1964.

——. *The Governance of Kings and Princes: John of Trevisa's Middle English Translation of the "De Regimine Principum" of Aegidius Romanus.* Edited by David C. Fowler, Charles F. Briggs, and Paul G. Remley. New York: Garland Publishing, 1997.

——. *Three Royalist Tracts, 1296–1302: Antiquam Essent Clerici; Disputatio inter Clericum et Militem; Quaestio in Utramque Partem.* Translated and edited by R. W. Dyson. Bristol, England: Thoemmes Press, 1999.

Gratian. *The Treatise on Laws (Decretum DD.1–20), with the Ordinary Gloss.* Translated by Augustine Thompson and James Gordley. Washington, DC: The Catholic University of America Press, 1993.

John of Paris. *On Royal and Papal Power.* Translated by Arthur P. Monahan. New York: Columbia University Press, 1974.

John of Paris (aka John Quidort). *On Royal and Papal Power.* Translated by J. A. Watt. Toronto: Pontifical Institute of Medieval Studies, 1971.

Marsilius of Padua. *The Defender of the Peace.* Translated by Annabel S. Brett. Cambridge: Cambridge University Press, 2005.

——. *Writings on the Empire: "Defensor Minor" and "De Translatione Imperii."* Edited and translated by Cary J. Nederman. Cambridge: Cambridge University Press, 1993.

Mommsen, Theodor, and Paul Krueger, eds.; Alan Watson, trans. *The Digest of Justinian.* Philadelphia: University of Pennsylvania Press, 1985.

Tierney, Brian. *The Crisis of Church & State, 1050–1300, with Selected Documents.* Englewood Cliffs, NJ: Prentice-Hall, 1964; Toronto: University of Toronto Press, with the Medieval Academy of America, 1988. (Includes excerpts from a wide range of primary sources, including canon jurists and decretalists.)

William of Ockham. *On the Power of Emperors and Popes.* Translated by Annabel S. Brett. Durham, UK: University of Durham Press, 1998.

——. *A Short Discourse on Tyrannical Government.* Edited by Arthur Stephen McGrade and translated by John Kilcullen. Cambridge: Cambridge University Press, 1992.

Secondary Literature

Bejczy, István Pieter. *Virtue Ethics in the Middle Ages: Commentaries on Aristotle's Nicomachean Ethics, 1200–1500.* Leiden: Brill, 2008.

Bianchi, Luca. "Felicità terrena e beatitudine ultraterrena: Boezio di Dacia e l'articolo 157 censurato da Tempier." In *Chemins de la pensée médiévale: Études offertes à Zénon Kaluza,* edited by Paul J. J. M. Bakker. Brepols: Fédération Internationale des Instituts d'Études Médiévales, 2002.

Blythe, James M. "Aristotle's *Politics* and Ptolemy of Lucca." *Vivarium* 40 (2002): 103–36.

——. *Ideal Government and the Mixed Constitution in the Middle Ages.* Princeton, NJ: Princeton University Press, 1992.

——. *The Worldview and Thought of Tolomeo Fiadoni (Ptolemy of Lucca).* Turnhout: Brepols, 2009.

Celano, Anthony J. "Boethius of Dacia: 'On the Highest Good.'" *Traditio* 43 (1987): 199–214.

——. "Peter of Auvergne's Questions on Books I and II of the *Ethica Nicomachea:* A Study and Critical Edition." *Mediaeval Studies* 48 (1986): 1–110.

Coleman, Janet. "Ockham's Right Reason and the Genesis of the Political as 'Absolutist.'" *History of Political Thought* 20 (1999): 35–64.

Condren, Conal. "Democracy and the *Defensor Pacis:* On the English Language Tradition of Marsilian Interpretation." *Il Pensiero Politico* 8 (1980): 301–16.

——. "Marsilius of Padua's Argument from Authority: A Study of Its Significance in the *Defensor Pacis.*" *Political Theory* 5 (May 1977): 205–18.

Davis, Charles T. *Dante's Italy and Other Essays.* Philadelphia: University of Pennsylvania Press, 1984. (Includes chapters on Ptolemy of Lucca.)

Donnelly, Dorothy F. *The City of God: A Collection of Critical Essays.* New York: P. Lang, 1995. (Includes essays by Peter Brown, Peter Burnell, R. A. Markus, Reinhold Niebuhr, Ernest Fortin, and Theodore E. Mommsen.)

Dyson, R. W. *Normative Theories of Society and Government in Five Medieval Thinkers: St. Augustine, John of Salisbury, Giles of Rome, St. Thomas Aquinas, and Marsilius of Padua.* Lewiston, NY: Edwin Mellen Press, 2003.

Finnis, John. *Aquinas: Moral, Political, and Legal Theory.* Oxford: Oxford University Press, 1998.

Flüeler, Christoph. *Rezeption und Interpretation der aristotelischen Politica im späten Mittelalter.* Amsterdam and Philadelphia: B. R. Grüner, 1992.

Fortin, Ernest L. *The Birth of Philosophic Christianity: Studies in Early Christian and Medieval Thought.* Edited by J. Brian Benestad. Lanham, MD: Rowman and Littlefield Publishers, 1996.

——. *Classical Christianity and the Political Order: Reflections on the Theological-Political Problem.* Edited by J. Brian Benestad. Lanham, MD: Rowman and Littlefield Publishers, 1996.

——. *Dissent and Philosophy in the Middle Ages.* Lanham, MD: Lexington Books, 2002.

Gewirth, Alan. *Marsilius of Padua, the Defender of the Peace.* Vol. 1, *Marsilius of Padua and Medieval Political Philosophy.* New York: Columbia University Press, 1951.

Gilson, Etienne. *Dante and Philosophy.* Translated by David Moore. New York: Harper Torchbooks, 1949. Also published as *Dante the Philosopher* (New York: Sheed & Ward, 1949).

——. *History of Christian Philosophy in the Middle Ages.* New York: Random House, 1955.

Goerner, E. A. "On Thomistic Natural Law: The Bad Man's View of Thomistic Natural Right." *Political Theory* 7 (1979): 101–22.

——. "Thomistic Natural Right: The Good Man's View of Thomistic Natural Law." *Political Theory* 11 (1983): 393–418.

Hackett, Jeremiah. "Aristotle, *Astrologia,* and Controversy at the University of Paris (1266–1274)." In *Learning Institutionalized: Teaching in the Medieval University,* edited by John Van Engen, 69–110. Notre Dame, IN: University of Notre Dame Press, 2000. (Discusses Bacon's views on astrology and theology.)

——. "Philosophy and Theology in Roger Bacon's *Opus Maius.*" In *Philosophy and the God of Abraham: Essays in Memory of James A. Weisheipl, OP,* edited by J. James Long, 55–69. Toronto: Pontifical Institute of Mediaeval Studies, 1991.

Hasse, Dag Nikolaus. "Averroica secta: Notes on the Formation of Averroist Movements in Fourteenth-Century Bologna and Renaissance Italy." In *Averroes et les Averroïsmes juif et latin,* edited by J.-B. Brenet, 307–31. Turnhout: Brepols, 2007.

Hissette, Roland. *Enquête sur les 219 articles condamnés à Paris le 7 mars 1277.* Louvain: Publ. Universitaires; Paris: Vander-Oyez, 1977.

Jaffa, Harry V. *Thomism and Aristotelianism: A Study of the Commentary by Thomas Aquinas on the "Nicomachean Ethics."* Chicago: University of Chicago, 1952; reprint, Westport, CT: Greenwood Press, 1979.

Mansfield, Harvey C. *Taming the Prince: The Ambivalence of Modern Executive Power.* Baltimore: Johns Hopkins University Press, 1989. (Includes sections on Aristotle, Thomas, Dante, and Marsilius.)

Marenbon, John. "Dante's Averroism." In *Poetry and Philosophy in the Middle Ages: A Festschrift for Peter Dronke,* edited by John Marenbon, 349–74. Leiden: Brill, 2001.

Markus, R. A. *Saeculum: History and Society in the Theology of St. Augustine.* 1970; rev. ed., Cambridge: Cambridge University Press, 1988.

McGrade, Arthur Stephen. *The Political Thought of William of Ockham.* London: Cambridge University Press, 1974.

Miethke, Jürgen. *De potestate papae: Die päpstliche Amtskompetenz im Widerstreit der politischen Theorie von Thomas von Aquin bis Wilhelm von Ockham.* Tübingen: Mohr Siebeck, 2000.

Nederman, Cary J. "Aristotelianism and the Origins of 'Political Science' in the Twelfth Century." *Journal of the History of Ideas* 52 (1991): 179–94.

——. *Community and Consent: The Secular Political Theory of Marsilio of Padua's Defensor Pacis.* Lanham, MD: Rowman and Littlefield, 1995.

——. "Nature, Sin, and the Origins of Society: The Ciceronian Tradition in Medieval Political Thought." *Journal of the History of Ideas* 49 (1988): 3–26.

Oakley, Francis. "Celestial Hierarchies Revisited: Walter Ullmann's Vision of Medieval Politics." *Past and Present* 60 (1973): 3–48.

——. "Medieval Theories of Natural Law: William of Ockham and the Significance of the Voluntarist Tradition." *Natural Law Forum* 6 (1961): 65–83.

Offler, H. S. "The 'Influence' of Ockham's Political Thinking: The First Century." In H. S. Offler, *Church and Crown in the Fourteenth Century: Studies in European History and Political Thought,* edited by H. S. Offler and A. I. Doyle. Aldershot, UK: Ashgate; Variorum, 2000. Also in *Die Gegenwart Ockhams,* ed. Wilhelm Vossenkuhl, Rolf Schönberger, and Otl Aicher (Weinheim: VCH-Verlagsgesellschaft, Acta Humaniora, 1990).

Peterman, Larry. "Dante and Happiness: A Political Perspective." *Medievalia et Humanistica* 10 (1981): 81–102.

——. "Dante's *Monarchia* and Aristotle's Political Thought." *Studies in Medieval and Renaissance History* 10 (1973): 3–40.

——. "An Introduction to Dante's *De Monarchia.*" *Interpretation* 3 (1973): 169–90.

——. "Reading the *Convivio.*" *Dante Studies* 103 (1985): 125–38.

Piché, David, with Claude LaFleur. *La condamnation parisienne de 1277.* Paris: J. Vrin, 1999.

Renna, Thomas. "Aristotle and the French Monarchy, 1260–1303." *Viator* 9 (1978): 309–24.

Rubinstein, Nicolai. "Marsilius of Padua and Italian Political Thought of His Time." In *Europe in the Late Middle Ages,* edited by J. R. Hale, J. R. L. Highfield, and B. Smalley. London: Faber and Faber, 1965.

Stone, Gregory B. *Dante's Pluralism and the Islamic Philosophy of Religion.* New York: Palgrave Macmillan, 2006.

Strauss, Leo. "Marsilius of Padua." In *History of Political Philosophy,* edited by Leo Strauss and Joseph Cropsey. 3rd ed. Chicago: University of Chicago Press, 1987.

Thijssen, J. M. M. H. "1277 Revisited: A New Interpretation of the Doctrinal Investigations of Thomas Aquinas and Giles of Rome." *Vivarium* 35 (1997): 72–101.

——. *Censure and Heresy at the University of Paris, 1200–1400.* Philadelphia: University of Pennsylvania Press, 1998.

Tierney, Brian. *The Idea of Natural Rights: Studies on Natural Rights, Natural Law, and Church Law, 1150–1625.* Atlanta: Scholars Press, 1997. (Includes discussions of Marsilius and Ockham.)

Torraco, Stephen F. *Priests as Physicians in Marsilius of Padua's Defensor Pacis.* San Francisco: Mellen Research University Press, 1992.

Watt, John A. *The Theory of Papal Monarchy in the Thirteenth Century: The Contribution of the Canonists.* New York: Fordham University Press, 1965.

Westberg, Daniel. *Right Practical Reason: Aristotle, Action, and Prudence in Aquinas.* Oxford: Clarendon Press, 1994.

Wilks, Michael. "Corporation and Representation in the *Defensor Pacis.*" *Studia Gratiana* 15 (1972): 251–92.

——. *The Problem of Sovereignty in the Later Middle Ages.* Cambridge: Cambridge University Press, 1963.

Wippel, John F. "The Condemnations of 1270 and 1277 at Paris." *Journal of Medieval and Renaissance Studies* 7 (1977): 169–201.

——. "Thomas Aquinas and the Condemnation of 1277." *The Modern Schoolman* 72 (1995): 233–72.

INDEX

Index does not include the names of God.

CPSIA information can be obtained
at www.ICGtesting.com
Printed in the USA
LVHW021508190123
737397LV00005B/102

9 780801 476815